IFIP Advances in Information and Communication Technology 480

IFIP – The International Federation for Information Processing

IFIP was founded in 1960 under the auspices of UNESCO, following the first World Computer Congress held in Paris the previous year. A federation for societies working in information processing, IFIP's aim is two-fold: to support information processing in the countries of its members and to encourage technology transfer to developing nations. As its mission statement clearly states:

> *IFIP is the global non-profit federation of societies of ICT professionals that aims at achieving a worldwide professional and socially responsible development and application of information and communication technologies.*

IFIP is a non-profit-making organization, run almost solely by 2500 volunteers. It operates through a number of technical committees and working groups, which organize events and publications. IFIP's events range from large international open conferences to working conferences and local seminars.

The flagship event is the IFIP World Computer Congress, at which both invited and contributed papers are presented. Contributed papers are rigorously refereed and the rejection rate is high.

As with the Congress, participation in the open conferences is open to all and papers may be invited or submitted. Again, submitted papers are stringently refereed.

The working conferences are structured differently. They are usually run by a working group and attendance is generally smaller and occasionally by invitation only. Their purpose is to create an atmosphere conducive to innovation and development. Refereeing is also rigorous and papers are subjected to extensive group discussion.

Publications arising from IFIP events vary. The papers presented at the IFIP World Computer Congress and at open conferences are published as conference proceedings, while the results of the working conferences are often published as collections of selected and edited papers.

IFIP distinguishes three types of institutional membership: Country Representative Members, Members at Large, and Associate Members. The type of organization that can apply for membership is a wide variety and includes national or international societies of individual computer scientists/ICT professionals, associations or federations of such societies, government institutions/government related organizations, national or international research institutes or consortia, universities, academies of sciences, companies, national or international associations or federations of companies.

More information about this series at http://www.springer.com/series/6102

Hamideh Afsarmanesh · Luis M. Camarinha-Matos
António Lucas Soares (Eds.)

Collaboration in a Hyperconnected World

17th IFIP WG 5.5 Working Conference on Virtual Enterprises, PRO-VE 2016
Porto, Portugal, October 3–5, 2016
Proceedings

Springer

Editors
Hamideh Afsarmanesh
University of Amsterdam
Amsterdam
The Netherlands

Luis M. Camarinha-Matos
Universidade Nova de Lisboa
Monte Caparica
Portugal

António Lucas Soares
University of Porto
Porto
Portugal

ISSN 1868-4238 ISSN 1868-422X (electronic)
IFIP Advances in Information and Communication Technology
ISBN 978-3-319-45389-7 ISBN 978-3-319-45390-3 (eBook)
DOI 10.1007/978-3-319-45390-3

Library of Congress Control Number: 2016948781

Printed on acid-free paper

This Springer imprint is published by Springer Nature
The registered company is Springer International Publishing AG Switzerland

Preface

Everyday life in societies is dramatically influenced by an exponential increase in connectivity, and we now talk of a hyper-connected world. Digital interconnection of people and things is expanding to anytime and anywhere. It is estimated that by 2020 over 50 billion networked devices will co-exist in the world. The hyper-connected world of the future would comprise environments transparently enriched with sensors, actuators, devices, machines, and computational elements that are interconnected and collaborating. Together with people, these provide complex collaborative environments with context sensitive interactions. The area of collaborative networks provides an important foundation for the emerging hyper-connected world, wherein humans, organizations, intelligent agents, and devices co-exist. These entities generate data, interconnect through data, and act together, potentially evolving toward an increasingly effective collective intelligence within an exponentially growing platform.

Profound and challenging social, political, economic and even cultural consequences are associated with such a vast level of heterogeneous connectivity. From the collaborative networks' perspective, it is therefore fundamental to first understand the structure and inter-relationships among entities within the hyper-connected world, and second design and develop collaborative support environments, tools, and systems addressing their functional/non-functional requirements.

There is already a base for ICT developments supporting this area. In the last two decades, advances in ICT, Internet, and cloud have led to the explosion of collaborative networks, both for networks of people, through social networks and virtual communities, and for networks of organizations through business ecosystems, dynamic supply chains, virtual organizations, and their breeding environments. This explosive trend is further amplified by the emergence of the Internet of Things and Cyber-Physical Systems, addressing a pervasive interconnection of and collaboration among physical and virtual objects. The challenges so far addressed by the collaborative networks community are however still touching only the tip of the iceberg. Many challenges in this area remain untouched and are waiting to be resolved.

Furthermore, models and support tools for new organizational collaboration structures, governance, and legal principles need to be envisioned and developed to deal with the large number of interconnected entities and their huge amounts of diverse data objects, enabling them to reach new levels of collective awareness and intelligence, facilitating new forms of evolution and co-creation, more effective problem solving, as well as collective decision making.

PRO-VE 2016 therefore addresses the timely topic of a hyper-connected world. It provides a forum for sharing experiences, discussing trends, identifying challenges, and introducing innovative solutions aimed at fulfilling the vision of a collaborative hyper-connected world. Understanding, modeling, and proposing solution approaches in this area requires contributions from multiple and diverse knowledge areas (social sciences, organization science, technologies, etc., which is well in line with the interdisciplinary spirit of the PRO-VE working conferences.

PRO-VE 2016, held in Porto, Portugal, was the 17th event in this series of successful conferences, including:

PRO-VE 1999 (Porto, Portugal), PRO-VE 2000 (Florianopolis, Brazil), PRO-VE 2002 (Sesimbra, Portugal), PRO-VE 2003 (Lugano, Switzerland), PRO-VE 2004 (Toulouse, France), PRO-VE 2005 (Valencia, Spain), PRO-VE 2006 (Helsinki, Finland), PRO-VE 2007 (Guimarães, Portugal), PRO-VE 2008 (Poznań, Poland), PRO-VE 2009 (Thessaloniki, Greece), PRO-VE 2010 (St. Étienne, France), PRO-VE 2011 (São Paulo, Brazil), PRO-VE 2012 (Bournemouth, UK), PRO-VE 2013 (Dresden, Germany), PRO-VE 2014 (Amsterdam, The Netherlands), and PRO-VE 2015 (Albi, France).

This proceedings book includes selected papers from the PRO-VE 2016 conference, providing a comprehensive overview of major challenges and recent advances in various domains related to collaborative networks and their applications, with a strong focus on the following areas, also related to the selected main theme:

- Hyperconnected Systems,
- Managing Data and Knowledge,
- Networked Business Processes,
- Collective Intelligence and Decision Making,
- Creating Supply and Production Networks,
- Operating and Management of Networks,
- Collaborative Engineering,
- Product-Services,
- Intelligent Product Ecosystems,
- Product Personalization,
- Service Orientation,
- Cloud Technology Aspects for VOs,
- Design Science Research,
- Business Models in Hyperconnected Context,
- Agribusiness Value Chain, and
- Collaborative Networks in Circular Economy.

We are thankful to all the authors, both from academia and research, as well as industry, for their contributions. We hope this collection of papers represents a valuable tool for everybody interested in research advances, emerging applications, and future challenges for research and development in collaborative networks. We very much appreciate the time spent and the dedication of the members of the PRO-VE International Program Committee who supported the selection of articles for this conference, and provided valuable and constructive comments to help authors with improving the quality of their papers.

July 2016

Hamideh Afsarmanesh
Luis M. Camarinha-Matos
Antonio Lucas Soares

Matthieu Lauras, France
Leandro Loss, Brazil
António Lucas Soares, Portugal
Patricia Macedo, Portugal
Nikolay Mehandjiev, UK
István Mézgar, Hungary
Arturo Molina, Mexico
Aurelie Montarnal, France
Simon Msanjila, Tanzania
Ovidiu Noran, Australia
Paulo Novais, Portugal
Adegboyega Ojo, Nigeria
Martin Ollus, Finland
Angel Ortiz, Spain
A. Luis Osório, Portugal
Hervé Panetto, France
Iraklis Paraskakis, Greece
Zbigniew Paszkiewicz, Belgium
Kulwant Pawar, UK
Adam Pawlak, Poland
Willy Picard, Poland
Jorge Pinho Sousa, Portugal
Raul Poler, Spain
Ricardo J. Rabelo, Brazil
David Romero, Mexico
João Rosas, Portugal
Hans Schaffers, Netherlands
Jens Schütze, Germany
Weiming Shen, Canada
Cristovao Sousa, Portugal
Chrysostomos Stylios, Greece
Klaus-Dieter Thoben, Germany
Lorna Uden, UK
Rolando Vallejos, Brazil
Elise Vareilles, France
Peter Weiß, Germany
Lai Xu, UK

Technical Sponsors

IFIP WG 5.5 COVE
Co-Operation infrastructure for Virtual Enterprises and electronic business

Society of Collaborative Networks

Organizational Co-sponsors

Universiteit van Amsterdam

Nova University of Lisbon

Contents

Hyperconnectivity and Interoperation - Hyperconnected Systems

Towards a Hyperconnected Transportation Management System: Application to Blood Logistics 3
Quentin Schoen, Matthieu Lauras, Sébastien Truptil, Franck Fontanili, and Anne-Ghislaine Anquetil

Collaborative Data Analysis in Hyperconnected Transportation Systems. 13
Mohammad Nozari Zarmehri and Carlos Soares

Applicability of Human-Robot Collaboration to Small Batch Production 24
Dario Antonelli, Sergey Astanin, and Giulia Bruno

Hyperconnectivity and Interoperation - Managing Data and Knowledge

Online Communities, Teams Characteristics, and Knowledge Quality 35
Amira Rezgui and Nicolas Jullien

Realizing the Innovation Potentials from Open Data: Stakeholders' Perspectives on the Desired Affordances of Open Data Environment 48
Adegboyega Ojo, Lukasz Porwol, Mohammad Waqar, Arkadiusz Stasiewicz, Edobor Osagie, Michael Hogan, Owen Harney, and Fatemeh Ahmadi Zeleti

Knowledge Sharing in Industrial Associations and Science and Technology Parks 60
Danielly Oliveira Inomata, Eric Costa, Solange Mazzaroto, Cláudio Santos, Ana Cristina Barros, António Lucas Soares, and Gregorio Varvakis

Using an Information Management Model as a Roadmap for Information Systems Implementation in Supply Networks 73
Cláudio Santos, Ana Cristina Barros, Tom Dawes, and António Lucas Soares

Hyperconnectivity and Interoperation - Networked Business Processes

Semi-automated BP Integration in Virtual Organizations 87
Katarzyna Adamiak, Hodjat Soleimani Malekan, and Hamideh Afsarmanesh

Connecting Business Processes and Sensor Data in Proactive Manufacturing Enterprises 101
Sobah Abbas Petersen, Rimmert van der Kooij, and Primoz Puhar

Positioning Collaboration in Business Process Model Consolidation in VOs . . . 110
Hodjat Soleimani Malekan, Mohammmad H. Rezazade Mehrizi, and Hamideh Afsarmanesh

Resilience Analysis of Collaborative Process Management Systems. 124
Paul de Vrieze and Lai Xu

Hyperconnectivity and Interoperation - Collective Intelligence and Decision Making

Collaborative Networks as Ways to Improve Cross-sector Collaboration in Social Innovation: An Exploratory Study 137
Michele Andréia Borges, António Lucas Soares, and Gertrudes Aparecida Dandolini

Collective Intelligence and Collaboration: A Case Study in Airline Industry . . . 148
Sónia A.C. Teixeira, Pedro Campos, Renato Fernandes, and Catarina Roseira

Big-Data and the Question of Horizontal and Vertical Intelligence: A Discussion on Disaster Management 156
Frederick Benaben, Aurelie Montarnal, Audrey Fertier, and Sebastien Truptil

Co-development and Co-working - Creating Supply and Production Networks

Towards a Gamified Approach for Enhancing VBE Preparedness for Establishing Virtual Collaborations. 165
Noor Jehan Rajper, Stephan Reiff-Marganiec, and Qurat-Ul-Ain Nizamani

An Information Management Perspective of Supplier Selection Process in Manufacturing Networks 178
Dario Messina, Ana Cristina Barros, and António Lucas Soares

Assessing the Suitability of Supplier Consortia for Public Procurement Contracts. 189
Andrew Crossley, Jane Lynch, Sue Hurrell, and Rhian Edwards

A Confidence Indicator Model for Virtual Organization Creation in Cloud Computing Environment. 200
Luís Felipe Bilecki and Adriano Fiorese

Co-development and Co-working - Operating and Management of Networks

Effects of Decision Synchronization on Trust in Collaborative Networks 215
Morice Daudi, Jannicke Baalsrud Hauge, and Klaus-Dieter Thoben

Decentralised Replenishment-Production Planning Optimisation Using Negotiation Rules in a Collaborative Network 228
Beatriz Andres, Raul Poler, Josefa Mula, Manuel Díaz-Madroñero, and Raquel Sanchis

Mapping Patterns of Co-innovation Networks...................... 241
Paula Urze and António Abreu

A Proposal of Performance Indicators for Collaborative Business Ecosystems.. 253
Paula Graça and Luís M. Camarinha-Matos

Integrated Smart Energy System Based on Production-Oriented Consumption 265
Ivan Popov, Alexander Krylatov, and Victor Zakharov

Industry 4.0 as Enabler for Effective Manufacturing Virtual Enterprises..... 274
Filipe Ferreira, José Faria, Américo Azevedo, and Ana Luísa Marques

Co-development and Co-working - Collaborative Engineering

Who Can Help to Review This Piece of Code?..................... 289
Noureddine Kerzazi and Ikram El Asri

Product Development in Collaborative Networks – An Expert View on Current Challenges and Future Trends......................... 302
Wei Min Wang, Pascal Lünnemann, Sebastian Neumeyer, Haygazun Hayka, and Rainer Stark

Collaborative Data Mining for Intelligent Home Appliances............. 313
Oliviu Matei, Giovanni Di Orio, Javad Jassbi, José Barata, and Claudio Cenedese

Advances in Production - Product-Services

A Step Towards Customized Product Realization: Methodology for Sensing, Smart and Sustainable Enterprise...................... 327
Dante Chavarria-Barrientos, Rafael Batres, Roberto Perez, Paul K. Wright, and Arturo Molina

Collaboration Driven Requirements for a Product-Service Engineering Platform... 340
Tapani Ryynänen, Iris Karvonen, Heidi Korhonen, and Kim Jansson

Competence Matching in Collaborative Consortia for Service-Enhanced Products 350
Ana Inês Oliveira, Mohammad Shafahi, Hamideh Afsarmanesh, Filipa Ferrada, and Luis M. Camarinha-Matos

Detecting Influencing Behaviour for Product-Service Design Through Big Data Intelligence in Manufacturing. 361
Michael Petychakis, Evmorfia Biliri, Angelos Arvanitakis, Ariadni Michalitsi-Psarrou, Panagiotis Kokkinakos, Fenareti Lampathaki, and Dimitrios Askounis

Advances in Production - Intelligent Product Ecosystems

Tools for Human-Product Collaborative Development of Intelligent Product Service Systems 373
Sebastian Scholze, Ana Correia, Dragan Stokic, Kevin Nagorny, and Philipp Spindler

A Novel Hybrid Engineering Methodology to Enhance Collaboration During the Design and Development of Meta Product Services. 385
Shamaila Iram, Terrence Fernando, and May Bassanino

Intelligent Product and Mechatronic Software Components Facilitating Mass Customization in Collaborative Manufacturing Systems 394
Majid Sorouri and Valeriy Vyatkin

Advances in Production - Product Personalization

Complexity Mitigation in Collaborative Manufacturing Chains 411
Vladimir Modrak and Slavomir Bednar

A Lean Set-Based Design Approach for Development of Customizable Products in Collaborative Networks. 420
João Bastos, Américo Azevedo, and Paulo Ávila

The Effects of Personalization on Collaborative Production Networks Location 433
Laura Macchion, Rosanna Fornasiero, Pamela Danese, and Andrea Vinelli

Services and Cloud - Service Orientation

Services Personalization Approach for a Collaborative Care Ecosystem 443
Thais Andrea Baldissera and Luis M. Camarinha-Matos

Information Governance as a Dynamic Capability in Service Oriented Business Networking 457
Mohammad R. Rasouli, Rik Eshuis, Jos J.M. Trienekens, Rob J. Kusters, and Paul W.P.J. Grefen

An Exploratory Method to Clarify Business Potential in the Context of Industrial Internet – A Case Study. 469
Maarit Tihinen, Marika Iivari, Heikki Ailisto, Marjaana Komi, Jukka Kääriäinen, and Irina Peltomaa

Services and Cloud - Cloud Technology Aspects for Vos

Do Cloud Computing Tools Support the Needs of Virtual Enterprises? 481
Andre F. Ruaro and Ricardo J. Rabelo

Towards Vendor-Agnostic IT-System of IT-Systems with the CEDE Platform 494
A. Luis Osório

Validating Policies for Dynamic and Heterogeneous Cloud Environments . . . 506
Simeon Veloudis, Iraklis Paraskakis, and Christos Petsos

Design Science and Business Models - Design Science Research

Managing Actors, Resources, and Activities in Innovation Ecosystems – A Design Science Approach. 521
Katri Valkokari, Cristina C. Amitrano, Francesco Bifulco, and Tiina Valjakka

Situating Case Studies Within the Design Science Research Paradigm: An Instantiation for Collaborative Networks 531
Eric Costa, António Lucas Soares, and Jorge Pinho de Sousa

Layout Design and Reconfiguration in a Collaborative Manufacturing Network. 545
Maria Manuela Azevedo, José António Crispim, and Jorge Pinho de Sousa

Design Science and Business Models - Business Models in Hyperconnected Context

Business Models Based on Co-opetition in a Hyper-Connected Era: The Case of 5G-Enabled Smart Grids 559
Sara Moqaddamerad, Yueqiang Xu, Marika Iivari, and Petri Ahokangas

A Collaborative Decisional System to Support a Business Model for the Development of Charging Infrastructure 569
Giuseppe Ianniello, Michela Piccarozzi, Ilaria Baffo, Giuseppe Stecca, and Pasquale Carotenuto

Business Model Boutique: A Prêt-à-Porter Solution for Business Model Innovation in SMEs 579
Sander Smit, Garyfallos Fragidis, Siegfried Handschuh, and Adamantios Koumpis

A Framework for Applying Data Integration and Curation Pipelines to Support Integration of Migrants and Refugees in Europe 588
Oya Deniz Beyan, Siegfried Handschuh, Adamantios Koumpis, Garyfallos Fragidis, and Stefan Decker

Emerging Applications - Agribusiness Value Chain

A Collaborative Architecture for Supply Chain Transparency Based on EPCIS Standard and MongoDB 599
Giulia Bruno and Vincenzo Viola

Modelling Pricing Policy Based on Shelf-Life of Non Homogeneous Available-to-Promise in Fruit Supply Chains 608
Hanzel Grillo, M.M.E. Alemany, and A. Ortiz

The Supply Chain Improvement Through Primary Collaboration. An Action Research Experience 618
Jesús García-Arca, J. Carlos Prado-Prado, and A. Trinidad González-Portela

Emerging Applications - Collaborative Networks in Circular Economy

Mapping Multidimensional Value(s) for Co-creation Networks in a Circular Economy. 629
Anna Aminoff, Katri Valkokari, and Outi Kettunen

Green Virtual Business Network for Managing and Reusing Waste Between Partner Organizations 639
Ahm Shamsuzzoha, Petri Helo, and Maqsood Sandhu

Establishing Networks for the Treatment of WEEE Components. 652
Mohammadtaghi Falsafi and Rosanna Fornasiero

Circular Economy in Shipbuilding and Marine Networks – A Focus on Remanufacturing in Ship Repair. 661
Kim Jansson

Author Index 673

Hyperconnectivity and Interoperation - Hyperconnected Systems

Towards a Hyperconnected Transportation Management System: Application to Blood Logistics

Quentin Schoen[1], Matthieu Lauras[1(✉)], Sébastien Truptil[1], Franck Fontanili[1], and Anne-Ghislaine Anquetil[2]

[1] Industrial Engineering Department, University of Toulouse – Mines Albi, Albi, France
{quentin.schoen,matthieu.lauras,sebastien.truptil, franck.fontanili}@mines-albi.fr
[2] Service Logistique, EFS Pyrénées-Méditerranée, Toulouse, France
anne-ghislaine.anquetil@efs.sante.fr

Abstract. Internet of Things, connected devices, and other wireless sensors networks offer a number of new opportunities to manage transportation flows. This is particularly interesting for critical Supply Chains like Blood Supply Chains. In this research work, we investigate how such new technologies can enhance transportation system by better managing hazards and changes. By developing an event-driven decision support system, we demonstrate how a hyperconnected solution could change the way to design and control transportation routes. This decision support system will both inform users in real-time with relevant information and propose appropriate behaviors. This system will also allow improving the whole collaboration that exists between the shippers, the carriers and the customers. A dawning application to the Blood Logistics in France is developed to highlight potential benefits of such an approach.

Keywords: Hyperconnected · Transportation · Event-driven system · Decision support system · Blood logistics

1 Introduction and Research Objective

During the last decade the world has been drastically changed with the arrival of an important number of connected technologies and devices. *Internet-of-Things* [1] or *Hyperconnected Systems* [13] are some concrete means of this major change. This new approach is now essential in the wireless telecommunications domain [1]. The concept is based on the fact that *things*, *objects* or *devices* able to interact with each other are today everywhere [5] as far as legacy systems like ERP, APS, WMS. A common characteristic of those systems is their ability to emit in real-time a huge number of data. They are used nowadays in various domains like home, industry, leisure or marketing. The field of Supply Chain Management and Logistics is also continuously evolving regarding these new opportunities and a new type of projects appears. A lot of them focus on the use of new connected technologies to better support goods traceability [2, 7] or resources tracking [11, 17]. A great majority of existing research works on

H. Afsarmanesh et al. (Eds.): PRO-VE 2016, IFIP AICT 480, pp. 3–12, 2016.
DOI: 10.1007/978-3-319-45390-3_1

connected logistics are focusing on data collection and transmission, but very few are studying the use of these data to support concretely decisions. As pointed by [4], this is an important lack of current uses of *Internet of Things* and *Hyperconnected Systems*. This work indicated that one major room for improvement consists in developing systems able to transform all this raw and dynamic data into contextualized knowledge able to concretely support decisions. Our research aim is to contribute to this objective by proposing an innovative Transportation Management System (TMS) module able to use the knowledge produced by connected device and systems to support routing decisions in real-time. The objective is to help practitioners to be more agile in their decisions by better considering disruption, variability and hazard. Thanks to this agility, the blood transportation must be optimized which is necessary to face with the sensitiveness of blood components, the products diversity and the urgency of some needs.

The paper is divided into four sections. The first one discusses some key points on literature about this subject. The second one develops the proposed decision support system architecture. The third one presents the solution to enhance the agility capability while the fourth one describes an application case about the shipment of blood pouches to French hospitals.

2 Literature Review

2.1 Flexibility and Agility Needs

Naim et al. [10] affirm that to be competitive and sustainable, modern logistics must increase their flexibility capabilities. They described the flexibility through three logistics categories. First, there is the *routine logistics service* that limits flexibility requirements. In such case, the carrier is competing on price and time. He has to be able to gather road traffic information in order to adapt to route disruptions. Such a carrier should propose vehicles that are flexible or at least a fleet that is composed of different types of vehicles. Second, there is the *standard logistics service*. Here, the carrier proposes higher flexibility regarding the delivery and the mix. The collaboration is no longer adequate, the cooperation between carrier and shipper is required in order to ensure good coordination of their activities. In such a situation, stakeholders have to share information, plans and schedules. If the carrier cannot propose such level of collaboration, he has to develop collaboration with another one. This partnership should at least ensure coordination of activities. This should make larger the potential flexibility capacity offers. Finally, there is *customized logistics service* that offers a complete set of flexibility options. Complementary to delivery and mix, volume and product, external flexibility types are proposed. A close collaboration agreement between the shipper and the carrier is necessary as they have to closely work at a strategic, planning and execution level, and as they have also to share data and information at all levels. If the logistics offers becomes critical then, such a kind of collaboration can conduct to the creation of a single company (like a joint-venture for instance).

As delivery processes usually discuss the dynamic adjustments of vehicle [15], other academics emphasized on the agility requirements for Supply Chain and logistics. According to [4], agility can be considered as the ability to perform detection and adaptation to events (in a rapid and efficient manner). [6] show that existing decision support systems are often a critical factor in applying agility in the Supply Chain. The authors have demonstrated that to develop the Supply Chain agility, the speed and flexibility capabilities must be enhanced through dedicated decision support systems. Existing systems are generally relevant for managing the business processes of a given organization [6]. They concluded that existing decision support systems were designed for internal logistics management and they missed to support the logistics coordination capabilities that are particularly critical for the management of agility in Supply Chains. Even such systems have allowed enhancing the performance of some organizations; they are not sufficient to really support the agility in logistics business processes [6].

As a consequence, future developments in matter of logistics decision support systems will have to consider agility capabilities.

2.2 Transportation Management System

Transportation Management System (TMS) assists companies with moving goods from a point A to a point B within a high level of performance (efficiency, reliability, and cost effectiveness). Such a system generally includes route planning and optimization, load optimization, execution, freight audit and payment, yard management, advanced shipping, order visibility and carriers management. TMS is not new and the literature on this subject is rich. One major concern is the Vehicle Routing Problem (VRP) as it represents the heart of a TMS. VRP formulation is a generalization of the Traveling Salesman Problem (TSP). Since 60's, academics have continuously improved the way to optimize the VRP as demonstrated by [12]. In their review, they explain that the VRP is generally a graph composed of a set of routes for K identical vehicles based at a depot (initial node of the graph), such that each of the customers (nodes of the graph) is visited exactly once, while minimizing the routing costs. They indicate also that various variants have been developed in the literature during the last decades:

- Capacitated VRP: customers have demand for freight and vehicles have finite capacity;
- VRP with Time Windows: customers have to be visited during a specific time frame;
- VRP with Pick-up and Delivery: freight has to be shipped in given amounts at nodes;
- Heterogeneous fleet VRP: same than previously but with vehicles that have different capacities.

More recently new kind of TMS research projects appeared. Most of them have been tried to develop sustainable and smart transportation solutions able to solve the ecological and fuel shortage issues. Suzuki [14] for instance proposed a new truck-routing approach for reducing fuel consumption while Mehar et al. [9] presented a survey on sustainable TMS that aim to reduce ecological impacts. Mehar et al. [9] reviewed the existing solutions for green transportation and described also the future elements that have to be developed for limiting the ecological impact of transportation. But the major trend is about the use of mobile and connected technologies within TMS. Authors like [16] have proposed the implementation of a smart onboard *Global Position System*

(GPS)/General Packet Radio Service (GPRS) system to be implemented into vehicles for tracking their speed. This allows sending in a real time a message including the location and the speed, in case of traffic speed violation. Other research works have developed real time vehicles monitoring and smart TMS using smartphones [8]. This research project was composed of four parts: (1) web system (2) TMS real time tracking application (3) real time tracking application for customer (4) salesman supporting application. Last but not least, authors like Kim et al. [8] have proposed Smart TMS to better support the coordination between the logistics stakeholders. Actually, as the authors mentioned, carriers' environment is more and more complex and the stakeholders have to manage an increasingly number of data flow. This imposes new kinds of TMS that better manage information between partners, increase goods traceability, better monitor involved business processes, and support improving dynamic routing and security [8]. If there is a strong trend to improve the transmission and the gathering of data through different technologies connected to TMS, very few research works seem to have studied the concrete use of this huge amount of data.

We consequently hold that if TMS are quite mature, a room for improvement still exists regarding the development of dedicated decision support systems able to benefit of the extreme wealth that connected devices produce.

3 Proposal

3.1 Approach

Based on previous literature analysis, we have decided to develop an event-oriented platform able to help TMS users to enhance their agility capabilities. In this study, agility is considered as a way to adapt the dynamic of the situation and can be defined as follow [3]:

$$\text{Agility} = (\text{Detection} + \text{Adaption}) * \text{Reactivity} \tag{1}$$

- The detection is the disclosure of a situation gap that makes the ongoing business processes not relevant to the running situation,
- The adaptation is executed, when a gap occurs, to change the current business processes to make them better relevant to the context,
- The reactivity is a property that has to ensure that detection and adaptation are done in a real-time (as fast as possible).

From this definition, it appears that agility permits to detect if the ongoing transportation process meets the requirements of the existing situation, and to adjust those processes in case of need.

3.2 Agility Services

Our detection module is based on [3]. In this paper, the authors proposed a step able to disclose a gap based on 3 main phases (see Fig. 1):

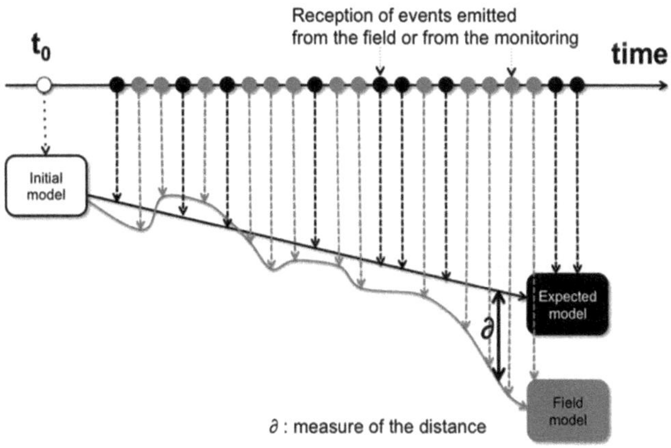

Fig. 1. Principles of divergence detection [3]

1. Establish a model of the situation in order to describe what should be the expected state when the processes will be applied and a model of the field to get a view of the current processes and real environment,
2. Identify potential gaps that might exist between the two models,
3. Calculate the distance that exists between the models to confirm or not the relevance of the ongoing business processes.

As mentioned earlier, agility needs both detection and adaptation. For the detection purpose, we propose to use connected devices and aggregate data they send continuously to create a contextualized knowledge and support concretely decisions. As for the adaptation purpose, we have developed a module that is able to measure the differences collected during the phase of detection. To reach such a goal, we define a set of business rules, which lists the different options that can be applied according to the nature of the detected difference. Then, the agility component is able to compare different options and select the best option(s) for adjustment to the TMS users. We have to remark here that the user always makes the final decision. The proposed solution is a decision support system that alerts on potential failures and suggests potential solutions. The system does not make automatic decisions instead of practitioners.

3.3 Architecture

The previous components have been implemented in a TMS platform that combines different technologies to manage collection, analysis and processing (decision-support) of events as real-time information. Figure 2 is a representation of this architecture that is divided into three parts: *Field*, *software architecture* and *monitoring*.

The *Field* aims at producing information about the situation without users' efforts. In order to be able to gather data about location and/or temperature of each product all the time, a possible solution consists in embedding sensors inside box and/or trucks (hyperconnection of containers). Indeed, these sensors are able to send data through

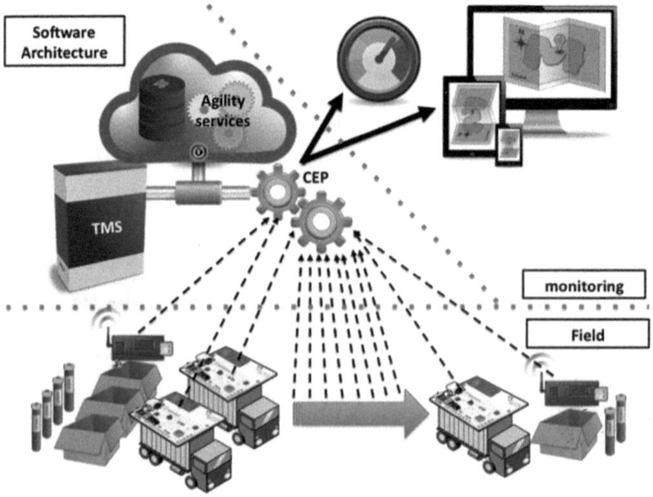

Fig. 2. Proposed hyperconnected TMS architecture.

several networks, as LTE, Bluetooth, ZigBee, Wifi or Sigfox, and thus it is possible to collect the information.

For now, TMS software is not able to collect and manage data producing by sensors. Therefore, the *software architecture* part provides a connected layer in charge of collecting, managing data from the *Field* and analyzing the situation thanks to an agility services describing in the previous section. This layer is based on Event Driven Architecture (EDA) and thus it is able to store, aggregate, forward events thanks to complex event processing (CEP) and database.

The last part aims at helping the user to *monitor* the situation thanks to Geographical Information System (GIS), indicators and result of the models comparison. Information visible on this layer is deduced from the TMS and the information from the *Field*.

4 Application Case

We develop in this section the case of French blood shipments to delivery centers. The French Blood Organization is split in 14 metropolitan regions. In each region, there are several places where people can donate their blood. In addition, the delivery centers are "blood supermarkets" where hospitals come to pick up the end products, derived from donors' blood, in order to treat patients. This donation and delivery places are often in the same site. In general, each region is made up of 20 to 30 sites.

The blood collected in donation centers have to be carried to the hub of the region where its components will be separated and filtered in order to make up end products. To ensure the use case accessibility, from now we only considerate the flow of end products (blood pouch) from the hub to the delivery centers.

In each region, daily rounds are planned to deliver the end products to the delivery centers. For instance, we consider that 5 sites, where the carrier has to deliver blood-derived product, constitute a round. Each site is around 40–80 km away from the other.

Currently, a truck leaves the hub with parcels that contain blood pouch for each site of its round. Because these products are very specific the French Blood Organization tries to deliver a broad range of products (blood pouch with different characteristics) to each site. However, it occurs often that a site needs as a matter of urgency a blood pouch that is not in its stock. In this case, the logistics department asks to one of its carriers it has a transportation contract with, for an urgent transport from the site (or the hub) that owned this blood pouch to the site that needs it.

Our idea is to be able to gather all the information linked with a round (sites, blood pouch ID, temperature, traffic jam, stock, etc.) to make it more efficient. The main goal is to be able to gather these data from all the sensors and databases to observe in real time the differences between the transportation process expected and the real one. Finally, we expect to save money and be able to manage with more efficiency the transportation activity. From this comparison, the proposed hyperconnected TMS will be able to suggest potential solutions. To permit this on going comparison and analysis, we have to define ad hoc business rules like:

- If a site of your round needs as a matter of urgency a product you will deliver it in more than 2 h, deliver it first to reduce this period.
- If there is an important traffic jam on the road between your site and the next one, deliver the third one first.
- If the temperature of the blood pouches in your truck is too high because of an unknown failure, go to the nearer site to stock these products.

Let us consider the following scenario as an illustrative example. In this scenario, there are one hub and five sites (Fig. 3). The carrier will drive 450 km and follow the following instructions:

- Start from the hub at 5 pm with the parcels prepared for the sites you are going to.
- Arriving at 5.20 pm to "Site 1", deliver parcels for this site, leave at 5.30 pm.
- Arriving at 6.30 pm to "Site 2", deliver parcels for this site, leave at 6.40 pm.
- Arriving at 7 pm to "Site 3", deliver parcels for this site, leave at 7.10 pm.
- Arriving at 7.20 pm to "Site 4", deliver parcels for this site, leave at 7.30 pm.

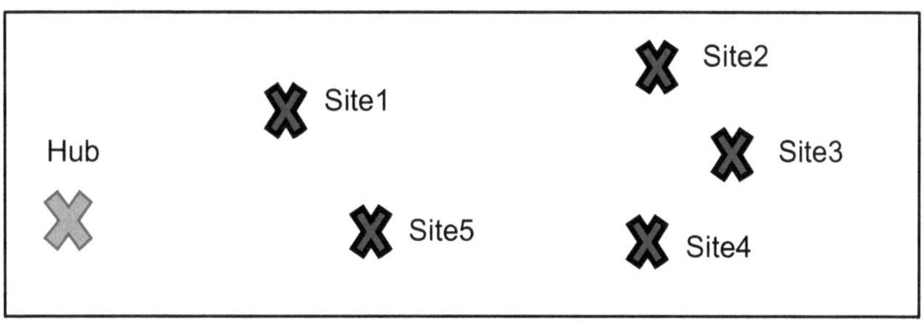

Fig. 3. Localization of the different delivery sites

11. Pérez, J., Seco, F., Milanés, V., Jiménez, A., Díaz, J.C., De Pedro, T.: An RFID-based intelligent vehicle speed controller using active traffic signals. Sensors **10**(6), 5872–5887 (2010)
12. Pillac, V., Gendreau, M., Guéret, C., Medaglia, A.L.: A review of dynamic vehicle routing problems. Eur. J. Oper. Res. **225**(1), 1–11 (2013)
13. Sallez, Y., Pan, S., Montreuil, B., Berger, T., Ballot, E.: On the activeness of intelligent Physical Internet containers. Comput. Ind. **81**, 96–104 (2016)
14. Suzuki, Y.: A new truck-routing approach for reducing fuel consumption and pollutants emission. Transp. Res. Part D: Transp. Environ. **16**(1), 73–77 (2011)
15. Taniguchi, E., Shimamoto, H.: Intelligent transportation system based dynamic vehicle routing and scheduling with variable travel times. Transp. Res. Part C: Emerg. Technol. **12**, 235–250 (2004)
16. Tarapiah, S., Atalla, S., AbuHania, R.: Smart on-board transportation management system using GPS/GSM/GPRS technologies to reduce traffic violation in developing countries. Int. J. Digit. Inf. Wirel. Commun. (IJDIWC) **3**(4), 430–439 (2013)
17. Yu-fang, D.A.N., Qing-lu, M.A.: Logistic transportation system based on integration of RFID, GPS and GIS technology. Appl. Res. Comput. **12**, 062 (2009)

d from a large-scale scenario [24], from taxis in the city of Porto. f 41.3 km^2, and contains 965 km of roads which make it the second gal. It has with more than one million inhabitants and is in a center ea. There are 441 taxis and 63 taxi stands in the city. Each taxi has can collect the log about each trip. The dataset consists of 5 months xis. The dataset contains 13 data features characterizing events [24]. of the scenario where the data is collected, Fig. 2 shows a snapshot of in the city of Porto. The green dots show the taxi positions in the city. range for two taxis (red and black) is also shown by purple circles.

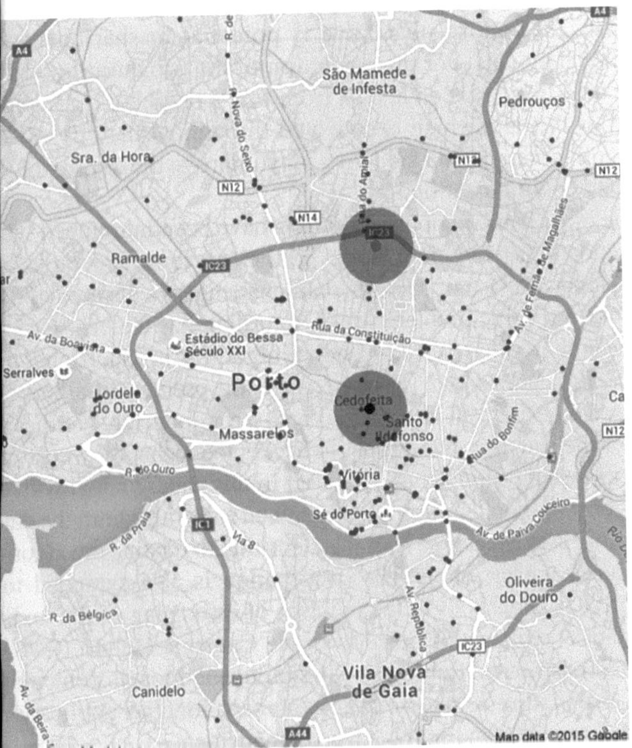

map of Porto, Portugal. The green dots are the initial taxi placement. The ge for the red and the black taxi is shown by a purple circle around them. (Color

months data in 2013. Table 1 shows the number of taxis and the average ations for each taxi in each month. There are around 440 taxis and on between 1238–1484 observations for each taxi. The fourth and fifth v the minimum and the maximum number of observations per each taxi, t can be seen, there are taxis with few examples (2–14 observations). In ggregation to use data from other taxis may be useful for modeling.

Collaborative Data Analysis in Hyperconnected Transportation Systems

Mohammad Nozari Zarmehri(✉) and Carlos Soares

INESC TEC, Faculdade de Engenharia, Universidade do Porto (FEUP), Rua Dr. Roberto Frias, 378, Porto, Portugal
{mohammad.nozari,csoares}@fe.up.pt

Abstract. Taxi trip duration affects the efficiency of operation, the satisfaction of drivers, and, mainly, the satisfaction of the customers, therefore, it is an important metric for the taxi companies. Especially, knowing the predicted trip duration beforehand is very useful to allocate taxis to the taxi stands and also finding the best route for different trips. The existence of hyperconnected network can help to collect data from connected taxis in the city environment and use it collaboratively between taxis for a better prediction. As a matter of fact, the existence of high volume of data, for each individual taxi, several models can be generated. Moreover, taking into account the difference between the data collected by taxis, this data can be organized into different levels of hierarchy. However, finding the best level of granularity which leads to the best model for an individual taxi could be computationally expensive. In this paper, the use of metalearning for addressing the problem of selection of the right level of the hierarchy and the right algorithm that generates the model with the best performance for each taxi is proposed. The proposed approach is evaluated by the data collected in the Drive-In project. The results show that metalearning helps the selection of the algorithm with the best performance.

Keywords: Hyperconnected world · Machine learning · Metalearning · Data mining · Intelligent transportation systems · Collaborative data analysis

1 Introduction

Hyperconnectivity is used to define the interconnectedness of people, organizations, and objects which result from different technology innovations like the Internet, mobile technology and the Internet of Things (IoT) [1]. The hyperconnectivity exists not only in the communication between people but also in the connectivity of cars [2]. In addition, to make the travel and transportation more efficient and more comfortable, the hyperconnectivity is the main driver of innovation [3].

On the other hand, the transportation system is clearly overloaded by congestion in the major cities. For example in the city center of London, the average speed of cars is 14 km/h [4] while the car's speed in the city center of Moscow is around 6 km/h [5]. Positively, this can be an opportunity to improve interconnectedness of cars in the city environment. These cars can be parts of the communication infrastructure for the Intelligent

H. Afsarmanesh et al. (Eds.): PRO-VE 2016, IFIP AICT 480, pp. 13–23, 2016.
DOI: 10.1007/978-3-319-45390-3_2

Transportation Systems (ITS) and also offer various opportunities for gathering data about a city by continually sensing events from streets and process sensed data.

Therefore, utilizing vehicular networks as an infrastructure for urban sensing is a cost-efficient way of deploying an urban monitoring system without actually deploying connected sensors [6] (Fig. 1 shows a snapshot of the communication between moving cars within the city of Porto). Vehicles typically do not have energy constraints. Therefore, cars can be equipped with powerful wireless transmitters, processing units, and sensing devices (vibration sensors, GPS, video cameras, detectors, acoustic detectors, car sensors, etc.).

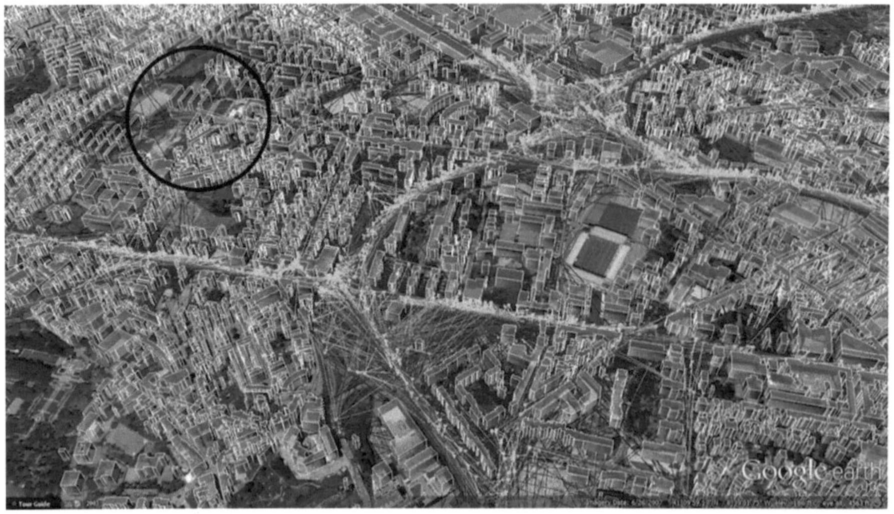

Fig. 1. A snapshot showing exchanged messages between taxis in the city of Porto [18]

Thousands of cars which are networked together using wireless communication are able to connect us to a seemingly unlimited data gathered from the city environment. The gathered data can be processed and visualized live, enabling monitoring activities (Fig. 1) and better decision making. However, this data can also be serve as the basis for predictive models that can be an informative tool for the decision support systems one step further. Given the availability of the massive amount of data which is geographically distributed, data mining approaches are being used to obtain models for all parts of the city that are integrated into ITS applications [7–14].

One of the interesting examples of ITS applications is the prediction of trip duration for public transportation [15–17]. Knowing the prediction of trip duration beforehand can be very instructive for taxi companies, passengers, and drivers to make the right decision for the route planning and scheduling by using the data collected about the taxi's trips by each taxi. Figure 1 shows a snapshot of exchanged messages between taxis in the city of Porto.

Machine learning algorithms by using the data collected by taxis relate the trip duration to several data features which describe the trip like the time of the trip, origin,

destination, the weather, and the week
vary from one taxi to another, due to dif
the driving habits, and the route.

In addition, taking advantage of the
of having a more specific model for an
taxis in the traditional data mining appr
transportation system.

However, this is not true for all ta
for creating an accurate model for all
like the area indicated in Fig. 1 with a
modeling. In this case, a collaborativ
improve the quality of the model by us
results [19, 20] confirm that there is
learning local models. For the predicti
different data like taxi's data, data fro
side unit, or the data which is collecte
Further, collaborative data modeling m
cost of data communication.

On the other hand, various algorithm
the prediction of trip duration. However,
several challenges. One of the important
discover for a specific problem which al
already been shown that there is no unique
for a broad problem domain [21]. Therefo
either based on expert advice or a trial-an
factory for the end user who wishes to ac

A metalearning approach [23] is used
which algorithm should be used, and (2) w
Metalearning uses a machine learning algo
to the data characterization. The contrib
collaborative data analysis to the problem
the taxi dataset which is obtained from th
DRIVE-IN (Distributed Routing and Infota
[24]. We also (4) discuss the use of this app
facturing of products and supply chain ma

The rest of the paper is organized as foll
and the results of the experiment. An exter
Finally, Sect. 4 concludes the paper.

2 An Example of Collaborative Transportation System

In this section, a collaborative data analysi
dataset from hyperconnected transportatio
approach is evaluated on the dataset and the

2.1 Taxi Data

The data is collect
Porto has an area o
largest city in Port
of a metropolitan a
a GPS receiver and
in 2013 for all the t

As an example
the taxis placement
The communicatio

Fig. 2. Illustrativ
communication ran
figure online)

There are five
number of obser
average, there ar
columns also sho
respectively. As
these cases, data

Collaborative Data Analysis in Hyperconnected Transportation Systems

Mohammad Nozari Zarmehri(✉) and Carlos Soares

INESC TEC, Faculdade de Engenharia, Universidade do Porto (FEUP), Rua Dr. Roberto Frias, 378, Porto, Portugal
{mohammad.nozari,csoares}@fe.up.pt

Abstract. Taxi trip duration affects the efficiency of operation, the satisfaction of drivers, and, mainly, the satisfaction of the customers, therefore, it is an important metric for the taxi companies. Especially, knowing the predicted trip duration beforehand is very useful to allocate taxis to the taxi stands and also finding the best route for different trips. The existence of hyperconnected network can help to collect data from connected taxis in the city environment and use it collaboratively between taxis for a better prediction. As a matter of fact, the existence of high volume of data, for each individual taxi, several models can be generated. Moreover, taking into account the difference between the data collected by taxis, this data can be organized into different levels of hierarchy. However, finding the best level of granularity which leads to the best model for an individual taxi could be computationally expensive. In this paper, the use of metalearning for addressing the problem of selection of the right level of the hierarchy and the right algorithm that generates the model with the best performance for each taxi is proposed. The proposed approach is evaluated by the data collected in the Drive-In project. The results show that metalearning helps the selection of the algorithm with the best performance.

Keywords: Hyperconnected world · Machine learning · Metalearning · Data mining · Intelligent transportation systems · Collaborative data analysis

1 Introduction

Hyperconnectivity is used to define the interconnectedness of people, organizations, and objects which result from different technology innovations like the Internet, mobile technology and the Internet of Things (IoT) [1]. The hyperconnectivity exists not only in the communication between people but also in the connectivity of cars [2]. In addition, to make the travel and transportation more efficient and more comfortable, the hyperconnectivity is the main driver of innovation [3].

On the other hand, the transportation system is clearly overloaded by congestion in the major cities. For example in the city center of London, the average speed of cars is 14 km/h [4] while the car's speed in the city center of Moscow is around 6 km/h [5]. Positively, this can be an opportunity to improve interconnectedness of cars in the city environment. These cars can be parts of the communication infrastructure for the Intelligent

H. Afsarmanesh et al. (Eds.): PRO-VE 2016, IFIP AICT 480, pp. 13–23, 2016.
DOI: 10.1007/978-3-319-45390-3_2

Transportation Systems (ITS) and also offer various opportunities for gathering data about a city by continually sensing events from streets and process sensed data.

Therefore, utilizing vehicular networks as an infrastructure for urban sensing is a cost-efficient way of deploying an urban monitoring system without actually deploying connected sensors [6] (Fig. 1 shows a snapshot of the communication between moving cars within the city of Porto). Vehicles typically do not have energy constraints. Therefore, cars can be equipped with powerful wireless transmitters, processing units, and sensing devices (vibration sensors, GPS, video cameras, detectors, acoustic detectors, car sensors, etc.).

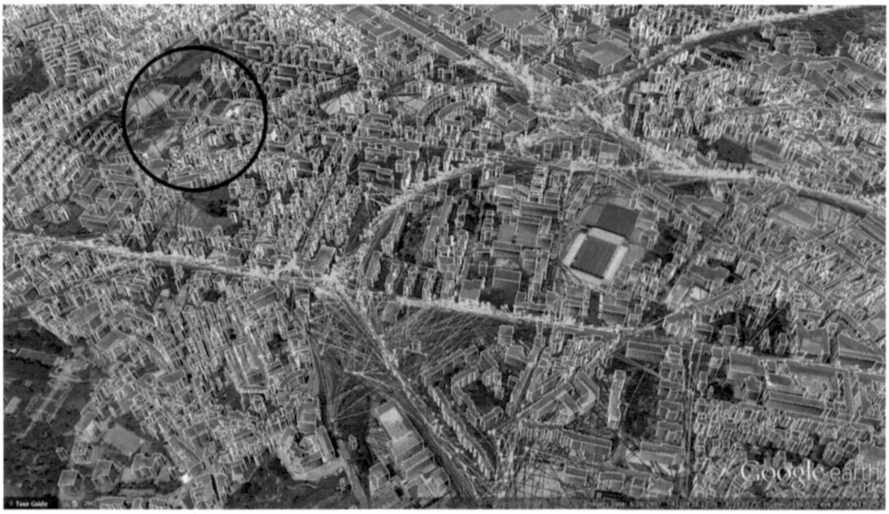

Fig. 1. A snapshot showing exchanged messages between taxis in the city of Porto [18]

Thousands of cars which are networked together using wireless communication are able to connect us to a seemingly unlimited data gathered from the city environment. The gathered data can be processed and visualized live, enabling monitoring activities (Fig. 1) and better decision making. However, this data can also be serve as the basis for predictive models that can be an informative tool for the decision support systems one step further. Given the availability of the massive amount of data which is geographically distributed, data mining approaches are being used to obtain models for all parts of the city that are integrated into ITS applications [7–14].

One of the interesting examples of ITS applications is the prediction of trip duration for public transportation [15–17]. Knowing the prediction of trip duration beforehand can be very instructive for taxi companies, passengers, and drivers to make the right decision for the route planning and scheduling by using the data collected about the taxi's trips by each taxi. Figure 1 shows a snapshot of exchanged messages between taxis in the city of Porto.

Machine learning algorithms by using the data collected by taxis relate the trip duration to several data features which describe the trip like the time of the trip, origin, destination, the weather, and the week's day. The prediction of duration of the trip may vary from one taxi to another, due to differences in the taxi usage, the brand of the vehicle, the driving habits, and the route.

In addition, taking advantage of the massive amount of gathered data, the possibility of having a more specific model for an individual taxi instead of a global model for all taxis in the traditional data mining approaches is a reality in the current hyperconnected transportation system.

However, this is not true for all taxis due to the lack of existence of enough data for creating an accurate model for all taxis. For example, in a sparse area of the city, like the area indicated in Fig. 1 with a circle, only a few observations is available for modeling. In this case, a collaborative data modeling would be a good solution to improve the quality of the model by using the data from other sources. The previous results [19, 20] confirm that there is potential in sharing data in the process of learning local models. For the prediction of the trip duration, different taxis can use different data like taxi's data, data from taxi's neighbors, data collected at the road-side unit, or the data which is collected throughout the city (different dimensions). Further, collaborative data modeling may improve the quality of the prediction in the cost of data communication.

On the other hand, various algorithms have been introduced which can be used for the prediction of trip duration. However, their performance varies and therefore causes several challenges. One of the important challenges in the area of data mining is that to discover for a specific problem which algorithm has the best performance. Yet, it has already been shown that there is no unique algorithm in which it has the best performance for a broad problem domain [21]. Therefore, the problem of algorithm selection is done either based on expert advice or a trial-and-error approach. Neither way is utterly satisfactory for the end user who wishes to access the technology cost-effectively [22].

A metalearning approach [23] is used in this paper to deal with these problems: (1) which algorithm should be used, and (2) when and with whom the data should be shared. Metalearning uses a machine learning algorithm to relating the algorithm's performance to the data characterization. The contribution is also extended to (3) applying this collaborative data analysis to the problem of estimating of the taxi trip duration using the taxi dataset which is obtained from the Carnegie Mellon (CMU) Portugal project, DRIVE-IN (Distributed Routing and Infotainment through Vehicular Inter-networking) [24]. We also (4) discuss the use of this approach for other applications including manufacturing of products and supply chain management.

The rest of the paper is organized as follow. Section 2 explains the proposed approach and the results of the experiment. An extension of the approach is discussed in Sect. 3. Finally, Sect. 4 concludes the paper.

2 An Example of Collaborative Data Analysis in Hyperconnected Transportation System

In this section, a collaborative data analysis (Sect. 2.2) is introduced and applied to a dataset from hyperconnected transportation system (Sect. 2.1). Then, the proposed approach is evaluated on the dataset and the results are presented in Sect. 2.3.

2.1 Taxi Data

The data is collected from a large-scale scenario [24], from taxis in the city of Porto. Porto has an area of 41.3 km^2, and contains 965 km of roads which make it the second largest city in Portugal. It has with more than one million inhabitants and is in a center of a metropolitan area. There are 441 taxis and 63 taxi stands in the city. Each taxi has a GPS receiver and can collect the log about each trip. The dataset consists of 5 months in 2013 for all the taxis. The dataset contains 13 data features characterizing events [24].

As an example of the scenario where the data is collected, Fig. 2 shows a snapshot of the taxis placements in the city of Porto. The green dots show the taxi positions in the city. The communication range for two taxis (red and black) is also shown by purple circles.

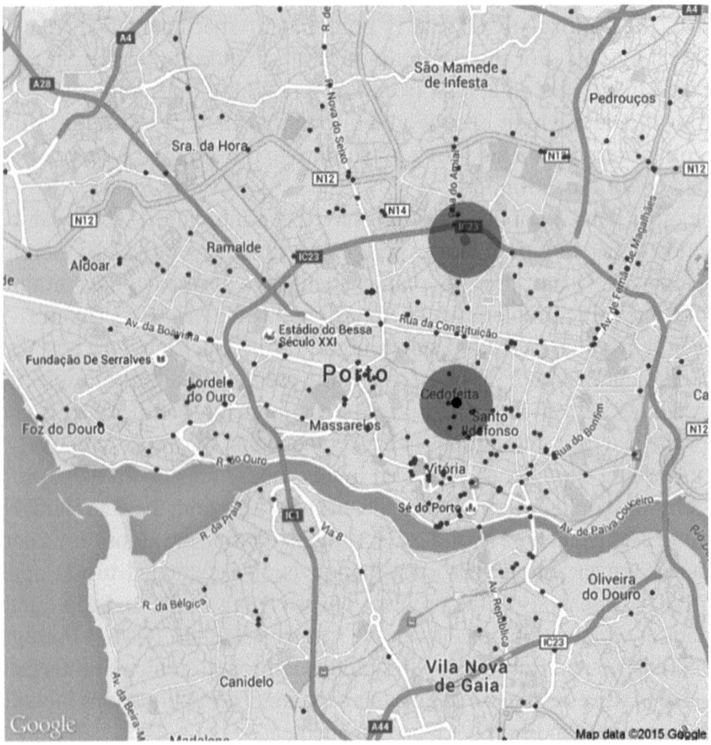

Fig. 2. Illustrative map of Porto, Portugal. The green dots are the initial taxi placement. The communication range for the red and the black taxi is shown by a purple circle around them. (Color figure online)

There are five months data in 2013. Table 1 shows the number of taxis and the average number of observations for each taxi in each month. There are around 440 taxis and on average, there are between 1238–1484 observations for each taxi. The fourth and fifth columns also show the minimum and the maximum number of observations per each taxi, respectively. As it can be seen, there are taxis with few examples (2–14 observations). In these cases, data aggregation to use data from other taxis may be useful for modeling.

Table 1. A simple statistics about Taxi dataset

Month	No. of taxis	Average number of observations per each taxi	Minimum number of observations per each taxi	Maximum number of observations per each taxi
201302	443	1238.5	2	2467
201303	443	1356.6	6	3452
201304	446	1302.7	14	2824
201305	443	1484.9	2	3165
201306	442	1385.7	6	3037

2.2 Collaborative Data Analysis

As mentioned earlier, to improve the problem of algorithms selection and collaborative data modeling, we propose a metalearning approach which helps to select the right algorithm and the right part of data space for each individual taxi. In this section, we briefly describe the methodology which is summarized in Fig. 3.

Fig. 3. Methodology used for a collaborative data analysis in hyperconnected transportation systems

The data collection is done within the DRIVE-IN project [24] (see Sect. 2.1). Then, the dataset is organized in hierarchy structure using two levels of hierarchy: the data associated with a taxi as local data and the data for the whole month as global data.

In the proposed model, at the first level, each taxi (T_i) makes a category, $C_i^1, \forall i \in \{1, \ldots, n_1\}$ where n_1 is the number of taxis. The level two has only one category joining all the data from 440 taxis.

After forming the dataset in a customized format, $DB = \{T_i, C_i^j, y_i\}, \forall i \in \{1, \ldots, 440\}, \forall j \subset \{1, 2\}$, it is passed to the base-level experiment. In the next step, each algorithm is applied on the data from both levels for each taxi.

At the base-level, four machine learning algorithms are applied to the data: support vector machines (SVMs) [25–27], random forest [25–27], decision tree [31–33], and linear regression [31, 32]. As a result, there are several performance indicators for each taxi: P_{ig}^k which indicates the performance of the algorithm g at level k for taxi i.

$$P_{iw}^j : \forall w \in \{1, \ldots, 4\}, \forall j \in \{1, 2\}, \forall i \in \{1, \ldots, 440\} \quad (1)$$

Where w indicates the algorithms, i shows taxis, and j stands for levels.

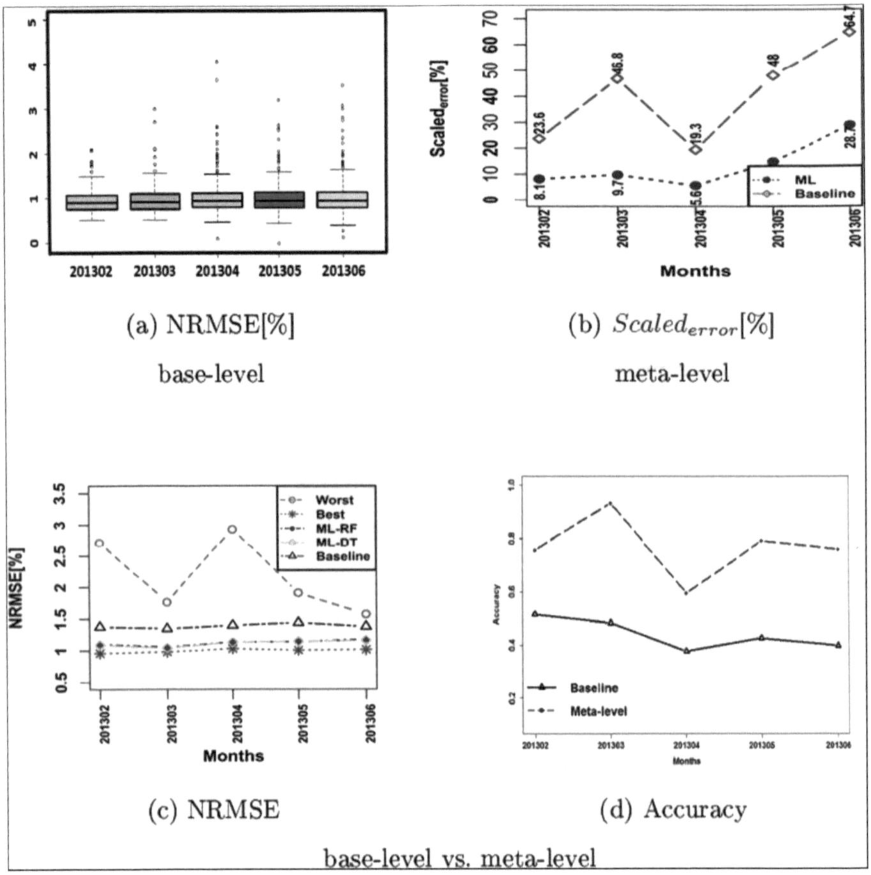

(a) NRMSE[%]

base-level

(b) $Scaled_{error}$[%]

meta-level

(c) NRMSE

(d) Accuracy

base-level vs. meta-level

Fig. 4. Evaluation results (Color figure online)

building a model. In this case, it is recommended to use the global model to have an accurate model.

Meta-Level vs Base-Level Results. The comparison results between the meta-level and the base-level show that the performance of the algorithms selected by the meta-model is near the best performance obtained at the base-level (Fig. 4(c)). The performance of the suggested solution by the meta-level (the blue and the cyan line) is almost close to the best performance at the base-level (the green line) while is better than the baseline performance (the black line). This satisfies our objectives.

Finally, the comparison of accuracy between the baseline (the black line) and the meta-level (the blue line) is illustrated in Fig. 4(d). According to these results, the performance of the meta-level exceeds the performance of the baseline for all months.

3 Discussion

The proposed approach in this paper helps to identify the best solution for the problem of prediction of taxi trip duration to improve the taxi utilization and passenger satisfaction. Using the hyperconnected intelligent systems, this proposal can be used by different applications including manufacturing of products by forecasting of product demands, supply chain management by predicting of the best location of stocks, and real-time optimization of supply chain networks by prediction of the best route for fleets, through networking machinery, sensors and control systems together.

All manufacturers have a desire to give their consumers exactly what they want. This can be done by using past data collected from sales and production lines and forecasting the demand for a product. Our proposed approach can be implemented in this case by organizing the past data into hierarchy structure. One of possible solution can be using three different hierarchy levels: the data associated with a product, the data related to a group of products which have the same type, i.e. foods, clothes, and so on, and all the data.

Another example is supply chain management where a poor stock's location can give low productivity, unreliable deliveries of materials, high costs, and poor customer service. The same approach can be done using the data that can be collected from the logistics and also stocks movement within the supply chain. The approach can help to deal with the uncertain and non-stationary demand with minimum cost.

The hyperconnected networks and IoT present excellent possibilities for businesses to conduct through evolution and innovation. For this purpose, companies need to be aware of the changing of the business dynamics caused by innovation.

4 Conclusion

The existence of hyperconnected networks can make a revolution in the public transportation systems. High resource utilization and customer satisfaction are two major metrics which can be achieved using hyperconnected networks and machine learning approaches. In this paper, a metalearning proposal is introduced for the prediction of taxi trip duration to improve the taxi utilization and passenger's satisfaction by using a collaborative data analysis. The proposed approach aims at assisting taxi companies, passengers, and the public authorities for better distributing taxis to the taxi stands and determining the best route for the taxi trips using appropriate learning algorithm for the prediction of taxi trip duration. The experiments are carried out on the data collected in the Drive-In project. Several models are obtained from two levels of granularity: taxi itself and whole taxis. The results demonstrate that the proposed metalearning framework can help recommending an algorithm with the best performance at the base-level with high accuracy and outperforms the baseline accuracy. Furthermore, the performance of the base-level is also substantially adequate. In overall, the metalearning forecasts the duration of the taxi trip with the error rate less than 5 %.

As interesting future works, this approach can be extended to other parts of the hyperconnected networks, i.e. manufacturing of products and supply chain management, as discussed in Sect. 3.

Acknowledgment. This research work has received funding from the ECSEL Joint Undertaking, the framework programme for research and innovation horizon 2020 (2014–2020) under grant agreement number 662189-MANTIS-2014-1.

References

1. T. E. I. U. Limited: The Hyperconnected Economy: Phase 2, Hyperconnected Organizations, London (2015)
2. G. S. M. A. for the SBD: 2025 Every Car Connected: Forecasting the Growth and Opportunity, London (2012)
3. T. W. E. Forum: Connected World Transforming Travel, Transportation and Supply Chains, Geneva (2013)
4. TfL: Performance Report Quarter 1 2012/13, London (2013)
5. Siemens: Pictures of the Future. Livable Megacities – Moscow and St. Petersburg, Russ (2007)
6. Englund, C., Chen, L., Vinel, A., Lin, S.: Future applications of VANETs. In: Campolo, C., Molinaro, A., Scopigno, R. (eds.) Vehicular Ad Hoc Networks, pp. 525–544. Springer International Publishing, Switzerland (2015)
7. Thill, J.-C.: Geographic information systems for transportation in perspective. Transp. Res. Part C: Emerg. Technol. **8**(1), 3–12 (2000)
8. Hauser, T.A., Scherer, W.T.: Data mining tools for real-time traffic signal decision support & maintenance. In: 2001 IEEE International Conference on Systems, Man, and Cybernetics (2001)
9. Chan, C.-Y., Marco, D.: Traffic monitoring at signal-controlled intersections and data mining for safety applications. In: 2004 Proceedings of the 7th International IEEE Conference on Intelligent Transportation Systems (2004)
10. Salim, F.D., Loke, S.W., Rakotonirainy, A., Srinivasan, B., Krishnaswamy, S.: Collision pattern modeling and real-time collision detection at road intersections. In: 2007 Intelligent Transportation Systems Conference, ITSC 2007. IEEE (2007)
11. Wang, F.-Y.: Parallel control and management for intelligent transportation systems: concepts, architectures, and applications. IEEE Trans. Intell. Transp. Syst. **11**(3), 630–638 (2010)
12. Qureshi, K.N., Abdullah, A.H.: A survey on intelligent transportation systems. Middle-East J. Sci. Res. **15**(5), 629–642 (2013)
13. He, W., Lu, T., Yu, C.Q.: A novel traffic flow forecasting method based on the artificial neural networks and intelligent transportation systems data mining. Adv. Mater. Res. **842**, 708–711 (2014)
14. He, Y., Blandin, S., Wynter, L., Trager, B.: Analysis and real-time prediction of local incident impact on transportation networks. In: 2014 IEEE International Conference on Data Mining Workshop (ICDMW) (2014)
15. Zhang, X., Rice, J.A.: Short-term travel time prediction. Transp. Res. Part C: Emerg. Technol. **11**(3–4), 187–210 (2003)
16. Rashed, T., Jurgens, C.: Remote Sensing of Urban and Suburban Areas, vol. 10, pp. 181–192. Springer, Berlin (2010)

17. Lee, U., Gerla, M.: A survey of urban vehicular sensing platforms. Comput. Netw. **54**(4), 527–544 (2010)
18. Boban, M., Barros, J., Tonguz, O.: Geometry-based vehicle-to-vehicle channel modeling for large-scale simulation. IEEE Trans. Veh. Technol. **63**(9), 4146–4164 (2014)
19. Zarmehri, M.N., Soares, C.: Improving data mining results by taking advantage of the data warehouse dimensions: a case study in outlier detection. In: Encontro Nacional de Inteligencia Artificial e Computacional, Sao Carlos, Brazil (2014)
20. Zarmehri, M.N., Soares, C.: Using data hierarchies to support the development of personalized data mining models: a case study in error detection in foreign trade transactions. Int. J. Data Warehous. Min. (2016, submitted)
21. Wolpert, D.H., Macready, W.G.: No free lunch theorems for optimization. IEEE Trans. Evol. Comput. **1**(1), 67–82 (1997)
22. Giraud-Carrier, C., Vilalta, R., Brazdil, P.: Introduction to the special issue on meta-learning. Mach. Learn. **54**(3), 187–193 (2004)
23. Brazdil, P., Giraud-carrier, C., Soares, C., Vilalta, R.: Metalearning: Applications to Data Mining, pp. 662–666. Springer, Heidelberg (2009). Sammut, C., Webb, G.I. (eds.)
24. Cmuportugal.org: DRIVE-IN: Distributed Routing and Infotainment Through Vehicular Inter-Networking (2014)
25. Hearst, M.A., Dumais, S.T., Osman, E., Platt, J., Scholkopf, B.: Support vector machines. IEEE Intell. Syst. Appl. **13**(4), 18–28 (1998)
26. Scholkopf, B., Smola, A.: Support Vector Machines. Encyclopedia of Biostatistics (1998)
27. Steinwart, I., Christmann, A.: Support Vector Machines. Springer Science and Business Media, New York (2008)
28. Amit, Y., Geman, D.: Shape quantization and recognition with randomized trees. Neural Comput. Mass. Inst. Technol. **9**(7), 1545–1588 (1997)
29. Breiman, L.: Random forests. Mach. Learn. **45**(1), 5–32 (2001)
30. Liaw, A., Wiener, M.: Classification and regression by random forest. R News **2**(3), 18–22 (2002)
31. Olshen, L.B.J.F.R., Stone, C.J., et al.: Classification and regression trees. Wadsworth Int. Group **93**(99), 101 (1984)
32. Safavian, S.R., Landgrebe, D.: A survey of decision tree classifier methodology. IEEE Trans. Syst. Man Cybern. **21**(3), 660–674 (1991)
33. Ripley, B.: Tree: classification and regression trees (2014)
34. Seber, G.A.F., Lee, A.J.: Linear Regression Analysis, vol. 936. Wiley, London (2012)
35. Montgomery, D.C., Peck, E.A., Vining, G.G.: Introduction to Linear Regression Analysis, vol. 821. Wiley, London (2012)
36. Zarmehri, M.N., Soares, C.: Using metalearning for prediction of taxi trip duration using different granularity levels. In: Fromont, E., De Bie, T., van Leeuwen, M. (eds.) IDA 2015. LNCS, vol. 9385, pp. 205–216. Springer, Heidelberg (2015). doi:10.1007/978-3-319-24465-5_18
37. Zambrano-Bigiarini, M.: hydroGOF: goodness-of-fit functions for comparison of simulated and observed hydrological time series (2014)
38. R. C. Team: R: A Language and Environment for Statistical Computing, Vienna (2015)

Applicability of Human-Robot Collaboration to Small Batch Production

Dario Antonelli, Sergey Astanin, and Giulia Bruno(✉)

Department of Management and Production Engineering, Politecnico di Torino, Corso Duca degli Abruzzi 24, 10129 Turin, Italy
{dario.antonelli,sergey.astanin,giulia.bruno}@polito.it

Abstract. In the past years, the use of industrial robots was on the rise. Today, they are used for mass production in large enterprises. On the contrary, deployment of robots in small enterprises is lagging behind. Programming time is usually two orders of magnitude larger than the cycle time, and this fact severely limits applicability of robots in small batch production. This work analyzes opportunities to profitably employ robots also in this case through the adoption of the human-robot collaboration. A collaboration paradigm is proposed, where the tasks are assigned to robotic and human workers based on the batch size, task programming complexity (time), and manual execution time. The validity of this approach is demonstrated in a case study conducted in a collaborative human-robot work cell.

Keywords: Human-robot collaboration · Collective ability · Manufacturing cell · Small batch production · Robotics

1 Introduction

For small production volume, some manufacturing operations (e.g., machine loading and unloading, part inspection, part cleaning, bin picking, kitting) are largely done manually [1]. In contrast, a lot of these operations are performed by robots in mass production lines, such as in the automotive industry [2, 3]. This fact clearly shows the potential of robots for the execution of certain manufacturing operations.

Significant efforts are needed to overcome the barriers that prevent SMEs from automating their processes, since many of the traditional industrial robots are not considered useful in this context due to high setup and maintenance costs, safety concerns, and lack of general-purpose capabilities [4]. Setting up purely robotic work cells is not a viable option for most SMEs, because the economic efficiency of robots' use is often undermined by (i) the costs of the implementation of a fully automatic work cell and (ii) the costs and the duration of robot programming for every new task.

Human-robot collaboration can address these issues by relying on human workers for the tasks which are expensive to automate. There are two kinds of human-robot collaboration: spatial collaboration (actors share the workspace but don't work simultaneously) and temporal collaboration (actors work simultaneously but in different

H. Afsarmanesh et al. (Eds.): PRO-VE 2016, IFIP AICT 480, pp. 24–32, 2016.
DOI: 10.1007/978-3-319-45390-3_3

spaces) [5]. Spatial collaboration is the easiest to implement using the off-the-shelf industrial robots, so this is the kind of collaboration this work refers to.

In this paper the issue of assessing the economic advantage of a collaborative human-robotic cell is addressed from the point of view of SMEs. They have to evaluate if the costs of setup and maintenance are affordable even for small batch sizes. Due to the fact that humans and robots share complementary strengths in performing the tasks commonly arising in small volume production, the idea is to decompose manufacturing operations into such tasks that humans and robots can perform those which are most suitable for each of them.

This allows to offset the greater part of the programming time, and it can be a viable strategy in small batch production. The validity of this approach is demonstrated in a case study conducted in a collaborative human-robot work cell. The comparison between the total time in a collaborative scenario and the total time in a fully manual production can be used as a criterion to evaluate the applicability of the human-robot collaboration for a specific batch size and task structure.

The rest of the paper is organized as follows. Section 2 revises the state of the art in literature. Section 3 describes the proposed human-robot collaboration paradigm and compares it to fully automatic and fully manual production scenarios. In Sect. 4, the validity of the proposed approach was shown in a collaborative human-robot work cell. Finally, Sect. 5 draws conclusions and states future works.

2 State of the Art

Collaboration between human and robotic workers is gaining traction in manufacturing [6]. Several works addressed the evaluation of collaborative robotic cells, especially in automotive industry, providing comparisons between conventional robotic cell and cooperating human-robot cell [7–9]. Optimal task assignment among workers and robots was studied in some use-cases [10]. Major efforts have also been devoted to the safety of human-robot collaboration [11, 12].

The programming time can be reduced by automatic inference of robot programs from observations of a human teacher or from executions controlled by a human. These methods are known as Programming by Demonstration (PbD) [13] or Learning by Demonstration [14]. Early PbD implementations, still dominant in the field of industrial robotics, were explicitly communicating the desired robot configurations [15]. However the configuration can often be inferred. It opens the way to goal-oriented imitation learning and programming of more complex motions [16]. A goal-oriented PbD system for a welding robot, used in this study, was presented in [4, 17].

Collaborative robotic cells are ripe to move from labs into the bigger world. Several approaches to facilitate robot programming exist. What's missing is a solid methodology to evaluate applicability of such cells. Criteria for high-level task partitioning to divide tasks between a human and a robot worker, have to be defined.

Our aim is to compute the total time T_{total} for the three different scenarios described above (fully automatic, fully manual and collaborative) to determine the range of batch sizes for which the collaborative scenario is the most efficient.

4 Case Study

The case study to prove the validity of the proposed approach was conducted in a collaborative human-robot work cell, which consists of a COMAU NS16 Robot, two laser scanners for human-robot collision avoidance, and several IR cameras for demonstration observation. The layout of the cell is shown in Fig. 2(a), and more details can be found in [4]. Safety issues have been completely avoided in this setup as only the programming phase was studied, and the operator was removed from the cell before test runs. The benchmark process model considered in the case study is composed by two tasks: (1) a welding task along a four straight line segments (a square) and (2) a welding task along an Archimedean spiral. The geometry of both paths are depicted in Fig. 2(b), and they have the same length of 643 mm.

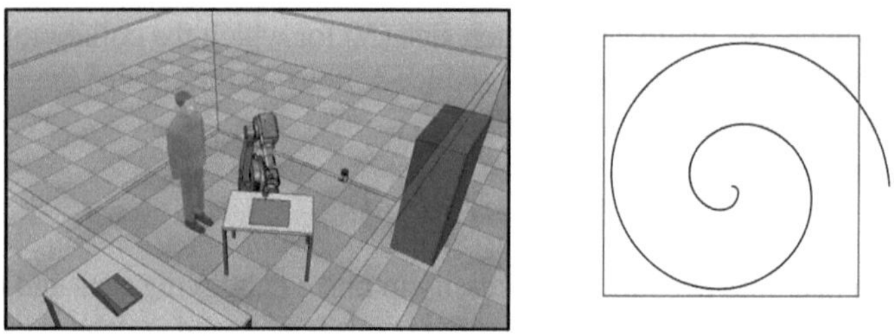

(a) (b)

Fig. 2. Layout of the collaborative human-robot cell (a), and benchmark trajectories to be programmed and executed (b).

The number of points, which the programmer has to indicate, is different for two trajectories. 5 points are enough to define the closed square trajectory. As the spiral doesn't have any straight line or circle arc segments, it is approximated by a polyline with 70 points on the curve. The square path is considered to be an easily programmable task (task A), conversely the spiral is considered to be the complicated one (task B).

In this benchmark, the following programming times are considered:

- the programming preparations time is the time required to switch the robot to programming mode, enter the robot cell, set appropriate robot movement parameters, position the end effector in the proximity of the work area, and return the robot to the starting position after the programming is done, leave the cell and disable the programming mode;
- the time for easily programmable tasks is the time needed to program the rectilinear path segments, which are defined by few distant points;

- the time for complicated programmable tasks is the time for programming the curvilinear paths, which may require to put many close points.

As robot programming is a creative, not a repetitive, activity, references and standard time tables for robot programming don't exist, to the extent of our knowledge. So the programming time had to be measured experimentally. We established that in our case the programming preparations time T_{prep} is 155 ± 20 s, programming of the straight lines requires 41.6 ± 5.6 s per point, and programming of the curvilinear path requires 13.3 ± 2.2 s per point. Thus the average programming time of the task A is estimated as $T_{prog\_E} \approx 170 \pm 11$ s, and the programming time of the task B is $T_{prog\_C} \approx 920 \pm 18$ s.

For the sake of simplicity, in this model we assume that the full length of the programming phase is K times longer than the time required to just record the trajectory. In the following we have assumed that $K \approx 10$.

The welding rate is assumed equal to 350 mm/min. This value is the welding rate for a wild steel tick from 1 to 2.5 mm, as reported by a producer of welding machines (www.fimer.com). This value can be substituted with the real rate of the manufacturing process under consideration. The welding rate is independent from the trajectory, thus both tasks have an operative time (T_{op}) of 110 s.

The non-value adding times are the set-up, the loading, the unloading, the tool maintenance, and the tool positioning. For human workers, the non-operative times (T_{nva}) are usually estimated as 80 % of the whole process, while for a robot, they are estimated as 30 % of the whole process. Thus, for both tasks, the non-value adding times are set 440 s when the tasks are executed by a human worker, and 50 s when the tasks are executed by a robot.

All the computed times are reported in Table 1, for the three considered scenarios. The total programming time is 1250 s for the fully automatic scenario and 330 s for the collaborative scenario. No programming time is required for the fully manual scenario. The cycle time is 320 s for the fully automated scenario, 1100 s for the fully manual, and 710 s for the collaborative one.

Table 1. Operation times in fully automated, fully manual and collaborative scenarios.

Times	Fully automated [s]	Fully manual [s]	Collaborative [s]
T_{prep}	160	0	160
T_{prog_E}	170	0	170
T_{prog_C}	920	0	0
$\boldsymbol{T_{prog}}$	**1250**	**0**	**330**
$T_{op}(taskA)$	110	110	110
$T_{nva}(taskA)$	50	440	50
$T_{op}(taskB)$	110	110	110
$T_{nva}(taskB)$	50	440	440
$\boldsymbol{T_{cycle}}$	**320**	**1100**	**710**

By applying (1), the total time depending on the batch size (*N*) was computed in the three scenarios, and the results are shown in Fig. 3. As expected, for very small batch sizes (from 1 to 8), the fully manual scenario is the more efficient due to the fact that no programming time is needed. For large batch size (*N* greater than 26), the fully automated scenario is the best, because the programming time becomes negligible with respect to the total cycle time. Collaborative approach is the most efficient for the batch size in the range between 9 and 25 units.

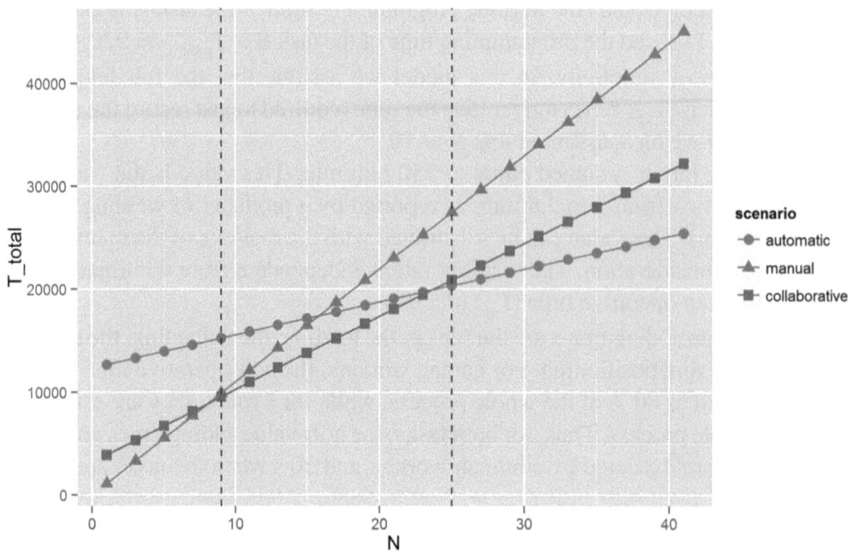

Fig. 3. Comparison of the total times in the three scenarios showing the range of the batch size in which the collaborative scenario is the most efficient. $K = 10$.

Notably, the range of batch sizes when collaborative scenario is the most efficient can be increased if the programming time of the task A can be further reduced. One of the possible approaches to reduce programming time even further is to employ programming by demonstration techniques proposed in [4]. Reduction of the programming time would shift down the line of the collaborative total cost in Fig. 3, thus increasing the efficient range of the collaborative scenario. However even users of the conventional programming approach can often benefit from collaboration as clearly shown above.

5 Conclusion

In this work, we propose a collaboration paradigm for assigning easily programmable tasks to the robot and the other tasks to the human operator. Robot programming time can prevail over other operations in small batch production, which is often the reason to avoid using robots altogether. We propose that eliminating only part of this time can open opportunities to employ robots in small batch production. The programming times of different tasks of an artificial use case were found experimentally in a real robotic cell. A basic model allowed to estimate the range of batch sizes for which the collaborative scenario was the most efficient.

Future works will consider the impact of rapid programming by demonstration techniques in order to further reduce the programming time and improve viability of collaborative scenarios.

References

1. Banerjee, A.G., Barnes, A., Kaipa, K.N., Liu, J., Shriyam, S., Shah, N., Gupta, S.K.: An ontology to enable optimized task partitioning in human-robot collaboration for warehouse kitting operations. In: Next-Generation Robotics II and Machine Intelligence and Bio-inspired Computation: Theory and Applications IX (2015)
2. Michalos, G., Makris, S., Papakostas, N., Mourtzis, D., Chryssolouris, G.: Automotive assembly technologies review: challenges and outlook for a flexible and adaptive approach. CIRP J. Manuf. Sci. Technol. **2**(2), 81–91 (2010)
3. Cherubini, A., Passama, R., Crosnier, A., Lasnier, A., Fraisse, P.: Collaborative manufacturing with physical human–robot interaction. Robot. Comput.-Integr. Manuf. **40**, 1–13 (2016)
4. Antonelli, D., Astanin, S., Caporaletti, G., Donati, F.: FREE: flexible and safe interactive human-robot environment for small batch exacting applications. In: Röhrbein, F., Veiga, G., Natale, C. (eds.) Gearing up Accelerating Cross-Fertilization Between Academic and Industrial Robotics Research in Europe, pp. 47–62. Springer, Switzerland (2014)
5. Bicchi, A., Peshkin, M.A., Colgate, J.E.: Safety for physical human–robot interaction. In: Siciliano, B., Khatib, O. (eds.) Springer Handbook of Robotics, pp. 1335–1348. Springer, Heidelberg (2008)
6. Tan, J.T.C., Duan, F., Zhang, Y., Watanabe, K., Kato, R., Arai, T.: Human-robot collaboration in cellular manufacturing: design and development. In: IEEE/RSJ International Conference on Intelligent Robots and Systems, pp. 29–34 (2009)
7. Morioka, M., Sakakibara, S.: A new cell production assembly system with human–robot cooperation. CIRP J. Manuf. Sci. Technol. **59**, 9–12 (2010)
8. Papakostas, N., Michalos, G., Makris, S., Zouzias, D., Chryssolouris, G.: Industrial applications with cooperating robots for the flexible assembly. Int. J. Comput. Integr. Manuf. **24**(7), 650–660 (2011)
9. Pedrocchi, N., Vicentini, F., Malosio, M., Tosatti, L.M. Safe human–robot cooperation in an industrial environment. Int. J. Adv. Robot. Syst. IJARS, **10**(27) (2013). doi:10.5772/53939
10. Ding, H., Schipper, M., Bjoern, M.: Optimized task distribution for industrial assembly in mixed human–robot environments – case study on IO module assembly. In: IEEE International Conference on Automation Science and Engineering (2014)
11. Harper, C., Virk, G.: Towards the development of international safety standards for human robot interaction. Int. J. Soc. Robot. **2**(3), 229–234 (2010)
12. Matthias, B., et al.: Safety of collaborative industrial robots: Certification possibilities for a collaborative assembly robot concept. In: IEEE ISAM (2011)
13. Billard, A., Calinon, S., Dillmann, R., Schaal, S.: Robot programming by demonstration. In: Siciliano, B., Khatib, O. (eds.) Springer Handbook of Robotics, pp. 1371–1394. Springer, Heidelberg (2008)
14. Argall, B.D., Chernova, S., Veloso, M., Browning, B.: A survey of robot learning from demonstration. Robot. Auton. Syst. **57**(5), 469–483 (2009)

15. Biggs, G., MacDonald, B.: A survey of robot programming systems. In: Proceedings of the Australasian Conference on Robotics and Automation, pp. 1–3 (2003)
16. Schaal, S., Atkeson, C.G.: Learning control in robotics. Robot. Autom. Mag. IEEE **17**(2), 20–29 (2010)
17. Antonelli, D., Astanin, S.: Qualification of a collaborative human-robot welding cell. Proc. CIRP **41**, 352–357 (2016)
18. Hopp, W.J., Spearman, M.L.: Factory Physics (2011)

Hyperconnectivity and Interoperation - Managing Data and Knowledge

network ties [6, 7] and social identity [8, 9]. In general, these studies highlight the reasons individuals participate in online communities and the manner in which these members are organized to reach group target. In particular they interested on the processes and the manner members coordinate their work. They are less prolix on members' characteristics, and how their diversity affects the quality of the knowledge produced by their virtual work.

To understand the production of article as common knowledge, we first base our analysis on the Institutional Analysis and Development framework described in Fig. 1. This framework distinguishes the characteristics of the community, or the "inputs" ("biophysical characteristics", "attribute of the community", "rules-in-use") from "the action arena" which constrain the way people interact, leading to "outcomes" [10].

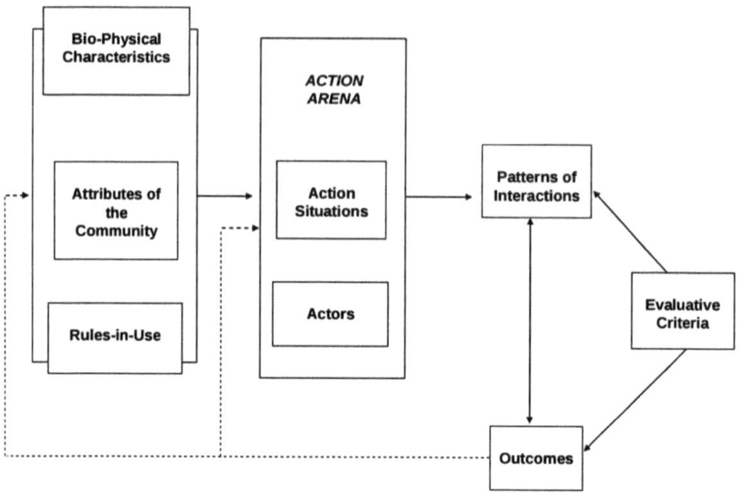

Fig. 1. Institutional analysis and development framework [10]

Based on this framework, we cannot overlook neither the effect of the process nor the effect of the community attributes on the quality of the articles. Before talking about the process and the action arena, we need to identify the appropriate group based on member attributes, because they affect greatly the manner members work together and how effective their collaborative efforts will be. In traditional organizations performance has been linked to members' characteristics and their diversity [11]. However, the negative effects of these factors could be restricted among teams using new collaborative technologies because of limited capabilities like visual anonymity and participation equality. Likewise, the positive effects can be improved due to coordination support and electronic use as additive capabilities. So in one side, two key factors are to be considered: group characteristics in general and member diversity. More specifically, the focus should be placed on characteristics reflecting the similarity or dissimilarity of members' attributes.

On the other hand, another specific characteristic of online groups is their nature of self-organizing. Contrary to work groups in virtual organizations where memberships are identified by management control and organizational model, online group in self-organization is coached voluntary involvement. So it is important to look at membership constitution based on the career of the contributors before the creation of the article. This factor plays also an important role in online collaboration success. However, this ideas is not developed in the case of Wikipedia as an online epistemic community. The majority of the existing studies on the subject focus on what happen after article creation. They link knowledge quality to group characteristics within the same project but neglect what may have happened before the studied project.

Our study will advance conditions under which this crowding group create high quality knowledge among online epistemic communities. In this paper, we inspect the following research questions:

1. What are the characteristics of a “good” team to produce new knowledge?
2. How does member diversity or similarity affect the outcomes that a group produced in an online epistemic community?

As a primary contribution of our work we developed a theoretical model about initial structure in terms of group composition and member diversity in virtual teams based on what happened before article creation. We further integrated various social theories to develop these propositions by considering how structure could be instantiated in shared mental models and the specific behaviors that contribute to building such models.

The paper is organized as follows: the next section reviews related work on group composition and core members. The following section develops hypotheses about the effects of group composition on the quality of produced knowledge. Then, we describe our research methods following with our results. Finally, we discuss our findings and highlight implications for both theory and practice, before our concluding remarks with possible future research directions.

2 Literature Review

There is a large body of literature that describes the structure in online communities. To develop our hypotheses, we follow two sets of literature. The first is the group composition literature where Tan et al. [12] shed light that group composition is an important factor of online community success. The second is the extensive core members and their relationships with knowledge quality [13].

2.1 Group Composition

Study research in team composition is based on members’ attributes and the effects of the combination of these attributes on action arena and outcomes [14]. Two important group composition dimensions were investigated in literature: the mean level of group’s characteristic, and the diversity within the group [13].

In one side, the mean level is considered as simple attributes combination of group members [15, 16]. Member attributes average is designed as a summary based on some measures of members’ characteristic [14].

On the other hand, diversity in group work is defined as heterogeneity or dis-similarity of individual attributes that arises from the difference of any attribute from others [9]. These attributes can be social demographic characteristics (age, gender, race, and nationality), informational ones (tenure, experience, education,…) or deeper individual differences (beliefs, values and personality). The relationship between team diversity and outcomes has been extensively [9].

This line of research has focused on the dimensions of the group's activity, based on what is done during article creation. It does not detail how member's previous activity, would determine group performance and quality results. To forecast knowledge quality, we use these group composition dimensions, focusing on the core members on the the basis of their previous behavior.

2.2 Core Member Constitution

Some studies on epistemic communities, especially in the case of open source software, stressed the importance of the core members [13, 17, 18]. In this context, they define the core-periphery structure by members' activity, where a set of high active members are accountable for the majority of project contribution and a large and loosely coupled group of periphery members support the others. Mostly, the core members are more active compared to others. Their presence is important for online communities success.

These studies conduct to making the hypothesis that in Wikipedia projects too, there is a core-periphery structure, similar to the one found in open software production, and that the initiators of the projects are its 'natural' core members, and are key to its success. In this study, we examine the question of how to identify core members of an article and if its characteristics impact the quality of the article produced.

3 Research Hypotheses

As mentioned above, most studies look at the contributions made after the first contribution. In our study, we are interested on what happened before. We define the "first contribution" as the first time an editor makes a revision and proposes a new article as a new and original knowledge.

Based on these definitions we define article creation life cycle as described in Fig. 2. The first contribution is a separator, allows us to define three main periods. "The learning period" is the period before the first contribution where we learn about the members attributes based on their history. "The teaming period" is the period of four months after the first contribution where we constitute the core members. "The active period" is the period just after the teaming period when teams start activities[1]. These definitions help to refine our main hypothesis:

H: "The teaming period carries important information about the initial group composition using what we learned about the members in the first period which impacts in turn the quality of knowledge produced by the group."

Our main hypothesis argued that group composition is responsible for the success of online epistimic community. The way in which groups self-formed, recruit and

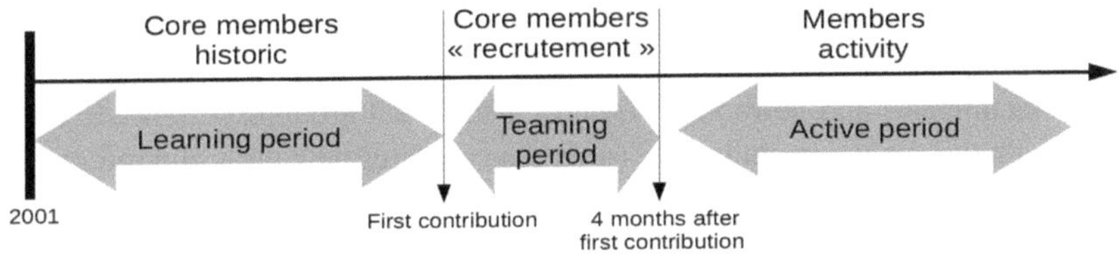

Fig. 2. Article life cycle among Wikipedia

attract participants automatically may affect group composition, which affects indirectly knowledge quality. In our study a key factor to consider is member characteristics, within the virtual work environment, at both individual and group levels. In addition, we provide valuable insights into their diversity which reflects wherever group members share different or similar attributes.

3.1 Effects of Initial Group Size on the Quality of Knowledge Produced by a Virtual Group

Many studies have been trying to determine whether small or large groups are more likely to cooperate on a project and produce knowledge. Group size affects quality differently. In one hand, wide groups ensure a large amount of knowledge and a faster time to corrected errors and discovered incomplete information [19]. On the other hand, small groups often lack the resources that large groups can extent. These limited resources, make difficult to give additional resources to producing article within Wikipedia as a collective action [20]. Ostrom suggested further research on collective action to focus on the hypothesized curvilinear effects of group size [10]. Based on Ostrom proposition we hypothesize that:

H1: "Group size in the teaming period is an important determinant of project success in online epistemic community which has a curvilinear effects on article quality."

3.2 Effects of Diversity of Member Characteristics Within the Virtual Group on the Quality of Knowledge Produced

Some studies on team dynamic, show that heterogeneous teams are more productive than heterogeneous isolated workers in the case of low-skilled worker. Our study of diversity in Wikipedia extends the literature of diversity in virtual teams. We test and confirm theoretical propositions of the effects of diversity to know if diversity should be encouraged or discouraged.

3.2.1 Effects of Experience Disparity on the Quality of Knowledge Produced by a Virtual Group

The members comprising a team may be classified according to their experience. Some agents are newcomers having a little experience and skills. The other are old-timers or incumbents, persons with identifiable talents named.

Evidence from virtual organizations has shown that, although old-timers are more experienced and skilled than newcomers, their effort is generally lower [21]. Having a blend of incumbents and newcomers ensures a sufficient group experience to establish and maintain task structure, and in the same time acquires new ideas and information to complete the task [9]. In the meantime, when experience disparity increases, old-timers and new-comers may have different collaboration work views. So experience diversity may reduce communication and social integration and thus it has been linked to increased conflicts. Therefore, our next hypothesis:

H2: "There is a non linear relationship between experience diversity and article quality. Article quality increases as experience diversity increases. However, beyond certain levels of experience diversity, article quality will decrease."

3.2.2 Effects of Reputation Diversity on the Quality of Knowledge Produced by a Virtual Group

User reputations are computed according to the number of their past contributions, the quality of produced articles and the quantity of succeeding edits (see [22]). Reputation systems are considered one of the primary factors for success of online communities [18]. By exploring German Wikipedia, [22] showed that high quality articles are not necessarily edited by a large number of people, but the most important is to be written by contributors with reputation for high quality contributions. On the other hand, [23] found that the highest quality contributions come from the large numbers of anonymous hardly contribute. So we must find an adjustment between user with high level reputation and anonymous users.

H3: "High-quality content in Wikipedia comes from means level of reputation distributed among members during the teaming period. In addition there is a non linear relationship between reputation diversity and article quality. Article quality increases as reputation diversity increases. However, beyond certain levels of reputation diversity, article quality will decrease."

4 Research Method

4.1 Wikipedia Case Study

To address our research questions and to verify the validity of the proposed hypotheses, we chose Wikipedia as data source. Wikipedia, is one of the most success stories of peer collaboration and the well-known example of the online epistemic community.

The first important characteristic of Wikipedia data availability. Many useful data records publicly available online, includes useful information about Wikipedia [24]. Furthermore, the case study will be Wikipedia, because of its connection with firms' knowledge management and production challenges. Another important aspect of Wikipedia is that MediaWiki site is maintained for every different language in Wikipedia.

4.2 Data Collection

The best way to retrieve large portions or the whole set of activity data from any Wikipedia language is using the database dump files. These dump files contain precise information about all actions performed in any Wikipedia language. Dump files can be retrieved from the Wikimedia Downloads center.

For our purposes, we are interested in French wikipedia. We first retrieve French Wikipedia XML database dump le "pages-meta-history.xml.7z" from the set of available dump files. We use data extracted on December 12, 2015. This data contains the complete meta data of every version of all French articles from the beginning of the online encyclopedia (January 2001) to December 2015.

Once dump file is loaded, we use WikiDAT and Media wiki API for data extraction. WikiDAT is a tool for Wikipedia data analytics, based on Python and R and using MySQL database. It is aim to create an extensible toolkit for Wikipedia using Python and R to automate the extraction of Wikipedia data into 5 different tables of MySQL database (page, people, revision, revision hash, logging).

The MediaWiki action API is a web service that allows the collection of data and meta-data from the latest Wikipedia's dump and it's available for several languages, in particular, French, the one we're concerned with. It is a project maintained by the Mediawiki and contains a well-structured documentation to be able to query data and can be returned as JSON. In our project, we used it to retrieve the articles that are part in the categories "Featured Articles" and "Good Articles".

4.3 Data Preparation

4.3.1 Data Selection

We preprocessed the XML records in the raw data using Wiki-DAT into a tabular data set representing 7833289 articles and 114907858 edits. We used MediaWiki API to retrieve article quality; a qualified article needs to belongs to one of two classes: "Featured Articles" and "Good Articles". There are 2920 qualified article (1 % of total number) and we randomly sampled 2500 non qualified articles. We finally analyzed these articles based on their revision and the historic of their members' revision on other articles. As a first contribution we start by analyzing 100 articles from 114907878 editors' revision made.

4.3.2 Variable Measure

In this part, Table 1 describes the different variables we consider for modeling our hypothesis.

4.4 Data Analysis

In this paper, we examined WikiProjects from 2001 to 2015 in order to understand how group composition and diversity characteristics affect the quality of created knowledge. For data analysis, we used Random Forest in order to select the most relevant group attributes leading to successful articles. We created a predictive model of random forest algorithm.

Table 1. Variables measure

Independent variables		
Variables		Metrics
Individual members' characteristics	# contribution	The number of edits made by each editors beyond current article
	length contribution	The length of edits made by each editors beyond current article
	# participation	The number of other article edited by each editors
	# Efficient contribution	The number of previous edits made by each editors in qualified articles(FA or GA) and beyond current article
	Length efficient contribution	The length of previous edits made by each editors in qualified articles (FA or GA) beyond current article
	# Efficient participation	The number of qualified articles (FA or GA) edited by each editors
	# Experience	The number of days from the first edit mad by each member in Wikipedia to his last revision [25]
	Reputation	The rate of a edit in excellent pages or the rate of participationp in successful projects [22]: $Reputation_{eb} = \frac{efficient_{contribution}}{Total_{contribution}}$ $Reputation_{pb} = \frac{efficient_{participation}}{Total_{participation}}$
Group members' characteristics	Group size	The number of editors contributing to the article during the teaming period (4 months after article inception) [20, 26]
	Maximum individual characteristics	Maximum of members' individual characteristics in each Wikipedia project
	Minimum individual characteristics	Minimum of members' individual characteristics in each Wikipedia project
	Average individual characteristics	Average of members individual characteristics in each Wikipedia project
	Diversity	Coefficient of variation of all members individual attribute in each Wikipedia project [27]: $diversity = \frac{\sqrt{attribute_i - attribute_{mean}}}{attribute_{mean}}$

(Continued)

Table 1. (*Continued*)

Independent variables	
Variables	Metrics
Dependent variables	
Article quality	Wikipedia's internal quality categorization schema which assigns articles to a set of 7 distinct categories (Stub->FA). We parse variables on article quality using the MediaWiki API. We used it to retrieve which articles are part of the categories "Featured Articles" and "Good Articles" [28]. For the quality variable, we use Wikipedia's own quality grading as our metric and we classify article on «Qualify Articles» (FA and GA) and «Non Qualify Article» (the rest)

This algorithm is a classification method that operates by constructing a many decision trees during training time, and take out ordered attributes by importance [29].

For our predictive model, we separated the dataset in train and test sets. The train set consisted in a random 70 % of all the articles and the test set contained the remaining 30 %. Then, the predictive model was trained on the training set and applied on the test set to predict article quality. We compared those predictions to the real value of article quality. To deduce the accuracy value of each predictive model we compute the rate of the good predictions over the total number of predictions. This process was done a 5000 times to smooth over the extreme cases.

5 Results

Descriptive statistics are presented in Fig. 3 for French Wikipedia. The random forest method gives values for quantifying the importance of an attribute for the quality of the prediction. The variable importance is a critical output of the Random Forest algorithm. For each variable it notes its importance to classify the data and predict the dependent variable. The plot presented in Fig. 3 shows each variable ordered top-to-bottom according to its importance from the most important to the least important. The estimation of their importance is given in the x-axis by computing the average decrease of accuracy of each tree in the forest in the absence of the given attribute. The most important variables are at the top. Higher this value is, more important is this attribute for the prediction. To choose the important variables, we look for a large break between variables. According to this metric Fig. 3 shows that the large break is between max_Nb_participation and diversity_participation_FA.

In our model there are many attributes and some of them may be useless, being very correlated to others. Hence, we calculated the Pearson correlation on all the attribute's pairs as mentioned in Fig. 4 and we removed one element of every pair for which the absolute value of the correlation is over 0.8. So the most important attributes

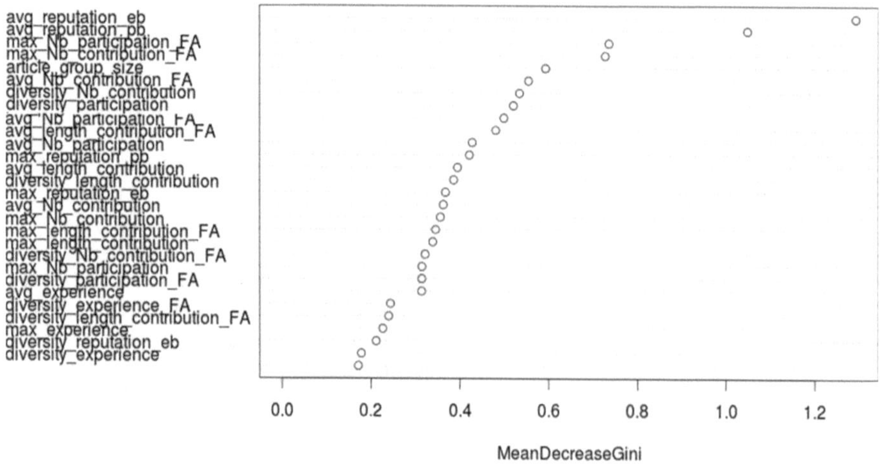

Fig. 3. Attributes' importance of French Wikipedia

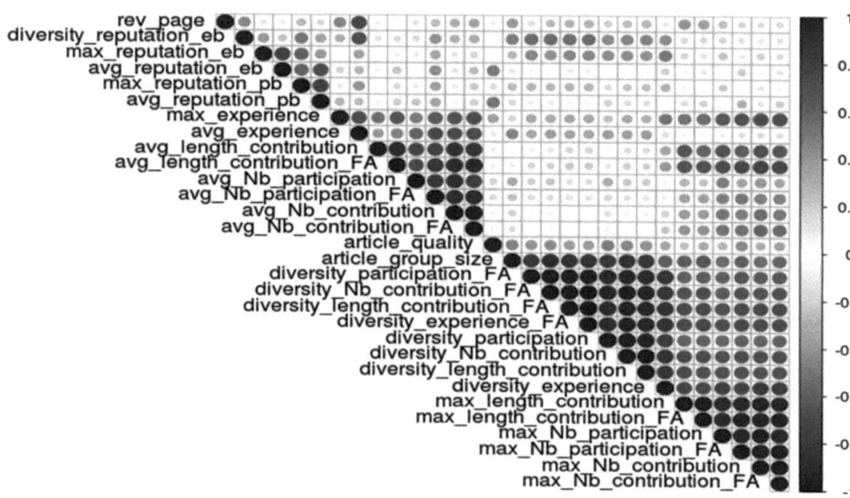

Fig. 4. Pearson correlation on all the attribute's pairs of French Wikipedia

in general and that standing out to predict a successful French Wikipedia project are average reputation, group size, diversity contribution and participation, average experience.

6 Discussion

The results detailed in Sect. 5 mention that the most important variable is average reputation. This means that the average effective participation of the authors who edit qualified articles is higher than the participation of authors contributing to other articles. Similarly, the editors who wrote the qualified articles participate during teaming periods of qualified ones. In the same time, average reputation is more important than maximum reputation. More specifically, average reputation is more important than reputation diversity which doesn't exert any significant importance to predict qualified articles. At the beginning of the core member recruitment process, recruiting editors with high or heterogeneous reputation is not necessary. But the most important is to recruit well-known editors based either on their edits or on the pages they edited.

The results of the experience effects are different to the findings of [9] which posit that high experience or tenure disparity leads to high productivity. Experience diversity does not have any significant impact article quality during teaming period. This means that core members do not need to have a diverse experience to produce a qualified article. In contrast, average experience distributed among core members have a slight importance article quality.

Experience in Wikipedia can generally provide a social status. Old editors and newcomers have the possibility to refer to each other, which may cause conflict in a WikiProject that reduces performance. In particular conflicts at the beginning of article creation, and during the teaming period, can be particularly damaging to online volunteer groups. As prior research on offline groups, high tenure diversity of core member increase conflict at the beginning. But, status inequalities during the teaming period can be less prominent in online groups. Therefore, in online volunteer groups like Wikipedia most editors should participate at the beginning with equal experience.

Furthermore, people in online volunteer groups are categorized based on experience and are treated them differently. But in a first step of teaming period, preferably having equal experience distributed among members lead to a high quality article.

Interestingly, we found that while diversity in experience and reputation has not an important impact on article quality, the amount of contributions, and their length, matter, in a single sense: the more diverse, the longer, the better. Our results show that group size is also an important attribute to qualify produced article. This can be understood as the fact that the team which rapidly attracts contributors (within this 4-months period) have a better chance of success, something to be related to the fact that a well-know indicator of article quality is the number of contributors who have participated in their redaction. This is coherent with the finding related to the control variable. Our results mentioned that article age exerted a positive effect on all constructs by generating the increase of teaming period on all article. The construction of an article of quality is, mainly a question of stock accumulation (here edits), and the longer the period is, the better the chance that new edits have been made.

7 Conclusion and Future Works

The first contribution of our work is to develop a set of theoretical models about structure involvement in term of group composition in a virtual team. We further integrate various social theories to develop these models taking into account the manner in which the structure can be instantiated in collaborative models.

We start by showing the importance of studying group composition in online open collaboration. In this context, existing research on online collaboration has focused mostly on social structure, governance and motivation. Unlike, our results suggest other attributes of group members that influences the group success. Our findings, on one hand, confirm the importance of identifying group composition in online collaboration basing on contribution history and, on the other hand, highlight the importance of diversity of some attributes.

As a second step in our model, we will work on the manner members organize their activities. We will study in particular the different kinds of leadership and their effect on article quality. Based on theoretical suggestions of leadership in virtual teams, we will present three order leadership that seems likely to be more effective.

References

1. Cohendet, P., Creplet, F., Dupouët, O.: Communities of practice and epistemic communities: a renewed approach of organisational learning within the RM. In: Workshop on Economics and Heterogeneous Interacting Agents (2001)
2. Rullani, F., Haefliger, S.: The periphery on stage: the intra-organizational dynamics in online communities of creation. Res. Policy **42**(4), 941–953 (2013)
3. Roberts, J.A., Hann, I.-H., Slaughter, S.A.: Understanding the motivations, participation, and performance of open source software developers: a longitudinal study of the apache projects. Manag. Sci. **52**(7), 984–999 (2006)
4. Butler, B., Joyce, E., Pike, J.: Don't look now, but we've created a bureaucracy: the nature and roles of policies and rules in Wikipedia. In: Proceedings of the SIGCHI Conference on Human Factors in Computing Systems, p. 1101. ACM (2008)
5. Stewart, K.J., Gosain, S.: The impact of ideology on effectiveness in open source software development teams. MIS Q. **30**, 291–314 (2006)
6. Daniel, S.L., Diamant, E.I.: Network effects in OSS development: the impact of users and developers on project performance. In: ICIS 2008 Proceedings, p. 122 (2008)
7. Grewal, R., Lilien, G.L., Mallapragada, G.: Location, location, location: how network embeddedness affects project success in open source systems. Manag. Sci. **52**(7), 1043–1056 (2006)
8. Bagozzi, R.P., Dholakia, U.M.: Open source software user communities: a study of participation in Linux user groups. Manag. Sci. **52**(7), 1099–1115 (2006)
9. Ren, Y., Chen, J., Riedl, J.: The impact and evolution of group diversity in online open collaboration. Manag. Sci. **62**, 1668–1686 (2015)
10. Hess, C., Ostrom, E.: Understanding Knowledge as a Commons. From Theory to Practice. MIT Press, Cambridge (2006)
11. Horwitz, S.K., Horwitz, I.B.: The effects of team diversity on team outcomes: a meta-analytic review of team demography. J. Manag. **33**(6), 987–1015 (2007)
12. Tan, Y., Mookerjee, V., Singh, P.: Social capital, structural holes and team composition: collaborative networks of the open source software community. In: ICIS 2007 Proceedings, p. 155 (2007)
13. Arazy, O., Nov, O., Patterson, R., Yeo, L.: Information quality in Wikipedia: the effects of group composition and task conflict. J. Manag. Inf. Syst. **27**(4), 71–98 (2011)
14. Mathieu, J., Maynard, M.T., Rapp, T., Gilson, L.: Team effectiveness 1997–2007: a review of recent advancements and a glimpse into the future. J. Manag. **34**(3), 410–476 (2008)

15. Moreland, R.L., Levine, J.M.: Group composition: explaining similarities and differences among group members. In: The Sage Handbook of Social Psychology, pp. 367–380. Sage, Beverly Hills (2003)
16. Moreland, R.L., Levine, J.M., Wingert, M.L.: Creating the ideal group: composition effects at work. Underst. Group Behav. **2**, 11–35 (2013)
17. Crowston, K., Wei, K., Li, Q., Howison, J.: Core and periphery in free/libre and open source software team communications. In: Proceedings of the 39th Annual Hawaii International Conference on System Sciences, 2006, HICSS 2006, vol. 6, p. 118a. IEEE (2006)
18. Bosu, A., Carver, J.C.: Impact of developer reputation on code review outcomes in OSS projects: an empirical investigation. In: Proceedings of the 8th ACM/IEEE International Symposium on Empirical Software Engineering and Measurement, p. 33. ACM (2014)
19. Surowiecki, J.: The Wisdom of Crowds. Anchor, Garden City (2005)
20. Yang, W., Liu, W., Viña, A., Tuanmu, M.-N., He, G., Dietz, T., Liu, J.: Nonlinear effects of group size on collective action and resource outcomes. Proc. Nat. Acad. Sci. **110**(27), 10916–10921 (2013)
21. Wang, L.S., Chen, J., Ren, Y., Riedl, J.: Searching for the goldilocks zone: trade-offs in managing online volunteer groups. In: Proceedings of the ACM 2012 Conference on Computer Supported Cooperative Work, pp. 989–998. ACM (2012)
22. Stein, K., Hess, C.: Does it matter who contributes: a study on featured articles in the German Wikipedia. In: Proceedings of the Eighteenth Conference on Hypertext and Hypermedia, pp. 171–174. ACM (2007)
23. Anthony, D., Smith, S.W., Williamson, T.: Reputation and reliability in collective goods the case of the online Encyclopedia Wikipedia. Ration. Soc. **21**(3), 283–306 (2009)
24. Ortega, F.: Wikipedia: a quantitative analysis. Ph.D. thesis, Universidad Rey Juan Carlos, Madrid, (Cit. on p.) (2009)
25. Chen, J., Ren, Y., Riedl, J.: The effects of diversity on group productivity and member withdrawal in online volunteer groups. In: Proceedings of the SIGCHI Conference on Human Factors in Computing Systems, pp. 821–830. ACM (2010)
26. Zhang, X.M., Zhu, F.: Group size and incentives to contribute: a natural experiment at Chinese Wikipedia. Am. Econ. Rev. **101**, 07–22 (2010)
27. Bedeian, A.G., Mossholder, K.W.: On the use of the coefficient of variation as a measure of diversity. Organ. Res. Methods **3**(3), 285–297 (2000)
28. Aaltonen, A., Seiler, S.: Cumulative growth in user-generated content production: evidence from Wikipedia. Manag. Sci. **62**, 2054–2069 (2015)
29. Breiman, L.: Random forests. Mach. Learn. **45**(1), 5–32 (2001)

Realizing the Innovation Potentials from Open Data: Stakeholders' Perspectives on the Desired Affordances of Open Data Environment

Adegboyega Ojo[1(✉)], Lukasz Porwol[1], Mohammad Waqar[1], Arkadiusz Stasiewicz[1], Edobor Osagie[1], Michael Hogan[2], Owen Harney[2], and Fatemeh Ahmadi Zeleti[1]

[1] Insight Centre for Data Analytics, Galway, Ireland
{adegboyega.ojo, lukasz.porwol, mohammad.waqar, arkadiusz.stasiewicz, edobor.osagie, fatemeh.ahmadizeleti}@insight-centre.org
[2] National University of Ireland, Galway, Ireland

Abstract. Despite the increasing number of datasets available on open data platforms, there has been limited adoption and use of open data by the public. This has consequently limited the innovation and transparency impact of open data on respective economies and governments. While literature is replete with articles on barriers to open data exploitation and use; these studies are yet to examine how affordances of open data platforms could help to overcome these barriers. This perspective is important since the platform directly mediates access to open data resources and their use. We describe a study carried out as part the Route-To-PA (Route-To-PA Project, Raising Open and User-friendly Transparency Enhancing Technologies for Public Administrations, H2020 Project, http://routetopa.eu/.) project to establish stakeholder's perspectives on barriers to effective use of open data and the desired open data platform affordances to address these problems. Our results provide details on what kinds of data are needed by stakeholders, the features required to support their interactions and collaboration around open data and features that could enhance the understandability of datasets available on open data platform.

Keywords: Open data · Transparency · Open data platforms

1 Introduction

Currently, there are over 519 open data portals or catalogs available globally[1] and over 8,000 datasets published in the European Union (EU) Open Data Portal [13] in response to calls for unprecedented government openness and the EU's Public Section Information directive [7]. Unfortunately, barriers such as limited access to open data by citizens and third-parties and lack of dedicated resources on the part of

[1] Data Portals – A Comprehensive List of Open Data Portals available around the world, http://dataportals.org/.

H. Afsarmanesh et al. (Eds.): PRO-VE 2016, IFIP AICT 480, pp. 48–59, 2016.
DOI: 10.1007/978-3-319-45390-3_5

government organizations to sustainably publish datasets of high value [17] has significantly limited the expected innovation and benefits of open data. While releasing data on processes and decisions of governments should, in general, improve transparency, recent studies have shown that transparency does not only depend on how visible information is made but also on how understandable the information is. Few studies like [23] have discussed the importance of open data platforms in enhancing transparency through features for accessing, using and collaborating on open data. In our opinion, the innovation potentials of open data are significantly impacted by the transparency-related affordances of the underlying open data platforms. Therefore, we believe that a good understanding of the limitations of existing platforms and the stakeholders' needs with respect to transparency-related affordances of open data platforms, is imperative for harnessing open data resources held on them. Albeit there are a few existing studies on Open Data Platforms such as [14], none of these studies explicitly address the affordances of these platforms regarding their explicit support for both data and organizational transparency. Building on our previous work reported in [1], the study presented here fills this gap by first reviewing the features of eleven open data platforms. The selected features are those that impact on the accessibility and understandability (or transparency) of datasets managed on the platforms. The eleven platforms were reviewed in this study include: CKAN [6], DKAN [11], Socrata [27], PublishMyData [24], Information Workbench [16], Enigma [12], Junar [18], OpenDataSoft [22], Callimachus [4], DataTank [8] and Semantic MediaWiki [26]. Next, the paper describes findings from the expert interviews and collective intelligence workshop co-organized with with the Dublin City Council to identify perceived shortcomings of current generation open data platform and the desired features of next generation ones from the perspectives of different categories of open data stakeholders. The rest paper is structured as follows: Sect. 2 provides an extensive review of existing platforms, Sect. 3 presents the methodology for the review and evaluation while Sect. 4 reviews the findings from the study, Sect. 5 discusses our findings, while concluding remarks are given in Sect. 6.

2 Review of Existing Platforms

Platform, in general, as a concept comprises three aspects: (1) a stable low-variety core, (2) a changeable set of complements and (3) interfaces which enable core and complements to operate as a single system [3]. In our study, we consider an Open Data Platform to be a software platform which comprises a software ecosystem that supports different end-user interactions with open data including search and discovery of datasets, publishing of datasets, analysis and visualization of datasets as well as sharing and development of stories from datasets. As part of the background study to our investigation, we reviewed eleven open data platforms based on some features which we considered pertinent for both data and organizational transparency. Data transparency is related to the accessibility and understandability of data. Organizational transparency relates to the degree to which both internal and external agents can observe or access different kinds of information about its functioning [19].

These platforms were selected based on their popularity and availability of them. A brief description of the features and our observations are explained as follows:

Metadata Schema and Data File Formats: open data platforms supports different metadata schema and a variety of data file formats. Metadata refers to information about the dataset which includes information such as the title, author, subjects, keywords, publisher, revision history, changes, and the source of data. Metadata also includes structural information about the data such as keys, indexes, columns. Metadata information enables search capabilities and enables interoperability between different open data platforms. Several file formats are associated with the datasets managed on open data platform. Example of file formats include CSV, JSON, XLS, RDF, PDF and HTML.

Search facility for datasets: contemporary platforms provide keyword-based search capability on metadata associated with the dataset and filtering of results; emerging platforms such as Enigma offer record-level search capability and information filtering at multiple levels.

Social Media and Collaboration: increasingly available platforms allow interaction between users through social sharing features. Specifically, the feature enables users to comment, share, review, and rate available datasets.

Dataset Publishing: supports dataset publishing process including dataset refinement, upload, and linking to other datasets.

Federation and Harvesting: Federation allows data replication across different instances of a platform; enabling seamless integration between the various independent platform instances. This allows searching across multiple instances of the platform. Harvesting allows automated extraction of data from different open data sources and catalogs into a one more more catalogs.

Extensibility mechanism: this feature enable adaptation and extension of the platform with complementary features through mechanisms such as APIs and libraries, connectors, plugins and extensions.

Data Analysis tools: features enables simple statistical operations, online analytical processing (OLAP) operations, use of dashboards and analysis widgets. It also provides access to external analytical tools such as R Programming Language.

Visualisation tools: feature enables the use of maps and charts in visualizing datasets. It employs existing maps services such as OpenStreetMaps, Google and Bing maps. Also, libraries such as D3.js and recline.js are supported.

Personalization tools: this feature allows users to modify the platform's look-and-feel for branding purposes and adopt specific portal view for different users based on desired preferences. This could include how datasets and search results are displayed.

Customization tools: feature allows the portal administrators to define the metadata schema, extensions to use and configuration of the data store and limits.

Dataset licensing service: feature allows licensing information to be added to the dataset as one of the metadata information.

Resource Accessibility: features enables access the data through APIs. These APIs provides clear specifications for external requests using protocols such as REST (Representational State Transfer) or SOAP (Simple Object Access protocol) services.

Technical Environment: describes the programming environment of the open data platform; a vital information for extension of platforms.

Others: We capture here all other features available on the platforms such as data download statistics that could impact on the accessibility of datasets.

Table 1 presents the summary of features for each of the eleven platforms reviewed. Summary of our observations on their features are discussed in Sect. 4 while the we refer the reader to [25] for detailed discussion.

Table 1. Summary of platform features

FEATURES	CKAN	DKAN	SOCRATA	PUBLISH MY DATA	INFO WKBENCH	ENIGMA	JUNAR	ODS	CALLIM	DATATK	SMWIKI
DATA, METADATA & FILE FORMAT	Full	Limited	Full	Limited	Limited	Limited	Limited	Full	Full	Limited	Limited
SEARCH & INDEXING	Full	Limited	Limited	Full	NO	Full	Limited	Full	NO	Limited	Full
SOCIAL MEDIA, SHARING &	Full	Full	Full	Limited	Limited	NO	Full	Full	Limited	NO	Full
PUBLISHING PIPELINE /	Full	Full	Full	Limited	Limited	Limited	Full	Limited	Limited	Limited	Limited
HARVESTING, FEDERATION &	Full	Full	Full	Limited	NO	NO	Full	Full	Limited	NO	Limited
DATA ANALYTICS	Limited	Full	Full	NO	Full	Full	Limited	Limited	NO	Full	NO
VISUALISATION	Limited	Limited	Full	NO	Limited	NO	Full	Full	NO	NO	Limited
PERSONALISATION	Full	Full	Full	Full	Full	NO	Limited	Full	Limited	Limited	Full
CUSTOMISATION	Full	Full	Full	Limited	Full	NA	Full	Limited	Limited	Limited	Full
DATASET LICENSING	Full	Full	Full	Full	NO	NO	NO	Full	NO	NO	Full
ACCESSIBILITY	Full	Full	Full	Full	Limited	NA	Limited	Limited	Limited	Limited	Full
EXTENSIBILITY	Full	Full	Full	Limited	Full	Limited	Limited	Limited	Full	Limited	Full
TECHNOLOGICAL ENVIRONMENT	Python	PHP, Drupal CMS	Scala	Ruby on rails	Java & Web apps	NA	Java & Python	NA	Java	PHP	PHP
OTHERS	Good manual Simple to use	Easy to use platform	Tracking & Measure of performance	Flexible, cloud-based, easy to use	R stat, support transparency, linked data	Reliable, scalable, large OD Analyses	Track & measures user impact on OD	Remote web services; easy deployment	Guides, videos, tutorial. Linked data	Deal with fraud, aids transparency	None

3 Methodology

3.1 Research Objectives

The aim of the study is to determine the needs of stakeholders regarding the desirable affordances of the next-generation open data platform that could reduce the barriers to the adoption and use of open data. The work explicitly aims at answering the following questions:

(Q1) To what extent are transparency-enhancing features supported on selected open data platforms? In answering this question, we adopted a set of criteria that enable direct and indirect support for dataset transparency and socialisation around datasets for evaluating selected platforms. These criteria were partly based on past studies [14]. The identification of remaining features (done iteratively) was based on whether the features will impact data and organizational transparency. Finally,

the twelve features elaborated in Sect. 2 were employed for the analysis - Metadata, Data and File Formats; Flexible search facility for datasets; Social Media, and Collaboration; Dataset Publishing; Federation and Harvesting; Data Analysis; Visualisation tools; Personalisation; Customisation; Dataset licensing; Accessibility and Extensibility mechanisms. We also reviewed extant literature on open data platforms.

(Q2) What are the perceived limitations of open data platforms? To tackle this question, we considered the barriers identified by stakeholders during the collective intelligence workshops and interviews that are related to data transparency and organizational transparency. We associated these barriers with specific stakeholder categories and specified the nature of transparency quality impacted by each barrier. We present the analytical model for Transparency Qualities in Sect. 3.2.

(Q3) What specific platform features suggested by Stakeholders? To answer this question, contributed solutions to identified barriers provided by stakeholders during interviews and workshops were analysed. The specific features were organized under three categories including (a) information needs of stakeholders – what kinds of datasets do stakeholders highlight as important for them? (b) social and collaboration needs – what features relate how stakeholders wish to interact and collaboratively make sense of the published data? (c) understandability, usability, and decision making needs – what platform features do stakeholders desire to be able to carry out inferences on datasets, enable easy sense-making of data and make decisions based on available data.

3.2 Analytical Framework

Our study is conceptually grounded in computer-mediated transparency characterized by Meijer in [21]. Computer-mediated transparency is characterised as unidirectional or one-way between parties involved in the transparency relationship and decontextualized regarding information being shared. As a necessary condition for any form of transparency, computer-mediated transparency should ensure that external or receiving parties are capable of processing the information that has been made available [15]. Thus, in our study, we argue, that open data platforms features should explicitly mediate effective transparency in terms of access and understandability. In particular, our study conceptualizes transparency as a *quality* which should be "satisficed" by an open data platform [5]. Specifically, we employ the deconstruction of the transparency construct described in [5] as shown in Fig. 1 to underpin our analysis of pathologies and platform-related barriers.

3.3 Data Gathering

We employed four data gathering methods in this study. The first source of information is extant literature on open data platforms. The second source of information is the survey of selected open data platforms through hands-on use and exploration of selected platforms in addition to review of accompanying documentations. Expert interviews are the third source of information. Lastly, we conducted a Collective Intelligence (CI) workshop involving stakeholders such as publishers, data intermediaries and wrangler, platform developers and end-users.

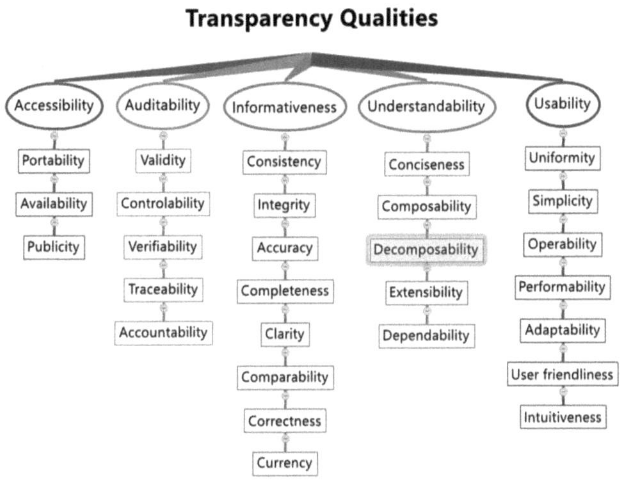

Fig. 1. Transparency Qualities and Sub-Qualities [5]

The CI workshop was co-organized with Dublin City Council in April 2015 to identify and to understand the perceived barriers and issues with using the current set of open data platforms and essential and expected features in the next generation platforms. There were ten participants in the workshop from different stakeholders' categories including data consumers, suppliers, mediators or intermediaries and Enablers. Data consumers are end-users of open data as the general public or apps developers. Data suppliers include all entities involved in the publishing of datasets, Non-Governmental organizations or private sector entities.

4 Results

4.1 Features of Existing Platforms

We studied the features available on the platforms by analysing extant literature and documentations about the platforms in addition to a systematic review of selected instances of these platforms. We observed that CKAN, DKAN, Sokrata and Semantic MediaWiki are clear outliers by providing fully-developed features that support between nine and twelve of the review criteria described in Sect. 2 (details presented in Table 1). Other solutions support between one and seven fully-functional features. Nevertheless, while the use of social media, personalisation and customisation of platform features are common in state-of-the-art platforms, the support for metadata schema adaptation, advanced visualisation of datasets and granular accessibility of datasets are limited. Features such as availability of publishing pipelines were also found to be relatively limited on existing platforms. Personalisation and customisation features are very common features of existing platforms and most of these platforms also support social media integration for social sharing and posting to social media pages. Table 1 provides a summary of features for the eleven platforms.

4.2 Platform Pathologies

This section presents our findings based on the analysis of the information captured from the interviews and workshop sessions about barriers and limitations of current open data platforms, and the desired affordances to address the identified shortcomings. The categories of stakeholders engaged include consumers, enablers, suppliers, and mediators of open data.

The findings show that the most common obstacle for using of open data platforms is *perceived the poor quality of open data provided on the platforms*. According to the stakeholders, poor data quality is largely characterised by poor metadata, failure to present data appropriately to different audience and difficulty in locating data of interest. Other barriers are related to irrelevancy of datasets, the poor usability of platforms and lack of examples of the prior use of available datasets. We highlight in Table 2 some of the issues identified by stakeholders. For each obstacle identified we specified a category for the problem such as "Non-relevancy" or "Poor awareness" and also associated the barrier with a high-level transparency quality attribute (such as Accessibility) and a more specific quality attribute like "Availability". This coding is underpinned by the model described in Sect. 3. Poor usability stood out as the most prominent shortcoming.

4.3 Desired Affordances

The desired essential features contributed by stakeholders for next generation open data platforms which were obtained from workshop and interviews were grouped under three related categories: (1) Information needs, (2) Social and Collaboration, and (3) Understandability, Usability and Decision making needs.

On the information need, stakeholders requested future platforms to ensure easy access to datasets related to their immediate environment and communities. They also requested the inclusion of datasets of interests: crime statistics, public health data as well as data about the environment. In addition, stakeholders demanded dataset rating, feedback comments on datasets, collaborative curation of datasets, prioritization and voting on dataset requests. Furthermore, stakeholders requested incentives for the use of platform through reward system and gamification under the social and collaborative needs. For better understandability, usability and improved decision-making on the upcoming platforms, stakeholders demanded customizable dashboards, custom visualization tools, data mining tools, support for linked data and map-based search. Some also demanded for a question and answering features. Details of the desired affordances are shown in Table 3.

5 Discussion

The contemporary open data platforms provide limited data cataloging features and largely lack interactivity, which implies low user engagement. While the design of the current open data platforms aligns well with the technical users needs (developers and data scientists); the findings from our study show that ordinary end-users (members of

Table 2. Shortcomings of selected open data platforms

Issue	Stakeholder	Problem	Transparency quality	Specific transparency quality
Available datasets not aligned to people's interest (low relevance)	Consumer	Non-relevancy	Accessibility	Availability
Problems with metadata	Supplier/mediator	Poor data quality	Informativeness	Clarity
Low data usefulness	Consumer	Non-relevancy	Accessibility	Availability
Difficulty in locating data, no good standard for cataloguing, describing and linking data	Consumer	Poor data quality	Understandability	Conciseness
Reliability of data feeds and keeping them updated; old data is gone off	Consumer	Poor data quality	Informativeness	Currency
Poor service design and management	Supplier/mediator	Poor platform usability	Usability	User-friendliness
Information spread out across multiple organisations, no single one-stop portal for open data access	Supplier	No one-stop consolidation	Understandability	Integration
Data is presented to user is a technical way and the use unfamiliar technical language is pervasive	Supplier/mediator	Poor usability	Understandability	Comprehension
Minimal publicity about available data leading to lack of awareness of its existence	Supplier/enabler	Poor information	Accessibility	Publicity

(*Continued*)

Table 2. (*Continued*)

Issue	Stakeholder	Problem	Transparency quality	Specific transparency quality
High density data that requires design input for better accessibility	Consumer	Technicality of data presentation	Understandability	Comprehension
No information on the circumstances of data production	Consumer	Poor data quality	Informativeness	Metadata quality and provenance
No user-friendly file-formats and interface	Consumer	Usability of data	Usability	Operability - data formats
Lack of relevant information (engagement support) for users browsing the website/service (without an explicit goal)	Consumer	Weak user engagement	Usability	User-friendliness
Lack of examples available for smart use of open data	Consumer	No smart use example	Usability	User-friendliness
Poor bandwidth to successfully access and interact with Open Data platforms	Enabler	Poor access to open data platforms	Accessibility	Resource constraints
Level of openness and licences for commercial use	Enabler	Openness of data	Usability	Openness
The level, the type and the granularity of data alignment to the target audience (spreadsheets for ordinary users and API for data developers)	Supplier	Poor data quality	Usability	User-friendliness

(*Continued*)

Table 2. (*Continued*)

Issue	Stakeholder	Problem	Transparency quality	Specific transparency quality
Poor usability with inadequate preview, mapping, visualisation, multiple data layering features	Consumer	Usability of data	Usability	User-friendliness

Table 3. Desired features in future open data platforms

Information needs
• Inventory of local business people —support local enterprise • Key indicators for my neighbourhood (social, crime, environment, health, etc.) for informed decision making • Local info of all kinds—planning, sports, cultural, commercial, social, councilors –
Social and Collaborative Needs
• Support for anonymity • Closed loop, share results of interactions & collaborations • Contact tools for finding Public Administration, forums, public participation, network, social media interaction, twitter, facebook • Dataset rating & ranking, Calendar, wall style fast feedback, live chat, comments on dataset, blogs, collaborative editing, curating, adding metadata for dataset • Support diversity of engagement , creative use of data, inclusion, new knowledge generation from data, viral travel of data, expert facilitation of conversations about data, live webcast with feedback, newsfeed for decision, prioritisation of data request based on needs/voting Project management tool Reward system, gamification, acknowledgement • Verification/traceability of account
Understandability, Usability and decision-making needs
• Modelling and simulations, Animations e.g. to illustrate changes, Interactive Visualisation and Predictive Analytics • Customizable Dashboards, Personalisation • Data availability over several portable devices; Customised display —pull in from other platforms + layer data • Support for integration of related datasets • Data mining tools & analysis tools for information extraction to support decision-making or interface to external tools • In-file data descriptors • Interactions, 'rate my dataset', submit suggestions on map get feedback • Interactive graphical representations as transparency enhancing tools, promote easy reading, understandability, making sense of data • Linked data for comparison • Map based search & queries • Tools for Metadata management • Modelling tools, layered maps • Personalisation —search with filter, especially with memory, notifications & updates • Polls and surveys on datasets • Public or anonymous profile options Q & A mechanism Question & answer, feedback mechanism monitored up-to-date Scheduling services— identify what is logged, actioned or closed Statistics under-pinning policies

the public) require more usability and user-friendliness as an imperative for improved transparency. We argue that the principle of citizen-centric and one-stop service design applied to e-government e-services portals should be mapped onto the next generation open data portals, in order to offer the public with a one-stop access to "data services". In particular, we argue that tools supporting social interaction between platform users are very essential for improved transparency in the context of monitorial, deliberative as well as participatory democracy [19, 20, 21]. Specifically, based on the feedback received from the interviewed experts and workshop participants, features like content sharing and possibility to discuss around datasets are pivotal. The integration of social media platform with an open data platform was one of the key subjects of the research reported in [2]. Moreover, the stakeholders expressed a strong need for anonymity while using open data. This observation supports the thesis that citizens perceive open data portals as a government-owned website and fear that their privacy may be endangered. Our findings are consistent with Open Data Barometer report [9, 10]. We argue that, the next generation open data platforms should augment and extend the existing solutions. Therefore, based on the review of the contemporary platforms we have identified platforms implementing open architecture that can be extended to accommodate new desired features. We observed that platforms like CKAN, DKAN and Semantic MediaWiki are the best candidates as they are most extensible, free and open source. Moreover the platforms provide a rich set of extension mechanisms with a set of guidelines for supporting developers in building new extensions. Callimachus and DataTank platforms are also open source and could be modified however considering no explicit extension mechanism implemented, any modifications would require significantly more effort. Thus, we believe that existing platforms provide a good foundation for next-generation platforms with the desirable set of affordances.

6 Conclusions

In this work we provide an elaboration on the shortcomings of the current generation and core affordances for future open data platforms. This study complements state-of-the-art knowledge on open data platforms from the perspective of different stakeholders groups. While related studies have dealt mainly with the technical aspects of the platforms, our findings provide deeper insight on socio-technical issues in general based on the direct contributions of different categories of stakeholders. Guided by our results, we argue, that some open data platforms such as CKAN, Socrata, DKAN, Semantic MediaWiki are extensible and provide suitable support for better data transparency of datasets. Specifically, CKAN, DKAN and Semantic MediaWiki are open-source platforms which standout regarding extendibility. Thus, we consider these platforms as plausible base infrastructure for building next generation open data platforms with significantly improved adoption and use potentials by public administration, citizens and other stakeholders.

References

1. Ojo, A., Porwol, L., Waqar, M., Osagie, E., Stasiewicz, A., Hogan, M., Harney, O., Riordan, R.: Pathologies of open data platform and desired transparency-related affordances for future platforms. In: 17th Annual International Conference on Digital Government Research (2016)
2. Alexopoulos, C., Zuiderwijk, A., Charapabidis, Y., Loukis, E., Janssen, M.: Designing a second generation of open data platforms: integrating open data and social media. In: Janssen, M., Scholl, H.J., Wimmer, M.A., Bannister, F. (eds.) EGOV 2014. LNCS, vol. 8653, pp. 230–241. Springer, Heidelberg (2014)
3. Baldwin, C.Y., Woodard, C.J.: The architecture of platforms: a unified view. In: Working Papers – Harvard Business School Division of Research, pp. 1–31 (2008)
4. Callimachus Project: http://callimachusproject.org/. Accessed 17 June 2016
5. Cappelli, C., et al.: Managing transparency guided by a maturity model. In: 3rd Global Conference os Transparency Research, Chung 2000, pp. 1–17 (2013)
6. CKAN Open Data Portal Platform. http://ckan.org/. Accessed 17 June 2016
7. Colpaert, P., et al.: A three-level data publishing portal (2014)
8. DataTank. https://www.iminds.be/en/technology/datatank. Accessed 17 June 2016
9. Davies, T.: Open Data Barometer. Open Data Institute and World Wide Web Foundation (2013)
10. Davies, T., et al.: Open Data Barometer Global Report. World Wide Web Foundation (2015)
11. DKAN Open Data Platform. http://www.nucivic.com/dkan/. Accessed 17 June 2016
12. Enigma Publich Data Search. http://enigma.io/. Accessed 17 June 2016
13. European Union Open Data Portal. https://data.europa.eu/euodp/en/data. Accessed 17 June 2016
14. Group, W.B.: Technical Assessment of Open Data Platforms for National Statistical Organisations (2014)
15. Heald, D.: Varieties of transparency. In: Proceedings-British Academy, pp. 25–43 (2006)
16. Information Workbench. https://www.fluidops.com/en/portfolio/information_workbench/. Accessed 17 June 2016
17. Janssen, M., et al.: Benefits, adoption barriers and myths of open data and open government. Inf. Syst. Manag. **29**(4), 258–268 (2012)
18. Junar Open Data Platform
19. Keane, J.: Monitory democracy and media-saturated societies. Griffith Rev. **24**(2009), 47 (2009)
20. Meijer, A.: Government transparency in historical perspective: from the ancient regime to open data in the netherlands. Int. J. Publ. Adm. **38**(3), 189–199 (2015)
21. Meijer, A.: Understanding modern transparency. Int. Rev. Adm. Sci. **75**(2), 255–269 (2009)
22. OpenDataSoft SaaS Platform. https://www.opendatasoft.com/. Accessed 17 June 201606-17
23. Peled, A.: Effective openness – the role of open data 2. 0 in a wider transparency program. In: 3rd Global Conference on Transparency Research, pp. 44–46 (2012)
24. PublishMyData Linked Data Publising Platform. http://www.swirrl.com/. Accessed 17 June 2016
25. ROUTE-TO-PA H2020 EU Project. http://routetopa.eu/. Accessed 17 June 2016
26. Semantic MediaWiki. https://www.semantic-mediawiki.org. Accessed 17 June 2016
27. Socrata Platform. https://www.socrata.com/. Accessed 17 June 2016

Knowledge Sharing in Industrial Associations and Science and Technology Parks

Danielly Oliveira Inomata[1,2(✉)], Eric Costa[2,3], Solange Mazzaroto[2,4], Cláudio Santos[2], Ana Cristina Barros[2], António Lucas Soares[2,3], and Gregorio Varvakis[1]

[1] Federal University of Santa Catarina, Florianópolis, Brazil
inomata.danielly@gmail.com, grego@egc.ufsc.br
[2] INESC TEC, Porto, Portugal
{eric.m.costa, solange.mazzaroto, claudio.a.santos, acbarros}@inesctec.pt
[3] Faculty of Engineering, University of Porto, Porto, Portugal
als@fe.up.pt
[4] Faculty of Arts, University of Porto, Porto, Portugal

Abstract. Knowledge management practices are used in collaborative networks promoting innovation in order to share critical knowledge among network members towards improving organizational results. This paper proposes to explore the channels and practices for knowledge sharing in collaborative networks, by means of an exploratory multiple case study carried out in two types of collaborative networks: (i) industrial associations; and (ii) science and technology parks. Empirical evidence has been collected from interviews with managers of the collaborative networks and of organizations participating in the collaborative networks. The contribution of this paper to the knowledge management literature is twofold: (i) it provides a characterization of the channels and technology used for knowledge sharing in collaborative networks based on empirical evidence and (ii) it describes knowledge sharing practices used among organizations to foster new forms of connectivity between groups and individuals.

Keywords: Knowledge sharing · Collaborative networks · Industrial associations · Science and technology parks

1 Introduction

Science and Technology Parks (STPs) have an impact in the economic growth and regional development [1, 2]. Companies in environments of STPs can benefit from the knowledge spillovers resulting from the research, ideas and experiences from both universities and research centers [3] or by the contact with other companies located in the park [4]. Industrial associations (IAs) also act as facilitators to provide critical knowledge for their associated companies, which can result in innovation and competitive advantages [5].

The discipline of Knowledge Management (KM) is concerned with the organizational knowledge as a process coming from individuals in a collectivity, providing benefits to individuals, employers, communities of practice and organizations [6].

H. Afsarmanesh et al. (Eds.): PRO-VE 2016, IFIP AICT 480, pp. 60–72, 2016.
DOI: 10.1007/978-3-319-45390-3_6

The challenge of this paper is to identify practices for knowledge sharing in networked innovation environments, such as STPs and IAs, contexts that to the best of our knowledge are still unexplored in the literature [7]. Previous research is related with how the process of KM is carried out in small and medium enterprises [8, 9], the dynamics of knowledge creation in inter-organizational cooperative networks [10], and the knowledge transfer in collaborations between companies from developed and underdeveloped countries [11]. This paper is focused on understanding knowledge sharing practices in STPs and IAs.

Knowledge sharing is described as a process that involves source, channel, message, destination and context [6, 11]. In this paper, the knowledge sharing in networks is defined as the behavior of individuals to pass along what they know to people with whom they interact (e.g. by means of product development, resource sharing, etc.), and vice-versa. Therefore, it is a mutual process of individual knowledge sharing to create a new knowledge in collaboration, where actors use multiple resources to this end, such as formal and informal channels, tools and technologies.

Regarding knowledge sharing in collaborative networks (CNs), previous research has been carried out in contexts such as internationalization of SMEs [12], services for industrial apprenticeship [13], socio-semantic collaborative platforms [14], social capital [15], or supply chains [16]. However, there is still a need to study knowledge sharing processes in different CNs and contexts, such as STPs and IAs. This gives room to the following research questions:

- How knowledge sharing practices occur among network members in IAs and STPs as collaborative networks?
- What have been the impacts for knowledge sharing?

Therefore, this paper proposes to explore the practices and channels for knowledge sharing in STPs and IAs, two different types of CNs. To this end, one STP and three IAs were selected to perform an exploratory multiple case study. The data sources used were semi-structured interviews with managers of the CNs and of organizations participating in these four CNs. This paper contributes to the literature of KM, with specific focus on the knowledge sharing process, as well as to the scientific knowledge of CNs. First, based on empirical evidence, it provides new insights about the channels and practices of knowledge sharing used in STPs and IAs. Moreover this study discusses how the establishment of CNs can facilitate knowledge sharing between companies associated with IAs, as well as startups incubated in STPs.

2 Literature Review

2.1 Collaboration and Collaborative Networks

The widespread concept of collaboration means "to work together towards a common goal" and involves mutual engagement of participants to solve problems in a process of sharing risks, resources, responsibilities and rewards [17]. In a context of inter-organizational networks, collaboration is considered as the process where two or more organizations perform tasks together to obtain collective results [18]. Therefore, in a collaboration process, autonomous actors interact with each other through formal and informal negotiations, creating together rules and structures to govern their relationships, as well as to define how they will act and make collaborative decisions [18].

Collaboration clearly impacts business performance and is recognized as a mechanism to increase competitiveness and, in many cases, the survival of companies [19]. So, many organizations are joining efforts using different collaborative models by joining complementary skills and capabilities, gaining new competitive advantages to deal with global market dynamics and environments [20]. Parung and Biticti [21] consider that the most important objective for establishing a collaboration is to become sustainable and create benefits for stakeholders in a competitive environment.

Many companies and organizations are forming collaborative networks with their partners for different purposes, such as to share risks and benefits [21] or to obtain important information and knowledge for their activities [12]. Camarinha-Matos and Afsarmanesh [22] define collaborative networks (CNs) as networks of organizations formed by different and autonomous entities that are geographically distributed and that are heterogeneous regarding operating environment, culture, social capital, and goals. Most of the times, interactions and collaborative processes in CNs are supported and mediated by information and communication technologies [18, 22]. Organizations can form different types of networks, such as supply chains, virtual enterprises, clusters or extended enterprises [21]. Despite the existence of many network forms, CNs differ in the fact that collaboration is "an intentional property that derives from the shared belief that together the network members can achieve goals that would not be possible or would have a higher cost if attempted by them individually" [22].

In this paper, two different types of CNs are considered: (i) industrial associations (IAs); and (ii) science and technology parks (STPs). We consider an IA as being both an organization that represents different companies of a specific industrial sector (sectoral IA) or an entity that act as an intermediary within a multisector network of companies in a specific area of activity (multi-sectoral IA). In both cases, membership for companies is voluntary and IAs develop an effective communication between their associated industrial firms with local governments [23]. Nevertheless, one of the main focus of IAs is to promote and improve collaboration among network members [24]. Regarding STPs, they are characterized by the physical facilities with buildings, laboratories, etc., combined with managerial support and with close access to research organizations [7]. Thus, they consider not only the university knowledge transfer for companies, but also the demand from these companies to the development of more effective knowledge to meet market needs [25]. Although there is no common definition of STPs, most of the literature emphasizes the importance of three dimensions [7]: (i) the physical location is in close proximity to a research institution; (ii) the knowledge or high-tech business is the core business; and (iii) there is a specialized managerial function to help the startups with new businesses (incubation).

2.2 Knowledge Sharing in Collaborative Networks

Knowledge is information that is combined with experience, interpretation and reflection, representing a high value form of information to be applied for making decisions or taking actions [26]. Knowledge sharing is considered as one of the more critical components for the KM success [27] and is the process when individuals exchange mutually tacit and explicit knowledge, creating new knowledge in collaboration [28]. Therefore, new knowledge is incorporated in an organizational knowledge only when is shared and assimilated using routines, documents and organizational practices [29]. This knowledge can be incorporated through action, contextualized in practice and subject to actors' interpretations [26].

In CNs, the knowledge sharing process happens at the individual and organizational levels. The individual knowledge is used to develop the organizational knowledge base but this organizational knowledge is not just the sum of the individual knowledge [30]. Technologies, techniques, and people create unique patterns of interactions to form the organizational knowledge. This knowledge is difficult to imitate by other organizations since the interactions are developed and shaped by the unique history and culture of organizations from a specific CN [30].

The ideal situation is obtained when network members share critical knowledge, exploit expertise and use resources for collective benefit [31]. Huang and Cummings [32] define critical knowledge as "the most influential information, know-how, or feedback that contributes directly to task outcomes". Cormican and Dooley [31] consider that an immediate access to the latest information, which includes information from external sources, allow organizations to reach a critical competitive edge.

Many practices can be adopted by organizations for the process of knowledge sharing. The Asian Productivity Organization (APO) presents a practical KM guide where an extensive set of knowledge sharing practices are indicated to be used by organizations [33], such as peer assist; communities of practice; collaborative physical workspaces; knowledge cafes; taxonomy; knowledge bases; social networking services; voice and VOIP; knowledge clusters; collaborative virtual workspaces; knowledge portal; mentor/mentee. This paper shows the knowledge sharing practices used between network participants of STP and IAs.

3 Research Methodology

Case research was used in this study because it enables an empirical description of a contemporary phenomenon within its real-life context [34]. Specifically, an exploratory multiple case study was used to explore the channels and practices of knowledge sharing in different types of CNs, i.e. IAs and STPs. The unit of analysis in this study is the collaborative network. Table 1 characterizes the case studies of this research.

Table 1. Case studies

ID	Type of CN	Area of activity	Network members	Interviews
STP	STP	(i) Technologies	84	9
		(ii) Biotechnologies	17	
IA1	IA (sectorial)	Aerospace industry	34	4
IA2	IA (multi-sectorial)	Production technologies	103	6
IA3	IA (multi-sectorial)	Innovation	367	4

These cases were selected by convenience sampling [35], i.e. access to data and contacts with companies was easier. Empirical evidence was collected using semi-structured interviews with managers of the CNs and of organizations participating in these four CNs. The aim was to obtain a good sample representing different types of organizations and CNs. Although the study included only one STP, two areas of its activity were analyzed, in a total of nine interviews. Regarding the IAs, one sectorial and two multi-sectorial were selected. Although also being multi-sectorial, IA2 was considered in this study since it presents a different type of association. In this case, different types of organizations were interviewed, such as technology providers, research institutes and universities, industrial associations, and end users.

Different management roles of the member organizations were interviewed, such as Presidents, CEOs, CFOs, Administrators, and people from technical departments, all of them with an active role in CNs. At the beginning of the interviews, the interviewees were asked to sign an informed consent document, allowing the interviewers to record the conversation for accuracy purposes. The duration of these interviews was between 10 min and 1 h, and were carried out personally or through voice/video call between March and April 2016. After that, all the interviews were transcribed and coded with the support of the qualitative data analysis software MAXQDA.

4 Findings

4.1 Within-Case Analysis

STP Case. The main collaboration objective of the STP is to create the means for companies that are in this environment to perform national and international networking activities, as well as to provide specific services to the network members, such as intellectual property and legal support. This is well reflected in the critical knowledge that is shared between network members and in the way they interact with each other. For example, the information channel prioritized is the personal contact and therefore events are realized in a way to guarantee that entrepreneurs can learn with mentors, specialists in intellectual property, investors, etc. The main impacts of this knowledge sharing are related with the own STP's dynamic, mainly in terms of networking and development of business plans. These aspects make sense due to the development stage of startups, i.e. they are starting to develop and grow their businesses, and searching for new investments.

IA1 Case. This IA promotes collaboration within its network through collaborative R&D projects, by performing two roles: (i) main promoter of R&D projects by inviting other companies to become project partners; or (ii) stimulator of member's participation in major R&D projects by disseminating information about R&D calls and opportunities. It is the understanding of the network manager that the sector represented by this IA is fragmented into several small businesses. Despite having recognized capabilities, their smaller size is perceived as an obstacle to access international value chains. Thus, this IA promotes collaboration as a mean to strengthen the value network capabilities, so that companies are able to deliver higher value added goods and services. Collaboration is accomplished through basic communication channels, such as telephone and e-mails. The efforts put forward by this IA have contributed to a regular and consistent presence of network members in the sector's main international fairs and exhibitions, thus providing greater visibility of the sector.

IA2 Case. The collaboration objectives of IA2 are to develop new processes and new products, elaborate R&D projects and promote the development of joint proposals. Therefore, the critical knowledge shared are the ones created by these collaborations. This is accomplished through Open Days, meetings, and organization and participation in events, such as national and international fairs. The main channel used is the personal contact, through visits and phone calls. Emails, tools for documents sharing, and the website of the IA are also used as the channels for knowledge sharing. All of these bring impacts for the network participants that are measured by the development of new investments and new projects, as well as by the establishment of partnerships.

IA3 Case. This IA promotes the collaboration between the network participants mainly through the use of a collaborative platform and Open Days. This platform is an exclusive channel for the associated companies that allow, for example, an intelligent search to understand the distribution of the different associates within the different markets. With this information, contacts and collaborations are established between the network participants. Regarding the type of critical knowledge shared, IA3 share knowledge about innovation practices and tools for innovation management, as well as some practical knowledge on how to develop R&D project proposals. The main practice for sharing this knowledge is through collaborative physical workspaces, such as events and conferences, and the channels used are the personal contact and the collaborative platform. From the perspective of this IA, the main impacts of the CN for the associated companies is the establishment of international contacts, the improvement of innovation capabilities and the public recognition.

4.2 Cross-Case Analysis

In order to be effective, KM practices must be related with the organizational strategic objectives [6, 33]. This study aims at identifying the collaboration objectives of the analyzed CNs and to link them to the practices and channels of critical knowledge sharing among network participants that impact their results.

With the cross-case analysis, it was possible to relate the collaboration objectives with the knowledge sharing practices used among the network participants. These collaboration objectives were uniformed and categorized in:

- **Create working groups:** interactions between different companies that gather together to discuss about strategic decisions;
- **Develop business relationships:** interactions between different business partners for the purpose of supporting the commercialization of a technology, product, or service;
- **Develop new products:** interactions towards collaborative product development;
- **Develop R&D projects:** interactions towards R&D projects development;

- **Share intellectual capital:** refers to the sharing of relational capital (customers), human (people) and structural (infrastructure, patents, etc.);
- **Share technological knowledge:** refers to the sharing of information about technologies;
- **Share business experiences:** refers to the sharing of knowledge on how to conduct business, e.g. information about investors, business plans, product launches, etc.;
- **Share information about events:** refers to the communications between network members concerning events for customers' prospection, new suppliers, etc.

The Collaborative Physical Workspaces was the knowledge sharing practice identified as the one that supports more collaboration objectives. This practice was not cited for the technological knowledge sharing or information sharing about events. In these cases, the Knowledge Cafes was the one prioritized, which is realized in an informal way by the network participants. Being in a Collaborative Physical Workspace allows to interact with other people through face-to-face communication to talk, discuss or simply ask a question. In well-conceived workspaces, human interactions happen, enabling knowledge sharing and creation [33].

From the collaboration objectives, three types of critical knowledge were identified and categorized as follows:

- **Technological knowledge:** refers to technological knowledge, scientific knowledge, technological solutions, patents (intellectual property), events about technology, etc.;
- **Market knowledge:** refers to knowledge about markets, investors and investments, business contacts, business opportunities, etc.;
- **Administrative knowledge:** refers to business plans, activities management, legal advice, certification, etc.

Table 2 relates the critical knowledge types and the channels for knowledge sharing used among network participants of the analyzed CNs.

In the analyzed STP, three types of critical knowledge were identified, which are mainly shared through personal interaction. This contact and interaction between network participants is facilitated by being in the same physical environment. Events and social networks were also cited as information channels to share knowledge.

Regarding the IAs, participants of IA1 and IA2 also share the three types of critical knowledge, using different channels. In the sectorial IA1, network participants use not only information and communication technologies (e.g. cloud, knowledge repositories, emails, and VOIP) to share both market and technological knowledge, but also the personal contact to share administrative knowledge. In the case of the multi-sectorial IA2 that has predefined technology providers and end-users, besides the channels supported by technology, critical knowledge (of all types) is shared through personal contact in meetings and events. Finally, in the multi-sectorial IA3 that does not have pre-defined end-users within the network, critical market and technological knowledge is shared with the support of a collaborative platform, but also using emails, phone and personal contact.

Table 3 summarizes the collaboration forms and the impacts of knowledge sharing for the organizational results of the network participants. In IAs, the impacts of

Table 2. Critical knowledge and channels for knowledge sharing

CN	Critical knowledge	Channels for knowledge sharing
STP	Administrative knowledge	People, social networks, events, emails, internet and VOIP
	Market knowledge	People, social networks, VOIP, emails, events and web site
	Technological knowledge	Emails, social networks, internet, events, people and VOIP
IA1	Administrative knowledge	People
	Technological knowledge	Emails, cloud and knowledge repositories
	Market knowledge	Videoconference, emails and VOIP
IA2	Administrative knowledge, Market knowledge and Technological knowledge	People, cloud, emails and web site
IA3	Market knowledge	Collaborative platform, phone and emails
	Technological knowledge	Collaborative platform, events, people, phone and emails

knowledge sharing are related with continuous improvement, technology development and increased product portfolio, attracting new projects, and increased knowledge base. This last one is much more evident in participants such as industrial associations and researcher institutes, rather than associated companies, which the main collaboration objective is to develop R&D projects. The process of continuous improvement

Table 3. Impacts of knowledge sharing for organizational results

CN	Organization type	Collaboration objectives	Impacts for organizational results
STP	Startup	Share technological knowledge Share information about events	New investments in business
	Startup	Share business experiences	Creation of opportunities and visibility. New investments in business
	Startup	Develop business relationships	New investments in business. Increased knowledge base. Increased networking
	Pre-incubated	Share business experiences	Business plan development. Increased networking
	Pre-incubated	Share business experiences	Customer acquisition. Increased networking
	Pre-incubated	Share business experiences	Business plan development

(*Continued*)

Table 3. (*Continued*)

CN	Organization type	Collaboration objectives	Impacts for organizational results
IA1	Company	Develop business relationships	Increased number of contracts. Increased networking
	Research institute	Develop R&D projects	Attracting new projects
IA2	Company	Develop new products	Increased product portfolio. Continuous improvement
	Association	Develop R&D projects	Increased knowledge base
	Association	Develop R&D projects Share business experiences	Increased knowledge base
	Company	Develop R&D projects Create working groups Share intellectual capital	Continuous improvement. Increased knowledge base. Costs reduction. Increased networking
	Company	Develop new products Develop R&D projects	Technology development. Increased networking
IA3	Company	Develop business relationships Develop new products	Customer acquisition
	Company	Develop new products Create working groups	Increased networking. Continuous improvement

mentioned by the participants is related with improvements in processes and technologies for the product development. Regarding the STP, in both pre-incubated and startups, the main impacts of being connected with the network are related with increased networking, business plan development, new investments in business, creation of opportunities and visibility. This result is very consistent and aligned with the main collaboration objective stated by the participants of sharing business experience.

5 Discussion

Socialization among different companies, both in the STP and IAs, is beneficial to the knowledge transfer, as it represents a strategy for sharing tacit knowledge within the group [36] and for increasing the knowledge base about markets, technologies and businesses. Besides this, it was clear that other results were experienced by the participants, such as increased number of contracts, contacts, and product portfolio, driven not only by the formal participation in these CNs but often also through the informal interaction with other network participants. Particularly, the benefits for companies is that a conversation between people can be the start for the development of trust, which is a critical factor to promote creativity [36].

According to Hansson [7], learning in organizations was mainly connected to acquire new knowledge about technical problems and their solutions, not knowledge for continuous learning and creativity. Moreover, this knowledge was most of the times managed by an isolated set of processes within the closed boundaries of an organization. However, specifically in the case of the analyzed STP, it became evident that interactions between network participants was facilitated by the formal events, but in addition to this practice, informal meetings or coffee hours are socialization practices cited as those that create better dynamics for knowledge sharing. There is a knowledge and experience sharing that are facilitated by being under the same physical space. Peña [37] state that these business incubation centers (STP in this case) offer a unique setting to develop an important relational capital element, where entrepreneurs overcome together some difficult moments regarding firms' gestation periods.

In IAs, there is evidence about the existence of physical workspaces of interaction that facilitate the knowledge sharing process. The events such as the Open Days have as main objectives to find solutions for a problem of a specific company or to identify innovative solutions for the routine activities of this company. For example, through these events, companies from the network "open their doors" for the other associates. During the event, a company presents its main constraints, needs and trends for the future, in terms of the level of its production processes and technologies. It is also carried out a visit to its facilities, where the invited associated companies present their solutions, which are jointly discussed or are presented individually to the organizing company. Regarding the collaboration objectives and the impacts in the organizational results, in IAs it is much more related with the process of product development and research process. In general, IAs articulates strategies and activities for the common benefit.

6 Conclusion

Sharing is the systematic exchange of knowledge between people, facilitated by the use of technologies or by face-to-face interactions. Results show that technologies such as websites, emails and VOIP are used in all analyzed CNs for information and knowledge sharing. Moreover, a collaborative platform is used in IA3. However, in this latter case there is a low adherence and acceptance from the network members due to the fact that they already use other applications and tools that replace the use of a platform, for example, intranet, task managers, etc. Interviewees suggest that this kind of collaborative platforms can have a great impact in their results but it must be considered as a means to reach an end, not as an end in itself. It is necessary to have face-to-face meetings, hear the companies and motivate them, i.e. meet their business needs.

An effective process of knowledge sharing, represented in this study by the collaborative physical workspaces, provides the creation of new knowledge, sharing of experiences and knowledge base increasing about businesses, markets and technologies. Results of this study show that the collaboration is facilitated by the formal process of participation in the network, but it seems that the informal and face-to-face interactions bring better results and more impacts in the companies' activities. Open Days was the knowledge sharing practice identified as one new form of socialization that can be practiced by other types of networks and that can contribute to the development of the KM area.

This paper has also practical relevance for innovation network managers and participants by allowing the decision-makers, for example, to verify the practices that occur informally and that can be implemented in the network, improving the knowledge sharing process. In the case of the STP, the Knowledge Café that happens informally within the participants can be intensified by understanding the need for formal and informal situations, allowing entrepreneurs to share experiences and know-how. In this kind of environments, results showed that the tacit knowledge sharing has impact in business development.

Empirical evidence has also shown the importance of physical workspaces in facilitating knowledge management practices. Future research could focus on the trade-off between knowledge dispersion and its assimilation, in other words, how knowledge from outside of the typical areas of actuation of organizations can be assimilated towards enlarging their knowledge base, when compared to the knowledge that is shared with the nearest neighbors.

This paper has some natural limitations. The adopted methodological approach is qualitative in nature where it is difficult to obtain a generalization of the results. The objective of this kind of research is not to generalize the results but the main value is the specific description, related to the particularity of a specific context. Therefore, the main contribution of this paper was in understanding the knowledge sharing practices adopted in CNs with the specific context of IAs and STPs, aspect not well explored in previous research.

Acknowledgments. This work was conducted during a scholarship supported by the Doctoral Sandwich Abroad Program CAPES/PDSE at the Federal University of Santa Catarina. Financed by CAPES – Higher Education Personnel Improvement Coordination within the Ministry of Education of Brazil. Additionally, this research was funded by the Portuguese funding agency, Fundação para a Ciência e a Tecnologia (FCT), through the Ph.D. Studentship SFRH/BD/110131/2015. It was also supported by the Project "TEC4Growth - Pervasive Intelligence, Enhancers and Proofs of Concept with Industrial Impact/NORTE-01-0145-FEDER-000020" financed by the North Portugal Regional Operational Programme (NORTE 2020), under the PORTUGAL 2020 Partnership Agreement, and through the European Regional Development Fund (ERDF).

References

1. Ratinho, T., Henriques, E.: The role of science parks and business incubators in converging countries: evidence from Portugal. Technovation **30**, 278–290 (2010)
2. OECD: Managing national innovation systems. Paris (1999)
3. Hansson, F., Husted, K., Vestergaard, J.: Second generation science parks: from structural holes jockeys to social capital catalysts of the knowledge society. Technovation **25**, 1039–1049 (2005)
4. Díez-Vial, I., Fernández-Olmos, M.: Knowledge spillovers in science and technology parks: how can firms benefit most? J. Technol. Transf. **40**, 70–84 (2015)
5. Wang, X., Kopfer, H., Gendreau, M.: Operational transportation planning of freight forwarding companies in horizontal coalitions. Eur. J. Oper. Res. **237**, 1133–1141 (2014)

6. Dalkir, K.: Knowledge management in theory and practice. Routledge, Abingdon-on-Thames (2013)
7. Hansson, F.: Science parks as knowledge organizations – the "ba" in action? Eur. J. Innov. Manag. **10**, 348–366 (2007)
8. Wong, K.: Critical success factors for implementing knowledge management in small and medium enterprises. Ind. Manag. Data Syst. **105**, 261–279 (2005)
9. Desouza, K., Awazu, Y.: Knowledge management at SMEs: five peculiarities. J. Knowl. Manag. **10**, 32–43 (2006)
10. Balestrin, A., Vargas, L., Fayard, P.: Criação de conhecimento nas redes de cooperação interorganizacional. RAE-revista Adm. Empres. **45**, 52–64 (2005)
11. Narteh, B.: Knowledge transfer in developed-developing country interfirm collaborations: a conceptual framework. J. Knowl. Manag. **12**, 78–91 (2008)
12. Costa, E., Soares, A.L., Sousa, J.P.: A new insight in the SMEs internationalization process. In: 16th IFIP WG 5.5 Working Conference on Virtual Enterprises, PRO-VE 2015 (2015)
13. Vallejos, R., Gomes, J., Lima, C., Nesello, P.: Combining collaborative networks and knowledge management: the SENAI case. In: 15th IFIP WG 5.5 Working Conference on Virtual Enterprises, PRO-VE 2014 (2014)
14. Soares, A., Alves, F.: Collaborative spaces as mediators for information sharing in collaborative networks. In: 13th IFIP WG 5.5 Working Conference on Virtual Enterprises, PRO-VE 2012 (2012)
15. Widen, G.: Social capital and knowledge sharing: lessons learned. In: 12th IFIP WG 5.5 Working Conference on Virtual Enterprises, PRO-VE 2011 (2011)
16. Buzon, L., Bouras, A., Ouzrout, Y.: Knowledge exchange in a supply chain context. In: 5th IFIP WG 5.5 Working Conference on Virtual Enterprises, PRO-VE 2004 (2004)
17. Camarinha-Matos, L., Afsarmanesh, H.: Concept of collaboration. In: Encyclopedia of Networked and Virtual Organizations, pp. 311–315 (2008)
18. Carneiro, L.M., Soares, A.L., Patrício, R., Azevedo, A.L., de Pinho Sousa, J.: Case studies on collaboration, technology and performance factors in business networks. Int. J. Comput. Integr. Manuf. **26**, 101–116 (2013)
19. Cao, M., Zhang, Q.: Supply chain collaboration: impact on collaborative advantage and firm performance. J. Oper. Manag. **29**, 163–180 (2011)
20. Romero, D., Galeano, N., Molina, A.: Mechanisms for assessing and enhancing organisations' readiness for collaboration in collaborative networks. Int. J. Prod. Res. **47**, 4691–4710 (2009)
21. Parung, J., Bititci, U.: A metric for collaborative networks. Bus. Process Manag. J. **14**, 654–674 (2008)
22. Camarinha-Matos, L., Afsarmanesh, H.: Collaborative networks: a new scientific discipline. J. Intell. Manuf. **16**, 439–452 (2005)
23. Bennett, R.: Business associations and their potential contribution to the competitiveness of SMEs. Entrep. Reg. Dev. **10**, 243–260 (1998)
24. Bell, S.: A victim of its own success: internationalization, neoliberalism, and organizational involution at the business council of Australia. Polit. Soc. **34**, 543–570 (2006)
25. Link, A., Scott, J.: The economics of university research parks. Oxford Rev. Econ. Policy. **23**, 661–674 (2007)
26. Davenport, S., Davies, J., Grimes, C.: Collaborative research programmes: building trust from difference. Technovation **19**, 31–40 (1998)
27. Kuo, F., Young, M.: A study of the intention: action gap in knowledge sharing practices. J. Am. Soc. Inf. Sci. Technol. **59**, 1224–1237 (2008)

28. van den Hooff, B., De Ridder, J.: Knowledge sharing in context: the influence of organizational commitment, communication climate and CMC use on knowledge sharing. J. Knowl. Manag. **8**, 117–130 (2004)
29. Cohen, W., Levinthal, D.: Absorptive capacity: a new perspective on learning and innovation. Adm. Sci. Q. **35**, 128–152 (1990)
30. Bhatt, G.: Knowledge management in organizations: examining the interaction between technologies, techniques, and people. J. Knowl. Manag. **5**, 68–75 (2001)
31. Cormican, K., Dooley, L.: Knowledge sharing in a collaborative networked environment. J. Inf. Knowl. Manag. **6**, 105–114 (2007)
32. Huang, S., Cummings, J.N.: When critical knowledge is most critical: centralization in knowledge-intensive teams. Small Gr. Res. **42**, 669–699 (2011)
33. APO: Knowledge management tools and techniques manual. Asian Productivity Organization. Tokyo, Japan (2010)
34. Yin, R.K.: Case study research: design and methods (2009)
35. Merriam, S.B.: Qualitative Research and Case Study Applications in Education. Jossey-Bass Publishers, San Francisco (1998)
36. Handzic, M., Chaimungkalanont, M.: Enhancing organizational creativity through socialization. Electron. J. Knowl. Manag. **2**, 57–64 (2004)
37. Peña, I.: Intellectual capital and business start-up success. J. Intellect. Cap. **3**, 180–198 (2002)

Using an Information Management Model as a Roadmap for Information Systems Implementation in Supply Networks

Cláudio Santos[1(✉)], Ana Cristina Barros[1], Tom Dawes[2], and António Lucas Soares[1,3]

[1] INESC TEC, Porto, Portugal
{claudio.a.santos,acbarros}@inesctec.pt
[2] Valuechain.com, Sci-Tech Daresbury, Daresbury, UK
tdawes@valuechain.com
[3] Faculty of Engineering, University of Porto, Porto, Portugal
als@fe.up.pt

Abstract. In the era of information overflow, the effective implementation of models for managing multiple information streams may contribute to organizations' decision-making capabilities. Even though literature has proposed several information management models, little has been described about their implementation in real-world settings. This paper presents a case study on the usage of an information management model in the implementation of a collaborative system in a supply network. The case application analysis reinforces the value of using information management models to account for cultural aspects in the mapping of information needs and in the analysis of multiple stakeholders' requirements.

Keywords: Information management model · Supply networks · Collaboration · Case study

1 Introduction

The methods employed by organizations to manage their information flows has been playing a critical role in the competitiveness of their businesses. Environmental turbulence requires that organizations have access to accurate information in real time in order to respond quickly to changes. Furthermore, and particularly observed in a number of sectors, organizations are focusing on their core competencies and thus, start establishing collaborations with partners to search for complementary resources and capabilities, this being an emerging paradigm for competitiveness of some industrial sectors [1].

Existing information management models in the literature describe the process by which information is managed by organizations internally and with other organizations, with little exploration of the implications about implementation of these models in particular organizational networks. This article aims at demonstrating, by means of a single case study, the importance of using an information management model during the implementation of information systems in supply networks.

Published by Springer International Publishing Switzerland 2016. All Rights Reserved
H. Afsarmanesh et al. (Eds.): PRO-VE 2016, IFIP AICT 480, pp. 73–83, 2016.
DOI: 10.1007/978-3-319-45390-3_7

This article is organized as follows: Sect. 2 reviews the literature on information systems and information management models, Sect. 3 describes the research methodology used in this study, Sect. 4 introduces a brief characterization of the case under study, Sect. 5 analyses the case application and, finally, Sect. 6 presents the discussion.

2 Literature Review

2.1 Information Systems

Information systems involve people, knowledge, organization and information technology that, by implementing an information management model, allow supply networks to collect, analyze, and disseminate information in order to improve decision making [2]. Information systems enable real-time communication between all partners within a supply network regardless their location and enable improving the quality of the information shared [2–5]. Table 1 provides an overview of research about information systems for supply networks.

Table 1. Information systems for supply networks

Information system	Description	Benefits	References
Data Warehouses (DW)	Combination of databases for the network relationships	Enables data integration and effective information management in a single system; lower costs in supply network integration; supports partners' relationships	[5]
Electronic Data Interchange (EDI)	Acquire the accurate information flow when information on electronic format is shared through different network computers	Improvement of information quality and operational efficiency; reduction of transaction cost	[4–7]
Enterprise Resource Planning (ERP) system	Efficient information system for a better integration of information and knowledge	Support information flow; information is entered immediately when changed, allowing the transfer of the changes to all partners; sharpest vision for supply network management	[8]

(Continued)

Table 1. (*Continued*)

Information system	Description	Benefits	References
Knowledge management platforms	Management of all available information and knowledge in one distributed knowledge base	Provides access to internal information models of supply network partners based on their competence profiles	[9]
Product Lifecycle Management (PLM) system	Provide product information to several regional ERP system and a global application systems	Information directly introduced into the receiving systems	[10]
Project Integrated Databases (PIDs)	Systematic infrastructure for project information sharing across supply network	Allows the sharing of project information to the network partners through a shared conceptual product/process model	[11]
Radio Frequency Identification (RFID) based information systems	Automatic identification technology that uses smart labels in order to trace products through the supply network and trace quality information	Product information stored in the tag ship; eliminate the delay of information sharing; information is gathered and stored into the product throughout its life cycle	[5, 6, 12–14]
Web-centric Extended Enterprise Knowledge Sharing (WEEKS) system	Intends to enhance performance of the supply network through the sharing of knowledge electronically	Assists the decision making, provides to managers alternatives to a problem after receiving pertinent information, provides a structured framework to aid the development of knowledge management	[15]
Web-Collaborative Extranets (WCEs)	Electronic management systems which in a secure and private network uses web protocols to share information	Cost efficiency, time efficiency, communication improvement, trust and transparency, knowledge base and learning organization	[11]

Table 1 shows the variety of systems that exist for accurate sharing of information among organizations. Effective information sharing is possible when the required information systems are implemented, providing accurate information to supply network partners that supports effective decision making [3, 5]. Still, the implementation of information systems alone will not be sufficient to improve the collaboration in supply networks. In fact, in order to develop information sharing capabilities companies have to work in parallel on the connectivity of information systems, on the willingness of companies to share information and on the capability of supply network partners to manage information effectively [2, 16].

2.2 Information Management Model

Information management is the management of the processes and systems that create, acquire, organize, store, distribute, and use information [17]. Thus, information management helps people and organizations access, process and use information efficiently and effectively. Organizations with information management capability are able to provide data and information to users with the appropriate levels of accuracy, timeliness, reliability, security, confidentiality, connectivity, and access [18]. Towards this goal, companies develop and implement information management models following a number of steps. Table 2 synthesizes the stages of information management models found in the literature. The first column presents the stages of information management models and is followed by its description, which is based on the references mentioning it as identified in the last four columns of the table.

Table 2. Stages of information management models

Stages	Description	[19]	[16]	[20]	[17]
Identifying needs	Identifying what and why information is needed, how it is going to be used, and the attributes that will enhance its value, quality, and usefulness	X		X	
Sensing	Detecting and identifying information concerning: economic, social and political changes; competitors' innovations that might impact the business; market shifts and customer demands for new products: anticipated problems with suppliers and partners		X		
Creating	Generating and producing new information				X
Gathering	Collecting relevant information from internal and external sources	X	X	X	X
Organizing	Indexing, classifying, and linking information to support its retrieval when it is needed		X	X	X

(*Continued*)

Table 2. (*Continued*)

Stages	Description	[19]	[16]	[20]	[17]
Storing and maintaining	Physically housing the information in databases or file systems in order to avoid the repeated collection of information and updating it to ensure that the best information available is used		X	X	X
Processing	Accessing, analysing, and presenting the information in a way that supports decision making		X	X	
Sharing	Distributing or disseminating to the adequate users according to the information needs	X		X	X
Using	Applying the information made available for better decision-making	X		X	X

3 Research Methodology

This paper reports a case study about the implementation of a collaborative system in a multi-tiered supply network. Insights from this implementation are discussed through the lens of the information management model framework introduced in Sect. 2.2.

Data was collected through a structured interview with the manager of the company in charge of the development and implementation of the system. Secondary data was collected from company reports and presentations. A brief overview of the company is presented in the next section.

4 Company Characterization

This study reports a UK-based information and communication technology (ICT) company engaged in the development of collaborative platforms for multi-tiered supply networks. The company has a wide range of solutions dedicated to promote the sharing of strategic, tactical and operational data between network members to support collaborative work and performance improvements.

The company develops solutions for SMEs, large Primes and Tiers 1, raw materials suppliers and industrial associations. These solutions support visibility and transparency among supply networks in several ways: (1) through the streamlining of operations, (2) the real-time monitoring of risks in the network, (3) the mapping of members' capabilities and (4) through collaborative platforms to support new product introduction, work package management, logistics, etc. In terms of operations, collaboration potentiated by the ICT company's solutions enable customers' relationship management, supply chain management, collaborative inventory management, aggregated procurement, collaborative tendering and collaborative project management. This system could be added to the information systems already reported in the literature and

Fig. 1. Display of collaborative project management features for New Product Introduction (NPI)

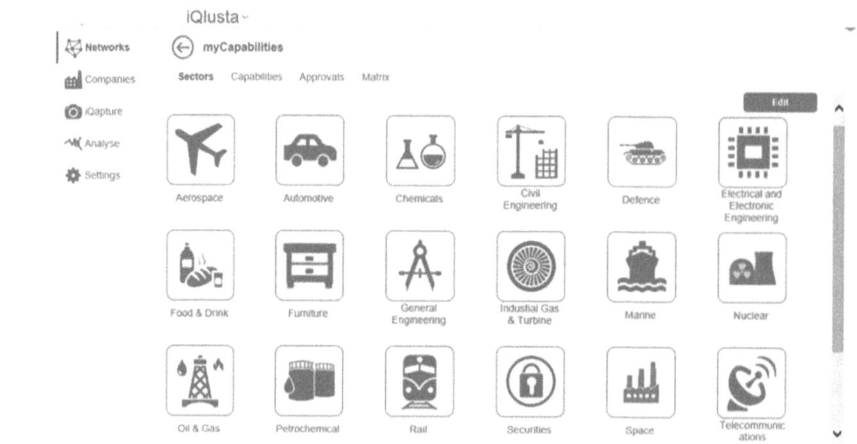

Fig. 2. Display of capabilities mapping features

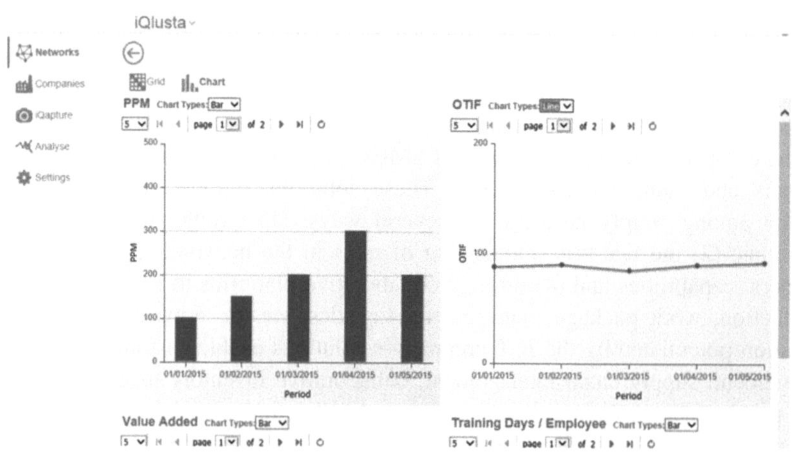

Fig. 3. Display of performance monitoring features

listed in Table 1. For a better understanding of the information systems in study, Figs. 1, 2 and 3 provide a snapshot of some of the functionalities embedded in ICT company's solutions.

5 Case Application

This section demonstrates that the information management model proposed in Sect. 2.2 can be used as a roadmap for information systems implementation in supply networks by describing the implementation of a collaborative system in a supply network in the UK. The case application refers to a national-level program promoted by a large trade organization, aimed to improve the competitiveness and performance of the supply chain of a particular UK industrial sector. This program supports several initiatives and projects with close interaction with small to large businesses. The following text describes the implementation, by the company, of a collaborative system in this network.

The objective of the implemented collaborative system is to promote, through a portal, the secure sharing of data between network members to ultimately support the development of network intelligence. The project had five stakeholders: the trade organization, regional alliances, training providers, suppliers of parts and components and customers. The trade organization is the main promoter of the project.

Addressing multiple, and sometimes conflicting, stakeholders' requirements was one of the key challenges of the project. Companies in different tiers of the supply chain have different business objectives. On a systems perspective, these companies present disparate system infrastructure, maturity and capabilities. Despite these challenges, the unifying objective is embodied in the mission of the main promoter of the project – improve overall supply network performance. This, according to the perspective of the trade organization, was possible by stimulating collaborative working methods in supply networks.

Contrary to a typical top-down and autocratic approach where suppliers have to conform to a system that is being pushed by a large organization, this project envisioned a collaborative system where all stakeholders voluntarily participate. As important as mapping information requirements, the cultural aspect, meaning how to engage people and align objectives, was critical.

After a period of mapping business processes, communication and information flows, organization by organization, workshops with groups of stakeholders were held to present the proposed set of features, the proof of concept and the expected benefits for each stakeholder group. This provided the basis for scoping the requirements that meet the expectations of every stakeholders' group.

The requirements were broken down into a mock-up of the features of the system. The refinement of requirements and functionalities was an iterative process, as data availability was largely dependent on the engagement level of stakeholders. The system was initially fed with data readily available from the trade organization concerning basic information such as members name, address, contacts, etc., which was then validated by the members.

Participation in the virtual network initiates by creating a passive network. A passive network is created by introducing basic network members' data into the information system in order to facilitate network members' enrolment in the future. The conversion of a passive network into an active network, where members are invited to connect, collaborate and share data, is the next step. Different types of data are maintained by different stakeholders: auditing data, for example, is generated by suppliers and training providers, but maintained by OEMs and Tiers 1 (the customers). Performance data is also generated by suppliers, and verified and validated by their customers. Financial and quality approvals data is generated by third party systems (e.g. credit checking systems and regulatory agencies), but companies are also able to complement with more detailed information. The system is currently not able to gather data from other third party systems, such as data concerning potential socio-economical risks in the supply chain.

Data is organized into six areas: basic information (contacts, addresses, documents, etc.), capabilities (technical and manufacturing capabilities, quality approvals, plant lists, etc.), collaboration (activities, projects, business opportunities, e-mail integration, etc.), auditing, performance and finance (credit check and accounts management). Data is stored in a third party cloud host, and its integrity is verified through an automated exception monitoring system.

Information processing supports collaboration between network members. The sharing permissions depends on data ownership, which is split between four parties: public (data that can be found in other sources, such as the internet); companies; network leader, which in this case application is the trade organization, and third party systems. Data owners decide which data they want to share and with whom. Table 3 presents a summary of the information management model stages from the case analysed above.

Table 3. Information management model stages from the case study

Stages	Implemented approach
Identifying information needs	• Multiple stakeholders' requirements analysis; • Different objectives and systems' maturity and infrastructures; • Need to understand cultural aspects from organizations; • Individual interviews: data, communications and business processes mapping; • Workshops with stakeholders' groups to present envisioned benefits and proof-of-concepts
Sensing	• Scoping the requirements and functionalities that meet the expectations of every stakeholders' group; • Iterative process with high stakeholders' involvement
Creating	• Data readily available from the Trading organization; • Passive network: data inserted but not online yet
Gathering	• Members invited to connect and share data: active network; • Performance, financial and capabilities data
Organizing	• Six areas: basic information, capabilities, collaboration, auditing, performance and finance

(Continued)

Table 3. (*Continued*)

Stages	Implemented approach
Storing and maintaining	• Stored in a third party cloud host; • Data integrity audits; • Data maintained by their owners, who decide with whom to share
Processing	• Data is processed through collaborative processes from the network members
Sharing	• Sharing permissions dependent on data owners willingness to share
Using	• Pilot stage: supply chain management and collaboration

Observing Table 1, the described collaborative system could be categorized as a Web-Collaborative Extranet, such is the emphasis put in building secure private networks to share information. However, features of Knowledge Management and Web-centric Extended Enterprise Knowledge sharing platforms can also be pointed out. This suggests a mixed-approach in the design of the information system that is embedded in the collaborative platform.

This collaborative system is in its pilot stage, however, it has been implemented in a network of approximately seven hundred suppliers, fifteen OEMs and Tiers 1, six regional alliances and eight training providers. By considering multiple stakeholders' requirements and organizational cultures, the envisioned benefits from the implementation of the collaborative platform include network intelligence and visibility of business opportunities.

6 Discussion

The case application analysis highlighted the importance of the organizational change needed to support the implementation of a collaborative system. Despite having a governance entity - the trade organization – the implementation of the collaborative system did not follow the typical top-down approach, where requirements are pushed down from a large organization. It was extremely dependent on members' voluntary participation and data inputs and, as such, understanding cultural aspects of organizations was important to engage them into the system.

The intention of this case study was not the analysis of a technical solution, simply mapping information flows and stakeholders' requirements, but rather on the insights about using information management models in the implementation of information systems in a multi-tiered supply network. Thus, information management models should put more emphasis in the understanding of multiple stakeholders' objectives and in benefits realization to promote a more effective implementation. The approach followed by the organization implementing the collaborative platform involved features from multiple information systems paradigms.

The empirical evidence collected in this research showed a number of benefits of using the information management model as a tool for the implementation of information systems in supply networks. The information model potentiates an ecosystem of intelligence, productivity and collaboration among supply chain partners at all tiers of the supply chain. The information model simplifies the capture, consolidation and analysis of multiple datasets from supply chain partners and allows for the creation of highly customisable user interfaces to meet diverse stakeholder requirements. By simplifying supply chain descriptive analytics, key stakeholders are able to redeploy data capture and focus on diagnostic analytics to identify root causes of supply chain risks and performance issues which will provide valuable insight for predictive and prescriptive supply chain analytics.

This study reports a single case study, which is a limitation for generalization. Future research should focus on extending the analysis to other implementations and consider literature on technology adoption to deepen our knowledge about information management models.

Acknowledgements. This work was funded by the Project CMUP-ERI/TPE/0011/2013 of the CMU Portugal Program, financed by the Fundação para a Ciência e a Tecnologia (Portuguese Foundation for Science and Technology), and by the Project "NORTE-07-0124-FEDER-000057", financed by the North Portugal Regional Operational Programme (ON. 2 – O Novo Norte), under the NSRF, through the European Regional Development Fund, and by national funds, through the Portuguese funding agency, Fundação para a Ciência e a Tecnologia.

References

1. Durugbo, C., Erkoyuncu, J.A.: Managing integrated information flow for industrial service partnerships: a case study of aerospace firms. Procedia CIRP **16**, 338–343 (2014)
2. Fawcett, S.E., Osterhaus, P., Magnan, G.M., Brau, J.C., McCarter, M.W.: Information sharing and supply chain performance: the role of connectivity and willingness. Supply Chain Manag.: Int. J. **12**, 358–368 (2007)
3. Baihaqi, I., Sohal, A.S.: The impact of information sharing in supply chains on organisational performance: an empirical study. Prod. Plan. Control. **24**, 743–758 (2013)
4. Li, S., Lin, B.: Accessing information sharing and information quality in supply chain management. Decis. Support Syst. **42**, 1641–1656 (2006)
5. Omar, R., Ramayah, T., Lo, M.-C., Sang, T.Y., Siron, R.: Information sharing, information quality and usage of Information Technology (IT) tools in Malaysian organizations. African J. Bus. Manag. **4**, 2486–2499 (2010)
6. Legner, C., Schemm, J.: Toward the inter-organizational product information supply chain – evidence from the retail and consumer goods industries. J. Assoc. Inf. Syst. **9**, 119–150 (2008)
7. Wilson, T.D.: Information sharing: an exploration of the literature and some propositions. Inf. Res. **15**, 1–11 (2010)
8. Toloie-Eshlaghi, A., Asadollahi, A., Poorebrahimi, A.: The role of Enterprise Resources Planning (ERP) in the contribution and integration of the information in the supply chain. Eur. J. Soc. Sci. **20**, 16–27 (2011)
9. Smirnov, A., Shilov, N., Kashevnik, A.: Developing a knowledge management platform for automotive build-to-order production network. Hum. Syst. Manag. **27**, 15–30 (2008)
10. Hüner, K.M., Schierning, A., Otto, B., Österle, H.: Product data quality in supply chains: the case of Beiersdorf. Electron. Mark. **21**, 141–154 (2011)

11. Ajam, M., Alshawi, M., Mezher, T.: Augmented process model for e-tendering: towards integrating object models with document management systems. Autom. Constr. **19**, 762–778 (2010)
12. Bindel, A., Rosamond, E., Conway, P., West, A.: Product life cycle information management in the electronics supply chain. Proc. Inst. Mech. Eng. Part B - J. Eng. Manuf. **226**, 1388–1400 (2012)
13. Bottani, E., Bertolini, M., Montanari, R., Volpi, A.: RFID-enabled business intelligence modules for supply chain optimisation. Int. J. RF Technol. Res. Appl. **1**, 253–278 (2009)
14. Da Xu, L.: Information architecture for supply chain quality management. Int. J. Prod. Res. **49**, 183–198 (2011)
15. Shih, S.C., Hsu, S.H.Y., Zhu, Z., Balasubramanian, S.K.: Knowledge sharing-a key role in the downstream supply chain. Inf. Manag. **49**, 70–80 (2012)
16. Marchand, D.A., Kettinger, W.J., Rollins, J.D.: Information orientation: people, technology and the bottom line. Sloan Manag. Rev. **41**, 69–80 (2000)
17. Detlor, B.: Information management. Int. J. Inf. Manag. **30**, 103–108 (2010)
18. Mithas, S., Ramasubbu, N., Sambamurthy, V.: How information management capability influences firm performance. MIS Q. **35**, 237–256 (2011)
19. Davenport, T.H., Prusak, L.: Information Ecology: Mastering the Information and Knowledge Environment. Oxford University Press Inc., Oxford (1997)
20. Choo, C.W.: Information Management for the Intelligent Organization: The Art of Environmental Scanning (2002)

Hyperconnectivity and Interoperation - Networked Business Processes

Semi-automated BP Integration in Virtual Organizations

Katarzyna Adamiak[1], Hodjat Soleimani Malekan[2(✉)], and Hamideh Afsarmanesh[2]

[1] Barbusselaan 72, 1102 TX Amsterdam, The Netherlands
adamiakkasia@yahoo.com
[2] Informatics Institute, University of Amsterdam, P.O. Box 94323, 1090 GH Amsterdam, The Netherlands
{h.soleimanimalekan,h.afsarmanesh}@uva.nl

Abstract. Organizations frequently form various types of partnerships, of which one form is the virtual organization (VO). In VOs, members share part of their capabilities and capacities to seize bigger market opportunities. For effective collaboration however, also sharing knowledge and details about their business processes (BPs) and services is required. If achieved, VO can act as a large and more capable organization, with a repository/pool of services. But to mimic large organizations, VOs need to both drop less optimized overlapping services from this repository and integrate similar services. Our stepwise semi-automated methodology facilitates creating a most optimized pool of BPs with clean and valid integrated processes/services for the VO. A chain of software tools is also introduced in the methodology next to some partially manual steps. The presented solution is applied and evaluated in a real construction industry.

Keywords: Virtual organizations · Business process integration

1 Introduction

Due to globalization and increased dynamism of industrial environment, organizations increasingly form partnerships, such as virtual organizations (VOs), in order to improve their performance and increase their competitive advantage. In VOs, organizations share knowledge, skills and resources to seize market opportunities, create innovative products, and provide value-added services [1]. As such they become a great enabler to increase enterprise agility, consequently ensuring better ability to survive in dynamically changing market conditions. In this research we adopt the following definition of the VO: "an association of legally independent organizations (VO partners) that come together and share resources and skills to achieve common goals, such as acquiring and responding to a market/society opportunity [1]". We further focus on addressing the BPs that are practiced by individual VO partners, and how they can be effectively shared, integrated, and used for the benefit the VO as a whole.

This paper introduces our semi-automated approach through one real example case of cooperation from the construction industry, which also serves as the proof of concept

H. Afsarmanesh et al. (Eds.): PRO-VE 2016, IFIP AICT 480, pp. 87–100, 2016.
DOI: 10.1007/978-3-319-45390-3_8

to validate our approach. In construction industry, partnership formation is traditionally a popular practice; however, often performed in an unstructured way. In a typical project, different organizations specialized in various disciplines are required to jointly fulfil multiple construction tasks. In our real example scenario, organizations co-work during the life time of every project, while they do not share and/or lend their business processes (BPs) to each other. In other words, each involved organization provides a set of own services needed for each construction project, and executes its services during different stages of the project. But currently organizations do not share/lend their processes, which prohibit them from working more efficiently together and/or delivering composed value-added services in the VO, as it typically happens among different departments within one large organization.

A collaborative operation in a niche market in construction industry is exemplified here, involved in construction of eco-friendly buildings. This type of projects is currently popular, with increasing number of interested investors. However, construction of eco-friendly buildings requires the use of novel technology, materials, and expertise from various disciplines. Through cooperation among a set of organizations however, a VO can successfully deliver such niche projects. This provides more opportunities and increases the reputation of the VO, consequently bringing more profit to the involved smaller organizations and increasing their chance of survivability in market turbulences. Continued collaboration among organizations and sharing all their abilities in the VOs create the base for partners to provide more efficient as well as a wider range of services and scope of operation. For instance, to enable proper management of their joint operations in VOs, participating organizations need to share their BPs. In the past, organizations who worked only in one project were reluctant to share and/or merge their BPs. They considered this against their autonomy and confidentiality concerns. However today, once negotiating a VO collaboration contract, organizations are more willing to do so; especially once realizing advantages resulted from their BP integration in VOs. BP integration helps organizations to standardize their practiced BPs and use each other's experiences and best practices. Furthermore, it helps with getting to know about the expertise of other organizations, which also underpins the potential of their additional collaboration in future. Another advantage that is the target of this paper is that the BP integration facilitates formation of an optimized and consistent repository of BPs at the VO level. Such processes can then support formalizing the VO collaboration plans among different organizations, so that together they can act as one larger organization. As such our approach guarantees the lack of redundancy in the BO pool, which can be resulted from simply storing all BPs of all organizations in one VO repository.

The main aims of our BP integration in VOs are twofold: (i) creating a shared BP repository while removing redundancies, thus reducing the size and enhancing common understanding about existing BPs by all VO organizations, and (ii) facilitating creation of composed value-added services. While the methodology presented in this research primarily addresses the former aim above, its last two stages are also applicable to the latter aim of supporting BP integration.

To build a reliable research background for the area of BP integration and to verify the existing approaches against requirements for our research, an extensive Systematic Literature Review (SLR) [2] is performed, identifying research gaps in the area.

Accordingly, it is shown that step-wise definition of a BP integration methodology is missing in approaches introduced in related research, such as in [10, 11]. The results of this extensive SLR, is the subject of a forthcoming paper. We therefore aim at introducing a semi-automated methodology needed to constitute the optimized set of processes in the VO context. Our general research question (RQ) is: *How to ensure successful co-creation of clean and valid integrated-processes among member organizations in a VO?* Three partial research questions follow this main RQ, as follows: RQ.1 *Which steps are needed to be taken by VO member organizations for creating a common set of integrated-processes?* RQ.2 *How to ensure the created integrated-processes are clean (i.e. syntactically correct)?* RQ.3 *How to ensure the methodology is valid and applicable to the VO context?*

The paper is structured as follows. Section 2 introduces the methodology applied for achieving an optimized pool of BPS and for BP integration. Section 3 addresses the suitability of our introduced methodology in an example case from construction industry. Finally, the paper is concluded, addressing a few areas of future research.

2 Methodology for BP Integration

This section addresses the RQ.1 and RQ.2 We design a semi-automated methodology, guiding the process of integrating BPs within a VO. The methodology consists of a set of practical steps that can be performed using the suggested tool chain, in order to successfully introduce a collection of clean and valid integrated-processes for collaborating organizations. Depending on some specific situations, when the BPs of an organization are already formalized, the steps 1 and 2 can be omitted (see Fig. 1). Also some other steps might need to be applied multiple times, e.g. the steps 4 and 5 that for instance need to be executed multiple times when a specific merge candidate group includes more than two BPs. Also, if more than one *merge candidate groups* are found in the VO, the part of the methodology from steps 4 to 6 must be executed multiple times. Please note that the steps in our methodology, while mostly automated, apply different methods varying among: manual, semi-automated and automated methods. All mentioned steps are captured in Fig. 1 that illustrates the BP integration methodology flowchart. Each step, from 1 to 6 in Fig. 1, is then described in more details in Sub-Sects. 2.1, 2.2, 2.3, 2.4, 2.5 and 2.6 respectively. We furthermore introduce justifications for design of our methodology based on its compliance to [3] – Design Science guidelines. Section 3 provides the validation of our proposed methodology, based on its application to a real construction case study.

2.1 Formalize Representations of BPs

Each VO member organization performs a number of business processes (BPs) within its individual operations. Those processes are not always formalised, and sometimes described only textually or in another ad hoc manner. For the purpose of processes' comparison, analysis, and integration, a collection of relevant BPs must be formalized in a consistent and common manner along all participating organizations. The formalization includes: process identification, process discovery and process model design [4].

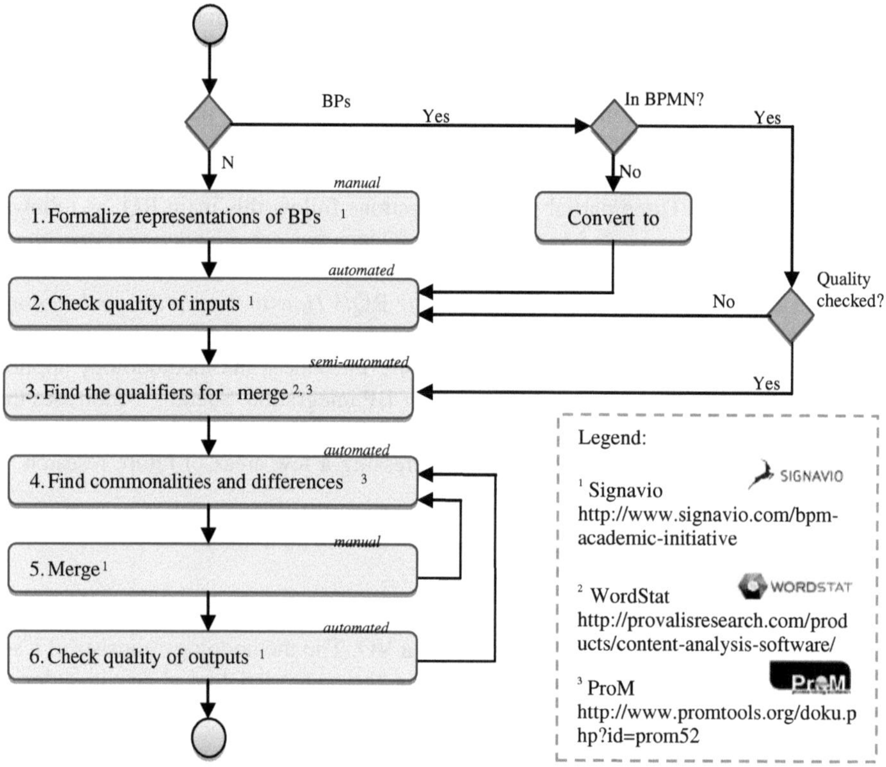

Fig. 1. BP integration methodology flowchart

In real-life, organizations formalize the design of their BPs in various ways, e.g. with use of workflow charts, UML Activity Diagrams, BPMN process models, EPC process models, etc. Different business process modelling languages (BPMLs) were evaluated in [5], who defined the Business Process Model and Notation (BPMN) as the most suitable BPML for use in CNOs. Therefore, BPMN is decided as the language used in our methodology. Varieties of tools are available for designing the BPMN process models. We indicate the web-based Signavio software, as one of the top tools and most used to support the BP design [6]. Please note that we use Signavio as the base environment to better represent the executed processes.

In summary, our *formalization of BP representations* includes following sub-steps:

- BP identification – presenting a list of relevant BPs performed by all VO member organizations and providing the appropriate naming of the identified BPs,
- BP discovery – collecting the data regarding each BP and investigating it to properly describe the overview of actions performed in the specific BP,
- BP design – illustrating the described BP by designing its graphical model representation in BPMN.

2.2 Check Quality of Inputs

The input BP models must be executable. This means, the XML logs of the entire designed BPs must be correct and readable by the software. Existence of any modelling errors disables the further comparison, analysis and proper integration of the BPs. Therefore, all the possible inconsistencies, including dead-lock or live-lock incidents, must be identified and removed at this early stage. Also we use Signavio, as it incorporates the functionality that provides the check of BP model's correctness.

2.3 Find the Qualifiers for Merge

Multiple similar BPs may exist among various organizations. In case of forming a VO, we need to collect all its member organizations' BPs in a shared repository, which may contain redundancy occurrence among the BPs in the repository. What is more, the repository may contain a number of BPs with repeated process instances, which are difficult to analyse. Therefore, as a first step we identify the similar BPs within a VO, to enable their merge in the further steps thus, aiming to reduce the size of the BP repository to the extent possible.

A number of process similarity evaluation algorithms are introduced by the researchers and a few are implemented in open source software. One such algorithm, in [7] provides the graph similarity calculation based on labelling, structural and behavioural analysis of the input processes. This algorithm is implemented in ProM 5.2 tool that is used in our methodology as the means for performing the BPs similarity check.

However, by only evaluating the similarity among all gathered BPs, the merge qualifiers' identification is not possible. In other words, here we are not searching for the similar pairs of processes, but the potential groups of BPs that are similar with each other and can be merged. To provide the more accurate semi-automatic merge qualifiers identification we identified two sub-steps. Those steps require pre-processing of BP collection, by word similarity checking on the names of processes.

A. *BP outliers potential*: Exclusion candidates identification
First sub-step aims at retrieving a set of BPs, which stand highly individual in the BP repository and can be excluded from the further analysis for similarity with other BPs. The main goal here is to potentially narrow the number of BPs included in the analysis.
B. *BP cluster potential*: Merge candidates identification
Second sub-step aims at providing a set of potential merge candidate groups that will be next analysed to consequently form a final set of BPs to be merged.

Both sub-steps are supported by semi-automatic identification of the BP clusters and BP outliers, based on the semantic distances related to their names. A function that displays the process names' map (illustrating the string semantic distances) is available in the WordStat software [8], trial version, which we have used. Based on the obtained word map, we can manually draw the circles around observable identified clusters, at the same time indicating the BP outliers.

2.4 Find Commonalities and Differences

The particular BP models located within the identified groups of BPs (the final merge candidates) at this stage must then be compared with each other to enable the merge. In [9] technique to compare BP models and indicate their differences is suggested, which is implemented in ProM 5.2 software. However, such detailed analysis can only be performed only on pairs of two BPs. Therefore, we approach both the differences identification and merging activities in hierarchical steps. In the provided hierarchy, we compare pairs of the most similar BPs with each other, define their differences, and at the same time their commonalities (containing the same fragments), and merge the processes as described in the next step. Next, one pair of merged processes is next compared with another pair of merged processes (or a single BP), their commonalities and differences are examined, and they are merged at a higher hierarchical step. This iteration lasts until we reach the top level of the hierarchy and all the BPs in a merge candidate group are integrated forming one final integrated-process. The abstraction of this approach is illustrated on Fig. 2.

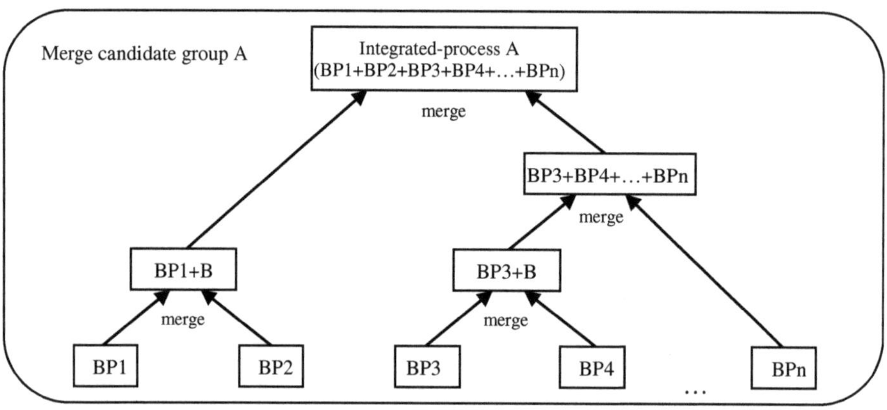

Fig. 2. Identifying differences in the merge hierarchy

2.5 Merge

Based on the information retrieved in the previous step, we can merge the processes by identifying the common fragments and resolving the differences. Some BP merging algorithms are available in research and implemented in an open source software, e.g. “EPC merge” function introduced in ProM 5.2 in [10]. We evaluate the identified automated merging algorithm, by comparing the automatically obtained result with the desired manually created integrated-processes. Based on evaluation of this algorithm, after applying it on our construction case study (see Sect. 3.5), we decided to provide this task manually. This was mainly due to the maturity level of the involved companies. The manual merging is performed mostly according to a method of [11] and is provided with the use of Signavio as the base environment. The main merging tasks include:

- Deciding on final labelling of equivalent nodes (e.g. deciding on using a more descriptive label)

- Adding a node (preceded by "XOR" split) that is not present on one of the merged models
- Rearranging the structure of fragments, which represent different sequence; e.g. if two nodes are provided in two BPs in an opposite sequence, we rearrange them into a parallel structure preceded by "AND" split
- Adding gateways where necessary, e.g. if two BPs contain different nodes placed on the same position, both nodes should be included in a merged process, preceded by an added "XOR" gateway
- Merging gateways, e.g. if two BPs contain different gateways ("AND" and "XOR") placed on the same position, these gateways should be merged into a configurable gateway ("OR")

The processes build upon each other, by adding the next BPs within the specific merge candidate group. After merging a pair of BPs, we return to step 2.4 to define the commonalities and differences of the next pair of BPs and merge this pair into one BP. This iteration lasts until all BPs in a specific merge candidate group are merged. Consequently, we obtain an integrated-process that includes all the nodes, structures and behaviours included in its entire set of initial BPs.

2.6 Check Quality of Outputs

This step together with step *2.2.* on *Check quality of inputs*, address concerns of RQ.2. Cleanness of the output processes is examined in the same way, as for the input processes, i.e. by Signavio automatic process quality check. The indicated errors and/or structure warnings must be reviewed, after which the process can be improved. After obtaining a clean integrated-process, we proceed to integrating the next merge candidate group's BPs, by returning to step 2.4. This iteration lasts until we obtain a complete set of integrated-processes.

2.7 Methodology Justification

The purpose of the presented solution is to contribute to development of the field by introducing a semi-automated BP integration methodology for organizations that co-operate in a VO. It is important to ensure that the presented solution is relevant and useful in practice. Therefore, the methodology was created in compliance with seven guideline criteria for proper design science research, as introduced in [3] and briefly explained below.

(1) *Design as an Artifact* – our methodology of BP integration is a viable academic artifact aiming to provide practical support in the operation phase of formed VO.
(2) *Problem relevance* – the solution supports an important and relevant business problem: sharing processes among partners in VOs, of special interest to SMEs.
(3) *Design evaluation* – our methodology is evaluated based on a real case study of ten individual organizations in a VO, to examine its usability and usefulness.
(4) *Research contributions* – the proposed methodology is innovative, effectively supports VO formation, and contributes to partners' BP sharing and integration.

(5) *Research rigor* – the rigorous research methods is applied to both: identifying the gaps and building research foundations, through the SLR, and evaluating every step of the proposed solution through the real case study in Sect. 3.
(6) *Design as a search process* – addressing the identified gaps, each methodology step is designed applying the state of the art in research, when it addresses the needs of the step, e.g. algorithms needed for the BP graph similarity evaluation.
(7) *Communication of research* – we aimed at designing a methodology that is understood and usable by both technical and managerial staff at the organizations for their effective BP integration in VOs. Additionally, we aimed to provide the base for software system engineers and designers that intend to develop software to support the automated BP integration in VOs, thus at providing a set of guidelines for building the new software architecture.

3 Evaluation of BP Integration Methodology

In this section RQ.3 is addressed by applying and thus evaluating the methodology introduced in Sect. 2 on a real large example case from building industry. This exercise proved fruitful, and the lessons learned and encountered limitations during this practical exercise, provides the base for future research in this area, as addressed in Sect. 4. This industry case concerns ten SMEs operating in the Polish market. These organizations have different complementary expertise, including: medium-size Construction (CC), Plumbing (P), Heating/Ventilation and Air-Conditioning (H), and Landscaping (LC), as well as some very small (one-person) SMEs including the Electrician (E), Carpenter (C), Surveyor (S), Excavator (EX), Tiler (T), and Roofer (R). Figure 3 provides a context model for their typical interactions in a construction project, where the ten companies are classified as contractors.

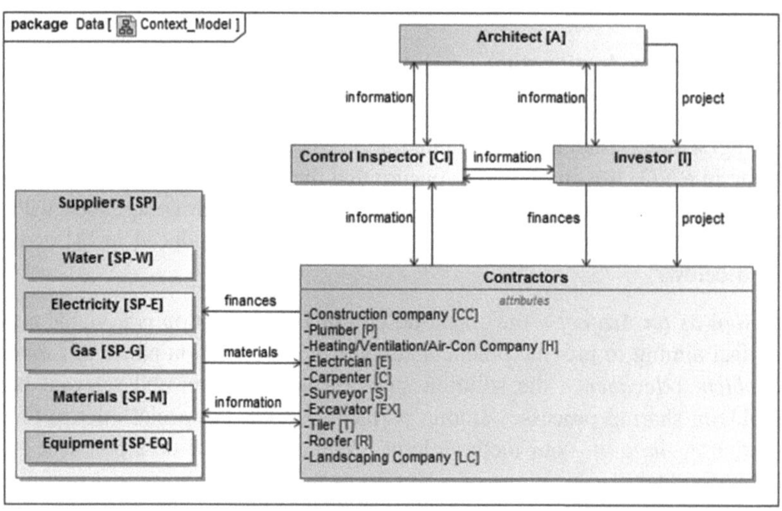

Fig. 3. Construction case study context model

A commonly used name for "customer" in building industry is investor. The investor is usually not a specialist in a construction domain, so the help of control inspectors is often needed during the project. Control inspector is a source of practical information for the architect and the investor, and is a representative of the investor on the construction site, controlling the quality of provided services.

At present, contractors operate individually at the construction site. While the same group of companies usually work together in similar projects, there is currently no long-term agreement for collaboration among the involved organizations. Therefore, the situation does not support process sharing and delivering value-added services by them. However, the construction industry remains increasingly competitive, and difficult to survive in, especially for SMEs that are analysed in our case study. They are continuously surpassed by large construction companies that offer fast services, which are cheaper but with lower quality. Therefore, the emergence of niche high quality construction projects enables SMEs collaboration through VOs, to increase their profitability, survival rate, and seizing more market opportunities. In the remaining of this section we briefly address in Subsects. 3.1, 3.2, 3.3, 3.4, 3.5 and 3.6, the application of the steps introduced in Sect. 2 for our BP integration methodology, to the real case study of ten collaborating contractor companies, as represented in Fig. 3.

3.1 Formalize Representations of BPs

For the ten contractor members in this VO, a total number of 82 BPs are identified. Using textual descriptions of these BPs provided by companies, their BPMN models are developed. One example such process, for "supplying materials" performed by the Electrician company [E], is presented in Fig. 4 and preceded by its textual description.

Electrician – supply materials [process E2]: *Supplying starts when a need for materials appears. Then, Electrician calculates the amount of needed materials, in parallel with searching other suppliers' offers. As an outcome of these tasks, a materials request is created and sent to another specific supplier. In the end, both the requested materials and an invoice are delivered and the process ends.*

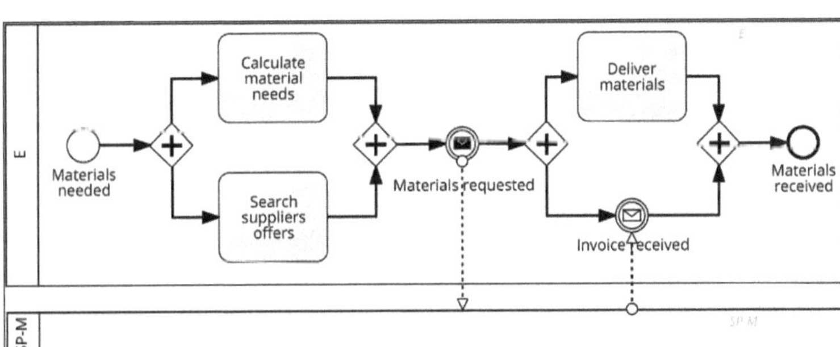

Fig. 4. E2 process formalization ("SP-M" – supplier of materials)

3.2 Check Quality of Inputs

All designed BPs are quality checked by Signavio software for potential syntactic problems. As an example, imagine that by mistake for E2 we generate the BP in Fig. 5. Running Signavio on it indicates some problems found for Electrician's "supplying materials" process (E2), as indicated in Fig. 5, with red "!" next to the XOR operation (in the center). The cleaned process is then produced to correct the syntactical errors, as shown in Fig. 4.

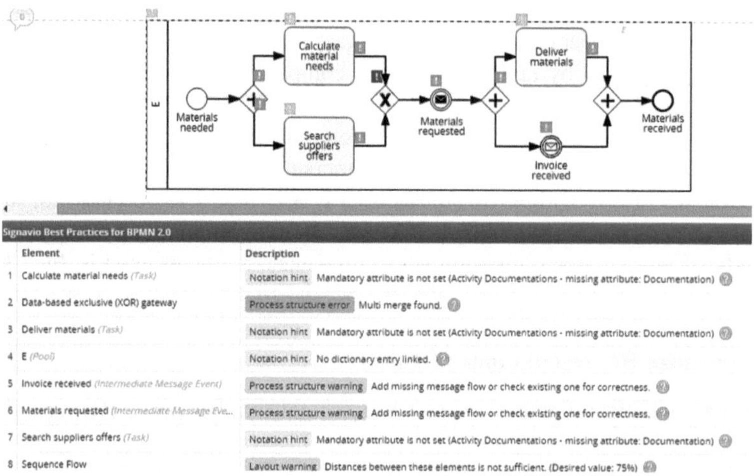

Fig. 5. Quality check by Signavio - process with error and warnings next to XOR

3.3 Find the Qualifiers for Merge

Analysing the formalized 82 BP models can spot several BPs that are more or less repeated by a number of organizations within this VO. Identification of the so called *merge qualifier processes* is the necessary first step in BP integration. Supported in semi-automated manner, this step identifies similarities among such processes.

Candidate BPs for both classes introduced in Sect. 2.3 – potential BP outliers and potential BP clusters – are identified based on two similarity checks: first on name similarity analysed with WordStat software, and second on graph similarity analysed with ProM 5.2 software. Note that only cross-organizational BP similarity is checked and not intra-organizational similarities. Then using the Link Analysis function a word map is created visualizing all similarities. Using the map, we first manually cluster potential candidate BPs for merge, as presented in Fig. 6. Each of the eight groups indicates a potential candidate for clustering and the rest are 27 potential outliers among the 82 BPs. The applied logic is explained further below.

Exclusion/outlier candidate identification – Running the two automated similarity checks identify that 27 out of 82 processes have little similarity (up to 6.7 %) to any other BP. Therefore these processes are 93.3 % different than others. Hence, produced results indicate BP outliers, and are excluded from further steps of this methodology.

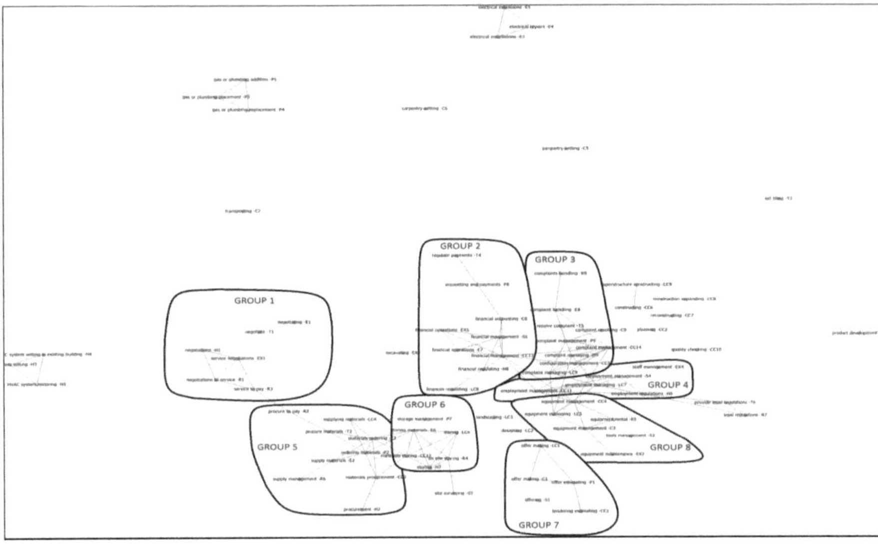

Fig. 6. Process names word map and clustering

Merge/cluster candidate identification – Eight groups are manually created on the results from running of the two automated similarity checks addressed above. In order to validate these clusters for merge purposes, we run automated graph similarity calculations once within each group, and once outside of these groups, with the use of ProM 5.2 tool. This task however requires a double conversion of the BPMN models (through Petri Net into EPC), since the automated comparison tool is only available for the EPC models, and to the best of our knowledge, there are no open source software that offers a single conversion between the BPMN and EPC languages. In practice, the first conversion (into Petri Net) was provided in ProM 6.4, and the second conversion (into EPC) was done in ProM 5.2. While this is the shortest possible way, we are certainly aware of the fact that the double conversion may cause some data loss, and thus may influence the results. For the similarity evaluation we used a threshold of 35 %, even higher than the acceptable estimation stated in [12] that uses 33 % similarity threshold. Table 1 shows positive (above threshold) and negative (below threshold) similarity results, inside and outside each merge candidate group.

Based on the right part of Table 1, we assess the usability of the proposed method. We can notice that inside all groups, the rates of their BPs being similar to any of the BPs outside of merge candidate groups (indicated in the 2nd column from right) is significantly lower than the rates of BPs that are not similar (indicated in the 1st column from right). In fact, the positive similarity with BPs outside the group is measured mostly under 25 %. Therefore, the method proves its applicability, by showing lack of similarity with other BPs, at a satisfactory level. By analysing the left part of Table 1, we can evaluate the internal group BPs and their candidacy for integration within the specific group. Furthermore, checking similarities inside each group, the similarity among BPs is larger than 50 % and sometimes 100 % (indicated in the 4th column

Table 1. Merge candidate groups' results overview

Merge candidate group:	Percentage of results that are: (inside the group)		Percentage of results that are: (outside the group)	
	Similar (result > 0,35)	Not similar (result ≤ 0,35)	Similar (result > 0,35)	Not similar (result ≤ 0,35)
1	57,14	42,86	26,43	73,57
2	100	0	12,50	87,50
3	77,14	22,86	13,75	86,25
4	100	0	23,56	76,44
5	61,43	38,57	8,00	92,00
6	100	0	22,47	77,53
7	55,00	45,00	10,76	89,24
8	86,67	13,33	14,81	85,19

from right). The main aim here is to identify and suggest to users groups of BPs as candidates for merging and those that are outliers in this process.

To assess the internal structure of each group, we must look closer into individual BP graph similarity check results. Groups 2, 4, and 6 show completely similarity internally, therefore they represent very good candidate for BP clustering. So we then analyse only each remaining group manually by domain experts, examining details of similarity checks among all their BPs, and deciding if they can or cannot be merged.

3.4 Find Commonalities and Differences

With automated software, we identify differences in the merge hierarchy for each of the eight groups, and resolve difference with manual help from experts. To give an example, consider merging of two BPs in group 5: C2 for "materials ordering", and T2 for "procure materials", which are identified as being highly similar (identified with 79.6 % similarity, in previous step), only 4 simple differences are identified by the software. The BP models of these two processes are presented in Fig. 7.

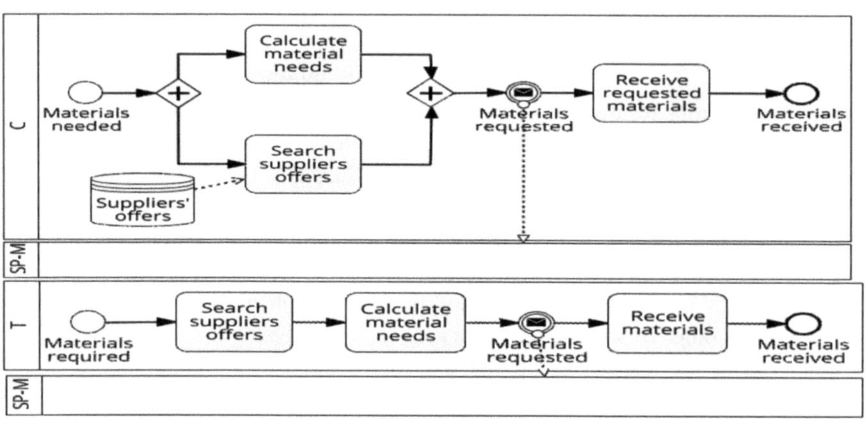

Fig. 7. BP models C2 and T2 before merging

3.5 Merge

At this stage common fragments are identified and differences are resolved manually to reach the merged BP, as described in Sect. 2.5. The manual merge is however provided step-wise, according to the merging hierarchy developed in Sect. 3.4. For the introduced example case (merging C2 and T2) we can notice that the process C2 actually contains the structure of process T2. The activities of "Searching suppliers offers" and "Calculating material needs" that are organized in a sequence in T2 can be therefore added to that sequence using additional AND split and join for them. However, for the needs of process C2, this sequence can be executed in parallel, as illustrated on its initial model. Concluding this merging instance, the process "C2 + T2" generates exactly the same as process C2, as in Fig. 8.

Note that, as mentioned in Sect. 2.5 we aimed at including all the nodes, structures and behaviours of the initial BPs. However, some additional decisions are always made by expert decision makers, e.g. regarding removal of a node and not including it in the model.

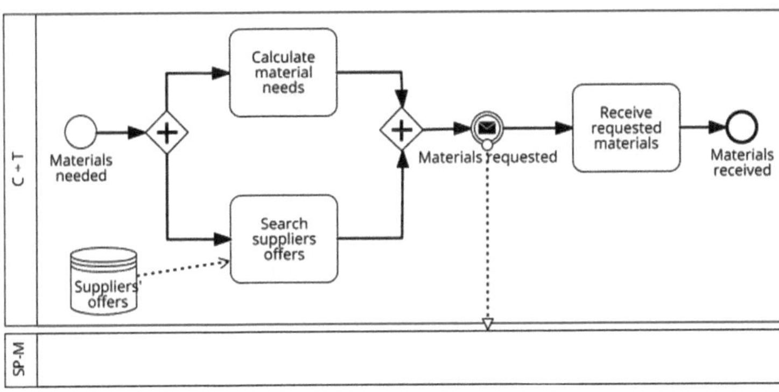

Fig. 8. Merged model C2 + T2

3.6 Check Quality of Outputs

Since our integrated-processes are also created in Signavio software, we provide the quality (i.e. the syntactical correctness) check the same way as introduced for the Sect. 3.2. In general, the integrated-processes are complex, so there is a higher risk of generating certain gateway inconsistencies, e.g. causing dead-lock errors in the resulted integrated BP. Therefore, it is essential to check if any resulted process includes such errors or ambiguities and if so, to disambiguate them. Semi-automated disambiguation of BP models is the subject of one of our ongoing research area, and will be reported in forthcoming publications.

4 Conclusions

The introduced BP integration methodology indicated the main tasks to be performed, and tools to be used by organizations, in order to integrate BPS in an established VO. We have identified that similarity checking based on BP names causes many difficulties for the software, and using shared BP names dictionary would increase the quality of this stage of the methodology. Another aspect indicated in research limitations is that the methodology needs a proper automatic merging tool that ensures a good quality of outcome processes that can be also disambiguated and executable. The step of merging the BPs is currently the most time-consuming task, highly influencing the methodology application time. Therefore, creation of an efficient and accurate merging tool is the next step of improving the BP integration methodology.

References

1. Afsarmanesh, H., Camarinha-Matos, L.: A framework for management of virtual organization breeding environments. In: Camarinha-Matos, L.M., Afsarmanesh, H., Ortiz, A. (eds.) Collaborative Networks and Their Breeding Environments. IFIP, vol. 186, pp. 35–49. Springer, Heidelberg (2005)
2. Kitchenham, B., Brereton, P.: A systematic review of systematic review process research in software engineering. Inf. Softw. Technol. **55**(12), 2049–2075 (2013)
3. Hevner, A., Chatterjee, S.: Design Science Research In Information Systems, pp. 9–22. Springer, Heidelberg (2010)
4. Dumas, M., La Rosa, M., Mendling, J., Reijers, H.A.: Fundamentals of Business Process Management. Springer, Berlin (2013)
5. Malekan, H.S., Afsarmanesh, H.: Overview of business process modeling languages supporting enterprise collaboration. In: Shishkov, B. (ed.) BMSD 2013. LNBIP, vol. 173, pp. 24–45. Springer, Heidelberg (2014)
6. Chrobak, P.: Overview of business process modelling software. Prace Naukowe Uniwersytetu Ekonomicznego we Wrocławiu **205**, 84–93 (2011)
7. Dijkman, R., Dumas, M., Van Dongen, B., Käärik, R., Mendling, J.: Similarity of business process models: metrics and evaluation. Inf. Syst. **36**(2), 498–516 (2011)
8. Pollach, I.: Software Review: WordStat 5.0. Organizational Research Methods (2010)
9. Dijkman, R.: A classification of differences between similar business processes. In: 11th IEEE International on Enterprise Distributed Object Computing Conference, EDOC 2007, p. 37. IEEE, October 2007
10. Gottschalk, F.: Configurable process models. Ph.D. thesis, Eindhoven University of Technology, The Netherlands (2009)
11. La Rosa, M., Dumas, M., Uba, R., Dijkman, R.: Merging business process models. In: Meersman, R., Dillon, T.S., Herrero, P. (eds.) OTM 2010. LNCS, vol. 6426, pp. 96–113. Springer, Heidelberg (2010)
12. Sirageldin, A., Selamat, A., Ibrahim, R.: Graph-based simulated annealing and support vector machine in Malware detection. In: 2011 5th Malaysian Conference in Software Engineering (MySEC), pp. 361–364. IEEE, December 2011

Connecting Business Processes and Sensor Data in Proactive Manufacturing Enterprises

Sobah Abbas Petersen[1(✉)], Rimmert van der Kooij[1], and Primoz Puhar[2]

[1] Department of Industrial Management, SINTEF Technology and Society, Sluppen, P.O. Box 4760, 7485 Trondheim, Norway
{sobah.petersen,Rimmert.VanderKooij}@sintef.no

[2] Hella Saturnus Slovenija, Letališka 17, 1001 Ljubljana, Slovenia
Primoz.Puhar@hella.com

Abstract. Real time sensor data is used often to monitor and control industrial applications. Such data is used to detect unexpected events and to take timely action to prevent industrial accidents or breakdowns. We introduce the concept of proactive sensing enterprises. The EU ProaSense project explores the use of real time sensor data and historical data to detect the likelihood of undesired events and to take proactive action to avoid undesired events and improve the resilience of the business. In this paper, we describe how enterprise modelling and process models may be used to connect the key performance indicators and business processes to data from sensors on technical components on the shop floor. We describe the benefits of connecting the business processes to sensor data and how modelling could contribute to reducing maintenance costs, improving proactive decision making and resilience in industry. An example from the manufacturing industry will be described.

Keywords: Proactive maintenance · Enterprise model · Real-time sensor data · Sensing enterprise · Proactive enterprise

1 Introduction

Enterprises face high demands to keep production and operations costs low while delivering high quality products and services. The need to deal with unexpected situations and resilience while complying with strict rules on safety aspects are a part of daily operations. The need for enterprises to anticipate what may happen in the future and proactively ensure smooth operations has become a necessity. The decisions that enterprises have to make are often influenced by the situation such as their production targets or their relationship with customers, requiring a careful analysis of the situation and making trade-offs. The need for technological solutions to support such decisions are a necessity for enterprises to meet their current needs. Among these, data and sensors are seen as revolutionary technologies for businesses [1].

H. Afsarmanesh et al. (Eds.): PRO-VE 2016, IFIP AICT 480, pp. 101–109, 2016.
DOI: 10.1007/978-3-319-45390-3_9

Collaborative Networks [2] have been considered as a means of supporting a network of enterprises where enterprises can maintain their competiveness and share knowledge, resources and sometimes risks among each other. Due to the changing nature of business situations, (e.g. the recent decline in the oil industry), enterprises have begun to focus on dealing with disruptions and increasing their resilience to such changes [3]. Enterprises have examined several approaches to maintaining their operations and dealing with disruptions and Collaborative Networks have been proposed as a means of effectively dealing with disruptions in enterprises and proposed as a proactive strategy [4]. Collaborative productivity, which can be interpreted as increasing the productivity by collaboration among the cyber (e.g. computing power) and physical (e.g. sensors and hardware) and the networks the enterprise operates within has been identified as important for Industry 4.0 [5]. In addition to maintaining their networks, enterprises also have a need to look within themselves and proactively work to ensure their operations. An important process in manufacturing companies is their maintenance process and the maintenance of their production equipment, as that affects their goals, such as keeping running costs low. Traditionally, maintenance was done at regular intervals or when something happens; reactive maintenance. More recently, predictive maintenance and condition-based maintenance has been practiced by careful inspection of equipment and specific parts. Proactive maintenance goes beyond these methods by taking a systematic approach and examining more than the equipment, but identifying the root cause of a problem and thus avoiding that in a timely manner [6]. Proactive maintenance models have been studied in engineering disciplines [7]. In this paper, we examine the proactive maintenance model of an enterprise, and how proactive decision-making could be supported in enterprises. An overview of proactive decision making models for maintenance is provided in [8].

In the EU ProaSense project, real time sensor data has been used to support proactive maintenance in industry. In this paper, we present ideas from Enterprise Models and how they could support proactivity in enterprises. We describe the maintenance process at HELLA and how real time sensor data on their production line could support proactive maintenance, which could lead to lower running costs and scrap rate. The main aim of the paper is to illustrate the benefits of enterprise models.

This paper is structured as follows: Sect. 2 describes the EU ProaSense project; Sect. 3 describes an example case; Sect. 4 describes the enterprise model and discusses the benefits of modelling and Sect. 5 summarizes the paper.

2 ProaSense Project

The work presented in this paper is a part of the European ICT research project ProaSense (The Proactive Sensing Enterprise) [9]. With the current demands on enterprises such as low production and maintenance costs and higher quality and safety, a new class of enterprise systems, proactive enterprises, that will be continuously aware of what "might happen" in the relevant business context and optimize their behaviour accordingly is essential. ProaSense aims to pave the way for an efficient transmission from Sensing into Proactive enterprises.

The central ideas of the project are focussed on the OODA loop for decision making which consists of Observing a situation, Orienting or making sense of a situation, Deciding on an action to take and Acting [10]. The action taken should also include feedback that is given to the observe phase. The Observe phase is supported by a system consisting of sensors in the environment to access the large amounts of data that are relevant to obtain a good overview of the situation. The Orient phase processes the large amounts of real time data as well as the historical data that is available using machine learning techniques. Complex Event Processing is applied to detect events that may indicate the need to act. The Decide phase anticipates events and recommends possible actions that could be appropriate and the Act phase keeps track of the business goals and Key Performance Indicators (KPIs) of the organisation. A software architecture has been designed and implemented (see [11, 12]) and is currently evaluated by two industrial companies in the oil and gas and manufacturing sectors. The aim is to support proactive maintenance of equipment in the enterprise using real time sensor data.

3 Manufacturing Industry – An Example Case

HELLA is a manufacturing company that produces large quantities of lighting technology, such as headlamps, in batches and delivers to the automotive industry. HELLA is interested in the proactive maintenance of their production equipment to support their KPIs, e.g. reduce the amount of downtime of equipment, maintain running stock and improve the quality of their products. The sensor data relevant for HELLA is from their manufacturing equipment on the production line such as the moulds, lacquering stations and ovens. HELLA's aim is to optimize production by reducing the downtime of their production equipment, securing delivery and reducing scrapped products, by detecting early warnings or indications and acting on them in a timely manner. There are several parts of equipment on the production line that could lead to a damaged product leading to scrap; e.g. incorrect parameters on moulding machines. The moulding machine are considered as controlled units as they could automatically correct values that are 'out of line' with the input given via a 'pre-set of golden parameters'.

To achieve proactivity in the maintenance of the equipment, there is a need to anticipate which parameters need to be adapted and when a parameter may deviate from the "golden set" by analysing the data that is available from the sensors and other sources and the trends and patterns to detect potential undesirable situations or events. A simple overview of HELLA's production and maintenance processes and how they relate is shown in Fig. 1. One of the sub activities in the maintenance process is to detect an anomaly or a deviation from the normal state, which is detected through the visual inspection of the product that is produced.

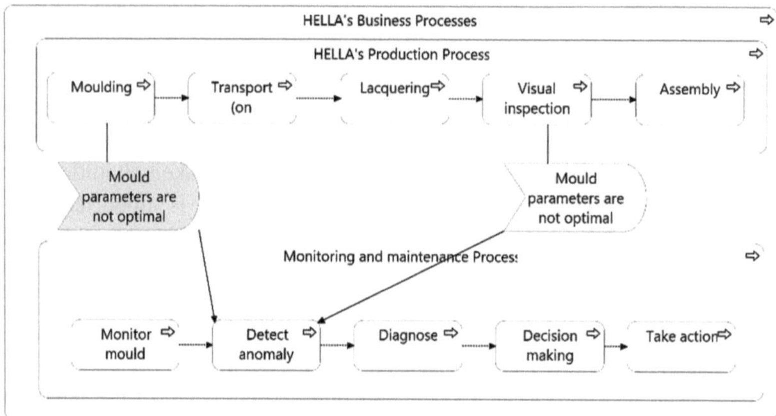

Fig. 1. HELLA's production and maintenance processes

Proactive maintenance using sensors placed on the moulding machines could provide input to identify the cause of a problem that could help to mitigate scrapped parts; e.g. the pressure and temperature of the mould or oil, or injection speed. Some of the relevant values could be obtained via real time sensors (hardware) placed on the equipment, while others could be processed or calculated by combining different data sources and through human observations. The latter two are called soft sensors, which include calculated values, values that are input by the humans and values that are derived from documents such as production plans or running stock.

In the Observe layer of the OODA conceptual architecture, sensors monitor and gather data on the relevant parameters of the machines which could be used in the Orient layer. The Orient layer detects anomalies based on Complex Event Processing. Here, contextual information is required to make a thorough analysis of the cause of the measured deviation. One of the defects in the products is the appearance of black dots on headlamp lenses. There could be at least three root causes; a jammed cooling line in the moulding machine, high dust level combined with high humidity, or a dirty mould. Sensor data, historical data and contextual information are used to determine the cause. Similarly, in the Decision layer, a set of actions are recommended based on the context such as the production plan, running stock, the product and the customer. For example, there is an upper limit of the scrap rate, which is determined by several factors such as the complexity of the product vs. the production cost, the customer and the status of the production schedule. The decision to take an action and which action to take often depends on the business context.

The enterprise model provides the contextual information that is relevant for the analysis. The model gives an overview of the nearest humidity sensor, the latest maintenance information available for the mould and how long it has been since the last time it was changed. As shown in Fig. 1, currently, the detection of defaults in the lenses take place at a later point in time in the production line when a visual inspection is done at the end of the production.

The main roles in the maintenance of HELLA's production line are, Operational Technologist and Setter who adjust and clean the moulds and other equipment, Engineer who fixes the equipment and Maintenance Engineer who is contacted if the problem is too complicated for the Engineer to fix. Depending on the severity of the problem, the level of skill and the number of engineers that are required and the time that will take to solve the problem could increase, leading to increased costs in maintenance and delays in production.

4 Enterprise Model

An information model has been developed to describe the case for HELLA to provide a quick overview of the use case and to provide the overview of the relevant contextual information. We have selected Archimate as our modelling language [13], as it provides comprehensive modelling support for all the perspectives of the proactive sensing enterprise: Business perspective (KPIs, Goals and Actors) and the sensing needs (technical equipment, applications and data).

One of the main business goals of HELLA that is relevant for proactivity is to maintain their running stock, see Fig. 2. Two of the KPIs that influence this business goal are the scrap rate of the products and the throughput according to plan (if the planned amount of products are produced during a shift). The scrap rate and the throughput are also related to the overall equipment efficiency such as minimising the downtime of equipment. These values are affected by the running stock for the products; e.g. if the running stock is low, then the tolerance for scrap rate can be higher. The model shows how the link between the business goal to maintain the running stock and how it can link to a particular product (e.g. head lamp and cover lens) and the customer (e.g. customer 1). This information is required to make decisions such as to stop a machine and correct the sub-optimal parameters, which would reduce the scrap rate.

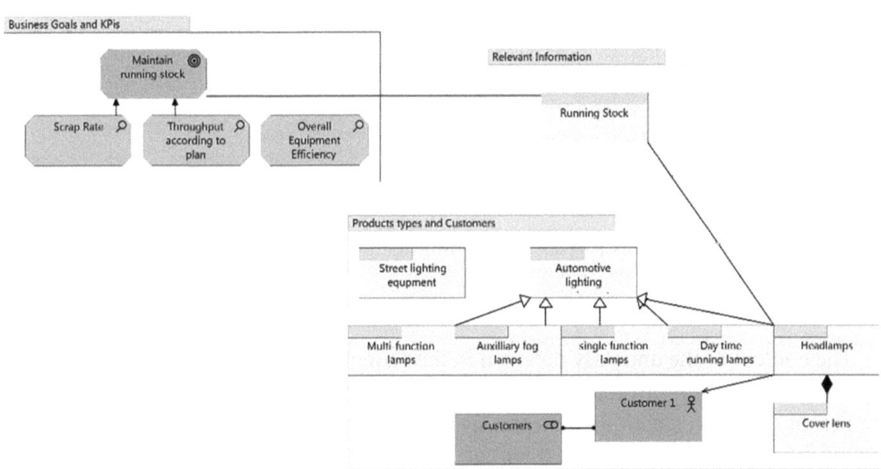

Fig. 2. Business goals and KPIs

An undesirable situation or an anomaly is detected by real time sensor data and other contextual information, see Fig. 3. The real time data from sensors is then analysed together with historical data, which can lead to new information and better understanding of the situation; e.g. through detecting patterns that could lead to an undesired event. The data is then used along with historical data (big data analysis) to diagnose the possible root cause and eventually to decide on the action to be taken. When this happens, e.g. as a non-optimal parameter value on a mould which may affect the scrap rate, decisions have to be made to either continue producing or to stop the production and attend to diagnose and correct the condition(s) that may lead to faulty products. This decision is based on the target for the production rate for that shift, the current running stock and the percentage of products that are scrapped. For example, the upper limit for the scrap rate is 20 % if the production plan's targets are met and if the production is under achieving (i.e. the production plan targets are not met), the upper limit for the scrap rate can be increased to 30 %. This approach takes the maintenance process beyond monitoring to anticipation of an undesired situation.

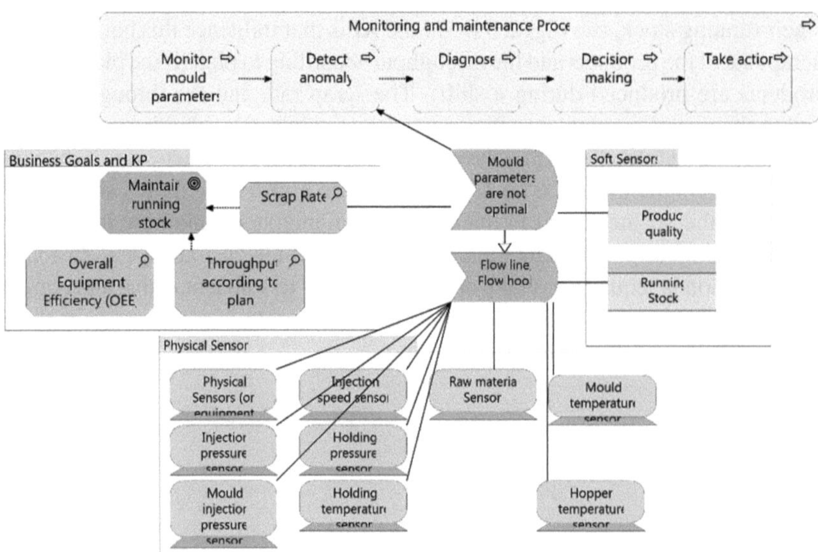

Fig. 3. Sensors and contextual information for detecting anomalies

The context of the anomaly detected in the Orient phase as shown in Fig. 3 is also a part of the contextual information that is relevant for the Decision phase. In addition to the sensor data, information about the sensors, such as their locations, and production related information, the actors that will be involved also influence the set of actions that will be recommended. For example, the Operational Technologist could fix adjustments on the mould while problems on the cylinder will require a Department technologist and their availability may vary.

The enterprise model served the purpose of establishing the relationships between business goals and the sensors and the relevant contextual information as described above. In addition, an Ontology model based on the WWW SSN Ontology [14] was developed for the sensors (physical, human and software) and their contexts, in Protégé. The WWW SSN Ontology was extended by modelling the sensors that are used at HELLA (e.g. sensors to measure humidity, mould temperature, etc.), the locations of sensors which were both on the production equipment (e.g. on moulding machines) and in the surrounding, the products and customers. Other relevant contextual information was modelled as "soft" sensors; e.g. production plan or running stock. To illustrate this, a small part of the Ontology Class structure is shown in Fig. 4.

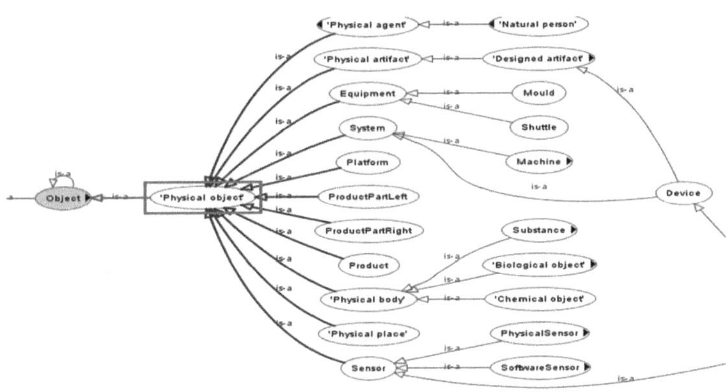

Fig. 4. Ontology to include contextual information

5 Discussion and Summary

The benefits of enterprise modelling is not new and has been the subject of several articles over the years, e.g. [15]. Modelling increases an enterprise's ability to make complex decisions for a number of reasons. It provides a better information and communications base; a property of an enterprise recognised as essential for agility. In the ProaSense project, this property of the enterprise is enhanced in the model by including detailed technical components such as sensors on equipment and how they relate to the business aspects such as the KPIs and business goals. As we saw from the HELLA case, when a potential undesirable event is detected, the decision to stop a machine to fix the anomaly is not always straightforward. It requires the careful consideration of many factors (the context) such as the running stock, the production plan for the shift, the availability of the technician to fix and the customer of the product. In addition, the actions taken must align with the business goals of the company. One of the challenges with data logs alone is to conceptualise them and to relate them to the other business and strategic aspects of an enterprise. The model can facilitate this to support the human in their understanding as well as to provide the relevant and contextualised information for supporting and automating the decision making process and providing recommendations wherever possible.

Proactivity, supported by modelling, can help enterprises improve their level of preparedness and minimise unexpected maintenance costs by avoiding failures and breakdowns. This can affect the Return on Investment (ROI). Proactivity, based on a number of contextual factors, can support better production planning and maintenance of equipment, which contributes to ROI, and return on production. The ability to obtain a better overview and understanding of the total enterprise and the connections within it and other relevant aspects support better decision and proactive maintenance.

The future work will involve the enhancement of the enterprise and ontology (OWL) models and developing the interface between the models and to the rest of the ProaSense software architecture to use the contextual information available from the models in the real time data processing.

Acknowledgements. The work was conducted in the EU FP7 project ProaSense. The authors wish to thank the project participants and HELLA for sharing their knowledge and example case.

References

1. Iansiti, M., Lakhani, K.R.: Digital Ubiquity: How Connections, Sensors, and Data are Revolutionizing Business. Harvard Business Review, Brighton (2014)
2. Camarinha-Matos, L., Afsarmanesh, H.: Collaborative networks: a new scientific discipline. J. Intell. Manufact. **16**, 439–452 (2005)
3. Camarinha-Matos, L., Benaben, F., Picard, W.: Risks and Resilience of Collaborative Networks. 16th IFIP WG 5.5 Working Conference on Virtual Enterprises PRO-VE. Springer, Heidelberg (2015)
4. Andres, B., Poler, R., Sanchis, R.: Collaborative strategies alignment to enhance the collaborative network agility and resilience. In: Camarinha-Matos, L.M. (ed.) PRO-VE 2015. IFIP AICT, vol. 463, pp. 88–99. Springer, Heidelberg (2015). doi:10.1007/978-3-319-24141-8_8
5. Schuh, G., et al.: Collaboration mechanisms to increase productivity in the context of industrie 4.0. Procedia CIRP **19**, 51–56 (2014)
6. EU Systems. The 4 Basic Maintenance Modes (2014). http://www.uesystems.com/mechanical-inspection/the-4-basic-maintenance-modes. Accessed 25 Apr 2016
7. Muller, A., Suhner, M.C., Lung, B.: Formalisation of a new prognosis model for supporting proactive maintenance implementation on industrial system. Reliab. Eng. Saf. Syst. **93**(2), 234–253 (2008)
8. Bousdekis, A., et al.: A proactive decision making framework for condition-based maintenance. Ind. Manag. Data Syst. **115**(7), 1225–1250 (2015)
9. Proasense. Proasence - The Proactive Sensing Enterprise (2012). http://www.proasense.eu/. Accessed 25 Apr 2016
10. Boyd, J.R.: The essence of winning and losing, 28 June 1995, a five slide set by Boyd (1995). http://www.danford.net/boyd/essence.htm. Accessed 25 Apr 2016
11. Magoutas, B., et al.: Anticipation-driven architecture for proactive enterprise decision making. In: CAiSE-Forum-DC 2014, Thessaloniki, Greece (2014)

12. Bousdekis, A., Papageorgiou, N., Magoutas, B., Apostolou, D., Mentzas, G.: A real-time architecture for proactive decision making in manufacturing enterprises. In: Ciuciu, I. (ed.) OTM 2015 Workshops. LNCS, vol. 9416, pp. 137–146. Springer, Heidelberg (2015). doi: 10.1007/978-3-319-26138-6_17
13. Lankhorst, M.: Enterprise Architecture at Work – Modelling, Communication and Analysis. Springer, Heidelberg (2013)
14. Semantic Sensor Network Ontology, 10 June 2011. http://www.w3.org/2005/Incubator/ssn/wiki/SSN
15. Leger, J.-B., Morel, G.: Integration of maintenance in the enterprise: towards an enterprise modelling-based framework compliant with proactive maintenance strategy. Prod. Plann. Control: Manag. Oper. **12**(2), 176–187 (2001)

Positioning Collaboration in Business Process Model Consolidation in VOs

Hodjat Soleimani Malekan[1(✉)], Mohammmad H. Rezazade Mehrizi[2], and Hamideh Afsarmanesh[1]

[1] Informatics Institute, University of Amsterdam, P.O. Box 94323, 1090 GH Amsterdam, The Netherlands
{h.soleimanimalekan, h.afsarmanesh}@uva.nl
[2] Faculty of Economics and Business Administration, VU University, Amsterdam, The Netherlands
m.rezazadehmehrizi@vu.nl

Abstract. Further to sharing their knowledge and information, organizations in a VO can also benefit from sharing and even combining/consolidating their Business Processes (BPs) in order to save costs, apply their best practices, and provide value-added services. A number of challenges are associated with the needed environment for BP consolidation. Our approach to tackle these challenges is two-fold. First part is addressed in this paper and deals with the human and procedural aspects of this problem and introduces an environment to support stakeholders of independent organizations with creating common understanding of each other's BPs and manually designing/testing consolidated BPs. The second part of our approach is however outside of the scope of this paper, which develops a semi-automated mechanism and algorithms to improve efficiency of defining and disambiguating consolidated BPs. Focused on first part, this paper presents results of an empirical study investigating performance and applicability of our approach, with about eighty participants.

Keywords: Business process consolidation · Merging organizations · Collaboration

1 Introduction

Companies select structured partnerships, such as Virtual Organization (VO) to reduce their costs, create innovative products, and provide optimized value-added services. The VO alliance represents a dynamic network, in which different companies share their knowledge, competences, and resources [1]. For instance, several travelling services can be integrated in a tourism VO, e.g. for buying the transportation tickets, reserving hotel rooms, reserving a rental car, purchasing travel insurance, etc., into a value-added service of a travel package.

A potential longer-term cooperation in VOs however, can create the base for partners to provide more efficiently a wider range of services and a wider scope of operation. When a set of companies intend to participate in a VO to operate for a long time, some of their Business Processes (BPs) can be merged/consolidated to deliver

H. Afsarmanesh et al. (Eds.): PRO-VE 2016, IFIP AICT 480, pp. 110–123, 2016.
DOI: 10.1007/978-3-319-45390-3_10

more efficient and optimized services. For example, the partners of the tourism VO mentioned above can standardize and run their reservation BPs on a cloud environment. As such, to save total cost of operation at the VO level, instead of each keeping a "reservation" or "purchasing" BP variants, they can start consolidating these BPs into two standard optimized BPs that all organizations can use. The consolidation procedure however must be performed by the people at these organizations, agreeing on intention, semantics, etc. of those BPS, which will then result in developing a merged BP.

Although, the VO partners usually may not tend to consolidate their BPs, they can benefit from it in several different ways. First, the BP model consolidation assists companies to standardize their BP models, use each other's experiences, and produce a high-quality BP model. Second, in the case of shared BP model repositories, the reduced size of merged BP models saves some maintenance costs. Third, knowing about the others companies BP models can underpin further future alliances among the VO members.

The main aims of supporting BP consolidation in VOs are twofold:

(1) Increasing the quality of the merged model that is the outcome of the consolidation process
(2) Increasing the efficiency and effectiveness of the consolidation procedure

However, because VO partners are highly heterogeneous, autonomous and usually geographically distributed, the BP model consolidation faces some difficulties and challenges: First, heterogeneities in the BP model representations, e.g. being graphically or textual, that can be found in different companies; Second, heterogeneities that can be found in the backgrounds and familiarity of the people who perform the consolidation job; Third, lack of a step-wise guideline for how to perform the consolidation. Consequently, a systematic approach is required to support and enhance the BP model consolidation procedure and products.

The existing approaches have mainly focused on merging graphical BP models, but lack the user centric perspectives [2, 3]. Therefore, the produced merged models are complicated to verify and difficult to understand by human users [4]. Additionally, the role of needed collaboration among organizations/agents in the BP model consolidation process is not addressed, while in practice, representatives from different companies typically gather together to decide how to combine their existing BP models and to develop merged models. Finally, no empirical study is performed to identify practical issues in the consolidation procedure, e.g. for identifying the importance of different business vocabularies used in the organizations for BP model consolidation in a VO context.

In this paper, we first describe and exemplify challenges in the BP model consolidation. We indicate the position of collaboration in increasing the efficiency of the consolidation procedure, as well as in enhancing the quality of the produced merged models. We then introduce a conceptual model with essential elements for successful establishment of collaboration in consolidating BP models in VOs. Then, we present the results so far achieved in our empirical experiment, which analyses our conceptual mode. Finally, the conclusions are addressed.

2 BP Model Consolidation in Practice

To develop an end-to-end business service, several BP models are used by VO members. This collection of BP models includes a number of BPs that are varied in different aspects, such as products they provide, purpose, locations, etc. For instance, two different insurance companies apply different "*claim handling*" BPs for *liability* or compensation cases. Thus, companies individually or collectively deal with their BP model variants [4]. Moreover, the proliferation of BP model variants in large collections and the need for developing inter-organizational BP models lead to an elimination of redundant and/or similar BP models through BP model consolidation.

In an inter-organizational BP model consolidation, the BP model variants of the involved companies are harmonized with their goals to produce added values. In other words, the BP model consolidation is about managing BP model variants [2]. However, reflecting to heterogeneities in the BP model variants makes the BP models consolidation a challenging task. To introduce the practical challenges in the consolidation procedure, an example is provided.

A set of companies, including the two insurance companies, called "ABC" and "MTTM", constitute a VO to produce insurance and financial services. The companies work to establish a long time collaboration, thus, they decide to consolidate some of their BP models. As a first step, *similar* and/or *equivalent* BPs must be identified. Suppose that one of these services, agreed to be consolidated, is the *claim handling service*, for which two variants exist in the pool of BPs from the two companies. A merger team is then formed of the representative of the ABC and MTTM companies to follow the consolidation procedure and develop a merged BP model for the *claim handling service*. The members of the merger team play the role of BP modelers. A set of potential challenges posed in this BP model consolidation process are addressed below.

Different representation modes. Companies document their BP models in different representation modes. They use textual descriptions or graphical depictions to represent their BP models. The two textual descriptions for this BP from the two companies are showed in Table 1. Moreover, in Fig. 1, the graphical representations of BP models from the ABC and MTTM companies are illustrated in Business Process Model and Notation (BPMN) language [5]. Selecting an appropriate modeling language for representing BP models requires a systematic method [6]. The BP modeling language used by different companies involved in a VO might be different. Thus, frequently we face with the challenge of different representation modes when consolidating BPs from different organizations.

Beyond the representation modes, some other model related challenges can emerge during the consolidation procedure. Here, we explain some of these other challenges in the following subsections, as they are also exemplified by "a" to "e" in Fig. 1.

a. Different modeling conventions: The modeling conventions, including modeling methods and modeling styles, (i.e. the combination of the modeling language's constructs) are diverse. This is considered by merger teams, when two similar tasks are modeled in two different forms. In Fig. 1(a), claim assessment and customer registration tasks are represented through a structured loop of exclusive gateways by the

ABC company, while a parallel construct comprised of two inclusive gateways is applied by MTTM for illustrating the same tasks. Additionally, the steps followed by the merger teams that start to design (or redesign) a BP model are often *emergent*, i.e. decided between modelers rather than conducted by any instruction or guidelines.

b. Similar business rules: The business rules are business decisions that lead the flow of a BP through different alternatives [5]. For instance, in Fig. 1(b) both BP models follow same decision of either *accepting* or *rejecting* a claim that are preceded by *assessing the claim*. Although identifying similar business rules in the current BP models of companies may seem to be trivial, determining whether they are and to what extent they are similar is difficult [2]. For instance, a business rule for accepting claims related to *car* compensation may differ from those for *personal* claims. This challenge further escalates when some modeling languages, such as the BPMN, have not provided efficient standard to accurately represent the business rules [7].

c. Conflicted Business Rules: In several cases the logical and temporal steps of performing a task is different, while the goals of tasks are the same. For example, in Fig. 1(c) the activities that succeed rejecting claims are executed sequentially in the MTTM Company. However, ABC synchronizes both activities of "*Updating customer's information*" and "*Inform customer*", in order to perform the same task.

d. Different level of granularity: Some tasks are provided in more and some in less details, corresponding to the modeler's opinion. Different levels of granularity represent the specific way of performing a task in a company. In Fig. 1(d), the compensation payment in the MTTM Company is depicted in one activity of "*Initiate payment*", however, the compensation payment task for ABC includes both "*pay out*" and "*Issue financial documents*" activities in parallel. The challenge here is to find the similarity threshold that specifies to what extent a BP model fragment, including one or more activities, are identical to the other one, in terms of fulfilling the same goal.

e. Different terminologies: Companies are communicating with their own business terminologies. Different companies need to converge their terms, business vocabularies, and semantics during the consolidation. In the represented BP models in Fig. 1(e), both companies run their service satisfaction evaluation activities, called "*customer satisfaction*" and "*quality of service assessment*" in ABC and MTTM, respectively. Since BP models, and particularly the graphical models, are commonly understood from the labelling in the models, selecting a correct, concise, and unambiguous terminology is necessary for successful consolidation of BPs.

In a similar manner, using different linguistic structures, such as words, verbs, sentences, and adverbs in a textual description imitates some of the same challenges as mentioned above. For example, the word "temporary customer" is used for new customers in the MTTM Company (step 4 of Table 1), while no specific word is used in the ABC company to address the customers.

In addition to the issues mentioned above, merger teams face another challenge, which is the heterogeneities among domain experts in practice. These are company representatives, with different backgrounds in modeling knowledge. Moreover, other roles such as consultant and mediator may be assumed to assist in BP consolidation procedure. Thus, the interactions and coordination of them are of importance to achieve best quality of consolidated BP model and efficient consolidation procedure. In brief,

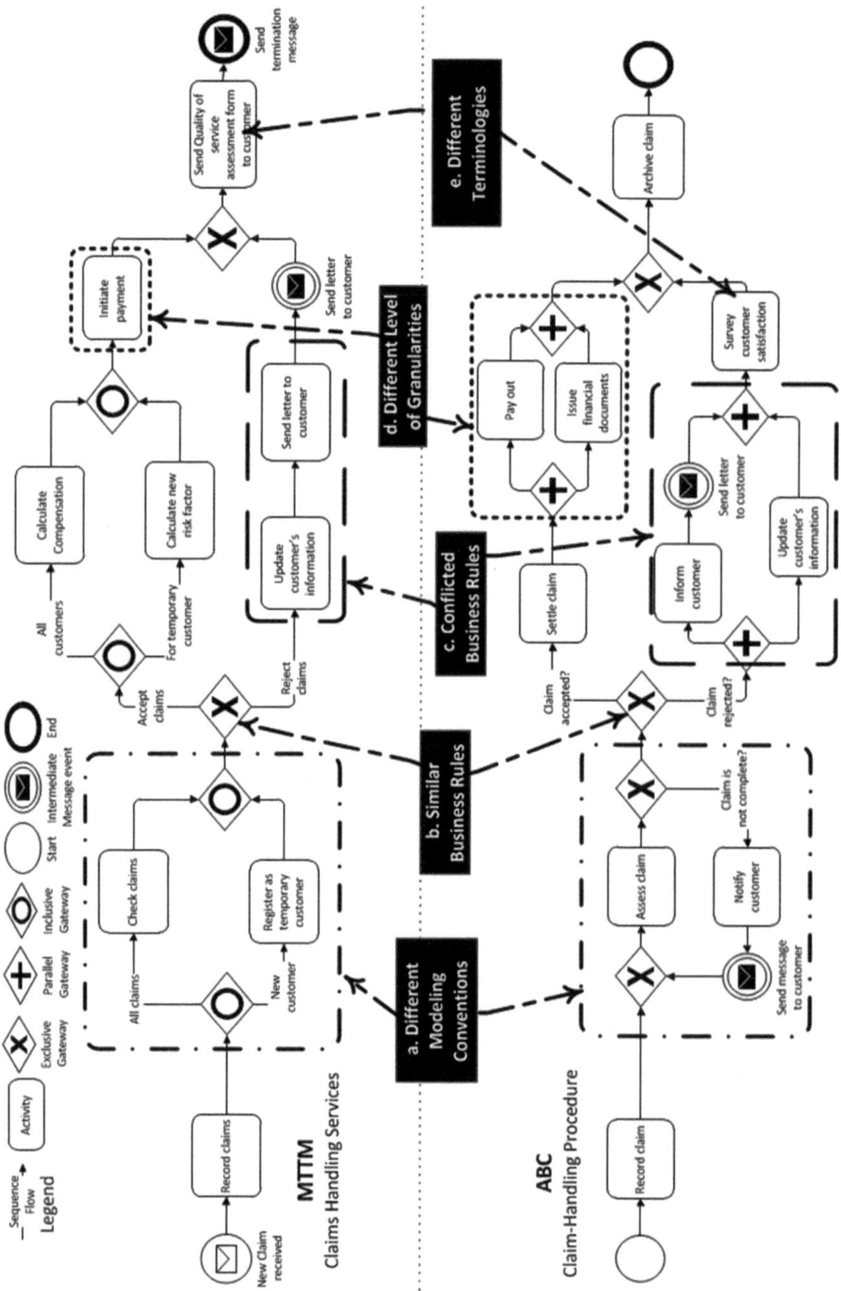

Fig. 1. Example of the graphical BP models in BPMN

Table 1. Example of textual description for two BP models in Fig. 1.

ABC company	MTTM company
Claim-handling procedure:	Claims handling services
1- Recording the claim is the first step in the ABC Company 2- Then, the claim is assessed. If the claim needs more information, such as new customer's information, a message is sent to notify the customer for more complete information. If the claim is assessed completely then it could be accepted or rejected 3- The accepted claims are settled to pay. Afterward, both the pay out and issuing the related financial documents are done by ABC 4- In case of rejected claims, the customer would be informed through sending a letter and the customer's information are updated in the system, at the same time. Afterwards, a survey is conducted to assess the satisfaction of the customer with rejected claim 5- The process finishes after archiving the claim	1- In MTTM Company, the process starts when a new claim is received. Each claim has to be recorded with enough details 2- All claims are checked accurately. Simultaneously, the claims and information of customers are checked. If it is a claim from an existing customer, its information already exists in the system. Otherwise, the information about the new customer will be registered as the temporary customer 3- Based on the claim's checking results, it would be either rejected or accepted 4- For the accepted claims, the compensation is calculated for all customers besides, if the claim is from a temporary customer, then a new risk factor is also calculated. After the calculations, the payment is initiated 5- While, if the claim is rejected, only the customer information gets updated accordingly, and afterward a letter will be sent to the customer 6- The process ends by sending "quality of service" form to the customer

several challenges of BP model consolidation for companies involved in a VO are tackled in our research. To address the mentioned challenges, we introduce a conceptual model to be delineated in regard to the VO specifications.

3 A Conceptual Model for Positioning Collaboration in BP Model Consolidation

The BP model consolidation is a collaborative-based procedure *per se*. In other words, various participants work together on achieving a shared understanding and developing a consolidated BP model. To show the collaboration position in our research, a conceptual model is illustrated in Fig. 2. This model visually describes essential elements that have influence on consolidating the two heterogeneous BP input models (i.e., graphically depicted or textually described), collaboratively in a VO context.

In this regards, we address both the consolidation procedure (i.e., certain steps to consolidate BP models) and the consolidation product (e.g., a merged BP model). Meanwhile, other elements which are essential to be incorporated in the consolidation procedure, in order to achieve a high quality consolidated BP model, are delineated. Additionally, their kind of relations such as *lead*, *support*, *enhance*, and *increase/decrease* are specified in Fig 2. Please note that the width of the arrow illustrates the strength of the relations, which we specifically address in this paper. Also, certain elements are specified from the insight we have gained from literature.

- *Consolidation procedure:*

The BP model consolidation is concerned with managing BP model variants. Depending on the number of BP model variants, five steps are often followed to consolidate BP models. First, step is *devising* the consolidation procedure, which specifies "*what to do"* and "*how to do it*". For instance, in the devise step, VO members decide on whether combining, synchronizing, or keeping their existing BP models. *Formalizing* of the existing BP models is the second step. Although the VO members work autonomously, the formalization is necessary to establish the communication among involved VO partners. However, the heterogeneities of the existing BP models are challenging for consolidation of BP models. The *merging* is the third step. In this step VO members, for instance combine their BP models into one merged model by identifying the similarities and resolving the conflicts. The fourth step is *correcting* the merged BP models, to assure that the merged BP model is in compliance with all syntax rules. Since during the merge steps, the BP models are restructured, there is a risk of some anomalies occurring, such as the deadlock and livelock, in the merged BP model. The last but not the least step is the *coevolving* step. This step is of great importance, because the BP merged models can be complex and large, therefore,

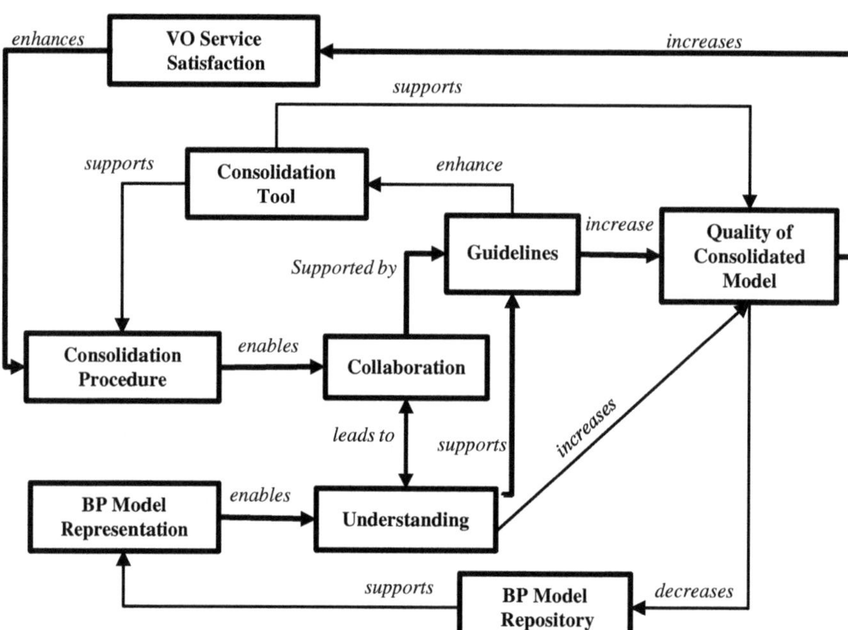

Fig. 2. Positioning collaboration in BP consolidation model

managing their changes are critical in the shared repositories or even the individual collections of the companies' BP models.

The above recommended steps have to be considered by the involved companies, in order to avoid inconsistencies and to increase efficiency and effectiveness in consolidation procedure. This steps primarily enable collaboration among VO members during the consolidation of their BP models.

- *BP model representation*:

BP model representation modes, e.g. the graphical depiction, enable knowledge acquisition from the BP models. Nevertheless, heterogeneities in the representation modes of the current BP models in companies, pose challenges for BP consolidation projects. Several of these challenges are already addressed in Sect. 2.

Today, different BP modeling languages are used to formalize BPs. The selection of a BP modeling language highly determines its capabilities and context. The *textual descriptions* and *graphical depictions* are identified as the two main representation modes used for BPs.

The textual documents, including reports, spreadsheets, and work instructions are the most dominant source of the business information. Additionally, the textual descriptions of BPs are easier for understanding by domain experts, since they usually do not require particular trainings or skills for their understanding by stakeholders. The textual representation can be (i) free-format, such as an English description of a BP, (ii) semi-structured, e.g. delineating a process steps in order of sequence, or (iii) structured texts, such as UML Use case descriptions. The textual descriptions of the two *claim handling* BPs are illustrated as examples in Table 1.

On the other hand the graphical depiction is preferred by modeling experts, due to the ease of communication and execution. Nevertheless, using graphical languages needs training and understanding the modeling languages. The BPMN language is the de facto standard for graphical depiction of BPs. Despite the suitability of BPMN for specific contexts [6], it still has certain problems, such as how it deals with ambiguities in some constructs, lack of formal semantics in its definition, and the arbitrary conventions that can be applied in modeling [7]. Two example BPMN Diagrams for the *claim handling* process are also depicted in Fig. 1.

- *Quality of consolidated BP Model*

In a consolidation project, the involved companies aim at producing high quality consolidated BP models. For this purpose, three aspects of BP model quality are addressed: "*syntactic*" [8], "*semantic*" [8] and "*innovativeness*" [9]. The syntactic quality aspect specifies to which extent a BP model adheres to the modeling language rules and grammar [8]. The semantic aspect of a BP model determines whether the existing model is consistent with what it intends to be in a real world context. In other words, it addresses how "good" the merged model is, in the existing context [8]. The innovativeness aspect however, reflects how well the model has chosen a convenient new way to express a BP model concept [9].

The selection of above mentioned three aspects are due to the following reasons: (i) Achieving a correct merged model is challenging [10] because the merged model is comprised of fragments of heterogeneous input BP models from different companies.

Thus, there is the risk of using incorrect BP model fragments from the existing input models, as well as the error-prone configuration of the consolidated BP models, e.g., the threat of deadlocks occurring [8]. (ii) Having errors in a BP model makes the model difficult to understand and therefore difficult to share and reuse [4]. (iii) Fostering innovativeness directly enhances the quality of the consolidated BP models. However, introducing innovativeness can also cause the consolidated model to have more errors [9], since creating new constructs beyond the existing structures pose the challenge of making mistakes or anomalies in the merged BP models. Consequently, discussing the quality assurance aspects of the consolidated model are necessary for producing innovative and valid outcome in the consolidation procedure.

Producing high-quality consolidated BP models however is not the only challenging objective of the consolidation projects, but also reaching high impacts on two other desired effects in the VO context, i.e. producing reduced size of the pool of consolidated BP models, as well as increasing the satisfaction of VO members.

- *BP model repository*

Managing a collection/pool of consolidated BP models itself brings new challenges, regardless of the size of the collections. For instance, a company, which is involved in the consolidation procedure, may demand for tractability of its BP model in the consolidated pool of BP models, for the sake of applying its internal changes in that model. The BP model consolidation, particularly by merging BP models, facilitates the maintainability of the BP model collections. Developing the consolidated BP model eliminates the collections redundancies. This is mainly because instead of the two BP model variants, one consolidated BP model is substituted and sustained/maintained.

It is noteworthy that consolidation, by focusing on similarities and reducing the differences, develops standardized BP models that impact on representation quality of the BP models in the VO.

- *VO service satisfaction*

The satisfaction of user is one aspect that is usually neglected in modeling tasks. The satisfaction of participants involved in consolidation procedures is defined as their attitudes toward factors that affect the consolidation procedure [11]. User satisfaction is triggered by the system quality and information quality. In our proposed approach, we follow the satisfaction triggered by the quality of the consolidated BP model.

- *Collaboration*

In theory, Malone and Crowston have introduced a multi-level collaboration on modeling tasks in [12]. At the base level of collaboration, especially through social interactions, “perception of common objects” is achieved by various actors. For example, defining shared tasks to achieve a common goal. At the next level, “communication” is established by a common language to facilitate sending and receiving common messages among the actors. Making “decision by group” is the next level, where actors in a collaboration have a set of alternatives aligned with their goal and make explicit choices, e.g. by voting or making a consensus. When a group of actors identifies their goals, schedule activities and allocate resources, they accomplish the “coordination” level. Through addressing collaboration in BP modeling, all levels mentioned above get behind the collaboration process in developing consolidated BP models, nevertheless organizing the collaborative tasks, such as "making consensus" is of critical importance

We distinguish between "*emergent*" and "*systematic*" collaboration procedures, more specifically, in the BP merging step. Systematic collaboration is associated with two or more individuals that are involved in a coordinated consolidation of BP models, when it is predefined beforehand. But emergent collaboration describes the situation when two or more individuals from different companies themselves define and follow their merge efforts process while it is happening [30]. More specifically, the systematic approach aims at drawing the consolidation team's attention into predefined important issues, by which the collaboration can be facilitated; whereas in the emergent approach, the consolidation process is led by the emerging consensus of the team members. Moreover, collaboration in either of its forms, facilitates the innovativeness due to asymmetry in the knowledge of the members of the merger team [9].

- *Understanding*

Understanding in the modeling process generally, and in the BP model consolidation specifically, refers to ability of knowledge acquisition from a BP model. The grammar of BP modeling assists modelers to better understand the content of a BP. In principal, modelers perform two major tasks: "*reading*" and "*writing*" [2]. When modelers read a model, they obtain information about its BP domain, while during the writing stage, a BP model is created to represent a real-world BP. Moreover, the collaboration and understanding of the BP models bilateral affect each other [13]. Furthermore, the quality of the merged model is increased, when the understanding of its modelers increases [8].

- *Guidelines*

At the heart of the BP consolidation approach there is a set of guidelines that support and enhance its different elements. The guidelines specify certain configurations that facilitate the collaboration positioning in a consolidation procedure.

The guidelines suggest solutions in regard to the type of collaborations and the modes of input. Further, it investigates the role of the outcome representation modes, e.g. producing a graphical or textual merged BP model.

These guidelines are not only applicable to companies for setting up their consolidation procedures, but also assist companies with increasing the quality of their consolidated BP models.

- *Consolidation tool*

Considering the correctness aspect of consolidation, a semi-automated tool is required to assure their correctness and generating anomaly-free merged BP models. The BP model anomalies, such as deadlocks and/or ambiguous constructs (e.g. OR-join patterns) cause difficulties in executability of the consolidated BP models [16]. Thus, the consolidation tool addresses the deficiencies and corresponding solutions, in order to provide a robust execution infrastructure for the consolidated BP models.

4 Experiment

In order to validate the inter-relations defined in the conceptual model described in Sect. 3, we have performed an empirical experiment with a group of students. The entire experiment is also recorded on videos.

The experiment was designed to study the following two main aspects:

(a) The joint effect that the "*consolidation procedures*" (i.e., systematic collaboration versus emergent collaboration) as well as the "*input representation modes*" (i.e., the textual BP model description or graphical BP model depiction) can have on increasing the quality of the produced merged BP models.
(b) The importance of the role played by the BP modeling knowledge of the collaborating partners, as the moderators from the two companies, in the consolidation procedure.

For the purposes of empirically investigating the two main issues mentioned above, 78 participants were recruited. The participants were students from the Faculty of Economics and Business Administration at the VU University. These were selected since in real-world companies, typically the staff with business administration degrees are assigned by companies to perform the tasks of BP modeling and/or BP merge. Moreover, short training in BP modelling is a part of the procedure that we apply for BP model consolidation, and using background expertise is not recommended in our experiment, e.g. for transferring between graphical and textual BP model representations [15], since the experiment could then be biased by the background knowledge.

The participants formed teams of two. Each set of two members worked together, each as the representative of one of the two companies in a merger team. We also divided the participants into four separate conceptual study groups, and assigned some of the teams into each of the following study groups.

- Study Group A: Systematic collaboration- graphical BP model inputs
- Study Group B: Emergent collaboration - graphical BP model inputs
- Study Group C: Systematic collaboration - textual BP model inputs
- Study Group D: Emergent collaboration - textual BP model inputs

For the systematic collaboration, the study groups "A" and "C" were suggested to fully adopt the following set of guideline steps:

(i) Reaching a mutual understanding of both input BP models.
(ii) Finding any and all similar fragments in the two input BP models.
(iii) Resolving any and all differences/conflicts over dissimilar parts of the merged BP model, with the original two BP models.
(iv) Verifying the correctness of the merged BP models.

On the contrary, the teams in the emergent study groups "B" and "D" did not receive any guidelines.

Additionally, two graphically depicted BP models from the two different companies were provided to the participants in study group "A" and "B" (See Fig. 1). Similarly, the equivalent textual descriptions of BP models were provided to the participants of the study Group "C" and "D" (See Table 1).

Then, all teams were asked to develop two consolidated BP models, including one graphical and one textual merged BP model. In total, we have received 60 merged BP models, half graphical and half textual.

This experiment has produced a valuable large set of data, which we have so far partially analysed applying the fuzzy set Qualitative Comparison Analysis (fsQCA) method. A set of promising results related to the BP consolidation approach in VOs are already induced and being gradually represented in a format similar to Fig. 3.

The presented results are used to evaluate the success and failure in achieving our desired outcomes. For instance, Fig. 3 represents some statistics about the results related to *Syntax Structural Correctness* of the produced merged BP models by teams.

Please note that the headers in the first 4 rows in Fig. 3 indicate the four criteria considered in this analysis. Also for each row, two values are considered, as mentioned in the header, and the solid circle and crossed circle respectively indicate these values for that row. The fifth row indicates the success or failure of the produced results in relation to the *Syntax Structural Correctness*. Please also note that each column represents one combination of cases that with a high percentage has produced either a success or a failure result.

Achieving the syntax correctness – as a quality aspect of – a merged BP is represented by SSCS1, and the syntax failure by SSCS2. Each of these solutions may

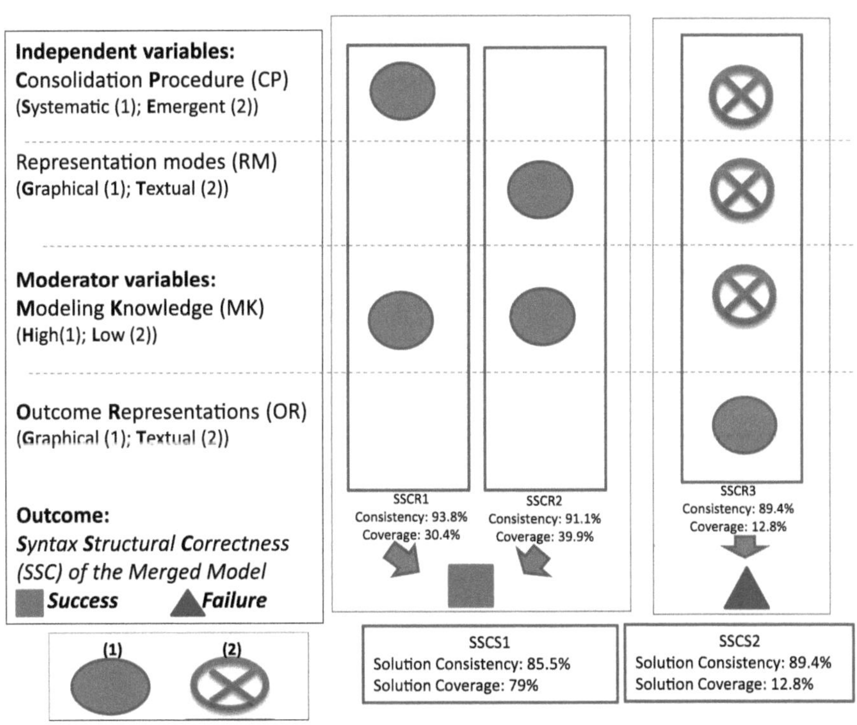

Fig. 3. The fsQCA analysis solutions for having syntactical correctness in the merged models

include a number of partial solutions. For instance, SSCR1 and SSCR2 are two partial solutions for having merged models with high level of syntactical correctness, i.e. the SSCS1 solution. Each of these solutions, as indicated by its respective column is due to a configuration of values for the four criteria represented by the rows.

For example, in the configuration of the SSCR3 partial solution, (i) given textual input BP models, (ii) while requiring the team to produce a graphical outcome, (iii) having low modeling knowledge of the participants, and (iv) applying an emergent consolidation procedure, while the produced result is highly consistent, it represents an 89.4 % of failures to achieve high quality merged BP model. Moreover, this configuration covers 12.8 % of solutions that results in having syntactical errors in their merged BP model.

Similarly in SSCR2, we observe that if (i) the input is graphical, (ii) the team members have high modeling knowledge, (iii) regardless of the type of outcome (i.e., graphical or textual merged BP model) and (iv) regardless of consolidation procedures (i.e., systematic or emergent) the syntactical quality correctness have high consistency and acceptable coverage. It is noteworthy that, the fsQCA is not symmetric, e.g. in case of the SSCR2, having textual input BP model and low modeling knowledge, does not necessarily ends in merged BP model with low syntactical quality.

5 Conclusion and Future Works

The presented research addresses the main challenging practical aspects of the BP consolidation in a VO context. Moreover, it positions and further conceptualizes the role of collaboration in the BP merge process. An empirical study is presented to investigate and validate the consistency of the introduced conceptual model, which can be used to provide a set of solutions for the VO partners involved in BP consolidation.

The results of this experiment will be applied to developing a set of guidelines for the process of for BP consolidation among companies, aimed both to increase the quality of the merged BP models, as well as for automating a part of the consolidation procedure in the VO context. At present we are in the process of analysing results from the empirical experiment. In the next step, we aim to study the quality aspects of the consolidated BP models, i.e. the syntactic, semantic, and innovativeness aspects.

References

1. Afsarmanesh, H., Camarinha-Matos, L.: A framework for management of virtual organization breeding environments. In: Camarinha-Matos, L.M., Afsarmanesh, H., Ortiz, A. (eds.) Collaborative Networks and Their Breeding Environments. IFIP, vol. 186, pp. 35–48. Springer, Heidelberg (2005)
2. La Rosa, M., Dumas, M., Uba, R., Dijkman, R.: Business process model merging: an approach to business process consolidation. ACM Trans. Softw. Eng. Methodol. (TOSEM) **22**(2), 11 (2013)
3. Gerth, C.: Introduction. In: Gerth, C. (ed.) Business Process Models. Change Management. LNCS, vol. 7849, pp. 1–12. Springer, Heidelberg (2013)

4. Dijkman, R.M., La Rosa, M., Reijers, H.A.: Managing large collections of business process models-current techniques and challenges. Comput. Ind. **63**(2), 91–97 (2012)
5. OMG: Business Process Model and Notation (BPMN), Version 2.0.2, December 2013. Last seen http://www.omg.org/spec/BPMN/2.0.2/
6. Soleimani Malekan, H., Afsarmanesh, H.: Overview of business process modeling languages supporting enterprise collaboration. In: Shishkov, B. (ed.) BMSD 2013. LNBIP, vol. 173, pp. 24–45. Springer, Heidelberg (2014)
7. Recker, J.: Opportunities and constraints: the current struggle with BPMN. Bus. Process Manag. J. **16**(1), 181–201 (2010)
8. Dumas, M., La Rosa, M., Mendling, J., Reijers, H.A.: Fundamentals of Business Process Management, pp. I–XXVII. Springer, Heidelberg (2013)
9. Figl, K., Weber, B.: Individual creativity in designing business processes. In: Bajec, M., Eder, J. (eds.) CAiSE Workshops 2012. LNBIP, vol. 112, pp. 294–306. Springer, Heidelberg (2012)
10. Schunselaar, D.M., Verbeek, E., van der Aalst, W.M., Raijers, H.A.: Creating sound and reversible configurable process models using CoSeNets. In: Abramowicz, W., Kriksciuniene, D., Sakalauskas, V. (eds.) BIS 2012. LNBIP, vol. 117, pp. 24–35. Springer, Heidelberg (2012)
11. Wixom, B.H., Todd, P.A.: A theoretical integration of user satisfaction and technology acceptance. Inf. Syst. Res. **16**(1), 85–102 (2005)
12. Malone, T.W., Crowston, K.: The interdisciplinary study of coordination. ACM Comput. Surv. (CSUR) **26**(1), 87–119 (1994)
13. Bernhard, E., Recker, J.C.: Preliminary insights from a multiple case study on process modelling impact (2012)
14. Ragin, C.C.: Fuzzy-Set Social Science. University of Chicago Press, Chicago (2000)
15. Burton-Jones, A., Wand, Y., Weber, R.: Guidelines for empirical evaluations of conceptual modeling grammars. J. Assoc. Inf. Syst. **10**(6), 495 (2009)
16. van der Aalst, W.M.: Business process management: a comprehensive survey. ISRN Softw. Eng. **2013**, 1–37 (2013)

Resilience Analysis of Collaborative Process Management Systems

Paul de Vrieze(✉) and Lai Xu

Faculty of Science and Technology, Bournemouth University,
Poole House, Talbot Campus, Fern Barrow, Poole, BH12 5BB, UK
{pdvrieze,lxu}@bournemouth.ac.uk

Abstract. Process management allows for the automated coordination of processes involving human and computer actors. In modern economies it is increasingly needed for this coordination to be not only within organizations but also to cross organizational boundaries. The dependence on the performance of other organizations should however be limited, and the control over the own processes is required from a competitiveness perspective. Overall, this indicates a federated process management approach instead of a centralized one. This paper analyses the resilience of automated process management overall and especially how the use of federated process management impacts that resilience.

Keywords: Collaborative process systems · Resilience · Federated process management · Process resilience

1 Introduction

Collaborative networks as a relative new scientific discipline [13] have been applied to application areas such as Factories of the Future [14], Manufacturing and logistics networks [15]. Organizations, enterprises, and communities are interconnected by networks in the new application areas. To support such collaboration in a hyper-connected world, existing technologies need to be improved and adapted in terms of larger scale integration and more intelligent devices, sensors and cyber-physical systems involvement.

The scope of business collaborations can be limited to a particular department in an enterprise, it may span multiple divisions within an enterprise or it may require inter-enterprise collaboration. In this research, we are especially considering how to manage interenterprise collaboration, i.e. collaborative business processes are executed among enterprises. In this work, we consider that (web) services and human interactions are coordinated through an automated process management system to form an SOA. In a traditional approach, the process management system forms a single point of failure. We defining resilience as the degree as to which the system can continue to meet its goals in the presence of errors. Based upon an analysis of different structures for federation we have analyzed how process federation can impact overall system resilience.

H. Afsarmanesh et al. (Eds.): PRO-VE 2016, IFIP AICT 480, pp. 124–133, 2016.
DOI: 10.1007/978-3-319-45390-3_11

In this paper we focus on federated control of collaborative business process systems as well as analysis of resilience related the federated collaborative business process systems. Federation in this context is the coordination of the execution of individual business process instances by multiple independent process engines. In the next section, we review challenges of collaborative networks and collaborative business process managements, federated control of information systems, large-scale systems, business process management systems/business services, and cloud services. In Sect. 3, different management types of federated collaborative processes are classified. Resilience of the federated collaborative processes is reviewed in Sect. 4. The paper is end with a summary of the paper and future research.

2 Related Work

Increasing importance of value chains and production networks, of interconnected organizations, collaboration dynamics, outsourcing, and the increasing potential of new ICT technologies supported innovations has driven research of collaborative networks [12]. Collaborative networks [6, 13] and collaborative business process management [11, 12] have been fostered by globalization over decades.

Federated control method has been applied into different areas. Federated information management architecture is provided to manage information across different organizations in virtual organization domain [3]. Different management level schemas of federated databases are specified for interoperation.

Systems control is another research area which federated control methods has been applied [6]. In this area, large-scale systems normally consist of several interconnected local systems, which conventional centralized control schemes are not suitable for due to global dynamic behavior complexity and computational difficulties. Many multi-agent based federated control systems are used to high performance computing area. Federated Cloud Services [8–10] emerges recently to deploy and to manage multiple external and internal cloud computing services for meeting business needs.

Paper [16] proposes a framework to create enterprise resilience using service oriented architecture approach. Antunes and Mourão consider a framework and related services for building resilient business process management [17]. Both works are not look at resilience of collaborative systems. Previous work on federated business process management [1, 2, 5] are proposed to handle the dynamic nature of collaborations among autonomous enterprises, which different structures are specified for different interactions among business partners.

Today we are facing to support enterprises' agility and resilience in turbulent business environments [4]. Advances in ICT, Internet, and cloud have led to the explosion of collaborative networks both people and organizational levels. A pervasive interconnection of and collaboration among physical and virtual objects provides opportunities of realization of manufacturing 2.0 (industrial 4.0) and sustainable development. Our previous work [7] provides a method to analyze resilience of a cloud-based collaborative process solution. We thus review federated collaborative process management and analyzing resilience of federated collaborative process management in the new context.

3 Federated Collaborative Process Systems

Processes that involve multiple parties may be collaborative. While it is possible for this to be limited to two parties, generally one would expect more than two parties. Various degrees of collaborativeness can be distinguished. At the lowest level of collaborativeness, collaborative processes have little differences to distinguish them from simple provision of (web) services. At the highest end there are complex interactions between the involved parties.

In addition to degrees of collaborativeness, there is the dimension of balance of power or control. Collaborations with dominant partners, as for example occurs in supplier networks for large manufacturers of cars or airplanes, are quite different from more peer-to-peer oriented collaborations where no partner is dominant.

3.1 Collaborative Processes

In terms of process management, it is convenient to make the distinction between service provision/consumption on the one hand and collaboration on the other hand. Starting from the precept that all processes have a single initiator, a process can be seen as collaborative if, at operational level (not purely on an intellectual basis with human owners) the initiator and executor have some awareness of each other's process and use this in some aspects of operations. The use of process nature can be limited, for example to monitoring, but there should be some use of the process nature.

In real terms we primarily consider automated processes that are managed through some form of workflow or business process management system. In this digital representation a process is represented as control flow as well as activities whose interaction is managed in line with the control flow to provide the process outcomes. Please note, that in this context we look at logical uniqueness and do not consider load balancing or replication of services or process management systems.

Centralised Process Management. Traditionally process choreography is seen as performed by a single process management system (or process engine). This system has a full view of the process and all components. In case that external components are involved, they are treated opaquely as service consumption where the system itself has no further knowledge of the underlying processes or possible interactions.

In this scenario, collaborative process management would imply that the management system requires quite some insight into and control over the implementation of activities within the collaborating organizations. While cloud computing makes this somewhat easier, many collaborators may object to this. In most cases, tight contractual arrangements are needed to allow this to happen [11, 12], and this is mainly seen in a context with dominant players.

3.2 Federated Process Management

Federated processes are distinguished from centralized process management in that process-aware collaboration occurs, but is controlled by multiple autonomous management entities. While federated process execution is normal when processes are managed and executed by humans (each person manages his own actions within the agreed boundaries), such coordination is not the norm for automated process management.

Federation as concept implies that there is some degree of meta-level coordination between the management agents that perform the service choreographies. Considering multiple copies of the same process (description) to be the same process (model), multiple instances of a single process model can, from a technical perspective, be instantiated on/coordinated by different management systems. For overall management it is however worthwhile that meta-information is coordinated to allow for overall statistics. Each process instance should have a single, eventually consistent, state.

When parts of a process are coordinated by different process management systems in a federation, there are different ways this can be organized. In this paper we only consider those approaches where at any point of time there is a single "master" or "owner" of the process instance. The coordination of a subset of the activities can be delegated to a different management engine. Ownership may also be transferred (voluntarily or in response to failure). While many real-world process would consist of combinations of these (descriptive) classifications, it is still worthwhile to consider them separately.

Hierarchical Federated Processes. Within federated process management, some processes are purely hierarchical. This means that the process is designed such that process instances are primarily managed by a single management system that delegates parts of the execution to other process management systems under control of a different collaborator. If we define an execution domain as those parts of a process managed and choreographed by a single management system, hierarchical federation is defined through a strict hierarchy of execution domains.

An example of a hierarchical federated process setup could be where a cooperative of specialized manufacturing companies is set up as collaborative network organization to be able to deliver more end-to-end solutions. As part of this collaborative network some centralized coordination is required and can be provided and managed by the cooperative. Individual manufacturers would however retain control over their own processes, but the overall process would be managed by the master process management system.

Sequential Federated Processes. A sequential federated process is a process where there is a clear transition from one locus of control to another, after which the original execution domain is no longer involved in the choreography of the process. Effectively this means that responsibility and control can be transferred.

Free-Form Federated Processes. In many cases, a strict hierarchy of execution domains is a significant restriction and sequential federation is also not applicable. Free-form federated processes as such are those processes where there are no restrictions are set on the relations between execution domains.

4 Collaborative Network Resilience

In determining resilience of a process system within a collaborative network it is first of all of import to define what degrees of resilience are considered. In this sense we only consider the resilience of the system, not the resilience of the network as a whole.

Resilience of a process system exists on four levels: the resilience of the system *overall*, the resilience of *individual processes* within the system, the resilience of *process instances* and the resilience of individual constituent *services*. In achieving resilience one would certainly require that failures at a lower level have minimal impact on the higher layers, but the failure forms do inform the achievement of resilience at a higher layer.

In this paper, resilience of the federated collaborative process systems can be defined as adaptive capacity and its ability to cope with, adapt to and recover after a disruption or failure. Thus we first look at failure model in Sect. 4.1 as well as service resilience (Sect. 4.2), process instance resilience (Sect. 4.3), process resilience (Sect. 4.4) and overall resilience (Sect. 4.5) respectively.

4.1 Failure Modes

The various process system aspects can fail in various ways, but they share many aspects of the ways in which they can fail. For the purposes of resilience, only the external aspects of failures are of interest. We are also looking at failure from a software perspective, where manufacturing failure modes inform the perspective taken, but are not sufficient to analyze interactions across levels of resilience or the kinds of systems. Overall we distinguish the following orthogonal dimensions (please note that these are not exclusive):

- **Temporal failure**: Along the time dimension a failure can be temporary (an independent temporary event, for example a network failure due to a power cut); failures can be intermittent based on a systematic issue (related failures for example due to insufficient capacity during nightly batch operations); Failures can also be permanent (the company providing the service has seized operation).
- **Failure detectability**: Some failures are easy to recognize such as those where error messages are provided, *signaled failure*. Other failures are detectable based on business rules or SLA's such as failure to respond within a certain time period, *detectable failure*. The final category of failure detection is are silent failures either in silent non-performance (i.e. the request is accepted but never actioned), *silent partial-performance* (i.e. some aspects of the request are not performed, but those aspects performed are valid. The final form of silent failure is *silent corruption* where the system provides incorrect state or results without signaling any error.
- **Partial failure**: Partial failure concerns the degree to which the system is failing. Full failure is a possibility, but partial failure can occur in various forms such as *degraded performance* (e.g. not meeting time expectations), *reduced quality* (the results are valid but not of the quality or precision normally provided, the range of the function is reduced) or *reduced provision* (the domain or image of the

functionality is reduced, i.e. not all inputs are supported, for example a weather service would have reduced provision for an area if the weather station in that area was unavailable for some reason).

- **Failure origin**: The origin of a failure can either be *internal* as in it is caused by issues within the logic control of a system, or *external* where the failure is outside of the control of the system. An internal failure could be a bug in a service implementation or process description. A bug in the process management system would be external from the perspective of a process. A network failure that causes a service to be unavailable would be external to that service. Both examples can, in circumstances, be seen as internal to the overall system. An internal failure can either be a *delegate failure* (a used component causes the problem) or a *direct failure* where the problem is not fundamentally in the delegate (although a delegate may return unexpected (but not invalid) results that trigger the issue).

4.2 Service Resilience

Services form the building blocks of a SOA based process system. The causes of their failures are therefore out of scope of this discussion, but they may exhibit all forms of these failures. These failures do impact the overarching resilience levels however as for the system to work, the failures need to be able to be handled.

4.3 Process Instance Resilience

Process instance resilience relates to how process instances can recover from failures. In this aspect, direct failures are normally due to incorrect assumptions or pure logic errors (bugs in the process model), and of less interest within the resilience discussion.

From a temporal dimension perspective, process instances are, due to their inherent nature as long-running, reasonably resilient to non-permanent failures. The lower the pressure on timing, the stronger the resilience.

From a detectability perspective, only signaled failures are normally handled by process instances, and higher resilience generally implies more complete failure management, that includes the availability of sufficient semantic information such as to allow automatic restarts or rerouting for failed paths/components. Silent non-performance can possibly be handled through monitoring and timeouts, but in many cases cannot be distinguished from other forms of silent failure.

In terms of partial failure, degraded performance may lead to timing issues on the process instance, but otherwise should not impact the performance of the process. Reduced quality of performance leads to reduced quality of the instance, and reduced provision would lead to some instances failing (those affected by the reduction) and some succeeding.

In relation to the location of failure, external failure is normally failure of delegates/activities, but can also be a failure in the execution environment (e.g. hardware failure). External failure of the execution environment could be compensated by regular replication solutions for the state of the execution environment (e.g. database replication/sharding etc.) that is not specific to process management. In terms of direct failure, there are two aspects to the resilience of process models. First is the ability of humans to interject in process instances and possibly modify them or provide "missing" data, this mainly a property of the management system and the used process language. The other aspect is the frequency of instances. In other words, while it may be technically feasible to intervene in a process instance and recover it, it may not be feasible for large amounts of instances that failed due to fundamentally the same cause.

4.4 Process Resilience

The resilience of processes is strongly related to the resilience of process instances. There are however ways in which the execution system can make processes be resilient even when individual instances fail. Conversely, timing and speed issues that are not problematic at instance level, may become so at process level.

Process resilience at a temporal level requires monitoring and (pre-emptive) intervention and/or rerouting. Processes are resilient when it is easy to (automatically) replace the providers of services for the process (activity execution or process management), but it requires a resilient system to actually make use of those possibilities. Obviously if these measures can be performed on already started process instances, this would even be better.

At process level, the detectability of failures is limited to the ability to express overall expectations, possibly at aggregate level. These process level specifications could then allow for pre-emptive intervention in the instantiation of new processes. Note that at process or system level it may also be feasible to determine some degree of likelihood of the various forms of silent failure by aggregating monitoring data and linking it to the expectations.

At process level partial failure of some instances would constitute partial failure of the process. A resilient process would allow the instance failures to be minimized and possibly corrected through re-execution along an alternative path. To do the latter, does require sufficient information to be available for the process components to be able to determine the semantic validity of doing so.

Locus of failure at process level implies some degree of process quality requirements as well as designs that minimize the impact of external failures. Again, monitoring of individual service and instance performance can help in detecting, mitigating and avoiding these failures or transitioning them from non-performance to degraded performance by for example choosing a lower quality service that does not have availability issues.

4.5 Overall Resilience

Overall the entire systems resilience is a combination of the resilience of the constituting processes. Many measures at overall level can however help to achieve this resilience. In particular the provision of fallback execution environments or services will improve the overall resilience of the system. Resilience in terms of fault tolerance mainly depends on the resilience of the components (services, processes) and sufficient provision of execution environments without single point of failure.

5 Resilience for Federated Process Management

Where the previous section discussed the resilience of the components that make up a federated process management system that is on a technical level rather than a utility level. The possibilities of federated process management can, on a theoretical level be seen as a subset of what single entity-controlled process management provides. On a practical level, there are resilience benefits to federated process execution (there are also disadvantages in complexity and management). In addition, in real-world business scenarios it is often not desirable to have centralized process control.

In terms of resilience, federated process management means that by implication, processes are managed by multiple independent execution environments. While these environments may have access to different components (such as company internal services) they would have similar orchestration capabilities. As federated processes allow parts of execution to be delegated to other execution environments this means that an overall master coordinator does not require direct access to all required components for process execution.

At system and process level, through a lack of single point of failure and lack of global coordination requirement, federation provides a strong level of resilience against total failure. Performance degradation, especially non-functional degradation, can be compensated for by additional provisioning elsewhere within the collaboration. Even the absence of certain unique resources, would only result in those processes being unavailable.

The services used by a system are independent of the form of process management, and their resilience is mainly a property that influences higher levels. Federation however brings some interesting perspectives to process instance resilience. In the case of sequential federation, given a well-defined ownership transition model, the failure of preceding execution environments would not lead to instance failure.

Within hierarchical federation it is possible that, beside the master execution environment multiple delegate environments are active concurrently. Fallback, if semantically valid within the process, would however still be possible as long as a strict order of fallbacks is known by all candidates. These candidates would also be required to have some degree of overall knowledge of the process, possibly under some sort of escrow approach.

6 Conclusion

From the discussion above, it is clear that beyond meeting business needs in providing the benefits of collaboration while safeguarding independence of control, federated process environments also bring interesting resilience properties. In particular, the independence of execution environments prevents the full failure at system level in the case of failure of individual execution environments. At process level, full failure is limited to those cases where no fallback to a component is available (a unique, mandatory, service only provided by a single partner). Instance resilience is no longer restricted to an ability to work around failure of single components, but also handle failure of execution environments.

Process resilience, in federated and other forms, does however require processes to be designed for resilience, to have additional information that specifies the semantic validity of cancellation and retries, and for there to be good, shared, monitoring of component performance and reliability.

References

1. Kutvonen, L., Ruokolainen, T., Metso, J.: Interoperability middleware for federated business services in web-Pilarcos. In: Agent and Web Service Technologies in Virtual Enterprises, vol. 31, p. 288, July 2007
2. Kutvonen, L., Metso, J., Ruokolainen, T.: Inter-enterprise collaboration management in dynamic business networks. In: Meersman, R., Tari, Z. (eds.) OTM 2005. LNCS, vol. 3760, pp. 593–611. Springer, Heidelberg (2005)
3. Afsarmanesh, H., Camarinha-Matos, L.M.: Federated information management for cooperative virtual organizations. In: Tjoa, A.M. (ed.) DEXA 1997. LNCS, vol. 1308, pp. 561–572. Springer, Heidelberg (1997)
4. Camarinha-Matos, L.M.: Collaborative networks: a mechanism for enterprise agility and resilience. In: Mertins, K., Bénaben, F., Poler, R., Bourrières, J.-P. (eds.) Enterprise Interoperability VI, vol. 7, pp. 3–11. Springer, Heidelberg (2014)
5. Leymann, F., Roller, D., Schmidt, M.T.: Web services and business process management. IBM Syst. J. **41**(2), 198–211 (2002)
6. Dong, Q., Bradshaw, K., Ferrese, F., Bai, L., Biswas, S.: Cooperative federated multi-agent control of large scale systems. In: ACTA Control and Applications Conference, June 2011
7. de Vrieze, P., Xu, L.: An analysis of resilience of a cloud based incident notification process. In: Camarinha-Matos, L.M., Benaben, F., Picard, W. (eds.) PRO-VE 2015. IFIP AICT, vol. 463, pp. 110–121. Springer, Heidelberg (2015). doi:10.1007/978-3-319-24141-8_10
8. Buyya, R., Ranjan, R., Calheiros, R.N.: InterCloud: utility-oriented federation of cloud computing environments for scaling of application services. In: Hsu, C.-H., Yang, L.T., Park, J.H., Yeo, S.-S. (eds.) ICA3PP 2010, Part I. LNCS, vol. 6081, pp. 13–31. Springer, Heidelberg (2010)
9. Demchenko, Y., Ngo, C., de Laat, C., Lee, CK.: Federated access control in heterogeneous intercloud environment: basic models and architecture patterns. In: 2014 IEEE International Conference on Cloud Engineering (IC2E), 11 March 2014, pp. 439–445. IEEE (2014)
10. Konstanteli, K., Cucinotta, T., Psychas, K., Varvarigou, T.A.: Elastic admission control for federated cloud services. IEEE Trans. Cloud Comput. **2**(3), 348–361 (2014)
11. Liu, C., Li, Q., Zhao, X.: Challenges and opportunities in collaborative business process management: overview of recent advances and introduction to the special issue. Inf. Syst. Front. **11**(3), 201–209 (2009)
12. Niehaves, B., Plattfaut, R.: Collaborative business process management: status quo and quo vadis. Bus. Process Manag. J. **17**(3), 384–402 (2011)
13. Camarinha-Matos, L.M., Afsarmanesh, H.: Collaborative networks: a new scientific discipline. J. Intell. Manuf. **16**(4–5), 439–452 (2005)
14. EFFRA: Factories of the Future 2020 Roadmap (2013). http://effra.eu/attachments/article/129/Factories%20of%20the%20Future%202020%20Roadmap.pdf. Accessed 8 Apr 2016

15. ALICE: Information Systems for Interconnected Logistics Research and Innovation Roadmap (2014). http://www.etp-logistics.eu/cms_file.php?fromDB=11627&forceDownload
16. Erol, O., Mansouri, M., Sauser, B.: A framework for enterprise resilience using service oriented Architecture approach. In: 2009 3rd Annual IEEE Systems Conference, 23 March 2009, pp. 127–132. IEEE (2009)
17. Antunes, P., Mourão, H.: Resilient business process management: framework and services. Expert Syst. Appl. **38**(2), 1241–1254 (2011)

Hyperconnectivity and Interoperation - Collective Intelligence and Decision Making

Collaborative Networks as Ways to Improve Cross-sector Collaboration in Social Innovation: An Exploratory Study

Michele Andréia Borges[1,2](✉), António Lucas Soares[2], and Gertrudes Aparecida Dandolini[1]

[1] Federal University of Santa Catarina, Florianópolis, Brazil
micheleandborges@gmail.com, ggtude@gmail.com
[2] Institute for Systems and Computer Engineering, Technology and Science – INESC TEC, Porto, Portugal
als@fe.up.pt

Abstract. Social innovation is presented as a viable alternative to incite systemic changes related to sustainability in its three dimensions (social, environmental and economic), to involve the government, companies and, above all, civil society. In order to understand the development of social innovation in Brazil and Portugal, and to promote cross-sector collaboration, we have conducted several case studies involving centers for social innovation in both countries. The data analysis demonstrates that collaboration between sectors and the construction of collaborative networks is as a key element in the development and sustainability of social innovation. In spite of this, in practice the construction of these networks is not trivial, there is the need to manage these networks innovatively. The literature review points out the key enablers for cross-sector collaboration in the context of social innovation, the alignment of values and goals, mutual trust, commitment and bridge leadership.

Keywords: Social innovation · Cross-sector collaboration · Collaborative network · Brazil · Portugal

1 Introduction

Society is undergoing great changes. Problems of environmental and social order that were (apparently) "silent" a few decades ago, are today shown to all. The saturation of a strictly economic view, causes the need for the involvement of social actors to think and act systemically. As stated by Dowbor, "this implies decision-making mechanisms and management that go beyond the immediate microeconomic interest" (p. 11) [1]. Corroborating this view, Hubert [2] says that the key global challenges of today (climate change, aging, migration, among others) are both from economic and social order.

According to UN data, developed countries are faced with a new growth of income inequality [1]. Among the EU countries, Greece and Portugal have been deeply affected by the global crisis. Santos [3] states that "studies show that Portugal is trapped in an austerity crisis and is the European country where austerity measures most affect the

H. Afsarmanesh et al. (Eds.): PRO-VE 2016, IFIP AICT 480, pp. 137–147, 2016.
DOI: 10.1007/978-3-319-45390-3_12

poor, which poses special challenges for the Santa Casa Misericordia de Lisboa" (p. 90). In developing countries, e.g. in Latin America, Brazil is located in the deepest pit of income inequality [1].

This situation has triggered initiatives and policies promoting entrepreneurship and social innovation in these countries. According to Santos [4], the Portuguese social sector has shown that the current models of adjustment aimed to address income inequality, although they have some positive results, are not enough to account for the complexity of the problem, needing urgently to "new form of social management based on a new creative social design" (p. 86) [3]. Social innovation is presented as a viable alternative to incite systemic changes related to sustainability in its three dimensions (social, environmental and economic), involving governments, companies and, above all, civil society.

> Innovation in the social sector generates productivity and economic value for the whole society. This value should be better recognised with new measurements of welfare beyond gross domestic product (GDP), as pointed out, inter alia, by the Economics Nobel Prize winner Daniel Kahneman in the American Economic Review and recently by the Stiglitz commission. According to this view, social innovations are innovations that respond to those societal challenges in which the boundary between social and economic blurs, and are directed towards society as a whole. (p. 28) [2].

The answer to these complex challenges will require the participation of actors at all levels, leading to proactive policies and an organized intervention of the various social groups [1]. Thus, more than isolated initiatives, collaboration among multiple stakeholders is the key to dissemination, effectiveness and sustainability of social innovation [4].

After a decade since the phenomenon of social innovation has established itself as a field of study [5, 6], the literature indicates that there is still a need for studies addressing the understanding of its concept, processes and diffusion [7, 8]. Studies focusing on the aspect of collaboration for social innovation are still incipient and require empirical studies in greater depth [9]. In this sense, one question emerges: how is cross-sector collaboration in social innovation initiatives developing?

In order to find preliminary answers to this research question, we explored two cases of social innovation centers, one in Portugal and the other in Brazil, aiming at achieving a preliminary understanding of cross-sector collaboration in the context of social innovation.

2 Cross-sector Collaboration for Social Innovation

A literature review on the subjects of collaboration and social innovation was conducted to further examine the content of the interviews. To map and analyze the literature the Proknow-C [10] methodology was adopted. This methodology encompasses two major steps: the selection and the filtering of a set of articles. In the first step, the bibliographic databases that have adherence to the research topic are selected. Then, keywords and their combination are chosen in accordance with the search axes. Finally, the search criteria are defined, i.e., the time the articles, article type, among others. The keywords, their combinations, the limiting criteria and the selection criteria of the articles are presented in the Table 1 below.

Table 1. Search strategy.

Keywords	Combination	Database	Search criteria
Social innovation Collaboration Alliance Partnership Cooperation	"Social innovation" AND (Collaboration OR Alliance OR Partnership OR Cooperation)	Scopus	Fields: Title, Abstract and Keywords Data range: 2010 to 2015 Document type: article
		Web of Science	Fields: topic Data range: 2010 to 2015 Document type: article

The second stage of filtering the paper set is cleaning the data, resulting in a total of 86 articles for reading the titles and abstracts. The reading was made based on the research objective and meeting the criteria of empirical studies. After reading the titles and abstracts, 14 papers remained for reading in full.

Collaboration is based on the notion that problems can be solved more effectively if done by partnerships, alliances and networks [11]. It is a process in which the parties involved observe a problem from different angles, exploring their differences constructively and seeking solutions that go beyond their own limited vision of what is possible [12]. It is also a process in which new arrangements are possible by sharing resources and knowledge [11].

The results of the literature review show that for social innovation, collaboration is an important resource in understanding their complex dynamics [13–15]. It is through it that the most effective transformations occur [16]. Social innovation and collaboration have a reciprocal relationship to the extent that the collaborative processes and methods influence the social innovation impact and, in turn, social innovation creates new shapes and designs for collaboration [9]. According to Sanzo et al. [9], the existence of new forms of collaboration between sectors (government, civil society and business) is a critical feature of social innovation practices.

Thus, the ability of an inter-agency team to produce results that have a major impact on society, is built from the fortress of inter-institutional networks that allow the emergence of a new meta-institution legitimacy, resources, knowledge and sufficient strategic alignment for proper harmonization efforts within each institution [17].

In this paradigm of collaboration and inter-sectorial partnerships, private companies have led many social issues in partnership with non-profit organizations and/or government. The union of the private sector with these other sectors, towards a social goal, has shown that it is possible to work side by side and not as opponents [16]. The opposite has also been valid. Non-profit organizations working collaboratively with other sectors have achieved more success in their social enterprises. According to Shier and Handy [15]: "collaborations are supportive because they help create capacity, align goals, and focus the efforts of a nonprofit's social change agenda" (p. 21). The government, in turn, moves away from the role of mere regulator. These changes in roles and relationships are central to the effectiveness of a range of social innovations [16].

An example presented by Selsky and Parker [18], about a poor educational system, illustrates how these sectors sighted and address social problems in different ways. For a business, a poor education system can represent a strategic challenge, since a failure education could result in shortages of skilled labor or training and training costs to develop a workforce. For the government, a poor educational system may reflect a lower tax revenues or managing them badly, the lack of political and administrative leadership and other impediments. For non-profit organizations, a poor educational system may indicate the need for development projects or public campaigns to keep local jobs. This example shows that when the actors from different sectors relate to the same question they are likely to think in different ways, are motivated by different objectives and employ different approaches to deal with what is in fact the same challenge. If they jointly focus efforts on this issue, a partnership project to address the poor educational system can develop. As a result, new learning can emerge and more innovative and effective solutions can be obtained as a result of the partnership and collaboration between these actors [18].

However, working together within the social action domain is not a trivial task. The process by which the cross-sector partnerships create social value is often not linear and full of weaknesses, difficulties and disappointments. Only a few partners can create social change constantly and cumulatively. Many collapse partnerships for bad account understood, incorrect allocation of costs and benefits, and distrust [19]. The challenge is to control the borders that are traded and handled within a cooperative relationship [11] so there is not only a cooperation state – "information exchange, adjustment of activities, splitting of resources and work while aiming at specific targets" (p. 1414) [20] – but also collaboration, which "involves mutual trust, in addition to being a process in which participants, working together, share information, resources, responsibilities and risks to achieve common goals" (p. 1414) [20].

When it comes to partnerships between businesses and non-profit organizations to create value and social innovation, empirical studies show that cross-sector partnerships should be cautious not to be affected by the heterogeneity of its values, missions and purposes, hampering knowledge sharing [11, 19, 21, 22]. In this sense, companies and non-profit organizations should measure efforts in aligning their partnership, since they "do not have the same agendas or the same ideological representation regarding human rights and consumer rights" [11] (p. 3).

This type of partnerships, civil-society-business, are more prone to tensions and conflicts due to their contractors institutional logic, which makes often problematic the development of the alliance [11, 19, 21, 22]. In the words of Le Ber and Branzei [19]: "Cross-sector partnerships follow nonlinear progression paths marked by constant adjustments and recombinations and punctuated by transient successes and temporary failures" (p. 145). But despite the different values and logic espoused by the authors, it is possible to innovate through cooperation and collaboration activities, without betraying the core value and the identity of the organizations [11]. This requires a collaboration between innovative multilevel, to be able to build bridges between different networks. Le Ber and Branzei [19] also suggest that the success or failure of the partnership between organization and nonprofit depends on the motivation of the partners to (re)iteratively align their roles, since the heterogeneity is inherent in this type of partnership. Moreover, they also suggest that partners sustain the momentum toward success by developing a stronger degree of relational link, especially when this relationship is emotionally charged, resulting in a greater exchange of knowledge and fostering co-creation for social innovation.

In this context, trust is a determining factor in the relational development of the partnership and in the sharing and dissemination of knowledge [9, 11, 23]; and that affective trust-based partnerships develop towards a greater success than those exclusively monetary [9]. Trust is nothing more than the belief in loyalty, sincerity, honesty and competence of others [24]. Sanzo et al. [9] relate to trust the three elements: capacity, honesty and benevolence. The capacity refers to the necessary experience and competencies in the partnership to carry out the work effectively. Honesty it is the fulfillment of the promises and adherence to the principles of the parties. Benevolence is the interest in the well-being that the parties have for each other [9]. The more you develop a trust in partnerships the more collaboration becomes intense and effective. This means a greater exchange of experiences and knowledge, which are favorable for innovation [11]. In other words, trust leads to a more successful collaboration which, in turn, creates more confidence in the partnership, which is then enhanced, leading to a virtuous circle of collaboration through the creation of new capital. This capital is made up of individuals moving between multiple networks and bring with them knowledge and influence of social ties that are leveraged to raise original solutions to complex problems [11].

Trust can be raised also by a Bridge Leadership. According to studies of Manning and Roessler, Mcmullen and Adobor and Raišienė collaborative partnerships they had a bridge leadership they were developed better than those who did not have [25–27]. A bridge leadership is an individual who connects through alternative ways, organizations can be widely disparate in wealth, power, culture, language, values, interests, and structural characteristics. This kind of leader has great ability to raise the confidence of the people and organizations in which he makes the bridge. This is due to their competence, integrity, perseverance and empathy, as well as their ability to involve different types of people, be open to compromise, have credibility with their constituents and an aptitude to learn to understand the language used by stakeholders [26].

Just as trust, commitment between partners is another key element to the success of cross-sector partnership [9]. Commitment is the belief that the relationship between the parties is sufficiently important enough to expend the maximum effort to maintain the partnership. There are two basic types of commitment [9]: calculative and affective. The first is based on a rational assessment of the benefits and costs of a particular relationship. The second takes an emotional predisposition to maintain the relationship because of an emotional bond with their partner, often as a result of the congruence of values that you have with him. Sanzo et al. [9] says that affective commitment is, for most researchers, the factor that has the greatest influence to maintain mutually beneficial relationships.

The existence of trust and commitment increases the attitudes and behaviors of participants, encouraging and promoting collaboration, creativity, information sharing and knowledge [9], the value creation and social innovation [11, 19].

Summarising, the alignment and realignment of values and goals, the achievement of higher levels of trust and commitment, and the role of the Leadership Bridge, are enablers that support cross-sector collaboration process. Figure 1 summarizes all those elements.

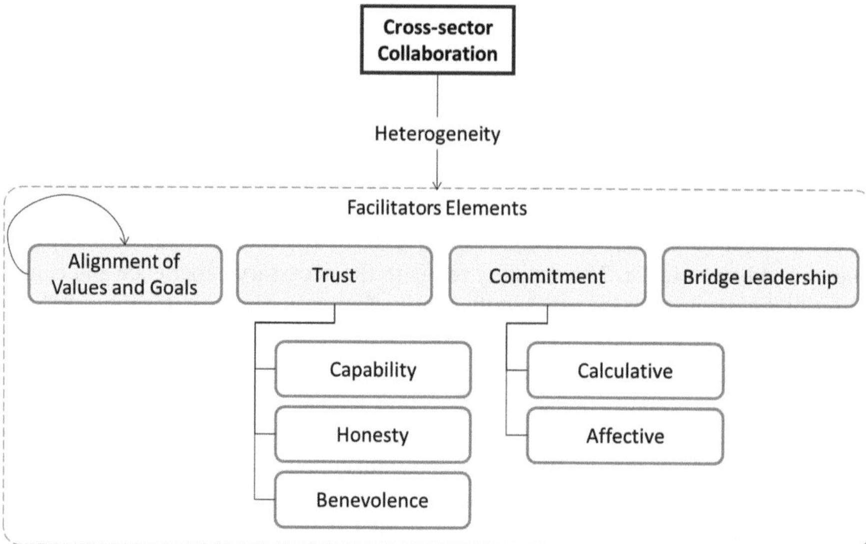

Fig. 1. Key enablers cross-sector collaboration.

The realignment, trust and commitment progress according to the maturity of the relationship over collaboration continuum, which can lead to a successful partnership [19] and creation or consolidation of collaborative networks. According Camarinha-Matos, the collaborative network is defined as:

> Is a network consisting of a variety of entities (e.g. organizations and people) that are largely autonomous, geographically distributed, and heterogeneous in terms of their operating environment, culture, social capital and goals, but that collaborate to better achieve common or compatible goals, and whose interactions are supported by computer network (p. 4) [28].

3 Exploratory Cases

In order to achieve a preliminary understanding of cross-sector collaboration in the context of social innovation, two cases were explored through the perception of managers of two centers for social innovation (CSI), one in Portugal and the other in Brazil. Data collection was conducted through face-to-face interviews.

The CSI investigated in Brazil is located in the south of the country and is characterized by supporting socially innovative initiatives, offering space and free services to people who want to make a difference in the region in which it is located. Born in 2011, from a demand from NGOs, social entrepreneurs, students, researchers and social investors who needed a place to think and act creatively in the public interest and the common good. Is inspired by the innovative models of the Centre for Social Innovation, Canada.

The CSI in Portugal is located in the north of the country and also originated in 2011, by a local authority and a social foundation. The goal of the CSI is to promote the implementation of innovation projects and social entrepreneurship in the city which it is based.

The average duration of interviews was 30 min. Although the interview had an open character, it was taken as based on three guiding questions, which include the focus and purpose of this study: How is developing the Social Innovation in Brazil/Portugal in particular regarding the collaboration between the different sectors of society involved (public, private, civil society)? What are the trends regarding to this in Brazil/Portugal?

For transcription and content analysis a qualitative and mixed methods data analysis tool was used MAXQDA™ref.

3.1 Cross-sectorial Collaboration in Social Innovation: The Vision of CSI Brazil

The interest of social innovation in Brazil, according to the CSI interviewed, has been growing. By analysing the activities in recent years in the Social Good Brazil social network (an organization that connects and supports individuals and organizations in the use of technology, new media and innovative behavior to contribute to solving social problems), an increasing number in the interest of the people by the theme social innovation has been observed.

Civil society organizations have been engaged in initiatives that promote the development of their communities. Private companies have also begun to work with the third sector organizations. However, when it comes to collaboration between sectors (private and third sector), the initiatives are still incipient.

At the core of CSI Brazil there is the issue of cross-sector collaboration and in this sense, they have worked in the union of collaborative partnerships, through the restructuring of a "Portal Transparência" project, whose goal is to make private companies aware of socially innovative ideas promoted by institutions of the third sector. The idea, organizational structure and impact of the action of third sector initiatives are evaluated in order to have a quality seal these initiatives, creating a relationship of trust with companies interested in collaborating.

This CSI project arose from the very necessity of non-profit organizations, once they realized the difficulty of private enterprises to trust and collaborate with their projects. CSI through a process of co-creation with the various social actors (organizations, entrepreneurs, students, etc.) is redesigning this "Portal Transparência" project.

While it is growing interest in the topic, the effectiveness of actions and the process of collaboration between the sectors challenges the future of social innovations in Brazil.

3.2 Cross-sectorial Collaboration in Social Innovation: The Vision of CSI Portugal

In the last five years there has been a setback for the development of social innovations. This setback is linked with some political discontinuities, since innovation projects in the social sphere were to be, in many cases experienced by the central government or the local government (municipal authorities).

However, 20 years ago, experiments with social innovation projects provided significant learning regarding the labor issues in public partnerships and private organizations from the third sector, as well as the tangible and intangible issues in the development of the territories. These experiments showed the need for networking and collaboration.

Under the perspective of the Portuguese CSI, the collaborative work between CSIs is an innovation in itself which demands overcoming many challenges and difficulties. The Portuguese CSI has, in this sense, experimented several models for innovation governance, integrating the various sectors (public, private and third sector).

> At this time the reality and complexity of the problems, the lack of funding, a crisis, in fact, require other types of innovation in governance models, much aiming at policy integration and integrated intervention in the territories rather than focused [in each of] different sectors" (manager of the CSI Portugal).

Thus, collaboration and inter-sectorial partnerships are key to a promising direction of social innovations. The partnership of CSI Portugal with international projects within the European Union (EU), demonstrates this fundamental quality of collaboration and sharing of knowledge in social innovation projects. "The EU in this respect is a super interesting work from the point of view of us put together" (manager of the CSI Portugal).

However, cross-sector collaboration and sharing of knowledge is a challenge to be overcome.

> It's hard to be able to share. And these issues of innovation, and we have some ability to be humble and to see what is what the neighbor be doing or trying to find that we are reinventing the wheel" (manager of the CSI Portugal). [...] Each one has a vision. Each of one us does not like to get out of its comfort zone. We share only up to a point. Either we change and we break with this logic or it is very difficult to innovate" (manager of the CSI Portugal).

3.3 Barriers and Future Challenges to Cross-sectorial Collaboration in Social Innovation

CSI Brazil and the CSI Portugal have a close view of the barriers and challenges in cross-sectorial collaboration in Social Innovation.

Barriers to social innovation and cross-sectorial collaboration:

- Difficulty in measuring the impact of initiatives.
- Many social interventions are deployed by associations and organizations whose volunteers frequently don't have some management skills.
- Social innovation can be seen as a hype. On the one hand, by becoming fashionable, the critical mass increases and the debate and discussion about the topic is encouraged. On the other hand, everyone ends up calling social innovation to any intervention that is made in the social sphere because it is fashionable to do so. There is no concern to understand and deepen the concept of what actually comes to be a social innovation.
- Difficulty working collaboratively. Everyone wants to be on your very confined space.
- Private companies want to be protagonists of the shares.
- The entrepreneurs think only from their perspective, without worrying about what people want to they will work want.

Future challenges for social innovation and cross-sectorial collaboration:

- Break up with the idea of many entrepreneurs in the social area and anyone can intervene or give feedback.
- Break away from the paternalistic vision.
- Empower citizens so that they are agents of transformation and that they can work collaboratively with the State for the promotion of public policies. The need of the institutions realized that they are a company that has to innovate within this social movement and it has to innovate in their management models in their entry strategies in the Market.
- Transform initiatives in social business.
- Work with the beneficiaries. Understand your needs and give fact they need an innovation.
- Working in collaboration with other sectors.

4 Discussion and Conclusion

Brazil and Portugal have an historical relationship of colonization and, although this has determined the adoption of some cultural aspects from the former colony, they are today countries that differ considerably in terms of economy and social development. However, global challenges and the global crisis have promoted the engagement of both the developed countries, as in the developments in driving new solutions to these challenges facing.

The content analysis of the interviews showed that these two CSI converge as ideas and as the perception of the development of social innovation. Both believe that collaboration and sharing of information and knowledge between the different sectors are the key to the direction of social innovations. Collaborative processes involving the sectors (governmental, profit and non-profit) the beneficiary communities can result in innovations that, in fact, contribute to the development of the territories. In this process, there is an exchange that fosters the process of improving project management by the organizations involved in social innovation.

Mechanisms of mediation and estimation of the impacts, and the professional management of initiatives through non-profit organizations are also challenges for social innovation. While the improvement in mediating the impacts and conduct of initiatives in social business aspect can cooperate in forming collaborative partnerships with other organizations, it provides the transparency of actions, generating more mutual trust between organizations.

The experiences of CSI investigated corroborate the empirical studies carried out at the international level. The research study indicate that collaboration is very important to bring solutions that go beyond the limited vision of a single individual, group or organization, and to transform the most effective and sustainable actions.

The culture for collaboration is relatively recent, it came with the era of knowledge and information and communication technologies [3]. In practice, the culture of collaboration demand efforts to establish itself in the daily lives of people and organizations, and it involves trust, commitment and alignment of values and goals. The higher the degree of trust and commitment will be greater knowledge sharing among actors [14].

Thus, this research contributes to the understanding of the challenges and key elements that can help advance the field as scientific knowledge, but also as shares of empirical reality.

Acknowledgment. This work was conducted during a scholarship supported by the Doctoral Sandwich Abroad Program CAPES/PDSE at the Federal University of Santa Catarina. Financed by CAPES – Higher Education Personnel Improvement Coordination within the Ministry of Education of Brazil. Furthermore, this work is financed by the ERDF – European Regional Development Fund through the Operational Programme for Competitiveness and Internationalisation - COMPETE 2020 Programme within project «POCI-01-0145-FEDER-006961», and by National Funds through the FCT – Fundação para a Ciência e a Tecnologia (Portuguese Foundation for Science and Technology) as part of project UID/EEA/50014/2013.

References

1. Dowbor, L.: Inovação social e sustentabilidade. Econ. Glob. E Gestão. **12**, 9–33 (2007)
2. Hubert, A.: Empowering People, Driving Change - Social Innovation in the European Union (2010)
3. Santos, R.T.: Social innovation oriented towards solving practical problems: the case of the Santa Casa da Misericórdia de Lisboa. In: Viñals, C.R., Rodríguez, C.P. (eds.) Social Innovation: New Forms of Organisation in Knowledge-Based Societies, pp. 84–107. Routledge - Taylor & Francis Group, London and New York (2013)
4. Klein, J.L., Fontan, J.M., Harrisson, D., Lévesque, B.: The Quebec system of social innovation. A focused analysis on the local development field. Finisterra **47**, 9–28 (2012)
5. Murray, R., Caulier-Grice, J., Mulgan, G.: The Open Book of Social Innovation. The Young Foundation/National Endowment for Science, Technology and the Art – NESTA, London (2010)
6. Mulgan, G.: The process of social innovation. Innov. Technol. Gov. Glob. **1**, 145–162 (2006)
7. Cajaiba-Santana, G.: Social innovation: moving the field forward. A conceptual framework. Technol. Forecast. Soc. Change **82**, 42–51 (2014)
8. Mulgan, G.: Collaboration and Collective Impact: How Can Funders, NGOs and governments Achieve More Together?. NESTA, London (2006)
9. Sanzo, M.J., Álvarez, L.I., Rey, M., García, N.: Business–nonprofit partnerships: a new form of collaboration in a corporate responsibility and social innovation context. Serv. Bus. **9**, 1–26 (2015)
10. Ensslin, L., Ensslin, S.R., Lacerda, R.T.O., Tasca, J.E.: Processo de Seleção de Portfólio Bibliográfico (2010)
11. Harrisson, D., Chaari, N., Comeau-Vallée, M.: Intersectoral alliance and social innovation: when corporations meet civil society. Ann. Publ. Coop. Econ. **83**, 1–24 (2012)
12. Gray, B.: Collaborating: Finding Common Ground for Multiparty Problems. Jossey Bass, San Francisco (1989)
13. Goldenberg, M.: Social Innovation in Canada: How the Non-Profit Sector Serves Canadians… And How It Can Serve. Canadian Policy Research Networks Inc. (CPRN), Ontario (2004)

14. Westley, F., Zimmerman, B., Patton, M.: Getting to Maybe: How the World is Changed. Random House of Canada Ltd., Toronto (2006)
15. Shier, M.L., Handy, F.: Social change efforts of direct service nonprofits: the role of funding and collaborations in shaping social innovations. Hum. Serv. Organ. Manag. Leadersh. Gov. **39**, 6–24 (2015)
16. Phills, J., Deiglmeier, K., Miller, D.: Rediscovering social innovation. Stanford Soc. Innov. Rev. Fall **6**, 34–43 (2008)
17. Hernández, I.D., Sánchez, O.: Innovación social abierta en el diseño de una política y estrategia de formalización sostenible: un caso colombiano de gobierno colaborativo. Rev. Fac. Ciencias Económicas **22**, 47–61 (2014)
18. Selsky, J.W., Parker, B.: Platforms for cross-sector social partnerships: prospective sensemaking devices for social benefit. J. Bus. Eth. **94**, 21–37 (2011)
19. Le Ber, M.J., Branzei, O.: (Re)forming strategic cross-sector partnerships: relational processes of social innovation. Bus. Soc. **49**, 140–172 (2010)
20. Ferreira, R.P., Silva, J.N., Strauhs, F.R., Soares, A.L.: Performance management in collaborative networks: a methodological proposal. J. Univers. Comput. Sci. **17**, 1412–1429 (2011)
21. Le Ber, M.J., Branzei, O.: Value frame fusion in cross sector interactions. J. Bus. Eth. **94**, 163–195 (2010)
22. Harrisson, D., Comeau-Vallée, M., Chaari, N.: Analyse d'une Pratique innovante Intersectorielle. Entreprise Publique et Associations de Défense des Droits des Consommateurs. Finisterra **XLVII**, 29–48 (2012)
23. Kolleck, N.: Innovations through networks: understanding the role of social relations for educational innovations. Zeitschrift für Erziehungswiss **17**, 47–64 (2014)
24. Zucker, L.G.: Production of trust: institutional sources of economic structure, 1840–1920. Res. Organ. Behav. **8**, 53–111 (1986)
25. Manning, S., Roessler, D.: The formation of cross-sector development partnerships: how bridging agents shape project agendas and longer-term alliances. J. Bus. Eth. **123**, 527–547 (2013)
26. Mcmullen, R.S., Adobor, H.: Bridge leadership: a case study of leadership in a bridging organization. Leadersh. Organ. Dev. J. **32**, 715–735 (2011)
27. Raišienė, A.G.: Sustainable development of interorganizational relationships and social innovations. J. Secur. Sustain. Issues **2**, 65–76 (2012)
28. Camarinha-Matos, L.M., Afsarmanesh, H.: Collaborative Networks: value creation in a knowledge society. In: Wang, K., Kovacs, G.L., Wozny, M., Fang, M. (eds.) PROLAMAT 2006. IFIP, vol. 207, pp. 26–40. Springer, Heidelberg (2006)

Collective Intelligence and Collaboration: A Case Study in Airline Industry

Sónia A.C. Teixeira[1,2](✉), Pedro Campos[1,2], Renato Fernandes[1,3], and Catarina Roseira[2]

[1] Faculty of Economics, University of Porto, Porto, Portugal
{sonia.c.teixeira, renato.s.fernandes}@inesctec.pt, pcampos@fep.up.pt
[2] LIAAD - INESC TEC, Porto, Portugal
croseira@fep.up.pt
[3] CPES - INESC TEC, Porto, Portugal

Abstract. In order to improve their competitive performance, airline companies often adopt as a strategy to establish arrangement between two or more organizations agreeing to cooperate on a substantial level. This strategy is often known as airline alliances. A paradigm to analyze the collective intelligence behavior which emerges from a group, as a strategic alliance, is the flocking behavior. Inspired by the Cucker and Smale algorithm (C-S) we propose a new version of the flocking behavior algorithm applied to airline alliances. Our goal is to understand the link between strategic alliances and flocks. For this new approach, metrics were obtained for the parameters of C-S algorithm, namely position, velocity and influence, where the latter uses cooperative games. Besides, reinforcement learning mechanisms have been explored. Some relevant outputs for airline alliances as the permanence rate and the growth rate were computed for each of the five configurations in analysis.

Keywords: Collective intelligence · Airline industry · Flocking behavior

1 Introduction

The evolution of markets induces a change in the way organizations act. Collaboration between organizations, as an alternative or in parallel to competition, allows them to get the edge over other competitors or potential new organizations of the same market [8]. In this work, we focus on airline industry and explore the emerging collective intelligence and collaboration in the perspective of flocking behavior. The nature of airline industry is different from other industries because it requires public reassurances and operating procedures that include a governmental involvement, which implicitly encourages collaborative working practices [5]. Collaboration in airline industry allows organizations to reduce costs from sharing operational staff, making investments or negotiating extra volume discounts, what can represent lower prices due to lowered operational costs for a given route [7]. In that way, organizations increase revenue and generate opportunities. What derives from the shared belief that together the network members can achieve goals that would not be possible or would have a higher cost if they try to

H. Afsarmanesh et al. (Eds.): PRO-VE 2016, IFIP AICT 480, pp. 148–155, 2016.
DOI: 10.1007/978-3-319-45390-3_13

achieve individually [2]. Social dynamics factors are important to understand fundamental economic questions, which can be compromised when social preferences are not taken into account, because it is not possible to understand adequately the laws that govern cooperation and collective action, or the effects and the determinants of material incentives or even the important forces which shaping social norms and market failures [6]. The algorithms of flocking behavior [3, 4, 10, 12, 16], are methods that use simple rules to describe the evolution of a flock and are appropriate to simulate the behavior of a group of organizations, such as airline alliances, that move in accordance to a common goal. We propose a new version of the flocking behavior of Cucker and Smale (C-S) algorithm [4] applied to airline alliances, taking into account a learning mechanism. The model is named AllFlock and the goal is to understand the link between strategic alliances and flocking behavior. The permanence rate of the alliances (computed for simulated and real data) and the growth rate of the alliances were computed for each of the five configurations in analysis, which can be important to evaluate the fitness and the structure of the alliance. The paper is organized as follows: In Sect. 2 we introduce collective intelligence, swarm intelligence and flocking behavior algorithms. Our case study in airline industry is described in Sect. 3. In Sect. 4 results are presented and finally Sect. 5 presents the conclusion.

2 Collective Intelligence, Swarm Intelligence and Flocking Behavior Algorithms

The terminology used by Saminen in [13] mentions swarm intelligence to refer to emergent collective behavior in simple agents. On another hand, collective intelligence in humans is a relatively new and multidisciplinary subject. Since the appearance of the name of collective intelligence many other approaches arose, as purely theoretical, conceptual, for simulations, case studies, experiences and systems architecture [13]. Areas such as psychology, complexity, cognitive studies, biology, computer science and the media also gave their contribution to this multidisciplinary theme [13]. Swarms algorithms [1] are based on social and collective behavior that is observed in ants, birds, insects, etc. Ant colony optimization (ACO), particle swarm optimization (PSO), as well as self-propelled particles algorithms (SPP) [16], are part of the class of swarm intelligence algorithms. The term self-propelled particles arises when flocking algorithm proposed by Vicsek et al. in [16], which describe a group of particles, each them which acts as an autonomous agent and each follows same simple rules as a way to regulate their behavior. The intelligence of these same systems are triggered by the collective behavior of individuals, that is, interactions between individuals lead to the emergence of a global intelligent behavior, named collective intelligence [9]. The flocking has been seen to Olfati-Saber [10], as "a form of collective behavior of a large number of agents that interact with a common group goal". This complex movement caught the attention of Reynolds, also, who in 1987 proposed a simulation-based approach to the flock movement [12]. This movement, very similar to a natural flock, is created by a distributed behavioral model in which each bird acts as an independent agent and chooses its course. The flocking behavior is the result of the interaction of simple behaviors of agents, represented by rules. The starting point for the Cucker and

Smale (C-S) model [4], one of the most important algorithms of flocking, arises from an extension of a work by the same authors [3], in which an analysis is made to the flocking model from Vicsek et al. [16]. Motivation for such extension was the observation that under certain initial conditions of the state the flock converge, i.e. all birds fly at the same velocity. The proposed development model [4], uses three important parameters namely: position, velocity and influence and aims at searching for the conditions for the state under which the convergence is established. We propose an innovative extension of the flocking algorithm of [4] where position is viewed as the choice of potential partner organization, velocity is the performance of the organization when compared to the alliance (measured as the growth of the net income between two time steps) and influence is measured through the Shapley Value [11, 14], with the aim of dividing goods gained by the cooperation among many organizations. We also consider that organizations learn through interactions within the alliances where they belong. Reinforcement learning [15] is the method we use to implement the learning mechanism in the flocking behavior. The permanence rate and the growth rate of the alliances were computed by each of the five configurations in analysis. The permanence rate was also computed for simulated and real data, by each alliance.

3 Case Study: *AllFlock* Applied to Airline Industry

Until September 2015, there were mainly three alliances in airline industry: *SkyTeam* (founded in 2000, with 20 members), *Oneworld* (founded in 1999, containing 15 members) and *StarAlliance* (1997, with 27 members). A new alliance, *Vanilla Alliance* started in September 2015, and *U-FLY Alliance* in January 2016, with 5 and 4 members respectively. Some annual results from three biggest airlines alliances are presented at Table 1.

Table 1. Results from StarAlliance, SkyTeam, Oneworld (adapted from Oneworld site, SkyTeam and StarAlliance annual report 2015)

	StarAlliance	SkyTeam	Oneworld
Passengers (million)	641.10	612	512.6
Countries	192	177	154
Employees	432603	481691	389788
Total revenue (US millions)	179.05	186.331	141.404
Daily departures	18500	16323	14313

Airline industry growing business, in terms of market prospects, once the traffic has been duplicating every 15 years. The AllFlock model (Flocking in Strategic Alliances) proposed in this paper intends to recreate the way as organizations act in order to analyze it in terms of flocking behavior. AllFlock models the intragroup behavior where each agent knows the decisions of the other agents (companies) belonging to the same alliance. There are two important decisions: 1) What company to follow (based on a combination of the utility function - Choice - and the Growth; 2) The decision of remaining in the alliance (based on Shapley value and the Growth). The pseudocode of AllFlock is presented in the following lines.

Pseudocode:

```
Initialize variables
    While don't converge
        For each organization i do
            Compute and update variables:
                Compute weight of Growth, Impact of the alliance and Choice
                Compute Growth expression
                Update net profit
                Compute Impact of the alliance on organization i
                Compute reward or punishment
                Compute learning velocity
                Compute Choice expression
            Take actions:
                Move forward with growth value
                Follow organization with the maximum value of choice expression
                Decide to remain or not, or evaluate to remain in the same alliance
        End for
        Verify if converge
    End while
```

The velocity in C-S is represented by the performance of an organization relative to the performance of alliance. Influence is measured by how much the organization considers to win with a specific alliance, which is the impact of a coalition could have on the organization. This is considered regardless of their physical location, unlike C-S. Simply put, each organization has to choose another organization to follow in each instant t, and this *choice* is dependent of *growth*, *choice* and *influence* (impact) of the alliance in previous moments. Regarding the position, we assume implicitly that organizations choose to collaborate with other organizations in order to maximize the gains. Following that idea, we compute choice value the result of tendencies by particular organizations. The *AllFlock* model considers that depending on their aspirations, at every time t, organizations give different importance to these three aspects. For that reason we included $pe_i(t)$, $ps_i(t)$ e $pc_i(t)$, as the weights with which organization i attaches *choice*, *influence* and *growth*, respectively. *Choice* considers which organization j the organization i wants to follow as a potential partner. When organization i is looking for the best direction to go, which means the organization that maximizes the *choice* expression, it collects information throughout their interactions in respect of previous choices. In our view, organization i is learning by trial and error, which is common in reinforcement learning situations. Collaboration is also taken into account in the reinforcement learning, where each company gives rewards or punishments to other companies for their attunement with choices. Let us denote the velocity at which the agent assimilates information by α, r the reward and the amortization rate by γ (the latter being defined by the user). Therefore, denoting by $E_{ij}(t)$, the *choice*, at time t; the *influence* of the alliance is $S_i(t)$, and the *growth* of the organization i at time t is $C_i(t)$, we have:

$$E_{ij}(t+\Delta t) = (1-\alpha) * (E_{ij}(t) * pe_i(t) + S_i(t) * ps_i(t) + C_i(t) * pc_i(t)) + \alpha * (r + \gamma \\ * E_{ij}(t) * pe_i(t) + S_i(t) * ps_i(t) + C_i(t) * pc_i(t))] \tag{1}$$

The Shapley Value $S_i(t)$ is used to measure the expectation of how much an organization can gain if it belongs to that alliance. Let a set of n companies $v = \{V_1, \ldots, V_n\}$, the function gain $v(.)$, and the subset $S \subseteq v$ [11]. The Shapley value is computed taking into account the value each company gains for being in the cooperation (2):

$$S_i(v) = \sum_{S \subseteq v} \frac{|S|!(|v| - |S| - 1)!}{|v|!} (v(S \cup \{V_i\}) - v(S)) \tag{2}$$

The impact of the alliance on the organization is given by the influence that affects the agent in its decision making. Organizations decide to remain (or not) in the alliance based on growth and on the impact of the alliance. If the organization is growing and has the expectation to improve its results for belonging to the alliance, then the organization will remain. When the organization is not growing and does not expect to have better results, then, it will go out of the alliance. If the organization has different indicators from the growth and the impact of the alliance, then the organization will evaluate what to do in the next period. In the case when a positive change happens then the organization stay, otherwise it exits. We assume that there is convergence in the flocking, when the organizations give the same reward in 80 % of time, in two different iterations of the algorithm. Exits and the permanence rate of the alliance are given by Eqs. 3 and 4, respectively.

$$Exits = \frac{initial\ number\ of\ organizations - final\ number\ of\ organizations}{initial\ number\ or\ organizations} \tag{3}$$

$$Permanence\ rate\ of\ the\ alliance = (1 - Exits) * 100 \tag{4}$$

4 Results

The *AllFlock* model that was created to simulate the flocking behavior has been developed in Netlogo [17].

The final results are the average of the 100 simulations for different number of iterations. In the analysis of the five configurations (Table 2), the evidence of convergence has the highest value at configuration 2, with the average of 106 iterations. The configuration that presents, on average, a fewer iterations occurs in the configuration 4. A Kruskal Wallis test was applied to verify if the distribution of iterations is the same between the configuration categories, as the permanence rate and the growth rate. The null hypothesis was rejected for a significance level of 0.05 in all three situations. Four different instants of simulation are possible to observe at Fig. 1.

Table 2. Configurations and combination of parameters

	Parameters (given by the user)				
	Initial number of organizations	Exploration rate vs. knowledge (sigma)	Delta	Discount	Evaluation time (time)
Configuration 1	Low	Low	High	High	Low
Configuration 2	Low	Low	High	High	High
Configuration 3	Low	Low	High	Moderate	High
Configuration 4	Low	Moderate	High	High	Low
Configuration 5	Low	Moderate	High	High	High

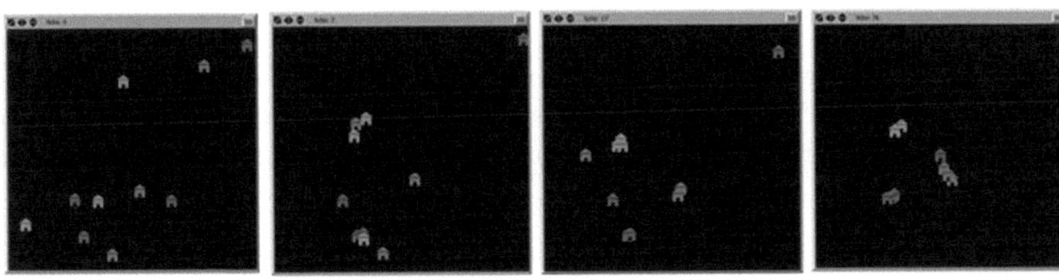

Fig. 1. Organizations behavior at four different instants of simulation (instants 0, 7, 17 e 76) for configuration 5 (Netlogo screenshots).

As we can observe at Fig. 2 the highest average permanence rate by alliance occurs at configuration 2 with 78.81 %, with 81.72 % at configuration 3 and at configuration 5 with 80.92 % and 79.73 %. The lowest average permanence rate by alliance occurs at configuration 1 with 54.95 % and at configuration 4 with 53.42 %. Average permanence rate between alliances in same configuration is not much different, in some cases is very close as in the alliances at configuration 1 (54.95 %, 57.62 % and 56.08 %) and between the Alliance0 and Alliance1 at configuration 4 (59.27 %, 59.37 % and 53.42 %).

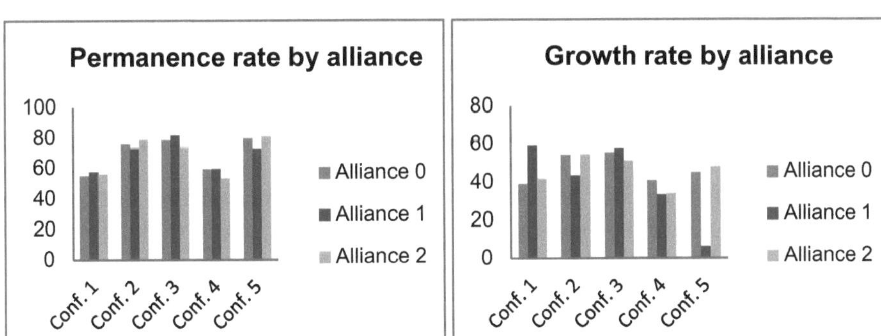

Fig. 2. Average permanence rate and average growth rate by alliance, for each configuration.

Average growth rate between alliances for configuration 3 (55.26 %, 57.78 % and 51.11 %) and configuration 4 (40.77 %, 33.34 % and 31.10 %) are very close, as is possible to observe at Fig. 2. The same does not happen in configuration 1, 2 and 5. In configuration 1 the average growth rate by alliance is 38.83 %, 59.17 % and 41.65 %, the average growth rate by alliance is 54.11 %, 43.26 % and 54.53 % at configuration 2, and for configuration 5 with 45.11 %, 6.37 % and 48.14 %. Average growth rate by alliance has the lowest value, 6.37 %, at alliance 1 in configuration 5 and the highest value for the same alliance at configuration 1.

Best result for average permanence rate by alliance with simulated data, using expression (4), occurs at Alliance0 with a rate of 69.69 %. The highest value in the air transport alliances, with real data, for the average permanence rate by alliance can be observed at *SkyTeam* alliance which has a rate of 79.17 %. *Oneworld* has the lowest value with an average permanence rate of 75 % and *StarAlliance* has an average permanence rate of 75.68 %. In the results for simulated data, (for which there is no correspondence with real data), the maximum number of organizations is in the initial instant.

5 Conclusions

Inspired on three C-S algorithm concepts: the position, velocity and influence, we used the same ideas concepts not always nearby, as in the case of the position and influence to construct the AllFlock model. The AllFlock model (Flocking in Strategic Alliances) proposed in this paper intends to recreate the way as organizations act in order to analyze it in terms of flocking behavior. We observed the evidence of convergence (existence of flock behavior).

In some configurations, such as, configuration 1 and configuration 4 companies remain in average less time in alliances, which can be explained by their need for good results ("time"). Was also observed that the average of permanence rate is closer between alliances than the average growth rate, which may be an indication of heterogeneous growth between companies. The AllFlock model does not allow for an organization to leave from an alliance and change to another. In addition, it does not consider other possibilities of sub-collaborations inside the companies of the alliance.

These are limitations of the AllFlock which are being considered for future work. With this evidence of flock behavior in strategic alliances, an analysis of typologies can be improved in future work (since there is some evidence that some typologies can be related with some parameters of simulation, like "time").

The proposed model can be seen as a first step to understanding the collective intelligence in organizations, namely in airline industries, by using flocking behavior.

References

1. Beni, G., Wang, J.: Swarm intelligence in cellular robotic systems, proceed. In: NATO Advanced Workshop on Robots and Biological Systems (1989)
2. Camarinha-Matos, L.M., Afsarmanesh, H.: Collaborative networks: a new scientific discipline. J. Intell. Manufact. **16**(4–5), 439–452 (2005)
3. Cucker, F., Smale, S.: Emergent behavior in flocks. IEEE Trans. Autom. Control **52**(5), 852–862 (2007)
4. Cucker, F., Smale, S.: On the mathematics of emergence. Jpn. J. Math. **2**(1), 197–227 (2007)
5. Evans, N.: Collaborative strategy: an analysis of the changing world of international airline alliances. Tourism Manag. **22**, 229–243 (2001)
6. Fehr, E., Fischbacker, U.: Why social preferences matter: the impact of non-selfish motives on competition, cooperation, and incentives. Econ. J. **112**(478), C1–C33 (2002)
7. Fernandez de la Torre, P.E.: Airline alliances: the airline perspective DSpace@MIT. http://hdl.handle.net/1721.1/68159
8. Johnson, G., Whittington, R., Scholes, K., Angwin, D., Regnér, P.: Exploring Strategy, 10th edn edn. Pearson, Harlow (2014). ISBN 978-1-292-00255-2
9. Lévy, P.: Collective Intelligence Mankind's Emerging World in Cyberspace. Challenges. Perseus Books, Cambridge (1997)
10. Olfati-Saber, R.: Flocking for multi-agent dynamic systems: algorithms and theory. IEEE Trans. Autom. Control **51**(3), 401–420 (2006)
11. Papapetrou, P., Gionis, A., Mannila, H.: A shapley value approach for influence attribution. In: Gunopulos, D., Hofmann, T., Malerba, D., Vazirgiannis, M. (eds.) ECML PKDD 2011, Part II. LNCS, vol. 6912, pp. 549–564. Springer, Heidelberg (2011). doi:10.1007/978-3-642-23783-6_35
12. Reynolds, C.W.: Flocks, herds and schools: a distributed behavioral model. SIGGRAPH Comput. Graph. **21**(4), 25–34 (1987). doi:10.1145/37401.37406
13. Salminen, J.: Collective Intelligence in Humans: A Literature Review. ArXiv preprint arXiv: 1204.3401, abs/1204.3, pp. 1–8 (2012). http://arxiv.org/abs/1204.3401
14. Shapley, L.S.: A value for n-person games. Ann. Math. Stud. **28**, 307–317 (1953)
15. Sutton, R.S., Barto, A.G.: Reinforcement Learning: An Introduction. Bradford Books, MIT Press, Cambridge (1998)
16. Vicsek, T., Czirok, A., Ben-Jacob, E., Cohen, I., Shochet, O.: Novel type of phase transition in a system of self-driven particles. Phys. Rev. Lett. **75**(6), 1226–1229 (1995)
17. Wilensky, U., Rand, W.: An Introduction to Agent-Based Modeling: Modeling Natural, Social and Engineered Complex Systems with NetLogo. MIT Press, Cambridge (2015)

Big-Data and the Question of Horizontal and Vertical Intelligence: A Discussion on Disaster Management

Frederick Benaben(✉), Aurelie Montarnal, Audrey Fertier, and Sebastien Truptil

Toulouse University, Mines Albi – Campus Jarlard, Route de Teillet, 81000 Albi, France
{frederick.benaben,aurelier.montarnal,audrey.fertier, sebastien.truptil}@mines-albi.fr

Abstract. Due to the unexpected context of disaster management (with heterogeneous and non-dedicated potential data sources), the classical Big-Data approaches within this business domain (schematically focused on data storage and pattern recognition) appear to be limited, especially when trying to get a situational level of such crises from data gathered from the field. That is why this article aims at discussing a specific vision of Big-Data for data management, in two steps: (i) analyzing this business domain to identify relevant characteristics, impacted or concerned by Big-Data, and describe the new key challenges that need to be tackled, and (ii) designing an innovative Big-Data framework dedicated to this particular business domain. After having highlighted the importance to push abstraction levels and especially data interpretation as a way to perform vertical intelligence in data analysis (instead of horizontal intelligence with usual approaches), the proposed Big-Data framework brings a layered approach according to three dimensions: gathering (data level), interpretation (information level), exploitation (knowledge level).

Keywords: Big-Data · Collaborative situation · Data interpretation · Metamodel · Modeling · Intelligence · Disaster management

1 Introduction

Just like any domain of human civilization, Disaster Management (DM) has to take into account the unavoidable increasing of generated and potentially accessible data. On any crisis site, heterogeneous and potentially not-dedicated data sources (sensors, opendata, witnesses and social networks, etc.) generate a deluge of data. Those emerging data could be very useful to characterize crisis situations and, thus, allow to better support DM and the decision-makers awareness. However, dealing with their specificities leads to raise new key challenges, and to the necessity of implementing a new Big-Data approach adapted to the needs of this business domain. That question of Big-Data is usually considered through the angle of emerging new technological solutions and platforms to manage this unprecedented amount of data. Though, the question of Big-Data definitely concerns so many human and social domains that it could be relevant to imagine that all domains do not require the same technological (or philosophical) approach for Big-Data management.

H. Afsarmanesh et al. (Eds.): PRO-VE 2016, IFIP AICT 480, pp. 156–162, 2016.
DOI: 10.1007/978-3-319-45390-3_14

Hence, this article aims at giving a vision of Big-Data applied to the DM, by exploring those various challenges raised both in terms of technological and philosophical points of view. Answering those issues leads to discuss the necessity to implement a 'vertical intelligence' and in particular, the ways and the means to bring levels of abstraction to the gathered data. Concretely, three main questions (and levels of abstraction) are addressed: (i) data gathering - how to extract data from unknown data sources and deal with their veracity and usability? (ii) data interpretation - how to transform datasets into exploitable models? and (iii) information exploitation - how to transform crisis situational models into actionable knowledge?

According to these objectives, this article is structured according to three sections: first section describes specificities and characteristics of DM from the Big-Data perspectives in order to define a particular profile for this domain. Second section uses this domain profile to infer what specific features of Big-Data management would be required in DM context (with regards to usual ways of tackle the question of Big-Data in other domains) and to introduce a Big-Data for DM framework. Finally a conclusion discusses the usage of this vision of Big-Data.

2 Specificities of Disaster Management on Social and Technological Perspectives

Based on [1] and [2, 3] the following definition for Disaster is suggested: *disruption within the state of a system, which reveals instability and discontinuity and which requires a specific treatment to deal with the unwanted consequences and to obtain a new acceptable state of the considered system.*

2.1 Social Dimension

Considering that consequences and impacts of Disasters are usually multi-dimensional and concern as various stakes as public health, politics, economics, etc., various types of stakeholders must be involved in DM (to cover all the involved multi-dimensional treatment actions). These responders should moreover be coordinated and smoothly synchronized to avoid conflicts and frictions due to pursuing heterogeneous missions and objectives. Consequently, dedicated collaborative networks must be established to perform efficient and adequate response. However, the usual questions related to the use of collaborative networks are exacerbated, due to five reasons:

- Critical stakes (consequences of crises may be heavy as far as they concern human lives and major societal stakes).
- Fickle kinetics (crisis is a fully dynamic system with cascading effects and potentially chaotic behaviour).
- Incomplete vision (stakeholders involved in crisis management only get a partial picture of the entire situation and its consequences).
- Unpredictable aspect (even if often expected, a crisis generally occurs at an unpredicted time that requires means and resources to be ready and available).

- Unheard of aspect (crisis management is not a mastered recurrent process and stakeholders, even if prepared at a micro-level are not a macro-level).

Furthermore, crisis management, as collaborative situation, concerns heterogeneous partners, which have their expertise area and are fully competent at a micro-level (besides it is their everyday-life activity). Consequently, and as described in [3], the main issue concerns coordination and collaboration of these stakeholders at a macro level. Finally, the main characteristic of DM from a **social perspective** is that *building efficient collaborative networks to support partners' coordination, although the supreme objective, is far more difficult in DM than in other domains*. This statement also includes all cultural barriers, rivalry and other human lows exacerbated by the critical context.

2.2 Technological Dimension

Another crucial element to be considered concerns the constantly increasing volume of available data. This is an indisputable matter of fact: today's world is numeric. This *cliché* also needs to be taken into account when considering DM: stakeholders are facing an increasing number of data sources, including non-dedicated ones. Practices, tools and usages regarding data management in crisis contexts are not appropriate to this situation anymore and must be adapted. Disaster managers must now deal with the following issues:

- In DM context, in addition to the (very classical) wide range of data types (sensors measures, photo, report, social network message), and in contrary to a lot of other domains, data sources are often massively unknown while starting the job.
- Credibility and trust of (potentially unknown) data sources must be evaluated [5, 6].

In [7] the authors particularly describes how big-data can be considered as a new challenge in crisis management, but not only in a "classical" way (mainly considering the increasing amount of data and dataflow): the way this large amount of data could be treated to become intelligible to exploit it relevantly (automatically or not) is at the heart of this new challenge. Finally, the main characteristic of DM from a **technological perspective** is that *performing Big-Data management implies to deal with unknown and heterogeneous data sources, potentially non-dedicated ones*. In DM, discovery of data sources and understanding of data is probably as important as exploiting data to support decision and action.

2.3 Conclusion of DM Characterization

The specificities of Big-Data management in DM can finally be summarized according to the following sentence: *The question is mainly about managing unknown data sources (rather than large amount of data coming from well-known data sources) to support solely and mainly coordination issues (rather than a multi-objectives exploitation)*. It is important to understand that both these specificities are really different from classical Big-Data problems:

- Data sources are generally well known: For instance, the industrial domain (from supply-chain to production) is based on a lot of data (such as the amount of stock, the location of a deliverer, the customer's invoice, etc.) that can be easily monitored. The only unexpected data sources could be some borderline examples, such as those related to weather forecast or traffic topics.

Data exploitation is generally covering a wide range of elementary purposes: For instance, in public transportation domain, Big-Data management may be dedicated first to ensure transportation continuity through management of inter-mode solutions (offering reactively palliative solutions in case of failure of one mode), second to manage customer relationship (CRM system), third to improve the network efficiency, etc.

3 A Specific Big-Data Framework for Disaster Management

Classical Big-Data problems can be summarized (from a very simple and schematic perspective) according to two main goals: it is mainly about (i) increasing the data storage capacity (to be able to collect and store as much data as possible, including historical consideration) and (ii) improving pattern recognition feature (to be able to parse the obtained gigantic data fields and find quickly and correctly specific patterns). Most technological progresses made these years in Big-Data domain are dedicated to one or both of these expectations (more storage or more parsing). Actually, this approach is perfectly adapted to most of the domains in which Big-Data is one perspective of improvement because: (i) data sources are well known and (ii) exploitation of data field through pattern recognition can serve a lot of simple objectives. However, as presented in the first section, this is exactly what DM is not.

In [7] the authors particularly describes how big-data can be considered as a new challenge in DM, but not in a "classical" way (mainly considering the increasing amount of data and dataflows): the way this large amount of data could be treated to become intelligible to exploit it relevantly (automatically or not) is at the heart of this new challenge. This article considers that Big-Data for DM should perform the following specific features.

3.1 Gathering: From Data Sources to Data Storage

Considering that data sources on disaster site might be unknown, randomly distributed and potentially doubtful in terms of veracity, the first layer of the Big-Data framework is in charge of identifying the data environment to be considered. This objective is a very innovative one and really arduous on a technological point of view; actually, Big-Data approaches are usually based on predefined data background with selected data sources.

The expectation is to perform *discovery* (of unknown data sources), *understanding* (of the emitted data), *trust and veracity evaluation* (of the understood data) and *subscription* (to discovered, understood and accepted data sources) mechanisms. It is absolutely necessary, in the connected world of DM, to make the gathering layer open, *i.e.* to allow Big-Data for DM to deal with a dynamical data environment involving incoming and outgoing unknown and non-dedicated data sources.

3.2 Interpretation: From Data to Information

The main stake for Big-Data in DM is probably the ability to interpret gathered data in order to automatically build situational models (such situational model might be considered as a common operational picture). This step is really the corner stone of Big-Data for DM. Actually, while classical Big-Data aims at exploring gigantic fields of data to detect patterns and thus at providing some direct results, DM Big-Data must insert an abstraction level between raw data and exploitation results. This intermediary level is in charge of combining and transforming collected data into intelligible concepts. This level is mandatory in the case of DM because data sources and data types may be unknown and consequently not directly exploitable.

The theory defended in this article states that this information level, to perform interpretation requires a situational metamodel (presenting concepts and relations inherent in DM domain). Such a metamodel (see the one described in [3]) provides the theoretical background to create a situation model by instantiating concepts and relations with gathered data.

3.3 Exploitation: From Information to Knowledge

Finally, the last level for Big-Data for DM is about the ability to exploit fruitfully the generated and formalized information, to support the coordination of responders. This level concerns mainly exploitation features to perform *decisions* and *actions*. Actually, there are a lot of DM tools covering coordination functionalities (such as first-responders alert, collaborative tasking, monitoring of coordinated actions, or orchestration of collaborative workflows), which would strongly benefit from such information base: these tools require real inputs to perform their service; consequently, providing these tools with consolidated information basis would remove this constraint and furthermore would ensure a higher quality of service considering that the collected and interpreted data would certainly supply robust and trustable situation models.

3.4 Big Picture of the Presented Big-Data Framework for Disaster Management

On the following figure, the three levels presented above are conceptually presented.

The most noticeable elements of Fig. 1 are the following:

- The abstraction path from data to information to knowledge inherent in the Big-Data for DM.
- Data level and Knowledge level are supposed to be open (allowing the use of emerging data sources and the exploitation of new DM tools).
- The central role of the Metamodel to perform data interpretation and information formalization.

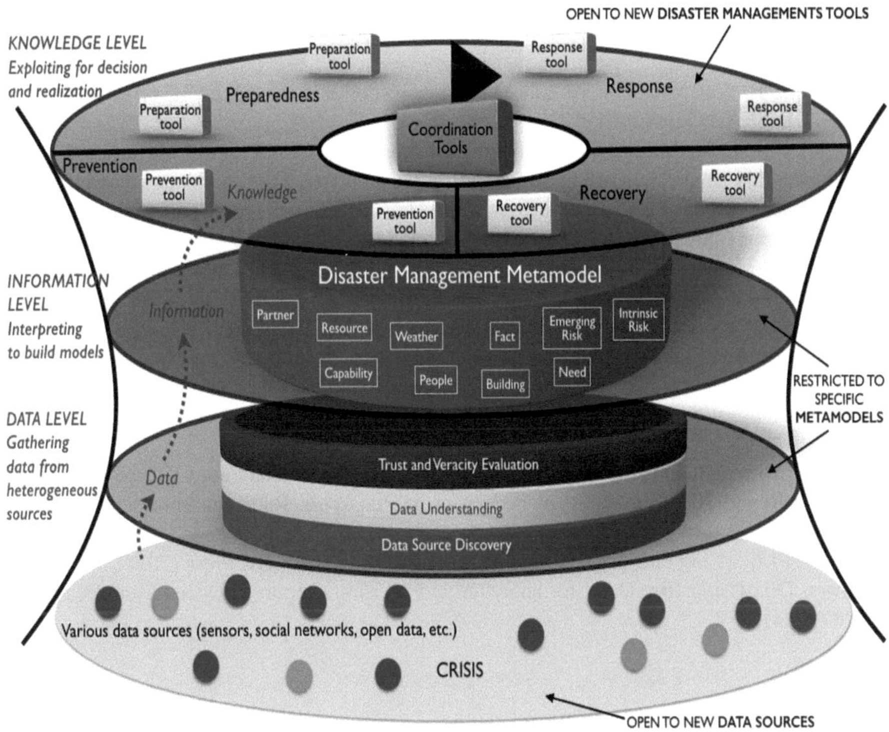

Fig. 1. Big picture of the big-data for DM framework.

4 Conclusion

This article aimed at presenting an original vision of Big-Data specifically dedicated to Disaster Management. Actually, this vision may be relevant for various domains as far as they match with criteria identified in first section. Big-Data is definitely a way to provide intelligence to data gathering. The main goal of big data as presented in [8, 9] is to facilitate the decision-making, through a swift analysis of large amount of data, of different types, from a variety of sources, to produce a stream of actionable knowledge. Consequently, it is dedicated to provide a computed system with the ability to exploit efficiently and relevantly large amount of data. However, the important aspect of the vision presented in this article is that it opposes an horizontal vision of this intelligence (mainly dedicated to increase on the one hand data storage and indexation capacities, and on the other hand, parsing and digging capacities) to a vertical vision of this intelligence (dedicated to stack up abstraction levels to improve interpretation capacity). The position of this article is to respect both these visions, but to claim that Disaster Management is a very specific domain, with a lot of particular characteristics (such as the unknown aspect of the impacted perimeter or the very wide potential origin of data from sensors to social networks). Consequently, one purpose of this article was to show that vertical intelligence in Big-Data is potentially better adapted to Disaster Management.

References

1. Tomasini, R., Van Wassenhove, L.N.: Logistics response in the 2002 food crisis in Southern Africa. INSEAD Case (2004)
2. Devlin, E.S.: Crisis Management Planning and Execution. CRC Press, Boca Raton (2006)
3. Benaben, F., Lauras, M., Truptil, S., Salatge, N.: A metamodel for knowledge management in crisis management. In: Proceedings of 49th Hawaii International Conference on System Sciences, pp. 126–135 (2016)
4. Camarinha-Matos, L., Afsarmanesh, H.: Collaborative networks: a new scientific discipline. J. Intell. Manuf. **16**(4), 439–452 (2005). Springer
5. Truong, B., Caragea, C., Squicciarini, A., Tapia, A.H.: Identifying valuable information from twitter during natural disasters. Proc. Am. Soc. Inf. Sci. Technol. **51**(1), 1–4 (2014)
6. Tapia, A.H., Moore, K.: Good enough is good enough: overcoming disaster response organizations' slow social media data adoption. Comput. Support. Coop. Work **23**(4), 483–512 (2014)
7. Meier, P.: Strengthening humanitarian information: the role of technology, Chapter 3 of World Disaster Report 2013, International Federation of Red Cross, Red Crescent Societies (ICRC) (2013)
8. Kalyvas, J.R.: A big data primer for executives. In: Big Data. CRC Press (2015)
9. Power, D.J.: Using 'Big Data' for analytics and decision support. J. Decis. Syst. **23**(2), 222–228 (2014)

Co-development and Co-working - Creating Supply and Production Networks

Towards a Gamified Approach for Enhancing VBE Preparedness for Establishing Virtual Collaborations

Noor Jehan Rajper[1], Stephan Reiff-Marganiec[2(✉)], and Qurat-Ul-Ain Nizamani[1]

[1] Institute of Mathematics and Computer Science, University of Sindh, Jamshoro, Pakistan
{nr76, qn}@usindh.edu.pk

[2] Department of Computer Science, University of Leiceter, Leicester, UK
srm13@le.ac.uk

Abstract. Formation of collaborative settings (virtual organizations, collaborative network organizations, etcetera) is hindered by the lack of trust between unfamiliar but potential partners. Gamification is the application of game design principles to non- game environments. We claim that incorporating the concepts of gamification into Virtual Organisation Breeding Environments (VBEs) leads to building trust between VBE members, as well as motivating them to be proactive members of the VBEs that contribute towards the flourishing of VBEs. This paper explores a novel gamified approach, supported by a suitable methodology, to address the relatively neglected concept of 'preparedness' of VBEs.

Keywords: Gamification · Virtual organizations · VO breeding environment · Motivation · Preparedness

1 Introduction

The organizations around the world are increasingly interested in opportunity-driven, timely and temporary collaborations and cooperation with other organizations [8]. Such collaboration, not only increase their profit but increase their survivability in today's turbulent and constantly changing business markets as well [2–4, 17]. However, different factors (such as lack of trust and the non-existence of basic infrastructure that allow for smooth transaction) play a critical role in the timely formation of such collaborations. To support this emerging tendency, long term alliances of autonomous and geographically dispersed organizations called Virtual organization Breeding Environments (VBEs) are being established among organizations, to serve as the base environments for creation of temporary and opportunity-driven collaborations [13]. Their main aim is to increase the preparedness of different organizations towards potential temporary collaborations (generally called Virtual Organizations (VOs)) [1, 11, 15]. However, in order to increase preparedness of VBEs the definition of the term must be unambiguously and formally

H. Afsarmanesh et al. (Eds.): PRO-VE 2016, IFIP AICT 480, pp. 165–177, 2016.
DOI: 10.1007/978-3-319-45390-3_15

defined first. At the moment, these terms mostly remain neglected and vaguely defined as per the situation.

Our hypothesis is that a deeper understanding of preparedness helps in designing applications that better capture the aspects associated with preparedness. Gamification is about capturing intrinsic innate human desires in a playful and fun way and motivating users to achieve certain objectives. We believe that it can provide great value to enhancing preparedness levels in VBEs. The main research questions that this paper addresses are:

- What does preparedness imply during different stages of VBE life-cycle?
- Who are the main players (actors) in VBEs with respect to preparedness?
- What are the behavioural characteristics of these actors in regard to their responsibilities?

The novel contributions of this paper are (a) answers to these research questions through an exploration of the feasibility of applying gamification concepts to enhance preparedness of VBEs, (b) design practices (guidelines) which enhance the preparedness depending on the stage of the VBE life-cycle and the actors involved and (c) a language to express objectives and the rules that contribute to their completion.

2 Background

VOs can be seen as concrete instances or configurations of partners that address a specific goal; VOs are generally seen as being created out of VBEs – which are essentially a pool of possible partners. Our aim in this work is to increase the preparedness of VBEs by tapping into the underlying behaviour shown by VBE members. We are proposing to use gamification as the solution for this matter. We now introduce the concepts of preparedness and gamification.

The success of a VBE depends on its own as well as its members' preparedness. VBE preparedness is generally defined as the agreement between members on common interests and general working principles. Interoperability between different infrastructures and processes of member organizations, provision of a basic VBE bag-of-assets to its members, and development of trust are some of the main facets [12]. The preparedness and readiness evaluation approaches suggested in the literature offer insights into evaluating VBE members suitability for a VBE and readiness to join a VO once accepted as a member.

While, preparedness of VBE members has been researched to an extent, so far focus has remained on the VBEs members only [15, 16]. However, a great role in enhancing the preparedness is played by those who actually create and manage the VBE as well.

We divide VBE preparedness into two phases (with respect to the VBE life-cycle): *Pre-joining* and *Post-joining* preparedness. Pre-joining preparedness refers to preparedness of potential VBE member organizations (with intention to gain business perks by joining in) that have shown their willingness to join a VBE. Post-joining preparedness applies to existing members of VBE whether business oriented members or those who are running the VBE. Our work utilizes the existing work on pre-joining preparedness [15, 16] but focuses on exploring the post-joining preparedness.

Gamification is fast emerging as a new trend to increase user engagement, motivation and participation in any system under consideration using game tactics to non-game environments [6, 7, 18]. Gamification is used for many different purposes such as behavioural adaptation of its users, skill development, or innovation (boosting positive competition between employees, resulting in coming up with new and innovative ideas proactively from employees). Game-like elements on top of business logic aim to transform mundane, repetitive and ordinary jobs to include fun and excitement for users. Rather than changing serious application to games a very subtly addition of game-oriented elements increases the acceptability and capture user's interest in using the application, leading to benefits for the organization such as increased job performance, employee satisfaction, or greater revenue generation.

Gamification mainly comprises of three parts, game mechanics, game dynamics and game rules. To implement gamification, we need to first identify the objectives that we want to achieve using gamification. The next step is to choose gamification mechanics and dynamics. Game mechanics represent the (visual) elements that we earn as we play (perform required tasks) such as badges, points, leaderboards, virtual or real goods. Game dynamics represent the behavioural aspect that is targeted by the game rule for motivating the player to act in a certain way. When the mechanics and dynamics have been decided, game rules are devised to proceed in a game like way (such as when player X achieve certain points, assign it a badge).

Users can show two types of behaviour: *altruistic* or *self-centered*. Altruistic behaviour captures all forms of selfless human attributes such as philanthropy, community association, or empathy. It is generally motivated by a will to achieve something for the sake of it rather than for gain. Selfish (self-centered) behaviour includes instincts to prosper, or surpassing everybody else. The majority of game mechanics and dynamics fall into this category: usually represented through rewards for actions and symbols to show achievements (e.g. badges). Gartner suggested that by 2014 70 % of the global 2000 organizations would have at least one gamified application[1]. They further predicted that out of those 80 % would have failed in the coming year or so due to lack of proper thought given in identifying the objectives and the mechanics selected to achieve them[2]. This failure occurs as gamification mechanics and the game rules are explicitly specified by the gamification providing platforms and specification languages, but the objectives are not explicitly specified. This leads to a plethora of game rules but no easy way to tell what objectives they accomplish or what game mechanics and dynamics are used by those rules. Without this understanding observations on actions cannot easily be traced back to the right rules. Besides explicitly specifying the objectives, we should be able to identify what behavioural attributes are targeted by the game rules. Associating objective with the right behaviour will allow for devised plans to achieve the goal to be more directed and hence more likely to succeed.

[1] Available at http://www.gartner.com/newsroom/id/1844115 (2011, November 9).

[2] Available at http://www.gartner.com/newsroom/id/2251015 (2012, November 27).

3 Methodology and Gamified VBE Preparedness Model

This paper explores the feasibility of providing a gamified solution for enhancing the preparedness of a VBE using gamification. We proposed the following general methodology to gamify any domain:

Step 1. Identify the main actors of the domain and the associated behavioural attributes with respect to a specific property being investigated.
Step 2. Once the domain actors have been identified identify different gamification approaches with similar characteristics as shown by actors identified in step 1.
Step 3. Map domain actors with gamification approaches with similar characteristics.

These mappings then act as a gamified domain model with respect to certain property for a particular domain. These mappings can be used as guideline while selecting game dynamics and mechanics for the game rules in the domain to enhance the concerned property. In our case the domain is a VBE and the property being explored is "preparedness". We will now consider the steps of the methodology in this context.

Step 1: Pre-joining preparedness applies to ordinary VBE members or simply members of a VBE that have joined a VBE to gain some benefit in their respective businesses (we call these businessMembers) and post-joining preparedness applies to business members as well as member managing the VBE (the latter will be called managementMembers). managementMembers are members that have created the VBE and taken up the responsibility of day to day management and smooth running of the VBE.

Considering post-joining preparedness in more detail we can distinguish two flavours: (a) *Structural* preparedness and (b) *Functional* preparedness. Structural preparedness encompasses smooth working and management of the VBE itself such as competency management, membership management, VBE bag-of-asset management, etc. It is not of direct interest to business members themselves that take the underlying infrastructure for-granted and join the VBE for sole purpose of gaining business opportunities. It could be said that management members are altruistic in the management tasks. Functional preparedness on the other hand is of direct interest to business members as it is related to currently available and emerging businesses opportunities. Business members have joined the VBE to gain access to more business opportunities or to overcome missing resources and skills. Clearly business members are selfish.

Step 2: Having identified two kinds of actors and their predominant behaviour (selfish business members and altruistic management members), we need to explore gamification approaches. The identified guidelines will help VBE policy developers to derive appropriate game rules (including mechanics and dynamics)

Gamification is designed to target humans' intrinsic behaviour in order to motivate them to strive, engage with others, or any other purposes. As such, at first it might not seem natural to apply the gamification concepts to the management of alliances of different entities most of which are organizations rather than individual users. However, members in VBEs can be different entities ranging from individual users to organizations and since even the interactions between the VBE and a particular organization can be traced down to an individual user representing the organization, the gamification concepts can readily be applied to organizations as well. Earlier we identified that both altruistic and self-centered gamification behaviours exist. These map very naturally onto the identified behaviour of our actors. Altruistic behaviour can be rewarded through for example badges (which have no material value, but reflect a reward for achievement).

We also identified that game rules and objectives are not usually defined in ways that link them explicitly and obviously together. However, we are able to be explicit the specification and development of gamification objectives, the rules that satisfy or accomplish those objectives and the mechanics and dynamics of those game rules. Furthermore, we are able to rewire game rules, game mechanics and dynamics, as well as the objectives they strive to achieve during application execution.

Step 3: We now map between the concepts from step 1 and step 2. The insights gained from exploring preparedness and gamification result in the proposed gamified VBE preparedness model. This model will act as guiding principle when designing rules for specific desired VBE behaviours.

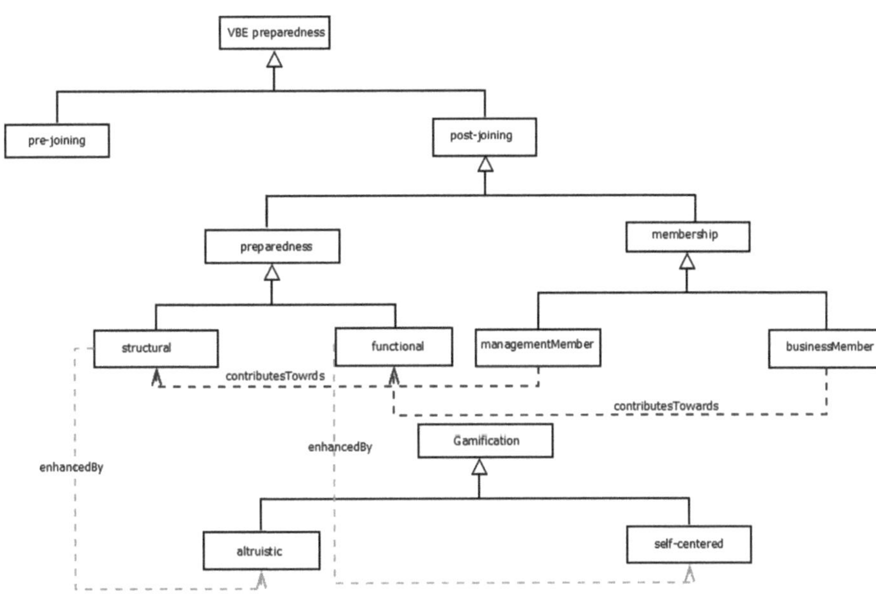

Fig. 1. Gamified VBE preparedness model

Figure 1 is a representation of the gamified VBE preparedness model. Recall that structural preparedness is for the strengthening the VBE itself and mainly the responsibility of management members which act altruistically. Therefore, the VBE should incorporate mechanics that raise altruistic levels for tackling the structural preparedness. The VBE will also incorporate self-centered approached to increase the functional preparedness of its business members.

4 GPSL: Gamified Policy Specification Language

The proposed gamified VBE preparedness model serves as a guiding principle while gamifying the VBE domain. However, we need a mechanism to specify, implement and execute the gamification concepts. The event-driven policy paradigm provides the most natural solution: we can easily add a gamification layer on top of the business logic of the domain (VBE). The policy paradigm is quite flexible and adaptable allowing for easy adaptation and change of the game rules at any time. Since, no policy language have built-in construct with concepts and elements of gamification, we have extended APPEL [14] policy language for gamification. APPEL follows the Event-Condition-Action (ECA) paradigm for policy specification. The basic building block of APPEL is a policy rule which consists of optional trigger(s), optional condition(s) and an action. A typical APPEL policy is as follows:

```
Policy policy-name When [trigger(s)]
If [condition(s)] Do action(s)
```

GPSL (Gamified Policy Specification Language) extends APPEL for the VBE domain through the inclusion of a VBEgoal construct. This construct allows for abstract specification of a VBE objective that is going to be achieved through gamification policies.

It has two attributes: a boolean-valued enabled attribute specifies if the VBE objective is currently enabled or disabled. If disabled, all the associated publishedBy and sinkedBy policies (explained below) are disabled as well, overwriting their localized enabled attribute. The effects attribute specifies what aspects of the VBE are going to be affected by the objective. The VBEgoal description further consists of one or more curly-bracketed blocks. Each block specifies a list of publishedBy and sinkedBy (policy references), preparedness, enabled and appliesTo attributes. The preparedness attribute specifies what preparedness category the VBE objective falls in, the enabled attribute specifies if the policies referenced by the block are currently enabled or disabled, and the appliesTo attribute describes what VBE actor type is going to be affected by the policies of the block. A typical VBEgoal looks as follow:

```
VBEgoal objective-id              enabled: boolean
effects : VBEaspectEffected    { appliesTo: VBE-actors
enabled: Boolean
 preparedness: preparednessType
publishedBy: policy1,policy2,..policyn
sinkedBy:  policy1,policy2,..policyn }
```

The only other construct of GPSL is the Policy construct. This construct is based on the APPEL policy rule, with one additional attribute: the supportsGoal attribute which links the policy to the VBEgoal it is contributing to.

The policies implement game rules. Each policy is either a publishing policy or sinking policy. A publishing policy is one that sets a gamified tasks for the player to accomplish, and entices them with the promise of a perk. A sinking policy is one that is triggered when the gamified task in the associated publishing policy is accomplished by the player. Whether a policy is publishing or sinking can be identified through publishedBy and sinkedBy attributes of VBEgoal description and the actions they execute.

Table 1 lists some of the actions defined by GPSL, each capturing a specific game mechanic and Table 2 lists actions for sinking policies giving a specified reward to the user. At this point, we are aware this list is incomplete and this aspect is being studied further.

Table 1. Publishing policy actions to gamify tasks

Action	Description
toEarnPoint (points, task)	Player is invited to earn the points, if he fulfills the task
toEarnBadge (badge-id, task)	Player is invited to earn the badge, if he fulfills the task
toReach (level-id, task)	Player is informed that in his current state, he gets eligible to reach mentioned level, if he fulfills the task
toUnlockChallenge (challenge-id, task)	Player is informed that the mentioned challenge can be unlocked for him to play if he fulfills the task
toSupportVBE (VBEhelpdBedge-id, task)	The player is notified that by doing the task he is contributing for the betterment of VBE and will be appreciated by getting VBEhelpdBedge-id
toAdvanceLeaderBoard (leaderboardGroup-id, task)	The player is enticed to do the task by improving his current position in the mentioned leaderboard group

Having VBE objectives explicitly specified and linking the policies that publish as well as sink the tasks associated with the objective allows to, have a structure gamified application. Instead of having a jumbled up mess of different policies, they are divided into separate groups with clear description of the purpose they serve. This allows the analysis of those policies while the application is in operation, and if the required aims are not achieved, the problematic policies can be readily identified and rectified.

The other benefit of this model is that having identified the nature of VBEgoal through its preparedness attribute, and the VBE actor type it applies to, not only helps policy developers in choosing appropriate game mechanics and dynamics, but it also contributes towards the development of policies editors that are able to suggest appropriate mechanics and dynamics to the policy developer, and in the development of automated analysis tools to assist in analysis if the chosen mechanics and dynamic contradict with the objective sought by the policies.

The concept of gamification is to make players act in a certain way without making them realize that they are actually working for some objective. The VBEgoal therefore is not visible to the player (VBE member in this case). They are only notified when a certain policy (published or sinked) applies to them and the motivation for them to act

Table 2. Sinking policy actions to gamify tasks

Action	Description
pointsEarned (points, member-id/group-id)	Mentioned points are given to the player or group of players. The reasons for this rewards are not specified here as sinking policies are only triggered if their associated publishing policy is satisfied
badgeEarned (badge-id, member-id/group-id)	Player or group of players earn a badge for fulfilling some criteria such as passing a threshold of points specified in the associated publishing policy
levelReached (level-id, member-id/group-id)	Player (or group) advances to next level for satisfying the task demanded by the associated publishing policy
challengeUnlocked (challenge-id, member/group-id)	The challenge gets unlocked, but the player (or group of them) has to overcome it yet
challengeAccomplished (challenge-id, member/group-id)	The unlocked challenge has been overcome by the player or group of them
VBESupported (hBadge-id, member-id/group-id)	Player (or group) gets some of helping VBE badge, for doing the mentioned task
advancedLeaderBoard (leaderboardGroup-id, member/group-id)	The player (or group) is advanced from its current position to the next position

according to the policy is the promised reward or consequence mentioned in the policy. The player is blissfully kept unaware of the burden of preparedness enhancement or VBE management or its flourishing.

5 Case Study

The case study revolves around a VBE in the tourism sector with members with a wide diversity of competencies such as accommodation providers, travel agents, tour guides, and many others offering services such as health insurance, entertainment or telecommunications. The VBE offers its services worldwide through different VOs for different cities.

The management members are responsible for the smooth day-to-day running of VBE. As the managers of VBE they focus on facilitating the creation of new business opportunities. Though they are by default business members as well in this case study we only focus on their role as VBE management providers. Therefore, all the gamification efforts must be focused at enhancing the VBEs structural preparedness through altruistic approaches according to the model (though there can be exceptions a well).

Business members on the other hand have joined the VBE to get more business, expand their reach, overcome their shortcomings, complements their skills and resources and tap into the VBE assets. Hence, the gamified VBE preparedness described these members as self-centered and their gamification policies incorporate self-centered dynamics and enhancement of functional preparedness (again there can be

Table 3. VBE specific list of some of GPSL triggers, conditions and actions

Trigger	Description
VOterminates (vo-id, success)	Triggered when a VO successfully terminates itself
VOstatus (vo-id, created)	Triggered when a VO has just created
CompMembersRecommended (managementMember-id, [businessMember1-id,competency-id], [businessMember2-id, competency-id]))	Is triggered when management member introduces two business members to each other that have complementary competencies, hence possibility for joint venture in future
VOformedWithUnaquintedMembers (vo-id, unAquinted- MemberLst)	Triggered when the recently formed VO-id has members that have no history of partnership with each other(represented by unAquintedMemberLst)
VOplannigRate (VOplanner-id, threshord.below)	Triggered when a management member's (acting as VO planner) performance falls below the threshold in terms of number of new VO planned by him
Condition	**Description**
memberVO (VO-id, member-id)	Returns true if member-id is (was, if has terminated) member of the VO represented by VO-id.
notAquainted (member-id, VO-id. members)	Returns true if members the VO-id are not acquainted to a member-id
friendOf (memberA, memberB)	Returns true if memberA is a friend of memberB
introducedBy (VO-id.memberLst, member-id)	Returns true if the member(s) (represented by VO- id.memberLst) were befriended by member-id
competencyComplements ([businessMember1-id, competency-id], [businessMember2-id, competency-id]))	Returns true when the competencies of two business members complement each other
Action	**Description**
introduceFriend (VO-id.members, friend-id)	This action is an invitation to the business member to which the policy applies, to introduce his friend (friend-id) to his partners of recently terminated VO
recommendCompMembers()	It is an invitation to the management member to which the policy applies, to introduce business members to each other if their competencies complements

exceptions as well). Let us consider an example Scenario: Creating a sense of community and bond between members. The aim is to introduce benefits for members to introduce their trusted friends to other members to allow future VOs to be able to tap into more partners. Given below is the excerpt describing the objective and related publishing and sinking policies.

```
VBEgoal communityBuilding
enabled: true                     effects :
VBEMembership,
{appliesTo: businessMember        enabled: true
preparedness: structural
publishedBy: introduceFriendToVOpartner
sinkedBy: VOformedWithUnaquintedMembers }
{appliesTo: managementMember       enabled: false
preparedness: Structural
publishedBy: recommendComplementatingMember, ...
sinkedBy: VOformedWithRecommendedMembers}
Policy   introduceFriendToVOpartner
supportsGoal communityBuilding, TrustDevelopment
When VOterminates (VO-id, success)
If memberVO (VO-id, member-id)
and friendOf(member-id, friend-id)and
notAquinted(friend-id, VO-id.members)
Do toEarnPoints(points, introduceFriend(VO-id.members,
friend-id))
```

The introduceFriendToVOpartner is a publishing policy that is triggered when a VO successfully terminates. This policy invites all the members of the successfully terminated VO to introduce their friends to the members of the recently terminated VO with the promise of gaining certain points when this acquaintance is realized in the form of new VO creation with at least one of the members from terminated VO and the newly acquainted friend.

```
Policy VOformedWithUnaquintedMembers
When VOformedWithUnaquintedMemebrs(vo-id,
unAquintedMemberLst)
If introducedBy(VO-id.unAquintedMemberLst,
pastPartnerOf(VO-id.unAquintedMemberLst)
Do pointsEarned(points,
  pastPartnerOf(VOid.unAquintedMemberLst))
```

The policy, VOformedWithUnaquintedMemebrs is a sinking policy that is triggered when a new VO is formed that has members that are doing business together for the first time. Once the policy is triggered, its associated condition is checked which in this case checks if the unacquainted members were introduced (befriended) to each other by their common friend (i.e. VO-pastPartnerOf(id.unAquintedMemberLst)). If that happens to be the case, the common friend is rewarded (pointsEarned() action).

```
Policy recommendComplementatingMember
supportsGoal communityBuilding, TrustDevelopment
When VOplannigRate (VOplanner-id, threshord.below)
Do toSupportVBE (VBEhelpdBedge-id,
recommendCompMembers()
Policy VOformedWithRecommendedMembers
supportsGoal communityBuilding, TrustDevelopment
When CompMembersRecommended (managementMember-id,
[businessMember1-id, competency-id], [businessMember2-
id, competency-id]))
    If competencyComplements([businessMember1-id, com-
petency-id], [businessMember2-id, competency-id]) )
   Do VBESupported (businessExpansionBedge,
managementMember-id)
```

Table 3 shows some of the VBE specific triggers and actions as used in the scenario. As can be seen from the case study, relatively complex constructs in terms of describing preparedness for VBEs – namely descriptions of how behaviour can be introduced through objectives that increase preparedness (here through having better links between possible partners as well as a wider field of available partners) can be readily captured in a goal description. More importantly, that goal description is linked to clear operational rules that describe how the goal is achieved.

6 Related Work

VBE preparedness has been rightfully acknowledged as one of the core benefits of VBEs [13, 15, 16]. In [15, 16], preparedness of potential VBE members has been discussed in depth. However, it mostly applies to evaluating business members (in our context) inclusion into a VBE. We attempt to further our current understanding of preparedness, in particular what it implies, once the business member has been added to a VBE as well as preparedness to members managing the VBE and the role of preparedness in the operational phase of a VBE.

Gamification is has been applied in different domains recently [5, 9, 19], but most of the applications target individual users (players) using the application. In this paper we have shown that gamification concepts can be trivially applied to situations where target players are actually organizations and not just an individual. Other aspects that distinguish our work from the current gamification implementation approaches is that current solutions do not explicitly specify the objective that is to be achieved through different game rules [10]. This has serious consequence when the size of the application grows, as it becomes increasingly difficult to identify what game rules are trying to achieve and which game rules collective achieve an objective. Our small policy based modelling language revolves around specifying game rules (policies) for an explicitly specified objective.

7 Conclusion and Future Work

In this paper we put forward a gamified model for enhancing the preparedness of VBEs. This model is obtained by following a methodology proposed in the paper: First of all we identify different actors of a VBE with respect to behaviour that emerges out of the type of responsibilities assigned to them. Then, gamification approaches are explored that relate to the behaviour of the different actors identified previously. This allows us to associate VBE roles to gamification approaches with similar behavioural characteristics. To gamify the VBE application we defined GPSL, a policy language capturing specific game mechanics. The GPSLs unique approach to explicitly specifying VBE objectives to be gamified and linking them with respective publishing and sinking policies have two immediate benefits: (1) the VBE objective is explicitly specified thus the purpose of the policies is immediately visible and (2) policies can be grouped with respect to the objectives they are contributing to.

In future, we will further validate our gamified VBE preparedness model against different VBEs to verify its applicability beyond the current case study. Other direction we are intending to investigate further are, applying the proposed methodology to develop gamified models for other domains. We are also investigating development of tools that suggest game dynamics for an objective at hand while designing policies that contribute towards achieving it.

References

1. Afsarmanesh, H., Camarinha-Matos, L.M., Msanjila, S.S.: On management of 2nd generation virtual organizations breeding environments. Ann. Rev. Control **2**(33), 209–219 (2009)
2. Camarinha-Matos, L.M., Afsarmanesh, H.: Creation of virtual organizations in a breeding environment. In: Proceedings of INCOM 6 (2006) 12th IFAC Symposium on Information Control Problems Manufacturing, Saint-Etienne, France, 17–19 May 2006
3. Camarinha-Matos, L.M., Afsarmanesh, H.: A framework for virtual organization creation in a breeding environment. Ann. Rev. Control **1**(31), 119–135 (2007)
4. Camarinha-Matos, L.M., Afsarmanesh, H., Ollus, M.: Ecolead: a holistic approach to creation and management of dynamic virtual organizations. In: Camarinha-Matos, L.M., Afsarmanesh, H., Ortiz, A. (eds.) Collaborative Networks and Their Breeding Environments, pp. 3–16. Springer, New York (2005)
5. Crowley, D.N., et al: Gamification of citizen sensing through mobile social reporting. In: IEEE International Games Innovation Conference (IGIC) 2012. IEEE (2012)
6. Deterding, S.: Gamification: designing for motivation. Interactions **4**(19), 14–17 (2012)
7. Deterding, S., et al: Gamification: using game-design elements in non-gaming contexts. In: CHI 2011 Extended Abstracts on Human Factors in Computing Systems. ACM (2011)

8. Foster, I., Kesselman, C., Tuecke, S.: The anatomy of the grid: enabling scalable virtual organizations. Int. J. High Perform. Comput. Appl. **3**(15), 200–222 (2001)
9. Hamari, J.: Transforming homo economicus into homo ludens: a field experiment on gamification in a utilitarian peer-to-peer trading service. Electron. Commer. Res. Appl. **4** (12), 236–245 (2013)
10. Herzig, P., et al: GaML-a modeling language for gamification. In: Proceedings of the 2013 IEEE/ACM 6th International Conference on Utility and Cloud Computing. IEEE Computer Society (2013)
11. Irigoyen, J., et al.: Virtual breeding environment: working and sharing principles. In: Konstantas, D., Bourrières, J.P., Léonard, M., Boudjlida, N. (eds.) Interoperability of Enterprise Software and Applications, pp. 99–110. Springer, London (2006)
12. Kasper-Fuehrera, E.C., Ashkanasy, N.M.: Communicating trustworthiness and building trust in interorganizational virtual organizations. J. Manag. **3**(27), 235–254 (2001)
13. Sánchez, N.G, Apolinar, D., Zubiaga, G., Atahualpa, J., González, I., Molina, A.: Virtual breeding environment: a first approach to understand working and sharing principles. In: Proceedings of First International Conference on Interoperability of Enterprise Software and Applications INTEROP–ESA (2005). http://interop-esa05.unige.ch/INTEROP/Proceedings/Interop-ESAScientific/PerPaper/I04-1%20456.pdf
14. Reiff-Marganiec, S., Turner, K.J., Blair, L.: Appel: the accent project policy environment/language. Technical report, TR-161, University of Stirling, December 2005
15. Romero, D., Galeano, N., Molina, A.: Mechanisms for assessing and enhancing organisations readiness for collaboration in collaborative networks. Int. J. Prod. Res. **17** (47), 4691–4710 (2009)
16. Rosas, J., Camarinha-Matos, L.M.: Modeling collaboration preparedness assessment. In: Camarinha-Matos, L.M., Afsarmanesh, H. (eds.) Collaborative Networks: Reference Modeling, pp. 227–252. Springer, New York (2008)
17. Sadigh, B.L., Unver, H.O., Nikghadam, S., Dogdu, E., Ozbayoglu, A.M., Kilic, S.E.: An ontology-based multi-agent virtual enterprise system (omave): part 1: domain modelling and rule management. Int. J. Comput. Integr. Manuf. 1–24 (2016)
18. Deterding, S., et al: From game design elements to gamefulness: defining gamification. In: Proceedings of the 15th International Academic MindTrek Conference: Envisioning Future Media Environments. ACM (2011)
19. Simes, J., Redondo, R.D., Vilas, A.F.: A social gamification framework for a K-6 learning platform. Comput. Hum. Behav. **2**(29), 345–353 (2013)

An Information Management Perspective of Supplier Selection Process in Manufacturing Networks

Dario Messina[1,2(✉)], Ana Cristina Barros[2], and António Lucas Soares[1,2]

[1] Faculty of Engineering, University of Porto, Porto, Portugal
up201406870@fe.up.pt
[2] INESC TEC, Porto, Portugal

Abstract. The past decades have been characterized by an increasing interest of companies in international trade and significant foreign direct investments, which led to a shift from localized manufacturing companies to global manufacturing networks. The main goal of this research is to analyze the management of information within the process of supplier selection in the context of manufacturing networks. The adoption of field study methodology allows understanding how the supplier selection process is carried out in Multinational Companies (MNCs) in different manufacturing sectors. In particular, this paper aims at identifying the information that mother company and their subsidiary companies share during the supplier selection process, and how they access to this information.

Keywords: Manufacturing networks · Supplier selection process · Information management

1 Introduction

Market globalization allows to broaden the potential base of customers worldwide but at the same time it leads to challenges in the management of suppliers and logistics. Moreover, the need for a quick reaction to the changes in demand, the decreasing production costs and the adoption of information and communication technologies (ICT) solutions leads to increasing level of uncertainty that organizations have to face [1–3].

Consequently, companies nowadays require increased efforts to manage their manufacturing plants from various locations and with different local requirements in order to maintain the service levels required by their customers [4, 5]. This paper aims at contributing with new research at the intersection of information management and manufacturing networks fields of research. Manufacturing networks (MNs) are networks of production plants that are wholly owned by a mother company, i.e. all factories are under full financial control of the Multinational Company (MNC) [6].

The main goal of this research is to analyze the management of information within the process of supplier selection in multinational companies. Particular attention is given to the information acquisition phase and usage of external information in the whole process. The activities considered in the supplier selection process in this study are namely: problem formulation, formulation of criteria, supplier qualification, and final

H. Afsarmanesh et al. (Eds.): PRO-VE 2016, IFIP AICT 480, pp. 178–188, 2016.
DOI: 10.1007/978-3-319-45390-3_16

selection [7]. For what concern the information management it is considered to being composed by the following processes: information acquisition, organization, distribution and usage [8].

Specifically, this paper addresses the following research question: How is information managed in the supplier selection process of MNCs?

2 Literature Review

This section introduces the topics of manufacturing networks and information sharing for supplier selection process. In particular, it analyses the context of global sourcing in which manufacturing networks operate and evidences the trends that global sourcing has experienced in the last decades. The main drivers for the adoption of global sourcing and the most common integration mechanisms are identified. The second part of the literature review describes the supplier selection process and the importance of information sharing within this process.

Global Sourcing. Manufacturing networks have their roots in the management of single manufacturing facility that has evolved to the management of several manufacturing facilities under the same overarching company [6]. The increasing interest on manufacturing networks and MNCs in general is linked with the internationalization of businesses. As environment becomes more complex and global, the management of an integrated international manufacturing network has become increasingly important for manufacturing managers [1]. Moreover, as manufacturing facilities of MNCs proliferate in the world, global sourcing has become a paramount function in these companies.

The adoption of global sourcing is not a new topic in management research field. It is possible to identify three waves that characterize the evolution of global sourcing in the last 30 years. Starting in the mid-'80s, firms showed an increasing interest in global sourcing related wit manufacturing activities [9]. Manufacturing firms start to look outside their local market in the search for more convenient sourcing opportunities abroad. Firms developed relationships with suppliers worldwide, mainly for raw materials and intermediate product, and consequently supply chains became more complex and global [10].

The '90s were characterized, substantially, by the growth of information technology (IT) departments that tried to respond to the complexity of organizational management. During these years firms considered IT departments as commodities, so outsourcing of this service to specialized providers was a common practice [11].

The third, and last, wave during the 2000s is characterized by an increasing adoption of the outsourcing strategy, not only related to IT as in the '90s, but in general to all the activities that do not represent the "core" of the firm, such as human resources, finance, and sales, among others [11]. Also, the massive diffusion of Internet and related services challenged firms in the way they see their business [4, 12] and enabled new functions and services such as, e-procurement, e-commerce, or more in general the e-business.

Nowadays, global sourcing is the integration of purchasing units across the globe searching for products, processes, technologies, and suppliers [3]; or more in general global sourcing is defined as the management of the activities that a firm has to undertake to serve both local and foreign markets, from the selection of supplier base to the identification of the different products that have to serve the different markets [10].

Drivers of Global Sourcing. The primary objective of global sourcing is to improve performance, by reducing production costs, increasing the quality of the final product, allowing the identification of resources and skills not available in the own country, and being more flexible to changes in local markets [11]. Global sourcing allows companies to exploit both its own competitive advantage and that of its suppliers, by identifying countries that show peculiarities useful for global competition [10].

As the global sourcing strategy evolved during the years, also the motivation underlying its adoption changed accordingly. At the beginning, the main driver was represented by cost effectiveness [13] so firms operating in developed countries started to outsource their production in countries with lower labor costs, such as China and India. Once this trend was consolidated, the presence of occidental firms in oriental countries increased substantially, which lead companies to consider additional aspects, as for example new market entry, availability of infrastructures, exchange rate fluctuation, cultural environment, and ease of working with foreign governments [1, 10].

What was initially considered as an opportunity generated also new barriers for firms adopting this sourcing strategy. One of the main problems is related with cultural distances between firms and hosted countries, this distance has repercussions in terms of quality due to cultural and idiomatic misunderstanding. Another problem is linked with exchange rate fluctuation that led in some cases to considerable profit's erosion. To face this situation many companies, firstly the Japanese, start to replicate their supply chains in United States and Europe. In this way, the problem related to the need of being closer to customer's markets in order to respond promptly to changes at local base is also overcome.

Trautmann et al. [3] synthesize the three main motives for implementing global sourcing, namely economies of scale, economies of information, and economies of process. Economies of scale, allow to bundle volume of production across sites in order to decrease their unit cost [14]. Level of uncertainty is high, due to the interdependencies among actors. Economies of information, relate to the sharing of all relevant information, across different sites and location, on suppliers, new technologies, markets, internal users, etc. [14, 15]. In this situation, the uncertainty is related to the limited availability of capable suppliers and the high heterogeneity of the offers. Finally, economies of process are related with the benefits derived from the establishment of best practices across different sites in different locations [14]. The uncertainty is relatively low, due to the standardization of processes across sites. The three kinds of economies are characterized by different organizational structures and integration mechanisms.

Organizational Structures and Integration Mechanisms. Organizational structure is defined as the network of relationships that exists among various positions and position holders to reach a common goal [16]. It includes rules and procedures and other planned attempts to regulate organizational behavior. Figure 1, shows a synthesis of the main organizational structures in which the circles with the "M" represent mother companies, while the other circles represent the network of subsidiaries regardless of their size, finally the lines identify the relationship between mother companies and their subsidiaries.

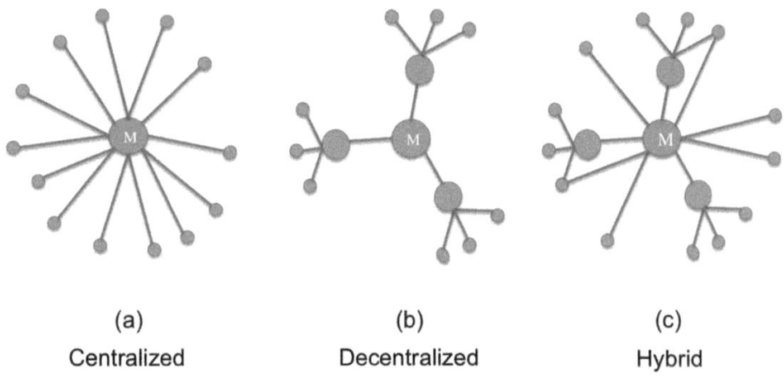

Fig. 1. Organizational structures

Major organizational forms include: centralized, decentralized, and hybrid structures. Centralized structure, Fig. 1(a), is generally adopted in manufacturing networks, in which different geographical units buy similar products [3]. In this form, the organization is divided into functions.

Decentralized structure, Fig. 1(b), is implemented when individual firms of the manufacturing network produce unique or significantly different products [3]. In this case the organization is divided into organizational units (or divisions). In their research Mourtzis et al. [17] study a European automotive manufacturer, simulating the production based on real data considering both structures, centralized and decentralized. The results showed that decentralized structure is more flexible compared with centralized, and also allows to reduce costs and lead-times [17].

Lastly, hybrid structure, Fig. 1(c), is adopted mostly in large multi-product organization, with the intention of managing in a most effective way the centralization–decentralization tradeoff [3]. At this purpose it maintain both functional and divisional partitions of the organization. A key challenge in this kind of structure is to distinguish between types of categories, to identify the ones with potential synergy and determining the most appropriate form of integration across geographical units [3, 14].

Once the organizational structure has been decided, firms belonging to the manufacturing networks need to identify the most suitable integration mechanism according to their goals. Integration mechanisms can be divided in two categories, namely vertical and horizontal integration. Each strategy has different implications for the internal relationships between parent companies and subsidiaries within the networks [2]. Figure 2 below presents the two integration mechanisms. As in Fig. 1, the circles with the "M" represent the mother companies and the other circles stand for the subsidiaries. In this case, the arrows are representative of the decision-making flows that have to be followed to take the final decision, in both mechanisms.

Vertical integration, Fig. 2(a), is a hierarchical authority structure in which the different levels of the organization have different responsibilities [18]. It is generally adopted to gain control over the entire supply chain. It also can be implemented upstream

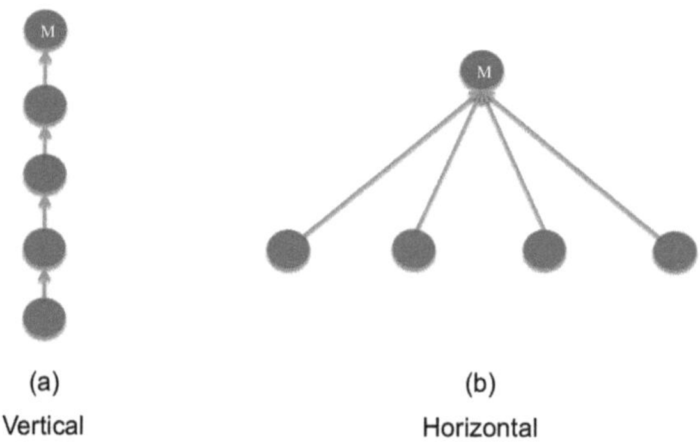

Fig. 2. Integration mechanisms

or downstream, depending if the mother company gains control over its supplier or over its distributors, respectively. Conversely, horizontal integration, Fig. 2(b), is a mechanism in which organizations belonging to the network are characterized by similar abilities cooperate to accomplish specialized tasks or to integrate each other [16]. It is adopted to reduce the competition in a market. The combination of the different organizational structures and integration mechanisms allow to characterize the possible decision-making patterns that a decision maker needs to follow to consistently support the supplier selection process.

Supplier Selection Process. The relevance of purchasing function increased considerably in the last decades. Some authors consider supplier selection as the most important process within purchasing and supply management, taking into account its direct impact on the quality, cost and lead-time of new products, and technologies needed to meet new market demands [7, 19].

Recent trends in purchasing and supply chain management have further emphasized the relevance of selecting the right supplier. The increased adoption of outsourcing strategy has led to more firms spending a significant portion of their total revenue on externally sourced goods and services [20]. The trend towards supply base reduction increases the need of a more accurate supplier selection process in order to include only suppliers that can contribute positively to business performance improvement.

Within this context, several authors have provided decision-making models that support the decision makers in the supplier selection process [7, 21]. These authors recognize the relevance of adding pre-phases to the supplier selection process, towards improving the quality of the final supplier selection. In particular, the supplier selection process has four phases: problem formulation, formulation of criteria, qualification, and final selection [7, 19, 22]. A synthetic explanation of the four phases proposed by De Boer et al. [7] is provided next.

Problem formulation is related with the needs leading the network to the selection of a new supplier or the replacement of existing ones. During the *formulation of criteria* phase, the decision maker identifies the criteria to be used in the selection of suppliers, e.g. capacity, availability, quality, cost, and lead-time. *Qualification phase* is related with the sorting of the supplier base into a smaller group of potential candidates. The last phase is the *final selection* of the supplier or suppliers that, among the reduced group generated in the previous phase, present the higher ranking.

In manufacturing networks, the supplier selection process is a joint effort among the various production sites. Therefore, information sharing between network partners for new supplier selection plays an important role within this process.

Information Sharing. If globalization allows to extend the selection of potential new suppliers worldwide, it also generates additional barriers to the integration and sharing of information [23]. These barriers may be characterized as legal, collaborative, organizational and informational. Legal constraints are related with the challenges due to the division of power among organizations and the adoption of information integration initiatives. Collaborative constraints refer to possible differences in terms of management that can obstacle cooperation and collaboration activities among partners. Organizational constraints are related with the need of business process standardization within the network. Finally, informational constraints are related with the different quality standards and possibility to share strategic information.

Information sharing is the action through which organizations share relevant, accurate, complete, and pertinent information with their partners, thus fostering connectivity with them and reducing information asymmetry [24–28]. The information shared can be grouped in two categories, namely internal and external information. Internal information, in this paper, is defined as any information present within the multinational, while external information is defined as any information that may be captured from outside the networks. Also, the distinction between internal and external is related with the means adopted to gather this information. External information may be gathered from institutional reports, stock market, public institutions, and consultancy reports, among others. Internal information is usually gathered from companies' IT systems, such as enterprise resource planning (ERP), electronic data interchange (EDI) or radio frequency identification (RFID) systems. The primary objective of information sharing is the improvement of network performance, since more visibility over others' operations lead to more informed and therefore better operational decision-making.

The decision-making models found in the literature [7, 19, 22, 23, 29], independently of the context of application and the approach (mathematical programming, rating/linear weighting, statistical etc.), take for granted that the information needed in the various steps of supplier selection process is available. This assumption is very strong because allows to overcome one of the major problem in real context, that is the need to have access to a conspicuous amount of valuable information to set the analysis. We consider information availability one of the focal point in all the information management process, independently from pursuing economies of scale, economies of information, or economies of process. For this reason, the analysis of how manufacturing networks have access to the information needed for supplier selection is an original aspect of this study.

3 Methodology

In this paper, the adoption of a decision making process contributes to understand how the information shared in manufacturing networks is organized. In particular, decision-making process is adopted with the purpose of supporting decision makers along the phases of supplier selection process.

Due to its exploratory nature, this work adopts field research [30]. In particular, case studies are developed in different manufacturing networks with subsidiary production plants installed in Portugal. Since the main purpose of this research is to understand how multinational companies in different sectors organize and share information among the network for supplier selection, the unit of analysis is considered at subsidiary level. The profiles of the interviewees are Purchasing or Procurement Managers. Data collection is carried out using semi-structured interviews at subsidiary companies, for a total of four interviews. Table 1 provides a summary of the empirical evidence gathered for the research.

Table 1. Companies data

Sector	Company code	Year of foundation	Company business	Number of employees of the plant	Number of production plants	Supply chain positioning	Position of the interviewee
Automotive	A	1991	Mechanical locking systems	338	17	1st Tier	Purchasing manager
Various	B	1998	Capacitors	160	16	1st Tier	Procurement managers
Automotive	C	1994	Elastomeric compon ents manufac turer	165	4	1st Tier/2nd Tier	Purchasing manager
Automotive	D	2014	Internal combust ion engine compon ents	720	56	1st Tier	Purchasing supervisor

The first aspect that stands out is related with the dimension of the firms belonging to the sample, in this case only Cases A and D can be classified as large business while Cases B and C are medium size business. The difference in terms of dimension is also associated with a broader coverage of different markets related with a massive presence of subsidiaries worldwide dispersed.

Only Case B operates in additional sectors aside the Automotive, such as Aerospace, Alternative Energy, and Telecommunication. All companies are positioning at Tier 1 level in the supply chain, except for Case C that is either Tier 1 or Tier 2 depending on their customers.

4 Findings

The research question leading this study is: How is information managed in the supplier selection process of MNCs? The results section is organized as follows: first, it presents how the supplier selection process is carried out in MNCs and which interactions exist between mother company and subsidiary, and second, it describes how information is managed in the supplier selection process in the context of a manufacturing network.

The results suggest a centralized organizational structure of the multinational companies with various levels of interdependency among partners along the supplier selection process. Companies A, B and C are vertically integrated while company D is horizontally integrated. Regarding this, companies A and B showed a higher level of dependency with headquarters during the whole process, while companies C and D are less dependent in terms of decision-making.

Taking into account the three steps of the supplier selection process namely, supplier identification, supplier evaluation, and supplier selection it was possible to identify that only companies C and D have complete autonomy, this level of autonomy allows them to be proactive in all the phases. On the contrary, companies A and B are involved in the first two steps, while mother companies are responsible for the final selection of new suppliers.

Another interesting aspect under analysis is the identification of the events triggering the need for a new or alternative supplier. Companies A and D showed a more strategic need for supplier selection process, while companies B and C more operational reasons. In particular, for company A the event leading to the adoption of a new supplier is related with the adoption of a new raw material for production, while for company D is related

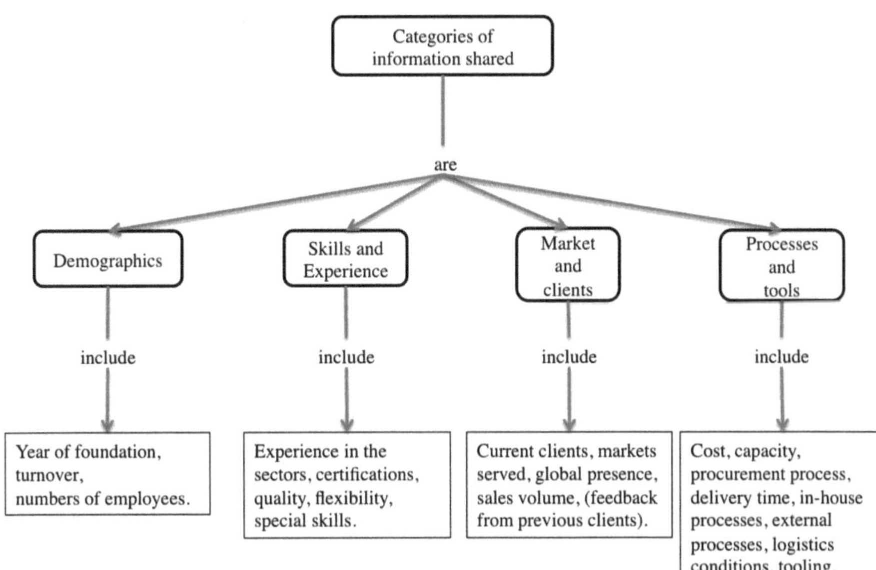

Fig. 3. Categories of information shared

with the introduction of a new technology or the availability of new market skills. Instead, for companies B and C the need of a new supplier is more related to its proximity with the existing plants, in order to be used as backup plants.

Considering now the information management aspect, the results are more homogeneous even if they present some difference in terms of the amount of information required to support the supplier selection process. For what concerns the information shared four categories were identified namely, demographics, skills and experience, market and clients, and process and tools. Figure 3 shows the categories and the related information shared collected during the interviews.

Table 2 summarizes the means used to gather and exchange the information shared among network members, external information is in bracket.

Table 2. Results of information gathering

	Company A	Company B	Company C	Company D
Information gathering and exchange	Visit/audit plant, platform, ERP	Visit/audit plant, platform, ERP, centralized compliance department	Visit/audit plant, e-mail, dropbox, ERP, (public events, workshop, fair etc.)	Visit/audit plant, platform

Two aspects related to the information shared are the most relevant. Firstly, company B requires from their suppliers evidence related to the procurement of raw material. Company B adopts a procurement policy which contrast direct and indirect benefit of armed groups in poor countries. The second and most important aspect is related to the use of external information. Only company C declares the adoption of external information, in bracket in Fig. 3, for the selection of new supplier. The drawback in this case is related with the fact that this information is the result of informal conversation in public events, and for this reason not systematized.

Regarding the information gathering, company B stated that the information is filtered by the presence of a centralized compliance department, that makes visible only the information relevant to the supplier selection process. Furthermore, contrary to the other cases company C is the only one that uses common means of information sharing, such as e-mail and Dropbox, instead of using a platform and/or ERP systems. The sole company satisfied with the performance of the actual information system is company D, but this could be associated with the fact that company was founded only two years ago. The other companies have a longer activity in the sectors and highlighted some problems related with the information systems adopted. Companies A and B affirmed the frustration related to the absence of linkage between the platform and a series of additional databases that allow the make comparison between potential suppliers. On the contrary, company C declared the incompatibility of the ERPs systems adopted in the different plants, and the lack of a platform enabling the management of the information entered in the ERPs systems.

Concluding, an additional difference in terms of visibility has been found in the four companies. Particularly, company A is the only case that showed local visibility of the information entered into the platform, whilst mother company has global and total visibility. For what concerns company B, C and D, once the information is shared, this become visible to all the network members.

Based on the evidence collected in the field, was possible to characterize the supplier selection process in the context of MNCs and to identify the information that need to be provided to support the decision-making process.

5 Conclusion

This work contributes in presenting how the supplier selection process is currently carried out in manufacturing networks. This research also sheds light on how the sharing of information influences the decision-making process according to the different perspectives of mother company and subsidiary company.

The main limitation of the paper is related to the low number of cases considered in the study Even so, from the analysis of the data is possible to deduce a lack of use of external information as support to the selection process of new suppliers. It is not possible to determine whether this is due to an absence of interest from subsidiary companies in using external information as support, or whether it is due to the fact that missing the perspective of mother companies. A further development of the research could be extending the analysis including mother company managers, and additional manufacturing sectors such as Aerospace, and Semiconductors.

References

1. Rudberg, M., Martin West, B.: Global operations strategy: coordinating manufacturing networks. Omega **36**, 91–106 (2008)
2. Shi, Y., Gregory, M.: International manufacturing networks—to develop global competitive capabilities. J. Oper. Manag. **16**, 195–214 (1998)
3. Trautmann, G., Turkulainen, V., Hartmann, E., Bals, L.: Integration in the global sourcing organization - an information processing perspective. J. Supply Chain Manag. **45**, 57–74 (2009)
4. Spina, G., Caniato, F., Luzzini, D., Ronchi, S.: Assessing the use of external grand theories in purchasing and supply management research. J. Purch. Supply Manag. **22**, 18–30 (2016)
5. Rebolledo, C., Nollet, J.: Learning from suppliers in the aerospace industry. Int. J. Prod. Econ. **129**, 328–337 (2011)
6. Rudberg, M., Olhager, J.: Manufacturing networks and supply chains: an operations strategy perspective. Omega **31**, 29–39 (2003)
7. De Boer, L., Labro, E., Morlacchi, P.: A review of methods supporting supplier selection. Eur. J. Purch. Supply Manag. **7**, 75–89 (2001)
8. Detlor, B.: Information management. Int. J. Inf. Manag. **30**, 103–108 (2010)
9. Kotabe, M., Omura, G.S.: Sourcing strategies of European and Japanese multinationals: a comparison. J. Int. Bus. Stud. **20**, 113–130 (1989)
10. Kotabe, M., Murray, J.Y.: Global sourcing strategy and sustainable competitive advantage. Ind. Mark. Manag. **33**, 7–14 (2004)
11. Kotabe, M., Murray, J., Mol, M.J.: Global sourcing strategy and performance: a "fit" versus "balance" perspective. Res. Glob. Strateg. Manag. **14**, 259–278 (2008)

12. Spina, G., Caniato, F., Luzzini, D., Ronchi, S.: Past, present and future trends of purchasing and supply management: an extensive literature review. Ind. Mark. Manag. **42**, 1202–1212 (2013)
13. Trent, R.J., Monczka, R.M.: International purchasing and global sourcing-what are the differences? J. Supply Chain Manag. **39**, 26–36 (2003)
14. Trautmann, G., Bals, L., Hartmann, E.: Global sourcing in integrated network structures: the case of hybrid purchasing organizations. J. Int. Manag. **15**, 194–208 (2009)
15. Faes, W., Matthyssens, P., Vandenbempt, K.: The pursuit of global purchasing synergy. Ind. Mark. Manag. **29**, 539–553 (2000)
16. Teixeira, R., Koufteros, X., Peng, X.D.: Organizational structure, integration, and manufacturing performance: a conceptual model and propositions. J. Oper. Supply Chain Manag. **5**, 69–81 (2012)
17. Mourtzis, D., Doukas, M., Psarommatis, F.: A multi-criteria evaluation of centralized and decentralized production networks in a highly customer-driven environment. CIRP Ann. - Manuf. Technol. **61**, 427–430 (2012)
18. Zhang, D.: The revival of vertical integration: strategic choice and performance influences. J. Manag. Strateg. **4**, 1–14 (2013)
19. De Boer, L., Van Der Wegen, L.L.M.: Practice and promise of formal supplier selection: a study of four empirical cases. J. Purch. Supply Manag. **9**, 109–118 (2003)
20. Luo, X., Wu, C., Rosenberg, D., Barnes, D.: Supplier selection in agile supply chains: an information-processing model and an illustration. J. Purch. Supply Manag. **15**, 249–262 (2009)
21. Weber, C.A., Current, J.R., Benton, W.C.: Vendor selection criteria and methods. Eur. J. Oper. Res. **50**, 2–18 (1991)
22. Wu, C., Barnes, D.: A literature review of decision-making models and approaches for partner selection in agile supply chains. J. Purch. Supply Manag. **17**, 256–274 (2011)
23. Scholl, H.J., Kubicek, H., Cimander, R., Klischewski, R.: Process integration, information sharing, and system interoperation in government: a comparative case analysis. Gov. Inf. Q. **29**, 313–323 (2012)
24. Li, S., Lin, B.: Accessing information sharing and information quality in supply chain management. Decis. Support Syst. **42**, 1641–1656 (2006)
25. Legner, C., Schemm, J.: Toward the inter-organizational product information supply chain-evidence from the retail and consumer goods industries. J. Assoc. Inf. Syst. **9**, 119 (2008)
26. Cao, M., Vonderembse, M.A., Zhang, Q., Ragu-Nathan, T.S.: Supply chain collaboration: conceptualisation and instrument development. Int. J. Prod. Res. **48**, 6613–6635 (2010)
27. Hung, W.H., Ho, C.F., Jou, J.J., Tai, Y.M.: Sharing information strategically in a supply chain: antecedents, content and impact. Int. J. Logist. Res. Appl. **14**, 111–133 (2011)
28. Baihaqi, I., Sohal, A.S.: The impact of information sharing in supply chains on organisational performance: an empirical study. Prod. Plan. Control. **24**, 743–758 (2013)
29. Kaipia, R., Hartiala, H.: Information-sharing in supply chains: five proposals on how to proceed. Int. J. Logist. Manag. **17**, 377–393 (2006)
30. Meredith, J.: Building operations management theory through case and field research. J. Oper. Manag. **16**, 441–454 (1998)

Assessing the Suitability of Supplier Consortia for Public Procurement Contracts

Andrew Crossley[1,2(✉)], Jane Lynch[3], Sue Hurrell[4], and Rhian Edwards[5]

[1] ServQ Alliance, Cardiff, Wales, UK
AndrewDCrossley@ServQ.com
[2] University of Bristol, Bristol, UK
[3] Cardiff Business School, Cardiff, Wales, UK
[4] Values Wales, Welsh Government, Cardiff, Wales, UK
[5] Wales Co-operative Centre, Caerphilly, Wales, UK

Abstract. This study offers a unique contribution to the existing research on collaborative working by exploring the buy side challenges facing public procurement teams when managing Collaborative Network Organizations (CNOs) termed 'supplier consortia' in this study. Two online management tools are proposed. A Procurement Assessment Model (PAM) guides buyers in assessing the suitability of public contracts for consortia bids. A Bid/No Bid model is offered to help suppliers align their CNO to the procurement and specification. This study is relevant for the public and private sectors but both tools proposed have been adopted by the Welsh Government (UK) and included as updates within the formal Joint Bidding Guide. The Joint Bidding Guide has been developed, published and tested by the Welsh Government since 2013.

Keywords: Supplier selection · Joint bidding · Consortia · Public procurement · Tendering process

1 Introduction

Significant technological advancements, such as the *internet of things* and *Cyber-physical systems* address the interconnection and collaboration among physical and virtual objects which expedites knowledge creation and growth opportunities for organizations [1]. The new competitive landscape [2] has enabled a significant rise in different forms of Collaborative Network Organizations (CNOs) operating through cloud computing, virtual communities, business ecosystems and other software [3].

Horizontal collaboration in the supply market, forming CNOS of *supplier consortia* leads to unprecedented organizational growth opportunities as commonly noted in logistics research [4] and e-commerce research [5]. Yet in the public procurement context there are many challenges and perceived barriers identified for Small and Medium Sized Enterprises (SMEs) when trying to compete against larger conglomerates for public contracts [6]. The purpose of forming networks or consortia is *"to build a*

H. Afsarmanesh et al. (Eds.): PRO-VE 2016, IFIP AICT 480, pp. 189–199, 2016.
DOI: 10.1007/978-3-319-45390-3_17

collaborative advantage in which multiple organizations together achieve something that individual organizations could not achieve alone" [3].

Using an abductive approach, and multiple methods which involve academics, public procurement practitioners and supplier case studies this paper explains the rationale and development behind the design and adoption of two powerful procurement tools. These relate to the suitability and selection of a supplier consortium and can be implemented during two critical stages of the public sector procurement process. During the first stage the client and procurement team assess whether bids from consortia are likely to be successful. During the second stage the tender opportunity is assessed as viable for delivery by consortium members working as a virtual network (VN) or using the lead model as a virtual enterprise (VE) [7].

The paper introduces the key influencing studies for horizontal collaboration, supplier selection, procurement assessment and related maturity models. Once the methodology has been explained, the findings are presented and the two models proposed as procurement tools form the main research contributions and conclusions.

2 Literature Review

2.1 Supplier Consortium Development

Aside from logistics research [4] and studies examining the e-commerce supply chain [5] much of the existing research on horizontal collaboration through consortia development has been applied to the buy side in procurement [7, 8] with limited research examining supplier consortia [8, 9]. Two key procurement studies were identified which highlighted the importance of selecting the appropriate organizational form for developing a consortium [8, 10]. Parallels were identified in the literature between recommendations for procurement and how these collaborative forms may apply to the supply market. Firstly, Bakkar et al. [8] established seven collaborative forms worthy of serious consideration: *professional network; piggy backing; shared services; lead-buying; third party advisory; third party joint purchasing* and *third party outsourced. Piggy backing*, *third party advisory* or the *lead buying model* can also be argued as the most suitable strategy designs for managing supplier consortia. Secondly, Cagnuzzo et al. [10] highlighted *Industrial Clusters, Districts, Virtual Organizations (VOs), Virtual Enterprises (VEs), Virtual Breeding Environment (VBE)* and *Collaborative Networks (CNOs)*. Governance is also reviewed in Rabelo et al. [11].

The practice of suppliers bidding jointly is not new, sometimes termed in the private sector as *bundling, clustering* or *co-option* [6]. Team building, staff engagement and trust were identified as key determinants for effective supplier consortia [9]. However, collaborative relationships are complex to manage as consortium members may be challenged with conflicting organizational cultures and approaches to leadership [3]. Further problems are likely when managing mutual benefit arrangements and information asymmetry [7].

2.2 Consortia and Economic Sustainability

The initiation of a public tender requires that the Client's 'make or buy' decision has been made at the outset. One important decision is whether the tender is suited to SMEs because there are social and economic community benefits for public contracts to be awarded to and delivered by smaller, local suppliers [12]. As the UK public sector faces times of increasing austerity, forced restructuring and centralization of procurement has meant that contract values have increased. This makes it difficult for SMEs to compete against larger conglomerates [6, 9]. SMEs bidding individually can also potentially represent higher financial risk to public buyers [6, 13]. Therefore, one solution for the Client to accept consortia bids is adapting either the *lead model* or *piggy backing* methods managed as a virtual enterprise (VE) [8, 10].

2.3 Procurement Assessment Models

The first of the assessment tools designed in Wales, called the Procurement Assessment Model (PAM), was created in 2013 for procurement teams to support efficient evaluation of the most relevant 'buy side' and 'supply side' factors influencing the likely success of consortium delivery [14]. The first PAM was designed as a *decision enhancing* tool rather than a *decision making* tool. This approach responded to the gap for appropriate research and evidence on collaborative procurement methods developed from case studies, highlighted by Cagnazzo et al. in their literature review. In 2013 supply side collaboration and virtual networks had not been actively encouraged by many client and procurement officers in Wales' public sector [13]. Hence procurement teams were inexperienced in developing consistent and fair supplier selection criteria to compare a consortium bid with one from a single organization. The software industry's Capability Maturity Model Integration (CMMI) and the newer international standards on software maturity assessment [15] were considered too specific for the PAM's assessment criteria. Instead, the first British Standard for Collaborative Working [16] offered a standard relationship maturity matrix using a four-point qualitative measurement scale ranging from limited application to high level of maturity, and this was a useful basis for the development.

2.4 Supplier Selection

The research on supplier selection is extensive[1]. Recent methods for determining supplier selection criteria seem to be weighted towards stochastic, analytical hierarchy process (AHP) and fuzzy AHP [17, 18]. Yet, studies relevant for public procurement are few. This is surprising given that procurement teams are pressured into using scoring mechanisms to ensure fairness, transparency and consistency [17, 19]. Increasingly the traditional lowest cost or "*Most Economically Advantageous Tender*" (MEAT) [19, 20] approaches to selection are being supplemented by value-adding sustainability

---

1 Google Scholar identified 37,400 published studies using "supplier selection" as the search terms [15/06/16].

criteria, for example by including social, economic and environmental community benefits [12]. Potential supplier consortia self-selection is also vital within an efficient procurement system, and a Bid/No-Bid model was also developed to facilitate this. It assesses five key areas: market positioning; bidding resource and availability; delivery competence; commercial acceptability; and risk [14].

2.5 Review Summary

Most of the existing studies examined for this review have focused more on different forms of collaboration in the procurement context. Yet, there are many lessons and transferrable concepts which can be explored for managing collaboration in the supply market. The review has emphasized that collaboration across SMEs improves performance through knowledge transfer and business growth opportunities [1, 6, 10]. Future research is invited exploring models for the private sector using *hard,* quantitative measurements rather than *soft*, qualitative measures [7, 19]. This provides the basis and rationale for the new PAM development.

In response to the economic tensions affecting public procurement in Wales and other parts of the UK, supplier consortia are being encouraged [9, 13, 14]. In 2012 the Welsh Government introduced a procurement policy statement which highlighted the importance of widening SMEs' access to public sector tenders. This led to the development of the Joint Bidding Guide (JBG) in 2013. The background to the Guide was published in 2015 [13], introducing the rationale for a successful series of Joint Bidding Demonstration Projects that ran between 2014 and 2015. Accepting important messages from the literature and research gaps as highlighted, this paper explores the key lessons learned from these Demonstration Projects, developing updated consortium models for procurement assessment and supplier bid selection.

3 Method

This study lends itself to an abductive research approach, established by Blaikie [21]. Abductive research is argued as offering a similar approach to inductive research or grounded theory as it relies primarily on existing prior knowledge and theory testing [21]. Theory, data collection and data analysis are managed simultaneously for developing new theory [22]. In total, six years of desk research (2010–2016), modelling design, field trials, feedback, review and updates have taken place. The subsequent Lessons Learned Report (LLR) published by Welsh Government in 2015 highlighted key development areas from Demonstration Projects [23]. The important Lessons Learned were based on the outcomes and experiences of managing twelve Demonstration Projects and the findings summarized from a series of interviews with senior procurement managers, procurement teams, procurement policy advisors, suppliers and steering group members. After publication of the LLR the Joint Bidding Steering Group agreed that enhancements were needed to the Procurement Assessment Model (PAM) designed for the original Guide. The Lessons Learned from the Demonstration

Projects were presented at Cardiff Business School in late 2015. The LLR and literature findings form the basis for the two new consortium models featured in this study.

4 Model Development – Procurement Assessment Model (PAM)

Prior to determining the new supplier selection criteria, four areas were considered from the LLR which highlights the suitability of a contract for consortium delivery:

(1) *Enhance Decision Making* - PAM should be used in the earliest stages of procurement planning; (2) *Maturity Indices* - The relationship management plan from BS 11000-1:2010 [16] was enhanced using the supporting guide for the British Standard (BS 11000-2:2011) [24]; (3) *Heat Map* - highlighting Red/Amber/Green (RAG) configuration. This format was readily accepted by senior decision makers in their risk analysis and management work; and (4) *High Level Characteristics of Suppliers* - strategy and operations covering location, production (or service provision), inventory and transportation/distribution were to be accounted for.

The procurement experts and suppliers interviewed emphasized the importance of pre-market engagement with the supply market as key to the success of consortium development and receiving joint bids. Specific tenders were advertised as suitable for consortium delivery using the online national tender e-portal and database known as Sell2Wales [25] along with early engagement meetings for potential suppliers.

Following the demonstration projects, feedback received from the interviews and field trials established that the PAM approach was potentially very effective. However, on closer review the LLR recommended that more detail was required to optimize the model's effectiveness. Key areas needing improvement include: (a) separation of the buy side and supply side factors; (b) introduction of summary descriptions guiding the PAM users on where their project or service sat on the horizontal continua; (c) expansion of the number of continua factors to twelve plus one additional option, and; (d) more introductory and explanatory text.

Steering group members questioned whether some form of weighting to score the overall model with pass/fail criteria was appropriate. This expert user group preferred the model to be used as an indicator of suitability. In principle, where there are a significant number of red and/or amber assessment points emerging, the procurement team should firstly review whether practical tactics can be used to reduce the RAG 'heat' such as repackaging the delivery location or size of lots (continua points 3 and 7 for example, in the Buy Side Factors). When this is possible the opportunity is better prepared for potential consortia.

At the time of writing, the web engineers appointed by the Welsh Government to manage the tender e-portal Sell2Wales were designing the relevant 'tick box' for highlighting suitability for consortia bidding and delivery. Ticking the advertisement's box stating '*the procurers believe that this opportunity is suitable for delivery by consortia*' gives a very strong indication to the market that the buy side is amenable to receiving joint bids. One of the most striking findings from discussions with successful consortium bidders on the Demonstration Projects was that this initial positive statement is one of the most important factors in encouraging bids from existing or newly-formed consortia. From the supply side's perspective, a positive endorsement on the Sell2Wales portal indicates that the PAM has been run and the opportunity is well suited to joint bidding. Conversely the buy side not ticking the box, to state the opportunity is suitable for joint bidding, could sensibly infer that the opportunity is considered as either marginal or not really suited for joint bidding.

For procurements subject to the UK Public Contracts Regulations 2015 [26], consortium bids must not be excluded, although consortia can be required to form a legal entity for contractual purpose. For procurements where the PAM shows red and amber indicators the procurement team may decide not to actively market the opportunity as consortium-friendly.

Figure 1 contains the upgraded PAM in response to points (a) separation of buy side and supply side factors and (d) including more introductory and explanatory text.

The upgraded PAM builds on both the literature findings and the findings of the Demonstration Projects. Using a RAG 'traffic light' approach for the continua factors, red zones (dark grey) indicate potential areas or issues with the procurement that make it less amenable to joint bidding. Amber zones (light grey) suggest that consortium delivery may pose some challenges, whereas green zones (white) suggest that the procurement is most suitable for consortium delivery. In this worked example the crosses (X) reflect the following assessment by the procurement team:

Buy side factors - There is time to prepare a framework tender; it is clearly specified; it is scalable; it is mainly service driven (time and location); it is a reasonable risk on performance (staff experience); it directly interfaces with end users (with access restrictions) and it is needed at many schools for a council.

Supply Side factors - There are incumbent providers who try and control the market via sub-contracting; a consortium can cover most locations within the council area; qualified teachers can create consortia (with access restrictions); with sufficient planning and infrastructure new consortia can compete effectively; the market is currently served by established suppliers; new members can add appropriate volume.

The conclusion from this PAM analysis is that the Supply Teachers contract, could be delivered by a consortium but there are some potential risks to be considered prior to contract advertisement. The PAM may also help buyers to consider re-packaging the demand to make it more attractive to consortia and/or smaller businesses. It is a useful model for identifying risk where red and amber indicators indicate that tender questions should ensure that supplier consortia have Relationship Management Plans [23, 24] and written agreements in place where necessary to manage risk of failure.

		Buy Side Factors				
1	**Short timeframe**	Less than 3 months.	Between 3 and 6 months to procure.	Between 6 and 12 months to procure.	Could take more than 12 months to procure.	**Extended timeframe**
				x		
2	**Readily specified**	Easily specified product/service.	Some expertise needed to specify the product/service.	Some external support needed to create the specification.	External expertise critical to creating a complex specification.	**Complex specification**
			x			
3	**Scalable delivery**	Highly scalable allowing a range of supplier sizes to bid.	A lotting approach is planned - which might enable consortia to bid for at least one lot.	The product/service can be split down into discreet stages.	A single very large scale product/service is required e.g. building and running a hospital or a high school.	**Unique and large**
			x			
4	**Product driven**	Can be broken down into packages of discreet products/services.	Requires some coordination between packages of delivery.	Service delivery appears seamless to end user.	The end user requires a high level of service integration involving multi-party programme management	**Service driven**
				x		
5	**Low risk on performance**	Performance of discrete packages can be managed separately.	Some coordinated performance management of separate packages in needed.	Robust quality management and systems are needed to ensure performance.	Delivery performance is critical to end user health, safety and/or security. A range of accepted standards may apply (ISO/BS etc).	**High risk on performance**
				x		
6	**Not end user facing**	The end user will not be interacting directly with the delivery team.	Some interaction between the end user and the delivery team is needed.	High standards of service delivery and compliance with good practices and/or regulations are needed.	The end user requires consistent and dedicated critical services. e.g Prisoner security or operating theatre cleaning.	**Critical to end user**
				x		
7	**Location-discrete**	The product/service is required in discrete location/s.	The product/service is needed in a confined geography within easy travelling distance of the consortium's base.	The product/service is required on a regional basis needing multiple bases or depots to fulfil requirements.	The product or service is required in multiple regions needing national levels of co-ordination.	**Geographically-networked**
				x		
		Supply side Factors				
8	**Suppliers of all sizes**	A full range of supplier sizes is available.	A competitive market exists, although some collaboration may be needed to increase scale.	Aggregation of suppliers may create high polarity, potentially limiting competition.	Large suppliers dominate the market with SMEs usually subcontracting.	**Polarised market**
				x		
9	**Portable supply**	Suppliers can deliver products/services anywhere, within reason.	Most products/services can be supplied to the end user's required locations.	A consortia could cover most locations.	The supplier must be collocated with the end user. E.g Court services.	**Fixed location**
				x		
10	**Easy to enter market**	No significant investment is needed to deliver the product/service to the market.	Some market entry costs.	With sufficient preparation and investment new consortia could be established to compete.	Barriers to entry are high requiring major capital or training, development and specialist certification to deliver the product/service.	**High entry cost**
				x		
11	**Collaborative market**	The market is used to collaborative working.	Suppliers can be flexible and sometimes work together effectively to meet user's requirements	The market is usually served by established suppliers operating familiar processes.	The market is dominated by discrete traditional firms with extensive experience, not used to (perhaps suspicious of) collaboration.	**Discrete 'Traditional' firms**
				x		
12	**Quality-led market**	Suppliers compete on quality more than on price, so may be willing to share price and cost information to improve quality through collaboration.	Established consortia can enhance their products/services with a limited number of new members. Members' Quality systems can be readily extended.	The costs associated with bringing in new members may remove any competitive advantage on price.	The price and margins within the market may make it unattractive to new entrants. Suppliers may be very reluctant to share price information that may impact future competitive advantage. High potential for collusive practices developing.	**Very price sensitive**
			x			
13	**Other (specify)**					**Other (specify)**

Fig. 1. Procurement assessment model (PAM) used for a supply teachers' tender

Assessment Templates

Mark each question from 0 to 5 or as Unknown (Unk) if not currently known

5	Excellent position for proposed Consortium
3	Good position for proposed Consortium
1	Basic position for proposed Consortium
0	Very weak position for proposed Consortium
Unk	Not currently known (we need to find out)

1 Consortium's Market Position

		Assessment (0-5)	Commercially Exposed? (Y, N)
1	Is this opportunity a good fit with our Consortium's goals?	3	N
2	Will winning enhance our Consortium's reputation and market positioning?	3	N
3	Will winning open up new market opportunities for our Consortium?	5	N
4	Are any members of our Consortium known to the key decision makers?	3	N
5	Does any member of our Consortium understand the imperative need or problem drving this opportunity?	Unk	N
6	Do we know the opportunity's evaluation criteria and how they will be weighted?	3	N
7	Do we know the proposal time frame?	5	N
8	Do our Consortium's features and benefits give it a distinct competitive advantage?	3	N
9	Can we compete if price is a major factor in selecting the winning bid?	5	N
10	Do any of our members have successful track records with similar opportunities?	3	N
11	Does our Consortium have differentiators that improve its odds of winning this opportunity?	3	N
12	Does the Consortium know who the other competitive bidders are, if any?	Unk	N
13	Can we win against a good competitor if it is currently in post?	3	N
14	Will winning this opportunity give our Consortium future business advantage over its competitors?	5	N
			# of Y's:
	1 Consortium's Market Position Score: (Maximum of 70 points)	**44**	**0**
	Percentage score:	62.9%	
	Total number of scores rated as 0 (Very weak position for Consortium):	**0**	
	Total number of scores rated as Unk (Unknown):	**2**	

Action to Improve Scoring: Need to get a better understanding of the requirements and demands that have led to this tender (5), At the moment we do not know who the competitors are likely to be (12). There is a meet the buyer event planned so we can see who is there.

2 Bidding Resource Availability

		Assessment (0-5)	Commercially Exposed? (Y, N)
15	Does the Consortium have a Bid Director qualified to manage this Joint Bid?	5	N
16	Can we deliver the final project without new Consortium members?	1	Y
17	Can any required new members be recruited in time?	3	N
18	Do we have sufficient resources and team budget available to bid?	1	N
19	Can we prepare a professional bid in the time allowed?	3	N
			# of Y's:
	2 Bidding Resource Availability Score: (Maximum of 25 points)	**13**	**1**
	Percentage score:	52.0%	
	Total number of scores rated as 0 (Very weak position for Consortium):	**0**	
	Total number of scores rated as Unk (Unknown):	**0**	

Action to Improve Scoring: We need to source an additional member with adult care home management skills in order to submit a bid as there is a requirement to maintain the new facility as well as construct it. Until this potential member is identified and signs a memorandum of understanding to form a consortium, we would be commercially exposed. That section of the bid also needs external expertise to complete it.

Fig. 2. Example of two key areas from a completed sell side go/no-go model

5 Model Development - The Bid/No-Bid Model

Chapter 9 of the JBG contains advice on how a potential consortium should review the opportunity: "*As the initiating member of a consortium you will need good quality tools and a basic opportunity assessment process to work out how to proceed. If you already have a consortium you should agree which of your members have the best tools for this stage.*" The Bid/No-Bid model uses 44 points of assessment in these 5 key areas:

(1) *Consortium's market positioning; (2) Bidding resource and availability; (3) Consortium's delivery competence; (4) Commercial issues; and, (5) Risk planning.*[2]

Figure 2 is a worked example of two key areas from a consortium Bid/No-Bid model. The other three areas have a similar form of evaluation. There is an overall dashboard with the key area scores mapped against an upper and lower boundary. An example of this is given in Chapter 9 Annex A of the Joint Bidding Guide.

Demonstration Projects feedback indicated that it was a very useful model but it would be more user-friendly if it were automated either as an on online tool or as a downloadable template. Due to the confidentiality of information shared by consortium groups the downloadable template option was the preferred solution and work was completed in early 2016 to create this template using Microsoft Excel.

6 Discussion and Conclusions

The development of the PAM and Bid/No Bid models started out as a field research project in 2012. This paper builds on the existing literature for managing consortium delivery in public procurement contracts. The results from the Demonstration Projects exceeded expectations and provided early feedback on the acceptability and usage of the new models included in the Joint Bidding Guide. Nine of the twelve procurements reached contract award stage during the study period and six of the contracts were awarded in part or fully to consortia. All but one of these consortia were newly-formed in order to bid for the procurements. If used appropriately alongside other advice in the Guide the two tools save resource and money for buyers and bidders, allowing better alignment of existing and new consortia to suitable opportunities.

Whilst this paper has explored the consortium concept and its application in the public procurement context, the findings are also relevant to the private sector. The study highlighted the importance of using a formal structured process for managing consortium delivery, taking account of the actions needed by both the buy and sell side. When managed effectively, using the tools available in the Joint Bidding Guide, business opportunities increase for SMEs and micro businesses working together as consortia networks (CNOs). This study provides empirical evidence that consortia can "*build a collaborative advantage*" [3]. The Welsh Government's Minister for Finance and Government Business endorsed this point by publicly highlighting the joint bidding programme's success in enabling small and micro businesses to win much larger public sector contracts than they could have accessed individually.

In 2016, the Welsh Government's procurement policy unit, Value Wales, and its collaborative procurement organization, the National Procurement Service won a highly commended award for innovation at one of the UK's national procurement awards. The Steering Group's lifespan has been extended to 2017 to capitalize on the program's

[2] The maximum score for each assessment point is 5. The model uses a semi-logarithmic approach to scoring (Unknown, 0, 1, 3, 5) to avoid 'mid-point' scoring bias from linear scales. A maximum score of 5 for each assessment point would yield a theoretical maximum total of 220 for the 44 points of assessment. Each key area has its own score to highlight which areas merit special attention.

overall success. All of the contracts awarded to consortia during the Demonstration Projects are still underway, and at the time of writing are being delivered successfully and creating significant community benefits. This bodes well for small businesses in the UK bidding for future public contracts and is an appropriate approach to the dispersed nature of a rural and mixed economy such as in Wales, where CNO members can be based far apart.

References

1. Stankovic, J.: Research directions for the internet of things. IEEE Internet Things J. **1**(1), 3–9 (2014)
2. Bettis, R., Hitt, M.: The new competitive landscape. Strateg. Manag. J. **16**(S1), 7–19 (1995)
3. Baker, E., Kan, M., Teo, S.: Developing a collaborative network organization: leadership challenges at multiple levels. J. Organ. Change Manag. **24**(6), 853–875 (2011)
4. Mason, R., Lalwani, C., Boughton, R.: Combining vertical and horizontal collaboration for transport optimisation. Supply Chain Manag.: Int. J. **12**(3), 187–199 (2007)
5. Dai, Q., Kauffman, R.: B2B e-commerce revisited: leading perspectives on the key issues and research directions. Electron. Mark. **12**(2), 67–83 (2002)
6. Walker, H., Preuss, L.: Fostering sustainability through sourcing from smaller businesses: public sector perspectives. J. Clean. Prod. **16**(15), 1600–1609 (2002)
7. Walker, H., Schotanus, F., Bakker, E., Harland, C.: Collaborative procurement: a relational view of buyer-buyer relationships. Public Adm. Rev. **73**(4), 588–598 (2013)
8. Bakker, E., Walker, H., Schotanus, F., Harland, C.: Choosing an organisational form: the case of collaborative procurement initiatives. Int. J. Procure. Manag. **1**(3), 297–317 (2008)
9. Jost, G., Dawson, M., Shaw, D.: Private sector consortia working for a public sector client-factors that build successful relationships: lessons from the UK. Eur. Manag. J. **23**(3), 336–350 (2005)
10. Cagnazzo, L., Taticchi, P., Bidini, G., Sameh, M.: Collaborative procurement within enterprise networks: a literature review, a reference framework and a case study. In: Camarinha-Matos, L.M., Paraskakis, I., Afsarmanesh, H. (eds.) PRO-VE 2009. IFIP AICT, vol. 307, pp. 351–360. Springer, Heidelberg (2009)
11. Rabelo, R.J., Costa, S.N., Romero, D.: A governance reference model for virtual enterprises. In: Camarinha-Matos, L.M., Afsarmanesh, H. (eds.) Collaborative Systems for Smart Networked Environments. IFIP AICT, vol. 434, pp. 60–70. Springer, Heidelberg (2014)
12. Lynch, J., Uenk, N., Walker, H., Schotanus, F.: Community benefits of public procurement: a comparison between Wales (UK) and the Netherlands local governments. In: Conference Proceedings for 25th IPSERA 2016, Dortmund, Germany (2016)
13. Crossley, A., Coles, G., Edwards, R., Hurrell, S., Ruddle, N.: The development and adoption of a new joint bidding system for public contracts in Wales. In: Camarinha-Matos, L.M., et al. (eds.) PRO-VE 2015. IFIP AICT, vol. 463, pp. 622–630. Springer, Heidelberg (2015). doi: 10.1007/978-3-319-24141-8_58
14. Joint Bidding Guide. http://gov.wales/docs/dpsp/publications/valuewales/151119-bidding-guide-en.pdf. Accessed 20 Apr 2016
15. BS ISO/IEC 30105-3. Information technology. IT Enabled Services-Business Process Outsourcing (ITES-BPO) lifecycle processes. Part 3. Measurement framework and organizational maturity model
16. BS 11000-1:2010 Framework specification for collaborative business relationships. BSi, Annex B & C, pp. 35–38 (2010)

17. De Boer, L., Labro, E., Morlacchi, P.: A review of methods supporting supplier selection. Eur. J. Purch. Supply Manag. **7**(2), 75–89 (2001)
18. Karsak, E., Dursun, M.: Taxonomy and review of non-deterministic analytical methods for supplier selection. Int. J. Comput. Integr. Manuf. **29**(3), 263–286 (2016)
19. Bergman, M., Lundberg, S.: Tender evaluation and supplier selection methods in public procurement. J. Purch. Supply Manag. **19**(2), 73–83 (2013)
20. Falagario, M., Sciancalepore, F., Costantino, N., Pietroforte, R.: Using a DEA-cross efficiency approach in public procurement tenders. Eur. J. Oper. Res. **218**(2), 523–529 (2012)
21. Blaikie, N.: Approaches to Social Enquiry: Advancing Knowledge. Polity Press, Cambridge (2000)
22. Mason, J.: Qualitative Researching, 2nd edn. Sage Publications, London (2007)
23. Lessons Learned Report 2015. http://gov.wales/docs/dpsp/publications/valuewales/151119-lessons-learned-en.pdf. Accessed 20 Apr 2016
24. BS 11000-2:2011 Collaborative Business Relationships – Part 2 BSi Table A1 (2011)
25. Sell2Wales. https://www.sell2wales.gov.wales/. Accessed 20 Apr 2016
26. Public Procurement: Public Regulations. http://www.legislation.gov.uk/uksi/2015/102/pdfs/uksi_20150102_en.pdf. Accessed 21 Apr 2016

A Confidence Indicator Model for Virtual Organization Creation in Cloud Computing Environment

Luís Felipe Bilecki(✉) and Adriano Fiorese

Department of Computer Science,
Santa Catarina State University, Joinville, Brazil
luis.bilecki@gmail.com, adriano.fiorese@udesc.br

Abstract. A Virtual Organization (VO) is a form of organization where a set of independent entities share resources, skills and risks in order to attend a collaboration opportunity. The integration between VO's concept and cloud computing seems promising since VO participants use or provide their services in a cloud computing environment. Nevertheless, in this context of integration, the problem of trust between VO partners and cloud providers is highlighted. This is noteworthy since it's necessary to select a reliable cloud provider for a VO business partner launch its service. Therefore, this work presents a confidence indicator model for cloud computing providers using the Data Envelopment Analysis (DEA) method. For the evaluation of this work, we used Quality of Service indicators of public cloud service providers. Results presented and discussed show the generated confidence indicator can be a good criterion to help the VO's manager to select reliable Cloud Computing providers to host VO partners during the VO creation process.

Keywords: Virtual organization · Confidence · Cloud computing

1 Introduction

In recent years, an increasing variety of collaborative networks have arisen because of the socio-economic challenges faced by society, such as globalization, competitiveness, variety of products and services, low cost, etc. [1]. The companies (entities) have been specializing and collaborating with others in order to survive to the competitiveness imposed by other members present in market. In this regard, the collaborative process has became easier due to the advances provided by the information and communication technology (ICT), providing alternatives to deal with the geographical arrangement of the entities [2].

Considering the forms of collaboration among enterprises, Virtual Organization (VO), is advantageous to incorporate flexibility and dynamism to handle the demands of the market [3]. A VO is the temporary alliance of autonomous, heterogeneous and geographically dispersed entities sharing skills and resources to attend a collaboration opportunity (CO). Given that, the VO's life cycle presents the following phases: creation, operation, evolution and dissolution [4]. This article focuses primarily on the creation phase, which is seen as a critical stage to ensure the success of the VO's operation [5].

H. Afsarmanesh et al. (Eds.): PRO-VE 2016, IFIP AICT 480, pp. 200–211, 2016.
DOI: 10.1007/978-3-319-45390-3_18

One of the problems observed during the creation of a VO is the necessary sense of confidence among the entities involved, particularly in the sub-process of search and selection [6]. In a VO and Cloud Computing (CC) integration model, cloud computing providers can host VO members' services. In this sense, a VO depends on the cloud providers who host its members' services. Thus, comprising the integration of VO and Cloud Computing, confidence is a key concept to be taken into consideration during the cloud provider search and selection step in order to form a VO. Moreover, regarding this integration model, the Quality of Service (QoS) delivered by the cloud computing provider plays an important role in the confidence assessment. Therefore, confidence also can help to avoid the dissolution of the VO during the operation phase. Namely, it seems plausible that the greater the confidence level in a cloud computing provider the lower the risk level during the attendance of the collaboration opportunity. This claim is partially supported by results from multi-criteria risk assessment works that take into consideration, among other indicators, the confidence one [3, 7].

Therefore, this paper proposes a model for the generation of the confidence indicator, through the application of the Data Envelopment Analysis (DEA) decision-making method. Considering that there are multiple inputs represented by Quality of Service indicators for several cloud computing providers, the proposed method assists to generate a single value of confidence for partners (e.g., a cloud computing provider). The developed indicator will consist of QoS indicators, represented by Key Performance Indicators (KPIs), available in Garg et al. [8] and Sun et al. [9]: availability, response time, stability, security and cost. Therefore the confidence value represents a level of trust in the service provided by cloud computing provider. Hence, a high level of confidence represents a greater probability of the service to be executed without failure during the several stages of VO's life cycle in the cloud. Thus, the proposed model, aims to support the decision process in several stages of VO integration with CC life cycle, such as the process of cloud computing providers' search and selection or during the operation phase. The generated indicator also can be used and integrated in a reputation service covering all the stages of the VO life cycle.

The remainder of this paper is organized as follows. Section 2 elaborates on the related work and concepts regarding the problem of trust concerning the various processes of a VO. Section 3 seeks to present the proposed model to generate the confidence indicator. Section 4 presents the results of implementation of the model. Finally, Sect. 5 presents conclusions and future work.

2 General Background

This Section presents related work, a definition of cloud computing concept and its relationship to virtual organization. It discusses the concepts of trust and reputation and methods of multi-criteria decision making, and it points out this work contribution regarding related works.

2.1 Related Work

Several works present approaches to support the decision making process to the VO Manager. In this regard, the process of search and selection of service providers based on competencies and candidates' skills occurs through different methods such as: multi-criteria decision making methods and others as optimization by swarm particles [10–12]. These works present methods to enhance the partner's search and selection step during the VO creation, but they do not use or generate a confidence indicator based on Key Performance Indicators (KPIs) belonging to the analyzed partners.

A study presents methods for classification and selection of reliable services based on QoS indicators and user ratings [13] returning a trust indicator. In other studies, services are evaluated according to the observations of users and also on a focused approach through the QoS indicators [14] as well as in satisfaction user ratings used for classification and selection of services [15, 16].

The work proposed by Squicciarini et al. [6] presents protocols for trust negotiation representing an effective way to select the best possible members during the several stages of the VO's life cycle. In Winkler et al. [5] it is proposed the generation of a confidence indicator for a reputation service, based on financial, organizational and operational indicators, among others. The developed confidence indicator has served as support for the decision-making tool for partner selection for the composition of the VO.

These aforementioned works seek to meet the purpose of supporting the VO manager in the decision making process in the VO creation phase, specifically in the partners' search and selection step. However, none of them provides an approach which defines a confidence indicator in the context of the virtual organization and cloud computing integration and also do not use this generated confidence indicator to support the several decision-making process presents in VO's life cycle, such as cloud computing partner search and selection and the VO's operation.

The application of confidence indicator on VO, during the integration with cloud computing providers, plays an important role, because the quality of service delivered by cloud providers is a key factor to ensure success in VO's operation. Therefore, the proposed model presents a confidence indicator based on QoS indicators for cloud computing providers, with the purpose to assist the several decision-making process presents in VO's life cycle.

2.2 Cloud Computing

The Cloud Computing (CC) paradigm provide access to computing resources (e.g., servers, networks, storage and applications) in a practical way and on-demand, where resources can be provisioned automatically to the user. For this purpose, the Cloud Computing Providers make available the necessary infrastructure so that users can run their services [17]. Also according to the National of Institute and Standards Technology (NIST) [17], CC has four deployment models (public, private, community, hybrid) and can provide three service models: Software as a Service (SaaS), Infrastructure as a Service (IaaS) and Platform as a Service (PaaS). Finally, CC has five essential characteristics (Resource pooling, rapid elasticity, measured service, on-demand self service and broad network access).

Due to the benefits offered by cloud computing, many entities have used their services to implement their applications, so being able to respond quickly and nimbly to a collaboration opportunity [2].

Despite the advantages that cloud computing offers, there are several concerns which fundamentally affect the service quality that providers offer to consumers. Some issues such as trust and security are defined as obstacles to the implementation of services delivered by the cloud computing provider [18]. Although the information related to QoS indicators present in the Service Level Agreement (SLA) is crucial to establishing contracts it is not enough to establish a trust relationship between the provider and the consumer [13], which in the context of VO and CC integration, the QoS indicators should be monitored, to ensure trust in VO's operation phase. Thus, in order to enhance the quality of the supporting mechanisms for trusting between the entities involved in the VO creation in a CC environment, it is necessary to develop a confidence indicator that can be automatically used by the business partners to make available their services through the resources provided by the cloud computing paradigm.

Particularly, during the several processes of a VO, this confidence indicator can be monitored and updated periodically allowing to identify whether a cloud computing provider continues meeting the needs of trusting regarding the established requirements by the collaboration opportunity. A reputation system using this confidence indicator can support and feed the whole trusting system [19].

2.3 Trust and Reputation

The trust concept originates from the social sciences, responsible for the study of the dynamic behavior of human society. Trust is a multidisciplinary concept, studied and applied in psychology, sociology, economics and technology. Psychologists study the trust as a mental attitude and brain behavior when the person trust or distrust someone. Sociologists claim that trust is the social relationship between people [20].

In the information technology area, the trust management problem was introduced by Blaze [21] defined it is and as a collective study of security policies, credentials and trust relationships. The Blaze's approach has resulted in a system, called PolicyMaker that manages and controls access to distributed environments. This system have leveraged several approaches to trust management applied to technological concepts such as e-business environments (Business to Business (B2B), Consumer to Consumer (C2C), Business to Consumer (B2C)), P2P (Peer-to-Peer) and collaborative networks (virtual enterprises) [5, 22, 23].

In addition to multidisciplinary, trust is also a complex concept that has no universally accepted definition. Each scientific area seems to have its own definition. In general, trust can be usually related with levels of confidence in something or someone. Therefore, when dealing with cloud computing paradigm, we can define trust as the level of confidence when using the services provided by the cloud service provider, from the consumer perspective [24]. It is worth noting that, in this work the cloud consumer perspective is associate with the companies that form a VO using cloud providers to host their services. Also, it is important to mention that other factors affect the trust of a cloud computing provider, quite often related to mechanisms for protect the user data and unauthorized access. Such factors can be summarized in: security, privacy, accountability and auditability [25]. With the purpose of assisting the trust in a cloud computing environment and other online services the reputation concept can be applied.

The reputation is closely related to the trust. Reputation can be defined as a set of feedback (comments) about the past behavior of the participants of a community, helping in the selection of virtual partners that are considered honest in the real world [26]. The reputation in VO context can be defined as a perception that each business partner has on each member of the VO. The perception is enhanced and developed based on past interactions and objective indicators used to evaluate the collaborative process. The reputation can be seen as a numerical value a participant A refers to a participant B. Thus, when considering that there is no past transactions, reputation may initially be defined as the value of the confidence indicator in the cloud computing provider.

2.4 Multiple Criteria Decision Analysis (MCDA)

Methods of multi-criteria decision-making have emerged as an important ally for solving problems presented by scientific, logistics, engineering and industrial areas. The MCDA can be defined as a collection of methods for matching, classifying and selecting multiple alternatives having multiple attributes whose application depends on the construction of a matrix called assessment matrix or payoff and can also be called scoreboard [27].

The Multiple Criteria Decision Analysis methods can be subdivided into two categories: Multiattribute Utility Theory (MAUT) and Outranking Methods. The MAUT looks for a function that reflects the usefulness of a particular alternative, where each action is assimilated with a level of utility, where the real number represents a preference level of such action. The outranking methods decide which alternative is most appropriate through a pairwise comparison [28].

Among the various MCDA methods presented in Velasquez and Hester [29], the Data Envelopment Analysis method (DEA) will be used because it is capable of handling multiple indicators as cloud providers inputs and outputs and the efficiency of this providers can be quantified and analyzed. DEA is a linear mathematical programming technique for production monitoring, which takes a group of companies and its production indicators (input and output) to assess the productive efficiency of each company decision unit (DMU). Furthermore, it focuses on measuring the efficiency of multiple DMUs in a multiple input and output units environment [30]. The Banker, Charnes and Cooper Data Envelopment Analysis (BCC-DEA) model was designed to measure the efficiency of units with variable returns to scale, i.e., increasing the input values of a unit does not affect proportionally the output values [31]. For this reason, the Banker, Charnes and Cooper (BCC) model is suitable for the problem in question and also to the proposed confidence indicator generation model presented in Sect. 3.

Unlike other usual methods to assess confidence, our approach uses DEA method because we claim the existence of a connection between efficiency and confidence.

3 The Proposed Model

Currently, cloud providers with similar characteristics and different prices have been emerging, eventually due to the competitiveness in the market [8]. In addition, given the diversity of services offered by cloud computing providers, there is a challenge for consumers and, particularly, to the VO Manager, to select a reliable cloud computing provider thereby not causing problems during VO operation. Thus, the proposed confidence indicator can assist the decision making process regarding the search and selection as well as other steps of the VO life cycle.

For this purpose, in the proposed model, Data Envelopment Analysis (DEA) is used to compose a confidence indicator that can be used as a criterion to support VO's manager decisions. Performance indicators that represent Quality of Service will be used for composing the confidence indicator. These indicators belonging to the cloud computing providers will be applied to DEA, which will generate an efficiency level. This efficiency level is reported as the confidence level of that cloud provider. Therefore, the proposed method associates confidence with the Quality of Service delivered by the cloud computing providers.

The rationale relating these concepts is summarized as the higher the efficiency of a cloud provider, the lower the possibility of offering a service that cannot be trusted, given that quality of service indicators will be used, the confidence is related to the quality of service provided by cloud provider. Thus, a high confidence level represents a greater probability of service does not fail, during the VO's operation stage. If the service provided by a cloud computing provider does not attend the need required by the VO's manager, this provider will be replaced preventing issues during the collaboration opportunity attendance.

Figure 1 depicts the proposed model. The proposed model consists of the following components:

- **Cloud Service Providers (CSP)**: Cloud computing providers that are input to the proposed model based on Quality of Service (QoS) indicators;
- **Service Directory**: Component responsible for the list of potential candidates as well as the association with the indicators to be used for classification;
- **KPIs**: Quality of Service indicators of the candidates;
- **DEA**: linear programming technique which calculates the level of efficiency through candidate KPIs;
- **Confidence Indicator**: The result of the application of the inputs in the DEA method is a confidence indicator of the cloud computing provider. This indicator can be integrated to the subprocesses present in the VO's creation phase, such as the search and selection step [6]. In that subprocess, the VO manager needs to select a reliable cloud computing provider for the business partner to make available its service in the cloud environment and thus compose the VO. We also foreseen that in addition to providing support in the VO creation phase, the confidence indicator

can be applied in the VO operation phase, where through a reputation system, it is possible to check if the confidence level of a cloud provider is maintained at an acceptable limit, allowing to perform the providers' change (VO evolution phase) in case the confidence level drops below that limit.

In order to explain the proposed model, Sect. 3.1 presents the Quality of Service indicators used as input and finally, Sect. 3.2 details DEA method.

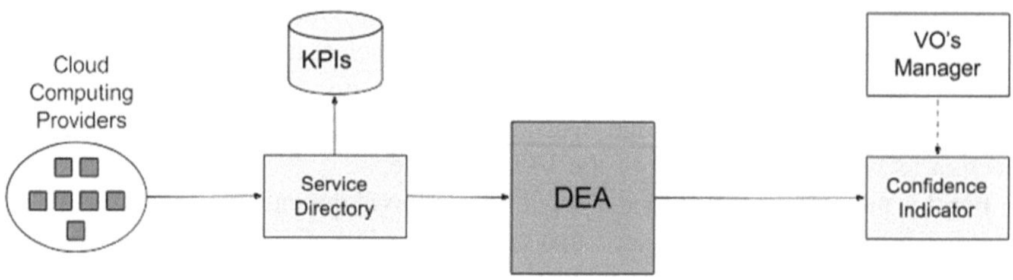

Fig. 1. The proposed model for the confidence indicator generation

3.1 Key Performance Indicators (KPIs)

Cloud computing providers can be evaluated using qualitative and quantitative indicators. Qualitative indicators are directly related to the user experience about a service provided. Quantitative indicators can be measured through hardware and software monitoring tools [8].

In order to calculate the confidence level to identify the most suitable service to the user, according to Tang et al. [13] the QoS properties are exploited, which are a set of non-functional attributes of services such as response time, stability, availability, security, etc. [8], and these attributes are applicable to all cloud computing service models.

The indicators that will be used to generate a confidence level of a cloud provider are presented in [8, 9]:

- **Response Time:** In the case of services provided in IaaS model, the response time refers to the time that a service is available for use. For instance, the user requests a virtual machine (VM) to the provider, the time is calculated from the moment of the VM creation until it is available for use.
- **Stability:** The stability of a service is defined as the variance in service performance. According to Garg et al. [8], for cloud storage service, stability is the variance in average time of read and write operations. For computational resources, it is the deviation of performance level specified in SLA, i.e., $\sum_{i=1}^{n} \frac{\frac{\rho_{avg.i} - \rho_{sla.i}}{T}}{n}$, where ρ is defined as resource unit (network, storage or computational resource); $\rho_{avg.i}$ is the monitored average performance of the cloud service leased by user i; $\rho_{sla.i}$ is the promised values in SLA; T is the service time and n is the total number of users;
- **Security:** The security level of a service is a major concerning factor for the protection of security and privacy. It is a qualitative indicator evaluated by service user, which is defined by a numerical value on a scale of 1 to 10;

- **Availability:** It represents the fraction of the time that the service is available to attend requests. Configured as a percentage of service access, given by $\frac{\text{total service time} - \text{total service time unavailable}}{\text{total service time}}$.
- **Cost:** Depends on two attributes: acquisition and on-going. Acquisition cost is used for SaaS services where users sign a service, paying monthly, weekly, among others forms. On-going cost refers to cost of resource usage (cpu, ram, bandwidth or storage) in a unit of time. However, in IaaS providers, cost can be defined as the amount charged for the time granted to use the resources of a VM.

3.2 DEA Application

Considering the number of service providers such as n (candidates with their level of confidence to be calculated) and the performance indicators used to evaluate the services, this section present the mathematical model used to calculate the confidence ratio.

Each cloud computing provider is modeled as a Decision Making Unit (DMU). The confidence measure takes into consideration the ratio between the input and output data set, where each input and output is multiplied by its corresponding weight.

Considering that the purpose of this model is the generation of the confidence indicator for cloud computing providers, the input data set corresponds to the Quality of Service indicators (response time, availability, security and stability) and the output data set is defined by the cost indicator. Therefore, we can define confidence as:

$$z_0 = \sum_{i=1}^{m} v_{i0} \times X_{i0} + v \tag{1}$$

Subject to,

$$\sum_{j=1}^{s} \mathrm{u}_{j0} \times \mathrm{Y}_{j0} = 1 \tag{2}$$

$$\sum_{i=1}^{m} v_{ik} X_{ik} - \sum_{j=1}^{s} u_{jk} Y_{jk} + v \geq 0 \qquad k = \{1, 2, 3, \ldots, n\} \tag{3}$$

$$u_j, v_i \geq 0 \,\forall \quad j = 1, \ldots, s \quad i = 1, \ldots, m \tag{4}$$

Where X_{ik} and Y_{jk} are the input i and output j of the DMU k respectively, v_i and u_j are the weights; v is a real scale factor; n are the number of cloud computing providers (DMUs);m and s, are the total number of input and output indicators, respectively.

Equation 2 sets that the sum of weights multiplied to the value of the output indicator must be equal to 1 due to the BCC-DEA model transformation of fractional to linear, in which confidence value is inversely proportional to output. Inequality 3 defines the confidence value must be positive. Inequality 4 defines the weight of inputs and outputs must be strictly positive. Using the classic BCC-DEA model, the real scale factor in this case is not considered because it determines a return on the production if it is increasing, decreasing or constant to a set of inputs and outputs [32]. Therefore, once calculated the weights, the Eq. 5 results the confidence level of the Cloud Computing Provider o:

$$Confidence_o = \frac{\sum_{j=1}^{s} u_{j0} \times Y_{j0}}{\sum_{i=1}^{m} v_{i0} \times X_{i0} + v} \tag{5}$$

4 Results

In this Section, the computation of cloud computing providers confidence indicator has been evaluated using QoS indicators of real public service providers: Amazon, RackSpace and Microsoft Azure, available at [8] and used to validate the classification method of cloud computing providers using a MCDA method.

Considering the indicators cited in Sect. 3.1, Table 1 presents data related to services offered by the following cloud computing providers: Amazon EC2 (CSP1), Rackspace (CSP2) and Azure (CSP3), with their respective values of Quality of Service indicators, weight values related to each indicator for cloud service provider.

Table 1. Offered services, their quality of service indicators and relative weight

KPIs	CSP1	W(1)	CSP2	W(2)	CSP3	W(3)
Response time	100 ms	0,05	600 ms	0,05	30 ms	0,05
Stability	38,5	0,02	43	0,02	49	0,02
Security	4	0,05	8	0,05	4	0,05
Availability	99.95 %	0,7	99,99 %	0,7	100 %	0,7
Cost	$ 0.68	1,47	$ 0.96	1,04	$ 0.96	1,04

The relative weights regarding input and output data sets coping with DEA must be set to define the preferences of the entity responsible for taking decisions regarding the indicators. In other words, weights should be as greater as they are judged as more relevant in the confidence analysis of the DMU. Therefore, only the weight of the cost indicator was set aiming to attend the restriction imposed by the Equality 02 present in the problem formulation and the other weights are randomly assigned to each QoS service attribute.

The application of the indicators in DEA method, returns for each cloud computing provider, the confidence level value related to presented indicators. In Table 2 are presented the results for the method application for each cloud computing provider.

Table 2. Confidence indicator for the presented cloud computing providers

Cloud computing providers	Confidence indicator
Amazon EC2 (CSP1)	14,49 %
Rackspace (CSP2)	3,13 %
Azure (CSP3)	29,54 %

According the presented results it is possible to note that a higher value for response time associated with others indicators which represents Quality of Service, cause a decrease in the confidence level.

Considering the VO's and cloud computing integration, where it is necessary to attend a collaboration opportunity, higher response time associated with lower stability of the service provided by the cloud provider, can become issues during the VO's operation. These issues fundamentally affect the collaboration, when it is necessary to respond quickly to a collaboration opportunity in order to follow the market competitiveness.

Moreover, based on the generated confidence indicator, the VO's manager can establish an acceptable confidence limit and then select the most reliable cloud computing provider to host the VO's members services,

5 Conclusion and Future Work

This article presents a model to generate a confidence indicator for cloud computing providers based on Key Performance Indicators comprising Quality of Service measures. Also, this model can be adapted to several scenarios that do not use cloud computing providers, just changing the indicators' set. The generation of this confidence indicator is driven by the problem observed during the subprocesses of VO's life cycle, where is necessary the establishment of confidence between involved members, so that the confidence is a crucial factor in VO and Cloud Computing integration.

The presented results show that the proposed method has the potential to generate a confidence indicator that can support cloud computing providers' selection in the VO creation stage. The VO's manager can see which cloud computing providers are most reliable and appropriate to integrate VO, based on generated confidence indicator from Quality of Service values. Furthermore, the proposed method can be customized by adding more indicators to compose the confidence indicator. Also, the VO's manager can choose weight values, giving priority to the desired indicators for every VO Collaboration Opportunity.

In a further work, we intend to integrate this confidence indicator model in a reputation architecture, composed of a reputation system that will carry out the monitoring and evaluation of each entity present in the Virtual Organization composed by services host in cloud providers. Also, it is intended to investigate how this reputed confidence indicator can support the Virtual Organization Manager in the several stages of VO's life cycle.

References

1. Esposito, E., Evangelista, P.: Investigating virtual enterprise models: literature review and empirical findings. Int. J. Prod. Econ. **148**, 145–157 (2014)
2. Camarinha-Matos, L.M., Afsarmanesh, H., Galeano, N., Molina, A.: Collaborative networked organizations – concepts and practice in manufacturing enterprises. Comput. Ind. Eng. **57**, 46–60 (2009)
3. de Lemos, F.S.B., Fiorese, A., Alves, O.C., Vieira Jr., R.G.: Using data envelopment analysis and fuzzy logic as intelligent risk-based decision making support for virtual organizations. Intell. Syst. Ref. Libr. **87**, 203–218 (2015)
4. Camarinha-Matos, L.M., Afsarmanesh, H.: The virtual enterprise concept. In: Camarinha-Matos, L.M., Afsarmanesh, H. (eds.) Infrastructures Virtual Enterprise, vol. 27, pp. 3–14. Springer, Heidelberg (1999)
5. Winkler, T.J., Haller, J., Gimpel, H., Weinhardt, C.: Trust indicator modeling for a reputation service in virtual organizations. In: Proceedings of the ECIS 2007, pp. 1584–1595 (2007)
6. Squicciarini, A.C., Paci, F., Bertino, E.: Trust establishment in the formation of virtual organizations. Comput. Stand. Interfaces **33**, 13–23 (2011)
7. Vieira, R.G., Alves-Junior, O.C., Rabelo, R.J., Fiorese, A.: A risk analysis method to support virtual organization partners' selection. Presented at the (2014)
8. Garg, S.K., Versteeg, S., Buyya, R.: A framework for ranking of cloud computing services. Futur. Gener. Comput. Syst. **29**, 1012–1023 (2013)
9. Sun, M., Zang, T., Xu, X., Wang, R.: Consumer-centered cloud services selection using AHP. In: 2013 International Conference on Service Sciences (ICSS), pp. 1–6 (2013)
10. Junior, O.C.A., Rabelo, R.J.: A KPI model for logistics partners' search and suggestion to create virtual organisations. Int. J. Netw. Virtual Organ. **12**, 149–177 (2013)
11. Sadigh, B.L., Arikan, F., Ozbayoglu, M., Unver, H.O., Kilic, S.E.: A multi-agent system model for partner selection process in virtual enterprise. Procedia Comput. Sci. **36**, 367–372 (2014)
12. Zhao, Q., Zhang, X., Xiao, R.: Particle swarm optimization algorithm for partner selection in virtual enterprise. Prog. Nat. Sci. **18**, 1445–1452 (2008)
13. Tang, M., Dai, X., Liu, J., Chen, J.: Towards a trust evaluation middleware for cloud service selection. Futur. Gener. Comput., Syst (2016)
14. Noor, T.H., Sheng, Q.Z., Ngu, A.H.H., Alfazi, A., Law, J.: Cloud armor: a platform for credibility-based trust management of cloud services. In: Proceedings of the 22nd ACM International Conference Information and Knowledge Management, pp. 2509–2512 (2013)
15. Yau, S.S., Yin, Y.: QoS-based service ranking and selection for service-based systems. In: Proceedings of the 2011 IEEE International Conference on Services Computing, SCC 2011, pp. 56–63 (2011)
16. Liu, X., Fletcher, K.K., Tang, M.: Service selection based on personalized preference and trade-offs among QoS factors and price. In: Proceedings of the 2012 IEEE First International Conference on Services Economics, SE 2012, pp. 32–39 (2012)
17. Mell, P.M., Grance, T.: SP 800-145. The NIST Definition of Cloud Computing. National Institute of Standards & Technology, Gaithersburg, MD, United States (2011)
18. Hwang, K., Li, D.: Trusted cloud computing with secure resources and data coloring. IEEE Internet Comput. **14**, 14–22 (2010)
19. Mashayekhy, L., Grosu, D.: A reputation-based mechanism for dynamic virtual organization formation in grids. In: Proceedings of the International Conference Parallel Process, pp. 108–117 (2012)

20. Cho, J.-H., Swami, A., Chen, I.-R.: A survey on trust management for mobile ad hoc networks. IEEE Commun. Surv. Tutor. **13**, 562–583 (2011)
21. Blaze, M., Feigenbaum, J., Lacy, J.: Decentralized trust management. In: 1996 IEEE Symposium on Security and Privacy, pp. 164–173 (1996)
22. Kerschbaum, F., Haller, J., Karabulut, Y., Robinson, P.: PathTrust: a trust-based reputation service for virtual organization formation. In: Stølen, K., Winsborough, W.H., Martinelli, F., Massacci, F. (eds.) iTrust 2006. LNCS, vol. 3986, pp. 193–205. Springer, Heidelberg (2006)
23. Resnick, P., Zeckhauser, R.: Trust among strangers in internet transactions: empirical analysis of eBay's reputation system. In: Baye, M.R. (ed.) The Economics of the Internet and E-Commerce. Advances in Applied Microeconomics, vol. 11, pp. 127–157. Elsevier Science, Amsterdam (2002)
24. Ko, R.K.L., Jagadpramana, P., Mowbray, M., Pearson, S., Kirchberg, M., Liang, Q., Lee, B.S.: TrustCloud: a framework for accountability and trust in cloud computing. In: Proceedings of the 2011 IEEE World Congress on Services, pp. 584–588 (2011)
25. Pearson, S., Benameur, A.: Privacy, Security and Trust Issues Arising from Cloud Computing. In: 2010 IEEE Second International Conference on Cloud Computing Technology and Science, pp. 693–702 (2010)
26. Comput, J.P.D., Hendrikx, F., Bubendorfer, K., Chard, R.: Reputation systems: a survey and taxonomy. J. Parallel Distrib. Comput. **75**, 184–197 (2015)
27. Rehman, Z.U., Hussain, O.K., Hussain, F.K.: Iaas cloud selection using MCDM methods. In: Proceedings of the 2012 IEEE Ninth International Conference on e-Business Engineering, ICEBE 2012, pp. 246–251 (2012)
28. Whaiduzzaman, M., Gani, A., Anuar, N.B., Shiraz, M., Haque, M.N., Haque, I.T.: Cloud service selection using multicriteria decision analysis. Sci. World J. **2014**, 10 (2014)
29. Velasquez, M., Hester, P.: An analysis of multi-criteria decision making methods. Int. J. Oper. Res. **10**, 56–66 (2013)
30. Chen, W.C., Johnson, A.L.: A unified model for detecting efficient and inefficient outliers in data envelopment analysis. Comput. Oper. Res. **37**, 417–425 (2010)
31. Banker, R.D., Charnes, A., Cooper, W.W.: Some models for estimating technical and scale inefficiencies in data envelopment analysis. Manage. Sci. **30**, 1078–1092 (1984)
32. de Souza, L.M., Fernandez, M.P.: Performance evaluation methodology for cloud computing using data envelopment analysis. In: Proceedings of the Fourteenth International Conference on Networks, ICN 2015, pp. 58–64 (2015)

Co-development and Co-working - Operating and Management of Networks

Effects of Decision Synchronization on Trust in Collaborative Networks

Morice Daudi[1(✉)], Jannicke Baalsrud Hauge[2,3], and Klaus-Dieter Thoben[1,2]

[1] International Graduate School for Dynamics in Logistics (IGS), University of Bremen, Bremen, Germany
mdaudi@uni-bremen.de

[2] Bremer Institut für Produktion und Logistik at the University of Bremen, Bremen, Germany
{baa, tho}@biba.uni-bremen.de

[3] School of Technology and Health, KTH, Royal Institute of Technology, Stockholm, Sweden

Abstract. In collaborative networks, individual and organizational entities encounter many disagreements over many decisions rights. These disagreements procreate conflicting preferences, which in turn, affect trustworthy amongst partners. To that end, it becomes necessary that partners assume a degree of fairness on decision rights by calibrating positions which they initially consider a final. This calibration involves synchronizing partners' conflicting preferences to a compromise. The objective of this paper, therefore, is to analyze and evaluate the effect of both, compromised and uncompromised preferences on trust. To achieve this, a corresponding behavioral trust model is proposed and evaluated empirically using a logistics collaboration scenario. This evaluation applies a multi-agent systems simulation method. The simulation involves 360 observations with three preferences set as predictor variables. Results show that irrespective of a degree to which conflicting preferences are synchronized, a magnitude of the generated effect on trust, depends as well on other factors like transport cost and extent to which vehicles are loaded. Additionally, if other factors are kept constant, compromised preferences affects trust more positively than uncompromised ones.

Keywords: Trust · Collaborative networks · Logistics collaboration · Decision synchronization · Conflicting preferences

1 Introduction

In today's world, Collaborative Networks (CNs) are increasingly becoming imperative and widely known about the support they provide to resource sharing. Meanwhile, global entities (partners/actors) are also establishing strong social-graphs, intensifying how critical CNs are. As a crucial requisite, partner relationships in CNs rest on a foundation of trustworthiness, particularly, to contexts where partners interact through socio-technical systems. As socio-technical interaction systems provide required support to CNs, they also raise a difficulty on trust management. This difficult, among

H. Afsarmanesh et al. (Eds.): PRO-VE 2016, IFIP AICT 480, pp. 215–227, 2016.
DOI: 10.1007/978-3-319-45390-3_19

others, is constituted by a lack of physical cues rich in physical interactions systems. As a consequence, uncertainty about an extent to which partners can uncover presumed consistency in their behavioral patterns becomes a challenge. This consistency relates to a degree of reliability by which partners can confidently rely upon one another. Rendering this confidence through "security primitives of Confidentiality, Integrity, and Availability (CIA) of data or information" [1] appears hard. This hardness originates from various angles, including the least ability of CIA protocols to accommodate partner's behaviors in CNs.

Unlike CIA mechanisms which protect computer-network resources by avoiding malicious agents, CNs emphasize on the confident assurance that partners will behave in a prescribed/expected manner. Fulfillment of this requirement includes investigating partner behaviors in the operational phase of CNs. In the operational phase, while interacting, partners exhibit a range of behaviors, which in turn can generate an effect on collaboration. To that end, understanding partner's behavioral uncertainties and the generated effect on network performance and trust are imperative. As much as various behavioral uncertainties exist in CNs, the present paper concentrates on behavioral uncertainty resulting from negotiation and decision making. In particular, the paper addresses behavioral discontents, which according to [2], are set of partners' disagreements over to a particular set of decisions [2]. Such disagreements can procreate conflicts, with the higher possibility to affect underlying trustworthy. Such disagreements are described in [3] as conflicts concerning partner's perspectives or beliefs. This paper refers to such disagreements as *conflicting preferences*.

Conflicting preferences on decision rights can affect network performance and underlying trustworthy differently. Context to resulting outcome, the effect can either strengthen or weakens trustworthy. In particular, a partner who enacts preferences to own interests can end up denying welfare of others. Such preference may have a high chance to decrease trustworthy. As a result, rather than remaining centric to own interests, partners urge to assume a degree of fairness in decision rights. Towards this required fairness, synchronizing partners' conflicting preferences is a necessary. While building on this assumption, unsynchronized decisions, according to [4], appear in forms of behavioral discontents, namely: rivalry and compromise. These discontents are further described in [4] as: (1) *rivalry*, a partner has high concern to own interests coupled with low concern for others' interests (*I win, you lose*); (2) *compromise*, a partner emphasizes on give-and-take bargaining (*we both win a bit and lose a bit*).

Whereas rivalry decisions can largely impede trust, compromised ones can facilitate its growth and sustainability. Therefore, the present paper investigates the effect of decision synchronization on trust. Alongside this objective, a model depicting behavioral trust has to be established as well. To that end, two research questions are specified: (1) *How can behavioral trust be modeled in CN and related domains?* (2) *How do compromised and uncompromised conflicting preferences affect trust in CN?*

The remainder of the paper is organized as follows. Section 2 discusses trust under computational and behavioral perspectives. While Sect. 3 presents research methodology applied by this study, Sect. 4 sheds light on agent preferences and confrontation analysis. In Sect. 5, a behavioral trust model applicable to CNs and related domains, comprising of trust propagation, measurement and assessment is proposed. Section 6 specifies a validation scenario in the domain of logistics collaboration. In Sect. 7, an evaluation consisting of implementation, experiment design, and setup, results and discussions are provided. The paper ends in Sect. 8 by providing conclusion and outlook.

2 Trust: Computational and Behavioral Perspectives

Trust is generally understood as a degree of confidence agent X develops in agent Y, while believing that Y will behave in ways X expects. Even though, this understanding is made contextual specific depending on application domain and discipline. In psychology, trust is conceptualized a psychological state comprising an intention to accept vulnerabilities [5]. In social relational exchanges, trust has a form of reputation aimed to deny betrayal aversion. In economics trust is associated with rational choices against risks aversions. Moreover, in computer science and engineering trust is categorized in groups of "system and user" [6]. System trust (hard-trust) addresses relationships among machine nodes, to protect computational systems according to CIA primitives. User trust (soft-trust) concerns a level of confidence trustor-agent has in numerous objects it interact and collaborate with. These objects are like machines, software-agents, humans, and organizations. In essence, user trust is conceived on a behavioral foundation of social, economic, and psychological primitives.

Trust requirements in CNs can largely be founded on social and economic behavioral primitives, with an attempt to reduce uncertainties and resulting vulnerabilities. Adding to these primitives, trust challenges in CNs stem from consortia structure. Structure-wise, CNs consortia are largely dynamic, sometimes engaging actors who are strangers, and configured in the partially seamlessly environment. Within these settings, there can rise a high possibility that partners exhibit behavioral inconsistencies. Such behavioral inconsistencies, can be related but not limited to how: agents share information; divide gains and costs; synchronize, both compatible and incompatible preferences (positions in decision rights); and deviate from goal congruence (opportunism). The present paper, however, concentrates on conflicting (incompatible) preferences.

3 Research Methodology

Investigation of decision synchronization applies a Multi-Agent Systems (MAS) as the main method, compared to the survey, normal experiments, and case study. On the one hand, the survey appears inappropriate due lack of a process (physical reality) and longitudinal observations. Normal experiments deny social-virtual environments in computational settings while case study might be expensive in terms of resources. On the other hand, relatively, usage of MAS achieves intended purpose. The MAS deploys social structures in computational settings while maximizing process and time under virtual reality.

Therefore, applied methodology follows this sequence. First, an approach to model conflicting preferences, especially those preferences resulting in a mode of conflict is discussed (Sect. 4). Secondly, a model of behavioral trust which integrates CNs life cycle, the definition of trust, and the analogy of human trust propagation is conceived (Sect. 5). To empirically evaluate and validate the model, and also forecast the effect of decision synchronization on trust, the MAS is used. Through MAS, a logistics collaboration scenario is conceived using Agent-Based Modeling (ABM) technique. The collaboration scenario evaluated by using a "PlaSMA Platform" [7]. PlaSMA is an event-driven simulation system which has been designed to solve and evaluate scenarios of the logistics domain[1].

4 Agent Preferences: Confrontation Analysis

It is common that agents engage in numerous relationships and dependencies, some of which ending up in dilemmas. Each singleton dilemma involves specific character behavior from participating agents. Highlighted in [8], agents face dilemmas at a point when each agent takes a position that it regards as final, called a *moment of truth*. The positions can be compatible (collaboration mode) or incompatible (conflict mode) [8, 9]. If positions are compatible collaboration proceeds. If they are incompatible, agents negotiate by synchronizing (calibrating) positions in their conflicting preferences. Although agents get into negotiation, it is not mandatory that always they end up into a compromise. Works in [8–11] address six dilemmas, two belonging to collaboration mode and the rest belonging to conflict mode. Collaboration mode is constituted by dilemmas of cooperation and trust; while the conflict mode is constituted by dilemmas of positioning, persuasion, rejection, and threat.

Whereas CNs comprehend on dilemmas of collaboration mode, in some situations, disagreements over the domain of decisions need to be compromised prior advancing to next stage. For example, in a collaboration between shipper and receiver, the shipper may prefer producing in fixed quantities while receiver prefers a production which is consistent with market demand. Such disagreement represents a conflict mode that must be responded to. To any occurring dilemma, according to [9], a character may respond in four ways: (1) by changing its position; (2) by amending its preferences for the possible outcomes; (3) by denying that the dilemmas exist, or; (4) by taking irreversible unilateral action. This study builds on the second and third responses and advances on dilemmas of persuasion and rejection respectively.

5 Modeling of Behavioral Trust

A proposed behavioral trust model (Fig. 1) is developed by conceiving an analogy of human trusting process, propagating in three stages: *intention, action,* and *reality*. This propagation conforms to a trust building framework in [12], generic understandability of trust, and trust definition in [13]. The human-agent trusting process begins by initiating an intention to trust, that depends on contextual characteristics. Upon satisfying this intention, human-agent engages in action to trust. The action to trust involves

[1] http://plasma.informatik.uni-bremen.de/.

establishing an expectation, corresponding to a degree of confidence human-agent develops in an object it desires to trust. The reality is a final stage in which a trust transaction become executed, providing human-agent a feedback through comparing expectation versus an outcome. In particular, the model is conceived by formalizing a dependency between two agents: *X* a trustor agent, and *Y* a trustee agent, although this relationship is symmetric. Moreover, as trust can be embedded within trustor or trustee, concordant to [12], conception draws on trust embedded within trustee.

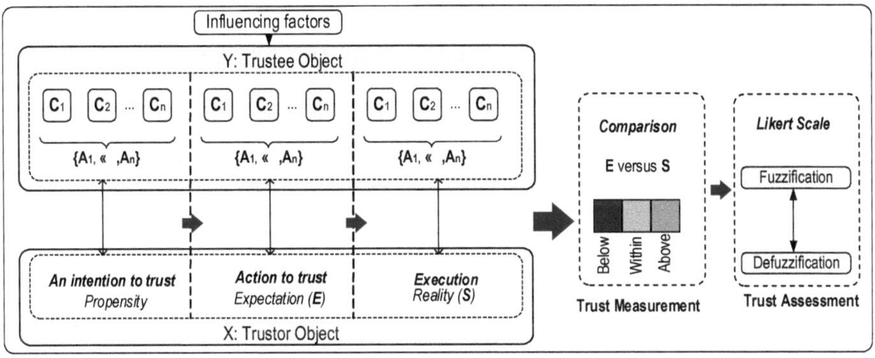

Fig. 1. Behavioral trust model

Under an intention to trust, X initializes its propensity to trust Y. Depending on preferred characteristics and a degree to which are fulfilled, X can commit its propensity to trust. If however, conflicting preferences arise, X and Y negotiate seeking a compromise. On passing the intention to trust, X propagates to an action to trust. In this stage, X utilizes existing factual data from Y to develop a degree to which it can trust Y (*expectation*). This expectation forms a level of confidence, assurance or reliability which X develops in Y. Alongside its decision, X can: (1) accept being vulnerable to Y's actions, or; (2) withdraw its action to trust if the payoff is perceived unsatisfactory. If X accepts vulnerabilities, for each underlying performance indicator, it specifies its range of expectation. Upon proceeding to reality stage, X loses control in hands of Y (during execution). Hereby, a transaction is executed and resulting outcome observed. Afterward, X measures trust (effect) by comparing resulting outcome to expectation it developed. In measuring and assessing trust, a specific level of trust is determined to depend on trust meter. For example, on applying a three scale meter, the outcome can be *below*, *within*, or *above* expectation.

6 Logistics Collaboration: A Validation Scenario

Validation of the behavioral trust model employs a collaboration scenario in logistics. The scenario is preceded by requirements definition as well as conceiving agents' interactive negotiations.

6.1 Collaboration Requirements

Logistics collaboration, among others, seeks to increase asset utilization, reduce costs, and improve customer services and efficiency. While exploiting these goals, confrontational preferences concerning issues like production, distribution and demand of goods can affect underlying trustworthy. As long as such preferences remain uncompromised, they threaten collaboration future, leading to the uncertain and vulnerable outcome. Although many preferences affect trust in logistics collaboration [14], this study concentrates on three preferences (Table 1); where shipper, carrier and receiver are collaborating agents. Shipper represents manufacturers, suppliers, sellers and individuals. Carrier agent represents transporters, moving goods to receivers. Receiver agent represents retailers, distributors, buyers, and end consumers. The three preferences are described as follows. Shipper prefers producing goods in fixed quantities (P1). Equally, carrier perceives delivering goods in fixed quantities (P2), and; full truck (P3). Each preference has a threatened future (conflict) to be synchronized to a compromise or rejection.

Table 1. A matrix of conflicting preferences and threatened future (adapted from [3])

Agent options	Positions			Threatened future
	Shipper	Receiver	Carrier	
Shipper – P_1	Fixed production quantities	Consistent with demand	Both options	Fixed production quantities
Carrier – P_2	Consistent with demand	Consistent with demand	Fixed delivery quantities	Fixed delivery quantities
Carrier – P_3	Both options	Both options	Full truck	Full truck

6.2 Agents' Interactions and Negotiations

Agent-Based Modeling (ABM) is applied to model, understand and prognosticate behavioral effect resulting from agents' decision synchronization in logistics collaboration. The ABM method is preferred because of its ability to capture emergent phenomena, and provide a natural description of a system [15]. Correspondingly, building on both, weak and strong agent notions as discerned in [16], collaborating agents are conceived autonomous, reactive, adaptive, with the ability to act socially. This implies, shipper, carrier, and receiver are limited to information related to planning and forecast of production, carriage and demand. As such they learn from previous experience, trying to match similar prospects. Moreover, each agent possesses objectives together with possible constraints. Among the constraints are conflicting preferences (Table 1). As such, shipper focuses on minimizing backorders and inventory, receiver focuses on increasing saving on transportation costs, and carrier seeks to maximize full truck.

While the behavioral description of the collaboration scenario (Fig. 2) draws from previous work in [14], its respective modeling proceeds as follows. A broker-agent invites shippers, carriers, and receivers (participants) by issuing a *Call For Proposal* (CFP).

In its CFP, broker-agent set required specificity, including an estimated number of pallets to be produced and demanded/consumed, and required carriage capacity. Upon receiving CFP, each participant performs own internal assessment on its capability to fulfill CFP requirements. Afterward, each participant replies to broker-agent by proposing or reject the CFP. If rejected, the CFP is brought to an end. If proposed, each participant sends a proposal reply to broker-agent. In turn, broker-agent assess the proposal against established specificity. Depending on assessment outcome (satisfactory specificity), broker-agent either accepts, adjusts or rejects the proposal. If found satisfactory, broker-agent engage participants in forecasting their orders, compromise conflicting preferences as well as developing expectations. Finally, during the execution of orders, goods are moved by the carrier from shipper to receiver. Along this execution, actions of each participant are observed subsequent to recording actual score (reality).

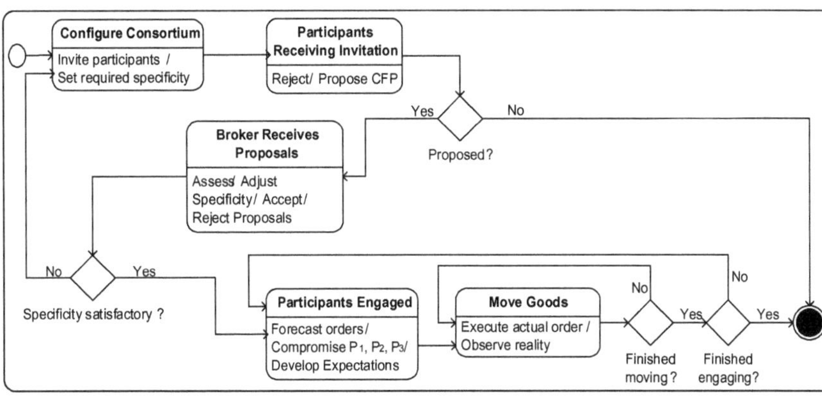

Fig. 2. Generic behavioral descriptions of agents in logistics collaboration

Specific to conflicting preferences, during negotiation, for each preference an agent takes a position that may differ to that of others, resulting in disagreements. These disagreements lead to a threatened future of a specific preference. To compromise disagreements, three alternatives exist *acceptance*, *persuasion*, and *rejection*. The acceptance alternative occurs if rival agents see that the threatened future is attractive. In this case, the preference changes to collaboration mode of a dilemma (cooperation or trust), thus, disqualified to constitute disagreements. If however the threatened future is unaccepted, the respective agent engages in persuading other agents to its position or reject the existence of the threat. The persuasion of the threatened future goes along with a provision of incentives to rivals, together with a promise that the agent whose future is threatened will act trustworthily (Table 2). Finally, if a threat is rejected, collaboration proceeds with a condition that associated vulnerabilities, if they occur, will bear a penalty to the agent which rejected the existence of that threat. Table 2 summarizes exemplified incentives as well as award and penalty to a persuaded and rejected preference.

Table 2. A matrix of preferences, award and penalty

Preference	Persuasion	Rejection
P_1	Pay receiver 10 % per pallet in case of backorder, and promise to be trustworthy	Charge 10 % per pallet as storage cost in case of inventory
P_2	Lower transportation cost by 10 % per pallet, and promise to be trustworthy	Charge extra 10 % of transportation cost per pallet
P_3	Lower transportation cost by 10 % per pallet, and promise to be trustworthy	Charge extra 10 % of transportation cost per pallet

7 Evaluation

This section details an assessment of applicability, usefulness and conceptual validity of the behavioral trust model. Secondly, it examines effect, compromised and uncompromised conflicting preferences generate on trust. Accordingly, details of implementation (Subsect. 7.1), experiment design and setup (Subsect. 7.2), experiment results (Subsect. 7.3), and discussions (Subsect. 7.4) are presented.

7.1 Implementation

A simulation prototype is set a centralized network configured and managed by a neutral trustee (broker). It comprises of 2 carriers, 6 shippers, and 6 receivers. All agents including the broker, exchange messages structured according to FIPA standards [17] using logistics collaboration ontology. The protocol type of negotiation is adapted from [18], such that owner of a preference whose future is threatened has to propose a persuasion which can either be accepted or rejected. Furthermore, all participating agents, upon being initialized, they register in a directory facilitator named as "collaboration", that provides yellow page services. Collaboration begins only when it is activated by the broker agent. The broker agent monitors collaboration by managing parameters exchanged, and it measures and evaluates trust levels.

7.2 Experiment Design and Setup

To examine the effect of decision synchronization on trust, MAS simulation experiment is designed as follows. Three predictor variables (P_1, P_2, and P_3), with each predictor having two levels (Persuasion, Rejection) are designed to affect response variables. The experiment employs two response variables: transportation cost and full truck. The response variables are used to determine the internal-oriented performance of logistics collaboration, and subsequently, the trust level. Moreover, while each experiment yields 6 observations, the same experiment is replicated 6 times to estimate experimental errors. Thus, 10 experiments are conducted, leading to 360 ($6 \times 6 \times 10$) observations.

The experiment setup involves three events, three experimental unit, generation of random numbers, as well as distinct approaches to verify the model. The events comprise changes in collaboration lifecycle: from planning to forecast, and finally to operation. The planning, forecast, and operation stages correspond to periods of one month, one week, and six days respectively. In view of experimental units, the setup employs shipper, carrier, and receiver. Additionally, various techniques including the use of trace and checking of simulation outputs for their reasonableness are applied to verify behavioral trust model. As the simulation uses randomly generated data, a care is taken on seed generation to assure that generated numbers do not affect final conclusion. To fulfill this requirement, linear-congruential generators are used. Furthermore, to verify that generated numbers are uniformly distributed, generated numbers are scrutinized by chi-square test. Uniquely, each predictor level is assigned own seed value to avoid wrong correlation. Finally, a confidence interval statistical technique is applied to determine conceptual validity of the behavioral trust model.

7.3 Experiment Results

Results obtained by conducting MAS simulation experiments are summarized in Table 3. In these results, preferences were combined in a form or code of ABC by using notations "P" and "R". Notations P and R denoted a persuaded and rejected preferences respectively. Similarly, the ABC combination corresponded to preferences P_1, P_2, and P_3 respectively. As an illustration, a combination PPR means shipper's preference (P_1) was persuaded, carrier's preference (P_2) was persuaded, while carrier's preference (P_3) was rejected.

Measurement and assessment of trust level applied parameters of cost saving and full truck. In particular, cost saving (reduction in transport costs) was benchmarked to a 15 % per pallet as remarked in [19]. Equally, an extent to which a truck is filled was benchmarked to a 95 % as remarked in [20]. That is, a truck is considered full if it is loaded to over 95 % of its capacity. Following these benchmarks, transportation cost and full truck were operationalized as follows. That, agent, develops an expectation of 15 % of cost saving on transportation cost and a 95 % of a full truck. Upon comparing these expectations and corresponding scores, one among the following outcomes occurred: (1) less than expectation, which implied "*less trustworthy*" with a trust level of 1; (2) very close to expectation, which implied "*trustworthy*" with a trust level of 2, and; (3) above the expectation, which implied "*more trustworthy*" with a trust level of 3. In addition, since there were two performance criteria (cost saving and full truck), corresponding trust levels were aggregated by using the mean average. Due to this aggregation, some results generated a trust level of 2.5 and were marked with an asterisk (*) (Table 3).

Alongside these results, and on top of verification approaches used, the study achieves a 95 % accuracy in determining model's validity as well as generated results (Table 4). Additionally, overall mean trust level of 1.890 is observed.

Table 3. A summary of results on synchronized preferences on performance and trust level

S/N	Combined preferences	Frequency	Cost saving	Full truck	Trust level
1	PPR	23	Less than 15 %	Less than 95 %	Less trustworthy
2	PRP	12	Less than 15 %	Less than 95 %	Less trustworthy
3	PRR	8	Less than 15 %	Less than 95 %	Less trustworthy
4	RPP	27	Less than 15 %	Less than 95 %	Less trustworthy
5	RPR	19	Less than 15 %	Less than 95 %	Less trustworthy
6	RRP	16	Less than 15 %	Less than 95 %	Less trustworthy
7	RRR	30	Less than 15 %	Less than 95 %	Less trustworthy
8	PPP	14	Above 15 %	Less than 95 %	Trustworthy
9	PPR	1	Within 15 %	Above 95 %	Trustworthy*
10	PRP	1	Within 15 %	Above 95 %	Trustworthy*
11	PRR	15	Less than 15 %	Above 95 %	Trustworthy
12	RPP	15	Above 15 %	Less than 95 %	Trustworthy
13	RPR	2	Within 15 %	Within 95 %	Trustworthy
14	RRR	36	Less than 15 %	Above 95 %	Trustworthy
15	PPR	18	Within 15 %	Above 95 %	Trustworthy*
16	PRP	17	Above 15 %	Above 95 %	More trustworthy
17	RPP	2	Within 15 %	Above 95 %	Trustworthy*
18	RPR	30	Within 15 %	Above 95 %	Trustworthy*
19	RRP	22	Within 15 %	Above 95 %	Trustworthy*
20	RPP	32	Above 15 %	Above 95 %	More trustworthy
21	PPP	20	Above 15 %	Above 95 %	More trustworthy

Less trustworthy = 1; Trustworthy = 2; Trustworthy = 2.5; More trustworthy = 3*

Table 4. A 95 % CI for 36 observations in each experiment

	Exp. 1	Exp. 2	Exp. 3	Exp. 4	Exp. 5	Exp. 6	Exp. 7	Exp. 8	Exp. 9	Exp. 10
Lower	1.46	1.70	1.60	1.47	1.52	1.90	1.79	1.73	1.75	1.58
Upper	1.96	2.14	2.18	1.90	1.98	2.32	2.29	2.24	2.22	2.09

7.4 Discussions

This research has focused on designing a behavioral trust model, and determine how compromised and uncompromised conflicting preferences affect trust. Concerning modeling of behavioral trust, the analysis indicates that confidence intervals overlap considerably to an extent that mean of each experiment falls in the intervals of others. In addition, the confidence intervals are within the overall mean trust level. At an accuracy of 95 %, it is established that there is no significant variation in results generated by the model. To that effect, theories and assumptions underlying the behavioral trust model, as well as its reasonableness are correctly valid.

Concerning how decision synchronization affects trust, the following are deduced. On the one hand, whether a preference is persuaded or rejected, its effect on trust depends as well on other existing factors. Reflecting on logistics and collaboration scenario, synchronized preferences are dependent on an extent to which the truck is filled. Taking serial numbers 3 versus 11 (Table 3) for example, preference combinations PRR affects trust in different magnitudes. Similar cases are also noted in serial numbers 7 versus 14; 6 versus 19; 2 versus 10 versus 16, and; 8 versus 21. In particular, more trustworthy is experienced in cases where both carriers' preferences are persuaded and the truck is at least filled to its full capacity. In such cases, shippers and receivers benefit lowered transportation cost by 20 % (Table 2), thus realizing a potential relief. On the other hand, if the full truck condition is held fixed, persuaded preferences generate better trust level compared to those in which preferences are rejected. This is observed in serial numbers 14 versus 21 as well as 9 versus 21.

The findings of this research have a number of crucial implications for practice. On the foremost, irrespective of the degree to which preferences are synchronized, a magnitude of the generated effect on trust is dependent on other contexts, if any. This dependence, however, is unlikely a guarantee to a partner who chooses to reject an existence of the threatened future. It has been demonstrated that other contexts (factors) can be in a position to favor or oppose the ignored threat future. Furthermore, under similar conditional settings, persuaded preferences are better than rejected ones (serial numbers 7 versus (8 and 21)). Finally, as collaboration seeks to compromise conflicts and build a foundation of trustworthy, it is prominent to persuade conflicting preferences than rejecting their existence. Remarking on a second research question, in the overall, compromised preferences in decision rights appear to be a better strategy than uncompromised ones.

8 Conclusion and Outlook

This paper addresses behavioral discontents resulting from disagreements collaborating partners encounter in decision rights. According to confrontational analysis, such disagreements occur when "each partner takes a position that it regards as final, called a moment of truth" [8]. Such disagreements are referred to as conflicting preferences. Appearing in the form of rivalry decisions, conflicting preferences affect trustworthy, especially when partners are denied of assumed fairness. This paper concentrates on investigating an extent to which synchronized and unsynchronized conflicting preferences affect trustworthy. In its first place, the paper contributes by devising a generic model that describes behavioral trust in CNs. Subsequently, the behavioral trust model is evaluated empirically using MAS method in logistics collaboration scenario.

In particular, a generic model of behavioral trust can be applied to CNs other than logistics in the operational phase. Concerning results presented in this paper, two critical insights are revealed. Firstly, synchronized preferences affect trust positively than unsynchronized ones. Secondly, irrespective of a degree to which conflicting preferences are synchronized, a magnitude of the generated effect on trust, depends as well on other factors. Future works will involve investigating a larger set of conflicting preferences in a combined form as well as effect generated by other collaborative processes, like incentive alignment and opportunism.

References

1. Robinson, R., Valeri, L., Cave, J., Starkey, T., Graux, H., Creese, S., Hopkins, P.: The Cloud Understanding the Security, Privacy and Trust Challenges. RAND Corporation, Santa Monica (2011)
2. Cruijssen, F.C.A.M.: Horizontal cooperation in transport and logistics. Dissertation, Tilburg University (2006)
3. Okdinawati, L., Simatupang, T.M., Sunitiyoso, Y.: A behavioral multi-agent model for Collaborative Transportation Management (CTM). In: Proceedings of T-LOG (2014)
4. Simatupang, T.M., Sridharan, R.: Supply chain discontent. Bus. Process Manag. J. **11**(4), 349–369 (2005)
5. Rousseau, D.M., Sitkin, S.B., Burt, R.S., Camerer, C.: Not so different after all: a cross discipline view of trust. Acad. Manag. Rev. **23**(3), 393–404 (1998)
6. Sherchan, W., Nepal, S., Paris, C.: A survey of trust in social networks. ACM Comput. Surv. **45**(4), 47 (2013)
7. Schuldt, A., Gehrke, J.D., Werner, S.: Designing a simulation middleware for FIPA multiagent systems. In: Jain, L., et al. (eds.) WI-IAT 2008, pp. 109–113. IEEE Computer Society Press (2008)
8. Murray-Jones, P., Howard, N.: Co-ordinated positions in a drama-theoretic confrontation: mathematical foundations for a PO decision support system. In: Proceedings of CCRTS (2001)
9. Bryant, J.: Drama theory: dispelling the myths. J. Oper. Res. Soc. **58**(5), 602–613 (2007). Special Issue: Problem Structuring Methods II

10. Bennett, P.: Confrontation analysis: prediction, interpretation or diagnosis? In analyzing conflict and its resolution. In: Proceedings of a Conference of the Institute of Mathematics and Its Application, IMA, Southend-on-Sea (2004)
11. Hermawan, P., Kobayashi, N., Kijima, K.: Holistic formal analysis of dilemmas of negotiation. Syst. Res. Behav. Sci. **25**, 637–642 (2008)
12. Laeequddin, M., Sahay, B.S., Sahay, V., Waheed, K.A.: Trust building in supply chain partners' relationship: an integrated conceptual model. J. Manag. Dev. **31**(6), 550–564 (2012)
13. Mayer, R.C., Davis, J., Schoorman, F.D.: An integrative model of organizational trust. Acad. Manag. Rev. **20**(3), 709–734 (1995)
14. Daudi, M., Baalsrud Hauge, J., Thoben, K-D.: A trust framework for agents' interactions in collaborative logistics. In: Proceedings of Dynamics in Logistics, pp. 49–60 (2016)
15. Bonabeau, E.: Agent-based modeling: methods and techniques for simulating human systems. Proc. Natl. Acad. Sci. **99**(3), 7280–7287 (2002)
16. Wooldridge, M.J., Jennings, N.R.: Intelligent agents: theory and practice. Knowl. Eng. Rev. **10**(2), 115–152 (1995)
17. FIPA: FIPA Communicative Act Library Specification (2002). http://www.fipa.org/specs/fipa00037/
18. Berndt, J.O., Herzog, O.: Anticipatory behavior of software agents in self-organizing negotiations. In: Nadin, M. (ed.) Cognitive Systems Monographs 29, 231-253. Springer, Heidelberg (2016)
19. Tseng, M.M., Yan, J., Cruijssen, F.: Position paper on compensation rules. In: Collaboration Concepts for Co-modality (2013). http://www.co3-project.eu/wo3/wp-content/uploads/2011/12/CO3-D-2-5-Position-Paper-on-Compensation-Rule.pdf
20. VICS Logistics Committee.: Collaborative Transportation Management White Paper, Version 1.0. CTM sub-committee of the voluntary inter-industry commerce standards. http://www.vics.org

Decentralised Replenishment-Production Planning Optimisation Using Negotiation Rules in a Collaborative Network

Beatriz Andres(✉), Raul Poler, Josefa Mula, Manuel Díaz-Madroñero, and Raquel Sanchis

Research Centre on Production Management and Engineering (CIGIP), Universitat Politècnica de València (UPV), Calle Alarcón, 03801 Alcoy, Spain
{bandres, rpoler, fmula, fcodiama, rsanchis}@cigip.upv.es

Abstract. This paper proposes a decentralised planning optimisation approach by using mathematical programming and negotiation mechanisms in a collaborative network. Two partners addressing the replenishment and production stages are considered. Concretely, production scheduling plans and material requirement plans, modelled by two mixed-integer programming models, are modified according to the established negotiation rules between the two collaborative partners. The main contribution of this paper is the improvement of the replenishment and production plans upstream of the network; proposing a decentralised collaborative planning process. The validation of the proposal is done using data based on an automotive industry.

Keywords: Decentralised planning optimisation · Mathematical programming · Negotiation mechanisms · Collaborative networks · Automotive industry

1 Introduction

Increasing competitive changes in the global market, combined with rapid advances in information technology have made that collaborative network planning is at the edge of the business practices of most of collaborative partners. Given the complexity of operations and the often-conflicting objectives [1] of the enterprises belonging to a collaborative network (CN), such as, purchasing, manufacturing, distribution and sales, it is essential to develop a unified and rigorous approaches to increase commitments and reduce discrepancies among the network partners. The effective integration of these different features is the main objective of the collaborative network planning [2]. Planning refers to the coordination and integration of key business activities undertaken by the network partners, from procurement of raw materials to distribution of finished products to the customer [3]. Nowadays, globalised markets are constantly changing, thus maintaining flexible, efficient and sustainable CN is essential to deal with the volatility prevailing in the business environment, which is constantly transforming, and with the variability of customer expectations.

H. Afsarmanesh et al. (Eds.): PRO-VE 2016, IFIP AICT 480, pp. 228–240, 2016.
DOI: 10.1007/978-3-319-45390-3_20

In response to the challenge outlined, this paper proposes a decentralised collaborative planning approach that focuses on the negotiation of replenishment-production plans. The proposed approach centres its attention on two levels of the CN: a manufacturer and its supplier supporting the decentralised collaborative planning between (i) the integrated scheduling and replenishment plan computed by the manufacturer, identifying the quantities of finished products to produce, the sequence of production, the quantity of components required to produce the finished products and the period in which the components are demanded; and (ii) the scheduling plan computed by the supplier, identifying the quantity of components to produce with the main aim of supplying them to the manufacturer, minimising the products shortages. In order to support such collaboration in the planning process, negotiation mechanisms are proposed, in which each collaborative partner defines decision-making rules that will allow exchanging results on plans until an agreement between the scheduling plans of both, the manufacturer and the supplier, converge; obtaining a beneficial solution for both.

In this regard, the paper is organised as follows. Section 1 introduces the problem to be solved, raises the research question, and describes the research approach carried out. Section 2 presents the literature review. Section 3 proposes a decentralised collaborative approach that consists of two mixed-integer programming models, for both the manufacturer and the supplier. Moreover, collaborative negotiation mechanisms are presented. A use case is proposed in Sect. 4. Concluding remarks and future research lines are drawn in Sect. 5.

1.1 Problem Description and Research Question

The operational planning process, such as replenishment, production, inventory management and distribution processes, is relevant for the establishment of collaborative processes among networked partners [4]. Collaboration can be seen as the mutual participants' commitment to jointly solve problems. The collaborative network management has associated a higher degree of complexity; due to heterogeneous and autonomous partners take part in [5]. This involves that each collaborative partner defines different goal-based objectives [1], making attractive the proposal of approaches devoted to integrate all the nodes through the network planning. Considering the importance of collaboratively perform the planning process, among the enterprises of the same network, in terms of improving the CN relationships, this paper proposes a decentralised approach to support enterprises on the operational planning, from a collaborative perspective. The collaborative planning is focused on the replenishment and production planning process upstream of the CN.

The following research question is raised to support the decentralised collaborative planning process, as the objective of this research: *What would be a decentralised and collaborative approach to adequately support enterprises on the modelling, assessment and resolution of the replenishment-production planning from a collaborative perspective?*

The constructive research approach (CRA) [6] is used to answer the research question defined. Five are the phases determined in CRA: (i) identify a relevant problem subject to study, the problem in this research is defined by the discrepancies among the network partners, given the complexity of operations and the conflicting objectives of the CN enterprises; (ii) consider the background to solve the problem, this research is based on the operations research, production planning and CN management fields; (iii) propose a solution to the problem in an innovative way. Accordingly, decentralised scheduling-replenishment plans, modelled by two mixed-integer programming formulations, are modified according to the established negotiation rules between the two collaborative partners; (iv) identify the theoretical relevance of the solution and the theoretical contribution, the proposed research focuses on improving the CN long term operation; and finally (v) validate the solution, in this research a use case is provided. In the current phase of this research, the main aim is to provide models and negotiation mechanisms to achieve coherence between the replenishment and production plans of the manufacturers and suppliers that take part in the CN, in order to promote sustainable collaboration.

2 State of the Art

Collaborative Planning. Different solutions have been proposed to jointly manage production, inventory and distribution planning activities [2, 7, 8]. The collaborative planning process can be considered as centralised (CDM) or decentralized (DDM) [9] decision models. Models that address the planning process according to the type of decision-making can be centralised [10] partially centralised [11] or decentralised [8]. To deal with uncertainty (in demand, materials, etc.) fuzzy approaches are proposed [12]. DDM allow the decision-making process to be more flexible [9]. To address the collaborative and decentralised planning process, the literature proposes multi-objective planning models [2].

Most of the models proposed in the literature focus on the centralised deterministic perspective, when dealing with collaborative planning. While decentralised models are focused on the downstream stages of the network, related with production-inventory management-distribution (third party logistics) planning processes. The main aim of this paper is to fill the gaps encountered with regards the decentralised collaborative planning processes, by focusing on the replenishment-production stages (upstream) of the network. In this context, they are pioneers the works by [13], who demonstrate the benefits of collaborative planning for improving material requirement plans by proposing a reference architecture, negotiation mechanisms and a collaborative multi-agent system as modelling approach. Related to these works, the main novelty of our proposal is the collaborative consideration between scheduling and replenishment plans. Additionally, it is important to highlight the use of mathematical programming formulations, traditionally used for centralised planning, as a modelling approach for collaborative and decentralised planning.

Negotiation. The establishment of DDM has associated the need for establishing negotiation mechanisms, defining pre-agreed business rules, and assessing and comparing planning alternatives using performance measurement techniques [11]. The literature review has allowed identifying different approaches dealing with non-hierarchical negotiations based on compensation schemes [13]. In this regard, it is worth to mention the work proposed by [8], which applies a non-hierarchical negotiation "a decentralised supply chain planning methodology (ADSCP)", allowing partners to create network plans by the simple exchange of information on the supply quantities. Here, the ADSCP methodology is adopted as the basis for the development of negotiation mechanisms.

3 Decentralised Planning in Collaborative Networks

The approach proposed to deal with the collaborative decentralised planning consists of the negotiation of two plans, each one pertaining to a different CN decision-maker, (i) the manufacturer that computes its scheduling plan (SP_M) and the material requirement planning (MRP_M); and (ii) the supplier that calculates its master scheduling plan (SP_S). In order to support the negotiation process, a collaboration mechanism is developed to link the two models from a decentralised and collaborative perspective [8].

3.1 Manufacturer Scheduling and Materials Requirement Planning Model

In this section, a mixed integer programming formulation for replenishment-scheduling planning based on [15] is described (see Table 1 for nomenclature). The first decision maker, the manufacturer, assumes the optimum scheduling planning and according to the quantity of products to produce, the manufacturer compute the MRP. Scheduling and MRP are integrated in the same model.

Table 1. Nomenclature model manufacturer

Index	
I	Set of products (finished goods and raw materials)
J	Set of finished goods
T	Set of periods
Parameters	
d_{it}	Demand of product i during time period t
ts_{ij}	Setup time from product i to product j
c_t	Production capacity during time period t
$INVMAX_i$	Available inventory capacity for product i
cv_{it}	Coverage inventory: Minimum inventory required for product i
INV_{i0}	Initial inventory of product i
SR_{it}	Scheduled receptions of product i during time period t
b_{ji}	Quantity of i to produce a unit of finished good j
tp_i	Required time to produce a unit of product i
cs_{ij}	Setup cost from product i to product j

(*Continued*)

Table 1. (*Continued*)

Index	
ci_{it}	Inventory cost of product i during time period t
co_t	Overtime cost during time period t
pcv_i	Penalty for soft inventory constraint violation for product i
b_{i0}	Backorders of product i during time period $t = 0$ (initial)
cb_i	Backorders cost of product i
$csup_t$	Production capacity of the supplier during time period t
M	Big number
N	Number of finished goods
Decision variables	
X_{it}	Amount of i to produce during time period t
Y_{it}	1 if product i is produced during time period t, 0 otherwise
S_{ijt}	1 if a setup occurs from product i to product j during time period t, 0 otherwise
INV_{it}	Inventory level of product i at the end of time period t
Q_{it}	Amount of product i to order to suppliers
TOV_t	Overtime hours during time period t
α_{it}	1 if product i is produced *first* during time period t, 0 otherwise
β_{it}	1 if product i is produced *last* during time period t, 0 otherwise
γ_{it}	1 if machine is setup for product i at the end of time period t, 0 otherwise
ω_t	Strictly positive when at least one product is produced in time period t, 0 otherwise
δ_t	0 if exactly one product is produced during time period t, an unrestricted non-negative number otherwise
V_{it}	auxiliary continuous variable to eliminate disconnected subtours
H_{it}	auxiliary variable to generate soft inventory constraint for product i during time period t
B_{it}	Backorders of the product i in time period t

Objective function

$$Min\, z = \sum_i \sum_j \sum_t cs_{ij} \cdot S_{ijt} + \sum_i \sum_t ci_{it} \cdot INV_{it} + \sum_t co_t \cdot TOV_t + \sum_i \sum_t pcv_i \cdot H_{it} + \sum_i \sum_t cb_i \cdot B_{it} \tag{1}$$

Constraints

$$INV_{i0} + X_{it} - INV_{it} - b_{i0} + B_{it} = d_{it} \quad \forall i \in J, t = 1 \tag{2}$$

$$INV_{i,t-1} + X_{it} - INV_{it} - B_{i,t-1} + B_{it} = d_{it} \quad \forall i \in J, t > 1 \tag{3}$$

$$INV_{i,t-1} + SR_{it} + Q_{it} - INV_{it} = \sum_j b_{ji} \cdot X_{it} \quad \forall i \in \{I\} \backslash \{J\}, t \tag{4}$$

$$INV_{i,t} \leq INVMAX_i \quad \forall i, t \tag{5}$$

$$INV_{it} + H_{it} \geq cv_{i,t} \quad \forall i \in J, t \tag{6}$$

$$X_{it} \leq M \cdot Y_{it} \quad \forall i \in J, t \tag{7}$$

$$\sum_{i \in J} tp_i \cdot X_{it} + \sum_{i \in J} \sum_j ts_{ij} \cdot S_{ijt} - TOV_t \leq c_t \quad \forall t \tag{8}$$

$$\sum_{i \notin J} tp_i \cdot Q_{it} \leq c\sup_t \quad \forall i \in J, t \tag{9}$$

$$Y_{it} \leq \omega_{it} \quad \forall i \in J, t \tag{10}$$

$$\sum_{i \in j} Y_{it} - 1 \leq (N-1)\delta_t \quad \forall t \tag{11}$$

$$\omega_t \leq \sum_{i \in j} \alpha_{it} \leq 1 \quad \forall t \tag{12}$$

$$\omega_t \leq \sum_{i \in j} \beta_{it} \leq 1 \quad \forall t \tag{13}$$

$$\alpha_{it} \leq Y_{it} \quad \forall i \in J, t \tag{14}$$

$$\beta_{it} \leq Y_{it} \quad \forall i \in J, t \tag{15}$$

$$\alpha_{it} + \beta_{it} \leq 2 - \delta_t \quad \forall i \in J, t \tag{16}$$

$$\sum_{i \in j} \gamma_{it} = 1 \quad \forall t \tag{17}$$

$$\sum_j S_{jit} \geq Y_{it} - \alpha_{it} \quad \forall i \in J, t \tag{18}$$

$$\sum_j S_{ijt} \geq Y_{it} - \beta_{it} \quad \forall i \in J, t \tag{19}$$

$$S_{ijt} \geq \gamma_{i,t-1} + \gamma_{jt} - \omega_t - 1 \quad \forall i \in J, i \neq j, t \tag{20}$$

$$S_{jit} \geq \alpha_{it} + \gamma_{j,t-1} - 1 \quad \forall i \in J, i \neq j, t \tag{21}$$

$$S_{ijt} \geq \beta_{it} + \gamma_{jt} - 1 \quad \forall i \in J, i \neq j, t \tag{22}$$

$$V_{jt} \geq V_{it} + N \cdot S_{ijt} - (N-1) - N \cdot \gamma_{i,t-1} \quad \forall i \in J, i \neq j, t \tag{23}$$

$$0 \leq \omega_t \leq 1 \quad \forall t \tag{24}$$

$$X_{it}, INV_{it}, \delta_t, TOV_t, B_{it}, H_{it} \geq 0 \quad \forall i, t \tag{25}$$

$$S_{ijt}, Y_{it}, \alpha_{it}, \beta_{it}, \gamma_{it} \in \{0, 1\} \quad \forall i, j, t \tag{26}$$

Objective function (1) minimizes all the performed setups, inventory holding, overtime costs, the penalty of finished goods inventory coverage violations, the backorders. Constraints (2) and (3) are typical inventory balance equations for finished goods allowing backorders and (4) for raw materials. Constraint (5) limits the inventory level for each product according to the available inventory capacity. Constraint (6) corresponds to inventory coverage extension for finished goods. In this case, and in order to avoid infeasibilities, it is set as a soft constraint with a penalty cost included in the objective function. Constraint (7) ensures that whenever $X_{it} \geq 0$, decision variable Y_{it} is set at 1. Constraint (8) establishes the production capacity limits by taking into account possible overtime decisions. Constraint (9) establishes the production capacity of the supplier. Constraints (10) to (17) determine which product is produced first and last during a given time period. They also find the product for which the machine is setup at the end of each time period. Constraints (18) and (19) apply whenever more than one product is produced during a single period. They force at least one S_{ijt}'s to be 1 per product i, except when this product is either the first or the last product in the sequence. Constraint (20) forces a setup during production-free periods when the machine's setup state at the end of the period is not the same as the setup status at the end of the following period. Constraints (21) and (22) are needed to properly count the setups between the periods during which the machine is not idle, while Constraint (23) ensures the subtours elimination. Finally, Constraints (24) to (26) correspond to the binary and non-negativity properties of the decision variables.

3.2 Supplier Master Production Scheduling Planning Model

In this section, a mixed integer programming formulation for scheduling planning based on [15], is described for the supplier master production scheduling planning model (see Table 2 for nomenclature).

Table 2. Nomenclature model manufacturer

Index	
I	Set of products (finished goods and raw materials)
T	Set of periods
Parameters	
d_{it}	Demand of product i during time period t
$INVMAX_i$	Available inventory capacity for product i
cv_{it}	Coverage inventory: Minimum inventory required for product i

(*Continued*)

Table 2. (*Continued*)

Index	
INV_{i0}	Initial inventory of product i
tp_i	Required time to produce a unit of product i
ci_{it}	Inventory cost of product i during time period t
co_t	Overtime cost during time period t
pcv_i	Penalty for soft inventory constraint violation for product i
$csup_t$	Production capacity of the supplier during time period t
csh_i	Shortage cost per unit of product i
M	Big number
Decision variables	
X_{it}	Amount of i to produce during time period t Inventory level of product i at the end of time period t
INV_{it}	Offered supply quantity of product i during time period t
Q_{it}	Overtime hours during time period t
TOV_t	Supply shortage of product i during time period t
SH_{it}	Auxiliary variable to generate soft inventory constraint for product i during time
H_{it}	period t

Objective function

$$Min\, z = \sum_i \sum_t ci_{it} \cdot INV_{it} + \sum_t co_t \cdot TOV_t + \sum_i \sum_t pcv_i \cdot H_{it} + \sum_i \sum_t csh_i \cdot SH_{it} \tag{27}$$

Constraints

$$INV_{i,t-1} + X_{it} - INV_{it} = Q_{it} \quad \forall i, t \tag{28}$$

$$INV_{i,t} \leq INVMAX_i \quad \forall i, t \tag{29}$$

$$INV_{it} + H_{it} \geq cv_{i,t} \quad \forall i, t \tag{30}$$

$$\sum_i tp_i \cdot X_{it} - TOV_t \leq c\sup_t \quad \forall t \tag{31}$$

$$X_{it} + SH_{it} = d_{it} \quad \forall i, t \tag{32}$$

$$X_{it} = Q_{it} \quad \forall i, t \tag{33}$$

$$X_{it}, INV_{it}, TOV_t, H_{it} \geq 0 \quad \forall i, t \tag{34}$$

Objective function (27) minimizes all the inventory holding, overtime costs, the penalty of finished goods inventory coverage violations and the supply shortage. Constraint (28) is typical inventory balance equation. Constraint (29) limits the inventory level for each product according to the available inventory capacity. Constraint (30) corresponds to inventory coverage extension for finished goods. In this case, and in order to avoid infeasibilities, it is set as a soft constraint with a penalty cost included in the objective function. Constraint (31) establishes the production capacity limits of the supplier by taking into account possible overtime decisions. Constraint (32) establishes that the quantities demanded by the manufacturer are the same as the products produced by the supplier plus the shortage quantity of products. Constraint (33) indicates what the suppliers produces is the same as what is supplied to the manufacturer. Finally, Constraints (34) correspond to the non-negativity properties of the decision variables.

3.3 Negotiation Mechanism for the Collaborative Planning Process

In this section a negotiation mechanism is proposed to support the network partners in the collaborative planning process. The negotiation mechanism is characterised by the decision-making rules, defined by the different partners involved in the collaborative planning. These decision-making rules allow to: (i) support the decision-making process and (ii) characterise the collaborative planning process by solving the differences among the planning activities of the parties involved. The decision-making rules should aim for a Win-Win outcome in order to meet the interests of all the sides involved. An example of decision-making rules is provided next with the main aim of guiding the enterprises, involved in the decentralised replenishment-production planning, in the collaboration process:

- Stockout Rule: This rule guarantees that at the end of the planning horizon the actual stock is higher than the minimum stock defined.
- Backorders Rule: It ensures that no demand delays are allowed at each period.
- Supplied quantity Rule: The quantity of components to be supplied (by the *S*) should be within a target range defined by the *M*.
- Inventory/Overtime/Setup costs Rule: The inventory/overtime/setup costs are defined in a bounded range.

Having identified the decision-making rules, the enterprises involved in the collaborative planning process start with the negotiation mechanism. The proposed negotiation mechanism, based on [8], is described next (Fig. 1):

Step 1. The manufacturer (*M*) starts to compute the integrated replenishment-scheduling plan (SP^0_M, MRP_M), given a planning horizon, depending on what to serve to the end customer (*end-customer demand*). According to the results obtained in the integrated replenishment-scheduling plan, *M* obtains the replenishment needs of the raw material or semi-elaborated components (MRP^0_M). *M* releases the replenishment needs to the supplier (*S*) (*manufacturer demand*).

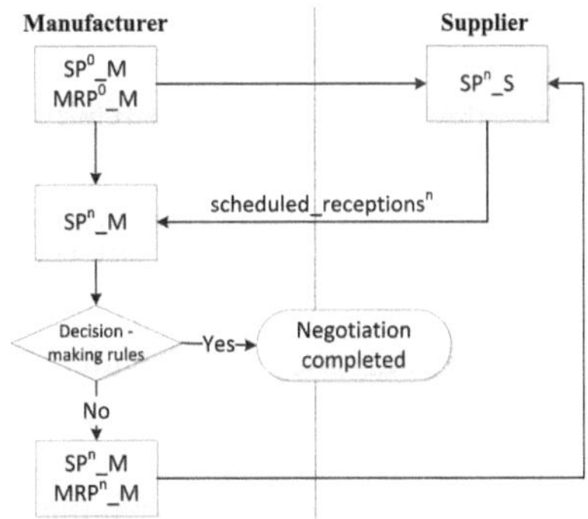

Fig. 1. Overview of the negotiation steps

Step 2. *S* computes its scheduling plan (SP^n_S), according to demand given by *M*. In case the *S* cannot satisfy the demand given by M, *S* communicates to *M* the quantities that can serve (Q_{it}: *Offered supply quantity of product i during period t*)

Step 3. *M* generates a scheduling plan for the given offered supply quantity and considering the *end-customer demand*, so as to minimize *M* total costs, and meet the demand; therefore no backorders are allowed. In this step, the obtained replenishment needs are limited by the amounts of components offered by supplier in the previous step.

Step 4.1. On the one hand, if the decision-making rules are achieved (end-customer demand reached, no backorders for the manufacturer, no shortages for the supplier, etc.) and the requested supply quantity of *M* d_{it} corresponds to the Q_{it} given by *S*, the negotiation procedure is completed.

Step 4.2. On the other hand, if the decision-making rules are not achieved, the negotiation process continues. Each iteration in the negotiation process is numbered as *n*. In this regard, *M* generates a new replenishment-scheduling plan (SP^n_M, MRP^n_M) considering a new input data as regards the sequence and the quantity of products to produce in each period that allows accomplishing the decision making-rules and satisfying the demand with no backorders. *M* reports to S the requested supply quantity in order to fulfil the given demand of end customer (*manufacturer demand*).

Step 5. *S* generates a new scheduling plan (SP^n_S), considering its internal production capacity and the *manufacturer demand*. *S* reports the new available supply quantity to *M*. Then the network nodes proceeds again with Step 3.

4 Numerical Example

This section presents the application of the proposed decentralized planning approach with a numerical example inspired in a real world automotive supply chain consisting of a supplier and a manufacturer. Both members by applying the proposed coordination mechanism achieve a compromise solution based on the coincidence of the amounts of components offered by supplier and the amounts of components requested by the manufacturer in order to meet the final customer demand following the stockout and backorders rules presented in the previous section, as well as a warehousing limitation rule for final products and components. Among them, the warehousing limitation and backorders rule in the last period are considered hard constraints while the stockout rule is considered as a soft constraint with a corresponding penalty. The mathematical programming models related to the supplier and manufacturer and the corresponding coordination mechanism have been in the MPL language V4.2. The resolution has been carried out with Gurobi 5.6.3 solver in a desktop computer with 4 Gb RAM. The input data and the model solution values were processed with the Microsoft Access database (2010) which was useful for the exchange of information between supplier and manufacturer models.

This study considers one finished good produced at manufacturer by processing one component obtained from the supplier in the same proportion over the four time periods considered. The demand levels at manufacturer are 3, 5, 11 and 0, respectively. The rest of manufacturer parameters are presented in Table 3. The initial backorders and scheduled receptions for each period are considered null and initial inventories are set according to stockout decision-making rule. The values for decision-making rules at manufacturer are presented in Table 4.

Table 3. Manufacturer parameters

Parameter	Value
c_t	24 h
tp_i	1 h/unit
$ci_{(i=1)t}$	10€
$ci_{(i=2)t}$	7€
co_t	100€
cb_i	1000€

Table 4. Values for decision making rules at manufacturer

Decision-making rule	Indexes	Values
Stockout	$i = 1, t$	3 units
Stockout	$i = 2, t$	3 units
Backorders	$i = 1, t = 4$	0 units
Warehousing space	$i = 1, t$	7 units
Warehousing space	$i = 2, t$	7 units

The supplier parameters are presented in Table 5. The initial inventories are also set according to the stockout decision-making rule. The values for decision-making rules at supplier are presented in Table 6.

Using this data set a total of three iterations of the proposed coordination mechanism are needed to obtain a satisfactory replenishment-production planning according to the hard (backorders and warehousing limitations) and soft (stockout) decision rules defined for each member of the considered supply chain. The results obtained after the third iteration are presented in Table 7.

As shown in Table 7, the coordination mechanism obtains a replenishment-production plan according to the established decision-making rules at each node of the considered supply chain with a minimum deviation. The possibility of introducing the stockout decision rule as a soft constraint allows to focus on strict

Table 5. Supplier parameters

Parameter	Value
$capsup_t$	10 h
tp_i	1 h/unit
ci_{it}	7€
co_t	100€
csh_i	1000€

Table 6. Values for decision making rules at supplier

Decision-making rule	Indexes	Values
Stockout	$i = 2,\ t$	3 units
Warehousing space	$i = 2,\ t$	7 units

Table 7. Results obtained from the proposed coordination mechanism

	Iteration 1	Iteration 2	Iteration 3
Supply chain member	Manufacturer	Supplier	Manufacturer
Decision-making rules matched	Stockout Backorders Warehousing space	Stockout Warehousing space	Stockout (with flexibility) Backorders Warehousing space
Exceptions	Infinite production capacity for supplier assumed		Inventory for product $i = 1$ in periods $t = 3$ and $t = 4$ is equal to 2 units

decision areas in the automotive industry such as maximum warehousing levels and backorders although minimum desired inventory levels are not obtained for only two periods.

5 Conclusions

In this paper, two decentralised scheduling models dealing with the replenishment and production stages of a CN have been used through a mathematical programming approach. The decentralised collaborative planning approach has been supported by a negotiation mechanism that allows modifying the quantities of components requested by the manufacturer and the quantities of supply offered by the supplier, with the main aim of minimising the shortages in the supply and the backorders to the final customer. The proposed approach allows promoting collaboration between the replenishment and production stages of the CN. In future research lines, negotiation could be performed using the multi-agents paradigm by programming them based on automatic decision-making rules agreed by both network nodes. Another future work could be led to apply the proposed approach in a real size CN.

Acknowledgments. "The research leading to these results is in the frame of the "Cloud Collaborative Manufacturing Networks" (C2NET) project which has received funding from the European Union's Horizon 2020 research and innovation programme under grant agreement No. 636909".

References

1. Andres, B., Poler, R.: Dealing with the alignment of strategies within the collaborative networked partners. IFIP Int. Fed. Inf. Process **450**, 13–21 (2015)
2. Gupta, A., Maranas, C.D.: Managing demand uncertainty in supply chain planning. Comput. Chem. Eng. **27**, 1219–1227 (2003)
3. Gupta, A., Maranas, C.D.: A hierarchical Lagrangean relaxation procedure for solving midterm planning problems. Ind. Eng. Chem. Res. **38**, 1937–1947 (1999)
4. Andres, B., Poler, R., Hernández, J.E.: An operational planning solution for smes in collaborative and non-hierarchical networks. Lect. Notes Bus. Inf. Process **164**, 46–56 (2013)
5. Camarinha-Matos, L.M., Afsarmanesh, H.: Collaborative networks: a new scientific discipline. J. Intell. Manuf. **16**, 439–452 (2005)
6. Kasanen, E., Lukka, K., Siitonen, A.: The constructive approach in management accounting research. J. Manag. Account. Res. **5**, 243–264 (1993)
7. Dudek, G., Stadtler, H.: Negotiation-based collaborative planning between supply chains partners. Eur. J. Oper. Res. **163**, 668–687 (2005)
8. Jung, H., Chen, F., Jeong, B.: Decentralized supply chain planning framework for third party logistics partnership. Comput. Ind. Eng. **55**, 348–364 (2008)
9. Schneeweiss, S.: Distributed decision making in supply chain management. Int. J. Prod. Econ. **84**, 71–83 (2003)
10. Alemany, M.M.E., Alarcón, F., Lario, F.C., Boj, J.J.: An application to support the temporal and spatial distributed decision-making process in supply chain collaborative planning. Comput. Ind. **62**, 519–540 (2011)
11. Pibernik, R., Sucky, E.: An approach to inter-domain master planning in supply chains. Int. J. Prod. Econ. **108**, 200–212 (2007)
12. Mula, J., Peidro, D., Poler, R.: Optimization models for supply chain production planning under fuzziness. Stud. Fuzziness Soft Comput. **31**, 397–422 (2014)
13. Hernández, J.E., Lyons, A.C., Mula, J., Poler, R., Ismail, J.: Supporting the collaborative decision-making process in an automotive supply chain with a multi-agent system. Prod. Plan. Control **25**, 662–678 (2014)
14. Mula, J., Poler, R., Garcia, J.P.: MRP with flexible constraints: a fuzzy mathematical programming approach. Fuzzy Sets Syst. **157**, 74–97 (2006)
15. Andres, B., Mula, J., Diaz Madroñero, F.M., Poler, R. Sanchis, R.: Capacitated lot-sizing and scheduling problem for second-tier suppliers in the automotive sector. In: CIO-ICIEOM-IISE-AIM International Joint Conference (IJC2016), 13–15 July 2016. TECNUN-School of Engineering, San Sebastian, Spain (2016). Forthcoming

Mapping Patterns of Co-innovation Networks

Paula Urze[1,2(✉)] and António Abreu[3,4]

[1] FCT/UNL – Faculdade de Ciências e Tecnologia, Universidade Nova de Lisboa, Caparica, Portugal
pcu@fct.unl.pt

[2] CIUHCT – Centro Interuniversitário de História das Ciências e da Tecnologia, Caparica, Portugal

[3] ISEL – Instituto Superior de Engenharia de Lisboa, Instituto Politécnico de Lisboa, Lisbon, Portugal
ajfa@dem.isel.ipl.pt

[4] CTS – Uninova, Faculdade de Ciências e Tecnologia, Universidade Nova de Lisboa, Caparica, Portugal

Abstract. In recent decades a significant research effort has focused on the role of innovation in giving enterprises a competitive advantage, and of socio-economic growth in general. Using the debate about systems as frameworks for innovation and the mapping of stages of innovation as our starting point, this paper aims to introduce an approach to understand the role of different types of co-innovation networks in terms of their capacity to generate novelty in terms of processes and products. The paper's empirical section is based on one case study about Portugal's largest highway concessionaire.

Keywords: Collaborative networks · Innovation · Types of co-innovation networks

1 Introduction

In recent decades a significant research effort has focused on the role of innovation in giving enterprises a competitive advantage, and of socio-economic growth in general. There is also a growing stream of literature analyzing models of innovation [1, 2]. Different perspectives have emerged associated to an effort to explain the social and institutional conditions of competitiveness in a collaborative environment such as industrial districts, industrial clusters, virtual organizations and collaborative innovation networks [3]. Recent research in socio-economic issues has also pointed out the role of networking as an element, which facilitates communication, thereby promoting increased information dissemination and knowledge sharing. One can detect a convergence of opinions from different schools of thought when attempting to study the factors that contribute to improving an innovative performance among enterprises and sectors [4]. Furthermore, a number of contributions on this same subject can be found in innovation literature.

In fact, cooperating and networking are essential assets in the search for an innovative growth path. Nonetheless, enterprises gain the crucial competitive advantage through the ability to coordinate resources and deploy them effectively, considering

Published by Springer International Publishing Switzerland 2016. All Rights Reserved
H. Afsarmanesh et al. (Eds.): PRO-VE 2016, IFIP AICT 480, pp. 241–252, 2016.
DOI: 10.1007/978-3-319-45390-3_21

knowledge as a key cornerstone for innovation and making sure it ranks first in the hierarchy of the organization's strategically relevant resources [5].

Networking may open the possibility, not only for the sharing of knowledge, but also for the launching of the knowledge-creation process itself. This may enable enterprises to strengthen their technological and innovative competencies. Within this assumption, the main purpose of this paper is to develop an approach for understanding the role of different types of co-innovation networks in terms of their capacity for generating new ideas, processes or services.

2 A Systemic Perspective of Innovation

Currently, there is a broad consensus among scholars of innovation that a systemic approach to innovation activities provides a more complete representation of reality, as opposed to the linear model. The systemic approach takes into account the need for a broader perspective of the innovation process, putting it within the framework of an innovation system [6]. The systemic perspective consists of a structure formed by a set of interdependent organizations in an institutional context, shaping the way systems work and determining the action of the systems.

The concept of innovation has been submitted to transformations over time, along with the development of models that attempt to understand the process. At first, it was thought that innovation was the result of a linear and hierarchical process, which starts with basic research, successfully going through consecutive stages, from applied research and development to production and marketing. Public intervention has a greater presence and intensity at the higher levels such as in universities and other public organizations, and it is more moderate, or does not take place at all, in the lower levels such as production and marketing [7, 8].

Contrasting with the 'linear model', the 'chain linked model' [9] developed in the 1980s considers that the innovation process takes place through a series of interactions and interdependencies. These occur within enterprises, between them and also through upstream activities, e.g. scientific and technological organizations, suppliers of goods, services, equipment and technology and in the downstream, e.g. distribution, industrial customers and end users. Moreover, the process is not hierarchical because innovative impulses can originate either from new scientific insights and technology or at the market level. Under this model, public intervention is different from the 'linear model'. The 'chain linked model' becomes less differentiated from one stage to another and does not contain the formal distinction between enterprises and other stakeholders [10].

The innovation process is influenced by several factors. Due to this complexity, enterprises rarely innovate alone. The innovation path interacts with other organizations to gain, develop and exchange different forms of knowledge, information and other resources. These may be other enterprises, suppliers, customers and competitors or also universities and research institutes [11]. Through their innovation activities, enterprises establish relationships among themselves and with other organizations. However, it makes sense to look for isolated innovative enterprises and individual decision-making units. Enterprise behavior is also shaped by institutions that constitute constraints or incentives for innovation, such as laws, cultural norms, social rules and technical standards. The interaction between various organizations operating in different institutional settings is important for the innovation process. The actors as well as the context factors are all important elements in the creation and use of knowledge for economic purposes [8, 12]. As a result innovation in such systems can emerge.

3 Stages for Mapping Innovation

As regards technological innovation, it is important to stress that one of the main concerns of enterprises is to measure the technological maturity of a new technology and capability (engineering or economic performance). Thus, the Technology Readiness Level (TRL) scale, developed in the 1970s and 80 s by NASA, has been largely used by different sectors and has often been adapted to the specific needs of organizations [13].

The initial scale contained 7 levels and has now been expanded to a 9-level scale that has broad acceptance through industry and public organizations. All levels describe the maturity in the development of a technology, from the idea to the implementation of the product in the market.

It is worth adding that the TRL scale uses a linear approach, which was usual in the early 1970s. The essential object of development is a component that is improved and integrated into a product. The possibility of delays in maturity as a critical feature of R&D activities was first incorporated through the 'chain linked model'. In contrast to the implicit linear logic of the TRL scale, these interactive models show that research is needed even at the higher TRL levels, i.e. an increase in maturity also requires further research. Thus, a technology in the pilot production stage can be thrown back temporarily to the technological feasibility stage, as defects in the product design emerge as result of problems in production. Despite having its defects, the TRL scale continues to be adopted by different institutions, including the Department of Defense, the European Space Agency and the European Commission, which uses this concept in Horizon 2020 [14]. There are several versions of the TRL scale, according to the entity or industry that uses it and where it is applied. For example, there are specific TRL ranges for the software, biomedical and energy industries, among others.

Grounded on literature [4, 15, 16] and considering the context of TRL scale, as a first approach, three dimensions have been proposed with a broader scope of analysis, which include the following perspectives:

Scientific Perspective – This perspective is focused on the basic principles of scientific research that transpose into applied research and development and the formulation of practical applications. Development and laboratory testing of technological modules are also implemented at this phase and the basic technological modules are set together to be experienced in a simulated environment.

Technical Perspective – This perspective addresses the prototype experiment in a relevant environment. The system or process demonstration is carried out in an operational situation. The driving force behind this level of development is to assure system engineering and foster management confidence. The goal of this stage is to reduce production risk.

Business Perspective – This phase refers to a complete and qualified system that is ready to be used in a real situation. It is a system that has been approved in operational conditions and is ready to be used in a real scenario. It includes documentation as well as the product, process or service that is launched commercially, and accepted by customers.

The Fig. 1 shows the relationship between the TRL and our proposal in terms of dimensions, taking into account the different resources and competences required in each stage.

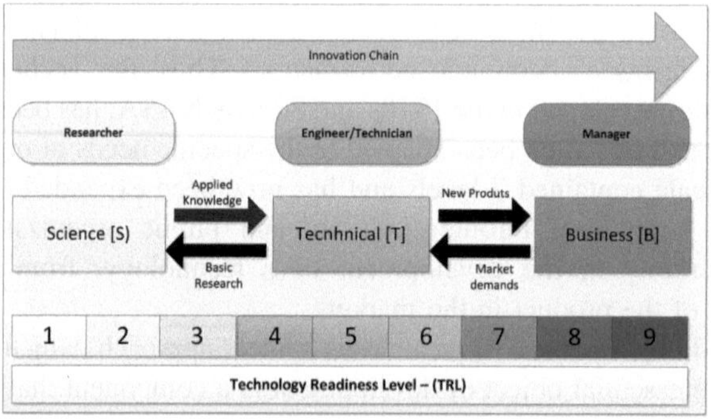

Fig. 1. Innovation chain

4 Co-innovation Patterns Model

In order to understand the role of a co-innovation network in the innovation chain, a model must be developed that supports the analysis of the relationships among enterprises and categorizes the knowledge that may be accessed through the collaborative network.

To do so, we start with the assumption that the contribution of an enterprise to an innovation process is related to the level of relationships that it establishes with other enterprises within a network under a co-innovation perspective. Therefore, as a first approach, using concepts from Social Network Analysis and adopting the model developed by Abreu e Camarinha-Matos [17] these relationships can be modeled using graphs, as showed in Fig. 2.

However, this simplification implies a partial view and consequently, a limitation of the model. In order to have a complete description of the patterns of innovation it is also important to consider what happens with other enterprises, which are connected with the main enterprise. For instance, other aspects as such as brokerage's roles and value systems should be taken into account [18].

The proposed model considers basic-maps and Innovation perspectives maps. The Basic maps are:

Map of collaboration – A graph showing the network of formal relationships for the purpose of exchanging knowledge to satisfy a request among enterprises belonging to the co-innovation network. In this map, the link's width represents the level of accessibility for knowledge transfer or level of co-innovation – (LC) between two

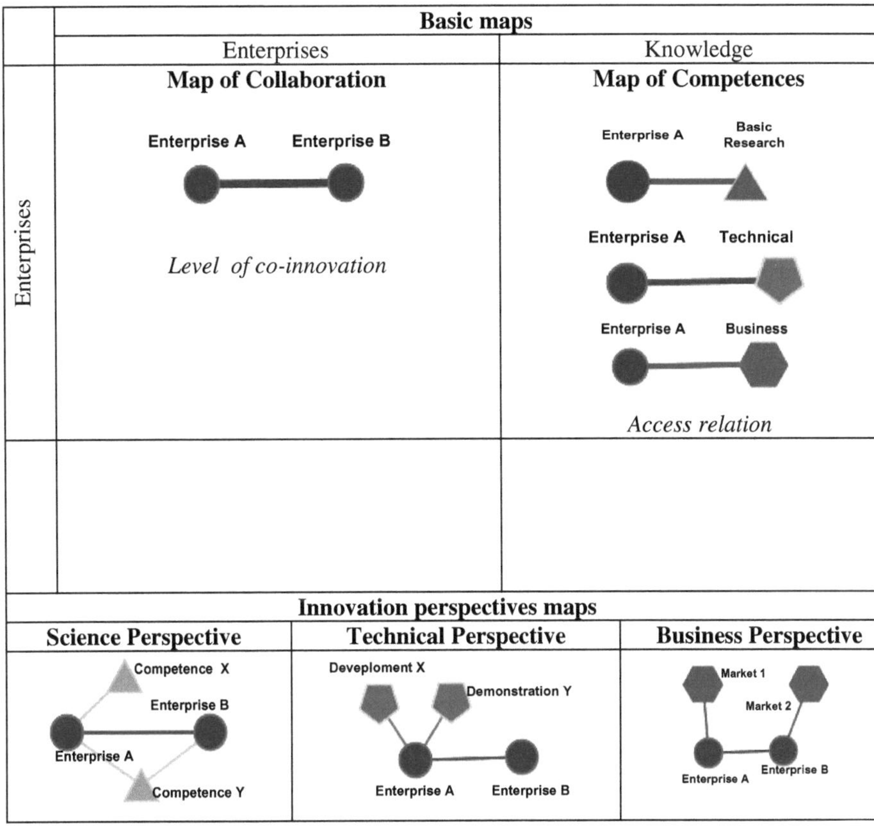

Fig. 2. Simple model to analyze co-innovation in CNs.

enterprises in a defined time interval. Taking into account the model developed by Urze and Abreu [19] its value can be given by the following equation:

$$LC_{ij} = w_1 \times TM_{ij} + w_2 \times CM_{ij} + w_3 \times NR_{ij}$$

$$\sum_{n=1}^{3} w_n = 1 \text{ and } w_n \geq 0$$

Where:

LC_{ij} – Level of co-innovation between enterprise i and enterprise j. It has a value over the interval [0, 3] where 0 means null collaboration and 3 means high collaboration. The level of co-innovation is assumed as an abstract quantifiable value based on past benefits in a defined time interval. Furthermore, at this research stage, the level of co-innovation represents only the positive side-effect of the relationships between enterprises in terms of accessibility to the knowledge that may be accessed through the network of contacts, and does not take into account the amount of time, effort and cost spent fostering the relationships.

TM_{ij} – The transfer mechanisms variable focuses on evaluation of distinct ways of "physical" interrelationship that support the process of knowledge transfer between enterprise i and enterprise j within a network in a defined time interval. It has a value over the interval [0, 3] where 0 means null transference of knowledge and 3 means the best use of knowledge transference.
CM_{ij} – The competences management evaluates the principles, policies, and governance rules that may facilitate or constrain the processes of searching for knowledge between enterprise i and enterprise j within a network in a defined time interval. It has a value over the interval [0, 3], where 3 means a high level of accessibility and dissemination strategy and 0 means a private and confidential strategy.
NR_{ij} – This variable evaluates the nature of the relationships between enterprise i and enterprise j within a network in a defined time interval, based on the identification and characterization of the various types of relationships (e.g. subordinate relationships, peer relationships), frequency and intensity of contact that enterprises may have with other enterprises within the co-innovation network. It has a value over the interval [0, 3], where 0 means a null relationship and 3 means a strong relationship.

The main difficulty is how to calculate each of the three variables mentioned above. Further research and development is required regarding how to collect and record the values without being intrusive in the network enterprises' "life". As a first approach, for instance, the assessment of the nature of the relationships might be determined based on the number and duration of collaborative co-innovation projects implemented over a period of time. The competences management evaluation might be based on the number of new competences that each enterprise acquired over a period of time and the evaluation of the knowledge transfer process might be based on the level of successful past co-innovation collaboration.

On the other hand, if the purpose is to design a simulation model to support the decision-making process, then the values of these components will be parameters of the simulation process.

Map of Competences – This graph shows the types of competences held by each enterprise and how the competences are shared or possessed by each enterprise. In this case, there are two sets of nodes: enterprises and competences. The nodes are connected by "*access*" relationships.

Innovation perspectives map – Graph showing how an enterprise may have access to competences held by another enterprise. It results from the aggregation of the map of collaboration and map of competences. Based on this map, it is possible to analyze the potential contribution of each enterprise through a visual representation. Therefore, this map consists of two sets of nodes: enterprises and competences.

Assuming that the competences are classified into classes in accordance with their position in the innovation chain then in this context it becomes possible to analyze the potential contribution of an enterprise according to different perspectives, such as:

- Scientific perspective – related to the ability to generate and produce validated knowledge.

- Technical perspective – related to the ability to develop and demonstrate new products in their final form, under the full range of conditions of the enterprise's operating mission.
- Business perspective – related to the ability to provide new products or services to customers.

Based on this approach it is possible to identify distinct co-innovation networks according to their focus. As illustrated in Fig. 3, there are co-innovation networks where the center of interest or activity is mainly on one perspective only – science, technical or business and mixed co-innovation networks.

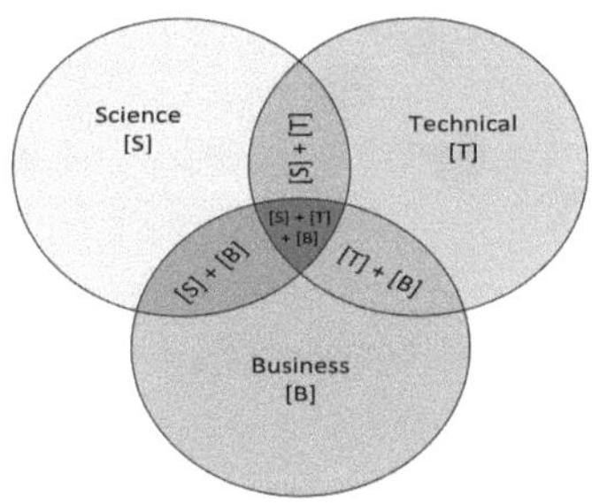

Fig. 3. Types of co-innovation networks

Example 1 Let us consider a scenario where we have a co-innovation network, which contains eight enterprises, as shown in Fig. 4. The purpose of this example is only to show the potential advantages of this model. In the network of collaboration, the level of co-innovation among enterprises (LC_{ij}), when is not null, is identical for all enterprises.

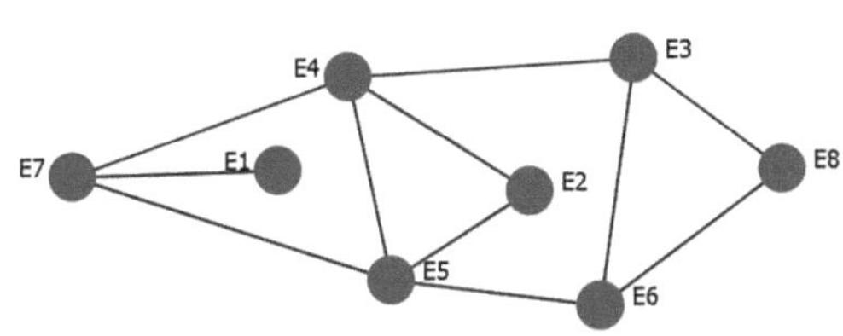

Fig. 4. Map of collaboration

Assuming that there are three distinct classes of competences (Basic Research, Technical, and Market), as shown in Fig. 5. Analyzing the graphs of Competences, it is possible to identify that in terms of basic research (graph 5A) only enterprises E1 and E2 have competences in this area and both enterprises have a competence exclusive to them alone: BR4 in the case of E1 and BR1 in the case of E2. On the other hand, according to the analysis of technical competences (graph 5C), it is possible to verify, for instance, that only enterprise E1 and E7 do not have any technical competences, and apart from the T4 competence, the others are shared by several enterprises.

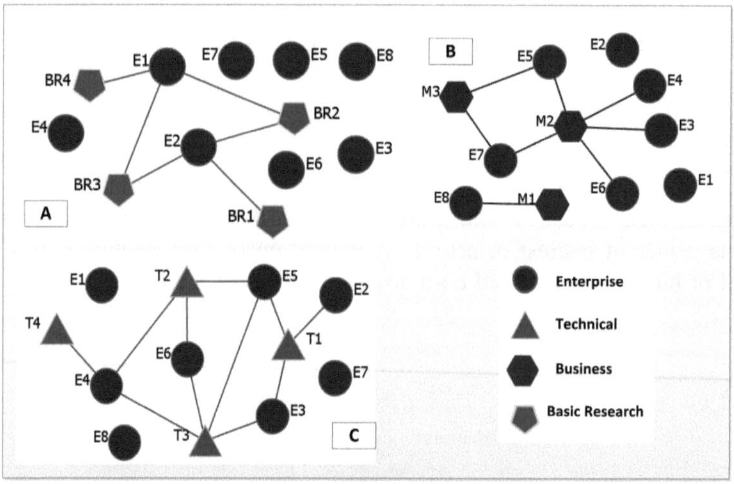

Fig. 5. Example map of enterprises' competences - (A) basic research (B) business and (C) technical

In order to analyze the innovation potential of a co-innovation network according to different perspectives, the following graphs can be created (Fig. 6). From the perspective of basic research (graph 6A), it is possible to verify that both enterprises E4 and E5 might have access to knowledge BR1 (exclusive competence in this network) through the enterprise E2. On the other hand, from the perspective of business competences (graph 6B) enterprise E6 might gain access to market competence M3 through enterprise E5 and might have access to market competence M1 through enterprise E8. From the perspective of technical competences (graph 6C) enterprise E4 might have direct access to all available technical competences in this co-innovation network through the enterprise E5, for example.

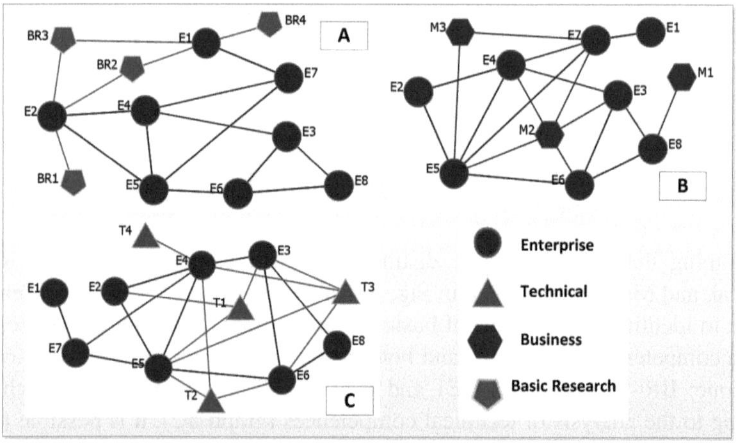

Fig. 6. Example of the potential of co-innovation analysis - (A) basic research (B) business and (C) technical perspective

5 Case Study

Brisa Case Study. Brisa is the largest operator of highways in Portugal. It is currently responsible for the monitoring and management of a network of eleven highways, representing the main part of the Portuguese road network.

In order to increase its operational efficiency and safeguard its leadership in providing new services to customers, Brisa has developed collaborative relationships with several enterprises and organizations (e.g. research institutions, universities, associations, government entities, start-ups, business angels) that have given rise to the emergence of a long-term co-innovation network.

Methodology. The research described in this paper is based on the two most relevant co-innovation projects in terms of innovation improvements carried out by the Brisa network.

The methodology used to develop the research comprises two steps. In the first step, the members who had taken part in innovation projects were identified and characterized. In the second step two techniques were applied in order to get empirical data: interviews with key actors and a questionnaire addressed to all members.

Taking into account the data collected, Table 1 shows the competences involved in the co-innovation projects under study. The number of "x's" represents the effort made in terms of basic research from the technical perspective.

Table 1. - Record of the competences identified

	Competences	Level of effort involved in	
		Basic Research	Technical
C1	Computer vision	xx	x
C2	Software engineering	xx	x
C3	Infrared illumination	xx	x
C4	Automatic pattern recognition	xxx	x
C5	Toll systems		x
C6	Information systems architecture	xx	x
C7	Industrial design		x
C8	Modelling of products		x
C9	Rapid prototyping		x
C10	Development of molds		x
C11	Plastic injection		x
C12	Functional tests		x
C13	Software development	x	x
C14	Software architecture	x	x
C15	Project management		x
C16	Functional analysis	x	xx
C17	Remote monitoring	x	x

(Continued)

Table 1. (*Continued*)

	Competences	Level of effort involved in	
		Basic Research	Technical
C18	Supplier of equipment for image capture		x
C19	Electronic toll collection (ETC) systems		x
C20	Information systems open to multi-vendor	x	
C21	Automatic vehicle identification systems	x	x
C22	Communication systems between vehicles	x	x
C23	Classification systems of vehicles	xx	x
C24	Short run production		x

The graphical visualization of competences provides a tool to evaluate in detail the 'sub-structures' that may be exist in a co-innovation network. Partitions of partners into cliques, i.e. sub-structures of a network in which the partners are more strongly linked to one another than they are to other partners of the co-innovation network can be important to comprehend how the process of innovation flows within the network.

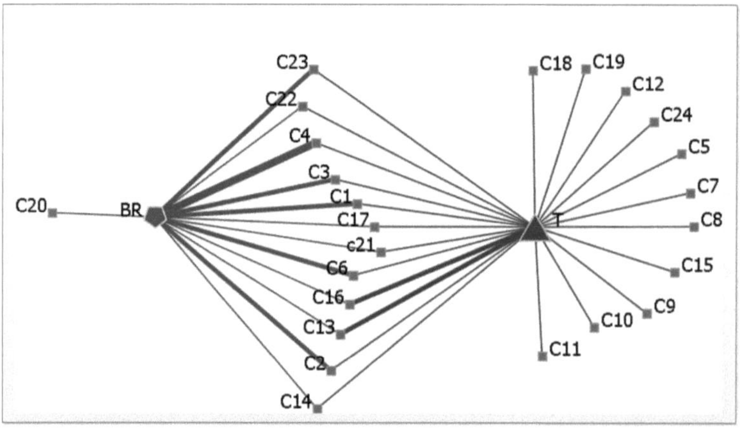

Fig. 7. Level of effort involved in the co-innovation projects under study.

In Fig. 7, the node size of Basic Research (BR) and Technical (T) represents the sum of competences used in the co-innovation projects and the node size of the competences is identical because they have no associated metrics. The link's width between competences and class of innovation, Basic Research or Technical, represents the level of effort based on each one perspective.

Figure 8 illustrates the distribution of competences by the partners of the co-innovation network.

Hence, the most versatile entities in terms of contribution to basic research and technical perspective are O1, E2 and E7 and O1 is the one with the greatest number of distinct competences. On the contrary, E5 and E3 are the members that alone contribute

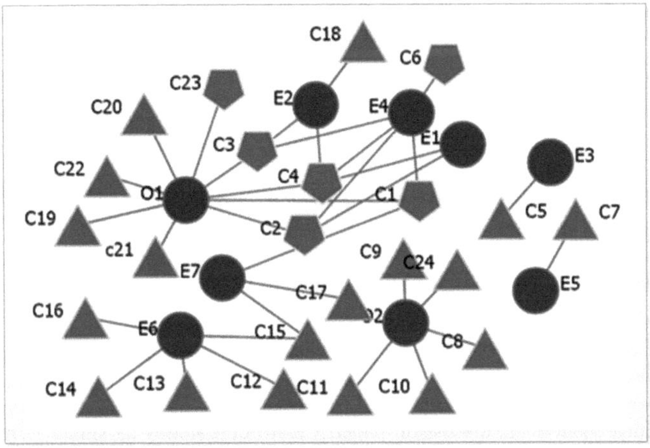

Fig. 8. Competences used by each partner in the co-innovation projects under study.

with only one competence, C5 and C7, to the innovation project. Additionally, some partners are the only ones to hold certain competences, for instance: E6, O1 and O2 which give them a dominant position within the co-innovation network.

6 Conclusions

The development of models to analyze co-innovation networks provides conditions for a broader adoption of the collaborative network paradigm. Furthermore, the development of research activities in this field has contributed to strength the scientific area by promoting new insights to enrich the theoretical debate.

As far as the presented co-innovation networks patterns is concerned, according to the empirical data we can conclude that BIT is a mixed enterprise in the sense that its performance is between the science and technical perspectives. In fact, BIT incorporates the ability to generate and produce validated knowledge and the ability to develop and demonstrate new products.

The application of this mapping to BIT co-innovation network has been a crucial step in terms of showing the use of the proposed approach. The case study gives us an overview about the performance of the different organizations in a collaborative environment, as a strategy to promote innovation flows.

Further research steps are essential regarding the consolidation of a more robust model as well as to strengthen its validation.

Acknowledgments. This work was partially supported by BRISA Innovation and Technology (BIT) through a research and development project.

References

1. Lundvall, B.-Å.: Innovation, Growth and Social Cohesion: The Danish Model. Elgar Publishers, London (2002)
2. Freeman, C.: The national system of innovation in historical perspective. Camb. J. Econ. **19**(1), 5–24 (1995)
3. Camarinha-Matos, L., Afsarmanesh, H., Galeano, N., Molina, A.: Collaborative networked organizations – concepts and practice in manufacturing enterprises. Comput. Ind. Eng. **57**, 46–60 (2009)
4. Fagerberg, J.: Innovation: a guide to the literature. In: The Oxford Handbook of Innovation. Oxford University Press (2005)
5. Grant, R.M.: Toward a knowledge-based theory of the firm. Strateg. Manag. J. **17**(Special Issue: Knowledge and the Firm), 109–122 (1996)
6. Marques, A., Abrunhosa, A.: Do Modelo Linear à Abordagem Sistémica – Aspetos teóricos e de política económica, discussion paper. Centro de Estudos da União Europeia, vol. 33. FE/UC (2005)
7. Edquist, C.: Systems of Innovation: Technologies. Institutions and Organisations, Printer/Cassel, London (1997)
8. Tidd, J.: Innovation Models. Imperial College London, Tanaka Business School, London (2006)
9. Kline, S.J., Rosenberg, N.: An overview of innovation. In: Landau, R., Rosenberg, N. (eds.) The Positive Sum Strategy: Harnessing Technology for Economic Growth, pp. 275–304. National Academy Press, Washington D.C. (1986)
10. Caraça, J., Ferreira, J.L., Mendonça, S.: A chain-interactive innovation model for the learning economy: prelude for a proposal. ISEG, WP 012/2007/DE (2007)
11. Godinho, M.M.: Inovação em Portugal. Lisboa Fundação Francisco Manuel Santos, Lisboa (2013)
12. Tidd, J., Bessant, J., Pavitt, K.: Managing Innovation: Integrating Technological, Market and Organizational Change. Wiley, Hong Kong (2005)
13. Mankins, J.C.: A technology readiness assessments: a retrospective. Acta Astronaut. **65**(9–10), 1216–1223 (2009)
14. EARTO: The TRL Scale as a Research & Innovation Policy Tool, EARTO Recommendations (2014)
15. Mankins, J.C.: White Paper, Advanced Concepts Office, Office of Space Access and Technology, NASA (1995)
16. OCDE: Oslo Manual: Guidelines for Collecting and Interpreting Innovation Data, 3rd edn. (2005)
17. Abreu, A., Camarinha-Matos, L.M.: Understanding social capital in collaborative networks. In: Ortiz, Á., Franco, R.D., Gasquet, P.G. (eds.) BASYS 2010. IFIP AICT, vol. 322, pp. 109–118. Springer, Heidelberg (2010)
18. Abreu, A., Macedo, P., Camarinha-Matos, L.M.: Towards a methodology to measure the alignment of value systems in collaborative networks. In: Azevedo, A. (ed.) Innovation in Manufacturing Networks. IFIP, vol. 266, pp. 37–46. Springer, New York (2008)
19. Urze, P., Abreu, A.: Knowledge transfer assessment in a co-innovation network. In: Camarinha-Matos, L.M., Xu, L., Afsarmanesh, H. (eds.) Collaborative Networks in the Internet of Services. IFIP AICT, vol. 380, pp. 605–615. Springer, Heidelberg (2012)

A Proposal of Performance Indicators for Collaborative Business Ecosystems

Paula Graça[1,2(✉)] and Luís M. Camarinha-Matos[1]

[1] Faculdade de Ciências e Tecnologia and Uninova CTS, Universidade Nova de Lisboa, Campus de Caparica, 2829-516 Caparica, Portugal
cam@uninova.pt

[2] Instituto Superior de Engenharia de Lisboa, Instituto Politécnico de Lisboa, Rua Conselheiro Emídio Navarro 1, 1959-007 Lisbon, Portugal
mgraca@deetc.isel.pt

Abstract. Business ecosystems enabled by the increasing use and improvement of communication networks, offer nowadays a powerful competitive advantage to business players and entrepreneurs. They form a collaborative new mean of economic and social value creation, addressing customers' needs, overcoming constraints of individual firms, increasing capabilities for new business opportunities, and accelerating learning and innovation. This paper proposes a set of performance indicators to measure some of these collaboration benefits, therefore motivating the sustainability and resilience of the business ecosystem. The presented results are based on simulation models, which intend to characterize the roles and interactions of a real life collaborative business ecosystem.

Keywords: Collaborative network · Business ecosystem · Digital business ecosystem · Performance indicators

1 Introduction

The increasing progress and use of information and communication technologies, namely computer networks, and collaboration platforms, have changed the ways of making business, which have moved from traditional industrial sectors to business ecosystems supported by collaborative platforms. The term Business Ecosystem was introduced by Moore [1], which used natural ecosystems as a metaphor to describe business environments. According to this author, a business ecosystem is "*an economic community supported by a foundation of interacting organizations and individuals - the organisms of the business world. This economic community produces goods and services of value to customers, who themselves are members of the ecosystem*". The players of the ecosystem "*coevolve their capabilities and roles*" [2] in a symbiotic business environment.

A recent business trends report [3] denotes the continued rise of business ecosystems as a highly relevant transition with substantial implications for the society, economy, and businesses. In fact, as argued by the author, a business ecosystem captures three main generic characteristics of any ecosystem: (1) Variety for a healthy

H. Afsarmanesh et al. (Eds.): PRO-VE 2016, IFIP AICT 480, pp. 253–264, 2016.
DOI: 10.1007/978-3-319-45390-3_22

ecosystem, due to the encouragement for participation of a diversity of organizations, that together can overcome the capabilities of any one of them; (2) Potential for ever more productive development of the ecosystem, due to the increasingly advanced ways of collaboration, boosted by high-tech tools of connectivity and interaction; and (3) Longevity and durability of the ecosystem, due to a collective awareness of its members to protect, foster, and sustain the ecosystem, motivated by common goals, benefits, and values. These characteristics of an ecosystem highlight and reinforce the purpose of this paper, which is driven by the following research question:

> ***"What is a reasonable set of key performance indicators to measure and assess collaboration benefits in a collaborative business ecosystem (CBE)?"*** [4]

In order to address the above presented research question, the following hypothesis is considered: "*Collaboration benefits can be evaluated and made explicit if a set of indicators is established through a holistic combination of concepts of value and benefit, derived from a number of research areas such as value systems, social networks analysis, supply chain performance, and complex adaptive systems*". This hypothesis guides this research, which proposes a set of performance indicators and related metrics to assess benefits in a CBE, promoting its sustainability and resilience.

The remaining sections of this paper are organized as follow: section two presents a brief literature review, highlighting contributions from a number of related research fields, section three proposes a set of performance indicators to assess CBEs, and section four shows results of some metrics based on simulation data, to assess the coherence of the models. The last section discusses the contributions and future work.

2 Literature Review

The research area of collaborative networks [5], in particular their established reference models and taxonomies [6], provide a significant contribution to understand the structure and dynamics of a business ecosystem. A business ecosystem, as described in [6], is a sub-class of a Virtual Organizations Breeding Environment (VBE), i.e. a source network of organizations founded as a long-term strategic alliance. As such, a CBE is modeled as a community of organizations, whose connections are created during a given period (for instance one year), resulting in the formation of Virtual Organizations (VOs), according to collaborative business opportunities.

In order to propose performance indicators for a CBE, a literature research shows that there are already well-established indicators for individual organizations, of which the balanced scorecard (BSC) [7] is the most common example. However, to measure collaboration benefits in a network of organizations, or more specifically in a CBE, there is still a lack of solutions, despite some efforts made in a number of research areas. One example is a conceptual model for VBEs value systems using a BSC to monitor the VBE performance [8]. Another example is the value systems proposed in [9, 10], which identify collaborative social and economic core values, suggesting mechanisms to assess the alignment of the value systems of the network members. These mechanisms allow identifying conflicts that may affect the performance of a CBE, although not suitable for performance measurement purposes. More concerned with collaboration benefits, an example presented in [11], identifies and characterizes benefits, such as innovation capacity, flexibility, agility, costs, and risks, among others, which constitute an important input for the establishment of the proposed metrics and associated performance indicators.

The research area of traditional supply chains, which have evolved to more collaborative platforms, known as supply chain collaboration (SCC), provides a wide number of performance models and metrics. For instance in [12], the authors made a comprehensive review of supply chain performance measurement methods comprising the period from 2000 to 2011, and found several techniques and models that were used, namely, AHP (Analytic Hierarchy Process), SCOR (Supply-chain Operations Reference Model), SEM (Structural Equation Model), BSC (Balanced Scorecard), Six Sigma, and combinations of two of them. In [13], more concerned with collaboration (SCC), the author conducted a survey in which he identified a number of mathematical and simulation models focused mainly on the performance evaluation. Some of these techniques and models can be adapted to CBEs; in particular, simulation models to characterize the business environment, and a subset of statistic models from SEM, widely used in the field of behavioral and social sciences.

Another related area is the social network analysis (SNA), which is currently a subject of much research work due to the growth of social networks. In SNA, the social structures are analyzed using network and graph theory, which provides measures of centrality (degree, betweenness, closeness, etc.), and cohesion (reciprocity, density, clustering, etc.). Inspired by SNA, several attempts have been made to apply these indicators to collaborative networks. For instance, a set of indicators to measure the value of social capital of a VBE [14], and a methodology for a network analysis of a business ecosystem [15], among others. However, the structural analysis of the network is limited when it comes to capture the value of the economic or social exchanges represented by the connections. To overcome these limitations, a value network analysis (VNA) model is proposed in [16], providing metrics to evaluate the complex dynamic exchanges of tangible and intangible values in the network. Even though these contributions, a solution to measure the performance of a CBE is not yet established.

The proposed performance indicators for CBEs described in the next section, are inspired mostly by these last presented approaches.

3 Metrics and Measures for Collaborative Business Ecosystems

The adopted research approach at this stage uses models with simulated data to assess the consistency and make a preliminary calibration of the measurement scale of the metrics and performance indicators proposed in this section. The approach is represented by the process depicted in Fig. 1. The analysis of the literature in a number of related research areas, such as enterprise performance indicators, value systems, collaboration benefits, social network analysis, and supply chain collaboration, inspired a set of metrics and measures with a potential applicability in CBEs. Then, several simulation models of CBEs are used to assess the metrics and calibrate the scales using ratios and standard normalization methods.

A CBE model is represented by a weighted direct graph, where nodes stand for organizations, and arcs correspond to the collaborative transactions between them. The weights of the arcs stand for the number of times the collaborative transactions were performed in a given period (by the creation of VOs in the CBE). In the used models, random series of data were also considered, to simulate existing (e.g. portfolio of competencies) or new value created by the organizations (e.g. products, services, or patents), resulting or not from the collaboration, therefore not directly characterized by the graph. Finally, the last step resulted in a first proposal of a set of performance indicators to assess CBEs.

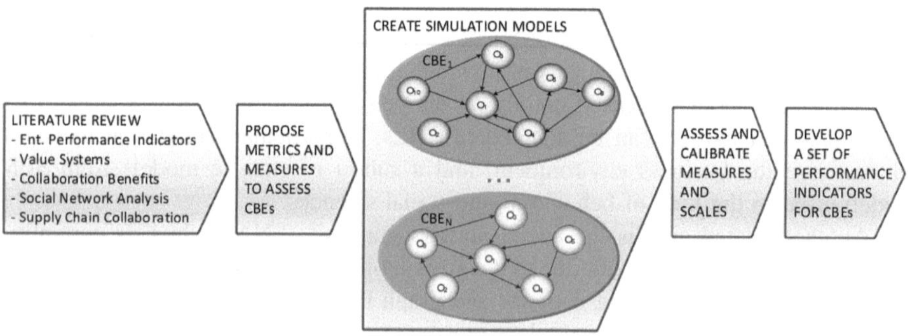

Fig. 1. Process representing the used methodology to develop a set of PIs for CBEs.

The performance indicators for CBEs introduced in this work and described in the following tables are: (1) Innovation Indicator (II), to measure the innovation potential of a CBE; (2) Contribution Indicator (CI), to evaluate the value creation of a CBE; (3) Prestige Indicator (PI), to assess the influence/prominence of each organization in the CBE; and (4) Resilience Indicator (RI), to assess the resilience of a CBE.

The choice of the above indicators is based on the performed literature analysis and mainly driven by societal, economic, and business concerns. The potential for innovation of a CBE reflects its health level, therefore contributing for social and economic value creation. On the other hand, in a business environment, the economic value is a strong argument for collaboration. As such, the contribution indicator is proposed to show the economic value of the collaboration, i.e. the value that an organization brought in the CBE, and the value that is gained by an organization from the CBE. The prestige indicator shows the distribution of collaboration among organizations in the CBE, revealing eventual prominence of one or more organizations, or even isolated organizations. A strong collaboration level enhances a common network identity, reinforcing collaboration trust, and increasing collaborative knowledge. At last, the resilience indicator in a business context assesses "*the capacity for an enterprise to survive, adapt, and grow in face of turbulent change*" [17]. Table 1 presents a brief description of these indicators, explaining their meaning for individual organizations O_i in the CBE, and for the CBE as a whole.

Table 1. A short description of the proposed performance indicators.

Performance indicators for CBEs		
Indicator	Definition (for each O_i)	Definition (for the CBE)
Innovation Indicator (**II**)	**II_i** - Measures the innovation potential of a member of the CBE	**II_{CBE}** - Measures the innovation potential of the CBE as a whole
Contribution Indicator (**CI**)	**CI_i** - Measures contribution for value creation of a member of the CBE	**CI_{CBE} = (CI_{CBE}t, CI_{CBE}d)** Measures the total value creation of the collaboration in the CBE as a whole (**CI_{CBE}t**), and the degree to which the most active member exceeds the contribution of the others (**CI_{CBE}t**)
Prestige Indicator (**PI**)	**PI_i** - Measures the influence/proeminence of a member of the CBE	**PI_{CBE}** - Measures the average difference between the most influent member and that of all members of the CBE
Resilience Indicator (**RI**)	______	**RI_{CBE} = f (Di, Ef, Ad, Co)**Assesses the resilience of the CBE, evaluating four main components: Diversity (**Di**), Efficiency (**Ef**), Adaptability (**Ad**), and Cohesion (**Co**)

Considering these performance indicators, a set of appropriate metrics had to be found in order to identify key measurable characteristics of each indicator. The suggested metrics are shown in Table 2, including mainly counting measurements (e.g. number of new products, services, or patents created by each organization or by the CBE as a whole), as well as measurements related to the network structure, such as centrality, which is a measure of the activity or level of influence in terms of relationships among the organizations of the CBE.

The metrics shown in Table 2 to assess the resilience of a CBE were inspired by the four fundamental characteristics of resilient living ecosystems considered in [18]: Diversity, Efficiency, Adaptability, and Cohesion, and were tailored to business ecosystems. In fact, the resilience of the CBE can be calculated as a function of these factors, if each of them can be translated in terms of one or more quantified metrics.

At this stage, the performance indicators can then be formulated as a function of the presented metrics. The suggested formulas described in Table 3, are calculated in terms of ratios (case of II), or measures of degree centrality (case of CI), and betweenness centrality (case of PI).

The measures of centrality are adopted from [19], but they will have to be reformulated in order to incorporate the weights of the connections, which represent collaborative opportunities and contacts towards potential collaborative opportunities. Then, the resulting indicators are normalized in relation to the size of the CBE (number of organizations). Finally, RI is calculated as a function of the factors (Di, Ef, Ad, and Co), in which the evaluating metrics are weighted by a value according to their relevance in the context of the CBE.

Table 2. A proposal of metrics to establish the proposed performance indicators for CBEs.

Metrics for Performance Indicators for CBEs			
PIs	**Org. O_i / CBE**	**Metrics**	
Innovation Indicator (II)	$\mathbf{II_i}$	$\#PortPd_i$	- Portfolio of products, services, or patents of the member O_i
		$\#NewPd_i$	- No. of new products, services, or patents generated by the member O_i
	$\mathbf{II_{CBE}}$	$\{\#VO_1, \ldots, \#VO_n\}$	- No. of VOs in which the members $O_1, \ldots, O_n$ participated
		$\Sigma_i \#PortPd_i$	- Total portfolio of products, services, or patents of the CBE
		$\{\#NewPd_1, \ldots, \#NewPd_n\}$	- No. of new products, services, or patents generated by the members $O_1, \ldots, O_n$
		$\Sigma_i \#NewPd_i$	- Total no. of new products generated in the CBE
Contribution Indicator (CI)	$\mathbf{CI_i}$ = ($\mathbf{CI_i}$ **in**, $\mathbf{CI_i}$ **out**)	$\#CoOp_i$ in, $\#CoOp_i$ out	- No. of collaborative opportunities the member O_i gained from or brought in the CBE
		Act in(O_i), Act out(O_i)	- Activity in/out of the member O_i in the CBE
	$\mathbf{CI_{CBE}}$ = ($\mathbf{CI_{CBE}t}$, $\mathbf{CI_{CBE}d}$)	$\Sigma_i \#CoOp_i$	- Total no. of collaborative opportunities created in the CBE
		$\{\#CoOp_1, \ldots, \#CoOp_n\}$	- No. of collaborative opportunities in which the members $O_1, \ldots, O_n$ participated
		$\Sigma_i [Act(O^*) - Act(O_i)]$	- Sum of the differences between the activity of the most active member (O*) and that of all members of the CBE Act(O*) = #CoOp of the most active member
Prestige Indicator (PI)	$\mathbf{PI_i}$	$\#CCoOp_i$	- No. of received contacts towards potential collaborative opportunities of the member O_i
		Inf(O_i)	- Influence of the member Oi, i.e., the likelihood of O_i to be contacted towards potential collaborative opportunities
	$\mathbf{PI_{CBE}}$	$\{\#CCoOp_1, \ldots, \#CCoOp_n\}$	- No. of receiving contacts towards potential collaborative opportunities of the members $O_1, \ldots, O_n$
		$\Sigma_i [Inf(O^*) - Inf(O_i)]/(n-1)$	- Average of the differences between the influence of the most influent member and that of all members of the CBE Inf(O*) = influence of the most influent member
Resilience Indicator (RI)	—	——	
	$\mathbf{RI_{CBE}}$ = **f (Di, Ef, Ad, Co)**	$\Sigma_i \#CoOp_i$	- Total no. of collaborative opportunities created in the CBE
		$\Sigma_i \#PortPd_i$	- Total portfolio of products, services, or patents of the CBE
		$\Sigma_i \#PortCp_i$	- Total portfolio of competences of the CBE
		$\Sigma_i \#ShIntgAs_i$	- Total of shared intangible assets (documents, processes, knowledge, etc.) in the CBE
		$\Sigma_i \#CCoOp_i$	- Total no. of contacts towards potential collaborative opportunities in the CBE
		$\Sigma_i \#RCCoOp_i$	- Total no. of reciprocated contacts towards potential collaborative opportunities in the CBE
		$\Sigma_i \#PCCoOp_i$	- Total no. of possible contacts between all pairs of members of the CBE

Table 3. Proposed calculation formulas for the performance indicators to assess CBEs.

Performance Indicators for CBEs		
PIs	**Calculation**	**Remarks**
Innovation I. (II)	$II_i = \frac{\#NewPd_i}{\#PortPd_i}$	Is measured by the ratio between the two variables #NewPd$_i$ and PortPd$_i$
	$II_{CBE} = \frac{\sum_i \#NewPd_i}{\sum_i \#PortPd_i} * r(\#VO, \#NewPd)$	The ratio of the totals is weighed by the correlation *r* between the two variables: (#VO, #NewPd)
Contribution Indicator (CI)	$CI_i = (CI_i\ in,\ CI_i\ out)$ $CI_i\ in = C_D(O_i)in = \sum_j O_{ij} \#CoOp_{ij}\ in$ $CI_i\ out = C_D(O_i)out = \sum_j O_{ij} \#CoOp_{ij}\ out$	Act in/out (O_i) can be measured by the weighted indegree/outdegree centrality (C_D) of the member O_i in the CBE, which stands for the sum of direct connections in/out of the member O_i to the n members O_j with weight #CoOp$_{ij}$ where $C_D(O_i)\ in/out = Act\ in/out(O_i)$
	$CI_{CBE} = (CI_{CBE}t,\ CI_{CBE}d)$ $CI_{CBE}t = \sum_i \#CoOp_i$ $CI_{CBE}d = C_D = \frac{\sum_i [C_D(O^*) - C_D(O_i)]}{(n-2)(n-1)}$	$CI_{CBE}d$ can be measured by the weighted degree centrality (C_D) of the CBE as a whole where $C_D(O_i) = Act(O_i) = \sum_j O_{ij} \#CoOp_{ij}$ $C_D(O^*) = Act(O^*) = max[C_D(O_i)]$
Prestige Indicator (PI)	$PI_i = C_B(O_i) = \sum_k \sum_j o_{kj}(O_i)$ $k < j$ $k \neq j \neq i$	Can be measured by the weighted betweenness centrality (C_B) of the member O_i in the CBE, assuming that connections between any member O_k and any other O_j have weight of #CCoOp$_{kj}$ where $C_B(O_i) = Inf(O_i)$
	$PI_{CBE} = C_B = \frac{\sum_i [C_B(O^*) - C_B(O_i)]}{(n-1)(n-2)(n-1)}$	Can be measured by the weighted betweenness centrality (C_B) of the CBE as a whole, assuming that connections between any member O_k and any other O_j have weight of #CCoOp$_{kj}$ where $C_B(O_i) = Inf(O_i)$ $C_B(O^*) = Inf(O^*) = \max[Inf(O_i)]$
	———	———
Resilience Indicator (RI)	$RI_{CBE} = f(Di,\ Ef,\ Ad,\ Co)$ $Di = \frac{\sum_i \#PortPd_i * W_i}{\sum_i W_i} + \frac{\sum_i \#PortCp_i * W_i}{\sum_i W_i}$ $Ef = \frac{\sum_i \#CoOp_i * W_i}{\sum \#CCoOp_i * W_i}$ $Ad = \frac{\sum_i \#IntgAs_i * W_i}{\sum_i W_i}$ $Co = \frac{\sum_i \#RCCoOp_i * W_i}{\sum_i \#CCoOp_i * W_i} + \frac{\sum_i \#CCoOp_i * W_i}{\sum_i \#PCCoOp_i * W_i}$	Can be measured in function of the factors: Di, Ef, Ad, and Co: (Di)versity = Port. Products + Port. Competences (Ef)ficiency = ratio of C. Opportunities over the Contacts towards potential C. Opportunities (Ad)aptability = Intangible Assets (Co)hesion = Reciprocity + Density where W_i is the weight of each metric according to its relevance in the CBE (which can be evaluated by questionnaires, interviews, literature, etc.)

4 Assessment and Calibration of the Performance Indicators

Among the performance indicators introduced in the previous section: Innovation Indicator (II), Contribution Indicator (CI), Prestige Indicator (PI), and Resilience Indicator (RI), II is chosen for the illustrative examples presented below. The II for a given organization O_i (II_i), measures the ratio between the new products, services, or patents created by that organization (#NewPd$_i$) during a given period, and its portfolio

(#PortPd$_i$). The same indicator for the whole CBE, measures the ratio between the number of total products, services, or patents created in the CBE ($\sum_i$ #NewPd$_i$), and the total portfolio of the CBE ($\sum_i$ #PortPd$_i$). However, this ratio does not give any indication about collaboration, i.e., the indicator does not reflect a measure of the improvement of innovation due to collaboration. Thus, the ratio II for the whole CBE (II_{CBE}) is weighted by a correlation coefficient (Spearman's or Pearson's) [20], denoted by r, between the number of VOs in which the organizations have participated (#VO), and the new products, services, or patents that they have created (#NewPd).

Pearson's correlation coefficient is a measure of the extent to which two quantitative variables (in this case #VO and #NewPd) are linearly related. It measures the strength of the association between the two variables, giving a value between +1 and −1 inclusive, where 1 is total positive correlation, 0 is no correlation, and −1 is total negative correlation. The Spearman correlation coefficient, is the usual Person r applied to data in the form of ranks, measuring how well the relationship between two variables can be described using a monotonic function. The process to rank data in order to calculate the Spearman correlation, consists of replacing each element of a set, by its ranking position according to its relative value (the lowest is rated one, and the higher the number of elements of the set). For instance, considering the set of data $S_1 = \{9, 2, 8, 5\}$, the resulting rank set is $RkS_1 = \{4, 1, 3, 2\}$. When the set contains repeating elements, for instance the set $S_2 = \{9, 2, 5, 5\}$, the repeated elements are rated with the mean of their raking positions, e.g., the mean for the element 5 is (2 + 3)/2 = 2.5), resulting in the rank set $RkS_2 = \{4, 1, 2.5, 2.5\}$.

To assess the metrics and coherence of the performance indicator II, as stated above, three simulated scenarios were created (CBE$_1$, CBE$_2$, and CBE$_3$), and described in Tables 4, 5 and 6. The three scenarios represent the same CBE composed of ten organizations, but showing different indexes of innovation, and collaboration

Table 4. Simulated scenario of the CBE$_1$ to assess the Innovation Indicator (II).

#N	#PortPd	#VO	#NewPd	II	Rk(#VO,#NewPd)	
O$_1$	1	2	2	**0,22**	3	6
O$_2$	2	2	2	**0,11**	3	6
O$_3$	3	3	1	**0,04**	5,5	2
O$_4$	2	4	2	**0,11**	7,5	6
O$_5$	3	5	3	**0,11**	9	9
O$_6$	4	3	2	**0,06**	5,5	6
O$_7$	5	6	4	**0,09**	10	10
O$_8$	1	2	1	**0,11**	3	2
O$_9$	2	4	2	**0,11**	7,5	6
O$_{10}$	3	1	1	**0,04**	1	2
10	26		20	**0,77** r_P:	**0,84** r_S:	**0,75**
				II_{CBE}:	**0,64**	**0,58**

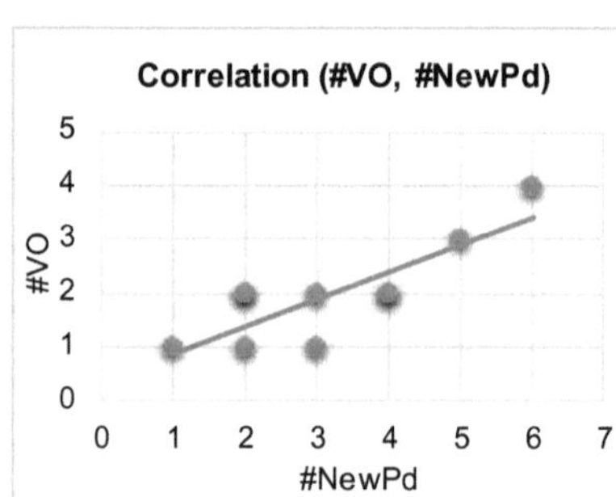

Notes: r_P and r_S denote Pearson and Spearman correlation coefficient, respectively
Rk(#VO, #NewPd) stands for rank data of #VO and #NewPd, used to find Spearman correlation coefficient

performances. The goal of the first two scenarios is to show the influence of the correlation coefficient over the same value of the ratio II of the CBE as a whole, i.e., the smaller the correlation coefficient, the smaller the value of the II_{CBE}. The third scenario shows how a high ratio II is pushed down caused by a very low correlation coefficient, meaning that the innovation capacity of the ecosystem was not due to collaboration.

Table 4 represents the simulated scenario CBE_1 exhibiting hypothetical series of data for the metrics #PortPd, #VO, and #NewPd, and the calculated ratio II_i, between 0 and 1, using linear normalization. The values of the II_{CBE} (0.64 and 0.58), are calculated by multiplying the ratio II (0.77) by the Pearson (0.84) and Spearman (0.75) correlation coefficients, respectively.

Table 5 depicts another scenario (CBE_2) showing the same ratio II for the whole ecosystem (0.77). However, the collaboration coefficients are lower (0.51 and 0.50), resulting in a lower value (0.39) for the II_{CBE}.

Table 5. Simulated scenario of the CBE_2 to assess the Innovation Indicator (II).

#N	#PortPd	#VO	#NewPd	II	Rk(#VO,#NewPd)	
O_1	1	2	1	**0,11**	3	1,5
O_2	2	2	2	**0,11**	3	5,5
O_3	3	3	2	**0,07**	5	5,5
O_4	2	5	2	**0,11**	8,5	5,5
O_5	3	5	2	**0,07**	8,5	5,5
O_6	4	6	2	**0,05**	10	5,5
O_7	5	4	3	**0,06**	6,5	9,5
O_8	1	2	2	**0,22**	3	5,5
O_9	2	4	3	**0,16**	6,5	9,5
O_{10}	3	1	1	**0,04**	1	1,5
10	26		20	**0,77** r_P:	**0,51** r_S:	**0,50**
				II_{CBE}:	**0,39**	**0,39**

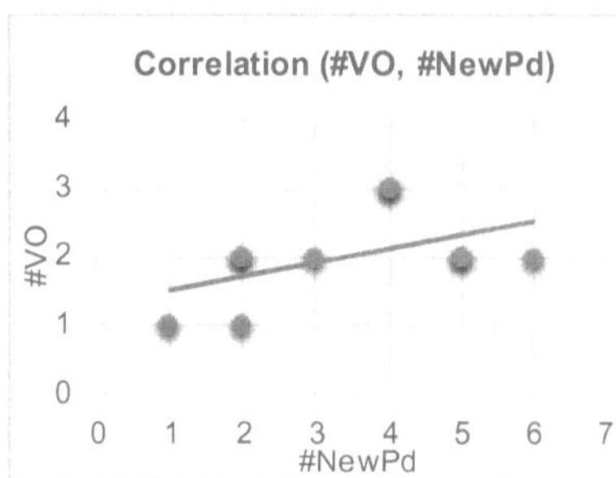

The last scenario (CBE_3), depicted in Table 6, exhibits a high ratio II (0.92), but a very low collaboration coefficients (0.13 and 0.10), resulting in equally low II_{CBE} values (0.12 and 0.09), meaning that the high improvement of innovation is not due to the collaboration in the CBE.

Considering the boundary conditions of the correlation coefficient ($r = 1$ and $r = 0$), the value $r = 1$ maximizes the result of the II_{CBE}, meaning that the innovation capacity is all up to collaboration. The value $r = 0$, pushes the resulting II_{CBE} down to 0, meaning that the innovation is not related to collaboration. A negative correlation coefficient is not considered, as it is not assumed that collaboration could influence negatively the innovation capability of the organizations.

The above analysis is based on simulated scenarios. For a further assessment of the proposed indicators, the ongoing work involves capturing real data from a concrete business ecosystem. This is being done for the ports area, a collaborative community offering integrated logistics and freight services. A port area is an interesting use case,

Table 6. Simulated scenario of the CBE_3 to assess the Innovation Indicator (II).

#N	#PortPd	#VO	#NewPd	II	Rk(#VO,#NewPd)	
O_1	1	5	3	**0,25**	8,5	7
O_2	2	6	1	**0,04**	10	2,5
O_3	3	2	2	**0,06**	2,5	5
O_4	2	4	1	**0,04**	6	2,5
O_5	3	4	1	**0,03**	6	2,5
O_6	4	5	5	**0,11**	8,5	10
O_7	5	3	4	**0,07**	4	9
O_8	1	2	3	**0,25**	2,5	7
O_9	2	4	3	**0,13**	6	7
O_{10}	3	1	1	**0,03**	1	2,5
10	26		24	**0,92**	**r_P: 0,13**	**r_S: 0,10**
				II_{CBE}:	**0,12**	**0,09**

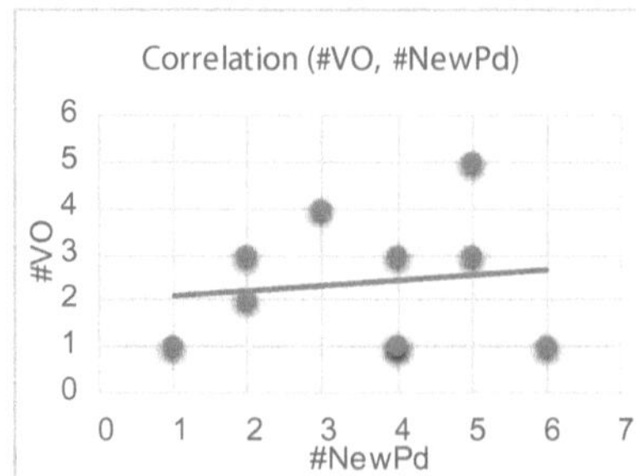

as it offers a wide diversity of players and services, such as port authorities, customs, freight forwarders, multi-modal transport entities (rail, road, and maritime), suppliers, and customers, collaborating through increasingly integrated technological platforms, effectively contributing to the growth of the local economy and social value.

5 Conclusions and Further Work

The metrics and associated performance indicators presented along this paper, contribute as a first approach to accomplish the research question and related hypothesis stated in the first section, by proposing a set of indicators to assess collaboration benefits. A set of metrics were also suggested to quantify those benefits, and different scenarios of CBEs represented by models with hypothetical data were used in order to assess the validity of the measures associated to the indicators. The ongoing work, as mentioned above, encompasses the continuation of the assessment of the proposed indicators, but capturing real data from concrete businesses ecosystems.

The future work is aimed at finding an answer to address the second research question, which consists of:

"How to promote collaboration sustainability and resilience within a business ecosystem?" [4]

In order to respond to this question, the following hypothesis is considered: "*Sustainability and resilience of collaboration in business ecosystems can be promoted if a system of incentives, combined with transparent assessment methods, is implemented at the ecosystem level*". This hypothesis will guide the next steps of this research, which will be mostly supported by models using system dynamics (SD) combined with agent based (AB) simulation. The AnyLogic Multimethod Simulation Software [21], will provide the methods and simulation tools to create and explore these models. SD is a method to improve learning in complex systems, somewhat a method to develop computer models, to help learning about dynamic complexity, understand the sources of policy resistance, and design more effective policies [22].

The goal of applying SD at this stage of the research is first to capture and represent the organization of a CBE, considered as a complex system, which, along with stocks and flows structures, feedback processes, time delays, and other structures, determine its dynamic behavior. In a second phase, the performance indicators should be introduced to affect the dynamic behavior of the agents. Finally, a third phase will be dedicated to simulation to observe the agents' behavior, playing with the introduction of incentives/penalizations, resulting from the decisions of the managers.

The explained research approach, aims to specify, validate and make accepted by experts and the scientific community, a set of indicators for CBEs, which not only allow to evaluate the performance of the system, but also contribute to motivate its sustainability and resilience.

Acknowledgment. This work benefited from the ongoing research within the CoDIS (Collaborative Networks and Distributed Industrial Systems Group) which is part of both the New University of Lisbon (UNL) - Faculty of Sciences and Technology, and the UNINOVA - Institute for the Development of New Technologies. Partial support also comes from Fundação para a Ciência e Tecnologia through the PEST program UID/EEA/00066/2013.

References

1. Moore, J.F.: Predators and prey: a new ecology of competition. Harvard Bus. Rev. **71**(3), 75–83 (1993)
2. Moore, J.F.: The Death of Competition: Leadership and Strategy in the Age of Business Ecosystems. HarperCollins Publishers, New York (1996)
3. Kelly, E.: Introduction: Business Ecosystems Come of Age (2015)
4. Graça, P., Camarinha-Matos, L.M.: The need of performance indicators for collaborative business ecosystems. In: Camarinha-Matos, L.M., Baldissera, T.A., Di Orio, G., Marques, F. (eds.) DoCEIS 2015. IFIP AICT, vol. 450, pp. 22–30. Springer, Heidelberg (2015)
5. Camarinha-Matos, L.M., Afsarmanesh, H.: Collaborative networks: a new scientific discipline. J. Intell. Manuf. **16**(4–5), 439–452 (2005)
6. Camarinha-Matos, L.M., Afsarmanesh, H.: Collaborative Networks: Reference Modeling. Springer Science & Business Media, Heidelberg (2008)
7. Kaplan, R.S., Norton, D.P.: The Balanced Scorecard: Translating Strategy into Action. Harvard Business Press, Boston (1996)
8. Romero, D., Galeano, N., Molina, A.: A conceptual model for virtual breeding environments value systems. In: Camarinha-Matos, L.M., Afsarmanesh, H., Novais, P., Analide, C. (eds.) Establishing the Foundation of Collaborative Networks. IFIP, vol. 243, pp. 43–52. Springer, Heidelberg (2007)
9. Camarinha-Matos, L.M., Macedo, P.: A conceptual model of value systems in collaborative networks. J. Intell. Manuf. **21**(3), 287–299 (2010)
10. Macedo, P., Camarinha-Matos, L.M.: A qualitative approach to assess the alignment of value systems in collaborative enterprises networks. Comput. Ind. Eng. **64**(1), 412–424 (2013)

11. Abreu, A., Camarinha-Matos, L.M.: A benefit analysis model for collaborative networks. In: Camarinha-Matos, L.M., Afsarmanesh, H. (eds.) Collaborative Networks: Reference Modeling, pp. 253–276. Springer, Heidelberg (2008)
12. Gopal, P.R.C., Thakkar, J.: A review on supply chain performance measures and metrics: 2000-2011. Int. J. Prod. Perform. Manag. **61**(5), 518–547 (2012)
13. Ramanathan, U.: Performance of supply chain collaboration–a simulation study. Expert Syst. Appl. **41**(1), 210–220 (2014)
14. Abreu, A., Camarinha-Matos, L.M.: An approach to measure social capital in collaborative networks. In: Camarinha-Matos, L.M., Pereira-Klen, A., Afsarmanesh, H. (eds.) PRO-VE 2011. IFIP AICT, vol. 362, pp. 29–40. Springer, Heidelberg (2011)
15. Battistella, C., Colucci, K., De Toni, A.F., Nonino, F.: Methodology of business ecosystems network analysis: a case study in Telecom Italia Future Centre. Technol. Forecast. Soc. Chang. **80**(6), 1194–1210 (2013)
16. Allee, V.: Value Networks and the True Nature of Collaboration. Digital edn. ValueNet Works and Verna Allee Associates, Tampa (2011)
17. Fiksel, J.: Sustainability and resilience: toward a systems approach. Sustain. Sci. Pract. Policy **2**(2), 14–21 (2006)
18. Fiksel, J.: Designing resilient, sustainable systems. Environ. Sci. Technol. **37**(23), 5330–5339 (2003)
19. Freeman, L.C.: Centrality in social networks conceptual clarification. Soc. Netw. **1**(3), 215–239 (1978)
20. Myers, J.L., Well, A., Lorch, R.F.: Research Design and Statistical Analysis. Routledge, New York (2010)
21. Multimethod Simulation Software and Solutions. http://www.anylogic.com/. Accessed 12 May 2016
22. Sterman, J.D.: Business Dynamics: Systems Thinking and Modeling for a Complex World, vol. 19. Irwin/McGraw-Hill, Boston (2000)

Integrated Smart Energy System Based on Production-Oriented Consumption

Ivan Popov[1], Alexander Krylatov[2,3](✉), and Victor Zakharov[2,3]

[1] Control Methods and Robotics Lab, TU Darmstadt, Darmstadt, Germany
ipopov@rmr.tu-darmstadt.de
[2] Saint Petersburg State University,
7/9 Universitetskaya nab., St. Petersburg 199034, Russia
{a.krylatov, v.zaharov}@spbu.ru,
info@iptran.ru
[3] Solomenko Institute of Transport Problems of the Russian Academy of Sciences, 13 12-th Line VO, St. Petersburg 199178, Russia

Abstract. Modern power grids are facing a number of challenges, such as ever-increasing consumption, development of alternative energy generators, and decentralization of energy markets. Renewable energy sources are strongly weather-dependent and, therefore, cannot provide reliable production profiles. This leads us to the concept of demand side management, where energy users modify their consumption patterns due to the availability of generation capacities. Additionally, power flow distribution should be carefully studied in order to avoid overloads in the grid. In this work, we describe a multi-supplier multi-consumer grid model and formulate a problem of an optimal energy contract assignment with respect to power flow constraints. Though generally energy consumers are selfish, we assume their readiness for collaboration within a smart energy system. We offer a cooperative solution for this problem on the assumption of appropriate coordination between agents. Finally, we provide an example illustrating the applicability of our methods.

Keywords: Demand side management · Multi-agent systems · Power grids · Congestion · Load flow

1 Introduction

The structure of power supply has been changing significantly in last two decades. A new vision of power grid structures has appeared due to set of reasons, firstly, such as ever-growing energy consumption and development of alternative energy sources. New requirements for power grid structures with generators of renewable energy exacerbate such a crucial problem in power grid management as imbalance between energy demand and supply. Hence, the power system should turn to the production-oriented consumption that leads us to the idea of demand side management (DSM).

Much work has been done in the field of demand side management and, more specifically, demand response. Basic pricing mechanisms for systems with single

H. Afsarmanesh et al. (Eds.): PRO-VE 2016, IFIP AICT 480, pp. 265–273, 2016.
DOI: 10.1007/978-3-319-45390-3_23

supplier and multiple consumers are studied by [1, 2]. Distributed generation and storage are considered in [3, 4]. Coalition formation for local networks is examined in various scenarios in [5, 6] with use of methods of cooperative game theory. However, the questions of power grid's topology and congestion in transmission lines are not taken into account in these works. In present paper we fill this gap since transmission network is a significant element of any power grid system.

Actually, the question of collaboration in energy market has long been irrelevant, and, in contrast to smart grid consumer collaboration, competitive market forces of power generation, consumption, and transmission have been deeply investigated [7–9]. Nowadays, the newly established circumstances force us to investigate collaborative mechanisms in power consumption. Due to modern technologies, generators and consumers are now able to be integrated spatially in a smart local (nodal) power system. Smart grid power system could guarantee the conditions of optimal nodal demand-side consumption by virtue of the agreement between consumers to collaborate in energy consumption.

In this paper we formulate a model of cooperating consumers in a power network. We show that an integrated smart energy system could reduce overall costs in congested networks with multiple producers. An example of a network with tree structure is considered in order to show the applicability of this idea.

2 Model Description

In this section, we formulate the power grid model with multiple generators and consumers. Each generator has a production cost function, and it depends on the total amount of energy this generator is assigned to produce. Consumers are price-taking agents with energy demand that they need to meet. Both production and transmission costs are covered by consumers. We now discuss all elements of this model in detail.

2.1 Network Structure

Consider a directed connected graph $G = (V, A)$, where V is a set of nodes and A is a set of arcs. Since energy current in a power grid can flow in either direction of any link, we assume that for any arc $(k, l) \in A$ there is also an arc $(l, k) \in A$. We also claim that only one of these two arcs can be used at the same time (i.e., energy current cannot proceed in both directions of a link simultaneously).

We enumerate nodes in V a specific way, so that set V consists of three subsets: a set of m consumer nodes $V_Q = \{1, \ldots, m\}$, a set of n producer nodes $V_P = \{m+1, \ldots, m+n\}$, and a set of all other nodes $V_O = \{m+n+1, \ldots, |V|\}$.

Consumers make bilateral energy contracts with multiple producers in order to meet their energy demands. By $e_{ij} \geq 0$ we denote a contract between a consumer $i \in V_Q$ and a producer $j \in V_P$, and $d_i \leq 0$ is an energy demand of consumer $i \in V_Q$. Let us also define $\overline{e}_i = \{e_{ij},\ j \in V_P\}$, consumer i's contract profile, and $\overline{e} = \{e_{ij},\ i \in V_Q,\ j \in V_P\}$, a contract profile of all consumers. Therefore, demand constraints take the following form:

$$d_i + \sum_{j=m+1}^{m+n} e_{ij} = 0, i \in V_Q. \tag{1}$$

For all other nodes $k \in V_P \cup V_O$, we also define d_k:

$$\begin{aligned} d_k &= \sum_{i=1}^{m} e_{ik},\ k \in V_P, \\ d_k &= 0,\ k \in V_O \end{aligned} . \tag{2}$$

Let us call d_k an energy input in a node $k \in V$. It is positive in producer nodes, negative in consumer nodes, and equal zero otherwise.

For each producer $j \in V_P$ we define a unit production cost $\alpha_j(d_j) \geq 0$, a function of an energy input d_j, the total sum of contracts assigned to this producer. Consumers share production costs proportionally to their contracts, and for a given contract profile $\overline{e}$ consumer $i \in V_Q$ pays to producer $j \in V_P$ the following price:

$$c_{ij}(\overline{e}) = e_{ij} \cdot \alpha_j(d_j) = e_{ij} \cdot \alpha_j\left(\sum_{i=1}^{m} e_{ij}\right). \tag{3}$$

Therefore, we can determine the overall production cost of each consumer $i \in V_Q$ for a given contract profile $\overline{e}$:

$$c_i(\overline{e}) = \sum_{j \in V_P} c_{ij}(\overline{e}) = \sum_{j \in V_P} e_{ij} \cdot \alpha_j\left(\sum_{i=1}^{m} e_{ij}\right). \tag{4}$$

2.2 Load Flow

Transmission costs are the second type of expenses covered by consumers. These costs depend on the load flow in a network, and we require to make several further definitions. By power flow $f_{kl} \geq 0$ in arc $(k, l) \in A$ we denote a non-negative value of current flowing in this arc. According to our assumption, f_{kl} and f_{lk} cannot be both positive. A flow profile $\overline{f} = \{f_{kl},\ (k, l) \in A\}$ is a set of flows in all arcs. We assume that each arc $(k, l) \in A$ charges a transmission fee $\beta_{kl}(f_{kl})$ that must be shared between consumers using this arc.

In order to determine the transmission cost of consumer i similarly to (4), we need to answer two questions: how does flow profile $\overline{f}$ depend on contract profile $\overline{e}$? And how should the transmission costs be shared between consumers?

The first question can be answered by applying Kirchhoff's laws to this power grid. Let us denote all neighbours of node k by $W_k = \{l \in V|\ (k,l) \in A\}$. Then the first Kirchhoff's law takes the following form:

$$\sum_{l \in W_k} f_{kl} - \sum_{l \in W_k} f_{lk} = d_k,\ \forall k \in V. \tag{5}$$

If $\Theta_{kl}(f_{kl})$ is a voltage change function for an arc $(k,l) \in A$, and π_k is a potential in node $k \in V$, we can formulate the second Kirchhoff's law for our model:

$$\pi_k - \pi_l = \Theta_{kl}(f_{kl}),\ \forall (k,l) \in A. \tag{6}$$

It is well-known that the flow profile can be found as a solution of a non-linear optimization problem (cf. Chap. 2.6 in [10]):

$$\min_{\bar{f}} \sum_{(k,l) \in A} \int_0^{f_{kl}} \Theta_{kl}(s) ds, \tag{7}$$

subject to

$$\sum_{l \in W_k} f_{kl} - \sum_{l \in W_k} f_{lk} = d_k, \quad \forall k \in V, \tag{8}$$

$$f_{lk} \geq 0, \quad \forall (k,l) \in A, \tag{9}$$

where contract profile $\bar{e}$ defines coefficients $\{d_k\}$ in (8).

By $\bar{f}(\bar{e})$ we denote the solution of problem (7)–(9) for a given $\bar{e}$. Mathematical programming formulation of the problem of finding equilibrium currents and voltages in electrical networks is an electrical network analogy of traffic equilibrium problem [10–12].

The second question is more complicated, since electricity is a homogeneous product, and unlike transportation problems it is not possible to track what portion of energy belongs to which consumer-producer contract. There are different methods used to determine transmission cost pricing, e.g. [13]. In general case, we define a set of functions $\{\delta_i^{kl}(\bar{e})\}$ that impose the cost sharing rule:

$$\begin{gathered} \sum_{i \in V_Q} \delta_i^{kl}(\bar{e}) = 1, \quad \forall (k,l) \in A, \\ \delta_i^{kl}(\bar{e}) \geq 0,\ \forall (k,l) \in A,\ \forall i \in V_Q. \end{gathered} \tag{10}$$

According to this rule, one can find transmission cost of consumer $i \in V_Q$ charged by arc $(k,l) \in A$ as follows:

$$t_i^{kl}(\overline{e}) = \delta_i^{kl}(\overline{e}) \cdot \beta_{kl}(f_{kl}(\overline{e})). \tag{11}$$

Thus, total transmission cost paid by consumer i is

$$t_i(\overline{e}) = \sum_{(k,l)\in A} t_i^{kl}(\overline{e}) = \sum_{(k,l)\in A} \delta_i^{kl}(\overline{e}) \cdot \beta_{kl}(f_{kl}(\overline{e})) \tag{12}$$

We are ready to formulate a network optimization problem for a system of cooperative consumers.

3 Integrated Smart Energy System

Usually, the participants of energy market are assumed to be selfish and independent, that leads us to a system formulated in terms of competitive games. However, if energy resources are scarce and/or uncontrollable (such as renewable energy generation) it may be more profitable for consumers to cooperate. This section formulates a total cost minimization problem for a power grid with multiple suppliers.

3.1 Total Cost Minimization Problem

In order to reduce total costs for energy production and transmission, we need to solve a total cost minimization problem. Let us consider the total cost of all consumers, according to (4), (12):

$$\begin{aligned} C(\overline{e}) &= \sum_{i\in V_Q} (c_i(\overline{e}) + t_i(\overline{e})) \\ &= \sum_{i\in V_Q} \sum_{j\in V_P} e_{ij} \cdot \alpha_j \left(\sum_{i=1}^{m} e_{ij} \right) + \sum_{i\in V_Q} \sum_{(k,l)\in A} \delta_i^{kl}(\overline{e}) \cdot \beta_{kl}(f_{kl}(\overline{e})) \\ &= \sum_{j\in V_P} d_j(\overline{e}) \cdot \alpha_j(d_j(\overline{e})) + \sum_{(k,l)\in A} \beta_{kl}(f_{kl}(\overline{e})). \end{aligned} \tag{13}$$

The minimization problem can be formulated in the following form:

$$\min_{\overline{e}} \sum_{j\in V_P} d_j(\overline{e}) \cdot \alpha_j(d_j(\overline{e})) + \sum_{(k,l)\in A} \beta_{kl}(f_{kl}(\overline{e})) \tag{14}$$

$$\text{subject to (1), (2),} \tag{15}$$

where flow profile $\overline{f}(\overline{e})$ is found as a solution of optimization problem (7)–(9).

Note that the solution of constrained optimization problem (14), (15) does exist. However, it is not a trivial task to define the uniqueness of the solution in general case. Nevertheless, the properties of a solution could be established via differentiating Lagrangian with respect to e_{ij} and using Kuhn-Tucker conditions. The only thing to be state is that Kuhn-Tucker conditions are necessary and sufficient when product $d_j(\overline{e}) \cdot \alpha_j(d_j(\overline{e}))$ and $\beta_{kl}(f_{kl}(\overline{e}))$ are convex functions. Generally, one could use most appropriate powerful numerical method for constrained nonlinear optimization [14].

3.2 Consumer Cooperation

There are different ways of fair cost sharing among consumers. Ideas of the cooperative game theory may be applied, such as the concept of Shapley value for a coalition of consumers (see, e.g., [15]). Another simplified policy to encourage the cooperation between consumers is to share the total cost proportionally to the demand of each consumer:

$$C_i(\overline{e}) = d_i \cdot C(\overline{e}), \quad \forall i \in V_Q. \tag{16}$$

In this case each consumer i minimizes the same function (up to a constant coefficient $\{d_i\}$.

In the following example we do not consider any specific rule of cost sharing, but rather the possible total cost reduction in the network without cycles.

4 Example and Simulation Results

This section shows how our methods can be applied to a specific example of a network with tree structure.

4.1 Example

Consider a network with 7 nodes that is depicted in Fig. 1. There are 3 consumers (red nodes), 3 producers (green nodes) and one intermediate node. Therefore, $V_Q = \{1, 2, 3\}$, $V_P = \{4, 5, 6\}$, and $V_O = \{7\}$.

All nodes are located in the same local area except for node 4 that depicts a conventional energy generator, e.g. a power plant. Hence, arc (4, 2) is longer than all other arcs, and transmission costs are higher for this arc.

Since there are no cycles in the network, we only need to check the first Kirchhoff's law (5). A flow on each arc is a linear combination of $\{e_{ij}\}$:

$$\hat{f}_{25} = e_{34} + e_{36} - e_{15} - e_{25}, \quad \hat{f}_{53} = e_{34} + e_{35} + e_{36}, \quad \hat{f}_{42} = e_{14} + e_{24} + e_{34},$$
$$\hat{f}_{27} = e_{14} + e_{15} - e_{26} - e_{36}, \quad \hat{f}_{71} = e_{14} + e_{15} + e_{16}, \quad \hat{f}_{67} = e_{16} + e_{26} + e_{36}.$$

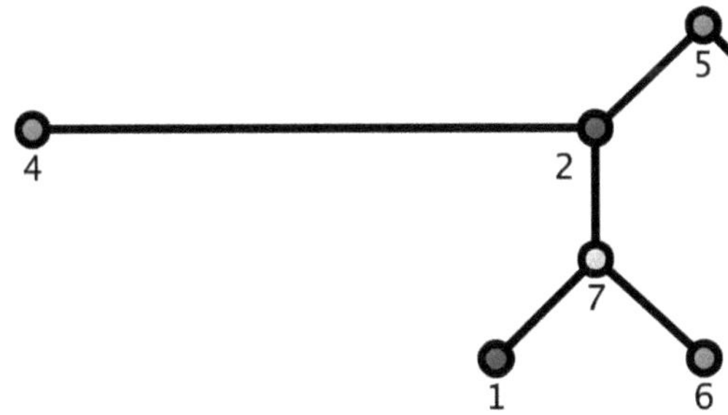

Fig. 1. 7-node network with no cycles (Color figure online)

The direction of flow in arcs (2, 5) and (2, 7) may differ depending on the values $\{e_{ij}\}$. If $\hat{f}_{25} < 0$, we assign $\hat{f}_{25} = 0$ and $\hat{f}_{52} = -\hat{f}_{25}$. The same is true for $\hat{f}_{27}$.

Let us assume that functions $\{\alpha_j(\cdot)\}$ and $\{\alpha_j(\cdot)\}$ have the following form:

$$\begin{aligned} \alpha_j(x) &= \lambda_j \cdot x^{1+\varepsilon} + \mu_j, \quad \forall j \in V_P \\ \beta_{kl}(x) &= \lambda_{kl} \cdot x^{1+\zeta}, \quad \forall (k,l) \in A, \end{aligned} \tag{17}$$

where all coefficients are non-negative. We now solve the problem (14), (15) with specific values of demands $\{d_i,\ i \in V_Q\}$ and coefficients in (17), and evaluate the total cost reduction.

4.2 Simulation

Let us assume that consumers have similar demand values, and that the transmission cost in arc (4, 2) is higher due to longer distance, while other five arcs have identical coefficients of transmission function (i.e., $\lambda_{42} > \lambda_a,\ \forall a \neq (4,2)$). We also assign $\varepsilon = \zeta = 0.2$.

We compute and compare minimal total costs of consumers in two different cases: $C_{\sin}$ if each consumer buys energy from a single supplier, and C_{opt} for a case, when consumers distribute their contracts between several producers (Table 1).

Table 1. Some of simulation results are given.

d_1	d_2	d_3	λ_{42}	λ_a	$\lambda_4,\ \mu_4$	$\lambda_5,\ \mu_5$	$\lambda_6,\ \mu_6$	C_{opt}	$C_{\sin}$	Gain
−20	−22	−23	0.005	0.001	(0.002, 0.2)	(0.001, 0.12)	(0.005, 0.1)	15.81	17.21	8.1 %
−10	−12	−9	0.005	0.001	(0.002, 0.2)	(0.001, 0.12)	(0.005, 0.1)	5.43	5.5	1.2 %
−10	−12	−9	0.005	0.001	(0.002, 0.2)	(0, 0.12)	(0.01, 0)	3.98	4.33	7.9 %

It is clear that the cooperative contract distribution reduces the total cost significantly (up to 8 %). However, this reduction strongly depends on the demand values of consumers and cost functions of producers.

5 Conclusion and Future Work

In this work, we described and studied a collaborative model of local area energy consumption in the presence of multiple producers. We showed that the distribution of power flow can be determined by solving an optimization problem based on Kirchhoff's laws, and we formulated the total cost minimization problem considering the congestion in the network arcs. We also considered an example of a network without cycles and presented promising simulation results. There are several possible extensions of this model. First of all, it is crucial to consider a dynamic setting over several periods of time (e.g., 24 h of a day). Second direction is the investigation of cost sharing techniques.

References

1. Mohsenian-Rad, A.H., Wong, V.W., Jatskevich, J., Schober, R., Leon-Garcia, A.: Autonomous demand-side management based on game-theoretic energy consumption scheduling for the future smart grid. IEEE Trans. Smart Grid **1**(3), 320–331 (2010)
2. Veit, A., Xu, Y., Zheng, R., Chakraborty, N., Sycara, K.P.: Multiagent coordination for energy consumption scheduling in consumer cooperatives. In: 27th AAAI Conference on Artificial Intelligence, pp. 1362–1368 (2013)
3. Atzeni, I., Ordóñez, L.G., Scutari, G., Palomar, D.P., Fonollosa, J.R.: Demand-side management via distributed energy generation and storage optimization. IEEE Trans. Smart Grid **4**(2), 866–876 (2013)
4. Atzeni, I., Ordóñez, L.G., Scutari, G., Palomar, D.P., Fonollosa, J.R.: Noncooperative and cooperative optimization of distributed energy generation and storage in the demand-side of the smart grid. IEEE Trans. Signal Process. **61**(10), 2454–2472 (2013)
5. Alam, M., Ramchurn, S.D., Rogers, A.: Cooperative energy exchange for the efficient use of energy and resources in remote communities. In: Proceedings of the 2013 International Conference on Autonomous Agents and Multi-agent Systems, pp. 731–738 (2013)
6. Mihailescu, R.-C., Vasirani, M., Ossowski, S.: Dynamic coalition adaptation for efficient agent-based virtual power plants. In: Klügl, F., Ossowski, S. (eds.) MATES 2011. LNCS, vol. 6973, pp. 101–112. Springer, Heidelberg (2011)
7. Chao, H.P., Peck, S.: A market mechanism for electric power transmission. J. Regul. Econ. **10**(1), 25–59 (1996)
8. O'Neill, R.P., Helman, U., Hobbs, B.F., Stewart, W.R., Rothkopf, M.H.: A joint energy and transmission rights auction: proposal and properties. IEEE Trans. Power Syst. **17**(4), 1058–1067 (2002)
9. Dolmatova, M.: Optimal nodal capacity procurement. In: Le Thi, H.A., Dinh, T.P., Nguyen, N.T. (eds.) MCO 2015. AISC, vol. 360, pp. 415–423. Springer, Heidelberg (2015)
10. Patriksson, M.: The Traffic Assignment Problem: Models and Methods. VSP, Utrecht (1994)

11. Zakharov, V.V., Krylatov, A.Y.: Competitive routing of traffic flows by navigation providers. Autom. Remote Control **77**(1), 179–189 (2016)
12. Zakharov, V., Krylatov, A.: OD-matrix estimation based on plate scanning. In: 2014 International Conference on Computer Technologies in Physical and Engineering Applications (ICCTPEA), pp. 209–210 (2014)
13. Bohn, R.E., Caramanis, M.C., Schweppe, F.C.: Optimal pricing in electrical networks over space and time. Rand J. Econ. **15**(3), 360–376 (1984)
14. Bertsekas, D.P.: Nonlinear Programming, 2nd edn. Athena Scientific, Belmont (1999)
15. Roth, A.E.: The Shapley Value: Essays in Honor of Lloyd S. Shapley. Cambridge University Press, Cambridge (1988)

Industry 4.0 as Enabler for Effective Manufacturing Virtual Enterprises

Filipe Ferreira[1(✉)], José Faria[1,2], Américo Azevedo[1,2], and Ana Luísa Marques[1]

[1] CESE - INESC TEC, Campus da FEUP, 4200-465 Porto, Portugal
{fdmf,almm}@inesctec.pt

[2] Faculdade de Engenharia da Universidade do Porto, 4200-465 Porto, Portugal
{jfaria,ala}@fe.up.pt

Abstract. Today, the variety of complex products, low volume and decreasing life cycles require a combination of multiple skills that, often, do not exist in a single organization. This raises the need to extend the traditional organization towards the extended virtual enterprise. During the last decade several research projects developed concepts, methods and tools to support the design and operation of the virtual enterprises. However, the impact in industry remains low mainly due to the lack of vertical and horizontal integration, both at business and technical level. Industry 4.0 may be the missing enabler for effective virtual enterprises, once it integrates both business entities and technical entities into a single concept - the Industry 4.0 component – thus enabling enhanced interoperability. This paper presents innovative Industry 4.0 approaches, concepts, methods and tools applied to real manufacturing environments, showing how they enable the creation of cyber-physical production systems leading to a flexible, efficient and seamlessly virtual enterprise.

Keywords: Virtual enterprise · Industry 4.0 · Internet of things · Cyber-physical systems · Intelligent product ecosystems

1 Introduction

During the last decades, increasing competitiveness pressure led companies to look at efficiency improvement opportunities obtained from a higher integration level between the design of the products, the design of production processes and the design of the value chains [1]. Mass customization and servitization are perhaps the most prevalent examples of responding to such competitive pressure [2]. Nowadays, companies seek to explore new organizational models such as virtual enterprises, in order to ensure a faster response to new business opportunities, and to offer differentiated products at competitive prices [3]. Sustainability, high variety, low volume and shorter product life cycles require a combination of multiple skills that is not easy to find in a single company. This raises the need to extend the organization, including skilled business partners, thus forming virtual enterprises [4, 5].

Collaboration is moving from the classical supply chain, with stable relationships between stakeholders with fully defined roles, to unprecedented dynamic structures.

H. Afsarmanesh et al. (Eds.): PRO-VE 2016, IFIP AICT 480, pp. 274–285, 2016.
DOI: 10.1007/978-3-319-45390-3_24

Some of these organisational forms are goal-oriented, that is, focused on a single project or business opportunity [6]. In this business context, virtual enterprises have been widely discussed over the past decades [7, 8]. In this research, the definition of virtual enterprise considered is based on the definition proposed by Camarinha-Matos, which states that "a virtual enterprise represents a temporary alliance of enterprises that come together to share skills or core competences and resources in order to better respond to business opportunities, and whose cooperation is supported by computer networks" [6]. A virtual enterprise is one form of Collaborative Networked Organisations that allows partners to exploit emerging business opportunities in a flexible way [9].

The effective implementation of a virtual enterprise raises several challenges: the integration of human and technical resources to enhance workforce performance and satisfaction; the need to instantaneously process information gathered from several sources into useful knowledge for an effective decision making and the ability to rapidly reconfigure manufacturing enterprises in response to changing needs and opportunities [10, 11]. Those challenges raise two main integration issues. The first is a business-oriented and addresses the integration of several business entities within a logistic value chain network. According to Reference Architectural Model for Industry 4.0 (RAMI 4.0), business entities can be represented as a component, exposing services, functions and implementing standard communication channels. The way how such business entities interoperate is typically described and analysed using a business process modelling notation such as BPMN. The second issue is mostly a technical one and addresses the interoperability of new and legacy resources (e.g., equipment, software, people) of the partners participating in the virtual enterprise so that cooperation can take place quickly, seamlessly and in a flexible way. Typically, a single task at the business process model is decomposed in set of tasks at the technical level (e.g. web services invocation). At the technical level, the interoperating entities are no longer companies, but equipment, software and people. However, in Industry 4.0, such resources are also considered entities that expose services and implements standard communication channels, as depicted in Fig. 1.

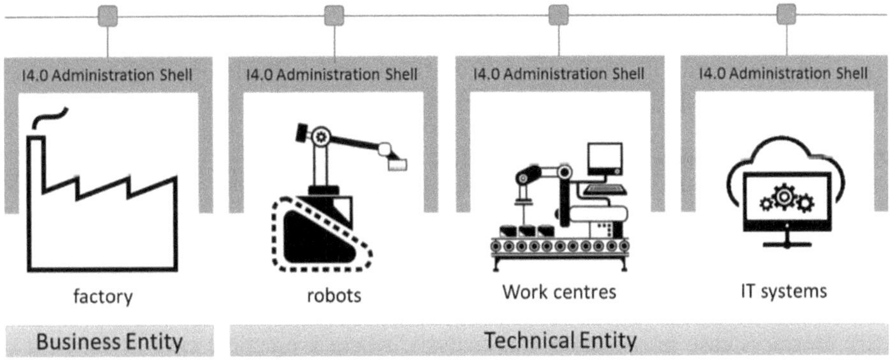

Fig. 1. Business entities and technical entities as Industry 4.0 objects

The Industry 4.0 paradigm seeks the complete digitalization and integration of the industrial value chain in order to produce goods using the most advanced information and communication technologies. The motivation behind this new paradigm stays on the increased digitization of the economy and society, which is changing the way the production will be held in the future. After the steam engine, the introduction of assembly lines and the use of electronic and computer systems in the production, the so-called smart factories with cyber-physical systems (CPS) come now to determine the fourth industrial revolution. The adoption of Industry 4.0 concepts, their related service platforms and innovation business models will help European SMEs to grow and boost European gross domestic product. Nevertheless the ability to adopt Industry 4.0 technologies by SMEs is still very scarce. Benefits of the adoption of these technologies include increased productivity and efficiency improvement, but obviously it is necessary to guarantee a return of investment [12]. Hence, there is the need for cloud based, scalable, secure and modular tools so that they can be introduced gradually and seamlessly in all manufacturing levels, from the shop floor, to the management level, without the need of a huge initial effort.

The essential issue tackled in this paper and the underlying research question refer to the Industry 4.0 concepts and technologies applied to virtual enterprise. In this research, it is of interest to face the following questions: (i) Which are the existing key enabling technologies to manage Industry 4.0 virtual enterprises? (ii) How to implement the Industry 4.0 technology in the European SMEs successfully?

This paper proposes an innovative cloud based framework to address these issues and enable collaboration in future Industry 4.0 compliant virtual enterprises. The rest of the paper is organized as follows: Sect. 2 presents the main phases considered in the research methodology. In Sect. 3, the current state of the art in the field of industry 4.0, including recent European project results are presented. Section 4 describes the considered business case. Section 5 present the implementation issues as well as the validation process. Finally, overall conclusions and further developments are mentioned in Sect. 6.

2 Research Methodology

The work presented in this paper has followed a research methodology that encompasses three main phases, as described hereafter:

(i) Industry 4.0 enabling technologies, where existing Industry 4.0 concepts and reference models as well as enabling technologies are presented and analysed. A comprehensive framework, founded on collaborative platforms, Internet of Things (IoT) and CPS is presented, answering the first research question (Which are the existing key enabling technologies to manage Industry 4.0 virtual enterprises?).
(ii) Business case presentation and analysis, where a practical case in the field of Automotive stamping planning is presented. Several workshops were conducted, in order to collect qualitative and quantitative data and relevant information, taking into account the expertise of all team members and experts. After analysing the as-is situation, current industrial challenges and issues and consequent

improvement opportunities were identified, the to-be business processes were designed and validated by the industrial partners, leading to the definition of requirements for the design, specification and development of new suitable and accurate supporting methods and tools. Industrialists, technology providers and researchers did participate in this task, bringing their multi-disciplinary expertise to the project.

(iii) Framework implementation and validation, where the framework was implemented and validated. In order to guarantee its sustainability, criteria for the framework evaluation were established and measured, paving the way for a successful exploitation and pointing out the strong points as well as aspects to be improved. This answers the second research question (How to implement the Industry 4.0 technology in the European SMEs successfully?)

The next three sections are directly related to the three stages of the methodology presented.

3 Industry 4.0 Enabling Technologies

The notion of enterprise systems architecture is crucial to understand and manage virtual enterprises. From an internal perspective, services are characterized by a modular structure with building blocks that are combined to create a Cyber-physical Production Systems (CPPS). From an external perspective, they are a part of a larger CPPS (i.e., a virtual enterprise), often found in industries where product design increasingly determines the organization of partners, such as high technology and automotive industry [13]. In this context, concepts such as Smart Objects (SO), Internet of Things (IoT), CPPS and finally Industry 4.0, have emerged over the past decade aiming at address the technological requirements imposed by virtual enterprises [4, 6, 14]. The concept of horizontal integration and decentralization of production processes push the boundaries of collaboration between organizations in the field of CPPS to an unprecedented dynamic level. According to the RAMI 4.0 [15], the paradigm of service-oriented architecture plays a key role in support to CPPS. SOA allows to describe and use services in any of the automation pyramid levels: from the sensors and actuators, machines, through work centres and production lines, up to enterprise management levels. These services encapsulate well defined functionalities implemented through software artefacts [12].

Recent research results from two major European Projects - ADVENTURE [16] and Apps4aME [17] - show how to introduce semantics to optimize and automate the modelling and execution of distributed production processes as an orchestration of such services. These research and innovation projects demonstrate that there are different approaches for managing virtual enterprises depending on its nature. For instance, Make-to-Stock (MTS) environments, where the factory and process configuration is inflexible and fixed to produce in large quantities, are suitable for totally automated processes, where typical workflow systems are able to manage and orchestrate the entire process. ADVENTURE project has developed a fully automated process manager [18]. On the other hand, an Engineering-to-Order (ETO) environment imposes, flexible, adaptive and knowledge based processes [19, 20]. Based on these concepts, Apps4aME project developed a hybrid process manager capable of manage knowledge intensive processes with high level of human interactions and decisions [17].

Process description languages like business process execution language (BPEL) allow the composition of various services to simple or complex processes and semantic annotations are designed to express the context of a virtual service functionality [2, 4]. This approach has been widely adopted, with the goal of providing companies with the ability to generate, adapt and control production processes in distributed organizational networks, integrating from the so-called smart sensors and machines to production and enterprise level management systems, or other legacy systems. Based on the definition of individual production steps such as services and making use of a production-oriented approach to services, it was possible to model manufacturing processes for assembly services based on the capabilities of real factories of different business partners. These physical services are combined in production processes and take advantage of SOA technologies [4]. The results of several projects were combined to develop a framework for integration and interoperability within organizational distributed networks that meets what is now the concept of horizontal integration described by RAMI4.0, reducing market access barriers for Small and Medium Enterprises (SMEs), which do not usually have the ability to control the entire production life cycle, neither the marketing strength to impose their own interfaces and standards. Thus, it becomes easier for SMEs to get involved in Industry 4.0 compliant distributed organizational networks [4]. If CPS are not in accordance with a common standard, the integration of systems in the decentralized and virtualized production environment will require multiple peer-to-peer interfaces, exponentially increasing complexity. With a SOA based platform, each entity publishes its services in a central repository in accordance with a common standard. When it is necessary to produce a specific product, a specific process model previously stored in the production support system is applied. This process relies on cyber services on the available physical resources (e.g. machines, work centres, software) [14]. Note that in the case of knowledge intensive processes such as engineering, people also play a central role as they are the main decision makers on the orchestration of the process [16].

The RAMI 4.0 introduces the concept of Industry 4.0 component as a model to describe in detail the properties of CPS, i.e. real objects in a production environment linked to virtual objects. The real objects (production systems, machines, systems and modules) necessarily need to contain a set of defined RAMI 4.0 properties in order to be considered compliant with RAMI 4.0 objects. One of the properties is the ability to communicate in real time and to expose its functions and data. This definition is aligned with the concept of SO developed under previous European projects such as ADVENTURE. An important Industry 4.0 requirement is that a component collects all the relevant data throughout its lifecycle, providing these data to the companies involved in the virtual enterprise. The data storage and respective communication are provided by the so-called administration shell [21]. An Industry 4.0 administration shell contains a large amount of data and information provided by manufacturers, such as CAD data, connection diagrams, datasheets, manuals, etc. Integrators and operators can add important information about the maintenance or connection with other hardware or software. The Industry 4.0 defines data security measures and ensures data availability, confidentiality and integrity. The administration shell also provides some functions such as planning, configuration, operation, maintenance as well as complex functions related to business rules. Data and functions are available within the component itself, inside a corporate network or even in the cloud. The advantage is that information is stored only once and may be provided in a transparent manner through IT services for any user in any use case. The horizontal and vertical integration is facilitated by a combination of Industry 4.0 compliant communication protocols [22].

In Summary, all information is fully available for the engineering as well as operation and maintenance. The data stored on the component can be expanded as desired. Intelligent systems vendors and integrators can implement services through the creation of new information, information models and technical functions. Thus, information can be provided to stakeholders within an Industry 4.0 network. This enables the intelligent virtual enterprise. In this context, companies should develop their new systems and adapt the existing ones taking into account these concepts in order to be aligned with Industry 4.0 standards [21].

Figure 2 shows a cloud based Industry 4.0 virtual enterprise management platform architecture based on Industry 4.0 concepts allowing vertical and horizontal integration that also includes the components described in the following paragraphs. The services repository provides a model and tools for representation, publication and discovery of companies and its services, required for the design, management and operation of virtual enterprises. The process manager orchestrates all the interactions within a virtual enterprise according to the process models defined in the process manager designer. Process manager interacts with the simulation and optimization tools, in order to ensure the highest efficiency. As described above, the process manager must suit the business

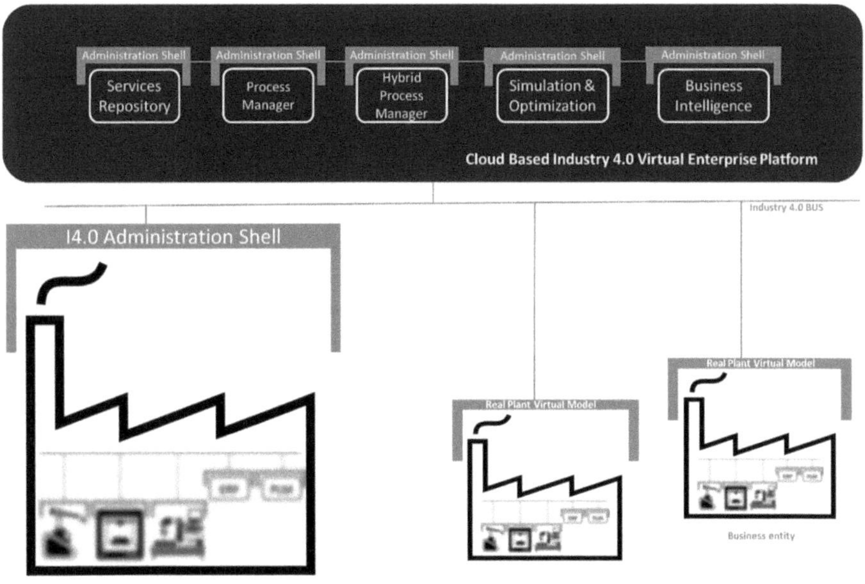

Fig. 2. Industry 4.0 virtual enterprise architecture

environment in terms of automation degree. In fact, lessons from industry tell us that many types of industry involve collaborative knowledge intensive processes (e.g. ETO equipment manufacturing considered in the next Section) where fully automation is not possible as process management depends on several human decisions taken on the fly. The simulation and optimization module relies on the process manager and uses Industry 4.0 shell services to get temporal and execution events from partners, supporting decision makers against particular partners. The optimization module provides a means to optimize virtual enterprises regarding the assignment of services to the business process steps and tasks. The business intelligence provides data extraction and transformation scripts and loading of real time and historical data relating to finished processes and instances. It also implements data mining techniques to generate useful information from big data sources towards a more proactive decision making in virtual enterprise environments [23–25]. All these software modules are also considered Industry 4.0 components and therefore are able to expose services and communicate using internet standards.

4 Business Case Presentation and Analysis

The business case presented hereafter was firstly considered in the context the FP7 apps4ame research project research project and you may find additional information about this project at http://apps4ame.eu.

The business case is based on a flexible automotive plant using a mixed production system (several models in one assembly line). During a new car model launch process, a set of stamping dies have to be planned, designed, produced and tested. Planning is a critical stage whose results directly impact the global performance of the virtual enterprise. This stage involves several activities, such as the setup of the team, process simulation, die set feasibility, resources assignment and die set design. Each technician handles a set of dies being allocated to several suppliers. At that point it is important to execute the right re-enactments and achievability tests, with a specific end goal to comprehend if the specialized particulars of every die are right from an item and assembling perspective. After validation of the technical specification for each DS, it is imperative to comprehend if the plant, where the DS will be utilized, has the assets to apply the composed DS.

Known and accepted the DS, and in addition the essential assets, it is possible to produce a 3D model of every DS, and also to arrange the DS development, as far as spending plan, time and quality. Here it gets to be basic to determine the quality norms to be approved toward the end of the procedure execution. In house try-out is likewise a basic assignment. The machining stage, is where the supplier needs to change the 3D model into a last and usable DS, proficient to create the parts as indicated by the item manager. The last stage must be centred on the assessment and change of the DS model produced, towards the effective creation of the admired parts. Therefore, as first activity, experts must form some model parts keeping in mind the end goal to approve if the DS satisfies the quality norms. After all item needs are approved, the assembling procedure is tried thought a pre-arrangement assessment.

Subsequent to breaking down the as-is procedures, it was possible to declare that the persistent reports on every DS status were expending a lot of time and assets, turning the process behaviour very reactive instead of proactive. It was additionally conceivable to see that the data was spread by various sources. The absence of business and specialized coordination is a major concern since it can be the reason for wrong or ease back choices because of falsehood in a procedure that is exceptionally time subordinate.

5 Implementation and Validation

After a detailed process analysis it was easy to recognise that many of the faults could be abolished by implementing Industry 4.0 key enabling technologies such as cloud based platforms, standard internet communication protocols and smart objects for manufacturing, in order to cope with the challenges and thus achieve a more pro-active approach in the die-set manufacturing process.

The aim of the proposed solution is to facilitate the flow of information among stakeholders, making it more reliable and actual, allowing a closer control and fast reaction. While collaborating with other departments and external partners, the stamping planning has to manage a package of DS, track the workflow process, schedule operations, state milestones, handle project changes, evaluate risks and define actions, keeping cost and available capacity controlled all along the project development. In order to successfully accomplish this mission, for each project the stamping department needs to collect and manage a huge amount of information and knowledge, coming from several heterogeneous data sources along the virtual factory. Indeed, managing all this information not only is intensively time consuming and slows down the decision-making processes, but also hinders project reliability. Cloud based Industry 4.0 virtual enterprise platform addresses the main challenges that are typical in this kind of environments by implementing horizontal and vertical integration: horizontal integration is addressed through a cloud based collaborative platform whereas vertical integration is accomplished using technologies from the IoT field, such as connected smart objects and

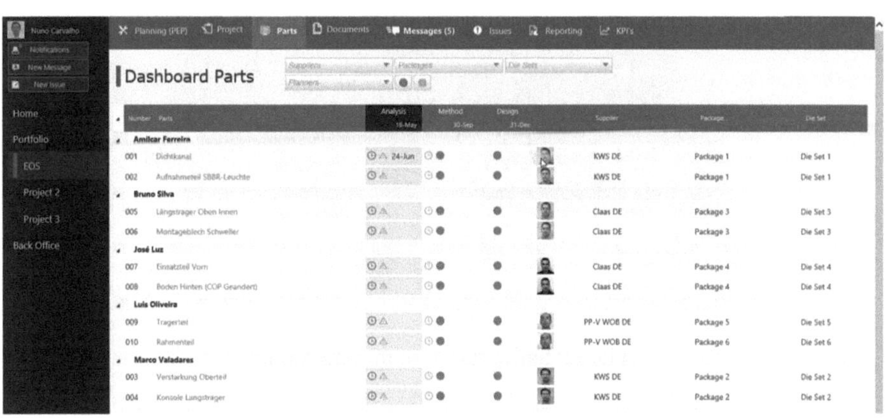

Fig. 3. Cloud based Industry 4.0 virtual enterprise platform dashboard

internet communication protocols. The total integration along these two axis leads to the development of a global dashboard (Fig. 3), enabling holistic view of project status, dynamic work planning and monitoring, real-time monitoring and control of ongoing work activities, knowledge and fully integrated document management and integrated communication/messages throughout the process.

Figure 4 depicts the architecture of the system, where the business process tasks are connected to the several resources along the value chain, including IT systems, industrial equipment, transportation as well as the product itself. The hybrid process manager orchestrates the flow, invoking services in the physical resources through the Industry 4.0 administration shell. The old equipment challenge has been overcome by the implementation of the smart object for manufacturing depicted in Fig. 5.

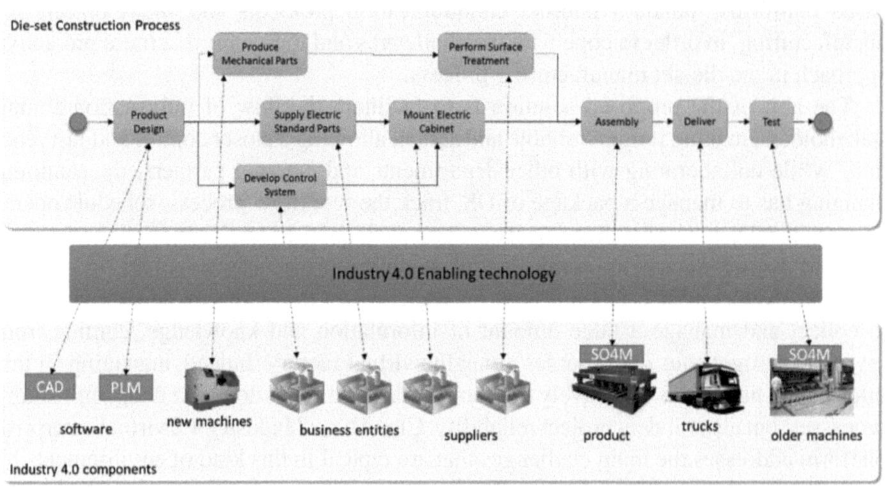

Fig. 4. Business and technical integration through process oriented approach

Fig. 5. Smart object for manufacturing

The cloud based hybrid process manager, supports company processes and enables a more reliable product development process. For instance, when a during the lauch of a new model, the chief manager defines some milestones that can be organised automatically. However, the real work tasks are not prone to be automated as they rely on intensive knowledge and decision tasks. The combination of well-defined and ill-defined activities is equally important in terms of leading a project to its success.

The communication tools that were developed allow linking all the stakeholders and interdisciplinary teams involved in the development of the product, guaranteeing real-time information regarding updated documents, machine breakdowns and quality related issues, thus saving time and improving the decision making processes. The platform was evaluated in real engineering environment, which involves part designers, die-set designers, planners, managers and suppliers in a unique virtual enterprise engineering environment.

Amid this assessment stage, a particular project has been utilized to test and check the functionalities implemented. Every partner has a particular certification to get to, test and approve the functionalities, giving criticism for persistent change [17]. This platform has proven to be very effective and efficient when applied in hybrid work systems and in particular in the automotive engineering collaborative processes.

This platform has ended up being exceptionally successful and productive when applied to this work frameworks and specifically in the car designing community oriented procedures.

The management system has also improved the communication, the cooperation and trust the exchanged information, which are key factors for a successful project. The virtual enterprise integration allow a proactive decision making, speeding up the product development process. The reaction time and resilience was also improved, making the process more responsive to unforeseen events.

6 Conclusions and Further Developments

Several technologies related to Industry 4.0 concepts have emerged during the past decade, however, due to the lack of technological maturity and also lack of capabilities for technology adoption, the supporting tools for virtual enterprises were not implemented successfully in industry, especially in SMEs. Now, with the new Industry 4.0 wave, several technologies from the fields such as IoT, interoperability, SO are being tested and introduced in industry. In this paper we presented several technologies and described the successful introduction of those technologies in a knowledge based manufacturing engineering environment. In summary, Industry 4.0 led us to the full automation world but lessons from industry show that there are several manufacturing environments where full automation is hard to achieve even with advanced technology. However, Industry 4.0 technologies, combined with flexible and suitable managing tools may be the missing enablers for effective virtual enterprise implementation and management.

Despite the success of the pilot business case implemented in the automotive industry, several challenges were identified related to the adoption of the technology and the with the enterprise interoperability, so that the entire CPPS can work seamlessly.

A large portion of today's IT frameworks are not completely integrated. Organizations, suppliers, and clients are once in a while connected. Capacities from the top management to the shop floor level are not completely coordinated. Indeed, even inside divisions, a full integration is as yet lost. Industry 4.0, is seen as the empowering influence to make organizations, divisions, capacities, and abilities more durable, as cross-organization, widespread information reconciliation systems develop and empower genuinely mechanized expanded virtual manufacturing plants.

Acknowledgments. This work is co-financed by the North Portugal Regional Operational Programme (NORTE 2020), under the PORTUGAL 2020 Partnership Agreement, and through the European Regional Development Fund (ERDF).

References

1. Fixson, S.K.: Product architecture assessment: a tool to link product, process, and supply chain design decisions. J. Oper. Manag. **23**(3–4), 345–369 (2005)
2. Azevedo, A., Almeida, A.: Factory templates for digital factories framework. Robot. Comput.-Integr. Manuf. **27**, 755–771 (2011)
3. Jovane, F., Westkamper, E., Williams, D.: The Manufuture Road: Towards Competitive and Sustainable High-Adding-Value Manufacturing. Springer, Heidelberg (2009)
4. Rojas, E.P.S., Barros, A.C., de Azevedo, A.L., Batocchio, A.: Business model development for virtual enterprises. In: Camarinha-Matos, L.M., Xu, L., Afsarmanesh, H. (eds.) Collaborative Networks in the Internet of Services. IFIP AICT, vol. 380, pp. 624–634. Springer, Heidelberg (2012)
5. Rojas, E., Azevedo, A.: Pillars and elements to develop an open business model for innovation networks. In: Camarinha-Matos, L.M., Afsarmanesh, H. (eds.) Collaborative Systems for Smart Networked Environments. IFIP AICT, vol. 434, pp. 317–326. Springer, Heidelberg (2014)
6. Camarinha-Matos, L.M., Afsarmanesh, H., Galeano, N., Molina, A.: Collaborative networked organizations – Concepts and practice in manufacturing enterprises. J. Comput. Ind. Eng. **57**, 46–60 (2009)
7. Cheng, Y., Farooq, S., Johansen, J.: Manufacturing network evolution: a manufacturing plant perspective. Int. J. Oper. Prod. Manag. **31**(12), 1311–1331 (2011)
8. Martinez, M.T., Fouletier, P., Park, K.H., Favrel, J.: Virtual enterprise – organisation, evolution and control. Int. J. Prod. Econ. **74**(1–3), 225–238 (2001)
9. Camarinha-Matos, L.M., Afsarmanesh, H.: Collaborative Networks –Reference Modeling. Springer, New York (2008)
10. Ferreira, F., Azevedo, A., Faria, J., Rojas, E.: Virtual enterprise process management: an application to industrial maintenance. In: Camarinha-Matos, L.M., Afsarmanesh, H. (eds.) Collaborative Systems for Smart Networked Environments. IFIP AICT, vol. 434, pp. 71–79. Springer, Heidelberg (2014)
11. Almeida, A., et al.: Process performance assessment in collaborative manufacturing environments: a role oriented approach. In: Advances in Sustainable and Competitive Manufacturing Systems, pp. 911–924. Springer International Publishing, Heidelberg (2013)
12. Barba-Sánchez, V., Martínez-Ruiz, M.P., Jimenez-Zarco, A.I.: Drivers, benefits and challenges of ICT adoption by small and medium sized enterprises (SMEs): a literature review. Prob. Perspect. Manag. **5**(1), 104–115 (2007)

13. Chandrashekar, A., Schary, P.B.: Toward the virtual supply chain: the convergence of IT and organization. Int. J. Logistics Manag. **10**(2), 27–40 (1999). RAMI 4.0. An Architectural Model for Industry 4.0, Dr.-Ing. Peter Adolphs - Berlin, 18 June 2015
14. Wang, L., et al.: Current status and advancement of cyber-physical systems in manufacturing. J. Manuf. Syst. (2015). doi:10.1016/j.jmsy.2015.04.008
15. Status Report Reference Architecture Model Industry 4.0 (RAMI 4.0), July 2015
16. D3.4 Conceptual Manufacturing Reference of Adventure Project - ADaptive Virtual ENterprise ManufacTURing Environment FoF-ICT-2011.7.3 – 285220 (2011)
17. Ferreira, F., Marques, A.L., Faria, J., Azevedo, A.: Large project management in the automotive industry: a flexible and knowledge based approach. In: Rocha, A., Correia, A.M., Adeli, H., Reis, L.P., Teixeira, M.M. (eds.) New Advances in Information Systems and Technologies. Advances in Intelligent Systems and Computing, vol. 444, pp. 455–464. Springer International Publishing, Heidelberg (2016)
18. Azevedo, A., et al.: A framework to support the lifecycle of virtual manufacturing enterprises. In: Proceedings of the 24th International Conference on Flexible Automation and Intelligent Manufacturing FAIM, DEStech Publications, Inc. (2014)
19. Faria, J., Silva, J., Marques, H.: Supporting the operation of semi-structured work systems. In: Quintela Varajão, J.E., Cruz-Cunha, M.M., Putnik, G.D., Trigo, A. (eds.) CENTERIS 2010. CCIS, vol. 110, pp. 416–425. Springer, Heidelberg (2010)
20. Faria, J.A., Nóvoa, H.: An agile BPM system for knowledge-based service organizations. In: Nóvoa, H., Drăgoicea, M. (eds.) IESS 2015. LNBIP, vol. 201, pp. 65–79. Springer, Heidelberg (2015)
21. Adams, M., ter Hofstede, A.H., Edmond, D., van der Aalst, W.M.: Worklets: a service-oriented implementation of dynamic flexibility in workflows. In: Meersman, R., Tari, Z. (eds.) OTM 2006. LNCS, vol. 4275, pp. 291–308. Springer, Heidelberg (2006)
22. PLM as Enabler for Industry 4.0 A NTT DATA Whitepaper as of May 2015
23. Shamsuzzoha, A., et al.: Business process monitoring and management in virtual enterprise through interactive user interface layer. In: Advances in Sustainable and Competitive Manufacturing Systems, pp. 451–464. Springer International Publishing, Heidelberg (2013)
24. Ferreira, F., Shamsuzzoha, A., Azevedo, A., Helo, P.: Virtual enterprise process management: an application to industrial maintenance. In: Selvaraj, H., Zydek, D., Chmaj, G. (eds.) Proceedings of the Twenty-Third International Conference on Systems Engineering. AISC, vol. 366, pp. 285–291. Springer, Heidelberg (2014)
25. Shamsuzzoha, A., et al.: Visualization functionality of virtual factories-an enhancement to collaborative business process management. In: 16th International Conference on Enterprise Information Systems (ICEIS) (2014)

Co-development and Co-working - Collaborative Engineering

Who Can Help to Review This Piece of Code?

Noureddine Kerzazi and Ikram El Asri(✉)

National Higher School for Computer Science
and System Analysis (ENSIAS), Rabat, Morocco
{n.kerzazi, ikram.asri}@um5s.net.ma

Abstract. Successful software projects require collaboration between team members. Efficient collaboration relies on both technical and social linkages. In this paper, we investigate whether a socio-technical analysis can support software contributors in identifying experts helping to review their source code. We mined the histories of five open source projects (OSS) from GitHub and examined both technical and socio-technical interactions based on Social Network Analysis (SNA). Mapping communication network to files co-edition network shows the existence of collaboration patterns between core teams and peripherals in the studied OSS projects. Our main contribution is the construction and mapping of three sources of social networks, in which contributors interact by co-editing, commenting or reviewing. We were able to identify behavioral patterns between core teams and peripherals related to the activity of code review. Our findings have implications on improving collaboration between contributors within virtual OSS communities witch drive teams' performance and software products quality.

Keywords: Collaboration · Coordination · Socio-technical relationships · Distributed development · Modern code review

1 Introduction

Software development is performed by development teams collaborating and interacting together on technical artifacts [1]. Lack of coordination, team cohesion, awareness, or misguided effort can all result in software failures or team performance decrease [2, 3]. To avoid collaboration breakdowns occurring at technical level, team members should communicate on dependencies between technical artifacts (e.g., source code files). Finding the right person to ask for help is a difficult task within a large organization [4]. Furthermore, prior studies showed that selecting unsuitable reviewers may delay the review process by an average of 12 days [5, 6].

Interactions between team members, through different channels, constitute the backbone of socio-technical[1] perspective which has gain increased attention over the past decade [7]. Social Network Analysis (SNA) has been used to capture and understand such information about relations among people [8] with the aim to enhance team performance, team members congruence, and software product quality.

[1] "Socio-technical" term refers to the interactions between individuals involved in a software project. It occurs because of collaboration needs due to technical dependencies.

H. Afsarmanesh et al. (Eds.): PRO-VE 2016, IFIP AICT 480, pp. 289–301, 2016.
DOI: 10.1007/978-3-319-45390-3_25

Most software development projects, including open source software (OSS), have adopted the practice of code review as a collaborative mechanism aiming at inspecting new code changes made by contributors to evaluate their quality and identify potential defects [6]. For instance, experience indicates that proactive software defect issues are best found by experts when reviewing the code [9, 10]. However, co-workers need to identify right persons to review their code, especially in virtual environments such as for open source projects. If we could support developers identifying the right person likely to perform good review, we can enhance the quality of the code [10] and improve the signal to noise ratio of comments on commits, witch decrease the team's performance. One way of localizing reputed domain expert, to ask for reviewing a piece of code, is to build contributors socio-technical networks and analyze them. Historically, SNA has been known to be effective in many areas [4].

In this paper, we examine the socio-technical interactions of five OSS using version control system data history. We construct contributors' networks based upon which files are commonly modified by contributors, commented, and previously reviewed by contributors. Using network analysis, we can uncover details of required collaboration/coordination and recommend a list of experts for assigning suitable reviewers to a given software change. The contribution of this paper is threefold: *(1)* the empirical evidence that we need to improve the delay of collaboration through code review within OSS communities; *(2)* a new approach SNA-base for identifying suitable list of persons, for source code review assignment, based on SNA metrics; and *(3)* a large-scale experiment on five OSS projects, namely: AngularJs, Docker, Ruby, Symphony, and JQuery, involving more than 1000 (JQuery 250) of virtual contributors. The main contributions of this work are:

- We empirically explore the source code review activity in five OSS aiming at uncovering unseen social interactions within a core-periphery structure;
- An approach to overlap different networks (files co-edition, reviews, commenters) aiming to localize contributors in one network on an another one;
- We demonstrated how contributors with a high centrality degree have more likely a shorter review interval than peripheral contributors.

The rest of the paper is organized as follows: Section 2 outlines our motivation and pinpoints our research questions. Section 3 surveys related work. Section 4 presents the methodology including projects description and data collection process. Section 5 provides our results. Section 6 discusses the threats of validity. Section 7 concludes and outlines future work.

2 Background and Motivation

2.1 Social Network Analysis

Social Network Analysis is a research domain studying the relationships between individuals [8]. These networks are typically modeled as graphs in which nodes represent individuals and edges represent relationships between these individuals. For instance, if two contributors have modified the same file, there is a co-edition relationship that can be represented as an edge. Similarly, if two developers comment on technical artifacts then we can represent this interaction (i.e., the list of comments) as an edge between those two nodes. These social interactions have an impact on group dynamics affecting collaboration and task efficiency performance. Therefore, previous research has shown that SNA techniques might help to understand different types of developer interactions in OSS projects. Bird et al. [1] mapped code commit interactions (co-edition files) to interactions in the mailing-list.

A wide range of SNA metrics can be applied for performing social analysis. Each metric looks at either specific properties of the networks or properties of the nodes. For our work we focused on centrality indices as detailed in Table 1.

Table 1. Social network centrality metrics

Metric	Definition	Meaning
Degree centrality	Number of edges incident upon a node. The degree centrality of a vertex v, for a given graph G is: $C_D(\vartheta) = \mathtt{deg}(v)$	Indication of how many other contributors each contributor interacts with. Core developers have a higher degree centrality because they interact with a large number of other contributors
Betweenness centrality	The number of shortest paths traversing a given node	Measure of the importance of a node within a graph. Contributors with a high betweenness centrality are broker nodes for communication with other contributors. Betweenness is useful as an index of the potential of a node for control of communication
Closeness centrality	Distance of an actor to all other nodes in the network	Gives an indication of how quickly a developer can reach the entire community. Used to assess the speed of information spread from a given node to other reachable nodes in the network
Eccentricity	Maximum distance from a node to all other nodes in the network	A high eccentricity means that the most distant vertex in the network is a long way away, and a low eccentricity means that the most distant vertex is actually quite close. A central developer should have lower eccentricity as they will have direct communication ties with many other developers

2.2 Motivation

Software development is performed by teams collaborating and interacting together on technical artifacts. Code review has been widely used in both companies and open source software projects [11] mainly to ensure the inclusion of only high-quality code into the project codebase. Typically, a developer submits a code change to a code review system and recommends a set of developers to review his changes. Then, the reviewers would provide comments and suggest improvements to the changes. Next, the developer improves the change according to the comments. Once those improvements have been applied and approved by reviewers they can be integrated to the mainstream branch of the version control. Figure 1 shows a concrete example of a list of pending changes waiting for the review process.

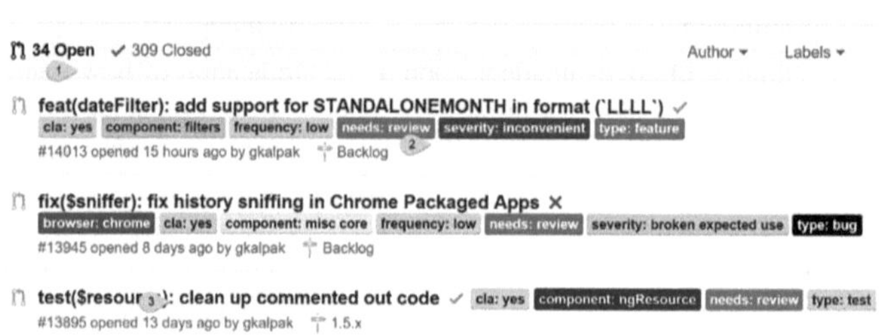

Fig. 1. A real example of requested needs for reviews (AngularJS project).

Preliminary analysis of data related to code review revealed a median delay ranging from 1 to 20 days. For instance, we found that for AngularJS project the review process takes, on average, 14 days ($\pm$ std. dev. 39.2) with a mean of 5 comments by review as illustrated in Fig. 2. Finding appropriate code-reviewers in OSS projects can be a tedious and time consuming task.

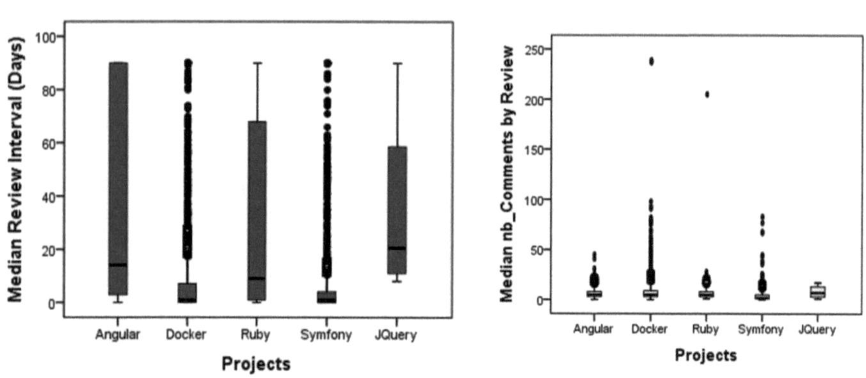

Fig. 2. Review intervals (left); nb_Comments by Review (right)

To speed up the code review process, contributors need to be supported with an automated approach seeking to find experts in the related source code. Thus, our exploration of code review using Social Network Analysis leads to the following research questions:

- ***RQ1.*** How does socio-technical interaction vary for various open source communities?
- ***RQ2.*** Does the socio-technical analysis make collaboration an actionable concept?
- ***RQ3.*** Contributors with a high centrality degree have shorter review interval than peripheral contributors?

3 Related Work

We address the related research areas with respect to socio-technical networks, source code review practice, and expert recommendation.

Socio-Technical Networks. It has been reported that higher socio-technical congruence usually correlates with higher developer productivity [2] and reduces integration failures [3]. Both researchers and OSS projects leads could use STC to diagnose project members' collaboration and improve team coordination. Prior work has shown that social networking contains plenty of information that can be leveraged for other purposes [8]. For instance, Bird et al. [1] studied code commit interactions and showed that developers who work on the same file are more likely to interact in the mailing-list. An SNA techniques can help an actionable graph of previous commit interactions providing new kind of metrics and patterns for a computational analysis.

Code Reviews Practice. Rigby and Storey [10] examined manually hundreds of reviews across five high profile OSS projects aiming to investigate the mechanisms and behaviors that developers use to find code changes they are competent to review. They found that the Apache project adopted a broadcast-based style of code review, meaning increasing the awareness of new changes, but annoying the community with a high amount of irrelevant notification. Prior work has analyzed the modern code review process used by the open source community. Baysal et al. [6] studied the factors that influence the outcome of the review process and found that review is positivity influenced by non-technical factors such as organization. Furthermore, a recent qualitative study at Microsoft [11] confirmed that identification of defects is not the only motivation for code review, but sharing knowledge among team members is also considered as an important motivation of modern code review.

Expert Recommendation. Xia et al. [12] proposed an approach, based on history of bug report and developer information, to recommend a developer for a new bug fix. Surian et al. [13] studied Sourceforge.Net attempting a cross-projects developer recommendation using developers' collaboration network. Authors try to recommend a list of top developers that are most compatible for a specific task based on their past projects they have worked on before. In the area of Question and Answer community (i.e., StackOverflow) using topic modeling and collaborative voting scores, Tian et al. [14] introduced an expert recommendation system in order to identify user expertise relevant to the topics of a given question.

4 Research Methodology

Our goal in this paper is to discover how SNA metrics can help to understand the source code review practice within OSS projects. Figure 3 illustrates our methodology regarding data extraction, processing and building different contributor's networks.

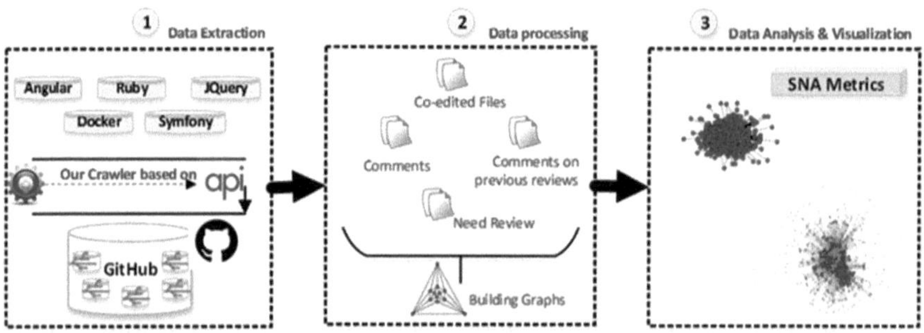

Fig. 3. Overview of our data extraction and processing approach.

Phase1 - *Data Extraction.* We focused our study on five large and rapidly-evolving open source systems. Height stared projects from GitHub. Our choice of projects was based on the following criteria: *(i)* project should be among the 100 most stared projects; *(ii)* should be still under active development; and *(iii)* involving at least 250 contributors. Table 2 summarizes the characteristics of our selected projects including the programming language, the total number of developers, number of releases; number of lines of code; number of requested reviews; and the total of commits.

Table 2. Overview of the studied systems

	Overview				Commits	
	Language	Contributors	Releases	LOF	Request review	Total
Angular.Js	JavaScript	1403	161	369.574	349	7534
Docker	Go	1301	129	670.722	2399	22318
Rails	Ruby	3000	283	387.862	750	56562
Symfony	PHP	1271	156	653.109	1193	25007
JQuery	JavaScript	250	134	62.566	10	6050

Phase2 - *Data Processing.* For each project, we use GITHUB API to extract detailed information about commits activity along with opened need reviews history. For each commit we were interested by the list of changed files (file name, status, author, churn) and comments (commenter, body, created at, etc.). When a collaborator opens a need review, conversation around the request is lunched. Thereby we were interested by contributors requesting reviews, carrying out a review, or simply commenting on it. We used these data to build three different graphs.

Phase3 - *Data Analysis and Visualization.* For each project we constructed three networks: The first is the collaborators' network based on coedited files. We generated social network graphs as undirected, weighted graphs where nodes represent contributors and edge weights represent the quantity of interactions between those contributors. The second is reviews commenters based on discussion launched after a review request. For example, if contributors C_1 and C_2 commented together on 20 code review requests posted by any contributor then the weight of the edge between their nodes would be 20. In addition, we used mapping option in order to construct sub networks of contributors that requested, resolved and closed reviews requests.

5 Analysis and Results

RQ1. *How does socio-technical interaction vary for various open source communities?*

Motivation. We are interested in understanding whether or not the open source community has an efficient underpin collaboration mechanism. The exploration of the collaboration topologies between contributors in such a virtual environment will provide more insights on how the communication flows and what would be the main patterns for an effective collaboration related to source code reviewing.

Approach. For each project, we constructed three networks: *(1)* contributors' collaboration network based upon co-edition files where nodes are contributors and vertexes are undirected and weighted links between contributors having modified together same files; *(2)* Comment's network representing contributors interacting trough comments on technical artefacts; *(3)* Reviewer's network representing previous interactions on source code reviews.

Results. Figure 4 (first column) illustrates the structure and density of OSS contributors' network. A clear visual distinction appears through the five projects regarding the density of networks and concentration of core/peripheral developers. We were able to observe the hidden structure and organization of the communities in OSS development [15]. The Core developers are generally involved in an OSS project for a relatively long period, and make significant contributions to the development and evolution of the Open Source System. While Peripheral developers contribute occasionally to a given project.

Figure 4 also shows (two other columns) the mapping of other useful information on top of the contributors' network to provide respectively the network location of commenters on review and contributors performing reviews. We were able to discover that commenters (green spots) might be in the core as well as in peripheral areas.

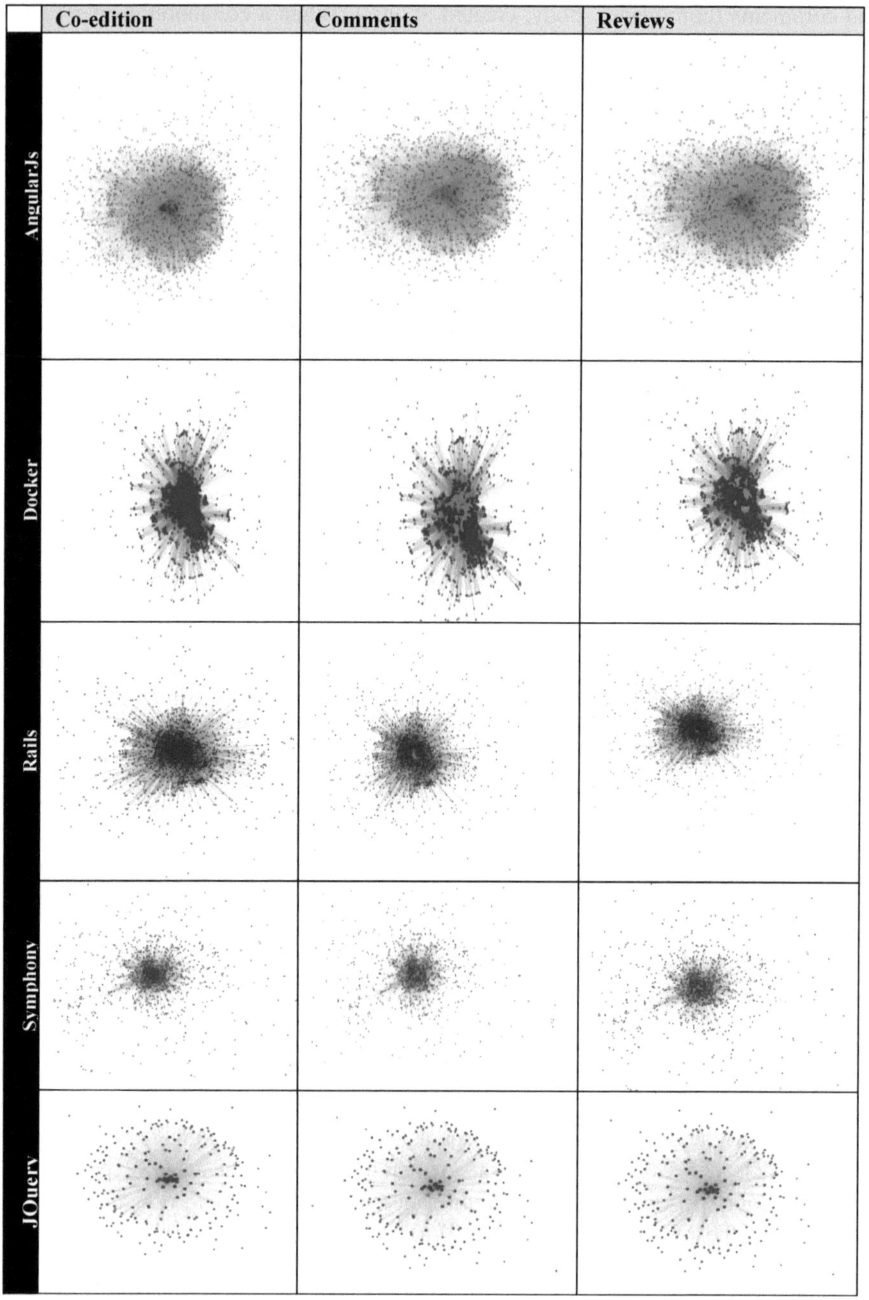

Fig. 4. Structure and density of OSS contributors' network (Color figure online)

However, reviews are carried out by contributors with high degrees of centrality (blue spots). We suspect that factors such as notoriety, awareness, and domain knowledge are of importance in this setting. A further topic analysis is required to get more insights regarding the density of core contributors.

RQ2. Does the socio-technical analysis make collaboration an actionable concept?

Motivation. Previous research examined the alignment between technical dependencies and social coordination within OSS projects [1]. Based on SNA, we try to confirm this correlation by examining connections between contributors in the context of work-related collaboration.

Approach. We used social network metrics to find patterns of collaboration needs. To do so, we manually analyzed interactions between collaborators through file co-edition, comments, and history of reviews. We then mapped our observations to our computed SNA metrics (Table 3).

Table 3. SNA metrics

	Clustering coefficient	Network centralization	Avg. # of neighbors	# Nodes	Network density	Network heterogeneity
Angular. Js	0.897	0.918	66.428	1393	0.048	1.674
Docker	0.874	0.794	81.385	1314	0.062	1.582
Ruby	0.855	0.876	207.242	3003	0.069	1.557
Symfony	0.866	0.952	63.425	1270	0.050	1.804
JQuery	0.834	0.725	61.197	244	0.252	0.837

Results. The core members across all projects play vital role of submitting reviews. For instance, we found that for AngularJs project, over 366 review requests (93 %) of closed reviews were resolved by core developers.

We found that not all reviews are assigned, furthermore, assigned ones are most often closed within lower average days than others.

RQ3. Contributors with a high centrality degree have shorter review interval than peripheral contributors?

Motivation. Previous research [16] has shown that there are experts reviewing technical contributions involved in most OSS projects. However, this past research does not explain where are those expert located in the contributors' network and what is the mechanism for assigning reviews to a list of predefined experts categorized by domain knowledge. We aim to assess the influence of contributors' position within the network on how long it takes for a code change patch to be reviewed.

Approach. A recent study showed that core developers play a major role in the evolution of OSS projects [15]. We further extend these results with social network visualization on review and collaborators' networks with respect to the lead time for the review process.

Results

Core Contributors are Source Code Review Brokers. Based on SNA metrics and visualization, we were able to identify central core contributors (see density core in Fig. 4 – co-edition). We segregate contributors according to the degree of centrality they have and then we mapped these data to our network of reviews. Our analysis shows that we can go further with SNA metrics to study the position of contributors in the network and their review activities. Figure 5 shows a comparative of the amount of reviews, comments, and time interval regarding the position of the contributors within the network (centrality degree) as well as the distribution of degree for contributors. Because of the space constraint, we show only the comparison between AngularJs and Docker.

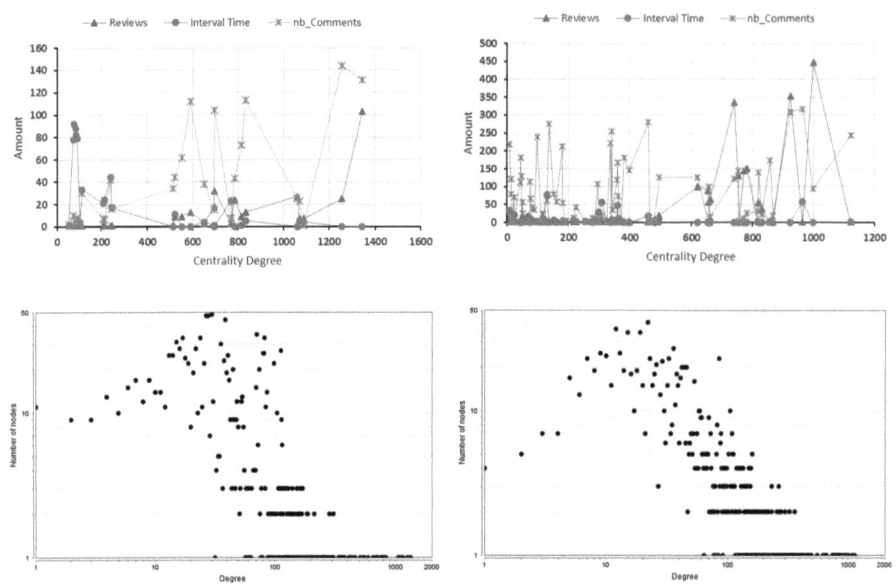

Fig. 5. Comparing networks metrics of angular and docker projects

For AngularJs, reviews are requested by core team and carried out also by the core team. Surprisingly, we observed that for changes coming from peripherals the comments on reviews flows from the core to the periphery and went back to the core for final acceptance. However, for code changes coming from the core team we observed a less amount of comments and less discussions. Consequently, **more a contributor is central in the network of contributors likely he has a shortest time for code revision and acceptance**.

In addition, Fig. 5b1 and b2 illustrates the distribution of centrality degree within AngularJS and Docker.

6 Threats to Validity

Construct Validity. First, we assume that all communications occur with comments either on commits or on code reviews. Developers on Github might use an external social media or mailing list to communicate. We are actively expanding the scope of our research to interview Github contributors, via a survey, in order to get more insights on factors that might improve collaboration on code review. Second, there may be number of unmeasured confounding factors that could influence a review outcome such as the projects architecture, the code complexity, and the availability of contributors. There is no evidence that our partitioning approach or our measurements would be systematically biased based on any of these confounding factors. Furthermore, the fact that the results were similar across all eight projects provides additional confidence that any confounding factors did not significantly impact the study results.

Internal Validity. We are aware that we might miss transitive dependencies between technical elements. For instance, changing the framework on which depends many files. Moreover, software development is dynamic, and as contributions are made over time, the nature of the socio-interactions changes. We mitigated this threat by studying multiple open source projects, using different languages, within the GitHub community.

External Validity. We focus our evaluation on five open source systems, which threatens the generalizability of our case study results, as with all empirical studies. However, we studied a variety of systems from different domains, various languages, and sizes to alleviate potential bias. Nonetheless, additional replication studies are needed.

7 Conclusions

In this paper, we used a Social Network Analysis approach aiming at studying the collaboration through code review practice within five OSS projects. We extracted and analyzed historical data of five large and long-lived OSS projects. We described collaboration between OSS contributors based on socio-technical analysis regarding files co-edition, comments, and reviews. The first key contribution of this study relates to our ability to visualize how contributors from the core team development interact with peripheral ones. Another key contribution of this study is our socio-technical analysis to make collaboration an actionable concept. Using a longitudinal data set which connects the same contributors over time in different interactions, we have been able to examine the backbone of code review practice within virtual communities, which we think is crucial for software products quality. Finally, we demonstrated how contributors with a high centrality degree have more likely a shorter review interval than peripheral contributors. Our study has important practical implications. As understanding the nature and types of collaborations in a virtual environment which provided some insights on the main patterns for collaboration related to source code reviewing. Our results suggest that core contributors play vital roles in carrying out review requests.

As part of our future work we want to inspect the temporal dynamics by which an OSS community structure grows and fades over time. For example, we could study temporal dynamics to determine patterns of how newcomers to an OSS project progress from the periphery to the core teams, how they gain their notoriety and how they lead and impact the trajectory of OSS projects.

References

1. Bird, C., Pattison, D., D'Souza, R., et al.: Latent social structure in open source projects. In: Proceedings of the 16th International Symposium on Foundations of Soft Engineering (FSE 2008), Atlanta, Georgia, pp. 24–35 (2008)
2. Cataldo, M., Herbsleb, J.D.: Coordination breakdowns and their impact on development productivity and software failures. Trans. Softw. Eng. **39**(3), 343–360 (2013)
3. Kwan, I., Schroter, A., Damian, D.: Does socio-technical congruence have an effect on software build success? A study of coordination in a software project. Trans. Softw. Eng. **37** (3), 307–324 (2011)
4. Yarosh, S., Matthews, T., Zhou, M., et al.: I need someone to help!: a taxonomy of helper-finding activities in the enterprise. In: Proceedings of the 27th International Conference on Computer Supported Cooperative Work (CSCW), Texas, pp. 1375–1386 (2013)
5. Thongtanunam, P., Tantithamthavorn, C., Kula, R.G., et al.: Who should review my code? A file location-based code-reviewer recommendation approach for modern code review. In: 2015 IEEE 22nd International Conference on Software Analysis Evolution and Reengineering (SANER), pp. 141–150 (2015)
6. Baysal, O., Kononenko, O., Holmes, R., et al.: The influence of non-technical factors on code review. In: Proceedings of the 20th Working Conference on Reverse Engineering, Koblenz, Germany, pp. 122–131 (2013)
7. Begel, A., DeLine, R., Zimmermann, T.: Social media for software engineering. In: FSE/SDP Workshop on Future of Software Engineering Research, Santa Fe, New Mexico, USA, pp. 33–38 (2010)
8. Kadushin, C.: Understanding Social Networks: Theories, Concepts, and Findings. Oxford University Press, Oxford (2011)
9. Meneely, A., Williams, L.: Socio-technical developer networks: should we trust our measurements? In: Proceedings of the 33rd International Conference on Software Engineering (ICSE 2011), Waikiki, Honolulu, USA, pp. 281–290 (2011)
10. Rigby, P.C., Storey, M.-A.: Understanding broadcast based peer review on open source software projects. In: Proceedings of the 33rd International Conference on Software Engineering (ICSE 2011), Waikiki, Honolulu, USA, pp. 541–550 (2011)
11. Bacchelli A., Bird, C.: Expectations, outcomes, and challenges of modern code review. In: Proceedings of the 35th International Conference on Software Engineering (ICSE 2013), San Francisco, USA, pp. 712–721 (2013)
12. Xia, X., Lo, D., Wang, X., et al.: Accurate developer recommendation for bug resolution. In: 2013 20th Working Conference on Reverse Engineering (WCRE), pp. 72–81 (2013)
13. Surian, D., Liu, N., Lo, D., et al.: Recommending people in developers' collaboration network. In: 2011 18th Working Conference on Reverse Engineering, pp. 379–388 (2011)

14. Tian, Y., Kochhar, P.S., Lim, E.-P., Zhu, F., Lo, D.: Predicting best answerers for new questions: an approach leveraging topic modeling and collaborative voting. In: Nadamoto, A., Jatowt, A., Wierzbicki, A., Leidner, J.L. (eds.) SocInfo 2013. LNCS, vol. 8359, pp. 55–68. Springer, Heidelberg (2014)
15. Geldenhuys, J.: Finding the core developers. In: 36th Euromicro Conference on Software Engineering and Advanced Applications, Lille, France, pp. 447–450 (2010)
16. Asundi, J., Jayant, R.: Patch review processes in open source software development communities: a comparative case study. In: 40th Annual Hawaii International Conference on System Sciences, p. 166 (2007)

Product Development in Collaborative Networks – An Expert View on Current Challenges and Future Trends

Wei Min Wang[1(✉)], Pascal Lünnemann[2], Sebastian Neumeyer[2], Haygazun Hayka[2], and Rainer Stark[1,2]

[1] Department for Machine Tools and Factory Management, Technische Universität Berlin, Pascalstr. 8-9, 10587 Berlin, Germany
w.wang@tu-berlin.de
[2] Department for Virtual Product Creation, Fraunhofer-Institute for Production Systems and Design Technology, Pascalstr. 8-9, 10587 Berlin, Germany
{pascal.luennemann,sebastian.neumeyer,haygazun.hayka, rainer.stark}@ipk.fraunhofer.de

Abstract. Cross-enterprise collaboration in product development has become a common practice in industry. Companies increasingly depend on collaborations with networks of partners from different tiers of value creation, various geographic locations and even from outside of their own sector. Moreover, there is a growing tendency to involve parties from later stages of the product's lifecycle in the product development phase. To face the challenges of the increasing complexity of collaborative product development a holistic approach of Product Lifecycle Management (PLM) has evolved. Although methods, processes and IT-systems of PLM proved to be beneficial in supporting the internal collaboration of industrial companies, they seem to have only little effect in the context of cross-company collaboration. Reasons and solution approaches for that were evaluated in an expert study with 40 experts from industry and academia. Results from that study and practical implications are presented in this paper.

Keywords: Product development in collaborative networks · Collaborative engineering · Product lifecycle management · Industrial collaboration practices · Expert study · Trends of collaborative engineering

1 Introduction

The development of modern products often requires interdisciplinary collaboration of several companies [1, 2]. This is partly a consequence of the increasing product complexity that is driven by trends such as Industry 4.0 and Product Service Systems (PSS) [2]. For example, cyber-physical products may be offered with accompanying services or even completely as a PSS. In both cases knowledge from various domains have to be combined. Furthermore, the expanding scope of product functions, their maintenance and repair often requires the knowledge of several companies to be merged to develop the product [1]. Hence, interdisciplinary and cross-company collaboration in

H. Afsarmanesh et al. (Eds.): PRO-VE 2016, IFIP AICT 480, pp. 302–312, 2016.
DOI: 10.1007/978-3-319-45390-3_26

product development has become a common practice in industry, causing companies to increasingly depend on collaborations with networks of partners from different tiers of value creation, various geographic locations and even from outside of their own sector [3]. Moreover, there is a growing tendency to involve parties from later stages of the product's lifecycle in the product development phase. The transformation of the enterprise-wide product development also requires an adaptation of the working environment in terms of tools, IT systems, technical infrastructure, information and data models, processes and organizational structures.

To meet these demands while achieving short development cycles, cooperation between enterprises will become even more intense. This and the widely dispersed allocation of the necessary expertise are driving the conversion of the former coordinated product development into a collaborative product development. To identify essential aspects of innovations and obstacles regarding planning and implementation of measures to realize this change, an expert study on product development in collaborative networks was conducted by the Fraunhofer Institute for Production Systems and Design Technology (Fraunhofer IPK) in cooperation with the CONTACT Software GmbH and the Association of German Engineers (VDI). In this study 40 experts from industry and academia with relevant experience in the field of Product Data Management (PDM)/PLM and engineering collaboration were asked to share their expertise on current challenges and future trends. The results of these interviews give insights to relevant drivers for cross-company collaboration from both the industrial and the academic perspective and combines empirical knowledge from industry and innovations from PLM system vendors, consultancies, research institutes and universities. Based on these insights, best- and worst-practices from industry and strengths and weaknesses of current collaboration approaches are discussed. Finally, expectations regarding collaboration processes, respective IT-tools and strategic goals are derived, especially with regard to PDM and PLM.

Comparing to other survey in the field of engineering collaboration this study focused on the value creating engineering activities performed by people in a multi-enterprise environment, their coordination through processes and benefits of used IT tools. Although the general motivation is comparable to existing studies (e.g. [4]) this study focuses more on the social aspect of collaboration. While several current studies analyze the collaborative software development (e.g. the controlling and tools [5, 6]) the presented study focuses mechatronic and cyber-physical systems as multi-domain products integrating different areas of product development.

Overall, it can detect that the collaborative product development is facing multifaceted challenges, in particular:

The change in the working situation, the increase of CPS, advancing globalization and related performance in data deployments and integration challenge the collaboration. As well as the coordination of very large and distributed development networks with nowadays' worse transparency in the procedures.

And the optimizations of the provided it-support, in particular in their alignment with the development activities and processes, as well as the data security, data availability and user friendly interface design need to be addressed. Especially these challenges are taken into consideration in the context of this paper.

2 Study Design and Implementation

2.1 Definition of Collaboration in Context of Product Development

There are numerous definitions of collaboration depending on the context of its application. Based on the definition of Lu et al. [7] this study regards collaboration in context of product development as an collective endeavor that "requires a team of individuals to work on tasks that not only have shared resources and shared outcomes, but, most importantly, a shared common goal". He distinguishes collaboration from coordination and cooperation as lower levels of collective endeavors. While coordination only requires sharing of resources to fulfil a collective task, cooperation also includes sharing of outcomes, but in both cases tasks designed to be disjunctive and are carried out independently. Whereas, collaboration explicitly requires combination of individual skills and collective efforts to fulfill tasks in order to reach a common goal. Therefore, organizational boundaries are neglected in favor of continuous exchanges of knowledge, information and resources [7]. Steinheider [8] further characterizes collaboration by the dimensions Coordination, Communication and Knowledge integration, each describing characteristics regarding one specific aspect of collaboration (see Fig. 1). As this study also evaluates IT-supported processes, the fourth dimension Information logistics was introduced, to provide a better understanding of information distribution within the product development process and throughout the lifecycle.

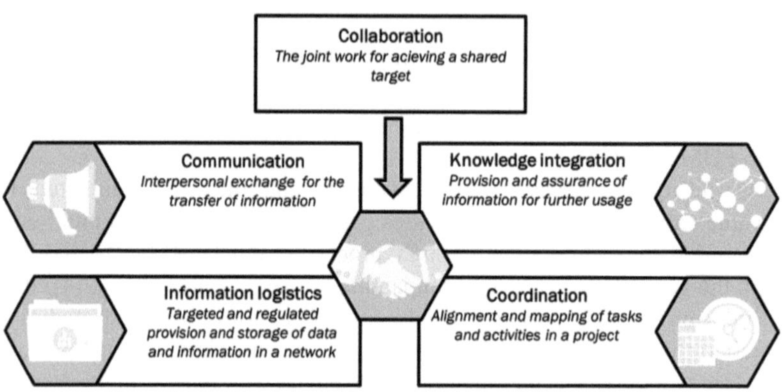

Fig. 1. Four dimensions of collaboration regarded in this study

2.2 Structure of the Study

The interviews were based on a standardized and structured questionnaire comprising closed and open questions, grouped in four sections (see Fig. 2). The first section focused on the evaluation of the current working situation and expected changes in collaborative product development with regard to the four dimensions mentioned before. In the second section, current practice and prospective future forms of cooperation are considered. Especially, the changing engineering environment and the related coordination aspects are considered there. In the third section, actual industrial practices and used tools are analyzed and best- and worst-practices are examined. In the fourth section, requirements regarding collaborative product development in the future are collected. These questions aim at the evaluation of both, current technological trends and organizational forms. Based on this structure, the study captures the current situation of collaboration in product development and shows a potential path for its development in the medium-term (i.e. in the coming five to ten years) from the surveyed experts' perspectives.

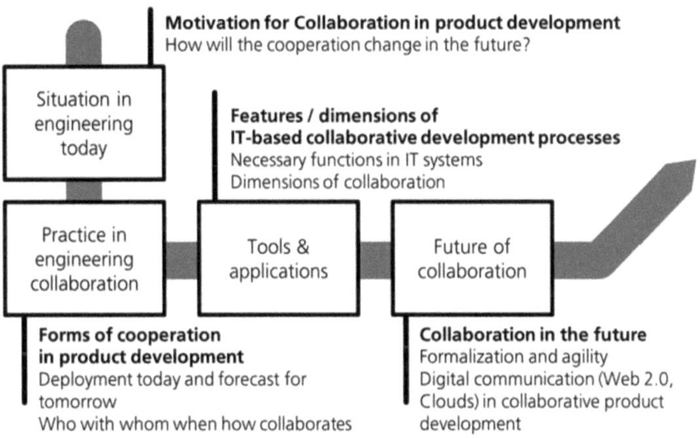

Fig. 2. General structure and core questions of the study

As part of the analysis of the responses recorded and protocolled conversations were analyzed on clusters and summarized in qualitative statements. According to the relatively small sample the responses were rated primarily qualitative and not quantitative. Even so in statistical reports for prioritizing statements equivalent weights were made (for example, placement weighting 1 to 5) and were taken in consideration accordingly in the qualitative analysis.

In total, 40 experts were interviewed using the structured questionnaire. The interviews were mostly conducted through phone calls and web-conferencing and took about one to two hours. In order to ensure a balanced mixture of practical industrial experience and innovative research, about one third of the interviewees are acquired from research institutes. Hereby, both an image of the current challenges and needs, as well as the currently under consideration innovations in research can be determined.

Two-thirds of the participants comprise representatives of the automotive industry, plant construction, consulting, aerospace and rail transportation (see Fig. 3a). With the aim of a possible heterogeneous and comprehensive picture of the challenges in enterprise-wide development, different roles were interviewed to get into the business. The models range from the experts in process management and information technology, corporate research and development departments (product-related), project managers and managers in departments, division and company boards. That way, both the practical work of community development as well as the strategic perspective of cooperation could be considered. Half of the participants from industry hold executive positions in their companies. With regard to the academic participants, the surveyed professors were counted analogously (see Fig. 3b). About half of the industrial participants work in OEMs, the other half in first-tier supplier companies.

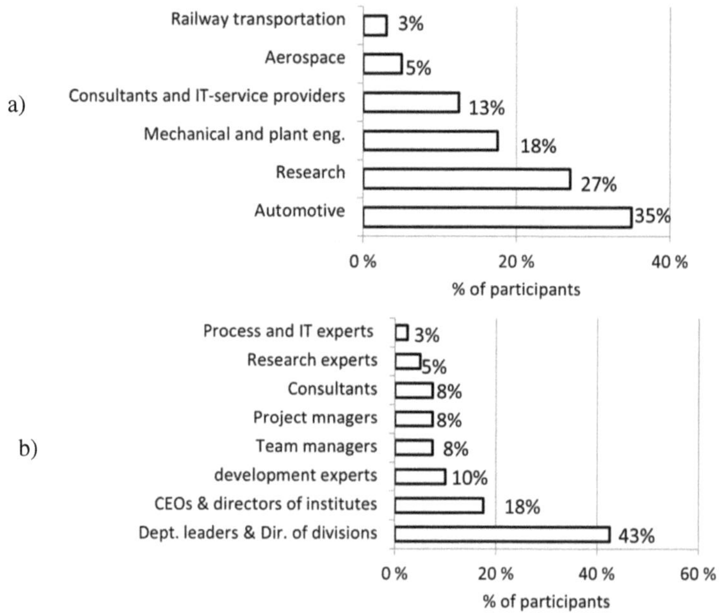

Fig. 3. (a) Branches of experts, (b) Positions held by the experts

3 Findings

3.1 Changes in Collaboration Practices

The increasing scope of product functions, new business models including product related services (e.g. PSS), the integration of software systems (e.g. user assistant systems) and communications to peripheral infrastructure (e.g. for condition monitoring) often require skills and expertise beyond the capabilities of one single company. In this respect, cross-enterprise and cross-sector collaborations are often seen as a way to acquire the necessary expertise [1]. This significance of this well-known driver is also confirmed by the answers of the surveyed experts. The acquisition of know-how, which is not or not sufficiently available in the own company, was ranked first by roughly 30 % of the respondents. The second main driver is Cost reduction that refers to both, outsourcing in low-wage countries as well as the national subcontracting of specialized engineering services.

With regard to the duration of collaboration, the experts expect that the current timeframes of joint development projects will rather remain in a similar scope or even decrease. This reflects the decreasing duration of development projects per se, which in turn results from the ever more rapid innovation-cycles. At the same time, the experts expect that the duration of partnerships between the companies will increase or at least remain stable. This opposing development is explained as consequence of overheads invested. As stated by the respondents, it is anticipated that long-term partnerships allow for "smoother" collaboration processes as mutual trust between involved engineers can be established and organizational structured harmonized.

Concerning the total number of partners within collaboration, two opposing developments are anticipated by the experts. On the one hand, there is a trend of consolidation of small and medium sized suppliers into larger system-suppliers (e.g. through merger and acquisition). On the other hand, a growing number of small and highly specialized component suppliers are entering the market. Which effect will outweigh depends could not be determined generally, but will depend on the tier-level and the industrial sector. However, more than the half of the experts is expecting a general increase in the amount of partners. Only twenty percent are assuming a decrease. Especially, experts from companies of second-tier suppliers/developers expect a general increase in consortia sizes.

In parallel, the experts also describe a globalization of their development activities, as local development centres for localized modules are established often near- or on-site of OEMs to compete with other global acting companies. As a consequence, intercultural work has to be increasingly considered in engineering collaboration. From the experts' viewpoint, the current mode of collaboration, where partners are only involved for the detailed engineering, will be extended to other lifecycle phases such as concept design, market analysis or later phases such as production planning and manufacturing as well as supporting services.

3.2 People are the Success Factors of Collaborations

As defined by Lu et al. [7], collaboration is the highest form of collective endeavour requiring the sharing and alignment of resources and goals, and the integration of knowledge. As it is also fundamentally a social process [9], the success of collaboration often highly depends on the involved individuals and their social relationships [10]. In the context of cross-enterprise collaboration, this aspect is even more important. Firstly, a huge variety of individuals with divers cultural and professional backgrounds will come together when organizations from different industrial sectors and geographic locations engage in collaboration. Secondly, there is an additional level of organizational culture and habits, which may influence the collaboration behaviour of individual persons [9]. Hence, the individuals engaged in collaborative projects are the key success factors. Still, the development of tools and IT-systems to support collaboration often tends to focus on technical requirements. This aspect was also stressed by the experts surveyed in this study. Various statements pointed out that the human is getting increasingly "lost" in the process of digitalization. One expert stated: "The IT-support for collaboration have reached a good maturity level, but the human factor within such processes have to be regarded. It is crucial to include direct communication on personal level to facilitate establishing a common base and building of mutual trust.[1]" Another

1 All citations are analogous translations of the statements made in German.

respondent from industry even said that "it has been forgotten, that every IT-system is used by humans". He pointed out, that the development of tools is often heavily dominated by technical requirements, while the human factor is totally neglected. In his opinion, this kind of focus led to "disastrous" user interfaces in all current PDM systems.

As confirmation of these statements, the summarized responses showed that personal discussions are the preferred best practice (20 % of total answers), followed by the realization if transparency (11 % of total answers) and communicative or spontaneous employees. Also the usage of multimedia as well as a frequent communication and a common language are success factors. The usage of email as main communication channel has been identified in a previous study conducted by Müller et al. in 2013 [11], and could be confirmed again in the current study (23 % of answers). In addition, video conferences have been mentioned (20 %), while the Phone as well as instant messaging tools, screen sharing and PDM-/PLM-Solutions for communication have been mentioned with 10 % or less(see Fig. 4).

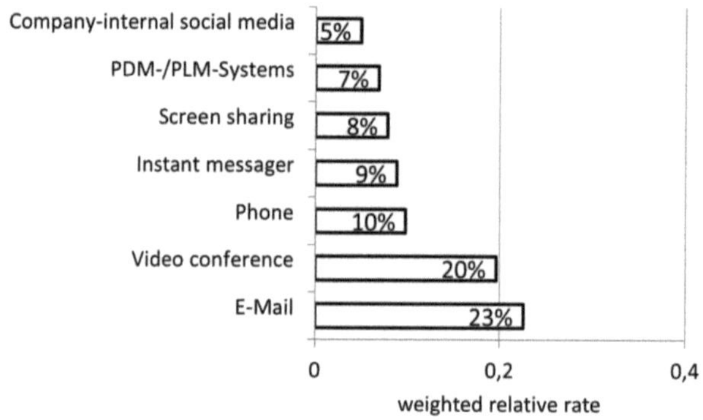

Fig. 4. Tools used for communication in industrial practice

The coordination of an engineering collaboration is due to different organizations, their different cultures and processes, always a challenge in projects. The previous study [11] revealed in this regard that coordination and communication are covering more than twenty percent of the working time of design engineers. This was also confirmed by the experts in the current study. As best practice for coordination, a shared comprehension of processes (18 %) as well as taking responsibility (11 %) and scheduled deliverables (10 %) have been highlighted by experts. In contrast, coordination is inhibited from the experts' point of view by unsuitable IT-solutions, bad leadership and missing process comprehension. These results again shows that the persons involved in the collaborative activities are of integral meaning to it's success.

Preferred IT-solutions in context of coordination are project management tools with nearly one third of mentioned answers (29 %). PDM- and PLM-solutions (15 %), workflow management (15 %) and project management functionalities in PLM-solutions (13 %) turned out to be less important as expected (see Fig. 5).

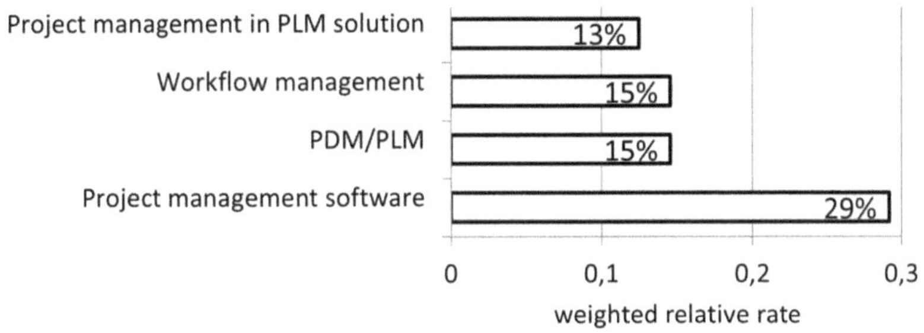

Fig. 5. Tools used for coordination in industrial practice

Beside coordination and communication, the information logistics in engineering collaboration need to be considered for a holistic view. To provide the engineer with the right information at the right time is the most important factor from the experts' viewpoint (16 % of answers). This aspect is followed by proper access privilege management (11 %), availability of the information (9 %) and clear specification (7 %) as best practice in information logistics (see Fig. 6).

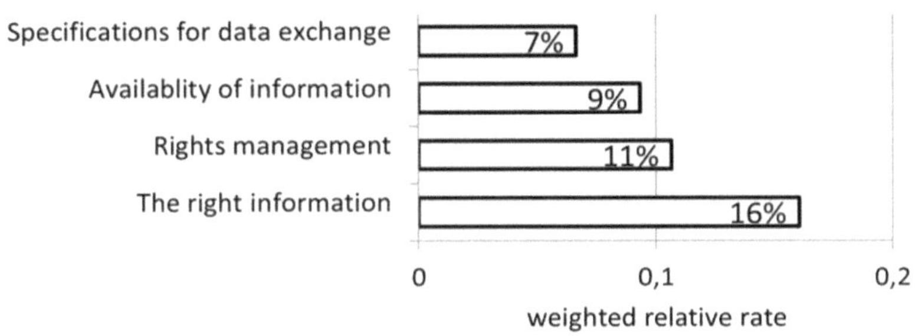

Fig. 6. Best practices in information logistics

Security concerns as well as unclear interfaces, unreliable IT-systems and missing information within an IT-system are show stoppers in this dimension. These IT-systems are in majority PDM-/PLM-Solutions (33 %), while only 6 % of the experts confirmed that direct partner integration in PDM-/PLM-solutions is given. Commonly used solutions for data exchange are dedicated Team Data Management (TDM) systems. Cloud-solutions were rarely mentioned in the answers (7 %) and are hence, considered exceptions in information logistics (see Fig. 7a).

The knowledge integration as the last building block is understood as methodological and procedural definition of the mode of operation and the securing of gained knowledge of an engineering collaboration. However, the current activities are focussing on documentation and transfer of explicit knowledge. Therefore, handbooks (14 %), guidelines (12 %) and IT-systems (12 %) are used. The use of Wikis for continuous documentation of group knowledge, the capturing of abstracted knowledge as well as lessons learned were only mentioned peripheral (7 % each). In this regard, the human factor proves to be a major hindrance, as one essential reason for insufficient knowledge integration is

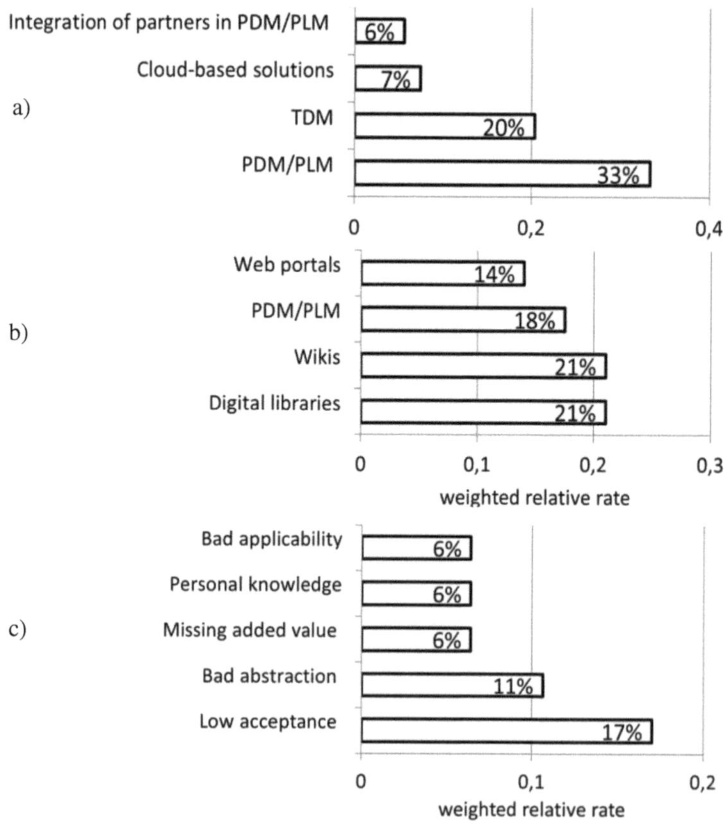

Fig. 7. (a) Tools used in information logistics, (b) Tools used in knowledge integration (c) Worst cases in knowledge integration

the lack of personal motivation share or provide knowledge. This is mainly due to a low acceptance of that activity per se (17 %), resulting partly from concerns about becoming easier replaceable and partly from a lack of defined processes. This in turn results in inadequate documentation and useless efforts. A further obstacle for knowledge integration is that the value of knowledge management is often not or not clearly defined in the working context of engineers (6 %). Hence, it is rather perceived as an overhead than as essential value creation activity.

4 Conclusion

The current situation in engineering collaboration is characterized by a wide variety of tools, interfaces, communication channels and process definitions. Due to security reasons, companies usually do not allow partners to access their central data sources, therefore the internal project members have to spend high efforts to search, extract and transfer data to portals so partners and suppliers can access them.

Partners have to deal with the challenge, that each customer provides different interfaces, individual processes and rules for the execution of collaboration. Information, data and processes need to be persistent though all the layers of developers, which hardly can be achieved by a high amount of interfaces and formats. While today engineers are already overwhelmed by the existing process instructions.

In addition, neither the currently implemented PLM-solutions provide the necessary flexibility and openness, so individual as well as different approaches for partner integration can be achieved. Nor the necessary human-to-human communication is adequately supported.

In consequence, collaboration needs to be planned and executed in a more holistic way and not treated only as a technical solution or a process definition. Due to the finding, that collaboration will extend, the number of partners will increase and the integration of non-sector specific partners is expected, collaboration need to be treated under multi-dimensional aspects with special emphasis on the human claims. Only by covering processes and organizations, tools and IT-systems as well as information and data models aligned with activities performed by people, the engineering collaboration will be a success.

With regard to the PLM-approach, the holistic consideration of all these aspects has to be covered to achieve a successful collaboration. Last but not least the most important element of collaboration has been mentioned: only with individual humans, who are motivated, communicative, upright and flexible with different situations, collaboration will finally succeed.

Acknowledgments. We thank all participants of the study for their contribution and support. Only by their individual commitment and their willingness to answer our questions patiently, even at early and late hours, this study could gained such in-depth insights about the present and future of collaboration in product development. We also want to thank Ms. Helena Rott (Fraunhofer IPK) and Ms. Barbara Scholvin (CONTACT Software GmbH) for their persistent contribution to the text editing and creation of graphics. Finally, we thank Dr. Heinz Bedenbender (VDI-GPP) and Ms. Sophia Rogge (TU Berlin) for proofreading.

A Appendix

Structure of the questionnaire and content summary:

1. Introduction:
   flow and content of the interview
2. Demographics:
   Information about the person, the company and the role
3. Drivers for cooperation:
   Key drivers in prioritization
4. Forms of cooperation:
   (Industry:) What forms are used, as these affect the daily life, as they affect the IT support

(All:) changes in collaboration situation (duration, form, size, accompanying processes, strategy and partnership)

5. Features of collaborative development processes:
   guarantee of success, show-stopper and IT support in the dimensions of communication, coordination, information logistics and knowledge integration.
   IT support in the areas of requirements management, risk management, project management, change management, BOM maintenance, data exchange
6. Cooperation in the future:
   process orientation and its flexibility, transparency in the collaboration, language barriers, technological trends, Clouds, mobile devices
7. Statement of the interviewee.

References

1. Krause, F., Hayka, H., Pasewaldt, B.: Efficient product data sharing in collaboration life cycles. In: ElMaraghy, H.A., ElMaraghy, W.H. (eds.) Advances in Design, pp. 365–375. Springer, London (2006)
2. Stöckert, H.: Fehlervermeidung an Schnittstellenprozessen der verteilten Produktentwicklung
3. Hayka, H., Staub, G., Thamburaj, V., Zhang, Q.: Kooperationsplattform fur mechatronische Produktentstehung. ZWF: Zeitschrift für Wirtschaftlichen Fabrikbetrieb **103**, 721–725 (2008)
4. Cisco Public. CISCO Collaboration Work Practice Study. Cisco Public, San Jose, California, USA (2013). http://www.cisco.com/c/dam/en/us/solutions/collaboration/collaboration-sales/cwps_full_report.pdf. Accessed 7 June 2016
5. IEEE International Conference on Software Quality, Reliability and Security - Companion; QRS; QRS-C; Information Assurance Workshop; Workshop on Information Assurance; Trustworthy Computing Workshop; Workshop on Trustworthy Computing; Workshop on Model-Based Verification and Validation; MVV; Workshop on Safety and Security in Cyber-Physical Systems; SSCPS Workshop; Workshop on Human and Social Aspect of Software Quality; HSASQ; Workshop on Software Engineering and Knowledge Management; SEKM Workshop. A Survey on Knowledge Management in Software Engineering, 3–5 August 2015, Vancouver, British Columbia, Canada: proceedings. IEEE, Piscataway (2015)
6. Marshall, C., Brereton, P., Kitchenham, B.: Tools to support systematic reviews in software engineering. In: 19th International Conference, pp. 1–6. doi:10.1145/2745802.2745827
7. Lu, S., Elmaraghy, W., Schuh, G., Wilhelm, R.: A scientific foundation of collaborative engineering. CIRP Ann. – Manufact. Technol. **56**, 605–634 (2007). doi:10.1016/j.cirp.2007.10.010
8. Steinheider, B.: Supporting the co-operation of R&D-teams in the product development process, Fraunhofer Institute for Industrial Engineering (2001)
9. Patel, H., Pettitt, M., Wilson, J.R.: Factors of collaborative working: a framework for a collaboration model. Appl. Ergon. **43**, 1–26 (2012). doi:10.1016/j.apergo.2011.04.009
10. Pennington, D.D.: Cross-disciplinary collaboration and learning. Ecol. Soc. **13**, 8 (2008)
11. Müller, P., Pasch, F., Drewinski, R., Hayka, H.: Kollaborative Produktentwicklung und digitale Werkzeuge: Defizite heute - Potenziale morgen. Fraunhofer IPK, Berlin (2013)

Collaborative Data Mining for Intelligent Home Appliances

Oliviu Matei[1(✉)], Giovanni Di Orio[2], Javad Jassbi[2], José Barata[2], and Claudio Cenedese[3]

[1] Department of Electrical Engineering, Technical University of Cluj-Napoca, North University Center of Baia Mare, Baia Mare, Romania
oliviu.matei@holisun.com

[2] UNINOVA-CTS, Department of Electrical Engineering, FCT-UNL, Caparica, Portugal
{gido,j.jassbi,jab}@uninova.pt

[3] Global Technology Center – GTC, Electrolux Spa, Pordenone, Italy
claudio.cenedese@electrolux.it

Abstract. The augmentation of physical devices and resources with electronics, software, sensing elements and network connectivity is a "hot topic" as confirmed also by the several research projects and activities on internet-of-things (IoT) and cyber-physical systems (CPS) research streams. It is obvious that intelligent products are taking more responsibility in future collaborative networks. Recent products are becoming more and more intelligent and connected by using the existing network infrastructure, meaning that products are becoming active agents in networks and valuable data sources that are capable to provide data continuously during their operation. This is leading to a massive amount of data that can be used by product manufacturers to be and remain competitive in market sharing. In this scenario, the application of collaborative data mining techniques, supported by machine learning algorithms, is aimed to enable the analysis of the data provided from multiple and above all distributed data sources in order to discover and extract useful knowledge about the behavior of the users along with the usage patterns of their devices and appliances.

Keywords: Collaborative data mining · Intelligent home appliance · Collaborative network

1 Introduction

Intelligent products are pushing more and more the Collaborative Networks (CN) discipline to a new level where the product itself is acting as an active and autonomous agent within an environment where people, processes, data, and things are connected together for designing/creating new products and services, while product manufacturers to more securely manage the risk and to extend the global reach by allowing higher collaboration from anywhere and at any time. In this scenario, the data continuously produced by intelligent products – if properly gathered and analyzed – can provide fundamental feedback information to product manufacturers about the products performance as well as products usage. This information can be used by the manufacturers

H. Afsarmanesh et al. (Eds.): PRO-VE 2016, IFIP AICT 480, pp. 313–323, 2016.
DOI: 10.1007/978-3-319-45390-3_27

for accelerating the product innovation process and increasing their competitiveness in market sharing. For these reasons, products have become an indispensable part of New Generation of Collaborative networks ([1]).

According to Sanou [2], the access to the Internet has grown from an estimated 10 million people in 1993, to almost 40 million in 1995, to 670 million in 2002, and to 2.7 billion in 2013. As the connectivity and Internet of Things penetrate the daily life, a reasonable concern of the producers is to monitor and understand the behavior of the users along with the usage patterns of their devices and appliances. This would bring up invaluable knowledge as a basis for further technical and marketing developments, both in industrial and business environment, as well as in home context.

Therefore, much research has been invested in determine these usage patterns, such as the ones reported in [4] and [5]. Both use data mining to fulfil this objective. The aim is to determine an expected behavior of the device or user based on some known sensors outputs.

Human Agent collectives (HACs), are interesting investment for companies. Home appliance market leaders are keen to build smart houses (including smart kitchens) with the collaboration of both humans and intelligent products. This means HACs are the heart of smart collaborative networks while Intelligent Products are playing crucial role and the advantage is the stream of available data through sensors in the products. To manage this data/Information in a productive way, different types of algorithm need to be employed. Collaborative Data Mining is a successful example of emerging algorithms to deal with "big data" collected from Collaborative Networks.

The term of collaborative data mining has been used several times, by Appleman in [6], Maimon in [7] and Moyle in [8]. But the term is not defined in a comprehensive manner that allows one to have a view of what are the advantages of such an approach compared to classical data mining, what are the benefits of such an approach, what are the underlying principles of such an approach and how this approach may be different compared to other approaches. Later on, in 2008, Zhan et al. [9] used the term collaborative as referring to using more data sources for mining.

As the connectivity is present in our daily lives [10], the quantity of available data is ever increasing and companies have real interest in understanding the behaviour of their customers [11], a trend is to collaborate all these data source for more accurate analysis [12]. The research questions are:

- *What is the influence of using the data from two sources to predict the behavior of one source?*
- *Is there any relationship between the accuracy of such predictions and the correlation between the two sources?*

2 Collaborative Data Mining

As stated in [8], collaborative data mining is a setting where the data mining effort and/or process is distributed among multiple collaborative agents that are autonomously executing actions in the environment. Collaborative data mining is based on the main assumption that collaborative data mining processes can better tackle the considered data mining process with respect to a data mining process built on the top of individual and non-collaborative agents. Data mining is the process of extracting information or better knowledge from large quantity of data. Collaboration is the act of a variety of entities to share information, resources and responsibilities to jointly plan, implement, and evaluate a program of activities to achieve a common goal [13]. As stated in [13], collaboration is a difficult process and typically its success depends on several requirements, namely:

(i) the main purpose for collaboration;
(ii) the initial baseline for collaboration;
(iii) the collaborative process (a set of generic steps);
(iv) the creation of a space for collaboration;
(v) and finally the definition of resources, rewards, commitment and responsibilities.

Despite these difficulties the main motivating point is that by using collaborative processes it is possible to reach results that cannot be reached by parties/entities/agents working alone. With this in mind, the proposed research is based on the assumption that there are similarities between usage patterns of the same devices or more in general agents [2]. In such a way, we propose a data mining model which takes into account also the behavior of other similar devices/agents in the region when doing patterns recognition. This extends the individual data mining with the input set of other devices/agents, while meaning that the size of the input set doubles with the data from the sensors of corresponding devices as shown in Table 1.

In the Table 1, the first 5 columns are the data from the devices/agents to be analyzed, namely the timestamp, from which the date of the week ("DW"), the date and the hour of the day ("Hr") are derived. The column "Door_close" shows the event of opening or closing the door, not whether or not the door is opened. That is why two successive records always have a true and a false value for "Door_close". The same data (shown in the main column "Similar device") is available for another device. While the classical data mining tries to predict the outcome as a Boolean value (column "Door_close") only based on the data from the same device/agent (main column "Analyzed Device"), the collaborative data mining take into account all available data, in this case both columns "Analyzed Device" and "Similar device".

Thus, in the context of this paper collaborative data mining is intended as the application of data mining techniques on multiple data sources (autonomous agents) to better understand the behavior of one of them as well as the correlation – if it exists – between them. The rapid progress on computer networks and the pervasive computing – supported by new computing paradigms and technologies such as IoT, CPS, web services (WS), cloud computing, Service Oriented Computing (SOC), etc. – is offering the technical infrastructure and foundation for new forms of collaboration in several context of application [14, 15], and where the proposed model can be easily deployed. In particular, for this research we have decided to use the technology and the infrastructure provided under the scope of EU-FP7 ProSEco[1] project, where intelligent products (intelligent autonomous agents) are providing data during their operation.

[1] https://www.proseco-project.eu.

This data is then used for applying the proposed collaborative data mining process i.e. as input to the data mining process. More specifically, we aim to combine the results generated by data mining processes – applied on isolated agents (i.e. devices) – in a collaborative manner, or better, the usage of the obtained results in order to refine and improve the outcome of the data mining process on a selected agent (see Fig. 1).

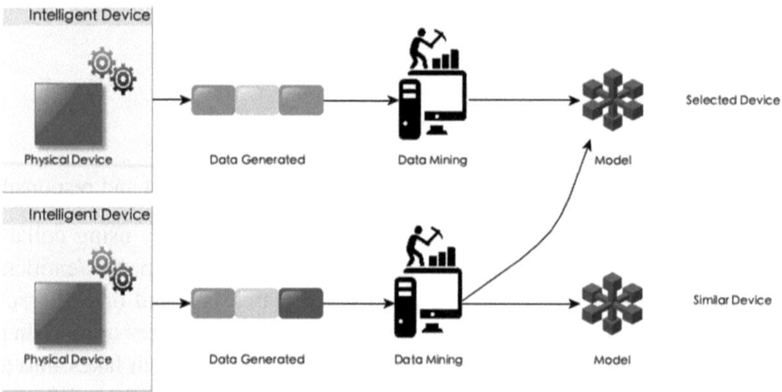

Fig. 1. Proposed collaborative data mining model flowchart

Table 1. Some samples of the data set in the case of collaborative data mining

Analyzed device					Similar device					Outcome
Time-stamp	DW	Date	Hr	Door_close	Time-stamp	DW	Date	Hr	Door_close
15.11.2013 00:28	6	15.11.2013	0	T	15.11.2013 00:49	6	15.11.2013	0	T
15.11.2013 00:28	6	15.11.2013	0	F	15.11.2013 00:49	6	15.11.2013	0	F
15.11.2013 01:11	6	15.11.2013	1	T	15.11.2013 02:15	6	15.11.2013	2	T
15.11.2013 01:11	6	15.11.2013	1	F	15.11.2013 02:15	6	15.11.2013	2	F
15.11.2013 01:40	6	15.11.2013	1	T	15.11.2013 02:45	6	15.11.2013	2	T
15.11.2013 01:41	6	15.11.2013	1	F	15.11.2013 02:45	6	15.11.2013	2	F
15.11.2013 01:44	6	15.11.2013	1	T	15.11.2013 03:18	6	15.11.2013	3	T

3 Methodology

We aim to compare the collaborative data mining with standalone data mining, hence we use the same research methodology as reported in [4]. The training data records are structured like in Table 1.

For collaboration, three devices have been selected randomly, along with the one used in [3] and [4]. The appliances are real ones, deployed by Electrolux to real customer in the United States, for tests. The monitored period is 13th of November 2013 - 25th of December 2013, with 1170 data records.

The objective is to determine the number of door openings per day. This process aims to determine how many times the device will be opened based on the number of openings in the previous days. This would be a good statistical indicator about the usage of the device and could help to manage internal functions (such as "Defrosting" procedure of refrigerators) in an efficient way. As the records are event-based, the data is aggregated over the day. The number of openings is a count of all records for which the value of "Door_close" is T (true).

The experiments have been done for the following benchmarks:

1. oven 1, 13, respectively oven 14 alone;
2. oven 13 using the previous data for oven 14, respectively oven 14 using the previous data for oven 13. The two ovens have been chosen because there is a high correlation between them. The mathematical foundations of the correlation are explained in Sect. 3.1.
3. oven 13 using the previous data for oven 11, respectively oven 1 using the previous data for oven 13. Between oven 1 and oven 13 there is a very low correlation (0.01).

The first set of benchmarks would provide a standard for comparing the results of the benchmark sets 2 and 3.

The methodology refers to the correlations between some ovens. The definition and the computations of the correlations are shown in the next section.

3.1 Correlations Between the Benchmark Appliances

Correlation between some benchmark appliances means correlation between some time series consisting of the usage patterns of the devices over the time [16]. The main challenge here is that the two series do not have the same time samples, although the tick is the same, e.g. one can be sampled at 15.11.2013 11:30:31; 15.11.2013 11:30:31 and the other one 15.11.2013 11:32:45; 15.11.2013 11:42:45 etc. Another challenge is that the two series may be correlated lagged in time. In this case, cross-correlation is the best function to be computed, according to Aarts et al. [17]. Considering two series *x(i)* and *y(i)*, where $i = 0, 1, 2, \ldots N\text{-}1$, Bourke [18] defines the cross correlation *r* at delay *d* as:

$$r(x,y) = \frac{\sum_i[(\mathrm{x(i)} - \mathrm{mx})(\mathrm{y(i-d)} - \mathrm{my})]}{\sqrt{\sum_i(\mathrm{x(i)} - \mathrm{mx})^2}\sqrt{\sum_i(\mathrm{y(i)} - \mathrm{my})^2}} \tag{1}$$

where *mx* and *my* are the means of the corresponding series.

Out of the 143 assets monitored by Electrolux, for which data is collected, only the ovens Kenmore Elite 97102 (counting up to 14 pieces) have the "Door_close" event, which is used in this research. Therefore we cannot talk about other correlations expect between the usage of these. Figure 2 displays graphically the collaborative network of the ovens over a period when most of the ovens were used, namely December 2013.

The nodes represent the ovens, denoted as numbers for a better comprehension. Their size is proportional with the total correlation for that respective oven, computed as:

$$r(i) = \sum_{i} \mathrm{r(i,j)} \quad (2)$$

The oven number "2" misses because that oven starts being used only in April 2014.

The vertices are inverse proportional with the correlation of usage of the respective ovens. The closer the nodes, the more cross-correlated the ovens. The cross-correlation factor is in absolute values, as the negative values represent a negative relationship (yet existent). Ovens "9" and "14" have a very similar behavior, which is why they overlap. On opposite, the farther the nodes (or the longer the vertex), the lower correlation between the usages of the respective ovens. If there is no vertex between two nodes, it means that the correlation between the nodes is almost zero and was not displayed in the network.

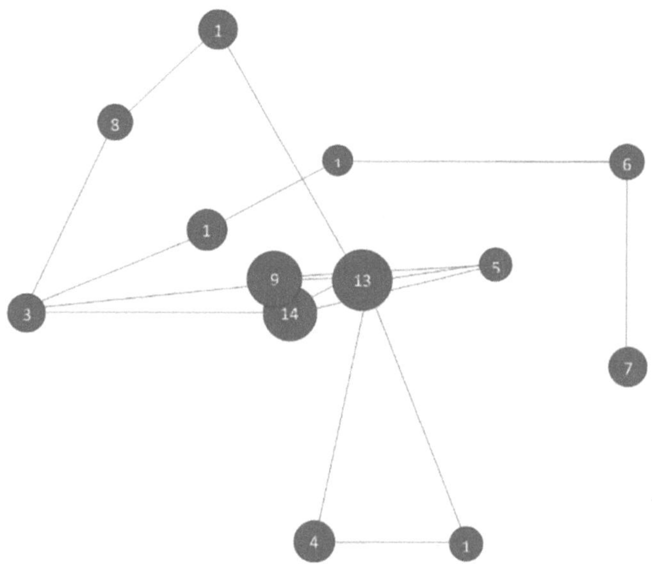

Fig. 2. Collaboration network based on the correlation between the usages patterns of the ovens

Figure 3 shows the correlations between usage patterns of the ovens over the whole period (November 2013 - April 2014) as a bubble chart. The larger the diameter of the bubbles, the higher the correlation. The smaller the bubbles, the lower the correlation. Please not that the positive and negative correlations are represented having the same diameters. The chart is symmetric as the correlation is symmetric. A missing bubble, like for the pairs (2, 4), (2, 5), (2, 6) and so on, means that the correlation is between the usage of the respective ovens is zero. It is the case of the oven 2 because it was used for a short period of time.

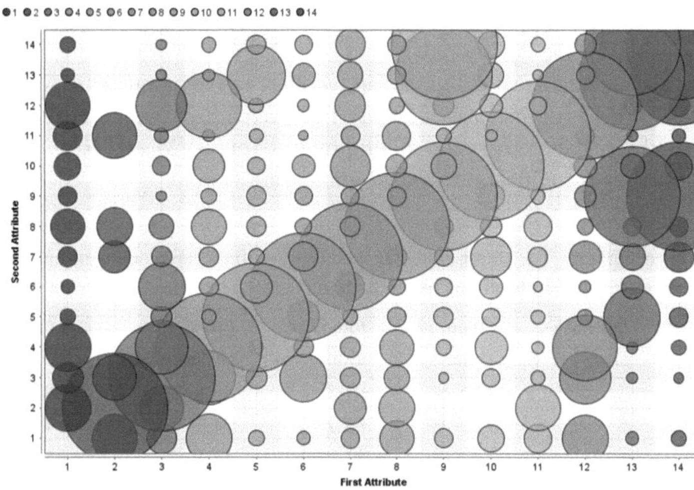

Fig. 3. The correlation between usage patterns over the whole period

The experimental results are summarized in the next section.

4 Experimental Results

Three sets of benchmarks have been experimented, as shown in Sect. 3:

- For three ovens (1, 13 and 14) independently;
- For oven 13, respectively 14, using the data from both 13 and 14, as the usages of the two ovens are correlated;
- For oven 1, respectively oven 13, collaboratively, as the usages of the two are not correlated.

The data mining tool is Rapid Miner because it provides also the libraries with which it can be embedded in any Java software. Therefore it can be used also in real field applications, as this research is meant to be a first step for introducing intelligent features such as predictive maintenance in electronic appliances.

Several algorithms have been used: LPR (local polynomial regression), SVM (support vector machine), NN (neural network) and k-NN (k-nearest neighbour). The results are summarized in Table 2. For avoiding overtraining, 20 % of the data was set aside for cross-validation.

The results are summarized in Table 2 for ovens 13 and 14, respectively in Table 3 for ovens 1 and 13. The first column displays the algorithm used, as the ones reported in [3]. The next two columns present the accuracy for each oven in the case of individual data mining. The last two columns present the accuracies for predicting the number of openings for each oven when applying collaborative data mining.

When the usage patterns of the ovens are correlated (see ovens 13 and 14, summarized in Table 2), the collaborative data mining got the best results (highest accuracies). In one case, the stand-alone and collaborative approaches had the same accuracy for oven 13 (in the case of SVM). For oven 14, in two cases the results were not improved by collaborative data mining (algorithms SVM and NN). However, the average accuracies for collaborative data mining are better.

Table 2. The accuracies for stand-alone, respectively collaborative data mining of ovens 13 and 14 (highly correlated in terms of usage patterns)

Algorithm	Window size	Oven 13 alone	Oven 14 alone	Oven 13 collaborative	Oven 14 collaborative
LPR	3	81.5 %	91.3 %	**80.0 %**	**92.0 %**
SVM	5	**91.3 %**	**95.7 %**	**91.3 %**	**95.7 %**
NN	1	46.2 %	**51.9 %**	**48.1 %**	**51.9 %**
k-NN	3	80.4 %	96.0 %	**92.6 %**	**96.2 %**
Average		**74.85 %**	**83.73 %**	**78 %**	**83.95 %**
Improvement				**4.21 %**	**0.27 %**

The second researched case is of collaborative data mining when there is a very low correlation between two ovens, in this case, ovens 1 and 13, with the correlation factor of 0.01. The experimental conditions are similar with the previous benchmark. In this case, the collaborative accuracies are lower than stand-alone ones with 8.91 % for the oven 1, respectively 1.4 % for oven 13 (see Table 3).

Table 3. The accuracies for stand-alone, respectively collaborative data mining of ovens 1 and 13 (loosely correlated in terms of usage patterns)

Algorithm	Window size	Oven 1 alone	Oven 13 alone	Oven 1 collaborative	Oven 13 collaborative
LPR	3	**48.1 %**	**81.5 %**	32.0 %	70.6 %
SVM	5	81.5 %	**91.3 %**	**91.3 %**	**91.3 %**
NN	1	**18.5 %**	46.2 %	14.8 %	**48.1 %**
k-NN	3	**36.0 %**	80.4 %	29.6 %	**85.2 %**
Average		**46.03 %**	**74.85 %**	**41.93 %**	**78 %**
Improvement				**−8.91 %**	**−1.4 %**

The improvements in accuracy of collaborative data mining has proven reasonable, but including context information, such as outside temperature and number of users could increase the accuracy even more. However, this kind of data is not available for now.

5 Conclusions and Discussions

We have shown that collaborative data mining means the use of data from two different data sources for determining the output of one source (in this case home appliances, but the specific embodiment of the source has no significance). We have proven that if the two sources are correlated, the accuracy of the data mining or machine learning process increases, whereas if the two sources are not correlated, the accuracy decreases. Eventually this could lead to predicting the output of a source using only the data from another, correlated source when the data from the former one is not available.

The main challenge of this work is dealing with information collecting from distributed system which would be recognized as Collaborative network. This information provided by real business cases from Electrolux using intelligent products. We have proven that there are varying similarities between usage patterns of the 143 electric appliances (refrigerators and ovens) in the field, studied in our research. Of course, those similarities influence the impact on the data mining results. This is why the average values displayed in Table 2 are quasi-equal, but the best values are significantly better in the case of collaborative data mining. Of course, those values are obtained when the data mining process takes into account devices with similar usage patterns.

This concept of "collaborative data mining", can be applied in any case when there are more devices with similar behavior which could be ideal tool dealing with huge amount of information in intelligent Products Ecosystem. Therefore, before using it, a correlation analysis must be performed. Such approach fits very well in the context of Industrial Internet (see also [4]), where the number of machines are relatively low, but with similar behavior. This could help to analyze distributed information from intelligent collaborative products.

6 Further Developments and Extensions

It is beyond the scope of this paper to research what is the (mathematical) relationship between the accuracies in the collaborative data mining and the series correlations described in Sect. 5.

Further research needs to be carried out on collaborative data mining with at least three devices, with various correlations. Another topic is how a series alone influences another series, relatively to the correlation factor. And yet, how can be handled the common case when the two series are not aligned temporarily.

As principle, collaborative data mining can be applied in any field, with any data arguments. However, the heuristics are obviously specific for each case, as well as the tuning of the parameters of the machine learning algorithm. Also extending the proposed methodology for analyzing the behavior of HACs could be interesting direction for future researches. Finally, from a more technical point of view further research is needed on identify a common representation for the data coming from the collaborative agents. As a matter of fact, as the number of collaborative agents are increasing more and more it is necessary to find a common way to represent the data in order to allow the data mining process to analyze get the data always in the same way, i.e. with the same syntax and semantic. It is a necessary issue that need to be considered and handled whenever new type of agents are considered and new context of application are studied.

Acknowledgments. This work is partly supported by the ProSEco project of EU's 7th FP, under the grant agreement no. NMP-2013 609143.

References

1. Picard, W.: Resilient and robust human-agent collectives: a network perspective. In: Camarinha-Matos, L.M., et al. (eds.) PRO-VE 2015. IFIP AICT, vol. 463, pp. 79–87. Springer, Heidelberg (2015). doi:10.1007/978-3-319-24141-8_7
2. Sanou, B.: "ITC Facts and Figures 2013", Telecommunication Development Bureau, International Telecommunications Union (ITU), Geneva, February 2013. Accessed 23 May 2015
3. Matei, O., Nagorny, K., Stoebener, K.: Applying data mining in the context of Industrial Internet. Int. J. Adv. Comput. Sci. Appl. (IJACSA) **7**(1) (2016). http://dx.doi.org/10.14569/IJACSA.2016.070184
4. Di Orio, G., Matei, O., Scholze, S., Stokic, D., Barata, J., Cenedese, C.: A platform to support the product servitization. Int. J. Adv. Comput. Sci. Appl. (IJACSA) **7**(2) (2016). http://dx.doi.org/10.14569/IJACSA.2016.070254
5. Matei, O.: Preliminary results of the analysis of field data from ovens. Carpathian J. Electr. Eng. **8**(1) (2014)
6. Appleman, K.H., et al.: Collaborative internet data mining systems. US Patent 5,918,010, 29 June 1999
7. Maimon, O., Rokach, L. (eds.): Data Mining and Knowledge Discovery Handbook, vol. 2. Springer, New York (2005)
8. Moyle, S.: Collaborative data mining. In: Maimon, O., Rokach, L. (eds.) Data Mining and Knowledge Discovery Handbook, pp. 1029–1039. Springer, Heidelberg (2009)
9. Zhan, J.: Privacy-preserving collaborative data mining. IEEE Comput. Intell. Mag. **3**(2), 31–41 (2008)
10. Haythornthwaite, C.: Social networks and Internet connectivity effects. Inf. Community Soc. **8**(2), 125–147 (2005)
11. Heierman III, E.O., Cook, D.J.: Improving home automation by discovering regularly occurring device usage patterns. In: Third IEEE International Conference on Data Mining, ICDM 2003. IEEE (2003)
12. Hajibandeh, N., et al.: Resemblance measurement of electricity market behavior based on a data distribution model. Int. J. Electr. Power Energy Syst. **78**, 547–554 (2016)
13. Camarinha-Matos, L.M., Afsarmanesh, H.: Collaboration forms. In: Camarinha-Matos, L. M., Afsarmanesh, H. (eds.) Collaborative Networks: Reference Modeling, pp. 51–66. Springer, Heidelberg (2008)
14. Camarinha-Matos, L.M., Afsarmanesh, H.: Motivation for a theoretical foundation for collaborative networks. In: Camarinha-Matos, L.M., Afsarmanesh, H. (eds.) Collaborative Networks: Reference Modeling, pp. 5–14. Springer, Heidelberg (2008)

15. Di Orio, G., Barata, D., Rocha, A., Barata, J.: A cloud-based infrastructure to support manufacturing resources composition. In: Camarinha-Matos, L.M., Baldissera, T.A., Di Orio, G., Marques, F. (eds.) DoCEIS 2015. IFIP AICT, vol. 450, pp. 82–89. Springer, Heidelberg (2015)
16. Wei, W.W.S. (ed.): Time Series Analysis. Addison-Wesley, Reading (1994)
17. Aarts, R.M., Irwan, R., Janssen, A.J.E.M.: Efficient tracking of the cross-correlation coefficient. IEEE Trans. Speech Audio Process. **10**(6), 391–402 (2002)
18. Bourke, P.: Cross Correlation, Auto Correlation—2D Pattern Identification (1996)

Advances in Production - Product-Services

A Step Towards Customized Product Realization: Methodology for Sensing, Smart and Sustainable Enterprise

Dante Chavarria-Barrientos[1(✉)], Rafael Batres[1], Roberto Perez[1], Paul K. Wright[2], and Arturo Molina[1]

[1] Tecnologico de Monterrey, Escuela de Ingeniería y Ciencias, Mexico City, Mexico
{dante.chavarria,rafael.batres,roberto.perez.cu, armolina}@itesm.mx

[2] University of California, Berkeley, Berkeley, CA, USA
pwright@me.berkeley.edu

Abstract. New trends such as mass customization have appeared, where production volumes are flexible, customers require One of a Kind production, and product variety is large. To accomplish these demands, there is a necessity of flexible enterprise operations and reconfigurable manufacturing systems. Enterprise models, integration frameworks, collaborative systems and flexible/reconfigurable manufacturing systems allow facing such challenges. This paper presents a methodology aiming to support the design, creation and implementation of sustainable, smart and sensing manufacturing systems. S^3 Enterprise (Sensing, Smart and Sustainable) Reference Model has been developed and used to create such systems. The S^3 Enterprise Reference Model uses a methodology based on action-research concept to pursue understanding and facilitating its implementation in Small and Medium Enterprises. The reference model is instantiated to define a Collaborative Networked Organization that is able to manufacture customized products. Finally, a case study is presented to demonstrate the usage and application of the methodology.

Keywords: Enterprise modelling · Sustainable manufacturing · Smart organization · Sensing enterprise · Collaborative networks · Instantiation methodology

1 Introduction

In mass customization, the manufacturing enterprises have to deliver low volume and customized products to satisfy the customer specific requirements. This is a complex task considering key characteristics of mass customization [1]. There are heterogeneous demand patterns due to dissimilar niches, low cost and high quality expectations, and short product life cycles. As a result, manufacturing systems need to be flexible and adaptive [1]. Conveniently, a list of enablers such as flexible manufacturing, Cyber Physical Systems, interactive computing technology, additive manufacturing can be

H. Afsarmanesh et al. (Eds.): PRO-VE 2016, IFIP AICT 480, pp. 327–339, 2016.
DOI: 10.1007/978-3-319-45390-3_28

used to generate such systems. However, such enablers need to be leveraged to be effective and implementable. One approach is through integration, collaboration and systematization. Integration among all levels of an enterprise support better decision making. Collaboration allows the union of multiple resources to fulfill a common end. Systematic design of manufacturing systems builds up know-how. Therefore, new developments include the learning from the previous designs.

Over the last three decades, the concept of manufacturing architectures has evolved to provide integration and systematization for the analysis and design of manufacturing enterprises. Early examples include the European ESPRIT project, ICAM architecture, ISO Manufacturing Automation Protocol, and GRAI architecture. Although they were an important step in the modeling of manufacturing companies, they were not aimed to implement different views. Then, a new set of architectures implemented the viewpoints concept: ARIS, CIM-OSA [2, 3], MOSES, Zachman's framework. The viewpoints allow focusing on particular aspects and therefore designing complex and large systems, such as enterprises [4].

Examples can be found in the literature regarding implementation of architectures. Monfared et al. [5] apply the CIM-OSA enterprise modelling approach to re-engineer the business process of an automotive industry. They create a reference model to develop new engine projects. Their study does not use the views as a central theme in the architecture. Nogueria et al. [6] proposes a new methodology based on action–research for the implementation of the business, system and technology models of the Zachman framework in Small and Medium Enterprises (SMEs). Because the case study was an IT enterprise, the methodology fall short in understanding the manufacturing implications. In the search of collaboration, Zwegers et al. [7] presented an architectural framework called VERAM. It has the purpose to structure to support collaborative networks. The study identifies the need of a reference model to build particular models. Bernus et al. [8] presented the use of Globemen reference model to create service virtual enterprises. An activity diagram showed the results, but the approach was not tested on a particular enterprise.

This paper proposes a methodology to define manufacturing enterprises. Such definition is achieved through an enterprise model. The concepts that support methodology are explained in Sect. 2. The methodology is presented in Sect. 3. Special considerations must be considered when the methodology is followed to build a Collaborative Networked Organization (CNO) for personalized products; such implications are discussed in Sect. 4. After that, to evaluate the methodology a case study is presented in Sect. 5. Finally, Sect. 6 provides conclusions.

2 S^3 Enterprise Reference Model + Action-Research

The research is based on two concepts mainly. The first concept is the Sustainable, Smart and Sensing Enterprise Reference Model (S^{3}E-RM) because it guides the analysis, design and implementation of an enterprise; and at the same time, it allows the adoption of the Sensing, Smart and Sustainable characteristics. These characteristics mean that the enterprise will be competitive in the digital economy [9]. The second concept is the action-research methodology to pursue understanding in a systematic way (which is a common characteristic in methodologies) and for its ability to implement frameworks in SMEs. The use of the S^3E Reference Model and methodology will enable the design of Sensing, Smart and Sustainable Enterprises through the creation of partial and particular models. Figure 1 illustrates this, where the S^3E-RM is used to create a partial model for Collaborative Networks that produce customized products; and subsequently the partial model is used to create the particular model for an enterprise of promotional articles. Both instantiations where achieved through action-research. Further explanation on how to make the instantiation appears in following sections.

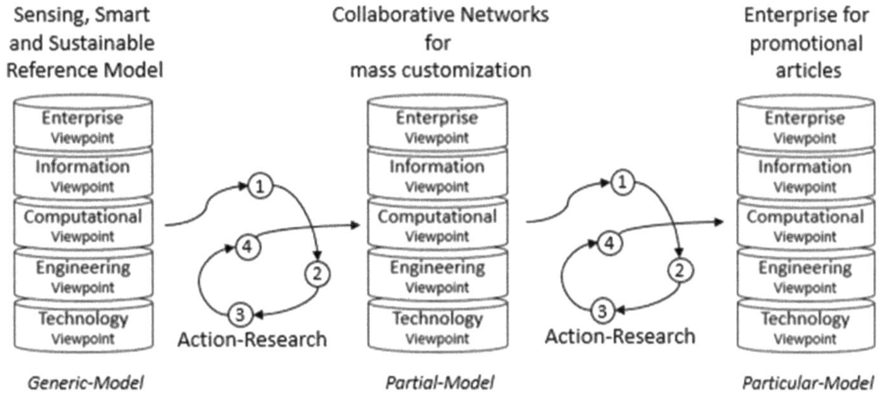

Fig. 1. Instantiation of the S^3 Enterprise (Sensing, Smart and Sustainable) reference model through action-research methodology.

2.1 Sensing, Smart and Sustainable Enterprise – Reference Model

The S^3E-RM is the evolution of the Smart x Sensing Enterprise Reference Model (S^2E-RM) presented in [10]. The S^2E-RM is an enterprise reference model that supports the concepts of smart and sensing. The S^2E-RM has been used to design and create manufacturing collaborative networks [10]. S^3E-RM is an evolution of S^2E-RM in which sustainability is considered. Sustainable manufacturing refers to a manufacturing execution where sustainability is guaranteed on its three pillars i.e. environmental, social and economic. The reference model aims at achieving three main tasks:

- Identify enterprise requirements that support the concepts of Sensing, Smart and Sustainable.
- Guide the analysis, design, planning and implementation of the enterprise system.
- Organize the process of implementation (people, methods and tools) to evolve the Sensing, Smart and Sustainable System towards the desired level of automation.

The S^3E-RM enlist five viewpoints (e.g. enterprise, information, computation, engineering and technology) based on the ISO/IEC 19439 ODP-RM standard [11]. The S^3E-RM has a list of tools and activities to define the each viewpoint (See Fig. 2). Further explanation is provided in [10].

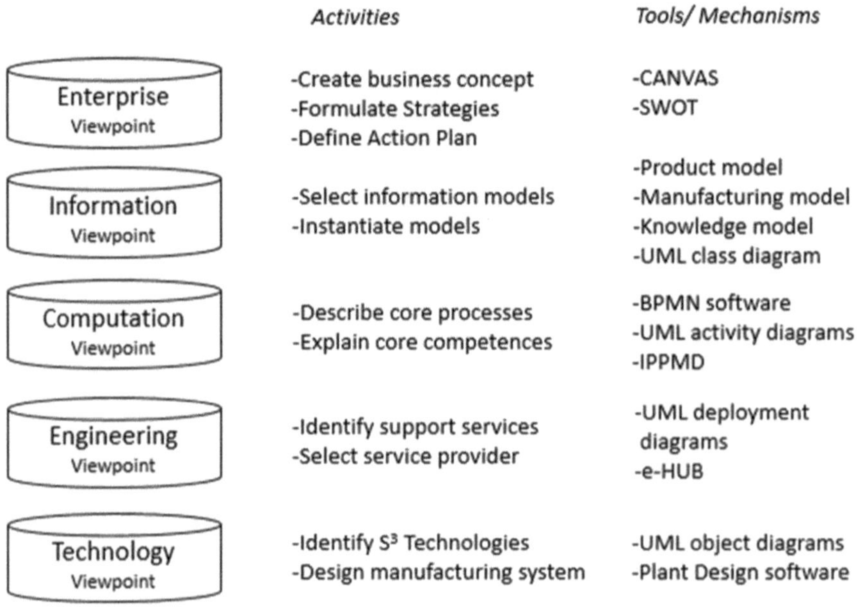

Fig. 2. Activities to be done on each viewpoint and tools that can be used.

2.2 Action-Research

Action-research is a family of methodologies that pursue a change and an understanding. The use of spiral processes or cycles alternating between action and reflection provides a refinement of methods [12]. In action-research the investigators test theories and then adjust them according to feedback [13]. Each cycle consists of four phases:

- Plan.- This phase establishes the action plan and must be originated from a future perspective considering risks.
- Act.- In this phase the action is taken based of the previous plan.
- Observe.- In this phase all the events that are happening need to be documented and a projection of a future is created.
- Reflect.- This phase is the result of the observation and it helps to construct a new plan if needed.

In 2012 the methodology was used by Nogueira et al. [6] to implement the Zachman Framework. They showed that action-research aids with the implementation of frameworks by SMEs.

3 Sensing, Smart and Sustainable Enterprise - Methodology

The proposed methodology in this paper has two structure levels. The external level includes the viewpoints defined in the S^3E-RM, and the internal level has the four phases of action-research.

The external structure is a sequence of action-research cycles, in which each cycle represents a viewpoint of the enterprise model. As seen in Fig. 3, the cycles start with the instantiation of the Enterprise viewpoint, and end with the instantiation of the Technology Viewpoint. The viewpoints can be modeled with UML diagrams [10] or other tools. When the five cycles end, the enterprise model is constructed.

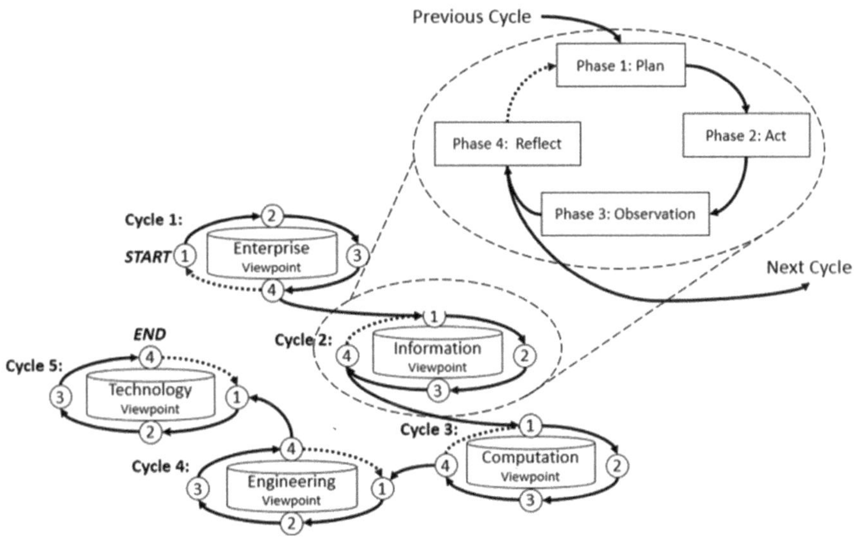

Fig. 3. Structure of the S^3E-Methodology. Five cycles for defining five viewpoints and four phases inside each cycle.

As seen in Fig. 3, the internal structure of each cycle consists of the action-research phases i.e. Plan, Act, Observe and Reflect. For this research, the first phase consists of defining:

- the objectives of the cycle, which include the Sensing, Smart and Sustainability (S^3) concepts,
- the information needed for this cycle,
- the series of steps to accomplish the objectives (activities shown in Fig. 2),
- the performers for the corresponding cycle,
- the tools for accomplishing the objectives (Fig. 2).

The second phase consists of the execution of the activities defined in the first phase. For some cycles, the set of activities include the development of other methodologies.

The third phase is an evaluation of the activities done during the second phase. The evaluation not only contemplates the consistency of information, but also the inclusion of elements for the adoption of the Sensing, Smart and Sustainable concepts.

In the fourth phase, the necessary adjustments are based on the results of the evaluation. Then, a decision is made to a decision is made, stay at phase one of the same cycle or continue to the next cycle.

To guarantee the adoption of the Sensing, Smart and Sustainable concepts, special considerations must be taken into account when instantiating each viewpoint. At the enterprise viewpoint, sensing entails the existence of megatrends implications in the business concept. The smart concept is realized by explaining how the business model canvas elements (building blocks) [14] provide reaction capabilities to cope with changes in the business environment. In addition, sustainability is realized by adding performance indicators that address social, environmental, and economical issues. At the information viewpoint, the sensing concept is realized by defining information models that support the information requirements identified at the enterprise viewpoint. The smart concept is realized by developing information models for representing product models and manufacturing models. Moreover, sustainability is realized by developing information models that support evaluation of environmental impact. At computation viewpoint, the sensing concept refers to processes for acquisition of information, for example, contact between the enterprise and the customer. The smart concept is realized in the structure of the processes; the processes should be defined to adapt to changes. To realize the sensing concept at engineering viewpoint, identification of possible partners is done. The smart concept is realized by recognizing the services needed to apply the process. In addition, social sustainability is realized by ensuring that the collaboration affect all members equally and fairly. Finally, at technology viewpoint the smart, sensing, and sustainable resources are identified.

The methodology can be used to create the partial or particular models. When the purpose is to create partial models, the users are creating structures that define more than one enterprise. The enterprises described share similar characteristics. And when the purpose is to create a particular model, the model describes a specific enterprise. Both applications are shown in the following sections.

4 Partial Model: Collaborative Networks for Mass Customization

As stated before, an instantiation of the S^3E-RM will be needed to fulfill two purposes: to develop a customized product, and to define a Collaborative Networked Organization. Mehrsai et al. [15] explains that isolated enterprises fall short in facing challenges of mass customization. Therefore, companies prefer to collaborate with others in order to achieve global reach and local responsiveness in the context of mass customization. In this paper, we explore the design of collaborative networks to manufacture mass-customized products. The key features of mass customization are identified in [1]: unpredictable demand pattern, heterogeneous niches, low-cost, high-quality, customized goods and services, short product development cycles, and short product life cycles. For Collaborative Networked Organization the main characteristics are explained by Camarinha-Matos et al. [16]: autonomous, distributed, heterogeneous entities, collaboration to achieve compatible goals and generate value; and interactions supported by computer networks. The results when using five cycles for creating the partial model, considering the above-mentioned characteristics, are presented next.

Cycle 1 – Enterprise Viewpoint

For this cycle, the objective is to create the business concept, define the strategies and select the core process and competences. The actors for this activity are identified, mainly marketing experts are needed. The tool for the realization of this viewpoint is the business model canvas (CANVAS).

- CANVAS concepts identified for the partial level:
  - Value proposition- mass customized product
  - Customer segments- all customer that wants a customized product
- Strategies:
  - Competitive strategy- mass customization – low cost
  - Value Chain strategy- Collaboration (Collaborative Networked Organization)
  - Production strategy- Build to Order, Make to Order, Configure to Order
- Core Process: product realization (customization), order fulfilment.
- Core competences: negotiation (Collaborative Networked Organizations), manufacturing of personalized products.

Because collaboration is pursued, an evaluation regarding open business models must be done. The Benson typology [17] can be used for such evaluation. Benson states eight types of business model, where the type I business model have complete internalization of the value system. As the type number increases, the externalization grows. Therefore, the type VIII is an externalized business model where the firm may not have any assets and the value generation depends on negotiation skills. The highest type is better for Collaborative Networked Organizations.

Cycle 2 – Information Viewpoint

The objective for this cycle is to define the Product Model, Manufacturing Model and Knowledge Model. The information needed is produced during the design of a customized product. The performers for this cycle are design and manufacturing engineers. The designing process can be supported with CAX (i.e. CAD, CAM, CAE) and PLM tools.

Two information models are selected. The product model proposed in [10] has function, solution and physical model. Usually the costs, dimensions and materials are described at the physical model. For allowing customization, those characteristics are included also in the solution model. Therefore, the function, and solution models act as restrictions to the customization at the physical model. The manufacturing model selected [10] has process, resources and strategies of the facilities, allowing a rapid configuration of process and resources for new and customized products. For the evaluation of this cycle, a prototype created from the physical model is presented. In addition, CAM software, can be useful to visualize the manufacturing process and evaluate the information models.

Cycle 3 – Computation Viewpoint

This viewpoint is for defining the core business processes. The performers for this phase are the industrial engineers and people that understand the nature of each process (e.g. marketing experts for obtaining customer commitment process). The modelling of the business process is done with ARIS modelling language because it incorporates different views (e.g. Organizational, Data, Control, Functional).

When product life cycles are short, product realization must be fast. This can be designed with the Integrated Product, Process, and Manufacturing systems Development reference framework [18]. The order fulfillment process must be done with the union of competences of enterprises, so negotiation activities must be considered to enhance co-design (with customer), co-engineering, and collaborative manufacturing.

Cycle 4 – Engineering Viewpoint

The objective of this viewpoint is to define where the Business Processes are going to be implemented. The list of possible partners with their competences and resources is the information needed. The performers are people with expertise in the specific e-services [10].

Two e-services are identified for the partial model. E-brokerage is needed to provide negotiation skills, and e-supply is used to add reaction capacity to changes in demand. The e-applications must include customer and supplier relationship management systems. Finally, CAD technologies must be included to provide personalization.

Because this viewpoint considers the distribution of the services, it must be evaluated as a network. The network characteristics proposed by Frankenberg et al. [19] can be used (See Fig. 4). For the partial model, customer centricity is high due to the mass customization strategy, so the configuration for high customer centricity is pursued.

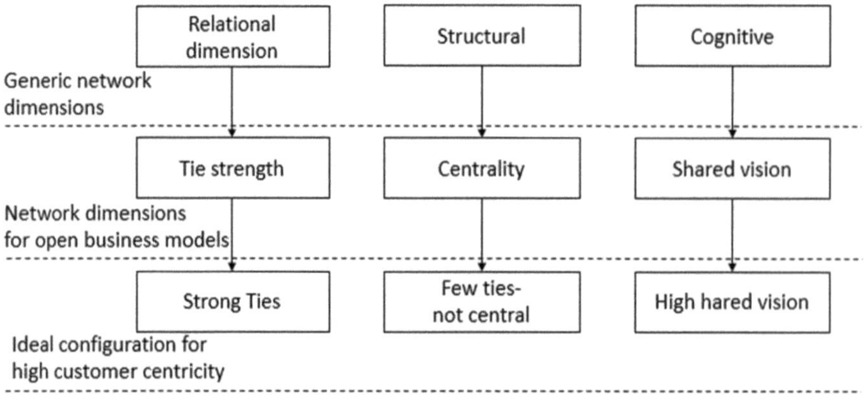

Fig. 4. Ideal network configuration for customer centric open business models.

Cycle 5 – Technology Viewpoint

Considering all the information described above, the manufacturing system is designed. Using the manufacturing model a network must provide the different activities form production to sales. To create the manufacturing network, first an identification of resources is needed. Technologies that support sensing are the ones that allow communication (collaboration) PLC, WSN, SaaS, CRM, SRM. The smart resources provide knowledge based execution of activities CNC, PLC, ERP. The efficient use of previous mentioned resources push sustainability.

5 Particular Model: Promotional Articles

The case study is an enterprise of promotional articles for Tecnologico de Monterrey. The mission of the enterprise is connect the final users with the product; this connection is possible by the belonging feeling with the Tecnologico de Monterrey symbols. Using the methodology a manufacturing system for promotional articles was developed. Two undergraduate students (Jessica Velázquez and Rebeca Cisneros) developed an example of promotional article in 2015. It is an iPhone cover case engraved with the Tec Logo and the user's nickname. They chose the iPhone 5 cover because it is the most used at Tecnologico de Monterrey. The outcomes are presented.

Cycle 1 – Enterprise Viewpoint

CANVAS:

- Value Proposition.- Mass customized product
- Customer Relationship.- Emotional and useful products
- Customer Channels.- on-line sales, Tec-Stores
- Customer Segments.- Alumni and workers at Tecnologico de Monterrey.
- Key Activities.- designing, manufacturing, marketing
- Key Resources.- Tec-stores, Milling Machines, CAD applications
- Key Partners.- Tecnologico de Monterrey (Tec stores), engraving and 3D printer Enterprises.

Strategies:

- Competitive strategy.- Mass customization & Low cost
- Value Chain Strategy.- Vertical Collaboration (Collaborative Network Organization)
- Production Strategy.- Built To Order

Core process: Order Fulfillment

Core competences: Negotiation and Manufacturing capabilities (Engraving, 3D-printing)

Cycle 2 – Information Viewpoint

Product Model: Fig. 5 shows the product presentation using CAD Software. It is an acrylic cover case, with logo engraved in aluminum.

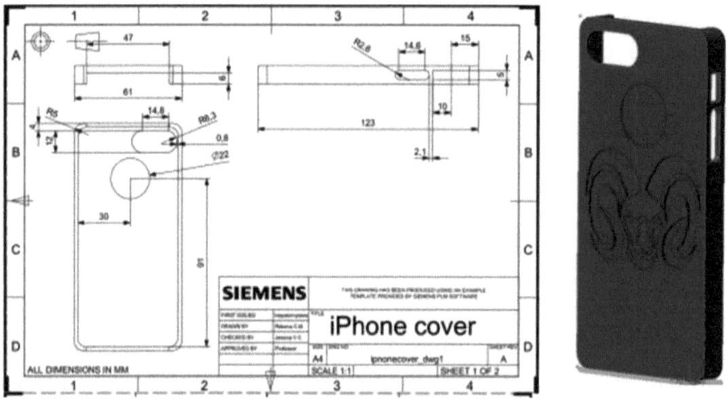

Fig. 5. Cover case presented in CAD tools.

Manufacturing Model:

- Process: Engraving, 3D-printing
- Resources: Reconfigurable Micro-Machine, 3D-printer
- Materials: Aluminum, plastics

Cycle 3 – Computation Viewpoint

The diagram for the core process was modeled with the ARIS modelling language. A detailed level of representation using, resources, organization and process representation was needed to correctly understand and evaluate the order fulfillment process. A representation of the core process is appreciated in Fig. 6. The process starts when the final users fill a template, which includes the information about the order. This process is done in Tec-Stores. Once the personalized order has been generated they pay the order. The order is sent to two companies, the company that manufactures plastics (Enterprise A) and to the one that engraves them (Enterprise B). While the manufacture is completed, enterprise B designs the personalization using CAD. After, when they receive the cover-cases they engrave them with the micro-machine [18] according to the design. Finally, the company ships the order to the Tec-stores where the final user can take up his personalized cover-case.

Cycle 4 – Engineering Viewpoint

In the engineering viewpoint, first the network was designed and then evaluated using the Frankenberg configurations. As seen in Fig. 6, the network has few and strong ties, and the enterprise share their vision that is to deliver the personalized product. The e-services to maintain the network configuration is e-brokerage. This service was offered with negotiation platforms (SRM and CRM). The e-Applications used for the core process are the following: PLM-CAD for design of the customization and ERPs for the planning. The interactions are done with and trough the e-HUB.

Cycle 5 – Technology Viewpoint

Finally, in the technology viewpoint manufacturing system is designed. As seen in Fig. 5, the collaborative network considers two micro-machines [18] and a 3D-printer. The smart resources are: CNCs for controlling the machines, the Customer Relationship

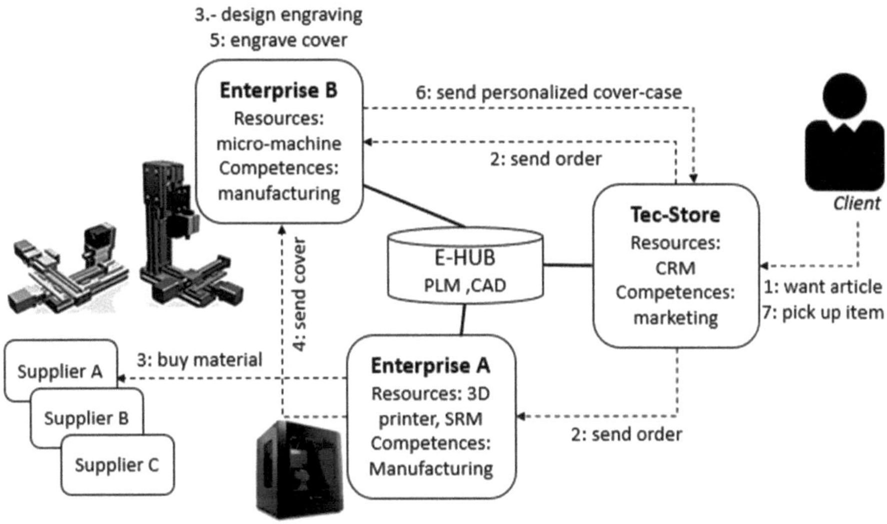

Fig. 6. Collaborative Networked Organization for customized promotional articles, and order fulfillment process.

Management system and the Supplier Relationship Management System and the relationship management systems. The sensing resources are WSN and Real-time systems, the interactions are supported with an e-HUB.

6 Discussion and Conclusion

A reference model to design and create sustainable, smart and sensing enterprises has been instantiated in order to define a partial model for a specific type of firm that could produce mass-customized products using a Collaborative Networked Organization as its integrated manufacturing system. In addition, a case study to create an instantiation of such partial model has been developed to demonstrate its usage in a real product and collaborative manufacturing system.

A methodology based on action-research has been used to support in a systematic manner the instantiation process. The methodology was easily adaptable to a specific case, and as a result, the five viewpoints were instantiated to satisfy the requirements of mass-customized products and use of a CNO for production. The action-research phases allowed the evaluation and learnings while applying the methodology.

When the methodology was used for partial modeling, only some specific outputs can be stated, especially in the enterprise viewpoint. However the definition of reference tools (methods) were selected (Benson typology and Frankenberg configurations for evaluation, and Canvas, IPPMD, ARIS for activities realization) in order to guide a designer to a more practical and faster instantiation.

Therefore the methodology for particular instantiation is easy of use, pragmatic and straightforward because constrains are already defined, and tools has been selected.

A Collaborative Network for Manufacturing was configured with the right processes and competencies to ensure quality, speed and delivery of the mass-customized product. The use of multiple core competences allowed the flexibility needed to achieve a Build To Order production system based on a collaborative network.

It is important to point out that the standardization in each viewpoint is different. In the case of the enterprise and computation viewpoint, due to the fact that models are available (e.g. Canvas, IPPMD, ARIS Core Process Models), the instantiation is more straightforward and structured. In the information viewpoint the existence of pre-defined information models (Product & Manufacturing) permits its correct instantiation. The Engineering viewpoint with an e-HUB of services, applications and technologies allows the configuration of an information system platform with will support the CNO execution. However, the networks implications must be further studied to have standards models and methods that aid CNO configurations in an automatic way. Moreover, sustainability was issued during the product development process, but it was not clear how to include it in all the core processes.

References

1. Tseng, M.M., Hu, S.J.: Mass Customization, Cirp Encyclopedia of Production Engineering, pp. 836–843. Springer, Heidelberg (2014)
2. Jorysz, H.R., Verndat, F.B.: CIM-OSA Part 1: total enterprise modelling and function view. Int. J. Comput. Integr. Manuf. **3**(3–4), 144–156 (1990)
3. Berio, G., Vernadat, F.: Enterprise modelling with CIMOSA: functional and organizational aspects. Prod. Plan. Control **12**(2), 128–136 (2001)
4. Hanneghan, M., Merabti, M., Colquhoun, G.: A viewpoint analysis reference model for Concurrent Engineering. Comput. Ind. **41**(1), 35–49 (2000). ISSN 0166-3615, http://dx.doi.org/10.1016/S0166-3615(99)00038-X
5. Monfared, R.P., West, A.A., Harrison, R., Weston, R.H.: An implementation of the business process modelling approach in the automotive industry. Proc. Inst. Mech. Eng. Part B: J. Eng. Manuf. **216**(11), 1413–1427 (2002)
6. Nogueira, J.M., Romero, D., Espadas, J., Molina, A.: Leveraging the Zachman framework implementation using action–research methodology–a case study: aligning the enterprise architecture and the business goals. Enterp. Inf. Syst. **7**(1), 100–132 (2013)
7. Zwegers, A., Tolle, M., Vesterager, J.: VERAM: virtual enterprise reference architecture and methodology. In: VTT Symposium, vol. 224, pp. 17–38. VTT (2003)
8. Bernus, P., Noran, O., Riedlinger, J.: Using the globemen reference model for virtual enterprise design in after sales service. In: VTT Symposium, vol. 224, pp. 71–90. VTT (2003)
9. Weichhart, G., Molina, A., Chen, D., Whitman, L.E., Vernadat, F.: Challenges and current developments for sensing, smart and sustainable enterprise systems. Comput. Ind. **79**, 34–46 (2015). ISSN 0166-3615, http://dx.doi.org/10.1016/j.compind.2015.07.002
10. Chavarría-Barrientos, D., Molina Espinosa, J.M., Batres, R., Ramírez-Cadena, M., Molina, A.: Reference model for smart x sensing manufacturing collaborative networks - formalization using unified modeling language. In: Camarinha-Matos, L.M., et al. (eds.) PRO-VE 2015. IFIP AICT, vol. 463, pp. 243–254. Springer, Heidelberg (2015). doi: 10.1007/978-3-319-24141-8_22
11. ISO ISO/IEC 10743-3. Information Technology – Open Distributed Processing – Reference Model: Architecture, International Standards Organization, Geneva, Switzerland (2009)

12. Baskerville, R.L., Wood-Harper, A.T.: A critical perspective on action research as a method for information systems research. J. Inf. Technol. **11**(3), 235–246 (1996)
13. Avison, D., Baskerville, R., Myers, M.: Controlling action research projects. Inf. Technol. People **14**(1), 28–45 (2001)
14. Osterwalder, A., Pigneur, Y., Tucci, C.L.: Clarifying business models: origins, present, and future of the concept. Commun. Assoc. Inf. Syst. **16**, 1–25 (2005)
15. Mehrsai, A., Karimi, H.R., Thoben, K.D.: Integration of supply networks for customization with modularity in cloud and make-to-upgrade strategy. Syst. Sci. Control Eng.: Open Access J. **1**(1), 28–42 (2013)
16. Camarinha-Matos, L.M., Afsarmanesh, H., Galeano, N., Molina, A.: Collaborative networked organizations–concepts and practice in manufacturing enterprises. Comput. Ind. Eng. **57**(1), 46–60 (2009)
17. Benson-Rea, M., Brodie, R.J., Sima, H.: The plurality of co-existing business models: investigating the complexity of value drivers. Ind. Mark. Manag. **42**(5), 717–729 (2013)
18. Pérez, R., Molina, A., Ramírez-Cadena, M.: Development of an integrated approach to the design of reconfigurable micro/mesoscale CNC machine tools. J. Manuf. Sci. Eng. **136**(3), 031003.3 (2014)
19. Frankenberger, K., Weiblen, T., Gassmann, O.: Network configuration, customer centricity, and performance of open business models: a solution provider perspective. Ind. Mark. Manag. **42**(5), 671–682.2 (2013)

Collaboration Driven Requirements for a Product-Service Engineering Platform

Tapani Ryynänen(✉), Iris Karvonen, Heidi Korhonen, and Kim Jansson

VTT Technical Research Centre of Finland Ltd., PL1000, 02004 Espoo, Finland
{Tapani.Ryynanen,Iris.Karvonen,Heidi.korhonen,
Kim.Jansson}@vtt.fi

Abstract. Modern manufacturing and business based on product service systems require software platforms capable of supporting offerings over their lifecycle thus securing long term customer value. Also a function to get and manage feedback from end users, customers and manufacturing is essential for design to build in functionalities and features that best enable efficient use and maintenance. The aim is to integrate the Product Life-Cycle Management (PLM) and Service Life-Cycle Management (SLM) concepts resulting in a coherent and collaborative Product-Service design and manufacturing engineering platform. The concept requirements were collected from four real world use cases and refined and combined to create final set of requirements. In this paper we present the facilitated requirement collection process and the final requirements in relation to engineering collaboration and product-service system characteristics.

Keywords: Product-service engineering · Requirements engineering · Platform for collaboration · Manufacturing intelligence · Use cases

1 Introduction and Objectives

Business based on Product-Services (P-S) is a reality today and such business continues to grow, both in the business-to-business sector as well as in the business-to-consumer sector. Car sharing is an example of this type of business that today is available in many cities. The same trend also takes place in the manufacturing sector, which is a phenomenon referred to as servitization. The EU H2020 Manutelligence project [1] aims at supporting this trend, allowing enterprises to develop sustainable innovative P-S efficiently addressing customer needs.

Some of these services can be provided only after punctual and accurate analysis of customers' product usage in order to acquire useful information for new product improvements or services provision. Often the misalignment between the product and service development processes and incapability for concurrent engineering between both processes arise due to the lack of information exchange among the product and service life cycle phases. Therefore more attention must be paid on P-S evolution along the entire value chain. The aim is to integrate the Product Life-Cycle Management

H. Afsarmanesh et al. (Eds.): PRO-VE 2016, IFIP AICT 480, pp. 340–349, 2016.
DOI: 10.1007/978-3-319-45390-3_29

(PLM) and Service Life-Cycle Management (SLM) concepts resulting in a coherent and collaborative P-S design and manufacturing engineering concept.

The collaboration platform in Manutelligence will build on an existing commercial PLM software solution enhanced with additional features for P-S engineering, Internet of Things (IoT) support and life-cycle assessment. The platform will enable designers and engineers to access data from both the traditional enterprise IT systems and IoT enabled systems. The objective is to manage manufacturing intelligence; all data, information and knowledge related to the P-S and its lifecycle.

An extensive requirements engineering and elicitation process has been undertaken in the Manutelligence project. The process and its justification as well as detailed data have been presented in the project deliverables [2, 3] and earlier articles [4, 5] and will not be studied in detail in this paper.

The user-centric perspective is important, both in terms of greater attention to the end customer requirements (use and goal oriented approaches) and an easier involvement of customers in the P-S co-design. A lack of user-centric perspective may easily lead to innovation resistance as the designed P-S does not fit customer needs [6]. Four real world pilot use cases form the basis for collection, structuring and analyzing user requirements for the P-S engineering platform. The cases that come from different industrial fields are of different sizes from multinational manufacturing companies to SMEs, the knowledge standards and the preparedness for adopting innovative approaches are on different levels. The pilots [2] cover some of the main European manufacturing sectors, e.g. automotive, marine, construction and additive manufacturing.

The paper will elaborate on and answer the following research question: What are the collaboration driven requirements for a product-service engineering platform? This is answered based on the data from the Manutelligence project.

The next Sect. 2 recaps on some previous research in the area of Collaborative Networked Organisations, P-S engineering, platform approaches for P-S, and Co-development. Section 3 presents the used requirements engineering methodology. The identified collaboration platform requirements are explained in Sect. 4. Conclusions and ways forward form the final Sect. 5.

2 Collaboration in Product Service Lifecycle

Collaborative engineering of P-S covering all life-cycle phases is an indeed demanding process. To come up with efficient solution we need a multi-disciplinary approach. State-of-the-art research progress and solutions must be capitalized from several fields of activity, e.g. Collaborative Networked Organisations (CNO), P-S engineering and P-S Life-cycle assessment, Internet of Things (IoT), Collaborative Platforms and Co-development. Manutelligence will improve the product and service development by connecting them together through cross-disciplinary feedback loops by means of modular collaborative secure ICT manufacturing intelligence platform. It will be possible to use the platform for the design of a product from the first life-cycle stage onward so that it acts as an enabler for multiple services on top, and for designing and developing new innovative services based on the existing products, for developing new products and tailored services based on product usage information and customer's wishes, and for collecting usage and operation data of the developed P-S. Thus the requirements identified in this paper are not the requirements of the P-S systems [7, 8] but the requirements for the platform used for their design and management. The paper presents the new case based user requirements to the platform. "The idea was not to collect all the potential functions that an engineering platform could cover, but to identify new needs with relation to their current tools and practices." [4]

2.1 Collaborative Networked Organisations

Much knowledge and understanding of CNO has been acquired through European Union supported research during the last decades. There have been a multitude of research initiatives in Europe in the field of CNOs [9] and also in the context of global co-operation [10]. The research objects span from traditional supply chains, collaborative networks and business eco-systems to virtual organizations.

In CNO research, two main concepts for inter-enterprise collaboration are often referred to. According to the objective and duration of the collaboration the two concepts are [11]:

- Network/Breeding environment which is a more stable, though not static, group of organisations which have developed a preparedness to co-operate.
- Virtual organisation (VO)/Virtual enterprise which is a temporary consortium of partners from different organisations established to fulfil a value-adding task, for example a product or service to a customer.

Accordingly, a VO is usually created within a network composed of organisations committed to collaborate. To achieve efficient collaboration, some degree of preparedness is needed. This preparation takes place within the Breeding Environment. The concept of the Breeding environment is used to characterise the network behind a VO. The Virtual organisation's Breeding Environment (VBE) represents a long-term "strategic" alliance, cluster, association, or pool of organisations that provides the needed conditions for collaboration [9].

The CNO concept has also been used for special purposes and application niches, for example; offering opportunities to provide aging care and elderly population assistance [12] and to promote the sharing and recycling of resources such as: information, materials, water, energy and/or infrastructure with the intention of achieving sustainable development in a collaborative way [13] as well as to effectively support the delivery of highly customized and service-enhanced products along their life-cycles [14].

2.2 Product-Service Engineering

The business approaches of service delivery as an integrated part of product is a vast research topic. Manufacturers are moving more towards the business approach of P-S in order to achieve new customers and increased sales. P-Ss have many advantages such as achieving closer customer connection and generating increased profit from manufactured products. The importance of services is also recognized in the marketing field. According to Vargo and Lusch [15] there is an emerging trend in the marketing and business thinking of firms where firms are moving from traditional goods-dominant logic (G-D) to service-dominant logic (S-D). In the G-D logic, customers are seen as targets for which value is created through transactions of products and services. In the S-D logic, customers are active participants in networks of value creation where value accrues to each actor as they integrate resources in their own use contexts. According to a study [16] based on broad empirical interview data, four types of open innovation with customers are identified to categorise product and service providers through their main business and innovation logics and relating customer involvement of companies. The types are customer-oriented providers, customer-solution integrators, developer partners, and facilitators of co-innovation.

According to [17] the following grouping of product/service systems is frequently used:

- Product-oriented Services: The product is owned by the user/consumer.
- Use-oriented Services: The product is owned by the service provider, who sells functions; for example, sharing, pooling and leasing.
- Result-oriented Services: The supplier provides incentives for the customer to consume services by using results orientated payment systems.

2.3 Platform Approaches for Product-Services

Globalization of production and growing level of outsourcing has been supported by information technology development. P-S over its lifecycle has been affected quite unevenly by this. The Beginning of Life (BOF) phase functions like R&D as well as End of Life (EOL) services like maintenance have been impacted less than more mechanistic production, especially in the goods industry. "The smiling curve" [18–20] is a term commonly used to represent this change of balance of value in favor of services over goods. Currently IoT and cloud based digital platforms are some of the most topical paths of progress, pushing servitization in industry.

Digital platforms are "information technology systems upon which different actors – that is, users, service providers and other stakeholders across organizational boundaries – can carry out value-adding activities in a multi-sided market environment governed by agreed boundary resources." [21].

Industry platforms are products, services or technologies that are similar to the former but provide the foundation upon which outside firms (organized as a "business ecosystem") can develop their own complementary products, technologies, or services [22].

2.4 Co-development

As brought up by von Hippel [23] in addition to manufacturers, development work and innovation is often carried out by suppliers and especially users. For this reason, companies have lately involved customers in their development efforts and instead of conventional market research many companies utilize the lead user method in their development efforts. Customers are often involved as informants, ideators and developers; but their involvement also helps (1) to shape the overall context where the value of P-S is created, (2) to foster network effects that guide the diffusion of P-S innovation, (3) to cope with contingency in P-S development and adoption, and (4) to engage customers in business that is meaningful for them [24]. However, involvement of customers in P-S development is costly both for providers and customers and it also leads to some extent of loss of power from the P-S provider to the customers. That is why many companies involve their customers in P-S co-development through innovation toolkits that reduce the costs of customer involvement and simultaneously limit the design scope. The design scope of innovation toolkits is also often limited to functionality offered by a single provider company alone. Co-development together with customers, suppliers and other stakeholders is particularly important when developing P-S for ecosystems contexts as the customer needs in an ecosystem depend on the actions of the other ecosystem members [25]. A collaborative platform like Manutelligence could provide many of the benefits of innovation toolkits with a wider design scope.

3 Methodology

The identification of collaboration needs and requirements for the intelligent platform is based on four industrial pilots. The process started with the creation of a "Pilot Story" for each pilot. The pilot story is a free text description of a fictive, future situation, when all the needed functional requirements are implemented and fully used, written in co-operation with the end users.

Based on the pilot stories more structured business scenarios and use case descriptions were created. A use case is an interaction with systems. The use cases describe the series of steps that take place during the interaction and include different ways that this interaction could play out. The scenarios and use cases were used as a starting point for requirement engineering.

The process to analyse the collaboration related requirements had two phases. First phase was for the requirements engineering (RE), resulting into aggregated requirements, and the second for identifying the collaboration driven requirements from the list of aggregated requirements. The chosen RE iterative model is based on the classical spiral methodology in which each iteration circle goes through the main four phases that compose the requirements process: (1) Elicitation, (2) Structuration, (3) Analysis and Refinements and (4) Validation, as illustrated in Fig. 1 [26]. In each phase of the RE process the P-S dimension is taken into account in order to ensure the integration of the services from the very beginning of the development.

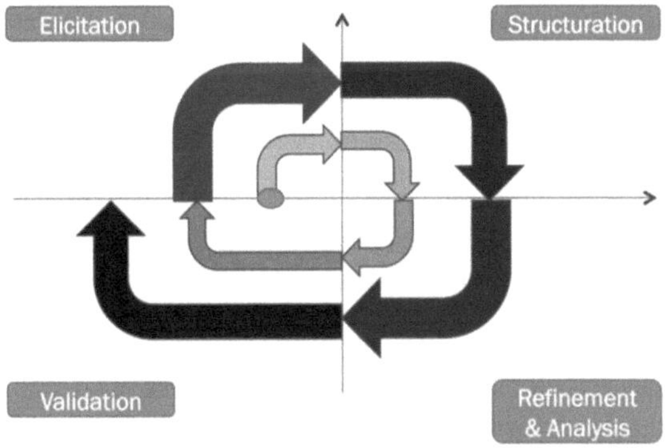

Fig. 1. Used requirements engineering process methodology. (Source: [26], p. 18)

All the cycles are the same except the first one because it has the role to initialize the process. Then the other cycles represent the continuous improvement of the requirements. This paper considers only the initialization phase because the further iteration cycles will be completed later on in the project. The four RE tasks of Manutelligence are:

- Elicitation: the elicitation is concerned with the identification and analysis of the real-world requirements. Heterogeneous opportunities coming from different stakeholders were identified. A list of unstructured requirements was created.
- Structuration: the main objective of the structuration was to unify and integrate the information collected in the previous step from disparate sources and organize them into a common structure that can be used for analysis.
- Refinement and Analysis: the target is to refine and verify the structured requirements. It consists of the assessment of the completeness, coherence and feasibility of the stakeholders' requirements. The refined technical requirements are subject to a prioritization process.
- Requirements validation: the validation purpose is to show the actual requirements to the use case stakeholders in order to understand if the actual definition fits their needs.

After these steps, the aggregated and validated requirements were retrieved. In the second phase the identification of the collaboration driven requirements was done by the authors. This took place in a group discussion and was based on two criteria a requirement had to fulfill: requirement had to be about collaboration between actors not just between an actor and the platform, and requirement was not to be focused on a single technical functionality but a systemic feature.

4 Platform Requirements Related to Engineering Collaboration

After the requirements engineering process 21 aggregated requirements were identified and listed. [27]. For the purpose of this paper the aggregated requirements were further analysed by the authors to select those mostly related to the engineering collaboration. The selected four aggregated requirements are presented below and unfolded including the most relevant topics originating from the unstructured requirements. The selection does not mean that there is no collaboration need in the remaining requirements.

4.1 The Collaboration Network and Community of Designers Shall Be Able to Support and Contribute the Design on the Platform

Design and engineering can be considered a multi-x activity: it requires the knowledge of multiple technologies (like mechatronics, electricity, software, services…), multiple partners are needed, it is performed multi-site. Products are often very complex and there is a pressure to shorten the design time. Efficient collaboration in the design process is needed to enable concurrency. The needs of collaboration in the design/engineering extend from being able to view the up-to-date design, through giving comments from another viewpoint to supporting the editing of the CAD design or product model. In some cases (like FabLab) an open community of designers may exist, which may guide the designer in product modelling. In distributed networks and organizations this requires efficient communication between partners and access to the same data. To make this collaboration effective the platform should provide access to the registered users to both support and contribute to the design.

4.2 The Customer Shall Be Able to View the Visual Product Model (Including Virtual Walk and Driving) and Give Feedback on It Using the Platform

When developing complex products and related services, it is important to get customer feedback to the design continuously along the design process. This requires that the P-S platform offers easy-to-use and illustrative visualisation of the design to the customer(s). Currently customers typically use only the traditional 2D drawings and they need to visualize the final product in their mind. The virtual reality 3D models are becoming more and more common in many industries but they are usually separate software packages. This requires discrete conversions and thus up-to-date drawings are not constantly available. A platform with integrated 2D/3D conversions and rendering provides a tool to accelerate customer collaboration over the design phase. To be useful the platform also has to provide user-friendly and efficient customer feedback reviewing tools. For example, the platform should allow the customer to give the comments and change requests directly to the visual product model. There are different types of P-S customers, like end users (not owing the product), product owners and service providers. These different roles may require and offer different viewpoints to the design which needs to be taken into account when developing the feedback mechanisms. Additionally, it is important to define the processes and responsibilities for how the customer feedback is handled in the design team.

4.3 The Production Personnel Shall Be Able to Use the Product Model on the Platform to Support and Monitor Production, Installation and to Give Feedback for the Design

Production personnel have both task specific knowhow and first row view to design implementation challenges. To enhance the exploitation of this immaterial capital the platform has to provide functionalities that support communication with design. There are multiple opportunities how the platform could support the production and the communication to design, using the visual product model. The production personnel may give comments to design related to the manufacturability, they may use the model to support the installation or to monitor the status of manufacturing, installation or inspection activities. To be efficient production personnel needs access via the platform to the supplier product data base (catalogues), production cost tracking and data linked to the model elements.

4.4 The Platform Should Support Sharing and Communication, also Remotely, Online and Off-Line

As a whole, the P-S lifecycle requires collaboration between different parties. In some cases open communities are built around the manufacturing activities. The platform needs to support the different levels of communication and sharing of data and information. Working life is moving towards networked organizations and place independent work. Remote work both online and off-line should be possible. Specifically off-line is critical since 24/7 online access to the system can often not be guaranteed nor be feasible also from the data transfer or security point of view.

5 Conclusion and Ways Forward

Though ICT platforms for design and manufacturing have recently evolved substantially, there are only few solutions that integrate all tools and phases over both product and service lifecycles. In Manutelligence many requirements based on use cases have originated from the challenges of accessing and sharing information across lifecycle phases. Especially design and design related tasks have been distributed globally. This trend has been enabled and pushed by the ICT. However the ability to transmit data from one continent to another as easily as within one office has not solved all challenges but actually created new ones. This new operational environment requires new ways of doing and sharing the work not just data.

Based on the findings presented in this paper the requirements are linked to several major elements of business; customer, design, manufacturing and ways of working. Thus it can be deduced that a holistic perspective is needed to secure maximum benefits from the new integrated platforms. If focus is on optimising individual tools and methods the efficiency of data and knowledge management processes required over lifecycle by an integrated P-S system is not attainable.

Our conclusion is that the ecosystem collaboration is essential in P-S lifecycle and it could be enhanced with a P-S platform which allows sharing, visualising and commenting manufacturing intelligence, including all information, models and data related to the P-S and its realization.

Acknowledgements. This work has been partly funded by the European Union's Horizon 2020 research and innovation programme under grant agreement no. 636951 (Manutelligence).

References

1. Manutelligence. Product Service Design and Manufacturing Intelligence Engineering Platform. EU H2020 project; Grant agreement no: 636951. http://www.manutelligence.eu/
2. Manutelligence Deliverable: D1.1 Elicitation of engineering and business requirements, H2020 project no 636951 (2015). http://www.manutelligence.eu/
3. Manutelligence Deliverable: D1.4 Structuration and organization of requirements, H2020 project no 636951 (2015). http://www.manutelligence.eu/
4. Karvonen, I., Ryynänen, T., Jansson, K., Korhonen, H.: Organizing end user requirements for product-service engineering platform. In: 14th International Design Conference, DESIGN 2016, 16–19 May, Cavtat, Dubrovnik, Croatia (2016)
5. Jansson, K., Karvonen, I., Ryynänen, T., Korhonen, H., Corti, D., Cerri, D., Cocco, M.: Processing requirements for a product-service engineering platform – a multiple use case approach. In: To Be Published in Proceedings of 2016 International Conference on Engineering, Technology and Innovation/IEEE International Technology Management Conference (ICE/ITMC), 13–15 June, Trondheim, Norway (2016)
6. Korhonen, H.M.E., Kaarela, I.: Corporate customers' resistance to industrial service innovations. Int. J. Innov. Manag. **15**(3), 479–503 (2011). http://www.worldscientific.com/doi/abs/10.1142/S136391961100343X
7. Qu, M., Yu, S., Chen, D., Chu, J., Tian, B.: State-of-the-art of design, evaluation, and operation methodologies in product service systems. Comput. Ind. **77**, 1–14 (2016)
8. Cavalieri, S., Pezzotta, G.: Product-service systems engineering: state of the art and research challenges. Comput. Ind. **63**, 278–288 (2012)
9. Camarinha-Matos, L.M., Afsarmanesh, H., Ollus, M. (eds.): Methods and Tools for Collaborative Networked Organizations. Springer, New York (2008). ISBN 978-0-387-79423-5
10. Putnik, G., Cruz-Cunha, M. (eds.): Encyclopedia of Networked and Virtual Organizations, vol. I-III. IGI Global, Hershey (2008). Print ISBN-13 978-1-59904-885-7
11. Kurumluoglu, M., Nostdal, R., Karvonen, I.: Base concepts. In: Camarinha-Matos, L., Afsarmanesh, H., Ollus, M. (eds.) Virtual Organizations, Systems and Practices, pp. 11–28. Springer, Heidelberg (2005)
12. Camarinha-Matos, L.M., Rosas, J., Oliveira, A.I., Ferrada, F.: A collaborative services ecosystem for ambient assisted living. In: Camarinha-Matos, L.M., Xu, L., Afsarmanesh, H. (eds.) Collaborative Networks in the Internet of Services. IFIP AICT, vol. 380, pp. 117–127. Springer, Heidelberg (2012)
13. Romero, D., Molina, A.: Green virtual enterprise breeding environments: a sustainable industrial development model for a circular economy. In: Camarinha-Matos, L.M., Xu, L., Afsarmanesh, H. (eds.) Collaborative Networks in the Internet of Services. IFIP AICT, vol. 380, pp. 427–436. Springer, Heidelberg (2012)

14. Camarinha-Matos, L.M., Afsarmanesh, H., Koelmel, B.: Collaborative networks in support of service-enhanced products. In: Camarinha-Matos, L.M., Pereira-Klen, A., Afsarmanesh, H. (eds.) PRO-VE 2011. IFIP AICT, vol. 362, pp. 95–104. Springer, Heidelberg (2011)
15. Vargo, S.L., Lusch, R.F.: Evolving to a new dominant logic for marketing. J. Mark. **68**(1), 1–17 (2004). ISSN 0022-2429, 01/2004
16. Paasi, J., Lappalainen, I., Rantala, T., Pikkarainen, M.: Challenges for product and service providers in open innovation with customers in business-to-business markets. Int. J. Innov. Manag. **18**(2), 1–27 (2014). Imperial College Press
17. Sakao, T., Lindahl, M. (eds.): Introduction to Product/Service-System Design. Springer, Heidelberg (2009). http://www.springer.com/978-1-84882-908-4
18. Veugelers, R.: Trends, challenges and prospects for manufacturing in Europe. In: Veugelers, R. (ed.) Manufacturing Europe's Future. Bruegel Blueprint Series, vol. XXI, pp. 7–47. Bruegel, Brussels (2013)
19. Baldwin, R.E., Evenett, S.J.: Value creation and trade in 21st century manufacturing. J. Reg. Sci. **55**, 31–50 (2015)
20. Pajarinen, M, Rouvinen, P., Ylä-Anttila, P.: Services: a new source of value. ETLA Briefs 11. The Research Institute of the Finnish Economy (2013)
21. Seppälä, T., Halén, M., Juhanko, J., Korhonen, H., Mattila, J., Parviainen, P.: The platform - history, characteristics, and the definition. ETLA reports 47, The Research Institute of the Finnish Economy (2015)
22. Cusumano, M.A., Gawer, A.: Platform Leadership: How Intel, Microsoft, and Cisco Drive Industry Innovation. Harvard Business School Press, Cambridge (2002)
23. von Hippel, E.: Sources of Innovation. Oxford University Press, New York (1988)
24. Korhonen, H.M.E., Kaarela, I.: Practices for involving organizational customers in service innovation. In: Agarwal, R., Selen, W., Roos, G., Green, R. (eds.) The Handbook of Service Innovation, pp. 591–615. Springer, London (2015). http://www.springer.com/br/book/9781447165897
25. Korhonen, H.M.E.: Organizational needs: a co-creation and human systems perspective. J. Bus. Mark. Manag. **6**(4), 214–227 (2013). http://www.jbm-online.net/index.php/jbm/article/view/65
26. Fiordi, P.: Proposal of a requirements process model for complex IT development projects. Politecnico di Milano, Facoltà di Ingegneria dei Sistemi, Corso di Laurea Specialistica in Ingegneria Gestionale (2012)
27. Manutelligence Deliverable: D1.3 - Requirements validation, H2020 project no 636951 (2015). http://www.manutelligence.eu/

Competence Matching in Collaborative Consortia for Service-Enhanced Products

Ana Inês Oliveira[1(✉)], Mohammad Shafahi[2], Hamideh Afsarmanesh[2], Filipa Ferrada[1], and Luis M. Camarinha-Matos[1]

[1] Faculty of Sciences and Technology, Universidade Nova de Lisboa/Uninova, Lisbon, Portugal
{aio, faf, cam}@uninova.pt

[2] Informatics Institute, University of Amsterdam, Amsterdam, The Netherlands
{m.shafahi, h.afsarmanesh}@uva.nl

Abstract. To exploit new market challenges in manufacturing industries, collaborative environments permit that different stakeholders achieve value creation and differentiated products when addressing the design and development of products that include associated business services (service-enhanced products). In order to facilitate a suitable context for networks of SMEs in the domain of highly customized and service-enhanced products, the GloNet project addressed collaborative networks with different configurations and purposes. In this context, this paper is focused on how a collaborative consortia for service-enhanced products can be created having into account the requirements for a new product and the necessary normalization of organization's competences.

Keywords: Service-enhanced product · Collaborative networks · Specification · Virtual organization

1 Introduction

In manufacturing, to meet customers' demands, the current tendency is to achieve highly customized products. Therefore, the idea of service-enhanced products represents a growing trend due to the fact that consumers more and more demand not only the manufactured products, but also services associated to the physical products. Examples of such services associated to products can be: insurance to protect it, expertise to install it, support to maintain its operation during its life cycle, etc. [1, 2]. Examples of service-enhanced products are: power plants, intelligent buildings, or complex technical infrastructures. As a consequence, if business services are associated to products in order to create and add value, then certainly that new business or collaboration opportunities can emerge. Hence, to achieve such services it is necessary to consider the involvement and collaboration of several stakeholders organized in collaborative enterprise networks [3]. Nevertheless, one obstacle that organizations typically face when creating a consortium to respond to a new business or collaboration opportunity is how to identify the needed competences to respond to the requirements. To achieve some solutions in this field, the GloNet project [4] (collaborative project funded under the Factories of the Future program of the European Commission) aimed

H. Afsarmanesh et al. (Eds.): PRO-VE 2016, IFIP AICT 480, pp. 350–360, 2016.
DOI: 10.1007/978-3-319-45390-3_30

"at designing, developing, and deploying an agile virtual enterprise environment for networks of SMEs involved in highly customized and service-enhanced products through end-to-end collaboration with customers and local suppliers".

Prior researches addressed the product specification and design such as collaborative CAD systems [5, 6]. In our previous work the requirements for a product specification system within a Coopetition environment like VBEs and goal oriented VOs [7] and how users can be guided through the specification process [8] were investigated.

In this line, the main challenge that is presented in this paper is twofold: (i) the description of the service-enhanced product specification that considers the customers' requirements and a mapping with existing standards of products classification; and (ii) considering the previous requirements and specification (product goals) with the corresponding mapping of product classification, match it with VBE members' competences to create a consortium. Section 2 briefly summarizes the main outcome of the GloNet project, Sect. 3 responds to the main challenges here presented and, Sect. 3 concludes.

2 GloNet Approach

In GloNet, depending on the type of required support and objectives, collaborative networks with different configurations and purposes were addressed. Those networks are summarized in Table 1.

Table 1. GloNet networks

Long term-strategic network	
Manufacturers network	Similar to a virtual organizations breeding environment (VBE), based on long-term alliances involving: manufacturers, project/product designers, service providers, and other relevant supporting stakeholders and entities
Customer network	Or "customer related community" – a part form the customer, it also includes, service providers, and a variety of local support entities. Although this network might not be fully structured, some principles are shared, such as geographical context, business domain, legal restrictions, culture, etc.
Goal-oriented network	
Product development network	Short-term VO related to the design and development of the physical product and its associated business services. This VO usually ends once the product is delivered
Product servicing network	Long-term VO with the aim to support the involved stakeholders in the required business services during the product life-cycle
Service co-creation network	Temporary VO with the aim of co-design and co-create innovative products and/or associated business services

For the above networks definitions, the adopted definitions for VBE and VO were:

- *"Virtual Organization Breeding Environment (VBE) is an association of organizations and related supporting institutions, adhering to a base long term cooperation agreement, and adopting common operating principles and infrastructures, with the main goal of increasing both their chances and preparedness towards collaboration in potential Virtual Organizations"* [9, 10].
- *"Virtual Organization (VO) is a temporary alliance of organizations that come together to share skills or core competences and resources in order to better respond to collaboration opportunities and produce value-added services and products, and whose cooperation is supported by computer networks"* [11].

The creation of a new service-enhanced product is therefore performed by a temporary goal-oriented network, in this case a *product development network*, whose formation is triggered by a new business opportunity brought in by the customer, and eventually found by a broker member of the VBE. The partners of the *product development network* (VO) are primarily selected from the *manufacturers network* (VBE) and if needed, additional partners, from the *customer related "community"* and other stakeholders from the geographical region of the customer, can be added.

The creation of the *product development network* is prepared *inside* the *manufacturers network*. After receiving the product order from the customer the member in charge of all the necessary arrangements for the creation of the VO (i.e. the VO Planner) begins the formation procedure, that: starts with the detailed specification of the product order; continues with the selection of the partners according to their competences against the skills and capacities that are necessary; and ends with the establishment of the necessary agreements and contracts to regulate the VO during its operation phase [12, 13]. Therefore, the product starts being developed under the supervision of the *product development network* and this network lasts the necessary time to have the product created.

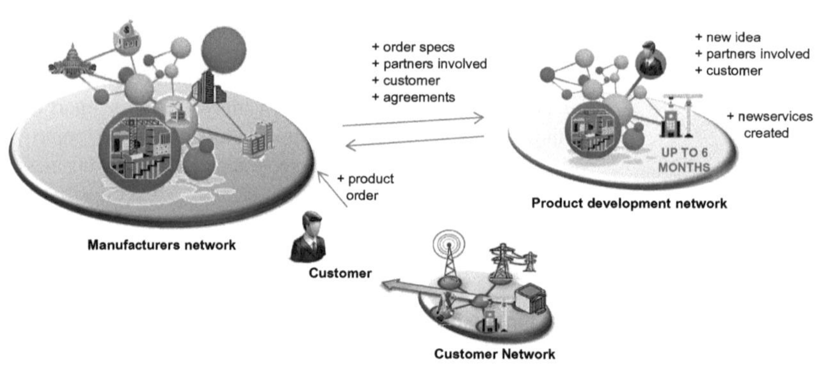

Fig. 1. Interplay of some GloNet networks

Meanwhile, new ideas for new business services might appear. These ideas need to be discussed and brainstormed with some of the *product development network* partners.

Thus, after choosing the most appropriate partners to the mission, a *service co-creation network* is created. This network (also a VO) has as its main purpose the co-design and co-innovation of novel value-added services to enhance the product being developed by the *product development network*. Considering that numerous new business concepts may occur, also numerous service *co-creation networks* might be formed. Once the product and its services are created, the *product development network* dissolves. Figure 1 illustrates the interplay among *manufacturers' network, customer networks,* and *product development network.*

The GloNet project developed an ICT support environment system comprising a cloud-based platform supporting various collaboration spaces and a collaborative networking framework that enabling the specifications of service-enhanced products and management of collaborative networks, which gives support to the networks presented before (Fig. 2). The work presented in this paper relies on two core components: the *Service-Enhanced Product Support* and the *Goal-Oriented Networks Management.*

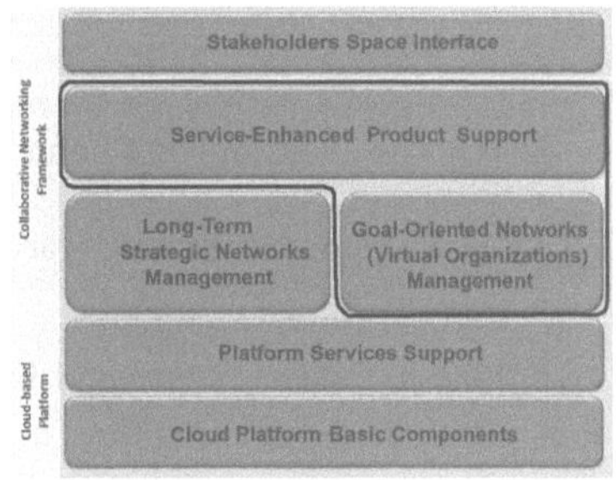

Fig. 2. GloNet system architecture

3 Matching Competences for Consortia Creation

One major challenge after the specification and design of a *product development network*, was how to map the specification of the service-enhanced product order with the corresponding required competences of the partners to be part of the VO. As a response to such challenge, the European standard NACE [14] was adopted as a match with organizations' competences. In this line, three main systems were designed and developed to provide an integrated solution: the *VBE Member Management*, of the VBE Management system; the *Products and Services Specification* System; and the *VO Formation* System.

Figure 3, exemplifies the flow of the creation and operation phases of a service-enhanced product. The creation phase corresponds to a *product development network*, and the operation and maintenance/monitoring (O&M) phase corresponds to a *product servicing network*. The dashed rectangle identifies the interactions of the mentioned three systems, and their description follows.

3.1 VBE Member Management System

A VBE's main aim is to provide commonality and support for interactions among its members [9]. Moreover, a VBE facilitates the collection and maintenance of members profile data, enabling refined selection criteria usage, comprising levels of

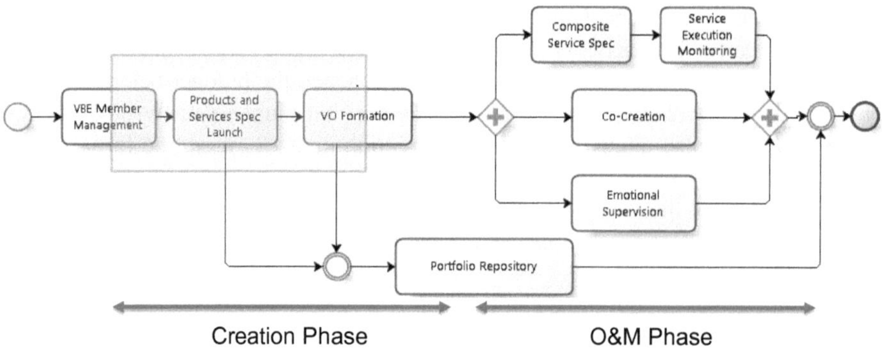

Fig. 3. Flow of the creation and operation & monitoring phases of a product

trustworthiness, value system, and historical collaboration performance. As such, the establishment of a VBE requires a proper management system that should provide functionalities to manage the members' profiles and VBE's competences, to enable performance management, and to facilitate trust building amongst VBE members. A strategic objective of a VBE is to increase preparedness of each member of the alliance concerning fast configuration of VOs in response to market opportunities.

The *VBE members management* system is intended to facilitate the VBE administrator with the management of the VBE members. It provides functionalities for VBE member admission and registration in addition to withdrawal. Furthermore, it contains functionalities that VBE members can use to list all other VBE members, and to permit searching for any VBE member and its profile. In both cases, the usage of these functionalities is conditioned by the permissions that the VBE members have. It is considered that the VBE administrator has fully access to all information of VBE members. The VBE members profile management permits the management of the VBE members' profiles. The profile contains a number of defining elements for each individual VBE member (e.g. business domain, name, address, capabilities, skills, etc.) about each VBE member. Moreover, the VBE member competences consists on the main part of the VBE member profile including the latest information related to each VBE member capabilities and capacities, and conspicuous information of their validity, making the VBE members involvement in actions and activities in the VBE eligible, and prepared to VO creation.

In order to have a common understanding within the VBE, a taxonomy of competences is included, consisting of a hierarchical classification of the competences foreseen for the VBE (i.e. the competences that the VBE would like to fulfill in order to be as competitive as possible in its domain of operation). Each taxonomy class includes a related informal description. To make this taxonomy as broad as possible, the representation of competences is based on the European standard NACE [14, 15].

3.2 Service-Enhanced Product Specification Tool

The service-enhanced product specification system supports two main functionalities of ***product/service specification*** and ***product/service registration***. This tool is designed and implemented to primarily assist the design & engineering phase of the service-enhanced product lifecycle (PLC). Nevertheless, it may also be needed from time to specify new sub-products within the operation and maintenance phase of the PLC.

The system facilitates specification of new customer-oriented service-enhanced products, and enables involvement of different stakeholders, e.g. equipment providers as well as the EPC designers. The service-enhanced product specification system primarily captures, handles, and manages the detailed meta-data about the product and all its sub-products/services, and assists users with their specification. The aims of the functionality provided in the product specification system are three-fold. The first goal is to support *gradual* specification of the products. This is needed to reflect the reality of products that are neither defined in one session and nor by one stakeholder. Therefore, detailed specifications that capture and transform customer requirements for a product into discrete sub-product specifications, can be gradually defined by the involved multi-stakeholders, using the developed service-enhanced product specification system. The second goal is to properly capture the classification of all relevant sub-products and enhancing services in a *granular and modular* manner in the product environment, e.g. distinguishing and capturing both the electrical and mechanical aspects of a sub-product. This will in turn support effective multi-perspective retrieval/discovery of information related to sub-products, as well as creating their concise presentation, needed for common understanding among different related stakeholders. The third goal is to capture all the details related to sub-products in a *reusable* from. As such, the existing specifications of already introduced sub-products can be either fully or partially (e.g. at the level of certain detailed feature-kind) be reused for the specification of other sub-products. Figure 4 demonstrates the overall flow for the specification process for complex products.

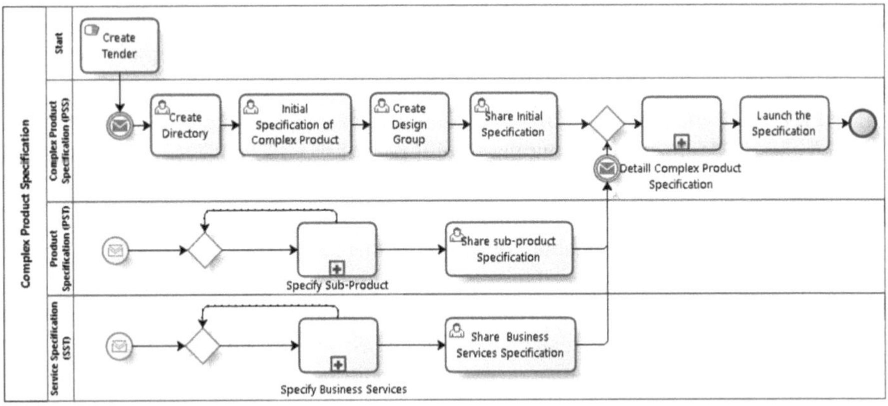

Fig. 4. Flow of the complex product specification

Other than the above mentioned functionalities sub-products specified using the product specification system are semi-automatically classified using the PRODCOM [16] convention for classifications, that are pre-defined in the system. The choice of PRODCOM suits this case because it is an extension of the CPA and as such compatible with NACE [14]. Furthermore, PRODCOM itself is accepted within the EU as a standard extendable coding system. The NACE Rev. 2 coding system, as suggested by its description of "Statistical Classification of ***Economic Activities*** in the European Community", classifies the economical activities preformed to realize a product or service. This provides valuable input when a specification is being realized by the VO formation sub-system and organizations need to be selected for the VO. A PRODCOM code is constructed by further extending the NACE activity code, and therefore embeds in itself the activity that is preformed to realize the product. If a product class is associated with at least one PRODCOM code, we can then use this coding in order to find suitable organizations that can realize this product class by focusing on the NACE part of the PRODCOM code and looking for organizations that have announced this NACE code as one competence.

3.3 Mapping of Service-Enhanced Product's Specification and Organizations Competences

As suggested before, the recommendation of a set of organizations that can produce or support a certain class of products can be achieved by looking at the NACE code of their competences, when related to the PRODCOM code of the product. If the class of some product is not directly associated with a PRODCOM code, then sub-products of the product can be used, were their classes are coded with PRODCOM, so that the competence of organizations standardized through the NACE [14, 15] coding convention can be used to build the link to that product. As such interlinking the sub-products of the product with the competences required from organizations to realize the sub-product, are established. As an example, the PRODCOM code "C27.11.43.80" refers to "Transformers, n.e.c., having a power handling capacity > 500 kVA" and its respective NACE code of "C27.11" refers to: "Manufacturing of electric motors, generators, transformers and electricity distribution and control apparatus". Now if a sub-product for instance is associated with this PRODCOM code "C27.11.43.80", then the suitable organizations that can realize and/or support this product can be identified by taking the NACE part of this PRODCOM coding which is "C27.11", and then looking for those organizations who have defined the NACE code "C27.11" as one of their competences.

The above mechanism enables our system to recommend a set of organizations capable of realizing and supporting a complex product. The approach suggested by Resnik [17] was used in order to further rank the suitability of a NACE code used as organization competency for realizing a product associated with a PRODCOM code. Clearly in the case when a product is associated with more than one PRODCOM code, and the organizations are associated with more than one competence (i.e. NACE codes), which is rather a typical case, then the most overlap between the interlinked NACE and PRODCOM codes are desired, in other words the more matches between an organizations set of competencies and the PRODCOM codes defined for a product, the more that organization is suited for realizing and support that product. Such a large number of matches in fact indicate that the sub-product and the organization belong to the same sector.

3.4 Consortia Creation

The formation of the VO for service-enhanced product development mostly involves the plan and scheduling of the work order consistent with the service-enhanced product specification, and selecting the appropriated partners considering the existent VBE competences. Nevertheless, to finish the VO formation, and assist the VO partners in attaining agreements, negotiation functionalities are also essential [13]. The VO agreements will serve as foundations for the VO governing principles through its operation phase [12]. Figure 5 exemplifies the main flow of the VO formation process. Nevertheless, as the focus of this work is on competences for consortia creation, this section highlights the three first services: *New order characterization*, *VBE members competences analysis*, and *Potential VOs assemblage*.

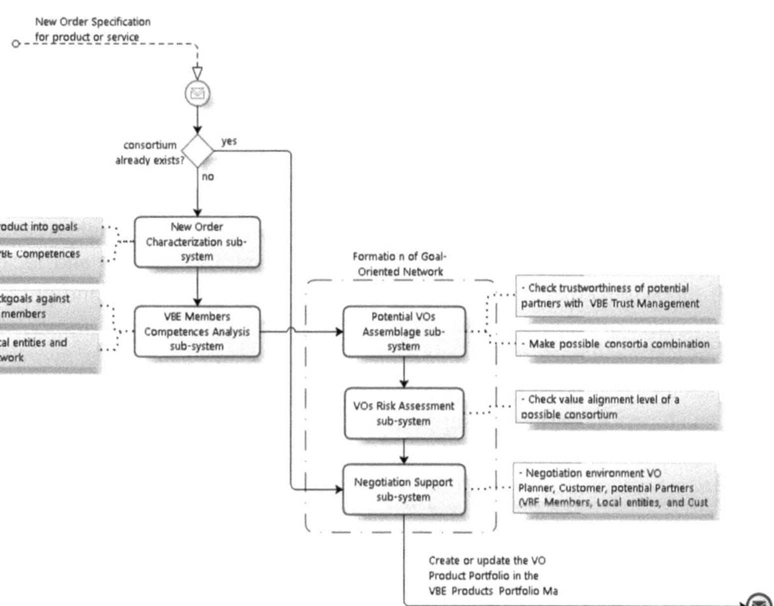

Fig. 5. Main flow of the VO formation process

As such, important services in the VO formation are:

New Order Characterization: to assist the VO planner in the characterization of the new order for products or/and services. Considering the identified requirements of the new order, the characterization relies on the decomposition of the new order into goals considering the outcome of the product specification tool and the VBE competences taxonomy.

VBE Members Competences Analysis: to support the VO planner in searching for the suitable partners for the VO. It allows checking how the *New Order Characterization* goals can be fulfilled considering the existing competences of the VBE members. Thus, the VO planner can properly detect the appropriated partners for the VO being created. The members are therefore searched within the VBE, the customer network, and also other relevant local entities or suppliers related with the VBE.

Potential VOs Assemblage: to assist the VO planner in making the conceivable consortia compositions considering the information already provided by the *New Order Characterization* and the *VBE Members Competences Analysis*. In this step, the VO planner already has a list containing the potential partners that can deliver, or are able to complete, the defined goals.

Moreover, the VO planner can make a VO risk assessment [18] using other VBE functionalities (such as evaluate the trustworthiness levels of partners [19], and their value systems alignment [20]). As mentioned, to finalize the VO formation, the VO planner starts the negotiation process [13] to achieve agreements among VO partners, and launch the VO.

4 Conclusions

One of the aims of the GloNet project was the design, development, and deploy of an agile enterprise environment for networks of SMEs involved in highly customized and service-enhanced products through collaboration with customers and local suppliers. One of the achievements was the specification of configurations and purposes of collaborative networks: *product development network, service co-creation network, product servicing network, manufacturers' network,* and *customer network.* This paper addresses the creation of a *product development network* focusing on three systems that were developed to permit its support, namely: the *VBE Member Management*, of the VBE Management system; the *Products and Services Specification* System; and the *VO Formation* System. The interaction of these three systems considered the normalization of the requirements of a new product and the necessary competences of organizations. Therefore, the challenges of addressing: *(i)* the service-enhanced product specification, mapping it with existing standards; and *(ii)* the consortium creation focusing on the VBE members matching, were achieved.

The approach was validated in the scope of the GloNet project, in a solar industry and intelligent buildings networks. As a general result, the solution was positively validated in terms of developed models and prototypes. Nevertheless, when evolving to commercial products, some improvements shall be considered, namely in terms of user interfaces.

Acknowledgments. This work was funded in part by the European Commission through the GloNet project (FP7 programme). The authors also thank the contributions from their partners in this project. Partial support also comes from Fundação para a Ciência e Tecnologia through the PEST program UID/EEA/00066/2013.

References

1. Shen, Q.: Research on organization mode selection of service-enhanced manufacturing enterprise. In: 3rd International Conference on Information Management, Innovation Management and Industrial Engineering (ICIII). IEEE, Kunming, China (2010)
2. Bitner, M.J., Brown, S.W.: The evolution and discovery of services science in business schools. In: Stauss, B., Engelmann, K., Kremer, A., Luhn, A. (eds.) Services Science, pp. 91–101. Springer, Heidelberg (2008)
3. Camarinha-Matos, L.M., Afsarmanesh, H., Oliveira, A.I., Ferrada, F.: Cloud-based collaborative business services provision. In: Hammoudi, S., Cordeiro, J., Maciaszek, L. A., Filipe, J. (eds.) ICEIS 2013. LNBIP, vol. 190, pp. 366–384. Springer, Heidelberg (2014)
4. GloNet: GloNet, Glocal Enterprise Network Focusing on Customer-Centric Collaboration. 2011–2015. http://www.glonet-fines.eu/
5. Li, W.D., Fuh, J.Y., Wong, Y.S.: An Internet-enabled integrated system for co-design and concurrent engineering. Comput. Ind. **55**(1), 87–103 (2004)
6. Li, W.D., Lu, W.F., Fuh, J.Y., Wong, Y.S.: Collaborative computer-aided design - research and development status. Comput. Aided Des. **37**(9), 931–940 (2005)
7. Shafahi, M., Afsarmanesh, H., Sargolzaei, M.: A coopetition space for complex product specification. In: Camarinha-Matos, L.M., Afsarmanesh, H. (eds.) PRO-VE 2014. IFIP AICT, vol. 186, pp. 83–97. Springer, Heidelberg (2014)
8. Afsarmanesh, H., Shafahi, M., Sargolzaei, M.: On service-enhanced product recommendation guiding users through complex product specification. In: International Conference on Computing and Communications Technologies ICT 2015, pp. 43–48 (2015)
9. Afsarmanesh, H., Camarinha-Matos, L.M., Ermilova, E.: VBE reference framework. In: Camarinha-Matos, L.M., Afasarmanesh, H., Ollus, M. (eds.) Methods and Tools for collaborative networked organizations, pp. 35–68. Springer, Heidelberg (2008)
10. Msanjila, S.S., Fsarmanesh, H.: A multi-model approach to analyze inter-organizational trust in VBEs. In: Camarinha-Matos, L.M., Afsarmanesh, H. (eds.) Collaborative Networks: Reference Modeling, pp. 195–214. Springer, Heidelberg (2008)
11. Camarinha-Matos, L.M., Afsarmanesh, H., Ollus, M.: ECOLEAD: a holistic approach to creation and management of dynamic virtual organizations. In: Camarinha-Matos, L.M., Afasarmanesh, P., Ortiz, L. (eds.) Collaborative Networks and Their Breeding Environments. IFIP, vol. 314, pp. 3–16. Springer, Heidelberg (2005)
12. Oliveira, A.I., Camarinha-Matos, L.M.: Negotiation and contracting in collaborative networks. In: Camarinha-Matos, L.M., Pereira, P., Ribeiro, L. (eds.) DoCEIS 2010. IFIP AICT, vol. 314, pp. 83–92. Springer, Heidelberg (2010)
13. Oliveira, A.I., Camarinha-Matos, L.M.: Electronic negotiation support environment in collaborative networks. In: Camarinha-Matos, L.M., Shahamatnia, E., Nunes, G. (eds.) DoCEIS 2012. IFIP AICT, vol. 372, pp. 21–32. Springer, Heidelberg (2012)

14. EurLex.: Regulation (EC) No 1893/2006 of the European Parliament and of the Council of 20 December 2006 establishing the statistical classification of economic activities NACE Revision 2 and amending Council Regulation (EEC) No 3037/90 as well as certain EC Regulations on specific statistical domains. http://eur-lex.europa.eu/legal-content/EN/TXT/?uri=CELEX:32006R1893. Accessed 27 Apr 2016
15. Eurostat.: NACE Rev. 2 - Statistical classification of economic activities. http://ec.europa.eu/eurostat/en/web/products-manuals-and-guidelines/-/KS-RA-07-015. Accessed 27 Apr 2016
16. Eurostat.: Your key to European statistics. http://ec.europa.eu/eurostat/web/prodcom. Accessed 28 Apr 2016
17. Resnik, P.: Semantic similarity in a taxonomy: an information-based measure and its application to problems of ambiguity in natural language. J. Artif. Intell. Res. (JAIR) **11**, 95–130 (1999)
18. Oliveira, A.I., Camarinha-Matos, L.M.: Negotiation support and risk reduction in collaborative networks. In: Camarinha-Matos, L.M., Tomic, S., Graça, P. (eds.) DoCEIS 2013. IFIP AICT, vol. 394, pp. 15–24. Springer, Heidelberg (2013)
19. Msanjila, S., Afsarmanesh, H.: Trust analysis and assessment in virtual organization breeding environments. Int. J. Prod. Res. **46**(5), 1253–1295 (2008)
20. Macedo, P., Camarinha-Matos, L.M.: A qualitative approach to assess the alignment of Value Systems in collaborative enterprises networks. Comput. Ind. Eng. **64**(1), 412–424 (2013)

Detecting Influencing Behaviour for Product-Service Design Through Big Data Intelligence in Manufacturing

Michael Petychakis, Evmorfia Biliri(✉), Angelos Arvanitakis, Ariadni Michalitsi-Psarrou, Panagiotis Kokkinakos, Fenareti Lampathaki, and Dimitrios Askounis

School of Electrical and Computer Engineering, National Technical University of Athens, Athens, Greece
{mpetyx,ebiliri,agg.arvanitakis,amichal, pkokkinakos,flamp,askous}@epu.ntua.gr

Abstract. The opportunity to gain insights from social media user generated data has triggered the interest of many companies who see in this a chance to better understand their customers' preferences and identify trends. However, the huge amount of such data is not always manageable. Identification of influencers for a specific industry and monitoring of their behaviour in social media could be proved of great importance towards the direction of reducing the amount of data for analysis and extracting more useful and targeted insights. In this context, the paper aims to present a platform that will provide data analysts and product-service designers with influencer identification functionalities per industry, topic and in time and will also visualise the correlation among influencers based on specific topics of interest. The platform was evaluated under a use case from the fashion industry.

Keywords: Influencer · Big data · Social media · Business intelligence · Manufacturing

1 Introduction

Influence is "*the power to change or affect someone or something, the power to cause changes without directly forcing them to happen*"[1]. Measuring influence and trying to predict how individuals influence one another in social media is of particular importance for enterprises looking to leverage social media communities not only for promotional and customer management purposes, but also as a means of inspiration towards creating enhanced products and services designed to appeal to a larger crowd.

The potential benefits of acting upon information regarding consumer preferences revealed from social media platforms is evident by the plethora of enterprises that invest in building a presence on social media (e.g. Facebook, Twitter, Instagram and Pinterest), but is also proved by numerous research studies, both academic and industry oriented.

[1] Merriam-Webster Dictionary http://www.merriam-webster.com/dictionary/influence.

H. Afsarmanesh et al. (Eds.): PRO-VE 2016, IFIP AICT 480, pp. 361–369, 2016.
DOI: 10.1007/978-3-319-45390-3_31

Electronic Word of Mouth postings were shown to be statistically significant in explaining changes in product sales [1]. Another study indicated that 19 % of all tweets mention an organisation or product brand and 20 % of those express a sentiment or opinion regarding this organisation, its products or services [2]. Image-based platforms are also very popular among organisations and enterprises that offer products which heavily depend on image and aesthetics. In fashion, statistics reveal 85 % Instagram adoption by top fashion brands [3]. As industry is beginning to realise the immense potential, targeted influencer identification platforms (e.g. TFI[2] for the fashion domain) emerge and tools are developed to support brands in extracting valuable insights from the huge amount of user generated data.

The present paper aims at presenting a brief overview of the current state of play in the influencer identification problem in the social media context, from the standpoint of product-service design. Academic literature and market analysis are presented in Sect. 2 to set the basis for our approach. Section 3 describes the core methodology on social media influencers identification in the manufacturing domain. Section 4 presents, the application of the methodology in the development Influencial platform. Finally, in Sect. 5 some conclusions and further steps are discussed.

2 Relevant Work

The theory that in every social network there are certain people, commonly referred to as influencers, that play a more important role in information diffusion is intuitive and supported by numerous studies. There has been some criticism on this theory, mainly on the following two axes: (1) Peers and friends may under circumstances influence behaviour more than general domain influencers and (2) The current state of the social network (e.g. readiness, openness) may also need to be considered [10]. However, in the social media ecosystem the role of influential users is considered very important, especially for content marketing, as shown by numerous academic works in the field, but also the abundance of commercial platforms that offer such insights.

Academic literature focuses on two aspects when it comes to influencer identification: what constitutes an influencer (i.e. definition and important attributes) and how can these users be identified. In the social media context, two differentiating factors are considered important for understanding influential behaviour: "Monomorphism vs. Polymorphism" which shows whether a person is active in one or multiple topics and "Spreader vs Inventor", which shows whether a person creates or only distributes information [4]. Regarding influence identification, most models are descriptive, rather than predictive and mostly rely on measuring and combining various social presence metrics, such as number of posts, number of followers, centrality etc. [4, 6]. There are also network-specific techniques developed and applied, i.e. targeting influencing bloggers based on detected follow-up activities relevant to blog content [5]. However, research studies focus on small-scale examples in order to showcase the

[2] Top Fashion Influencers http://www.topfashioninfluencers.com.

proposed methodology on a given dataset and are not meant to be directly applied in other cases, hence do not offer implementation details.

On the other hand, numerous commercial platforms offer influencer identification functionalities, usually combined with other social media analytics. Table 1 presents some of the most known such platforms. The vast majority of commercial platforms aims to enable content marketing through influential social media users, hence address the middle and end stages of product-service lifecycle. Moreover, it is usually unclear how influencers are identified, e.g. Kred defines its own scoring system, Keyhole uses Klout score which is in turn computed in an unknown way from the overall online presence. None of them offers adjustable computations and the user may only view the computation results. It should also be stressed that there are currently no completely free offerings of these platforms.

Table 1. Social media influencer tools and platforms.

Tool/Platform	Supported social networks	Free (pricing)	Primary focus
Kred (http://home.kred/)	Twitter, Facebook	No	Influencer measurement
Klout (https://klout.com/home)	Multiple (all major)	Yes (limited)	Influence measurement
Traackr (http://traackr.com/)	Multiple (all major)	No	Marketing
LittleBird (http://www.getlittlebird.com/)	Twitter	No	Marketing
Followerwonk (https://followerwonk.com/)	Twitter	Yes (limited)	Followers influence measurement
Buzzsumo (http://buzzsumo.com/)	Multiple (all major)	No	SEO, marketing
Keyhole (http://keyhole.co/)	Twitter, Instagram	No	Content tracking with influence measurement
GroupHigh (http://www.grouphigh.com/)	Multiple + Blogs	No, Free Trial	Marketing, blogger outreach measurement
Appinions (http://www.appinions.com/)	Multiple	No	Marketing
Klear (http://klear.com/)	Twitter, Facebook, Instagram	No, Free Trial	Influencer marketing

The common conclusion by both academic and commercial approaches in influencer identification is the need to apply big data techniques, in order to handle the variety (multiple network structures), volume and velocity of social media data (indicatively: Every second, on average, around 6,000 tweets are tweeted on Twitter[3]).

However, the dual analysis shows that the available commercial solutions mainly focus on identifying influential social media users for marketing purposes and academic work does not discuss scalability and implementation. Hence, there is currently a gap in providing influencer identification functionalities in the context of product-service BOL, i.e. developed to be leveraged by design teams towards creating better products

[3] Internet Live Stats, Twitter Usage Statistics http://www.internetlivestats.com/twitter-statistics/.

and services. The purpose of this paper is to present InfluenCial, a new web platform offering an intuitive interface for product-service design teams to explore fine-grained online trends and get inspiration for future creations.

3 Methodology

The first step towards tackling the described problem was to formally define what constitutes influencing indication and how it should be measured in the social media context. The core methodology builds on the premise that ideas expressed by influencers are more probable to turn out into new trends that may affect the product-service design phase. As already explained, the definition of an influencer may vary depending on the context and may, indicatively, include:

- People often mentioned in other people's discussions, e.g. in social media.
- People whose expressed opinions are commonly referenced by others, e.g. in social media this is expressed in the form of retweets, Facebook shares etc.
- People whose expressed opinions are widely adopted and liked, e.g. through up-votes or likes.
- People popular in a network, e.g. expressed as a large number of followers.
- Friends of influent people for a specific topic should also be influent and typically talk about the same or similar topics, e.g. in Twitter, Instagram, Blogs [7].

Acknowledging the validity of different definitions for social influencers, InfluenCial aims to offer decision maker teams the ability to experiment with various techniques and select the most appropriate according to specific user interaction patterns, which may differ in diverse networks but also inside the same network across different industries. Therefore, a number of algorithms for link analysis and association rule learning will be implemented to offer this flexibility. More specifically, in the first iteration presented in this paper, the InfluenCial Platform ranks user behaviour in terms of influence indications, applying the PageRank algorithm [8]. However, through the provision of this one algorithm, a larger number of options is essentially provided, since the platform user can choose to apply it on various network edge types (e.g. user mentions, follower relations etc.).

The notion of a hyperlink is extended to a social media account where "reference" attribute is now the "follows" attribute. The relation is again anti-symmetric and irreflexive and thus PageRank works in the same way, assigning social media users that have been analysed with the corresponding algorithm a score from 1 to 10.

The proposed InfluenCial platform is a big data infrastructure to analyze "social" data (i.e. indicating interactions between stakeholders) in order to identify influencers and point the product-service design team towards the most popular/trending ideas. It will provide data analysts, product-service managers and generally the product-service design team with the ability to: (a) Detect influencers: Identify and rank influencing behaviour per industry, topic and in time with the help of the PageRank algorithm. (b)Track and cluster interactions: Visualize the correlation between different influencers on specific topics of interest.

In general, the envisioned procedure towards achieving these goals includes the following high-level steps: (a) Import data that contain or imply the importance of a user in a certain network/communication channel; (b) Extract the interactions that indicate influencing behaviour (e.g. likes, follower relations, retweets, etc.) and model them in a predefined format; and (c) Apply importance measuring algorithms and identify influencers' graphs (clusters of influencers or independent graphs). When the information retrieved is in the form of text, mentions of specific predefined entities are extracted and algorithms to detect entities commonly appearing together are applied. When the influencers along with the associated topics are calculated, the InfluenCial Platform starts investigating what is the correlation between trends and influencers to identify who is talking about what in the specified time period. Such an extensive calculation also classifies hashtags to topics and explores link propagation in time, in order to result into the daily impact of each influencer on each topic category.

In order to fully support the described functionalities in a way that provides actionable insights to designers regarding future products and services, a large volume of user generated content from various social sources will be retrieved and analysed, a process that involves application of various correlation computations and link analysis methods. In the first release of the InfluenCial platform, presented in the following section, the selected social sources are Twitter and Instagram which were considered as most relevant for the application and evaluation of the platform in a fashion related use case.

4 Implementation

In this section, the approach followed for the development of the InfluenCial platform is described, which currently implements core parts of the aforementioned methodology and is tested and evaluated in a use case taken from the fashion industry.

The architecture upon which the InfluenCial Platform is built can be split into 4 discrete parts that rely upon a set of state-of-the-art, open technologies:

- The **Pre-Processing Layer** of the platform leverages ElasticSearch as an indexing repository that allows fast and complex queries on unstructured data, allowing real-time data and analytics. Retrieval, processing and modeling of social media data is based on the Anlzer engine [9].
- A **Cluster Computing Engine** build on top of Hadoop and Spark is used in order to conduct the necessary big data processing activities and run the algorithms for the identification of social influencers and their graph interrelations.
- A **Results Storage Layer** to store the structured results of the big data analysis conducted on the selected social data.
- A **Post-Processing, Export and Visualization Engine** which uses JavaScript-based visualization frameworks to present in a meaningful and user-friendly way the results of the analysis (Fig. 1).

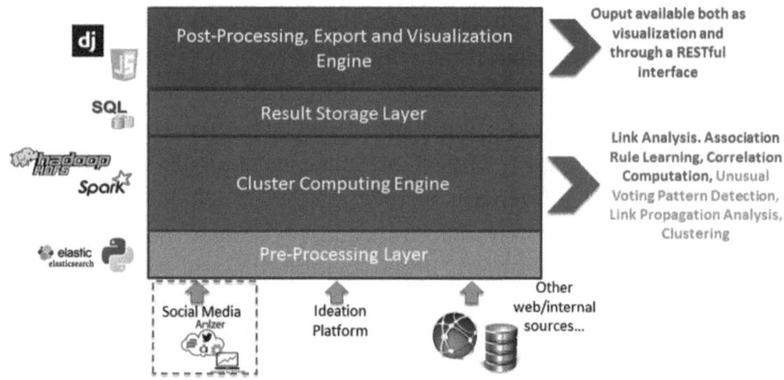

Fig. 1. InfluenCial platform: high-level architecture showing the complete envisioned system

Upon logging in the InfluenCial platform, the user views the landing page that presents various topics for which he may retrieve the top influencers. For each influencer, the platform user is presented with a profile picture taken from the influencer's Twitter or Instagram account, the name, a PageRank score (depicted in a 5-star scale) and a list of the five (5) topics mostly associated with him. The PageRank score is a simple metric derived from the InfluenCial algorithms in order to denote the social importance of the user by analysing the traffic in his social accounts; specifically, his posts and the sharing/retweeting of his posts by others. This score is normalized in a scale of zero (0) to five (5) and is presented through a star system (Fig. 2).

Fig. 2. InfluenCial platform: landing page for topics selection and presentation of domain influencers

By clicking on an influencer's image, the user is provided with the top three topics of this social media user, followed by two types of charts, a **timeline chart** (Fig. 3), depicting the intensity of the user's social activity throughout the past weeks for each of the topics that he influences, and a corresponding **mean-average** chart.

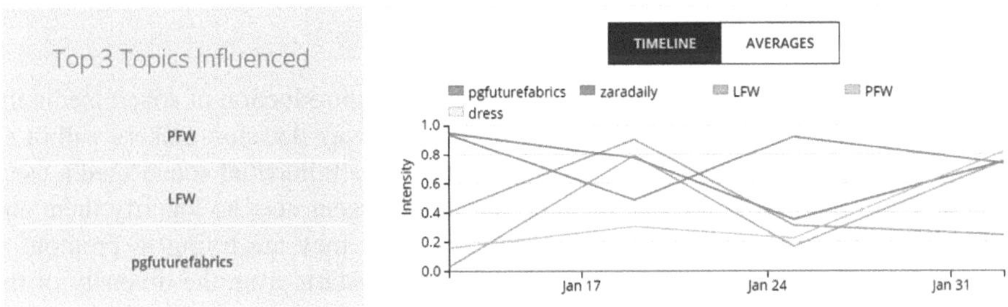

Fig. 3. InfluenCial platform: influencers' details - timeline chart

The influencers' page allows for navigation to the most socially dominant people, who are filtered out based on the topics that they influence. It is accompanied by a dedicated discussions page that provides an easy way to view the correlation between different influencers on the same topics. The user is prompted to enter a list of topics that he/she is interested in, and a graph will denote the correlations between the influencers on the topics that the user has selected. The system also recommends topics based on the topics that the user has entered.

Finally, the output is a graph where the nodes represent the influencers and the edges signify different topics (each topic has its own unique colour). Thus, an edge between two nodes is in fact a correlation between these two influencers on the specific topic. In other words, these two users have mentioned each other (or are someway related to each other) on their social activities (Fig. 4).

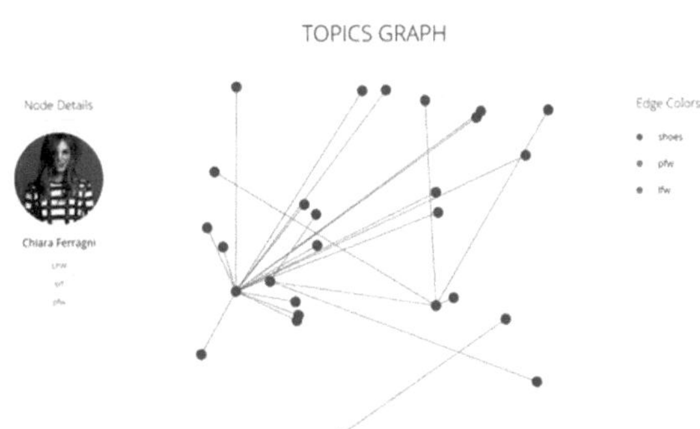

Fig. 4. InfuenCial platform - discussion topic selection and graph visualisation

The platform was validated as part of the EU funded project PSYMBIOSYS. We started with 40 Twitter and 30 Instagram accounts in the fashion domain and the system started collecting tweets from accounts they follow and having as a starting point those accounts, iteratively, apply the same methodology to all accounts they follow as well. This concluded in hundreds of thousands Twitter and Instagram accounts and millions of statuses to process. The results were validated in fashion by experts in the domain.

5 Conclusions

Both the flourish of the web and more specifically the introduction of social media the last decade have established a paradigm shift in the way decision makers within an industry make their conclusive judgements. Nowadays influential social media users play a vital role driving the market and there is an urgent need to identify them and understand their interests and more specifically what they are trying to promote at specific periods of time. One of the major challenges starts from the diversity of the sources, the media platforms as well as the influencers themselves.

The InfluenCial architecture and implementation are motivated by the presented research challenges. It has been currently evaluated in a fashion use case and the retrieved feedback will be leveraged towards enhancing the provided functionalities.

In the next release, a deeper integration with more data sources is going to be pursued, e.g. more social media channels, blogs and personal pages, and an expansion of the definitions of influencers by adopting even more algorithms and more visualisation options. Ultimately, an admin interface will be implemented where each stakeholder can choose their own definitions of an influencer, algorithms and their preferred sources of information. Thus, a customisable solution that would fit innumerable scenarios and needs could be delivered to the decision makers.

Acknowledgments. This work has been funded by the European Commission through the FoF-RIA Project PSYMBIOSYS: Product-Service sYMBIOtic SYStems (No. 636804). The authors wish to acknowledge the Commission and all the PSYMBIOSYS project partners for their contribution.

References

1. Davis, A., Khazanchi, D.: An empirical study of online word of mouth as a predictor for multi-product category e-commerce sales. Electron. Mark. **18**, 130–141 (2008). Routledge
2. Jansen, B.J., Zhang, M.: Twitter power-tweets as electronic word of mouth. J. Am. Soc. Inf. Sci. Technol. **60**, 2169–2188 (2009). http://www.cs.rochester.edu/twiki/pub/Main/HarpSeminar/Twitter_power-_Tweets_as_electronic_word_of_mouth.pdf
3. Simply Measured: State of Social Marketing Report (2015)
4. Li, J., Peng, W., Li, T., Sun, T., Li, Q., Xu, J.: Social network user influence sense-making and dynamics prediction. Expert Syst. Appl. **41**(11), 5115–5124 (2014)
5. Keller, E., Berry, J.: One American in ten tells the other nine how to vote, where to eat, and what to buy. They are Influentials **25**(5), 1–8 (2003). New York
6. Cha, M., Haddai, H., Benevenuto, F., Gummadi, K.P.: Million follower fallacy. In: International AAAI Conference Weblogs Social on Media, pp. 10–17 (2010)
7. Swanson, A.: The Washington post. The 100 most influential economics bloggers on Twitter, charted. http://knowmore.washingtonpost.com/2015/04/13/the-100-most-influential-economics-bloggers-on-twitter-charted/. Accessed 27 Apr 2016
8. Winograd, L.P.B.M.: The PageRank citation ranking: bringing order to the we. Technical report, Stanford InfoLab, vol. 9, no. 1, pp. 1–14 (1999)

9. Biliri, E., Petychakis, M., Alvertis, I., Lampathaki, F., Koussouris, S., Askounis, D.: Infusing social data analytics into future internet applications for manufacturing. In: 2014 IEEE/ACS 11th International Conference on Computer Systems and Applications (AICCSA), vol. 2015-March, pp. 515–522 (2014)
10. Domingos, P., Richardson, M.: Mining the network value of customers. In: Proceedings of the Seventh ACM SIGKDD International Conference on Knowledge Discovery and Data Mining, pp. 57–66. ACM

Advances in Production - Intelligent Product Ecosystems

Tools for Human-Product Collaborative Development of Intelligent Product Service Systems

Sebastian Scholze(✉), Ana Correia, Dragan Stokic, Kevin Nagorny, and Philipp Spindler

Institut für angewandte Systemtechnik Bremen GmbH, Wiener Str. 1, 28359 Bremen, Germany
{scholze,correia,dragan,nagorny,spindler}@atb-bremen.de

Abstract. Intelligent products, having cyber physical features, are best candidates for building Intelligent Product Service Systems (IPSS), in which integrated products and services provide a higher level of intelligence. Such IPSS may actively provide feedback on their use, which in turn may support the development of new IPSS. The objective is to develop a set of tools to establish a Collaborative Network, where both human actors and products themselves can collaborate and contribute to the development of such IPSS. The tools support involvement of various stakeholders within the Collaborative Networks. Several tools, such as a tool to select sensors and intelligent features at the products, a tool to model context under which IPSS is used, as well as tools to provide feedback on the IPSS use are defined. The paper presents as well the application of the proposed concept in machine industry.

Keywords: Intelligent products · Collaborative development · Product service system · Cyber physical features · Collaborative network

1 Introduction

Modern products include more and more cyber physical features as a basis for their intelligence. Cyber physical features allow to build various intelligent services encompassing such products to build for example Intelligent Product Service Systems (IPSS). IPSS provide a new quality of offers to customers as the products and services are integrated and built with a higher level of intelligence. Such systems can communicate and provide information within Collaborative Networks. Many Cyber Physical Products in manufacturing industry, such as vehicles, home appliances etc., are already used or can be used to build such IPSS. Modern machines are probably one of the most promising products to build IPSS.

Such IPSS are innovative results of the fourth industrial revolution [1, 2], as a collective term covering a number of modern technologies in manufacturing, automation and data exchange. The forth industrial revolution is 'a collective term for technologies and concepts of value chain organization' consisting of loosely coupled Cyber-Physical Systems (CPS) in an Internet of Things and Internet of Services [3–6], it includes all resources needed for developing IPSS.

H. Afsarmanesh et al. (Eds.): PRO-VE 2016, IFIP AICT 480, pp. 373–384, 2016.
DOI: 10.1007/978-3-319-45390-3_32

IPSS is an evolutionary step to smart manufacturing. Loosely coupled cyber-physical systems realize comprehensive cross-level and cross-domain collaboration and analyzation possibilities. Furthermore, in manufacturing environments such services improve the volatile and dynamic. This continuously rising ramification generates also a demand on Collaborative Development approaches to manage those future highly complex IPSS and to exploit new potentials.

IPSS, having the ability to communicate within Collaborative Networks, may actively contribute to the development of new IPSS or re-design of the existing ones. The objective of the research shown in this paper is to develop Collaborative Networks, comprising both humans and IPSS, whose aim is to (re-)develop IPSS. Within such networks, besides different stakeholders normally involved in the development of IPSS (product designer, process designers and shop-floor experts, service providers, various suppliers, as well as business customers, consumers etc.), IPSS can play an active role. They may pro-actively provide information about the product use and by this support the development of intelligent products and/or services. Such an approach requires new organization and definition of processes for IPSS development. However, collaborative environments and tools to support such Collaborative Networks in which human stakeholders and IPSS collaboratively "work" together on the development of IPSS are currently missing, based on the literature review carried out for this research.

The paper presents the vision of the human-product Collaborative Network and Environment, which shall support the operation of such Network and focuses upon three tools.. The paper also discusses the application of the approach in machine industry where development of IPSS is specifically complex. The paper focuses on the environment and tools while organizational aspects will be implicitly addressed.

2 Overview of State of the Art

Cyber Physical Systems/Products: CPS are systems that include seamlessly integrated and closely interacting hardware (physical) and software (cyber) components sensing and to controlling (in real-time) the state of them and their environment. A high degree of complexity of such systems at a numerous spatial and temporal scale generate highly networked communications for integrating with their computational and physical components. As such CPS refer to information and communication systems (computing, communicating, actuating, sensing, etc.) seamless integrated in physical objects, interconnected through a unified network technology including the (Industrial) Internet (of Things/Services), providing several innovative applications based on digitized data and virtualized models, services and information. Therefore, CPS can also be referred to as emerging ubiquitous computing embedded cyber-physical applications that is bridging the physical and virtual worlds and share all kind of collaborative networks [7–11].

Product/Service-System (PSS): PSS has evolved in different geographic locations and has different motivations, e.g., one of the most spread concept is closely coupled sustainability and the reduction of environmental impact [12]. There are many research communities that deal with similar concepts, e.g. services sciences [13]. Product-service bundles enable to extend the product's life-cycle. The concept of extended products [14] provides a suitable model to conjunct products, product related services and the needs of users. The meta-product plays a decisive role in this process. The more a manufacturing enterprise is getting closer to a highest level of servitisation, the more the meta-product has knowledge about a service embedded in itself and the more it is becoming "service-aware", thus smarter. Products based on CPS are especially appropriate for building PSS, because they allow to combine the intelligence of the cyber physical products themselves with the intelligence of services built using sensors and intelligent features of the product, which in turn build higher level of system intelligence, namely Intelligent PSS (IPSS).

Collaborative Development Environment: Collaborative Networks and Environments for complex service-enhanced products are subject of intensive research activities [15, 16]. One of the most important topics in research relevant for IPSS is related to generic software frameworks allowing developers to integrate services for products to create specific improved/extended industry solutions. Still promising approaches in this area are the "Common Object Request Broker Architecture (CORBA)", the Grid computing infrastructure (e.g. Globus, Legion and SNIPE) and the Common Component Architecture (CCA). This work has now led to the concept of Service Oriented Architecture, Cloud Computing etc. Some commercial collaborative systems are coming from CAD/CAM/PLM vendors which are more specific for the manufacturing industry and others are more tailored towards more general forms of collaboration (Webex, GoToMeeting, MS Messenger). Similarly, much research work has been done to develop virtual distributed environments resulting in advances in the area of collaborative virtual environment. Still a lot of work is needed to realize in real engineering settings collaborative workspaces covering the whole view of a product life cycle and intensive collaborative engagement of all the stakeholders that could lead to services, ecological products and related processes in production.

Many leading industries related to CAD are now offering in some form features for collaboration into their CAD/PLM products/services. The fundamental motivation for this evolution is to enable CAD/PLM products and services using remote teams to come together for their own product to work collaboratively to improve productivity (reduce costs and time consumption in product design and development while increasing quality). This indicates that major CAD/PLM vendors currently providing some forms of collaboration capabilities focused on collaboration related to their products so that one of the key limitations of their systems is the collaborative restriction on detailed CAD design but less on PSS. Although these systems tend to support some form of distant collaboration, they lack the ability to integrate various contributions from both humans and products that can expand the IPSS life cycle analysis involving multi-functional teams.

Context Sensitivity: With recent advances in context-aware computing, an increasing demand for formal context modelling and reasoning techniques arises. To enable the development of context-aware applications in first step a well-designed Context Model (CM) is necessary. As context merges different sources of knowledge and associates knowledge to a user to guarantee a consistent understanding, context modelling is extensively studied within research of Knowledge Management. Research related to context can be categorized in two areas: (1st) proactive context-based delivery of knowledge, and (2nd) capturing and utilization of contextual knowledge. CMs enable the understanding of user's activities in relation to situational conditions for applications. Traditional techniques for context modelling include object oriented and key-value models, as well as ontological methods [17]. Ontologies as base for the modelling of context is the most suitable approach for realizing context sensitive IPSS; context reasoning and context provisioning are some of the main topics for context extraction: how to inference high-level context information from low-level raw context data [18, 19]. Using context awareness in IPSS has not yet researched in a sufficient magnitude. In the case of IPSS the notion of context is related to capabilities of the equipment, process preferences of products and process features of devices and also environmental conditions. In this case the modelling of context shows a further challenge, as IPSS solutions are highly dynamic and working in environments which are distributed and often in a continuous change.

3 Vision of an IPSS Collaborative Environment

As the development of IPSS around products with CPS features requires involvement of all stakeholders from the whole value chain, there is a need for building innovative Collaborative Networks where collaboration paths can be extremely complex. The main idea of the research presented in this paper is to build Collaborative Networks, where besides human stakeholders, IPSS can be actively involved and where IPSS are able to actively provide information on use in real-time and conditions under which the products and services are used. By this, they actively support building new IPSS or extending/re-development existing ones.

Such human-product Collaborative Networks require an ICT Environment to support effective and collaborative development of IPSS as shown in Fig. 1. The Environment includes a range of engineering tools covering various life cycle phases of the IPSS development process starting from idea generation and conceptual phase up to the deployment and re-design phases based on the feedback obtained from customers and consumers [20]. The tools that may be included are e.g. simulation tool to simulate/predict the behavior on new IPSS and by this investigate different design options, Product Data Management/Product Lifecycle Management (PDM/PLM) tools for IPSS (i.e. IPSSDM/IPSSLM) which may in real time monitor the configuration of IPSS and allow for real-time reconfigurations of IPSS [21], tools for idea generation, tools for engineering of data mining algorithms for various services etc. These tools allow for collaborative work of various human stakeholders in the network such as product designer, manufacturing process designer and shop floor leaders, service designer and providers, marketing experts, component designer from various suppliers (both hardware and software components), management from all stakeholders, as well as business customers, consumers etc. The main innovative characteristics of these tools are that they allow for active participation of the IPSS themselves. In many of these tools, IPSS actively provide data needed for the engineering tasks covered by the tools. The key rational behind the environment is that the IPSS may provide the inputs needed for the engineering tasks based on the requests from human actors involved in the development of IPSS. Furthermore, IPSS may pro-actively provide inputs whenever they observe that the engineering is dealing with tasks for which the IPSS products may provide additional data/knowledge.

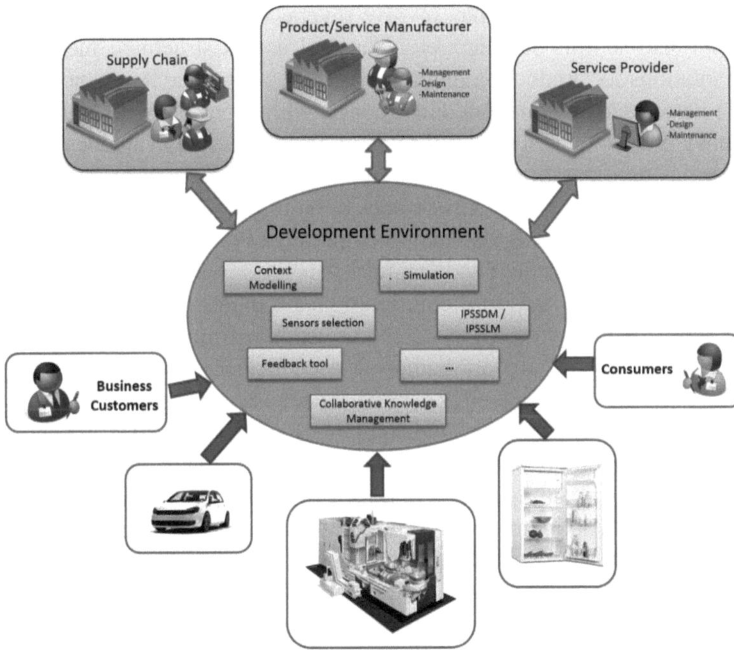

Fig. 1. Development environment for IPSS human-product collaborative network

4 Tools to Support Human-Product Collaborative Development

As indicated at Fig. 1, the Development Environment may include diverse engineering tools. In the text to follow three tools typical for human-product collaboration in the Network, are briefly described. The key approach to integrate information flowing from various sources (IPSS products, human actors, different systems in supply chain, etc.) is semantical enrichment of all data using the agreed ontology for IPSS. This allows to effectively correlate data/knowledge from various sources. The visual analytics approach is planned to be applied for delivery of such integrated knowledge to various actors in the environment.

4.1 Tool to Select Sensors and Intelligent Features

The objective of this engineering tool is to support the design/development of IPSS by allowing a selection of sensors and diverse intelligent features, or propose to the designer which sensorial and smart feature/technology could be used in the product to allow for building of IPSS and which information on the designed product one could obtain from such smart systems/sensors. The sensors and intelligent features integrated in IPSS are sources of information which can be effectively (re-)used to build various services and/ or new intelligent features. The tool offers to the designing team the list of sensors/ features which are currently available at the product and which may be used for building diverse services. The selection may involve several stakeholders: product and service designer but also sensors suppliers etc. The tool uses a structured methodology for sensorial solutions for production industry based on a so-called Ambience Intelligence solutions reference model integrated in products with cyber-physical features [22].

IPSS may provide in real time information on sensors and available smart features used in various configurations of the products and services and by this supports the designer to select the most appropriate ones to build new IPSS or extend the existing IPSS with the new services. It also may provide sets of data obtained by these sensors allowing to design new services and features.

The tool and method support the designing team in designing/selecting of sensors and other kinds of measurement systems and extended monitoring and services for decision support, may also support to improve eco efficiency during life cycle operation and product manufacturing, as well as to provide useful knowledge to enhance the design of processes and products in an ecological point of view. One critical RTD issue is for example, how to select the mentioned measurement systems or sensors with potential information on ecological impact relevant for (further) design of a product and which potentially support an optimum for eco-impact in life cycle operation and manufacturing of a product. The tool proposes to the designer which sensorial system/technology could be used in the product under design and which information on ecological impact of the designed product one could obtain from such sensorial systems.

4.2 Tool to Model Context of IPSS Use

IPSS offer to users' diverse opportunities to use products and services aiming to adjust both product and services to the specific customers' needs and specific conditions under which a user is using IPSS. In other words, the use of IPSS is context sensitive, i.e. the IPSS adjust its offer to the specific current context of the user. On the other hand, sensors integrated in IPSS provide information usable to extract context under which the products and services are currently used and by this allow for making IPSS context sensitive. Context sensitivity requires a definition of context model (CM). One of the tools in the IPSS Development Environment enables the user to model the context of the user and use of IPSS.

In most cases, the user uses this tool in a combination with the Sensors Selection tool, starting by selecting the sensors/signals (signals related to the Products) and using the Context Modelling tool to add signals to identify the user behavior and needs and user environment. In order to be able to extract the context of IPSS use, CM has to be created using the context modelling tool. The full description of context of an IPPS use is not provided by a CM, but the indexing of context to support the identification of the current context. Essentially, CM defines three models: generic, sector-specific and company specific CM. All three CMs exist to model the knowledge by the use of context (including information of user, product, resource, activity, goal, etc.).

As shown in Fig. 2, the tool is a web based application for defining context models (ontologies). The free software solution Protégé is applied. The tool allows to define/select concepts which will be included in CM as well as their mutual relations. The tool allows for an effective maintenance of CM.

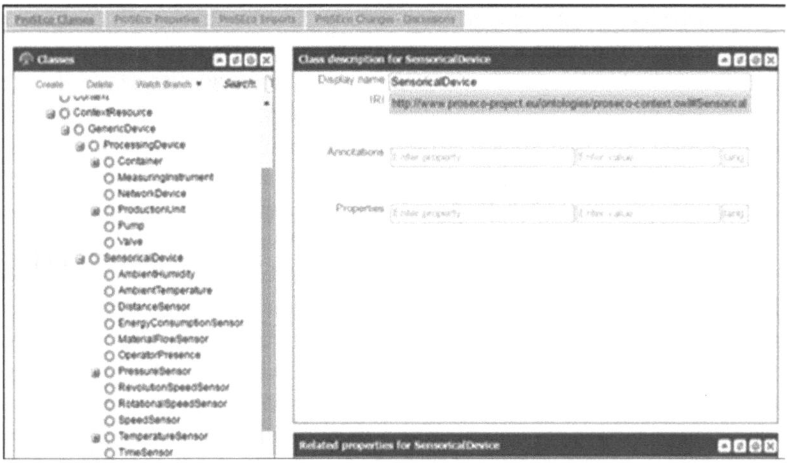

Fig. 2. Context modelling tool

Once the model is defined and deployed in IPSS environment, it can be updated based on the feedback on IPSS use. IPSS provide, based on sensorial system, information on CM use: e.g., by detecting how the user accepts the product and/or services under different context, one may conclude whether the context models is appropriate or has to be updated. Therefore, IPSS may actively provide inputs on CM use and by this contribute to definition of new CMs (for new IPSS) or to update of the already deployed models.

4.3 Feedback Tool

The tool includes three basic functionalities: (1) feedback from business customers, (2) feedback from consumers, (3) feedback provided by the IPSS themselves.

1. The customers of many IPSS are business organizations: e.g. machine industry normally sells their IPSS to various manufactures with whom they build various business partnerships. From such customers the companies get either direct feedback (e.g. on problems with the products, etc.) or get feedback about various joint activities. In the proposed tool, the feedback from business customers is captured via social software which serves as a platform for cooperation of the manufacturers, service providers and their business customers. As IPSS have to exhibit very high flexibility and require multidisciplinary expertise, experience in using and building services.

Collecting feedback is a very difficult task, when using classical PDM/PLM solutions. Social software such as Wikis etc. allows for very flexible capturing and presentation of knowledge/experience of different actors and provision of feedback from the business customers. Social software, however, often suffers from missing structures limiting reuse of these experiences and feedback. These solutions allow non-IT experts to provide their experience/feedback in any form it fits them. For example, problems in manufacturing of parts or assembly can be documented by the shop floor in a form which best suits specific manufacturing line/machine (each group can define its own 'form'). The feedback from customers on the IPSS use can be also provided in any form which suits specific customer and/or service experts.

2. Social media networks allow the gathering off feedback in very "free" form. Feedback is thereby often indirectly expressed by opinions/experiences of consumers. The tool analyses such feedback from social media networks, such as LinkedIn, Facebook, Twitter, Pinterest, Instagram, etc., by applying various data mining algorithms, and provides it in the form re-usable by the actors.
3. As explained above, IPSS can directly provide feedback on their use as well as other information which can be used for (re-) development of IPSS. For example, IPSS may provide feedback serving for continuous ecological impact improvement (including monitoring of ecological impact patterns using sensors based information). Feedback could also be used for "eco-optimal condition based maintenance" of products (including e.g. setting observers to predict possible negative ecological impact patterns etc.), or design recommendations based on "eco-knowledge" as feedback for continuous "eco-improvement" of the products itself, in a form of so-called feedback or monitoring services integrated in IPSS. In order to have an accurate measure and monitoring mechanism to gather feedback from IPSS e.g., on the environmental impact, the tool for the selection of sensors, as explained above, supports the definition of appropriate sensors on the products. Special attention is e.g., paid to monitoring the resources (energy and water) consumption during the use stages. This ensures a critical component performance to optimize IPSS operation and improving sustainability by extending product life.

   One of the most critical questions is how the monitoring services identify feedback patterns within use and provide design recommendations in appropriate form that can be effectively used in the future design. The tool applies a method (under development) for modelling such feedback patterns, which is continuously improved based on self-learning approach using measurement data and data obtained from the selected sensors. As self-learning approach genetic algorithms, Reinforcement Learning methods (adequate to support adaptation based on experience) or Supervised Learning techniques (require a set of training samples to start with) are under consideration [23]. In this way, the selected sensors are embedded within the product during the use in order to collect the required data and feed them back to the Development Environment. In addition, the tool includes the mechanisms to capture the behavior of the users to provide a feedback loop to the Environment to provide the Network with the ability to conceive and understand the needs of the market to provide solutions to these unexpressed new requirements and evolving needs. The data mining algorithms are under consideration to capture the behaviors of the users and by this provide feedback to the Development Environment in a form which can be effectively used by various actors in the Collaborative Network. It is assumed that IPSS may provide such feedback proactively: whenever the Network starts to deal with the services and products which are same or 'similar' the IPSS may 'offer' the available data/knowledge to the Network.

5 Potential Applications

Machine industry is the most typical sector in a need for new methods and tools for development of innovative IPSS, as machines are the most typical products with cyber physical features and this industrial sector is rapidly turning from solely manufacturing to servitisation. The manufacturing companies in the machine sector, producing machines and equipment for various sector, to be delivered to the global market require new solutions for effective collaboration and knowledge exchange among various stakeholders within IPSS Collaboration Networks. For such companies the design of IPSS is even a more complex process than for mass product manufacturers. Manufacturing companies are today facing a new paradigm, called "Mass Customization". This new paradigm intends to move from classical production to production of highly customized products in large numbers. Companies can interact with customers, following different approaches, to determine the features of a product/service that they really need or firms can produce a standardized product that will be customizable by consumers. One of the most distinctive features to achieve mass customization is to provide customizer the ability to involve customer in the design of products and services. However, to meet requirements of mass customization, the manufacturers of machines for production of mass customized products need feedback from their business customers to whom they sell their equipment as well as from the final-product users/consumers. For example, the German company producing machines for shoe industry, involved in the research on IPSS development environment, needs to combine feedback from their business partners (shoe manufacturers) and feedback from the shoe buyers in order to improve their machines and various services around machines and allow for mass customization of shoes, which is one of the key requirement in today's global shoe market [24].

This company aims at both products performance/usability improvements as well as a reduction of the lifecycle CO2 footprint of new/enhanced machines-services within IPSS. They intend also to use the services (e.g., remote diagnostics and predictive maintenance) to automatically collect the overall equipment efficiency of their machines, used at their customers. Goal is thereby enhancement of the design of the machines and services. On the other hand, in order to improve the design of the machines and reduce CO2 footprint in manufacturing of machines, they feedback along the whole machine life-cycle (from design to machine usage). Their machines have cyber physical features and a number of services collect high volume of data on the machines usage, which allow to establish direct feedback from the IPSS to the Development Environment.

Besides data which is collected by automatic measuring overall equipment efficiency (hardware and software), especially the knowledge of people involved in these processes is of key importance. For example, the knowledge of service teams as well as business customers (shoe manufacturers), which are distributed all over the world (mostly Far East, South America etc.) is of key interest. In order to allow the people involved in these value chain, taking into account diverse aspects, such as cultural differences, education level of operators and highly variable machine usage conditions, they need a support system allowing for easy documentation of actors experience. Therefore, they intend to build a unique system where machines and services are delivering automatically feedback over the tools described in Sect. 4 and knowledge/experience from both machine designers, process designers, shop-floor experts and customers from different world regions. The feedback is collected and structured to be re-used for optimization of IPSS design. However, as explained above, in order to cope of mass customization requirements in shoe market, and upgrade their machines and services to achieve flexibility required by such approach (but in the same time reducing prices of machines, assuring their reliability), the company needs to obtain feedback from 'shoe consumer'. This will allow for better identification of mid-term customization requirements of consumers in different parts of the world. To achieve the upcoming trend for consumer driven customization, they intend to build shops (both physical and internet based) where the consumers may design/customize their own shoes and by this implicitly and automatically provide knowledge on their needs. Therefore, feedback from own manufacturing, business customers and shoe consumers will be collected in real time and provided to machine and service designers within the new Development Environment. On mid-term, it is expected that also the final products (shoes) will include sensors and cyber physical features which may be used to gather feedback to the Environment.

The company is currently testing several services built within the new IPSS Development Environment and using the tools described in Sects. 3 and 4, and investigate the feedback from the machines in order to establish continuous improvement of IPSS and especially address environmental aspects. The senor data as a feedback from machines is automatically flowing in the environment and used to identify potentials for improvements. The feedback from the business customers is obtained over wiki and semantically enriched to be correlated with the products knowledge. Based on the current testing by this company, as well as by several other companies involved in the research, it is expected that the environment and tools will allow for a reduction of time and efforts needed for development/update of IPSS by 25–35 %, and allow for an increase in number of innovative personalized services by more than 40 %. It is expected that the proposed solution will contribute to reduction of time to market of IPSS for products with cyber physical features by at least 10 %.

6 Conclusions

The paper introduces the new concept of Intelligent PSS (IPSS), i.e., PSS developed around products with cyber physical features. The research presented in this paper is one of the first attempts to establish the Development Environment and set of tools for human – product cooperation on the development of IPSS. The three tools presented are typical examples of novel engineering functionalities needed for the development of IPSS, which allow for effective collaboration among various stakeholders in the IPSS values chains and IPSS themselves. Such tools, together with a set of other tools for engineering of IPSS, may facilitate building of new forms of Collaborative Networks within which humans and products may effectively collaborate on (re-)development of IPSS.

The Development Environment and the tools are currently under development and they are tested by several companies both in machine industry (as presented in Sect. 5) and by several mass product manufacturers (automotive and home appliance industries). The current version of the Environment and of the tools is limited to active provision of data/knowledge by IPSS. This means that the Collaborative Environment and the tools "inform" IPSS distributed over the world that a new IPSS is under development and IPSS then may provide appropriate knowledge. Future research it will be investigated how IPSS may more proactively take part in the development process: e.g., they may initiate re-development of certain services or components. For example, based on the identification of the needs of the customers, new services to improve the use of the product may be proposed etc.

The benefits of the proposed concept and tools are expected in terms of more effective building of intelligent product-services which better fit to the users' needs.

Acknowledgment. This work is partly supported by the PROSECO (Collaborative Environment for Eco-Design of Product-Services and Production Processes Integrating Highly Personalized Innovative Functions) project of European Union's 7th Framework Program, under the grant agreement no. NMP2-2013-609143 and DIVERSITY (Cloud Manufacturing and Social Software Based Context Sensitive Product-Service Engineering Environment for Globally Distributed Enterprise) project of EU's H2020 framework, under the grant agreement no. 636692. This document does not represent the opinion of the European Community, and the Community is not responsible for any use that might be made of its content.

References

1. Schwab, K.: The Fourth Industrial Revolution: World Economic Forum (2016)
2. Nagorny, K., Scholze, S., Barata, J., Colombo, A.W.: An approach for implementing ISA 95-compliant big data observation, analysis and diagnosis features in industry 4.0 vision following manufacturing systems. In: Camarinha-Matos, L.M., Falcão, A.J., Vafaei, N., Najdi, S. (eds.) DoCEIS 2016. IFIP AICT, vol. 470, pp. 116–123. Springer, Heidelberg (2016). doi:10.1007/978-3-319-31165-4_12
3. Hermann, M., Pentek, T., Otto, B.: Design principles for Industrie 4.0 scenarios: a literature review. Technische Universität Dortmund, Dortmund (2015)
4. Jasperneite, J.: Was hinter Begriffen wie Industrie 4.0 steckt 19 December 2012. https://tinyurl.com/jubuvjh. Accessed 11 Mar 2016
5. Kagermann, H., Helbig, J., Hellinger, A., Wahlster, W.: Recommendations for implementing the strategic initiative Industrie 4.0: securing the future of German manufacturing industry. Final Report of the Industrie 4.0 Working Group: Forschungsunion (2013)
6. Wermann, N.K., Colombo, A.W., Moraes, E.C.: Impact of new ICT trends for the educational curriculum in the area of Industrial Automation and engineering. In: 41st IEEE Annual Conference on the Industrial Electronics Society, IECON 2015 (2015)

7. Colombo, A.W., Bangemann, T., Karnouskos, S., Delsing, J., Stluka, P., Harrison, R., Jammes, F., Lastra, M.: Industrial Cloud-Based Cyber-Physical Systems: The IMC-AESOP Approach. Springer, Heidelberg (2014)
8. Sundmaeker, H., Guillemin, P., Friess, P., Woelfflé, S.: Vision and Challenges for Realising the Internet of Things. European Commission, London (2010)
9. Marron, P.J., Karnouskos, S., Minder, D., Ollero, A.: The Emerging Domain of Cooperating Objects. Springer, Heidelberg (2011)
10. Road2CPS project: http://www.road2cps.eu
11. Colombo, A.W., Karnouskos, S., Bangemann, T.: A system of systems view on collaborative industrial automation. In: IEEE International Conference on Industrial Technology (ICIT 2013), Cape Town, South Africa, 25–27 February 2013
12. Pezzotta, G., et al.: A service engineering framework to design and assess an integrated product-service. Mechatronics **31**, 169–179 (2015)
13. Chesbrough, H.: Open Business Models. Harvard Business School press, Boston (2006)
14. Thoben, K.-D., Jagdev, H., Eschenbaecher, J.: Emerging concepts in E-business and extended products. In: Gasos, J., Thoben, K.-D. (eds.) E-business Applications - Technologies For Tomorrow's Solutions. Advanced Information Processing Series, pp. 17–37. Springer, Heidelberg (2003)
15. Camarinha-Matos, L., Juan-Verdejo, A., Alexakis, S., Bär, H., Surajbal, B.: Cloud-based collaboration spaces for enterprise networks. In: Proceedings of ICCCT 2015 - IEEE International Conference on Computing and Communications Technologies, pp. 185–190, 26–27 February 2015, Chennai, India (2015)
16. Camarinha-Matos, L.M., Oliveira, A.I., Ferrada, F.: Supporting collaborative networks for complex service-enhanced products. In: Camarinha-Matos, L.M., et al. (eds.) PRO-VE 2015. IFIP AICT, vol. 463, pp. 181–192. Springer, Heidelberg (2015). doi:10.1007/978-3-319-24141-8_16
17. Strang, T., Linnhoff-Popien, C.: A context modeling survey. In: Workshop on Advanced Context Modelling, Reasoning and Management as Part of the Conference on Ubiquitous Computing - The 6th International Conference on Ubiquitous Computing, Nottingham (2004)
18. Stokic, D., Scholze, S., Kotte, O.: Generic self-learning context sensitive solution for adaptive manufacturing and decision making systems. In: ICONS 2014, Nice (2014)
19. Scholze, S., Barata, J.: Context awareness for flexible manufacturing systems using cyber physical approaches. In: Camarinha-Matos, L.M., J. Falcão, A., Vafaei, N., Najdi, S. (eds.) DoCEIS 2016. IFIP AICT, vol. 470, pp. 107–115. Springer, Heidelberg (2016). doi: 10.1007/978-3-319-31165-4_11
20. Di Orio, J., Matei, O., Scholze, S., Stokic, D., Barata, J., Cenedese, C.: A platform to support the product servitization. (IJACSA) Int. J. Adv. Comput. Sci. Appl. **7**(2), 20 (2016)
21. Müller, P., Kickstein, J., Gregorzik, S., Goppelt, F., Tracing requirements in PLM environments from use cases to design verification tasks. In: 7th Grazer Symposium Virtuelles Fahrzeug, May 2014, Graz, Austria (2014)
22. Stokic, D., Kirchhoff, U., Sundmaeker, H.: Ambient intelligence in manufacturing industry: control system point of view. In: The 8th IASTED Conference on Control and Applications CA 2006, Montreal, Australia (2006)
23. Scholze, S., Stokic, D., Kotte, O., Cândido, G.: Reliable self-learning production systems based on context aware services. In: 2013 IEEE International Conference on Systems, Man, and Cybernetics (SMC), Manchester, UK (2013)
24. Stokic, D., Scholze, S., Decker, C., Stöbener, K.: Engineering methods and tools for collaborative development of industrial cyber-physical based products and services. In: 12th IEE Conference on Industrial Informatics, 27–30 July 2014, Porto Alegre, Brazil (2014)

A Novel Hybrid Engineering Methodology to Enhance Collaboration During the Design and Development of Meta Product Services

Shamaila Iram(✉), Terrence Fernando, and May Bassanino

School of the Built Environment, THINKlab, University of Salford, Greater Manchester, UK
{S.Iram,T.Fernando,M.N.Bassanino}@salford.ac.uk

Abstract. Since the Product-Service System (PSS) is accompanied by a paradigm shift towards the sustainability of the production process, it demands an advanced level of collaboration throughout the design and development process. This poses new challenges to enhance collaboration among cross-sectional, multi-disciplinary design teams in order to incorporate a variety of interdisciplinary services in a complex service-oriented system. Therefore, a new collaboration methodology is needed to reduce barriers to collaboration in a cross- organizational structure domain. This research work aims at highlighting the collaboration challenges that Meta-Product design teams face and also proposes a novel methodology to enhance collaboration among multi-disciplinary teams. The proposed methodology is a hybrid engineering model designed by integrating an Information Delivery Manual approach with a traditional software development process along with three interlinked collaboration services.

Keywords: Meta products · Product Extension Services · Product-Service Systems (PSS) · Information Delivery Manual (IDM) · Business Process Model Notation (BPMN) · Collaboration

1 Introduction

The need to adopt sustainable and environmentally-oriented production and consumption processes led to the idea of transferring the physical products to digital platforms, or to intelligent products and services, called "Meta Products" and "Meta Services" respectively. Essamlali *et al.* [1] and Rubino and Hazenbergy [2] defined the concept of Meta Products as "*dedicated networks of four elements: services, products, people, and environments*". Alongside Meta Products, the Product-Service System (PSS) has recently emerged as a competitive, added value strategy to impel manufacturers to offer a set of products and services as a whole [3], called Product Extension Services (PES). These services offer to achieve sustainable growth by providing high value service solutions based on the product, such as product maintenance, support, repair, energy management, upgrading and recycling [4].

The complexity and diversity of the PES design and development process, however, demand the integration of diverse skill sets and a wider span of expertise in

H. Afsarmanesh et al. (Eds.): PRO-VE 2016, IFIP AICT 480, pp. 385–393, 2016.
DOI: 10.1007/978-3-319-45390-3_33

product design teams. This requirement is by no means surprising since strong collaboration among team members, in the end, defines the quality of PES. The production of large and complex systems usually requires coordination and collaboration among many individuals including designers, developers, marketing staff, standards' experts and customer representatives. Often, these individuals are spread among the numerous divisions of a corporation or amongst different sectors. Collaboration among these actors is extremely crucial in order to synchronize various system development activities. Therefore, collaboration among multidisciplinary teams is recognized as one of the challenges in creating complex product extended services.

In the same line of thinking, Rubino *and* Hazenbergy [2] highlighted "*connection among stakeholders*" as a critical challenge to the exchange of information among potential stakeholders. Similarly, researchers from different domains [1, 5, 6] articulate that due to the involvement of multidisciplinary design teams in creating complex products, an advanced level of collaboration is required to incorporate a variety of diverse services to accelerate the product development process.

Therefore, in order to enhance and promote collaboration in the design and development of complex product services, this paper proposes a novel collaboration methodology with integrated advanced communication services to facilitate the effective exchange of information across all domains.

2 Literature Review

Recent research work, underpinning the concept of complex Meta Products or Meta Services, highlights *collaboration* as a main challenge in the enhancement of coordination among multi-disciplinary teams [5]. Lots of methods and infrastructural technologies have been developed and applied to support system integration and collaboration for Collaborative Product Development (CPD). For instance, Szykman *et al.* [7] proposed a product model to make design information accessible to users in a Web-based system. Similarly, Kim *et al.* [8] developed an ontology-based assembly design method that aims to make heterogeneous modelling terms semantically processed both by design collaborators and intelligent systems. Moreover, Chu *et al.* [9] implemented a 3D design environment where information with different levels of detail is transferred to different design engineers.

In addition, various examples of frameworks have also been proposed, such as the Multi-disciplinary Collaboration Simulation Optimization Platform for complex product design [10], the Multi-domain Collaboration Model [11] and Complex Product Development based on Concurrent Engineering [12]. However, what is still missing from the literature is the mapping of tools and actors to their corresponding design phases in the complete workflow process, the integration of advanced collaboration services (such as communication, cooperation and coordination in one development platform) and, finally, the integration of process, information, organization and technology in one comprehensive collaborative portal to support complete Meta product development ecosystems.

The work presented in this paper provides a new approach to overcome the barriers to communication and leverage the enhancement of collaboration between different domain experts by continuously exchanging the ideas at each stage of the development process. It also offers an opportunity for the industrial partners to continuously engage with the production process, to frequently discuss the achievements and milestones, regularly monitor the current status of the development process and eventually, approve the final product.

3 Research Approach

The work that is presented in this paper conducted as part of EU research project, ProSEco. The objective of the research is to provide a novel methodology and a set of ICT solutions for collaborative design of cyber-physical based product-services. Collaboration among multi-functional teams is identified as one of the main issues towards the design and development of complex products and services, such as, Cyber-Physical Systems (CPS), Product Service Systems (PSS), and Product Extension Services (PES). This section articulates the steps that have been followed to propose a solution to solve collaboration issues in the design and development of PES. Since, this study is directly related to the industrial partners who are the key stakeholders of the project; the starting point for this research is the analysis of real industrial cases than theoretical study. However, to relate the work with the existing knowledge, the authors conducted search in relevant academic databases to find peer reviewed papers in the area of PES, collaboration, collaborative process, and barriers to collaboration in the design and development of PES. In the course of finding relevant material they studied available collaboration models, commercial as well EU projects, tools and platforms available in the market with the aim of capturing state of the practice solutions that claim to enhance collaboration for PES design process.

At more advance level of research, face-to-face meetings have been arranged with industrial partners who are involved in this project as well as research and development (RTD) teams to capture basic requirements of the collaborative PES development platform. The purpose of the meetings was to capture those collaboration issues that were not anticipated before and also to discuss the best possible solutions to overcome the collaboration barriers.

Later, in order to propose a new collaboration model, the authors studied the traditional Software Development Life Cycle (SDLC) methods, Agile framework, and Information Delivery Manual (IDM) approach together with Business Process Modelling Notations (BPMN). The initial prototype of the framework is designed, developed and agreed among the team member at this stage of the project. However, further, improvements are expected along the progress of the project when more advance level of requirements will be identified.

4 Collaboration Services

Collaboration services were identified in the CoSpaces project [13] as three distinctive yet interlinked services required within a collaboration service platform. These services are: communication services, coordination services and co-operation services. These services form an important part within the PES collaborative development portal.

4.1 Communication Services

Communication is an important attribute to define the quality of team work which is highly dependent on information exchange, knowledge acquisition and knowledge representation. Communication helps to get deep understanding of the evolving ideas, to discuss the complicated issues, to develop new solution and at the end to approve results.

In this context, as part of the communication services, the proposed PES collaboration methodology provides advance integrated communication tools that help users to develop a mutual understanding of the project. The proposed collaboration methodology facilitates all different modes of collaboration such as, co-located/synchronous (same place, same time), distributed/synchronous (different places, same time), co-located/asynchronous (same place, different time) and distributes/asynchronous (different places, different time). The communication services that are provided in the proposed collaboration methodology are; audio/video conference tool, brain storming session through eco-observation wall, and project management through Oobeya tool as presented in Fig. 1.

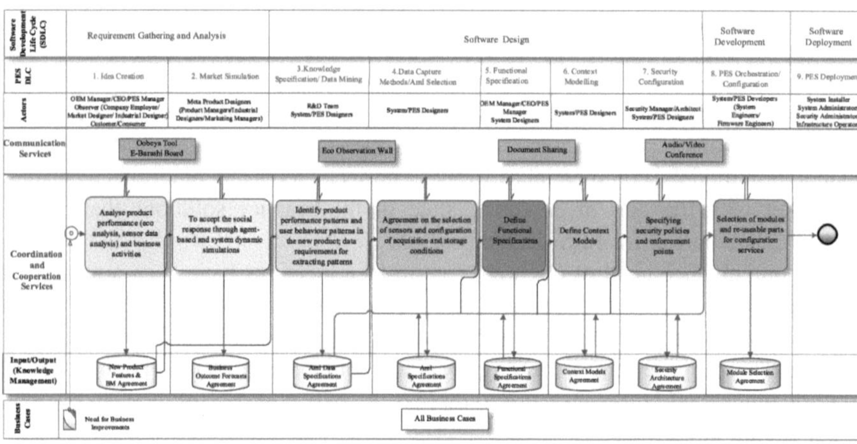

Fig. 1. The PES collaborative development portal

4.2 Coordination Services

Coordination is defined as exchanging information and altering process activities for mutual benefit and for a common purpose [14]. Coordination builds on networking (the exchange of data/information) by adding behaviour, and modifying activities and foci, bringing forward mutual benefits and a common purpose. Coordination increases the efficient use of resources and the ability to meet community needs.

The proposed collaboration methodology provides coordination services through integrated workflow engine. Assigning roles to the corresponding users who are responsible to initiate and complete the workflow activities are part of workflow services. Workflow services are designed to configure and customize PES workflow process. This also helps to trace the current status of the ongoing development process.

Furthermore, workflow services also control events by notifying the development team about the current status of the process or the actions that need to be taken to accomplish a task. Step-by-step workflow activities that are needed to develop a complete PES are illustrated in Fig. 1.

4.3 Cooperation Services

Interaction among all the participants, who may belong to different sectors or different functional groups, to achieve a common task defines cooperation services. Cooperation services in the proposed methodology will be provided in terms of:

- Managing actors according to their roles, and
- Managing activities corresponding to each engineering tool

The proposed collaboration methodology is designed to manage all the users according to their roles and it also ensures the seamless integration of all the engineering tools into the portal to provide comprehensive support for the design and development of PES solutions.

The cooperation services encapsulate the engineering tools' services, the sharing of data between tools and also the brain-storming services where ideas raised by participants can be discussed.

Figure 1 demonstrates a comprehensive PES Collaborative Development Portal with an integrated proposed collaboration methodology that facilitates the design and development of a sustainable PES solution for industrial sectors.

5 Modelling PES Collaboration Environment

This proposed collaboration methodology (designed by the integration of the IDM approach and traditional software development methods) presents a process model which details the steps, milestones and phase dependencies where several functionalities are integrated corresponding to a particular phase of the ongoing PES development process.

The PES Development Life Cycle (PESDLC), described in this paper, is tailored to the traditional standard Software Development Life Cycle (SDLC) approach which starts from requirement gathering to software deployment. A traditional software development life cycle (Waterfall [15], Spiral [16], Agile software development [17], rapid prototyping [18], incremental [19], and synchronize and stabilize) is composed of a number of clearly defined and distinct workflow phases which are applied by system developers to plan, design, develop and deploy software systems.

However, due to the complex service-oriented nature of the project and also to incorporate a variety of services in terms of knowledge management, context modelling, intelligent data analysis, security enhancement etc., it has not been not possible to follow the exact sequence of a traditional software development life cycle (SDLC). Also, to keep the software applicability traits aligned with the business orientation, where a number of actors/participants will be involved from different organizations/

backgrounds, it has been decided to follow an interdisciplinary approach. This approach combines the IDM methodology with the traditional software life cycle approach to provide a mutual understanding of the model in all sectors.

Information Delivery Manual (IDM) Methodology. The Information Delivery Manual (IDM) methodology specifies the process and the actors that are involved in creating, consuming and benefitting from the information as well as what information is created, exchanged and consumed [1]. It intends to help software vendors to cope better with the specified individual process-related information requirements of the clients [15, 16].

While creating a PES, the exchange of requirements defines exactly which artefacts are created during which activities, who (actor) is responsible for the tasks, and what the consuming activities are. So, the IDM methodology, in the case of PES development modelling, will help to reduce the communication gap among PES solution providers and the business partners and allow them to exchange information smoothly and flawlessly.

The IDM methodology is deployed by using a standard notation called Business Process Model and Notation (BPMN).

Business Process Model and Notation (BPMN). The Business Process Model and Notation (BPMN) is a standard for expressing process maps which are flow-oriented representations of business operations. This provides a common tool and method for process modelling and mapping. BPMN aims to bridge the communication gap that frequently occurs between business process design and implementation [17]. BPMN models are mainly used to facilitate information exchange and communication between project participants to support decision-making based on various analysis techniques and to provide input to software development projects. Furthermore, the BPMN models are also used to specify the information nuggets being shared or exchanged in the process map; subsequently, it would be possible to identify the required software features in the systems' development effort [18].

Software Development Life Cycle (SDLC). At a higher hierarchical level, the main stages of the software development life cycle (SDLC) are: Requirement Gathering and Analysis, Software Design, Software Development, Software Deployment/Impleme ntation and Software Testing and Maintenance. However, due to the complexity of the PES design and development process, these traditional phases of the model are tailored and mapped to the phases of the PES development process as shown in Fig. 1. Since, the informal testing of the software development will be carried out, in a collaborative session, at the end of each phase of the PES development life cycle; therefore, testing and maintenance phase of the traditional software development life cycle is not included explicitly as a separate phase in the PES development life cycle.

Comparing to the traditional software development life cycle phases, PES development phases are more advanced and complicated. This implies that design and development phases, in the PES development life cycle, are further divided into sub-phases due to the nature of the functionalities required to create a PES. However, these phases are tailored and mapped to traditional SDLC phases to keep the software development traits similar to the traditional development life cycles, as demonstrated in Fig. 1.

PESDLC constitutes of following stages:

- **Idea Creation:** this phase helps to analyse the existing products to find the hot-spots, to realize the problem, to propose new ideas, and finally to conceptualize new business model.
- **Market Simulation:** this phase is to simulate the importance of proposed solution against its market value.
- **Knowledge Specification/Data Mining:** this phase helps to define new data that is required to be captured in developing the proposed model. This also helps to find the useful patterns to take better future decisions.
- **Data Capture Method/AmI Selection:** once datasets are identified in the previous sections, this phase will support to find the corresponding sensors that are needed to capture data.
- **Functional Specifications:** this phase will create the documentation of the specifications of the new products or services.
- **Context Modelling:** This phase helps users to model the context for the product or service using ontologies and ontological reasoning methods.
- **Security Configuration:** this will enforce the security parameters during the design and development of services.
- **PES Orchestration:** this phase helps to specify the sequences of services in which they are going to be deployed.
- **PES Deployment:** at the end of PESDLC, all the services will be executed in the deployment phase.

Other extended attributes of the proposed collaboration methodology are: integrated advanced *engineering tools' services*, potential *users/actors* that are responsible for completing each particular phase of the whole process, and *output visualization* of each service with integrated advanced visualization tools.

As case studies, the proposed collaborative PES development environment with integrated advanced ICT services would serve in different sectors, such as, automotive, home appliances, shoe manufacturing companies and automation equipment to provide effective extensions to their existing products. For instance, in case of automotive company, collaborative PES development environment will be used to improve vehicle's design based on user's behaviour. This will be done by directly analyzing data patterns related to user's behaviour, weather, and pollution level over time and space in a given local and global context. This will help the design teams to discuss the possibility of changing car design that can lead to better driver performance. This can also help to reduced CO2 emissions as well as possible policy change that can enforce positive driver behavior or engine performance configurations and also can reduce pollution levels in the city.

6 Conclusion and Future Work

The proposed collaboration methodology, presented in this paper, acts as a bridge to minimize the communication gap between the technical solution providers and the rest of the stakeholders and allows them to exchange information smoothly and effectively in intelligent products' development ecosystems. The main advantage of the proposed collaborative PES development environment is to provide a comprehensive single platform with seamlessly integrated advance collaborative, engineering and visualization services at one place. It also provides integrated workflow engine based on collaboration design principles to coordinate the concurrent workflow activities. Furthermore, it correlates the workflow activities with its corresponding design and development phase and recognizes the actors who are responsible to accomplish that phase. It provides the opportunity to analyze a designed artefact with one of the integrated visualization tool and discuss the results and future possibilities in a collaborative session to improve it further.

Moreover, depending on the functional capabilities/responsibilities of each particular participant, the overall workflow process shows the dependencies of business partners and technical expertise on each other, making the whole process a "Cross-Organizational Business Process Model". The PES development process does not initiate until an input is received from the business partners wherein they analyse the product requirements with technical team members who, at the end, provide the software solutions. However, one of the limitation of the proposed framework is it requires users to have proper relevant technical skillset to use the platform.

The first prototype of the collaborative PES development portal is achieved. Currently, the initial testing of the first prototype is being carried out in a laboratory environment. For this initial testing, the proposed solution will be tested for its functional capabilities, usability and likeability. Business benefits, however, will be tested in an industrial environment when a complete prototype will be achieved. The proposed solution will be validated using "Goal Question Metric" (GQM) approach [20] together with the "McCall Quality Model" approach [21].

Acknowledgments. The research leading to these results has received funding from the European Union's Seventh Framework Programme (FP7/2007–2013) under Grant Agreement n° 609413. This document does not represent the opinion of the European Community, and the European Community is not responsible for any use that might be made of its contents.

References

1. Essamlali, M.T.E., Sekhari, A., Bouras, A., Santiteerakul, S., Ouzrout, Y.: The methodology for collaborative development of intelligent wearable meta-products. In: 2014 8th International Conference on 2014 Software, Knowledge, Information Management and Applications (SKIMA), pp. 1–8 (2014)
2. Rubino, S., Hazenbergy, W.: Meta Products Meaningful Design for Our Connected World. BIS Publishers, Amsterdam (2011)
3. Geng, X., Chu, X., Xue, D., Zhang, Z.: An integrated approach for rating engineering characteristics' final importance in product-service system development. Comput. Ind. Eng. **59**, 585–594 (2010)
4. Song, W., Wu, Z., Li, X., Xu, Z.: Modularizing product extension services: an approach based on modified service blueprint and fuzzy graph. Comput. Ind. Eng. **85**, 186–195 (2015)

5. Jiaqing, Y., Jianzhong, C., Yiping, L., Nan, L., Shasha, Y.: Meta-service oriented collaborative design platform for complex product. In: 2008 IEEE International Conference on Industrial Engineering and Engineering Management, pp. 629–633 (2008)
6. Büyüközkan, G., Arsenyan, J.: Collaborative product development: a literature overview. Prod. Plann. Control **23**, 47–66 (2012)
7. Szykman, S., Racz, J., Bochenek, C., Sriram, R.D.: A web-based system for design artifact modeling. Des. Stud. **21**, 145–165 (2000)
8. Kim, K.-Y., Manley, D.G., Yang, H.: Ontology-based assembly design and information sharing for collaborative product development. Comput. Aided Des. **38**, 1233–1250 (2006)
9. Chu, C.-H., Wu, P.-H., Hsu, Y.-C.: Multi-agent collaborative 3D design with geometric model at different levels of detail. Robot. Comput.-Integr. Manuf. **25**, 334–347 (2009)
10. Fan, W., Wang, W., Xiao, T.: Multidisciplinary collaboration simulation optimization platform for complex product design. In: 2nd International Conference on Pervasive Computing and Applications, ICPCA 2007, pp. 174–178 (2007)
11. Fan, W., Wang, K., Xiong, G.: Multi-domain collaborative simulation platform: an integrative framework for complex products design. In: 2006 10th International Conference on Computer Supported Cooperative Work in Design 2006, pp. 1–6 (2006)
12. Junjie, X., Xiaolan, J., Zhong, W., Huahui, C.: Research on green design of complex product based on concurrent engineering. In: 2006 7th International Conference on Computer-Aided Industrial Design and Conceptual Design 2006, pp. 1–5 (2006)
13. Patel, H., Pettitt, M., Wilson, J.R.: Factors of collaborative working: a framework for a collaboration model. Appl. Ergo. **43**, 1–26 (2012)
14. Himmelman, A.T.: On coalitions and the transformation of power relations: collaborative betterment and collaborative empowerment. Am. J. Commun. Psychol. **29**, 277–284 (2001)
15. Wix, J., Karlshøj, J.: Information delivery manual guide to components and development methods (2010). http://iug.buildingsmart.org/idms/development/IDMC_004_1_2.pdf. Accessed June 2016
16. Breit, M., Häubi, F., Raps, M., Arnold, N.: Process oriented model based information exchange between architecture and fabrication in early project phases. In: International Conference in Computing in Civil and Building Engineering, p. 156. Nottingham University Press (2010)
17. van der Aalst, W.M.P.: Business process modeling notation. In: Liu, L., ÖZsu, M.T. (eds.) Encyclopedia of Database Systems, pp. 293–294. Springer, Heidelberg (2009)
18. Ouyang, C., Dumas, M., van der Aalst, W.M.P., ter Hofstede, A.H.M.: From business process models to process-oriented software systems. ACM Trans. Softw. Eng. Methodol. **19**, 1–37 (2009)
19. OMG: Business Process Modeling Notation (BPMN) Version 1.0. OMG Final Adopted Specification (2006)
20. Basili, V.R.: Software modeling and measurement: the Goal/Question/Metric paradigm. University of Maryland at College Park, p. 24 (1992)
21. Cavano, J.P., McCall, J.A.: A framework for the measurement of software quality. SIGMETRICS Perform. Eval. Rev. **7**, 133–139 (1978)

Intelligent Product and Mechatronic Software Components Facilitating Mass Customization in Collaborative Manufacturing Systems

Majid Sorouri[1(✉)] and Valeriy Vyatkin[2,3]

[1] Science and Research Branch, Islamic Azad University, Tehran, Iran
majidsorouri@srbiau.ac.ir
[2] Luleå University of Technology, Luleå, Sweden
vyatkin@ieee.org
[3] Aalto University, Helsinki, Finland

Abstract. The intention of this research is to propose a uniform architecture for control software design of collaborative manufacturing systems. It introduces software components known as Modular, Intelligent, and Real-time Agents (MIRAs) that represent both products (C-MIRA) and mechatronic components (O-MIRAs) in a production system. C-MIRAs are in constant interaction with customers and operators through human machine interfaces (HMIs), and are responsible for transforming products from concepts up to full realization of them. It is demonstrated that desired services of a number of machines and mechatronic components can be dynamically allocated to a C-MIRA using a fully decentralized scheduling and operation control. This architecture also envisages the machines' control to be composed of a set of modular software components, with standardized interfaces. This makes them intuitive and easy to install, to create the desired behavior for collaborative manufacturing systems. A simplified food production case study, whose control is synthesized using the proposed approach, is chosen as an illustrative example for the proposed methodology.

Keywords: IEC 61499 · Mass customization · Collaborative production systems

1 Introduction

Mass customization is exceedingly beneficial for both customers and manufacturers, as on the one hand, customers can personalize products according to their preferences. On the other hand, manufacturers can enhance their customer satisfaction, and worry less about relying on marketing predictions and dealing with a large amount of stock. Up to the present day, manufacturing factories have been using fixed production lines; as a result, any change in the plant layout poses significant costs and efforts for adoption of the existing production system into the desired condition. Therefore, with the current need for individual product customization, the achievement of the ability to rapidly design, control and reconfigure manufacturing systems is inevitable, and manufacturing enterprises are continuously striving to address this need by implementing collaborative manufacturing systems.

H. Afsarmanesh et al. (Eds.): PRO-VE 2016, IFIP AICT 480, pp. 394–407, 2016.
DOI: 10.1007/978-3-319-45390-3_34

2 Research Background

In the past two decades various research approaches have promoted the notion of production through collaboration among main role players in manufacturing industries such as a wide range of devices, resources, machines and robots. In this section, a number of recent practices are mentioned.

Merdan et al. [1], look at the possibility of matching a Machine Agent (MA) to each physical component and applying it in a production line where, for instance, each conveyor, diverter and pallet is represented by an agent and transportation of a product will be achieved through collaboration of the agents. Gouyon et al. [2] proposed a product-driven approach in which product plays a pivotal role in manufacturing rationale. This method is mainly based on the collaboration between product controllers and resource controllers, through exchanging requests (by product controllers) and reports (by resource controllers). Simao et al. present a holonic control solution in which causal knowledge is embedded as individual rules in Rule holons. They receive facts from Resource holons and decide on the appropriate actions to be taken. This method also resembles the product-driven approach, in that the Rule holons are in charge of regulating the collaboration between Product holons and Resource holons [3].

A comprehensive review of the previous implementations of collaborative manufacturing systems, along with some of the future challenges ahead of their implementation is provided in [4–7]. Although these methods have overcome many of the industrial concerns such as decentralization of control as well as increasing intelligence and flexibility that are essential for mass customization, due to the inherent complexity of such systems their industrial applications are still very limited.

2.1 The IEC 61499 Standard Facilitating Distributed Control of Production Systems

The IEC 61499 is an open standard for design of distributed control systems [8]. This architecture allows encapsulating intelligence into structured and modularized control logic blocks known as Function Blocks (FB) and distributing them into various control devices. The IEC 61499 FB software architecture is used as an implementation platform for this research and the key features of the proposed approach are: reusability, compatibility and autonomy of modular software components, which require limited dependence on human intervention. The results of this research add design flexibility to collaborative manufacturing systems while minimizing their costs and efforts.

2.2 IMC Concept

The IMC architecture was originally proposed in [9] and then formally defined in [10] to facilitate developing modular and reusable control software for industrial automation systems. The concept of IMC is to encapsulate hardware and software models of mechatronic devices into a single-design artefact. Similar to FB concept, an IMC can be viewed as a black box that is only accessible by its interface [11]. Simple IMCs can be hierarchically composed to form more complex ones. The final automation system is thereby a network of collaborating IMCs. By generalizing the IMC approach, the bottom-up control synthesis of machines, and at a higher level, production systems, becomes conceivable.

3 MIRA Design Approach

MIRA follows the concepts of IMCs along with Intelligent Product Software components (IPSC) and elaborates on three expected characteristics from them, namely *Modularity*, *Intelligence* and *Real-Time* behaviour in a collaborative network. It certainly inherits some of its features from current approaches. However, it enhances the simplicity of the control system design, and makes the solution more engineer/operator friendly. This design approach is applicable to a wide range of production systems, regardless of their size: from a small automated shop which receives its orders directly from customers, to large manufacturing systems, where all the information, regarding production rules and equipment, is provided from the enterprise level. The MIRA approach for control software design of customized production system has been described in [12, 13], and in this paper the collaboration aspect of MIRAs is elaborated.

MIRA considers a trio of main role players in a collaborative manufacturing system: *Human*, *Operator (O)* and *Client (C) MIRA,* and particular tasks are allocated to each of them. MIRAs can either participate individually or as a group in a manufacturing system. Figure 1 shows an example of a bottom-up approach that is applied in a simple food production system.

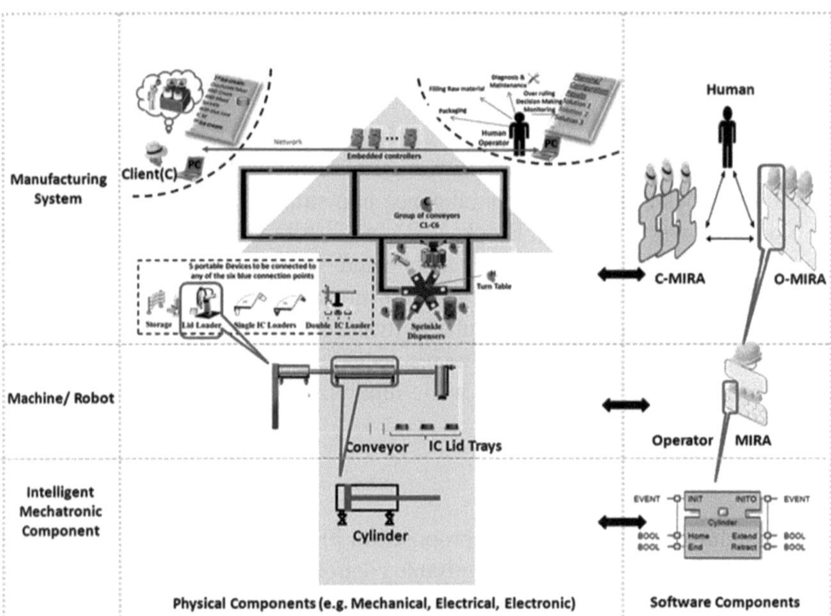

Fig. 1. An example of a bottom-up approach for the design and implementation of a food production system.

3.1 Human

Humans can provide a deeper knowledge of the problem domain that is not already captured by the agents. They adapt the system if problem specifications alter over time [14]. Humans can also play a supervisory role, and, whenever needed, overrule MIRAs' decisions, as they are given a higher priority. In addition to the above roles, a human can act as an operator/technician supporting the system with different activities (i.e. collaboration, maintenance, supplying raw material, and so on).

3.2 O-MIRA

O-MIRA represents a machine/robot in a manufacturing system and consists of one or a group of IMCs in a bottom-up approach. An O-MIRA includes sensors, actuators, software components, controllers and power sources. The layout of a manufacturing plant follows the physical structure of its constituent O-MIRAs. Each O-MIRA it is able to be rapidly plugged into an existing manufacturing system. However, it is vital for every two or more cooperating O-MIRAs to ensure that both their physical and software components are compatible with each other. The compatibility check between two O-MIRAs can be either done manually or determined through their communication and decision-making. O-MIRAs receive tasks from Client MIRAs (described below) and in return, inform them about their availability and task fulfilment. An O-MIRA may be capable of serving several C-MIRAs simultaneously and also can respond to their requests differently based on its operation capacity. For instance, a machine may be available to handle a few C-MIRA requests and send a "Ready" message to them, but as it reaches its operation capacity, it may temporarily reject other requests.

A task that is received by an O-MIRA is normally deconstructed into numerous subtasks and is performed through collaboration with the constituent IMCs. An O-MIRA is also responsible for maintaining human safety according to its predefined vendor specifications. If an O-MIRA is considered hazardous, then sensors to detect human presence, and procedures on safety maintenance, must be provided.

3.3 C-MIRA

C-MIRA is an intelligent product software component that has a thorough knowledge of a product including: raw materials; cost; due date; order quantity; recipe (manufacturing process); machinery that is capable of producing its components, and so forth. C-MIRA receives an order from a customer interface and breaks it down into a sequence of operations. Then it requests those operations from O-MIRAs. When a C-MIRA receives information about the available O-MIRAs, if there is more than one O-MIRA capable of performing a task, then the C-MIRA selects one among others, based on different criteria which are either directly identified by customers or have been received from the enterprise level. Some of the criteria by which O-MIRAs can be distinguished and the manufacturing process can be optimised include: operation cost; transportation distance; operation performance, and bottleneck avoidance. In cases where there are multiple criteria that must be considered for determining the optimum

O-MIRAs, then multi-variable optimization techniques as described in [15] can be applied by a C-MIRA to precisely determine the best solution. After the production is completed, C-MIRA sends a completion report to the customer interface.

Direct communication between C and O-MIRAs is a convenient solution for relatively small manufacturing systems. However, in larger applications, O-MIRAs with similar functionalities can be grouped together and managed by a Coordinator O-MIRAs to minimize the number of interactions among MIRAs. Coordinators can receive requests from C-MIRAs instead of individual O-MIRAs, and manage operations among them.

3.4 Knowledge Representation of MIRAs

The way MIRAs' knowledge is shaped for manufacturing is similar to IMCs and is based on the STEP method [12] as illustrated in Fig. 2.

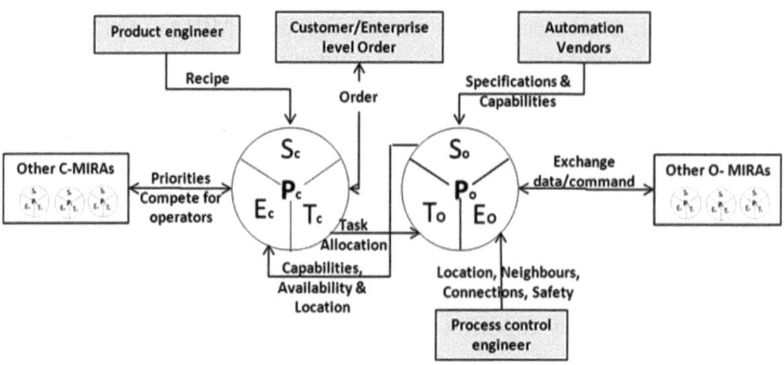

Fig. 2. Knowledge representation of C-MIRA and O-MIRA based on STEP approach in manufacturing systems.

The Knowledge of C-MIRAs and O-MIRAs can be defined as:

P_c: $\{S_c, T_c, E_c\}$ and P_o: $\{S_o, T_o, E_o\}$, where

P_c: C-MIRA's knowledge perception;	P_o: O-MIRA's knowledge perception;
S_c: C-MIRA's self-perception;	S_o: O-MIRA's self-perception;
T_c: C-MIRA's task-perception;	T_o: O-MIRA's task-perception, and
E_c: C-MIRA's environment-perception;	E_o: O-MIRA's environment perception.

S_c is provided to a C-MIRA by product designers who define a detailed specification of the production by an orderly set of operations (or recipe) that a product has to undergo to be produced [2]. T_c consists of the knowledge that specifies which task (order) is to be managed by an O-MIRA. T_c is provided to C-MIRA by the enterprise level or through a customer interface. E_c includes the information that C-MIRAs receive from O-MIRAs regarding their capabilities, availabilities and locations to be able to navigate the physical product through several production stations. Furthermore, a C-MIRA has to negotiate with other C-MIRAs to sort out order priorities. For instance, if a production strategy is on a first-come, first-served basis, the second

C-MIRA has to communicate (i.e. through a Block-Permit approach) with the first O-MIRA to be able to access resources for production.

S_o is an integration of the characteristics and functionalities of the IMCs that construct an O-MIRA. T_o is provided by a C-MIRA and identifies which task an O-MIRA has to perform for an order. Next, the O-MIRAs' constituent IMCs will break it down into detailed tasks to be accomplished in a distributed way. For example, if a "placing work piece" task is assigned to a pick-and-place robot, it creates a set of detailed tasks (for example, extend/retract cylinder and turn vacuum on/off) to be performed by its horizontal and vertical cylinders and vacuum unit. For a Transport O-MIRA, T_o will be the source and destination of the product at each stage, and the constituent conveyors will collaborate to transport the product. During the manufacturing process, if an interruption occurs because of machinery failure, a C-MIRA will allocate the task to the next available O-MIRA. If no alternative O-MIRA is available, the C-MIRA will halt the operation to avoid product waste. E_o includes: O-MIRAs' location; raw materials status; safety (e.g. whether a human is present); the other MIRAs it is collaborating with, and so forth. Some of this information (such as positions) has to be provided manually by the process control engineer because they are specific to a manufacturing environment; others will be gathered through negotiation with other O-MIRAs.

4 A Case Study

To demonstrate MIRAs' collaboration in a manufacturing environment, a simplified case study of an automated and customized Ice Cream Production System (ICPS) is selected for implementation at a laboratory scale, using available equipment in the Industrial Informatics lab at the University of Auckland. The list of raw materials used to make customised ICs includes:

- Two IC flavours: vanilla and chocolate IC cups (IC makers and cup fillers are not included in the case study);
- IC lid;
- White cream;
- Two sprinkle colours, and
- Six types of IC sauces represented by six colours.

4.1 Ice Cream Controller (C-MIRA)

A variety of toppings enables customers to choose their desired IC among various combinations. Customers' choices range from the simplest (and the cheapest) IC, which consists of an IC cup, to the most expensive IC, which includes three toppings (that is, cream and a choice of sauce and sprinkle). A customer order is received through a graphic user interface and is fed into a C-MIRA as an IC production controller. A C-MIRA acts as an intelligent product, in the sense that it contains a thorough representation of the IC recipe. It negotiates with the available devices that perform the required production operations. This negotiation will result in the creation of specific solution/s (routings and sequences) for the production of each IC order, based on various production conditions, such as particular order requirements, the availability of certain devices, and their locations (Fig. 3).

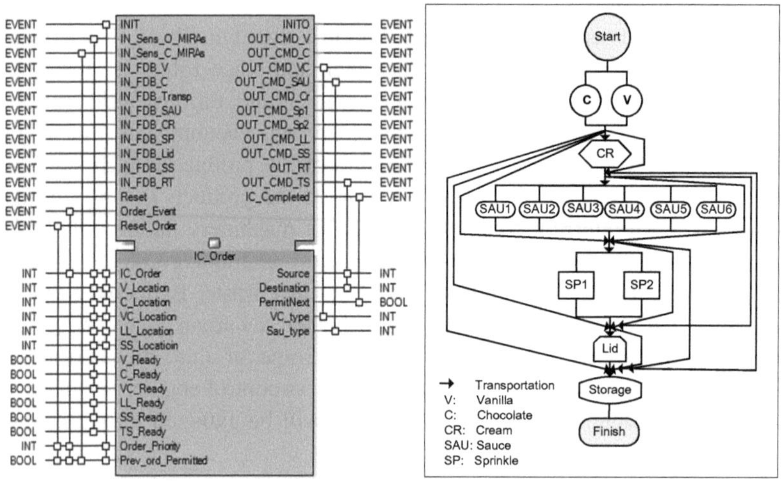

Fig. 3. IC production FB (C-MIRA) and IC production flowchart.

Figure 4 shows four C-MIRAs (each representing one IC production controller) that are populated in the IC control application. IC controllers receive orders from the customer HMI and communicate with O-MIRAs through Merger FBs. Each Merger FB acts as a medium between the C and O-MIRAs. It is associated with one O-MIRA and receives commands from C-MIRAs, then passes them to an O-MIRA and after the task completion, forwards the O-MIRA's feedback to the C-MIRA which had sent the command.

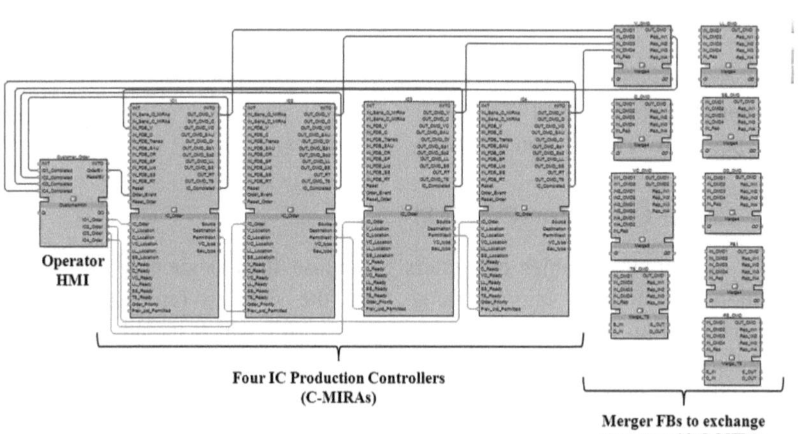

Fig. 4. Operator HMI, IC Controller FBs and Merger FBs populated in IC production control application.

4.2 Mechatronic Devices (O-MIRAs)

O-MIRAs intermittently advertise their operation status via a Boolean variable "Ready" (true when it is ready, false when it is not ready), to the C-MIRA, operator interface and the O-MIRAs with which they are collaborating.

There are two types of devices: *Stationary* and *Portable*. Stationary devices, which are assumed to be permanently available in the production process, include:

- Two sprinkle dispensers;
- A rotary sauce dispenser;
- A cream dispenser;
- A rotary table, and
- A group of conveyors for transportation (C), comprising four bi-directional conveyors (C1–C4) and two one-way conveyors (C5 and C6). There are six positions on the conveyors (identified with blue squares P1–P6 in Fig. 6a) that have optical sensors, allowing them to be used in any order as entry or exit connection points for the other portable devices that are depicted in Fig. 6 including:
- A storing station: to store ready ICs to be delivered to customers (last production stage);
- A pick-and-place device to place lids on IC cups;
- Two semi-rotary loaders with stack magazines, each of which supplies an IC flavour. In this case study it is assumed that these two IC loaders have priority over the dual IC loader in supplying IC. If they are unavailable (that is, either. faulty or out of IC cups), the C-MIRA will send a request to the handling station, and
- A handling station that has a pick-and-place robot, along with two sliders, to supply both IC flavours.

4.3 Transport System

Conveyors allow IC cups, as raw materials for this production system, to be transferred from one station to another to receive the desired IC dressings, and finally to guide them to the storing station. Although each conveyor operates independently, communication between them is necessary to direct the IC to the right station.

Each conveyor is equipped with one or more photo eye sensors (PS) to identify the presence of ICs at particular locations. It is assumed that the travel time for ICs between every two adjacent photo eye sensors is measured in advance by the control engineer and provided to the conveyor O-MIRA. In addition, some conveyors are equipped with diverters (D) to pass ICs to their attached conveyor.

Apart from the inherent flexibility of choice that is provided to customers in selecting ICs on the production side, the intended reconfigurability of the system allows the five portable devices to be freely located in any order around the fixed conveyor network and be connected to any of the entry/exit points. The through beam (photo eye) sensors mounted underneath the connection points allows the transport system to detect a portable device that is connected to its connection point. Providing the source and destination locations of an IC to the Transport O-MIRA enables it to calculate the travel time between two stations through possible routes and chose the fastest (and the shortest) path.

4.4 Customer and Operator HMIs

The customer interface gives customers multiple options to customize the IC to their preference. The customer has the choice to select between two flavours and a number of dressings (Fig. 5). This information is then sent to the C-MIRA and based on that, the O-MIRAs will operate.

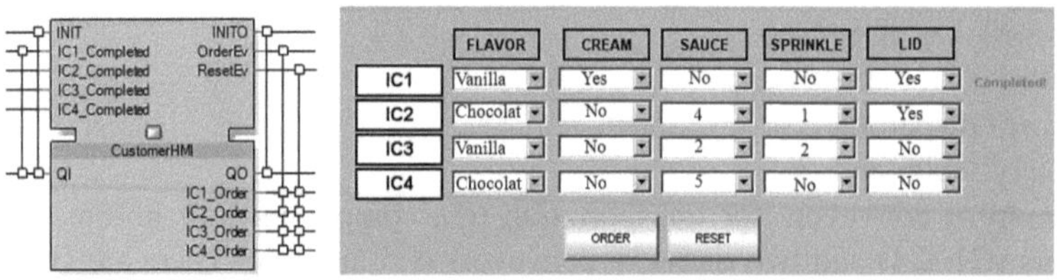

Fig. 5. Customer FB and HMI by which customers can select the desired IC flavours and dressings and be informed about the production progress.

The operator interface displays all the related production information to the operator. All HMI FBs are executed on a virtual PLC on a PC. Similar to other controllers, a virtual PLC communicates with other controllers through standard TCP/IP communication.

4.5 Control Design of O-MIRAs

In this case study, C-MIRAs are served on a first-come, first-served basis; however, in general, C-MIRAs may compete for resources based on their predefined priorities. In this approach, as is expected in agent-based manufacturing systems, each mechatronic component has only a minimal understanding of the whole system operations. For instance, an IC loader has no information about how many topping dispensers are available at the plant, or a conveyor does not know about the toppings that the IC may receive. The type of object (e.g. an IC or a metal work piece) that a conveyor is carrying is not important, so long as that object does not violate its predefined self-perception (the capability of carrying objects up to a certain size and weight). Therefore, decision making is systematically distributed across all IC production devices,' and each of the devices will behave autonomously.

Figure 6 shows a configuration of an ICPS and an example of how C- and O-MIRAs exchange messages in order to make a vanilla IC with cream topping. First, the user places their order through the user HMI, and all O-MIRAs inform the C-MIRA of their positions and readiness for operation. Next, C-MIRA sends a set of separate requests to O-MIRAs according to its recipe, and receives their report (through Merger FBs) after each task's completion. Meanwhile the adjacent O-MIRAs, whose concurrent operation is not allowed, exchange Block-Permit messages to avoid conflict. For example, once an IC loader is placing an IC on a conveyor, it blocks the conveyor operation to avoid it being used by other C-MIRAs. Similarly once the cream dispenser is operating, the rotary table must not rotate. Finally once the last O-MIRA (storing station) has accomplished its task and reported to the C-MIRA, the C-MIRA will report on the IC production to the user interface.

As it is illustrated in Fig. 6b, the total time taken for production of the IC order can be calculated as:

$T_{Tot} = \sum_{i=1}^{n} t(i)_{OM}$ where
T_{Tot} = Total production time of an IC order
$t(i)_{OM}$ = Operation time of an O-MIRA

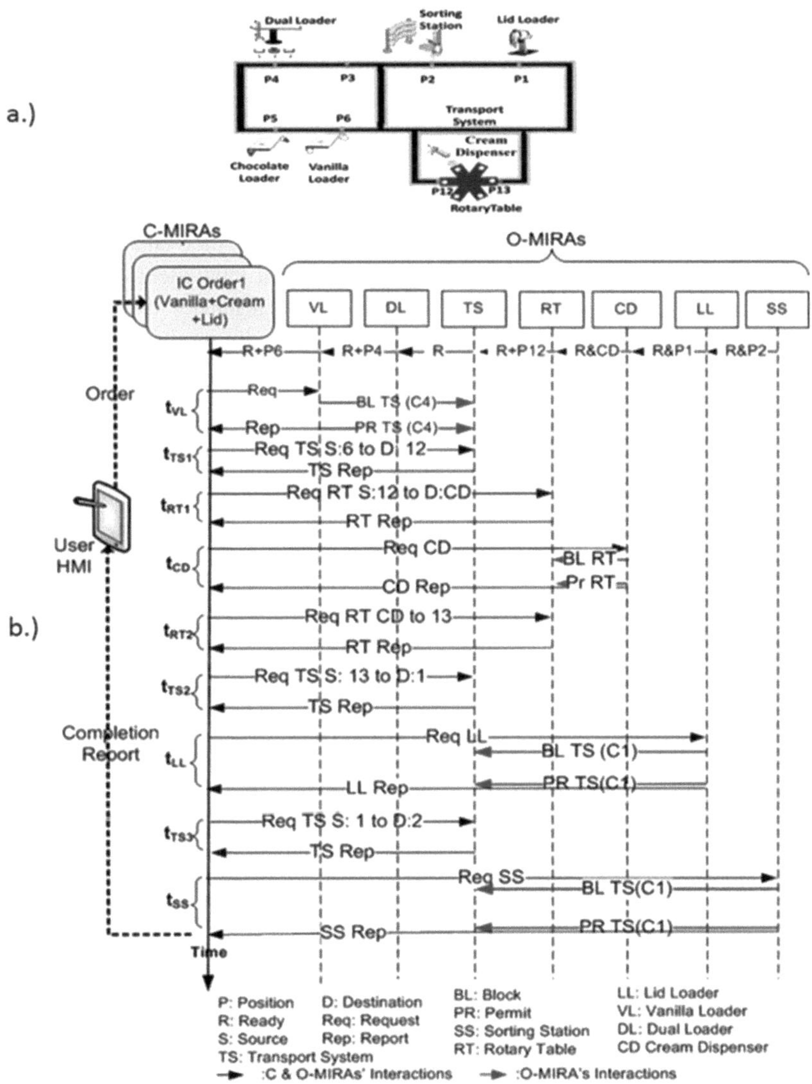

Fig. 6. (a) A configuration of O-MIRAs in ICPS, (b) message exchange among C and O MIRAs for producing a vanilla IC with cream topping

n = Number of O-MIRAs in the production including transport system i = 1, 2 … n
Therefore, the total production time for the IC with cream topping will be:
t(PT) t = t(VL) + t(CD) + t(LL) + t(SS) + t(TS) + t(RT) where
Total Transport Time: t(TS) = t(TS1) + t(TS2) + t(TS3)
Total Rotary Table Operation time: t(RT) = t(RT1) + t(RT2)

In general, communication among O-MIRAs results in increasing the throughput of the system. For, instance, while the first IC is receiving cream topping at the cream station, the second IC can be loaded on the C4 conveyor and transferred to the turntable. However, handling multiple IC orders simultaneously introduces the risk of collision. This situation is avoided by the conveyor system, through a permit-block communication technique between O-MIRAs. To this end, the conveyor controllers (as well as other devices) periodically advertise their availability (with a Ready or Not Ready message), and, based on their availability, issue permit-block messages among themselves to prevent others from overloading them. Through this method, each device will only handle one IC (or other objects) at a time.

Apart from O-MIRAs' autonomous behaviour, their other characteristic is that devices with similar components and functionalities will have identical control modules. For instance, the two single IC loaders use two instances of an identical FB, regardless of being placed in different locations within the production system. Conveyors are another example of the use of modular and identical software components.

The ICs can be observed and tracked by 14 photo eye sensors at various positions on the transport system. Distributed scheduling among conveyors is similar to the methodology reported in [13] for scheduling in modular automated machines. At first, the cylinder which contains the source node will start the scheduling procedure by searching for destination node. If destination node also exists in the same conveyor, then completion task will be sent to other conveyors and depending on the position of destination node with respect to the source node, the conveyor may chose forward (FW) or Backward (BW) movement to transfer an IC. However, if the destination node is located in other conveyors, the conveyor which has the source node firstly assumes its direction to be FW and based on that, sends requests (one at a time) to the output nodes along the way. The output node can be the conveyor which is connected to the end of this conveyor, or the one which is attached to its middle nodes and receive IC by diverter's actuations. Such algorithm will be followed by the consequent conveyors until the destination becomes reachable and then the "Scheduling Success" message will be broadcasted from the last conveyor which contains the destination node to the previous conveyor and cascaded to the first conveyor. If FW assumption for the first conveyor does not lead to a successful transportation path, the conveyor will again assume its movement direction to be BW and asks upstream output nodes to find a path to destination node. This procedure will enable the conveyors to find a solution to transfer an IC between two of the eight locations identified on the conveyors (i.e. positions 1–6). After the scheduling process is completed and the required actuators (conveyors and diverters) for IC transportation are identified, the conveyors involved in operation will become unavailable to other C-MIRA's and each conveyor will enable its actuators for operation. When the photo eye sensor at the destination node detects the IC, the operation is complete and conveyors will be ready for the next transportation task.

4.6 Control Hardware and Software Design Tool

The control hardware utilized for control of the production system consists of 12 Adam PLCs from Advantech Company. The PLCs control every conveyor, portable and stationary device used in the ICPS (Fig. 7). The whole software, including control and visualization, is implemented in IDC Builder environment by NxtControl company as one of the compliant tools to the IEC 61499 standard [16]. The entire control software was distributed and deployed to various hardware configurations, and in each case, the production system had identical performance.

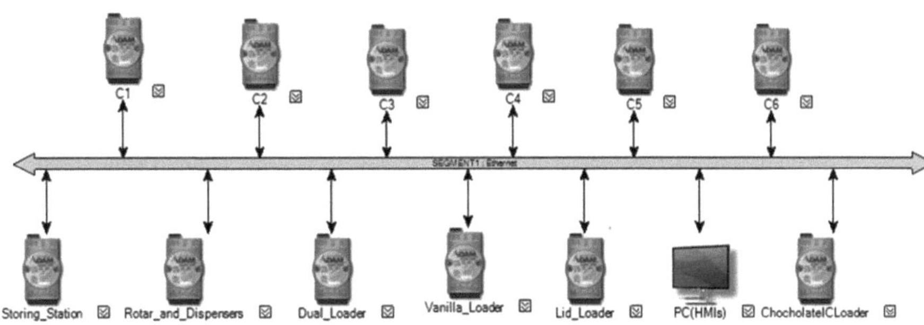

Fig. 7. Collaboration among Adam Controllers through the network.

4.7 Fault Tolerance

One of the notable benefits of the collaborative decision making when using MIRA is that it eliminates any unnecessary critical point and the system can cope with faults without human intervention. If an O-MIRA is unavailable, the C-MIRA will send a request to the next available O-MIRA.

The ICPS implementation was tested under the following fault scenarios:

- The vanilla IC loader was unplugged (representing a fault condition) and became unavailable, while the dual loader station (VC) received the command from the IC-Order FB and took charge of loading an IC.
- The cream dispenser was unplugged. Since there was no counterpart for that in the ICPS, the operation did not proceed, to avoid wasting IC.
- Conveyor 3 was unplugged (representing a fault condition) while the IC was supposed to be transferred from the position 5 to the position No. 2. The rerouted transportation path is illustrated in Fig. 8.

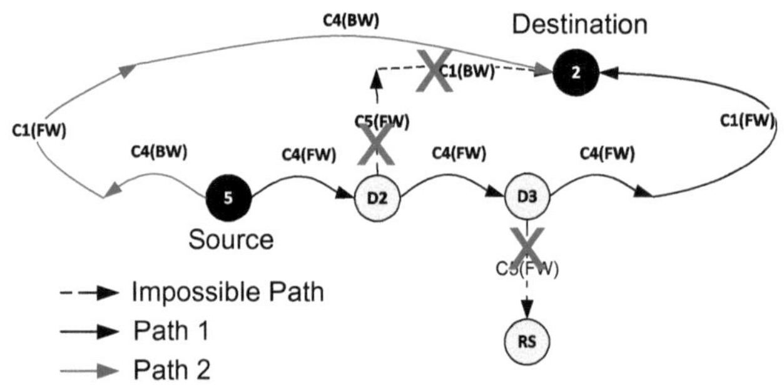

Fig. 8. Transportation paths explored in distributed scheduling between conveyors to move an IC from position 5 to position 2 while conveyor 3 is unplugged.

Among the three examined fault scenarios, in the first and the third cases, because the ICPS had other production alternatives, was able to successfully maintain its operation and produce the desired ICs.

4.8 Discussion

Before the design and implementation of ICPS, the same machinery had been used in a similar production application and for the control software development; the IEC 61499 FBs had been used. However, because of code's centralized nature, it was not feasible to reconfigure the production layout and add more components to it. Considering the shortcomings of the previous development, the ICPS control design was undertaken, based on the MIRA approach, which allowed reuse of devices in ICPS and thorough reconfiguration of the system. The new collaborative approach resulted in a significant reduction in control development time when compared with the previous implementation and the achievements will be more meaningful, bearing in mind that this method eliminates further development time in future expansions.

5 Conclusions

Future manufacturing will not just be concerned with satisfying a customer's straightforward requirements, but rather making their more ambitious aspirations come true. As an extension of the IMC design concept, MIRA was introduced at the manufacturing level, which represented intelligent products and machine controllers that can cooperate with one another without human intervention to achieve mass customization in manufacturing systems. Furthermore, MIRA architecture was studied and evaluated on a simulated food production case study in a laboratory environment.

References

1. Merdan, M., Lepuschitz, W., Hegny, I., Koppensteiner, G.: Application of a communication interface between agents and the low level control. In: 4th International Conference on Autonomous Robots and Agents, ICARA, pp. 628–633 (2009)
2. Gouyon, D., Pétin, J.-F., Morel, G.: A product-driven reconfigurable control for shop floor systems. Stud. Inform. Control **16** (2007)
3. Simao, J.M., Tacla, C.A., Stadzisz, P.C.: Holonic control metamodel. IEEE Trans. Systems Man Cybern. Part A: Appl. Rev. **39**, 1126–1139 (2009)
4. Vrba, P., Tichy, P., Marik, V., Staron, R.J., Maturana, F.P., Kadera, P.: Rockwell automation's holonic and multiagent control systems compendium. IEEE Trans. Systems Man Cybern. Part C: Appl. Rev. **41**, 14–30 (2011)
5. Leitao, P., Marik, V., Vrba, P.: Past, present, and future of industrial agent applications. IEEE Trans. Ind. Inform. 1 (2012)
6. Shen, W., Hao, Q., Yoon, H.J., Norrie, D.H.: Applications of agent-based systems in intelligent manufacturing: an updated review. Adv. Eng. Inform. **20**, 415–431 (2006)
7. Leitão, P.: Agent-based distributed manufacturing control: a state-of-the-art survey. Eng. Appl. Artif. Intell. **22**, 979–991 (2009)
8. Vyatkin, V.: IEC 61499 as enabler of distributed and intelligent automation: state-of-the-art review. IEEE Trans. Ind. Inform. **7**, 768–781 (2011)
9. Vyatkin, V.: Intelligent mechatronic components: control system engineering using an open distributed architecture. In: IEEE Conference on Emerging Technologies and Factory Automation, ETFA 2003, vol. 2, pp. 277–284 (2003)
10. Pang, C.: Model-driven development of distributed automation intelligence with IEC 61499. Ph.D. Electrical and Computer Engineering, The University of Auckland (2012)
11. Zoitl, A.: Real-Time Execusion for IEC 61499: OSA & O3neida (2009)
12. Sorouri, M., Vyatkin, V., Salcic, Z.: MIRA: enabler of mass customization through agent-based development of intelligent manufacturing systems. Paper presented at the IEEE International Conference on Robotics and Automation (ICRA), Hong Kong (2014)
13. Sorouri, M., Patil, S., Vyatkin, V., Salcic, Z.: Software composition and distributed operation scheduling in modular automated machines. IEEE Trans. Ind. Inform. **11**, 865–878 (2014)
14. Rachlin, J., Goodwin, R., Murthy, S., Akkiraju, R., Wu, F., Kumaran, S., Das, R.: A-teams: an agent architecture for optimization and decision-support. In: Papadimitriou, C., Singh, M. P., Müller, J.P. (eds.) ATAL 1998. LNCS (LNAI), vol. 1555, pp. 261–276. Springer, Heidelberg (1999)
15. Lim, M.K., Zhang, D.Z.: An integrated agent-based approach for responsive control of manufacturing resources. Comput. Ind. Eng. **46**, 221–232 (2004)
16. *NxtOne 2.0* (2014). www.nxtcontrol.com. Accessed April 2016

Advances in Production - Product Personalization

Complexity Mitigation in Collaborative Manufacturing Chains

Vladimir Modrak and Slavomir Bednar(✉)

Faculty of Manufacturing Technologies with a seat in Presov, Technical University of Kosice, Bayerova 1, 08001 Presov, Slovakia
{vladimir.modrak,slavomir.bednar}@tuke.sk

Abstract. Collaborative manufacturing chains (CMSs) are understood as networks of manufacturing units that are highly specialized, cooperation-independent and economically autonomous. CMSs are becoming ever more complex in today's global market and one pertinent task for supply chain designers/managers is to handle outsourcing decision-making problems, by which such complexity can be reduced. In this paper, we propose to solve this problem through generation of alternative collaborative manufacturing chains that are benchmarked using topological complexity metrics. For this purpose, firstly supply chain structures are modelled. Subsequently, topological complexity measures for each possible configuration network are quantified. Finally, optimal supply chain configurations are selected.

Keywords: Mass customization · Entropy · Axiomatic design · Topology · Decision-making

1 Introduction

One of the main challenges for original equipment manufacturers (OEMs) is transformation of their business strategies into mass customization (MC). This trend is pulled by the growing demand for tailor-made mass produced products and pushed by rapid development of modern supporting technologies such as information technologies, additive manufacturing, 5th generation mobile networks, identification technologies and others. Companies aligned with this strategy will need to adopt collaborative manufacturing network models. As it is known, this leads to an increase in manufacturing complexity. Therefore, companies with higher degree of customization might focus on reducing the complexity of the production processes, since complexity problems not only affect the production processes, but also managerial processes [1, 2]. Although this objective is quite clear, the way to achieve it is not. Then, the following research questions can be stated. RQ_1: Can suitable alternative supply chain (SC) structure(s) be modelled? RQ_2: If yes, how to identify the least complex structure?

An identification of complexity metrics is the first precondition for solving such problem. Prior to this task, it would be helpful to have a basic understanding of what factors affect the manufacturing complexity. Typical feature for MC is that products

H. Afsarmanesh et al. (Eds.): PRO-VE 2016, IFIP AICT 480, pp. 411–419, 2016.
DOI: 10.1007/978-3-319-45390-3_35

consist from several modules and each module can have a certain number of variants. Combinations of these variants contribute to high product variety that triggers high manufacturing complexity [3]. The supply chain creates a network of interconnected producers. At each producer, selected components according to customer needs are assembled onto the partially finished product. Finally, end product is finalized at the OEM. The goal of paper is to propose a framework for modelling of alternative collaborative supply chain (CSC) structures and to provide a description of possible complexity mitigation in collaborative manufacturing chains.

2 Generating Alternatives to Collaborative Manufacturing Structures

Generating the alternatives of CSC structures is useful especially when obtained structures can be utilized for practical guidance, and applied in conjunction with a selection of optimal collaborative manufacturing models. Moreover, it helps layout designers, among others, to increase productivity and to reduce costs and complexity. Especially, the network complexity reduction is recently in the centre of managers' attention as assembly SC systems are becoming increasingly complex. On the other hand, high flexibility of supply chains is required to obtain short delivery times.

Commonly for this purpose, graph theory is applied. Assembly SCs can be represented by tree directed graphs, in which each node in the chain has at most one successor, but may have any number of predecessors. Convergent SCs are divided into two basic types: modular and non-modular. In the modular structure, the intermediate sub-assemblers are understood as assembly modules while the non-modular structure consists of only original suppliers and a final assembler (root node). Steps to identify optimal assembly SC structures have been clearly specified by Zhu et al. [4] in the following steps:

(a) Generation of all possible SC structures;
(b) Quantification of topological complexity values for each possible configuration;
(c) Selection of the optimal SC configurations.

The same authors outlined the way forward to model possible SC structures depending on the number of original suppliers *i*. If a SC has from two to four original suppliers, then we obtain one, two, five different assembly SCs. In the case of five suppliers $i = 5$, 12 different assembly SC networks can be generated, as can be seen in Fig. 1 (Class #5).

Analogically, it is possible to generate topological structures of assembly SC networks for any number of original suppliers, starting from $i \leq 2$–∞). From here on, assembly SC structures are further considered are CSC structures.

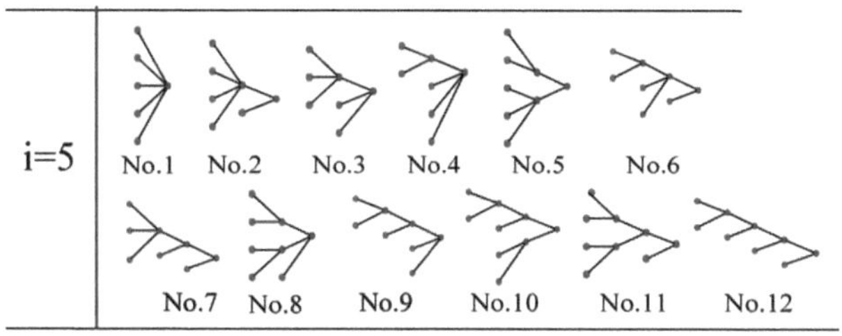

Fig. 1. All possible SC networks for five original suppliers (Class #5) [5].

3 Complexity Mitigation in CSC Structures

In the previous Sect. 2, SCs have been modelled by unlabeled graphs. However, CSCs correspond with labelled graphs. Therefore, in order to mitigate complexity of CSC structures, it is advisable to follow these steps:

1. Firstly, to transform a realistic SC system into a labelled graph and subsequently to assign a corresponding SC structure to that graph. A simple example is shown in Fig. 2.

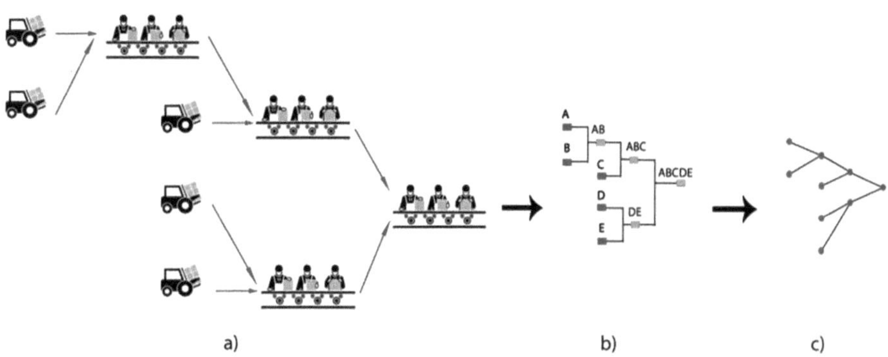

Fig. 2. (a) CSC realistic layout; (b) transformation into a labelled graph; (c) transformation into the SC network No. 10 in *Class #5*.

2. Identify alternative SC structures to the corresponding SC considered as the original one. Such alternative structures are available in all lower classes "*i*" of the SC structures than the class of the given assembly SC structure. As an example, original SC structure from Fig. 2(c) can be used.

Then, all alternative CSC networks can be identified as depicted in Fig. 3 below. Such alternative CSC structures are empirically less complex and at the same time they keep the predefined assembly sequence unchanged. From the graph theory viewpoint, obtained alternative graphs in the lower topological classes are then homeomorphic to the original labelled graph. From a practical point of view, such alternatives of CSC systems can be achieved based on outsourcing method that often allows company's clients to reach better, faster, and more sustainable results.

3. Finally, substitute intuitive methods for complexity comparison of benchmarked CSC structures by appropriate and effective indicators of topological complexity.

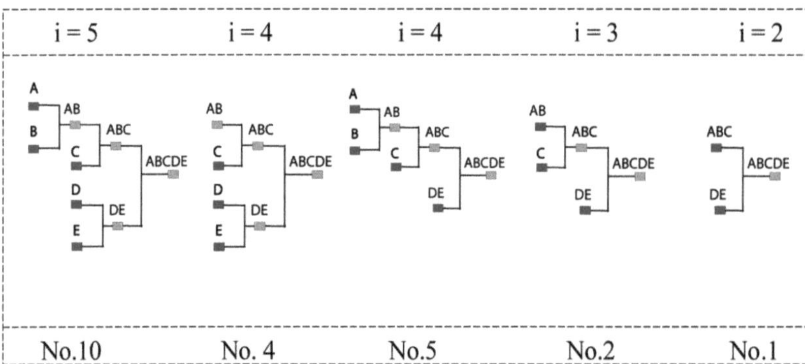

Fig. 3. Original CSC structure with $i = 5$ and related alternative SC networks

Coming back to Fig. 3, four alternative CSC structures are taken from SC topological Classes of #4, #3 and #2. Then, when considering, e.g. the CSC structure taken from the topological Class #4 (namely, graph No. 5), it is assumed that node DE with two external suppliers is substituted by one external supplier of the DE module. It is also evident that in alternative CSC models, the predefined sequences are unchanged. Arrangements of other two alternative CSC structures (graphs No. 4, No. 2, and No. 1) are analogical. In the next step, it is useful to benchmark the complexity of original CSC structure (graph No. 10) against the four alternative CSC networks. For this purpose, in the next section two alternative complexity indicators are described.

4 Approaches to Structural Complexity of CSC

Metrics of structural complexity for specific or general networks can help companies not only design SC structures but also to better understand their topological properties. Layout design complexity metrics can be effectively used especially when comparing two or more CSC structures. Several studies in the literature, e.g. [6–15] can be found dealing with complexity indicators for structural complexity measurement of manufacturing and logistics systems.

Since there are several types of assembly supply chain models, not all the complexity indicators are equally effective for different groups of networks. Based on the literature review aimed at current developments in assessment of SC complexity, the following gap has been identified: So far, there is no SC framework that identifies structural relationship among the system vertices.

Respecting this fact, two complexity indicators are proposed to satisfy the need for effective SC complexity assessment.

4.1 Vertex Degree Index I_{vd}

According to Shannon's information theory [16], the entropy of information $H(\alpha)$ in describing a message of N system elements, distributed according to some equivalence criterion α into k groups of $N_1, N_2, \ldots, N_k$ elements, is calculated by the formula:

$$H(\alpha) = -\sum_{i=1}^{k} p_i \, log_2 p_i = -\sum_{i=1}^{k} \frac{N_i}{N} log_2 \frac{N_i}{N}, \quad (1)$$

where p_i specifies the probability of occurrence of the elements of the i_{th} group.

Since it is of interest to characterize entropy of information of a network according to [16], it is possible to substitute symbols or system elements for the vertices.

In order to define the probability for a randomly chosen system element i it is possible to formulate general weight function as $p_i = w_i/\Sigma w_i$, assuming that $\Sigma p_i = 1$. Considering the system elements, the vertices, and supposing the weights assigned to each vertex to be the corresponding vertex degrees, one easily distinguishes the null complexity of the totally disconnected graph from the high complexity of the complete graph. Shannon defines information as:

$$I = H_{max} - H, \quad (2)$$

where H_{max} is maximum entropy that can exist in a system with the same number of elements.

Subsequently, the information entropy of a graph with a total weight W and vertex weights w_i can be expressed in the form of the equation:

$$H(W) = W \, log_2 W - \sum_{i=1}^{V} w_i \, log_2 \, w_i, \quad (3)$$

where the total number of vertices within a SC is V. Since the maximum entropy is when all $w_i = 1$, then

$$H_{max} = W \, log_2 W. \quad (4)$$

By substituting $W = \sum_{i=1}^{V} \deg(v)_i$ and $w_i = deg(v)_i$, the information content of the vertex degree distribution of a network called as Vertex degree index (I_{vd}) is derived by Bonchev and Buck [17] that is expressed as follows:

$$I_{vd} = -\sum_{i=1}^{V} deg(v)_i log_2 deg(v)_i. \quad (5)$$

An explanation of the $deg(v)_i$ and I_{vd} calculations are depicted in Fig. 4.

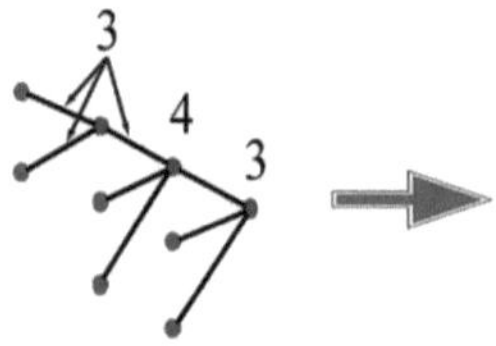

$$\deg(v)_i=4;3;3$$
$$I_{vd}=(4(\log_2 4))+(3(\log_2 3))+(3(\log_2 3))=17{,}51$$

Fig. 4. Information content I_{vd} of the case SC structure with $i = 6$

Following the procedure obtaining I_{vd} information content, Table 1 summarizes values of I_{vd} indicator for all CSC structures in Classes #2–5, while suitable alternative CSC structures are highlighted.

Table 1. I_{vd} values of CSC structures for the related topological classes.

Class #	I_{vd} values for individual CSC structures											
	No. 1	No. 2	No. 3	No. 4	No. 5	No. 6	No. 7	No. 8	No. 9	No. 10	No. 11	No. 12
#5	11,61	13,61	12,75	12,75	14,75	14,75	14,75	14,26	14,26	**16,26**	16,26	16,26
#4	8,00	10,00	9,51	**11,51**	**11,51**	-	-	-	-	-	-	-
#3	4,75	**6,75**	-	-	-	-	-	-	-	-	-	-
#2	**2,00**	-	-	-	-	-	-	-	-	-	-	-

4.2 Axiomatic Design-Based Complexity - Systems Design Complexity (SDC)

The main definition of Axiomatic design [18] states that any process can be seen in four main domains: process, functional, customer and physical. The process consists of several steps and at the end results with structured relations between customer needs, functional requirement (FR) and selected design parameters (DP). These relations or dependencies between FRs and DPs within any design hierarchy can be expressed by the relation: $FR = [A]\ DP$. This relation can be expressed as each FR on the product component depends on the specific design parameter (DP) of the product specified by customer, so that each such dependency [*A*] can be understood as existing relation of FR on DP. If in the design matrix of any process element A refers to "0", then FR is not in relation with DP. And vice versa for "1", where there is relation between the DP and FR.

According to the SDC approach, we indicate each initial node of the CSC model as a FR (for example FR_1 to FR_{10} at Class *#10*) and each sub-assembly vertex as DP (for example DP_1 to DP_3 depending on the specific CSC structure shown in Fig. 5. This is because initial nodes practically represent company requirements on suppliers and specify the number of initial nodes into CSC. This way, the transformation of all repeated CSC is possible and valuable. Analogically, we can transform each CSC structure into an axiomatic design matrix. For such matrices it is characteristic that individual elements *[A]* are mostly non-zero and thus the FRs cannot be satisfied independently.

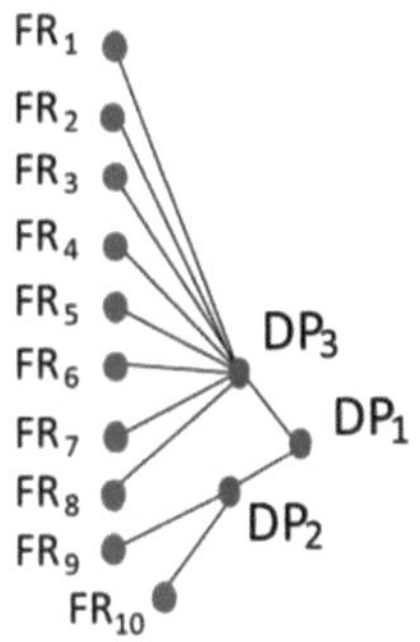

	DP_1	DP_2	DP_3
FR_1	1	0	1
FR_2	1	0	1
FR_3	1	0	1
FR_4	1	0	1
FR_5	1	0	1
FR_6	1	0	1
FR_7	1	0	1
FR_8	1	0	1
FR_9	1	1	0
FR_{10}	1	1	0
	N_1=10	N_2=2	N_3=8

SDC=(10(ln10))+(2(ln2))+(8(ln8))=41,05 *nats*

Fig. 5. CSC structure with 10 FRs and 3 DPs transformed into a design matrix.

We propose the following SDC measure (in *nats*) based on the Axiomatic Design (AD) expressed as follows:

$$SDC = \sum N_j \, ln \, N_j \tag{6}$$

where the volume is equal to unity and '*Nj*' is interpreted as number of direct relations per single DP of the design matrix. Case transformation of the design matrix into a coupled design including calculation of SDC complexity is depicted in Fig. 5.

Subsequently, the following Table 2 summarizes the values of SDC for all CSC structures, while suitable alternative structures and their SDC complexity values are highlighted.

Table 2. SDC values of all and suitable alternative CSC structures for the related topological classes

Class	SDC values for individual CSC structures											
#	No. 1	No. 2	No. 3	No. 4	No. 5	No. 6	No. 7	No. 8	No. 9	No. 10	No. 11	No. 12
#5	8,05	13,59	11,34	9,43	12,73	14,98	16,89	10,82	12,73	**14,12**	16,36	18,27
#4	5,55	8,84	6,93	**8,32**	**10,23**	-	-	-	-	-	-	-
#3	3,30	**4,68**	-	-	-	-	-	-	-	-	-	-
#2	**1,38**	-	-	-	-	-	-	-	-	-	-	-

5 Comparison of the Approaches to Structural Complexity

The above presented indicators can be assessed in the view of their applicability:

In the case of I_{vd} indicator and its application, 12 graphs in the same SC Class #5 can be divided into six levels of structural complexity (see Table 1). The mentioned complexity indicator is therefore not an optimal measure of structural complexity of CSCs.

On the other hand, AD-based indicator SDC considers graphs links as interactions between nodes. Then, complexity values of SDC indicator for the same CSC structures in Classes from #2 to #5 differ for each of the graphs (see Table 2).

Concluding the computational analysis using three structural complexity indicators, we may state that AD-based complexity suits best for the given purpose.

6 Conclusions

Complexity topology analysis of the CSC structures in this paper revealed potential tools to optimize any SC structures to be used in mass customization environment. Moreover, it has been found that modelling of all possible SC is purposeful because any existing structure can be simplified using the approach presented above to obtain less complex SC alternative(s). Secondly, the two complexity metrics, namely I_{vd} and SDC to capture structural properties of all possible CSC networks have been benchmarked. The SDC indicator fits best for the decision-making about the optimal collaborative chain as it considers also links between nodes and their interoperability.

Subsequently it was shown that the proposed approach to model CSC networks can be effectively used in MC manufacturing environment. Finally, a draft concept to product variety quantification has been outlined as a precondition for posterior solutions of product variety complexity mitigation.

References

1. Stump, B., Badurdeen, F.: Integrating lean and other strategies for mass customization manufacturing: a case study. J. Intell. Manuf. **23**(1), 109–124 (2012)
2. Brosch, M., Beckmann, G., Krause, D.: Approach to visualize the supply chain complexity induced by product variety. In: Proceedings of 18th International Conference on Engineering Design (ICED 2011), Impacting Society through Engineering Design, p. 10. TU Denmark, Copenhagen (2011)
3. Blecker, T., Friedrich, G., Kaluza, B., Abdelkafi, N., Kreutler, G.: Information and Management Systems for Product Customization, vol. 7. Springer Science & Business Media, New York (2004)
4. Zhu, X., Hu, S.J., Koren, Y., Marin, S.P.: Modeling of manufacturing complexity in mixed-model assembly lines. J. Manuf. Sci. E-T ASME **130**(5), 1–10 (2008)
5. Modrak, V., Marton, D., Bednar, S.: Modeling and determining product variety for mass-customized manufacturing. Procedia CIRP **23**, 258–263 (2014)
6. ElMaraghy, H., AlGeddawy, T., Samy, S.N., Espinoza, V.: A model for assessing the layout structural complexity of manufacturing systems. J. Manuf. Syst. **33**(1), 51–64 (2014)

7. Crippa, R., Bertacci, N., Larghi, L.: Representing and measuring flow complexity in the extended enterprise: the D4G approach. In: Congress For Research in Logistics (2006)
8. Modrak, V., Bednar, S., Marton, D.: Generating product variations in terms of mass customization. In: 2015 IEEE 13th International Symposium Applied Machine Intelligence and Informatics (SAMI). IEEE (2015)
9. Wang, H., Zhu, X., Hu, S.J., Koren, Y.: Complexity analysis of assembly supply chain configurations. In: ASME 9th Biennial Conference on Engineering Systems Design and Analysis, pp. 501–510. American Society of Mechanical Engineers, Michigan (2008)
10. Koren, Y., Heisel, U., Jovane, F., Moriwaki, T., Pritschow, G., Ulsoy, G., Van Brussel, H.: Reconfigurable manufacturing systems. CIRP Ann. Manuf. Technol. **48**(2), 527–540 (1999)
11. Wang, H.: Product variety induced complexity and its impact on mixed-model assembly systems and supply chains. Doctoral dissertation, General Motors (2010)
12. Frizelle, G.: Measuring complexity as an aid to developing operational strategy. Int. J. Oper. Prod. Manag. **15**(5), 26–39 (1995)
13. Deshmukh, A.V., Talavage, J.J., Barash, M.M.: Complexity in manufacturing systems, Part 1: analysis of static complexity. IIE Trans. **30**(7), 645–655 (1998)
14. Espinoza Vega, V.B.: Structural complexity of manufacturing systems layout. M.Sc. thesis, University of Windsor, Canada (2012)
15. Németh, P., Foldesi, P.: Efficient control of logistic processes using multi-criteria performance measurement. Acta Technica Jaurinensis **2**, 353–360 (2009)
16. Shannon, C.E.: A mathematical theory of communication. Bell Syst. Tech. J. **27**, 379–423 (1948)
17. Bonchev, D., Buck, G.A.: Quantitative measures of network complexity. In: Bonchev, D., Rouvray, D.H. (eds.) Complexity in Chemistry, Biology and Ecology, vol. 1, pp. 191–235. Springer, Heidelberg (2005)
18. Suh, N.P.: Complexity in engineering. CIRP Ann. Manuf. Technol. **54**(2), 46–63 (2005)

A Lean Set-Based Design Approach for Development of Customizable Products in Collaborative Networks

João Bastos[1,2(✉)], Américo Azevedo[1], and Paulo Ávila[2]

[1] INESC TEC – INESC Technology and Science and FEUP - Faculty of Engineering, University of Porto - Campus Da FEUP, Rua Dr. Roberto Frias, 4200-465 Porto, Portugal
{jsbastos,ala}@fe.up.pt

[2] ISEP/IPP - School of Engineering, Polytechnic Institute of Porto, Rua Dr. António Bernardino de Almeida, 431, 4249-015 Porto, Portugal
psa@isep.ipp.pt

Abstract. In nowadays competing market, companies are constantly challenged to reduce the lead time for new products design process by diminishing the time response that goes from the arise of the market opportunity to the satisfaction of the customer need. Simultaneously, companies and networked organizations face a growing number of product configurations, lower product volumes, a continuously growing appetence for personalized products, pressing the decision makers into adopting more efficient product development processes. The present paper addresses the main collaborative product development issues by proposing a responsive and efficient use of knowledge on networked environments through a lean-based framework for collaborative networks. In particular, this work describes the main lean concepts and tools that are enhancers of an efficient and distributed customizable product development process in networked environment.

Keywords: Product development · Collaborative networks · Product customization · Set-based design · Lean

1 Introduction

Manufacturers and sellers of a multitude of products from simple t-shirts to luxury woman purses and even more general consumer packaged products are finding out the value of letting customers creating and customizing their own unique products. Retailers use intensively market analysis tools to understand and cope with the market trends and be prepared to present a personalized set of "one-of-a-kind" products to their customers. Fast fashion retailers such as Zara have dramatically reshaped their business processes on designing, manufacturing and distribution to respond to current and emerging market trends by adapting their product collections as quickly and effectively as possible. Similarly, a driving force behind Amazon's success has been the company's customer experience pillar based on providing the "earth's biggest selection" with its biggest focus on product personalization.

H. Afsarmanesh et al. (Eds.): PRO-VE 2016, IFIP AICT 480, pp. 420–432, 2016.
DOI: 10.1007/978-3-319-45390-3_36

In reality, an increasing number of brands are now taking personalization and customization in their offer a step further by resorting to a new paradigm, such as co-design approach aligned to mass customization practices, a production strategy focused on the broad provision of personalized products. These companies are discovering that they can raise customer interest, commitment and loyalty in the nowadays volatile global markets.

Several web-based manufacturers have used product customization practices to boost sales on their own websites and gain share on retailer's sites. For example: bivolino.com provides on its site custom tailored man shirts and woman blouses with several thousand of possible product combinations selectable by the customers; in jawbone.com customers can configure their own Jambox speakers, and Brooks Brothers (brooksbrothers.com) allows men to custom their own shirts and suits.

However, despite the obvious advantages of manufacturers offering customized products, its acceptance by the majority of companies has been very limited. Past examples have shown that in order to a company embrace the customization game it is necessary to enhance their capabilities in three areas: product development capabilities; efficient processes design practices and supply chain integration.

The research performed in the recent years have shown that the customization transformation of a company's offer is achieved through modularized product/service design, flexible and efficient processes, and integration & collaboration between supply chain members [1–3].

In parallel to the customization game, companies area facing in their quest for innovation an increase in the complexity of their products, designing processes and manufacturing activities. Coupled with the complexity increase, managers are constantly challenged to reduce the lead time for new products technical design, diminishing the time interval that goes from the arise of the market opportunity and the satisfaction of the customer need with full-rate production of marketable products.

In overall, the current trend is forcing companies to be faster, more flexible and increasingly efficient in the design approach of new products and simultaneously taking into consideration the customer aspirations of more personalized products. The growing number of product configurations, lower product volumes, a continuously diminishing response time in designing and delivering new products have a significant impact on the company operations management strategy and is changing the landscape of collaborative networking.

This paper addresses the multidisciplinary complexity of personalized product development processes in customer-driven value chains, in particular, by tackling the main collaborative business processes on the operational level, namely on its competencies, resources and processes dimensions tailored for responsiveness and efficient use of knowledge on customized manufacturing environments through a lean-based framework proposal.

The proposed approach transposes the lean basic concepts and practices, historically implemented in in-doors manufacturing operations, to a networked and extended environment of Collaborative Networks (CNs) through a set of tools and methods aimed to support the design, modeling and implementation of the necessary development processes for customizable products.

The remaining of this paper is organized as follows: first the existing related literature and research questions are presented, followed by the description of the lean set-based principles in collaborative networks. Afterwards, the concepts, methods and tools of the framework are presented. Finally, conclusions and future developments are detailed concerning the framework instantiation and further improvement.

2 Background and Research Topics

The last decades have shaped the context on manufacturing consumer goods with a tendency to an increase in the number of product variants, a dramatic reduction of products life-cycle and a shorten in the expected response time from market requests. Furthermore, paradigms such as mass customization and personalization are changing the traditional relationship with the customer from "made-to-stock" to "made-to-order" [3]. The shift from mass production to a more complex and highly demanding "high-variety-low-volume" production is defying the traditional product development processes and supply chain management policies forcing companies to increase their flexibility in order to produce small batches - till one-of-a-kind product - in order to satisfy customer demand [4].

2.1 Design for Personalization

In order to support the new paradigm resulting from the personalization process, the company should rethink the whole value chain from the front-end to the back-end in order to consider four factors: efficiency, time-to-market, variety, and economy of scale.

All these issues pose a challenge for manufacturing companies: how they can cope with the consumers demand for personalized value-added products and simultaneously assure high quality, innovative functionalities and responsiveness?

In fact, in order to the manufacturing value chains be able to address this new challenging kind of market demand with efficient development processes, they need to resort to new collaborative methods and tools. These new forms of networked organizations fitted with efficient product development processes present a promising approach to deal with the need to customer driven focus, reduced time to market of new products and cost effective manufacturing in a cooperative and collaborative environment [5].

The development value stream produces operational value streams which run from suppliers through factories, into product features and out into the customers. Design for product customization is to consider economy of scale at the early stage of product development process, seeking efficiency in all the stages of this value stream [6].

From a traditional approach, product development processes, including the case of customized products, usually follow a "waterfall" approach or "V" methodology. With this approach, after the business opportunity identified, it is created a concept specification, which in turn is translated into a system design. This overall system design, which in the case of customizable products is modular, in reality freezes the interfaces between the different modules or subsystems, allowing the next phase of independent and in many cases parallel design of the subsystems. This hierarchical design process follows a top-down approach during the design phase and bottom-up approach during testing and prototyping [7].

Due to its independent subsystem designs in autonomous modules, this "waterfall" approach is widely used in collaborative networks. Even though abundantly used, this traditional approach, has significant drawbacks. By following a modular and top down approach, this means that critical systems decisions about module or subsystems interfaces are made on the basis of early insufficient data and wishful thinking of the designers of what the final product will be. As several studies point out, this distributed product development process is performed mostly from draft designs of products, processes and network configurations. Hence, these drafts designs are usually vague, leading to inconsistent final solutions, resulting in problems that are discovered late or in advanced phases of the design process. Another reported drawback of this traditional approach is the low levels of reutilization of parts, manufacturing systems or reconfiguration of networks [8–10]. These problems observed in advanced phases of the product development process force design loopbacks and network reconfigurations (see Fig. 1) which often consumes 50 to 75 % of engineering resources [6].

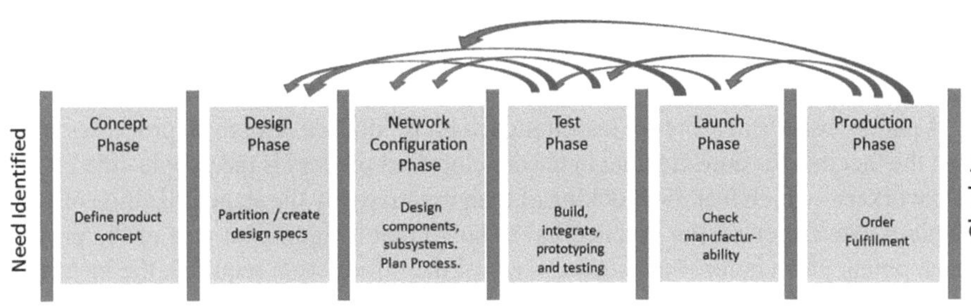

Fig. 1. Waterfall approach for collaborative networks product development process

Therefore with the traditional "waterfall" approach it is observed the following disadvantages [7]:

- **Inefficient resource usage** - due to the late discovery of design problems which require loopbacks and rework;
- **Discard of knowledge** - due to the early commitment to rigid product design specifications, the knowledge acquisition is restricted and the network partners involvement and knowledge generation is suppressed;
- **Poor and unreliable solutions** - since every new product development project only aims in attaining a single feasible solution in terms of products specs and network configurations, usually there is insufficient domain knowledge that results in a good or optimal solution.

In summary, the traditional networked product development approach, presents efficiency, knowledge acquisition and responsiveness shortcomings that demand for an overall rethinking of the product development process in collaborative networks.

2.2 Lean Principles and Tools for Product Development

Womack and Jones in "Lean Thinking" stated that "lean companies figure out what value is (what customers actually want) and concentrate on 'value streams', the connected activities that create value" [11]. These authors argue that conventional companies often get so engaged with their internal way of doing business that lose sight of what is actually creating value and instead produce waste. On the other hand, lean companies are focused on ways to add value by eliminating non-value creating activities. Lean is defined as an efficient and systematic approach to maximize value by minimizing waste, and by pull flowing the products through the resources at the customer demand pace. In order to achieve this goal, it is useful to outline the characteristics of a lean approach in manufacturing systems. Lean enterprises are always looking for ways to cut the use of any of these resources anywhere in the company [12].

Despite the lean started from the improvement of physical production processes, since the beginning, the lean pioneers accepted the challenge of extending the lean philosophy to the product development process. The effort for creating an efficient product development process struggled with the high variability and mostly immaterialized flow of activities present in any product development process.

A major obstacle in using the lean approach for product development processes arises from the fact that the core element in the development process is the people - the knowledge workers - which fear the blocking of their creativity by the standardization of work practices. Nevertheless, the practice have shown that a significant part of the product development effort comprises the discovery of the information required, the identification of the information sources, and what to do with this information since it is collected. These are all activities that can be simplified and standardized using lean practices. Afterwards, once these processes have been simplified and all the data collected, often the development team finds out that they have more time for actually creative and innovative activities [13, 14].

Although the novelty of this research area, there are very few examples of published works that studied and documented the use of lean principles in product development. The most significant was published by Morgan and Liker in 2006. In this book, the authors identify 13 principles that distinguish the lean product development process in three categories: the process; the skilled people; and tools and technology [15]. The lean principles identified by the authors show that the challenge in product development is to reduce variability while conserving the creativity that is necessary to the product design process.

From the analysis of selected manufacturing success cases, it was possible to identify in addition to the main principles which are the methods and tools that support the lean product development system. In Table 1 it is summarized the most significant tools used by lean companies in their product development process.

Although in recent years it was observed a disclosure of lean practices, methods and tools to support the product development process, yet very few companies followed the lean approach in this critical process for competitiveness. This is especially true for Collaborative Networked organizations that need to undergo in a series of alliances as part of their strategy to obtain new technologies, enter new markets and, in general, increase responsiveness to customers by enhancing their flexibility and efficiency.

Table 1. Lean tools used in product development process

Lean tool	Use in the product development process
SBCE (set-based concurrent engineering)	The SBCE tool take into consideration several possible designs and technical solutions at the beginning, and as the process progress, the workable solutions are narrowed as more information from development, testing, the customer, and across the organization is obtained in order to obtain the most efficient solution
VSM (value stream mapping)	Through mapping of the development value stream, it is analysed the set of all actions required to develop a specific product or service through the critical management tasks in order to eliminate the waste
QFD (quality function deployment)	Methodology used to capture the customer perspective and translate the customer needs into design requirements and specifications. QFD consists of a series of interlocking matrices that transform the customer needs into product and process characteristics
Pugh matrix (criteria based matrix)	It is a matrix used to compare several different design concepts under consideration allowing the developer team to compare the different concepts, create strong alternative concepts from weaker concepts and arrive to an "optimal" concept, which may be a combination the best aspects of other designs
DOE (design of experiments)	DOE is statistical technique to increase the effective use of the information generated through experimentation. It can help the designing team understand the dependency or relationships between different critical variables

The question is, what is still missing? How can networked organizations, often with poorly defined existing development processes, redesign it in order to achieve higher efficiency and get their arms around the lean thinking?

To start, Collaborative Network managers need a reference model or a step-by-step methodology that they can apply, in a practical way, to their own networked development processes. This is especially true, because despite the abundant information on the appliance of lean method in indoors product development, there is still missing from the literature practical guides and references that assist collaborative networks practitioners into the goal of becoming efficient product development networked organizations.

3 Set-Based Design in Networked Product Development

The extension of the lean principles from a mostly in-house scenario to a network environment, especially in the case of Collaborative Networks, poses some challenges. In reality, it is necessary to adapt some of the lean basic principles and include some new methods and tools to support the redefinition of the basic concepts.

Let's take the example of *waste*. Ohno and Shingo defined the seven principal manufacturing wastes as: overproduction; waiting; transporting; over-processing; excessive inventory; excessive motion; rework and defects [11].

Since in the case of the CNs product development processes, most of the activities are dematerialized, the equivalent examples of waste need to be identified from the customer perspective of the net added-value of the activity. Therefore, based on the assumption that the customer is only willing to pay for an activity in the development process if it sees its value, it was possible to characterize waste in a networked product developing process in its different forms according to Table 2.

Another adaptation successfully implemented of extending the lean principles to a collaborative network environment, was the concept of lean set based thinking. This concept resulted in the adaptation of the principles behind the lean tool called SBCE (Set-Based Concurrent Engineering) [7, 8].

The concept derives from the Toyota's product development practices. This automobile manufacturer is the industry leader and presents the most reduced lead time for new product launches and product development. In order to achieve this performance, Toyota values the knowledge it can collect from the different actors involved in the development process.

Similarly, in the case of collaborative networks, due to its dynamical nature, the effort to collect and reuse knowledge during the product development process is a critical factor to the success of the business opportunity. This assertion is especially true when it is considered the case of innovative and customized products with an increased emphasis in the time constraints and the usual complexity of the task.

The knowledge focus in the development of new products in CNs starts immediately at the customer request early definition. Traditionally, when using the "waterfall" approach, the customer requirements are frozen at the beginning, followed by a more detailed design system with a fixed interface specification of the subsystems. This in turn allows the independent development phase of the subsystems between the different members of the collaborative network.

This traditional approach in many cases results in inconsistent final solutions, due to problems that are discovered late or in advanced phases of the design process. It has also the drawback of low levels of reutilization of knowledge and a suboptimal regarding the network configuration.

In contrast, with the set-based approach, the development process begin with a set of possibilities that comply with the customer requirements, then through a series of tests and experimentation, an intensive acquisition and combination of knowledge occurs, which results in the elimination of the unfeasible solutions narrowing the set of solutions until arriving at an unique solution supported in a final network configuration (see Fig. 2).

Table 2. Waste examples in a networked product development process

Type of waste	Examples
Overproduction	- Over-engineering - Over-complex solutions from poor designs - Completing design elements that are not needed before time - Develop features that the customer does not see as a value - Dividing the developing tasks and letting each network partner duplicate what others are doing
Waiting	- Unnecessary approvals from other partners in the network - Waits for other partners to process their tasks - Queuing to use an overloaded partner facility - Waiting from customers inputs - Waiting for partner responses - Waiting for completion of other design elements
Transportation	- E-mailing information to other partners - Multiple hand-offs between partners - Circulating paperwork for signatures - Reports distribution among network
Overprocessing (nonvalue-added processing)	- Preparing reports or paperwork that aren't used - Creating features the customer doesn't want - Re-entering data for each partner - Re-designing products or components that already have been designed - Most network engineering support services
Excess inventory	- Poorly organized projects that take too long to complete - Working on projects that are not commercially viable - Batch processing transactions among partners - "Large" design releases
Excess motion	- Searching for information that has not been, often across partners - Going to meetings - Travel
Rework and defects	- Design errors - Data service failures or data missing - Engineering change orders due to design errors - Missing or not understanding customer needs - Missing or incomplete information
Underutilized people	- Limited authority and responsibility for basic tasks inside the network; - Not sufficiently sharing knowledge; - Not involving partners early in the development process

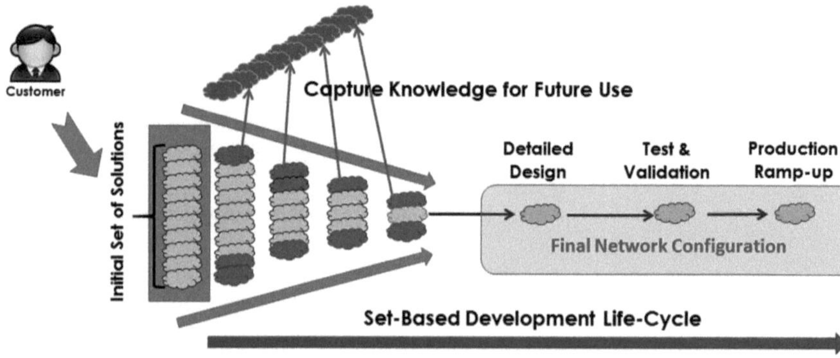

Fig. 2. Set-based development life-cycle in collaborative networks

This set-based development process occurs simultaneously with a collaborative planning construction and is oriented to address the demand planning and demand fulfillment activities for new personalized and innovative products. This integrated tool allows each partner of the collaborative network to contribute to the value-added knowledge acquisition process. After the detailed design approvable and the selection of the final network participants, the tool also allows each partner to collaboratively negotiate the collaborative production plan by directly proposing delivery dates, production lead times and costs, via a web-based planning graphical tool which is available and shared by all supply network partners [16].

Ultimately, through negotiations undertaken between all the core partners and potential partners of the collaborative network it is reached a feasible and efficient manufacturing plan for the supply network, where all the necessary operations are defined in terms of lead times, time overlaps, minimum cost, and other relevant negotiation indicators defined at the beginning of the negotiation.

In summary, a set-based development approach offers remarkable opportunities for efficient learning and knowledge acquisition before decision making. By allowing delayed decision-making, till the moment where enough knowledge is available, enables intelligent decisions and minimizes mistakes. Another advantage derived from this approach is the support for collaborative decision-making, facilitating robust product designs that take into consideration the best solutions in terms of products configurability as well as the need for fast response to market requests.

A third adaptation of extending the lean principles to a collaborative network environment, is the value stream mapping. Value stream mapping (VSM) is an effective and confirmed tool to analyze existing business processes and to help redesigning them based on lean concepts.

The VSM uses lean concepts to analyze the current state of a process, in this case the development process, and seeks to improve its performance, which means to develop the "future state" (the to-be), and creates a plan for implementing the new efficient process. When using the VSM on the customizable product development processes in CNs, the key is to focus the analysis on the work flow and on the waste in its different forms as presented in Table 2. The practitioner when analyzing a specific development project has to focus is eyes on the different forms of waste, seeing specific activities for what they truly are - waste or nonvalue-added activities.

For the current case of establishing a more efficient product development process in collaborative networks, the VSM tool prototype developed inside the framework offers a way to assess the overall efficiency of a development project, based in lean principles (see Fig. 3). The approach is proving to be a very powerful tool towards an easy and intuitive interpretation of the relevant indicators of the aggregated efficiency in the management of customizable product development processes. The VSM collaborative analysis tool is also very helpful to handle the common trade-offs that arise in development projects so that the managers can see the consequences of a decision that has multi-criteria impacts.

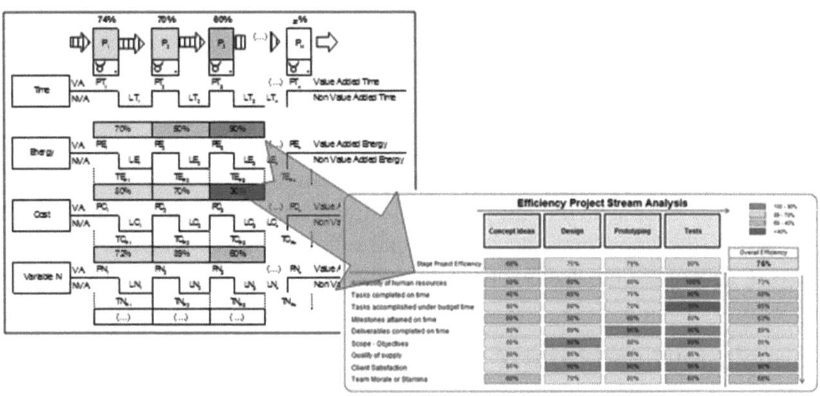

Fig. 3. Value stream mapping in collaborative designing analysis

In order to test and validate the lean concepts addressed in the proposed set-based framework, it was developed the two prototype tools described previously: a set-based collaborative development tool and a value stream mapping collaborative designing analysis tool. These two tools were included in a previously developed Collaborative Portal aimed to support the formation and the operation of collaborative networks for production of innovative and personalized products.

The Collaborative Portal is an ongoing research project that includes industrial manufacturing companies and it is aimed to help managers in face of business opportunities to form and configure collaborative networks. Figure 4 represents the business process definition of the Collaborative Portal which now includes the set-based product development toolset.

By using web-based technology, the current prototype implementation of the Collaborative Portal allows the network managers in CNs to interact dynamically and in real-time in order to deal with the complexity of addressing the demand of innovative and personalized products in a efficient and responsive way.

The Collaborative Portal is intended to provide a comprehensive set of tools aimed to cover the full life-cycle of collaborative networked organizations from the arise of

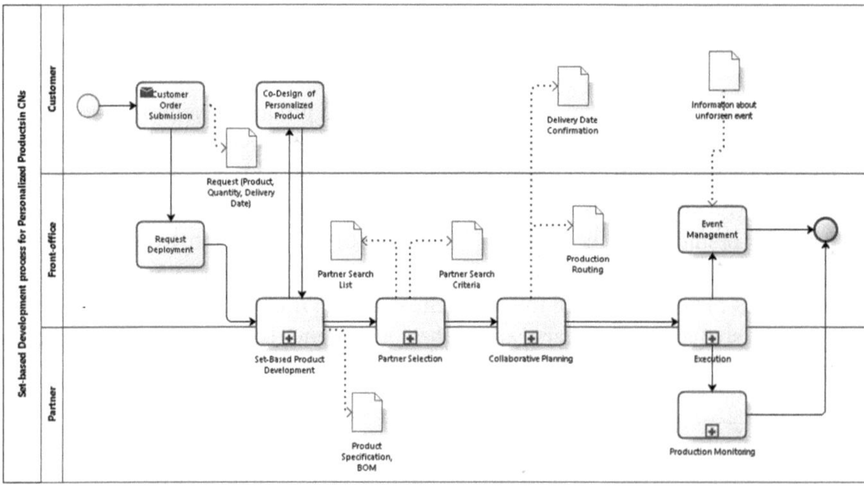

Fig. 4. Business process of set-based development process in CNs

the business opportunity to the execution and the delivery of the product. With the set-based product development module latest inclusion it was possible to tackle more clearly issues such as the knowledge acquisition and efficient development of personalized products in networked environments.

4 Conclusions and Future Developments

The present work proposes a lean set-based design approach for development of customizable products in Collaborative Networks. This approach intended to support the creation of efficient collaborative environments that enable manufacturing companies to produce customizable high value-added products. The main concept that mobilized this approach was the effort to address the "time to market" issue or responsiveness for innovative and personalized products inside collaborative networks. This critical factor of responsiveness is assuredly associated with the efficient use of resources and the preservation of the knowledge inside the companies. Therefore in order to guarantee full compliance with these objectives it was selected a lean inspired knowledge-based engineering approach.

In particular, the approach represents a translation of the lean manufacturing principles, tools and methods. Using this approach, the objective is to provide companies with the necessary means to develop and manufacture collaboratively customizable products with increased efficiency. Despite the immediate obstacle in using the traditional lean approach for product development due to the inexistence of material flows and the main element involved in the development process correspond to the human element, nevertheless the implementation of standard work practices and other lean concepts bring to this knowledge intensive activity great benefits.

The proposed approach aims to facilitate collaborative networks managers in achieving more efficient and faster responses to customer request of personalized products through: the use of lean principles such as waste reduction; the support of a innovative knowledge engineering design of new products through a lean inspired set-based approach; and through the assessment of the overall efficiency of the development projects by using the value stream mapping analysis tool.

The conceptual model of the approach, developed from previous and ongoing R&D international and national projects with industrial partners has been translated into prototypes applied to the real cases of textile and clothing industry.

The proposed approach of a lean set-based design approach for development of customizable products in Collaborative Networks represents a contribution towards the definition of adequate business models addressing responsiveness and efficient use of knowledge on customized manufacturing and collaborative environments.

As future developments, it is planned for the research team to continuing testing the current prototype Portal through the contributions of the industrial users. Simultaneously seeking to add to the current set of tools other lean methods and tools that contribute to the ongoing effort to deliver a more efficient and reliable knowledge-based framework designed to assist companies in operating in collaborative networked environments.

Acknowledgments. Project "TEC4Growth - Pervasive Intelligence, Enhancers and Proofs of Concept with Industrial Impact/NORTE-01-0145-FEDER-000020" is financed by the North Portugal Regional Operational Programme (NORTE 2020), under the PORTUGAL 2020 Partnership Agreement, and through the European Regional Development Fund (ERDF).

References

1. Piller, F.T., Tseng, M.M.: New directions for mass customization. In: Tseng, M.M., Piller, F.T. (eds.) The Customer Centric Enterprise, pp. 519–535. Springer, Heidelberg (2003)
2. Fogliatto, F.S., da Silveira, G.J., Borenstein, D.: The mass customization decade: an updated review of the literature. Int. J. Prod. Econ. **138**(1), 14–25 (2012)
3. Tseng, M.M., Hu, S.J.: Mass customization. In: Laperrière, L., Reinhart, G. (eds.) CIRP Encyclopedia of Production Engineering, pp. 836–843. Springer, Heidelberg (2014)
4. Zangiacomi, A., et al.: Reference model framework for production of small series of innovative and fashionable goods in manufacturing networks. In: Azevedo, A. (ed.) Advances in Sustainable and Competitive Manufacturing Systems, pp. 1291–1303. Springer, Heidelberg (2013)
5. Carneiro, L., et al.: Reference model for collaborative manufacturing of customised products: applications in the fashion industry. Prod. Plann. Control **25**(13–14), 1135–1155 (2014)
6. Kennedy, M.N., Harmon, K.: Ready, Set, Dominate: Implement Toyota's Set-Based Learning for Developing Products and Nobody Can Catch You Author: Mich (2008)
7. Bastos, J., Azevedo, A., Ávila, P.: Towards a customer-driven value chain framework – a set-based oriented approach. In: Camarinha-Matos, L.M., et al. (eds.) PRO-VE 2015. IFIP AICT, vol. 463, pp. 1–14. Springer, Heidelberg (2015). doi:10.1007/978-3-319-24141-8_19
8. Ward, A., et al.: Toyota, concurrent engineering, and set-based design. **8**, 192–216 (1995)
9. Liker, J.K., et al.: Involving suppliers in product development in the United States and Japan: evidence for set-based concurrent engineering. IEEE Trans. Eng. Manag. **43**(2), 165–178 (1996)

10. Inoue, M., et al.: Collaborative engineering among designers with different preferences: application of the preference set-based design to the design problem of an automotive front-side frame. Concurr. Eng. 1063293X13493447 (2013)
11. Womack, J.P., Jones, D.T.: Lean Thinking: Banish Waste and Create Wealth in Your Corporation. Simon & Shuster, London (1996)
12. Bruun, P., Mefford, R.N.R.N.: Lean production and the internet. Int. J. Prod. Econ. **89**(3), 247–260 (2004)
13. Locher, D.A.: Value Stream Mapping for Lean Development: A How-To Guide for Streamlining Time to Market. CRC Press, Boca Raton (2008)
14. Radeka, K.: The Mastery of Innovation: A Field Guide to Lean Product Development. CRC Press, Boca Raton (2012)
15. Morgan, J.M., Liker, J.K.: The Toyota Product Development System Integrating People, Process, and Technology. B&T, Charlotte (2006)
16. Fornasiero, R., Bastos, J., Azevedo, A., Zangiacomi, A., Coscia, E.: Collaborative services for customized production in networked companies. In: Camarinha-Matos, L.M., Scherer, R.J. (eds.) PRO-VE 2013. IFIP AICT, vol. 408, pp. 363–372. Springer, Heidelberg (2013)

The Effects of Personalization on Collaborative Production Networks Location

Laura Macchion[1(✉)], Rosanna Fornasiero[2], Pamela Danese[1], and Andrea Vinelli[1]

[1] Department of Management and Engineering, University of Padova, Stradella San Nicola 3, 36100 Vicenza, Italy
laura.macchion@unipd.it
[2] Institute of Industrial Technologies and Automation, National Council of Research (ITIA-CNR), Via Corti 12, 20133 Milan, Italy

Abstract. This paper focuses on the identification of proper localization for collaborative production networks for personalized products. By the analysis of five case studies of the Italian footwear industry, the research provides the relationship between the type of personalization and the required supply network configurations by considering the production location issue, which is a topic not addressed in the literature.

The research demonstrates that since personalization is most of the time managed in parallel with mass production thus companies should be able to manage different network configurations by developing a local or global network based on the level of product personalization.

Keywords: Fashion industry · Personalization · Location · Supply chain · Supply network configuration

1 Introduction

Personalization represents an important market-niche, which accounts for about 10 % of the entire fashion industry and leads to greater consumer satisfaction and a decrease in unsold products and inventories along the supply chain [1]. But the introduction of product personalization in manufacturing activities is not an easy task because it requires the realization of small batches of products (or even single products) with unique features that implies not only radical changes in the way to organize production but also requires o reorganize the location of production network in order to provide these personalized products in reasonable times with the required cost and quality levels.

This study concerns the footwear industry, strongly influenced by variation in product styles and customers' preferences, thus providing a suitable context in which to explore the personalization. Moreover, very different and complex supply chains characterize the footwear system in terms of both fragmentation of production activities and geographical dispersion of the actors involved. However, previous literature still lacks of an extensive analysis that could link the personalization issue with the location

Published by Springer International Publishing Switzerland 2016. All Rights Reserved
H. Afsarmanesh et al. (Eds.): PRO-VE 2016, IFIP AICT 480, pp. 433–440, 2016.
DOI: 10.1007/978-3-319-45390-3_37

decision of production facilities within the supply chain. In this context, this research aims to analyse how a production network's configuration should be designed according to different types of personalization by suggesting the use of local or global networks based on the types of personalization.

A recent study established that more than 3 million visitors each month access the site www.Nikeid.com to try to personalize their own shoe [2]. Personalization brings many advantages for companies in terms of increased sales, improved customer satisfaction and loyalty and, thanks to the application of premium prices to products, the possibility of avoiding competition based on low prices [3]. A company may decide to offer just some personalized products (or just some options), or it could adopt a fully made-to-measure approach within its production. Moreover, according to this decision, companies will develop also proper information and communication technologies (ICTs), such as product virtualization and configurators, 3D scanning tools and computer-aided design technologies, to collect customers' data, identify and test in real time many personalization opportunities and also support manufacturing processes [4–8]. Therefore available literature still approaches the personalization issue by underlining the importance for the modern industry to catch the personalization possibility to enlarge their business but it lacks in debating how personalization impacts on the reorganization of production networks. In fact, even if companies have the possibility to buy the technologies necessary to implement personalization (such as 3D scanning tools) they should also be able to reorganize their production networks in order to ensure that customers can have the required personalized products in the required times.

1.1 Collaborative Production Networks

Growing competitiveness in the global market encourages manufacturing companies to form alliances among them for mutual benefit. Many forms of collaboration emerged as response to business environment transformations and the rapid developments in ICTs [8–10]. Collaboration in the form of stronger business relationships are a powerful instrument to achieve strategic objectives such as short lead time, high quality, and cost competitiveness especially for SMEs which need to create critical mass to stay competitive and collaborative networks represents a combinations of improved inter and intra-organizational business processes [8, 11]. In this paper we mainly analyse the organizational perspective of collaborative networks. From the perspective of SMEs, the collaborative business improves traditional supply chains, since they can manage the business better and increase their added value [12, 13]. In regional or sectorial Business Communities, trust can be built and communication streamlined, creating an environment suitable for the fast and efficient creation of partnerships or collaboration projects to respond to specific business opportunities [8, 10]. Moreover, the location of the companies participating to collaborative networks seems to have some strong influence on the final result of the relationship especially with customization strategies since it allows to better streamline the information and product flow [11].

1.2 Configuration of Collaborative Production Networks in Terms of Location

Even if the personalization benefits in terms of sales improvements are well known by companies and encourage these companies towards adopting customization practices, much care should be taken in the organization of production aspects. Developing personalized products requires a reorganization of processes, both internally within companies and externally with production network partners, to be able to create and produce new, small personalized collections (or even just one personalized product) with compressed lead times. Therefore, the issue of production network location assumes a crucial relevance [14–17] in particular for collaborative networks [18]. Indeed, personalization within the footwear sector remains a challenge considering the complexity of production processes connected to the assembly of the many parts composing a shoe, which are created with different materials and manufacturing technologies that may be located far-away countries. Production activities are assigned to many actors who are responsible for specific phases of the process requiring higher level of cooperation to be established among them. In the Italian footwear industry, this production network complexity drove companies to establish strong relationships with partners in the supply chain and, since the 1950s, led to the birth of local industrial districts characterized by peculiar inter-company synergies each specialized in the production of shoes typologies (sneakers, formal, fashionable woman, etc.). However, since the 80ies, a significant percentage of footwear production is outsourced and localized in other countries and widespread networks, making the realization of customized products more difficult. In this scenario, some companies have undertaken a backshoring path, shifting production from countries characterised by low labour costs to Italy (or to areas closer to their European headquarters) so that they can both respond quickly to changing customer requirements and control production quality [14–17]. Hence, for Italian footwear companies, the latest strategic challenge seems to be the identification of a new trade-off between delocalized (and distant) activities and local ones in order to produce the personalization of products in shorter times for customers but, at the same time, to produce traditional collections, with longer wait times, that could require different collaborative production network structures. Therefore, where and how to locate production in a global scenario are critical decisions to achieve competitive advantage with a personalization approach and have become an increasingly important part of firms' competitive priorities [8, 14, 16–21].

1.3 Research Objectives

New models and solutions for collaborative production network configuration are thus required, both from a scientific and an industrial point of view, to be able to catch customers' personalization necessities and to increase companies' capability to quickly react to mutable market demand [16]. This is particularly true in very complex and fluctuating environments such as the footwear industry.

Despite the importance of the personalization issue within the footwear industry, literature lacks of studies that deepen the relationship between personalization and the proper supply chain location. The literature highlights the need to study the personalization issue in relation to production network configurations, particularly in terms of production location decisions (e.g., [16, 17]). Examples of such reorganization can include backshoring delocalized activities and searching for a new trade-off between international and local activities to compress market lead times [14, 16, 17, 19–21]. Given these considerations, many authors have recognised the centrality of the issue of geographical production diversification and how it is linked to personalization, but none have focused on the footwear industry. The introduction of different types of personalization strongly changed the production processes of the footwear industry, making decisions of production network configurations very critical. Thus, the research question is as follows:

RQ. How production network should be located accordingly to different types of personalization in the footwear industry?

2 Methodology

Considering the explorative nature of the research question, data collection and analysis were conducted accordingly to the multiple case study methodology [22]. Theoretical sampling and replication method were adopted to structure the research [23]. Moreover, the focal companies of the supply chain were selected as unit of analysis accordingly to the following criteria: the focal company holds the brand licence; it controls the entire supply chain and is responsible for the realization of the final product and for the location of the production within the entire supply chain; the focal company should occupy different market positions to provide a complete overview of the footwear market. Five companies agreed to participate in the study (Table 1).

Table 1. Companies' collection selection criteria

	Company A	Company B	Company C	Company D	Company E
Owned brand	✓	✓	✓	✓	✓
Market positioning	Luxury	Luxury	Mass market	Mass market	Luxury

To adopt an accurate case study approach and ensure data triangulation, we used different sources of observation, including data derived from direct observation during company visits, systematic interviews with company managers, and archives and documents shared with the interviewers. Industrial and operations managers and entrepreneurs were interviewed during company visits in 2015. We selected these profiles since they have a deep knowledge about the firms' processes and strategies. An interview protocol was developed for the research and information were collected during company visits; email or telephone contact were used where necessary [24]. In particular, the interview protocol was divided into three areas. The first area was dedicated to the main collection of data related to the company (such as turnover, employees and main economic indicators). The second area was dedicated to studying companies' ongoing decisions regarding personalization. The third area dealt with determining production networks' configurations in order to identify business relationships with supply partners and different production configurations. The interviews were recorded with the permission of the respondents [24].

Analysis of the collected data was based on two main components: within and cross case analysis [15]. The within case analysis was useful to study for each supply chain in the presence of personalization, and then the cross case was used to compare the constructs of interests in other settings [22]. In particular, within case analysis was used to reduce and manage data to structure, define, reduce and organize of collected information and avoid bias. It explored the relations between different types of production networks (i.e. the unit of analysis of the research) and the personalization issue in footwear production networks. Then, the cross-analysis was used to underline these differences among the cases study in order to identify how supply chain should be organized accordingly to different personalized products. The process of data analysis was based on the achievement of full agreement between the research team also doing a check and a thorough discussion of any individual author's biases that could have obfuscate the analysis.

3 Results: The Relationship Between Personalization and Production Network Configurations

This research identifies the collaborative production network configurations in terms of locations that can support different types of personalization within the Italian footwear industry (RQ). In particular, first it was analysed how production networks are structured by identifying the presence of different production areas: the first is located in the Far East, mainly for reasons of low cost (companies C and D); the second is in Italy or near the Italian headquarters to take advantage of specific manufacturing specialization (company C) and lead time compression (companies A, B, C, E). However, the research shows a growing push for the footwear industry to open new factories in or near Italy. This aspect is particularly interesting in relation to the backshoring phenomenon (e.g., [16, 21]), which is assuming an increasing importance in the footwear sector and within the fashion industry in general since it allows a strong reduction in delivery times and logistical costs, as well as the avoidance of cultural differences and communication problems easing the collaboration mechanisms with suppliers. For instance, companies C and D are building their new plants in Italy and in Eastern Europe for, respectively, 20 % and 10 % of their production. In these new plants, they will realize either the complete production processes (as in the case of company C) or just the final assembly (company D), but in both cases, these production relocations will allow the companies to deliver even personalized productions with compressed lead times. The new manufacturing plants opened by companies C and D will be used, in particular, to improve their segmented personalization by reinforcing the realization of new collections personalized for market trends. This is based on a different collaboration approach where, upon a strategic framework, suppliers are asked to quickly answer to specific requests of the focal company needs of the customer.

Moreover, the case studies reveal that the production network location is linked to the personalization typology offered to customers. For the highest personalization achievable, the production network structure must ensure speed within processes by developing fast delivery times through the design of the local production network (located in Italy or in areas near Italy, such as East European countries). In fact, made-to-measure and configured products require that collaboration is based on flexibility of suppliers and the companies A, B, C and D produce their collections in local production networks. By developing local networks, companies can better communicate with suppliers and other partners to share information obtained from markets and customers and provide the right product for the specific needs of the final consumer. Moreover, in this type of production network, raw materials and components are obtained locally when possible, always with the idea of decreasing lead times. Production capacity for individual personalization is, in fact, strongly affected by demand peaks, which companies try to cope with through collaboration with partners (subcontractors and raw materials suppliers) to achieve, through personalization, a real competitive advantage towards cheaper imported products. The re-localization of the production networks is occurring particularly among the highest market segments of the footwear industry as they attempt to reduce lead times of production and to better control the quality of the final products. In fact, customers asking for personalization may often be willing to pay a higher price for products, but this price must be supported by fast delivery times and adequate quality in manufacturing. Therefore, the reason for localizing is not only the need to achieve high product quality but also the necessity of shortening the market response time.

For mass products, the production network can be organized locally but also internationally depending on the type of position that the company has in the market: luxury companies will continue to choose local networks (mainly located in industrial districts) to achieve the advantages of using a "made in" label and to maintain high quality in their products (such as company A), but to companies belonging to the low-medium level market segment, the choice of production network localization may fall on countries in the Far East for cost benefits (such as company D). However, it is interesting to note that new product development phases are all produced within the Italian territory (for both companies locate production in Italy and in other countries) that aim to design products characterised by the "Italian style".

4 Conclusion and Discussion

This study has helped to deepen the understanding of the personalization issue by identifying what configurations of production networks in terms of location can support personalization (RQ). The case studies revealed that there are substantial differences in the definition of production networks by identifying the presence of two different production areas: the first located in the Far East, mainly for reasons of low cost, and the second characterized by local networks to take advantage of specific manufacturing specialization and lead time compression. The research highlights that to approach the personalization issue there is a strong need to shorten the required lead-time within the collaborative production network to be successful and give strength to the return of productive activities (previously outsourced) in the European territories (i.e., the back-shoring or reshoring issue). In this way, personalization provides openings for a "new industrialization" of the European countries, even if companies must be able to radically reorganize their production processes by focusing on. Thus, for Italian footwear companies, the current challenge seems to be the identification of new trade-offs among delocalized and local activities in order to produce personalized products in short times but, at the same time, to produce traditional collections, with longer production times, that could require different production network structures. The results of this study may contribute to both theory and practice since the identification of different types of personalization and their deployment into different production network configurations are key determinants in overcoming ongoing market challenges. In this way, the research contributes not only to the identification and formalization of different types of personalization within the footwear industry but also identifies a clear correspondence between different types of personalization and supply chain configurations. Also, for managers, this work may represent a significant contribution to the identification of new ways to compete in the footwear industry and, at the same time, to define the best approach to production networks in line with their type of personalization. Moreover companies aiming at approaching the personalization issue can have the possibility to achieve a higher margin. In fact, the use of local suppliers would enable companies to justify the higher price on the finished product first of all in terms of improved quality features but also to prove the sustain of the company to national labour market (that normally in European Countries have a higher labour cost to be sustained by companies). However, given that the personalization issue is a trend that is also growing in other industries, this paper contributes to extend the managerial and academic debate on this theme and further research are encouraged to investigate personalization in other sectors. Starting from this preliminary analysis, it is possible to define a quantitative model to evaluate the impact of new location of production networks with performance indicators linking the increase of flexibility, the level of personalization and the location of the companies to the overall performance of the systems. Moreover future works could consider the impact of personalization on sales and operations plans since they are extremely relevant processes that must be taken into consideration when a company decide to implement personalization.

References

1. Bain & Company 2013, Making it personal: rules for success in product customization. http://www.bain.com/publications/articles/making-it-personal-rules-for-success-in-product-customization.aspx
2. Yeung, H.T., Choi, T.M., Chiu, C.H.: Innovative mass customization in the fashion industry. In: Cheng, T., Choi, T. (eds.) Innovative Quick Response Programs in Logistics and Supply Chain Management, pp. 423–454. Springer, New York (2010)
3. Piller, F.T.: Mass customization: reflection on the state of the concept. Int. J. Flex. Manuf. Syst. **16**(4), 313–334 (2004)
4. Christopher, M., Peck, H., Towill, D.R.: A taxonomy for selecting global supply chain strategies. Int. J. Logistics Manage. **17**(2), 277–287 (2006)
5. Fiore, A.M., Lee, S.E., Kunz, G.: Individual differences, motivations, and willingness to use a mass customization option for fashion products. Eur. J. Mark. **38**(7), 835–849 (2004)
6. Dong, B., Jia, H., Li, Z.: Implementing mass customization in garment industry. Syst. Eng. Procedia **3**, 372–380 (2012)

7. Fogliatto, F., da Silveira, G.J.C., Borenstein, D.: The mass customization decade: an updated review of the literature. Int. J. Prod. Econ. **138**, 14–25 (2012)
8. Carneiro, L., Shamsuzzoha, A.H.M., Almeida, R., Azevedo, A., Fornasiero, R., Ferreira, P.S.: Reference model for collaborative manufacturing of customised products: applications in the fashion industry. Prod. Plann. Control **25**(13–14), 1135–1155 (2014)
9. Camarinha-Matos, L.M., Afsarmanesh, H.: Collaborative networks: a new scientific discipline. J. Intell. Manuf. **16**(4–5), 439–452 (2005)
10. Camarinha-Matos, L.M., Afsarmanesh, H., Ollus, M.: Methods and Tools for Collaborative Networked Organizations. Springer, US (2008)
11. Claudia-Melania, C., Azevedo, A.L.: Multi-perspective challenges on collaborative networks business environments. In: Camarinha-Matos, Luis M., Afsarmanesh, H., Ortiz, A. (eds.) Collaborative Networks and Their Breeding Environments. IFIP, vol. 186, pp. 25–32. Springer, US (2005)
12. Ignatiadis, I., Briggs, J., Svirskas, A., Bougiouklis, K., Koumpis, A.: Introducing a collaborative business model for European ERP value chains of SMEs. In: Camarinha-Matos, L.M., Afsarmanesh, H., Novais, P., Analide, C. (eds.) Establishing the Foundation of Collaborative Networks. IFIP, vol. 243, pp. 505–512. Springer, US (2020)
13. Carneiro, L.M., Almeida, R., Azevedo, A.L., Kankaanpaa, T., Shamsuzzoha, A.H.M.: An innovative framework supporting SME networks for complex product manufacturing. In: Camarinha-Matos, L.M., Boucher, X., Afsarmanesh, H. (eds.) PRO-VE 2010. IFIP AICT, vol. 336, pp. 204–211. Springer, Heidelberg (2010)
14. Poulin, M., Montreuil, B., Martel, A.: Implications of personalization offers on demand and supply network design: a case from the golf club industry. Eur. J. Oper. Res. **169**, 996–1009 (2006)
15. Montreuil, B., Poulin, M.: Demand and supply network design scope for personalized manufacturing. Prod. Plann. Control **15**(5), 454–469 (2005)
16. Macchion, L., Moretto, A., Caniato, F., Caridi, M.: Production and supply network strategies within the fashion industry. Int. J. Prod. Econ. **163**, 173–188 (2015)
17. MacCarthy, B.L., Jayarathne, P.G.S.A.: Supply network structures in the international clothing industry: differences across retailer types. Int. J. Oper. Prod. Manage. **33**(7), 858–886 (2013)
18. De Maggio, M., Gloor, P.A., Passiante, G.: Collaborative innovation networks, virtual communities and geographical clustering. Int. J. Innov. Reg. Dev. **1**(4), 387–404 (2009)
19. Şen, A.: The U.S. fashion industry: a supply chain review. Int. J. Prod. Econ. **114**, 571–593 (2008)
20. Taplin, I.M.: Restructuring and reconfiguration: the EU textile and clothing industry adapts to change. Eur. Bus. Rev. **18**(3), 172–186 (2006)
21. Kinkel, S.: Trends in production relocation and backshoring activities: changing patterns in the course of the global economic crisis. Int. J. Oper. Prod. Manage. **32**(6), 696–720 (2012)
22. Yin, R.: Case study Research: Design and Methods, 5th edn. Sage publications, Thousand Oaks (2013)
23. Eisenhardt, K.M.: Building theories from case study research. Acad. Manage. Rev. **14**(4), 532–550 (1989)
24. Voss, C.: Case research in operations management. Int. J. Oper. Prod. Manage. **22**, 195–291 (2002)

Services and Cloud - Service Orientation

Services Personalization Approach for a Collaborative Care Ecosystem

Thais Andrea Baldissera(✉) and Luis M. Camarinha-Matos

Faculty of Science and Technology and Uninova-CTS,
Universidade NOVA de Lisboa, Campus de Caparica, Portugal
{tab, cam}@uninova.pt

Abstract. Ageing entails several limitations, calling for assistance services adapted to particular elderly's needs and life style. Provision of such may involve many stakeholders, including relatives, caregivers, professional care people, suppliers and other support entities. The use of collaborative networks has been proposed as a mean of integrating contributions from distinct service providers and promoting collaboration to seek the best options among multiple services. Despite of advances in collaborative networks for elderly care, current research and development in care services are chiefly focused on the development of isolated services, considering only a single service provider, emphasizing excessively techno-centric solutions. The need for dealing with personalization of care services in a collaborative environment is rising in importance and, thus, requires a flexible way to guide the process of ranking and selecting services. In this paper, a method based on fuzzy logic to identify services and corresponding providers thought service adherence criteria is presented. To show the feasibility of the method, an illustrative scenario of elderly life style in which services are ranked based on multiple views, from single to composite services, to show how distinct integrations may result in different recommendations.

Keywords: Collaborative business services · ICT and ageing · Collaborative networks · Personalization · Fuzzy logic

1 Introduction

In recent years, one of the most important changes in the history of humanity has been taking place: the increasing demographic shift related to elderly population. Current trends suggest that the global elderly population above 80 years old will increase by 217 % in 2050 when compared to 2015. Also, the elderly population is supposed to surpass young people in many regions of the world, according to the *Help Age International Organization* [1], which accentuates the importance of research on aging-related matters in our society [2–4].

As people age, additional needs are required to maintain individuals healthy, and within good quality of life. In this process, classifying an individual as elderly goes beyond the use of age as a determinant factor. Indeed, individual aging aspects, such as the living context, personal capabilities and competences also contribute to better characterize an elderly individual. Each elderly individual may require very specific services (e.g., care and assistance) in accordance to this/her life context. As a

H. Afsarmanesh et al. (Eds.): PRO-VE 2016, IFIP AICT 480, pp. 443–456, 2016.
DOI: 10.1007/978-3-319-45390-3_38

consequence, a particular service may be perfectly adequate for an individual and completely useless for another one. Therefore, a relevant issue refers to the need of integrated and personalized services.

The notion of personalized service means that the service is tailored to each individual [5–9]. For several authors [5, 6, 10], personalizing a service involves an agreement between customers and providers (and all other involved stakeholders) through which they share information to be organized in an intelligent and adaptive way. This collaborative agreement allows reaching best experiences by those involved in providing personalized services, relevant and attractive to each customer, respecting the characteristics and the context of life of each one.

In this sense, care services should then be integrated, since they usually have influence on each other. The notion of collaborative business ecosystem for elderly care can assist on the integration of different services from distinct providers [11]. In addition, finding the best combination of services and service providers that cover customer's desires and life context, and following a collaborative network strategy is a though process. Many criteria for service composition can influence decisions, and frequent contextual analysis for service personalization and evolution. To facilitate the process of finding best composite service in the context of CBE, we propose: (i) an approach to model the main CBE stakeholder′s requirements, and (ii) a mechanism to personalize services based on fuzzy cognitive maps.

The remainder of this paper is organized as follows: the introduction the research backgrounds in Sect. 2. Section 3 presents the CBE stakeholder's requirements that supports the approach. A fuzzy cognitive maps in the context of collaborative network environment to rank care services is presented in Sects. 4. A practical application of the approach is shown in Sect. 5. Finally, the conclusion in Sect. 6 with a discussion on the main future work and conclusions.

2 Research Background

The main research question addressed in this work is: *How to provide personalized and evolutionary collaborative care services for elderly in an effective and reliable way?* And the pursued hypothesis is: *Effective and reliable personalized and evolutionary services for elderly care can be provided if a suitable set of multi-provider business services are composed and integrated in the context of a collaborative network environment and supported by context awareness methods, mechanisms and systems.*

The research is organized according to the following phases: (1) Collaborative Business Ecosystem Model and Personalization Mechanism Development; (2) Personalization Mechanism Refinement; (3) Personalization Mechanism Consolidation; (4) Evolution Mechanism Development; and (5) Collaborative Business Ecosystem Model and Evolution Mechanisms Consolidation.

This work follows the initial ideas presented in [11], where the proposed a Collaborative Business Ecosystem (CBE) was proposed for elderly care. The main goal of CBE is delivery of personalized and evolutionary care services. In the elderly care domain, personalization involves the analysis of the senior's life context for personalized service composition. For each change in the customer's context it is necessary to analyze the situation (in collaboration will all relevant stakeholders), and evolve the service to fit that context.

The simplified view of a support system for the CBE is presented in Fig. 1. In such ecosystem, the main intervenient actors are divided into two groups: (a) *Elderly Living Environment (ELE),* representing the elderly costumers and their ambient and context, including informal caregivers, such as family and friends, and all applications and devices with which they interact such as context aware devices; (b) *Service Providers Environment (SPE),* representing the care provision stakeholders, which has the goal of providing care and assistance services, facilitating support and companionship, all based on community participation with established trust.

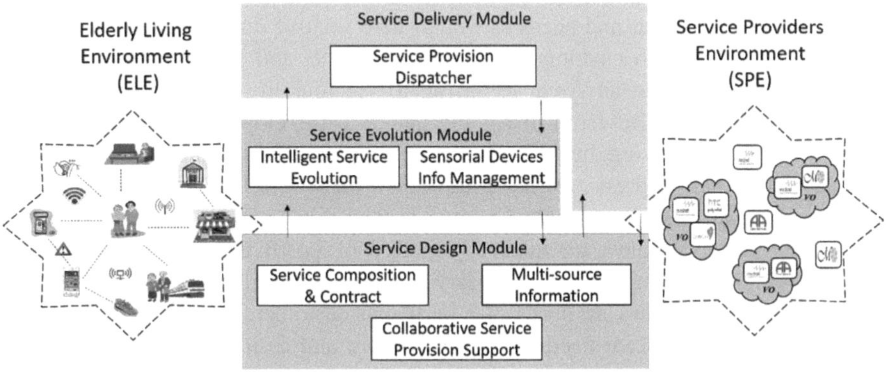

Fig. 1. Simplified view of the CBE system

To operate the CBE, three main modules are considered: (1) Service design module: responsible for receiving service requests from seniors and family and searching the providers and best services available for the senior and his/her living environment (*ELE customer*); (2) Service evolution module: responsible for analyzing context information and proposing a personalized and evolutionary care and assistance service for ELE customer; and (3) Service runtime module: responsible for notifying the *SPE* and delivering to *ELE* the care and assistance services according to the corresponding agreed terms.

This paper focuses on the first research phase (Collaborative Business Ecosystem Model and Personalization Mechanism Development) and proposes a mechanism based on fuzzy cognitive maps to identify the required services and corresponding providers.

3 Elderly Care Ecosystem Stakeholders

A Collaborative Business Ecosystem (CBE) may involve many elements, covering customers (elderly) and their preferences and needs, care and assistance services, and service provision organizations [11]. The organization of this ecosystem is according to four main areas: customer, care needs, service, and service providers. *Customer* is related to relevant information about elderly as a customer within the CBE. *Care needs* represent the major groups of necessities of individuals within the elderly community. A *service* represents a care service available within the ecosystem. *Services* are provided by *service providers*. In more detail:

- *Customer:* an accurate customer's profile is fundamental to identify the best option of care services. In CBE, a customer is characterized by personal attributes, constraints and life style. Personal attributes include gender, age, personality, family members, address, etc. Constraints refer to customer's physical and cognitive restrictions, and current and historical diseases. Life style captures customer's preferences, such as wishes, religion, social activities, technology usage, etc.
- *Care Need:* when requiring some care services, it is important to identify what are the customer's wishes and needs as well as their relative importance. A care need is directly connected to customer's profile, constraints and life style. In CBE, each care need belongs to an Area. Referring to the four life settings defined by the BRAID - Bridging Research in Ageing and ICT Development - roadmap project [12]: independent living, health and care, occupation in life, and recreation in life as areas. Customers express care needs through a fuzzy scale to indicate their priority regarding each need, i.e., ranging from no to very high priority as shown in Fig. 2. A care need may have an impact (negative or positive) on other care needs. Identifying such impacts is necessary to provide adequate level of services according to multiple care needs of a particular customer.
- *Service:* to cover a care need, one or more care and assistance services might be available in the collaborative ecosystem. A fuzzy scale is associated to these services to indicate their level of coverage of a care need (from no coverage to very high coverage as shown in Fig. 2). CBE considers that service descriptions are kept in a *Service Catalogue*, to be consulted whenever is needed.

Care needs and services are linked to a taxonomy to classify what is required from the customer and what is provided by service providers. The taxonomy is important during the matching process, where CBE module seeks for services to attend a set of care needs. Both services and care needs can be linked to distinct levels in the taxonomy, which may enlarge or restrict the searching process. For example, consider the following snippet of a taxonomy for health and care (Fig. 3). A service can be linked to *Remote monitoring*, which means it attends care needs related to *Follow-up monitoring* and *Regular monitoring*. However, a care need linked to *Physical compensation* does not match a service that is assigned to *Neurocognitive compensation* in the taxonomy.

- *Service Providers:* have the goal of providing care and assistance services, facilitating support and companionship. Service providers include support and regulation

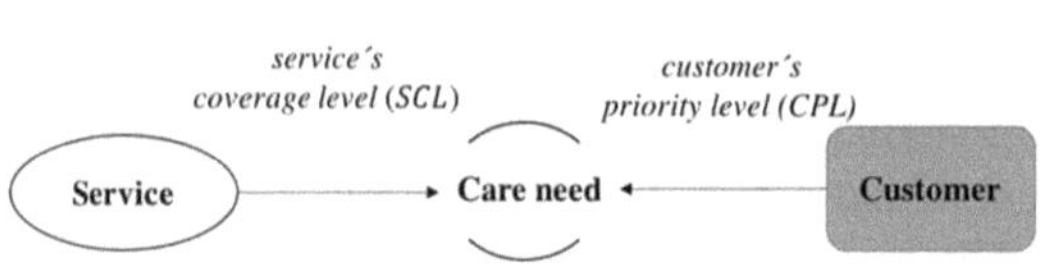

SLC	Fuzzy Scale	*CPL*
no coverage	0	no priority
very low coverage	0.2	very low priority
low coverage	0.4	low priority
moderate coverage	0.6	moderate priority
high coverage	0.8	high priority
very high coverage	1	very high priority

Fig. 2. Fuzzy scale level for service, care need and customer

entities, private companies, and/or governmental institutions. CBE can include several service providers, each one delivering its own services. It is supported by a virtual space or collaboration platform in which members (service providers) agree to create composite services as soon as good opportunities arise. This platform shall also facilitate the fast, dynamic, (desirably) on-the-fly partnership formation [13, 14]. As members of the ecosystem, partners remain prepared to engage in a composite service. When a market opportunity for a new personalized service appears, they engage in fast partnership creation (leading to a Virtual Organization - VO). The partnership remains while the package is still being delivered [15].

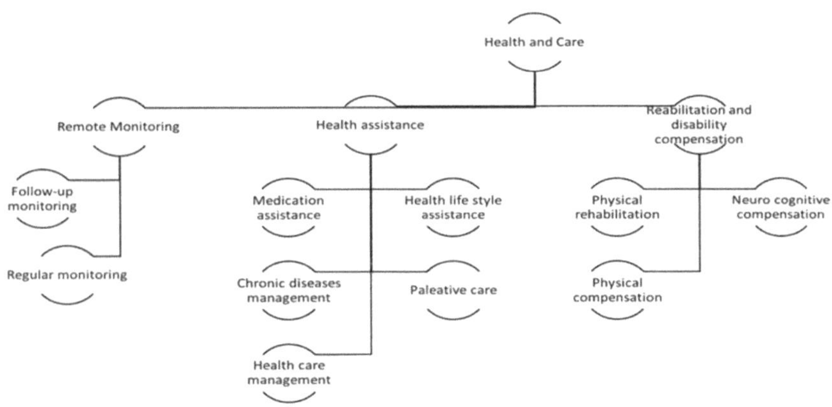

Fig. 3. Partial example of health and care taxonomy

Figure 4 illustrates the stakeholders and their relationships within the CBE.

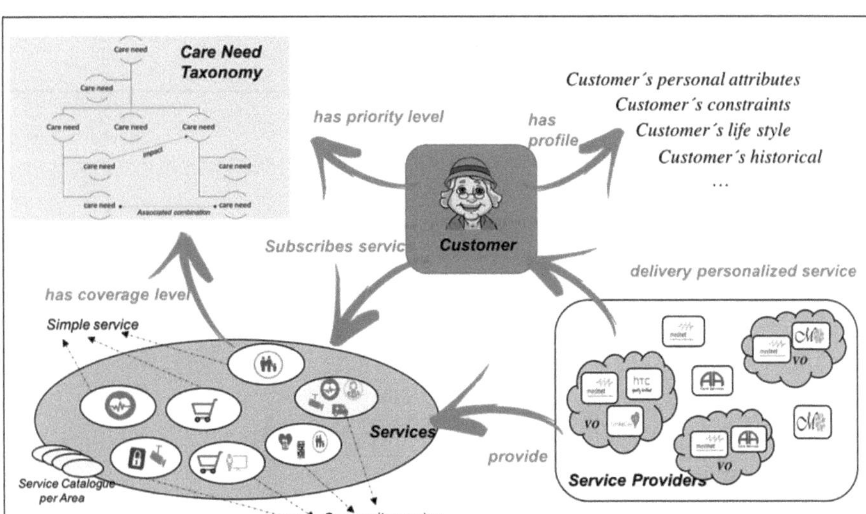

Fig. 4. CBE stakeholders and their relationships

4 A Fuzzy Cognitive Map for Elderly Care Service

Based on the relevant concepts of the elderly care ecosystem described in previous section, a causal network was designed to support the computation of a ranking of care services. The proposed causal network is inspired on the Fuzzy Cognitive Map (FCM) Kosko [16]. However, it was enriched with utility and decision nodes to support the decision process. When selecting services within the CBE, distinct factors can influence positively or negatively this decision. Additionally, decisions are often not based on precise criteria. Thus, the use of a FCM is an appealing choice to support the approach. FCMs are fuzzy directed graphs with feedback, covering many nodes and directed edges that connect and represent the causal relations between those nodes, so nodes in FCM represent concepts while edges are causal connections. A positive edge from node A to node B means A causally increases B. Intuitively, a negative edge from B to C means that node B causally decreases C. Causality is expressed in terms of a fuzzy degree, such as very low, low, moderate, high, very high, etc.

Building the Fuzzy Map Network

The proposed fuzzy causal network (FCN) has three types of nodes [17]: *chance nodes* representing uncertain domain entities, significant for causal reasoning (denoted by

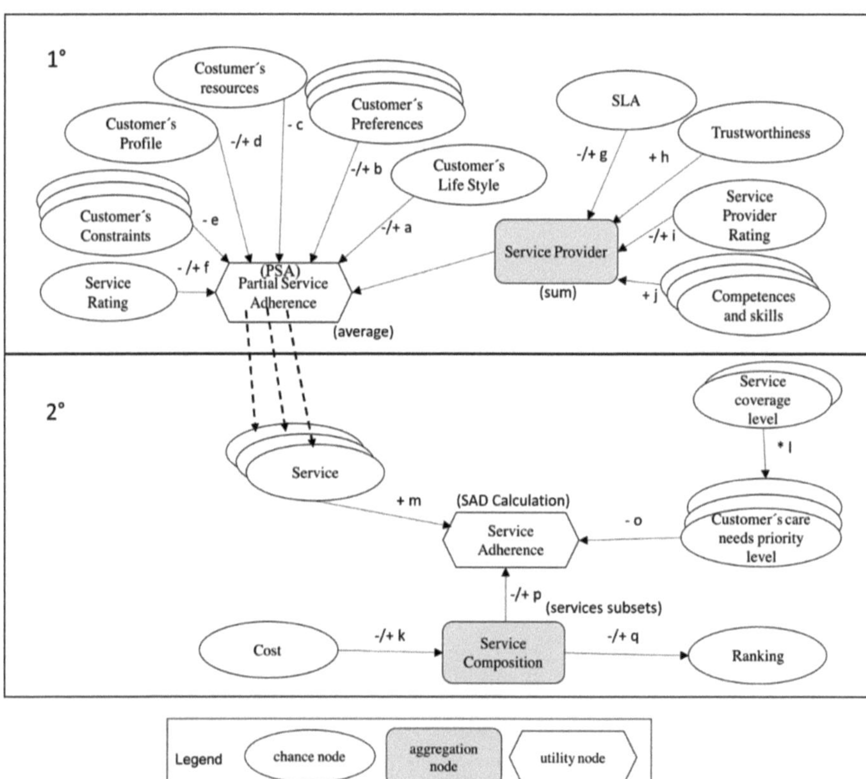

Fig. 5. The abstract model of the fuzzy causal network

ovals), *aggregation nodes* indicating partial computation (denoted by rectangles), and *utility nodes,* corresponding to the fitness value of the map configuration (denoted by a hexagon). Figure 5 presents the abstract model of fuzzy causal network, which is built in two layers. The first layer computes a partial service adherence without deeming the care needs (for each care service). The second layer takes into account the services ranked in the first layer and the customer care needs to compose multiple service options. The outcome of this layer is a ranking with service composition options that best fit the service provision.

Table 1 briefly describes the nodes of FCN. Except for utility node (*Partial Service Adherence* and *Service Adherence*), and aggregation node (*Service Provider* and *Service Composition*), all the others are represented by fuzzy variables in the range [0, 1]. This allows to initialize and analyze nodes whose values are imprecise.

Table 1. Nodes in the causal network

Node	Semantics	Type
Service Rating	The rating given by the ecosystem for a service	Chance
Customer's constraints	The constraints expressed by the customer	Chance
Customer's profile	The properties representing a customer profile	Chance
Customer's resources	The resource set possessed by a customer	Chance
Customer's preferences	The preference set expressed by the customer	Chance
Customer's life style	The properties that characterize the customer life style	Chance
SLA given by the provider	A value (0 to 10) representing the level of agreement a provider states about a service	Chance
Organization trustworthiness	The trustworthiness level given by the ecosystem to an organization	Chance
Service provider rating	The rating given by the ecosystem to a service provider	Chance
Competences and skills	The list of competences of a provider for a particular service	Chance
Service provider	A aggregator for provider characteristics	Aggregation
Partial service adherence	The adherence of a service without considering the customer care needs	Utility
Cost	A total cost of a composite care service	Chance
Partial service adherence	A value of partial adherence that was calculated in the first layer	Chance
Service coverage level	The SCL given by the service to a care need	Chance
Customer's care needs	The care needs set of a particular customer	Chance

(*Continued*)

Table 1. (*Continued*)

Node	Semantics	Type
Service adherence	The adherence of a service with care needs	Utility
Service composition	The composition of services	Aggregation
Ranking	Ranked list of services	Chance

- *Chance nodes.* They are qualified using fuzzy variables ranging from 0 to 1. These nodes and their respective degrees are determined by rules established by the services. For example, consider a service s_1 inserted in the service catalog represented by a node in the FCN. This service provides a particular resource that requires from the customer good knowledge on advanced smartphone features. The node representing this service will positively influence the service adherence whether the customer owns advanced knowledge on smartphones. On the other hand, if the customer is not familiar with this technology, the node will be considered negative.

For valued nodes, such as service rating and trustworthiness, a degree scale according to the value intervals is considered. For example, service rating may correspond to values between 0 to 10, separated in two intervals [0, 5] e [5.1, 10]. The first interval represents negative influence and the second interval is the positive influence. The degrees are also established in subintervals. Figure 6 illustrates the service rating influence scale. For example, if the rating value is 8.6, the influence is positive and the corresponding fuzzy scale is +0.8.

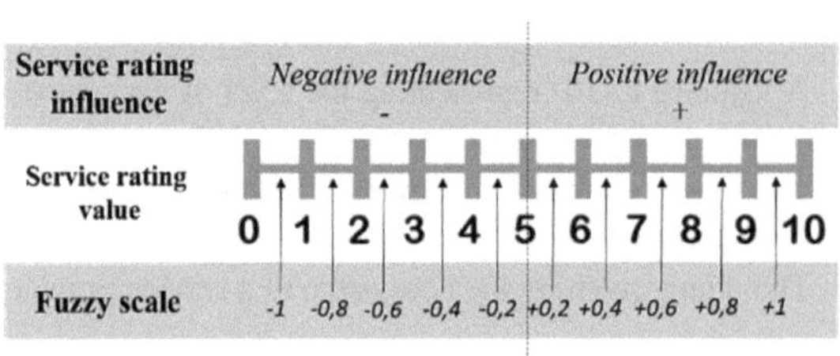

Fig. 6. Example of service rating influence scale example

When there is more than one node for an information, the influence degree is computed by the average among the nodes. For example, a customer constrained by health complications and memory disability will have the final constraint computed by the average between them.

- *Aggregation node. Service Provider* is an aggregation node because multiple providers can provide the same service. This aggregation sums the received influences. The same concept is applied to *Service Composition*. Thus different kinds of composition are built to create the service ranking.
- *Utility node.* For each service, the *partial service adherence (PSA)* is calculated. The value of *PSA* is the starting point for the second phase, where the partial service

adherence will become a chance node. It receives a service partial adherence value. Service has a positive influence on *Service Adherence* node.

Service adherence (SAD) combines *partial service adherence (PSD) and service coverage level (SCL) of* the *customer's care needs*. SAD is calculated by multiplying these values.

SAD considers a service and all customer's care needs. However, *service composition* can bring even better solutions to attend the elderly and it should be taken into account. As such, for each service composition, the service composition node represents the maximum coverage of the composite services for each customer's care needs.

5 Service Personalization Process

The proposed service personalization process is divided into four phases (Fig. 7).

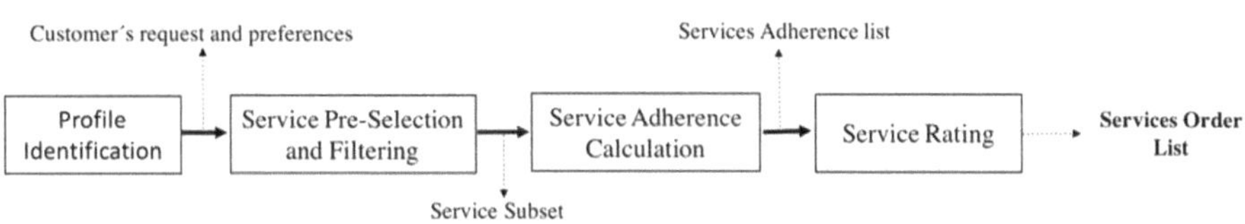

Fig. 7. Personalization Mechanism Steps

Profile Identification. Initially the customer's profile identification and customer's requests are collected, representing a preliminary step.

Service Pre-selection and Filtering. In sequence, services that cover customer's wants are selected in phase 2. Selected services are filtered through restrictions. For instance, the customer's geographical area will constrain the searching to available services in a particular region. Customer's constraints determine the best ranked (and also the not eligible) care services for attending the senior. Life style information and personality [18] can suggest customer's preference for service choice and service evolution.

Service Adherence Calculation. Service adherence represents a compatibility index between the service, customer's profile and customer's care needs. The larger the *service adherence* is, the more personalized the service is for the customer's profile. Adherence represents a potential decision criteria to rank care services. A composite business service is a collection of related and (to some extent) integrated business services that provide a specific business solution. Service composition can bring even better solutions to attend elderly and it should be taken into account.

Service Rating. The main considered parameter is *service adherence* that covers customer's requests, human constraints, preferences, etc. However, financial constraints and management strategies must also be considered for rating. For instance, service's cost and number of services providers.

6 Case Study

In this phase, the purpose is to evaluate the feasibility of the model. As a preliminary validation, we applied some illustrative scenarios-examples to give us confidence to move on to more complex cases. Thus, enlarging studied scenarios with non-trivial cases and new validation strategies will reinforce the applicability of our approach.

To guide the fuzzy map network application, let consider the following Mary's scenario. Figure 8 shows the first stage, profile identification and care needs request.

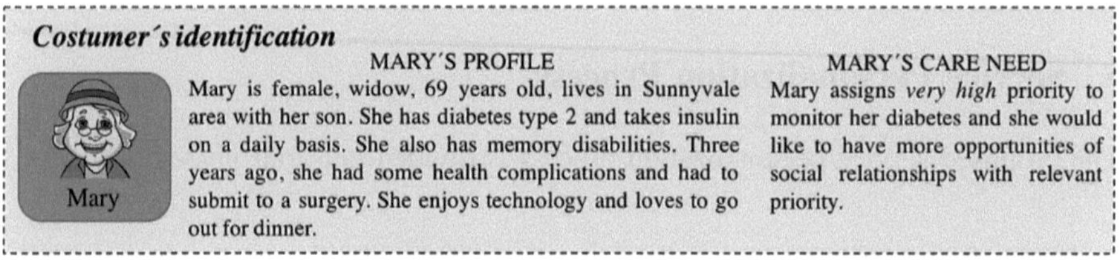

Fig. 8. Mary's identification

After customer's profile acquisition, the next step is service subset selection. Let´s imagine that five potential services to attend Mary's care needs are found. Among these services, the filtering process verifies that two of them are not available for Mary. The first one because it is not delivered in her geographical location and the second one because it is not suitable for diabetics. So, the available services for Mary's request are three services called s1, s2, and s5.

The causal network is then started. Considering service s1 like a regular health monitoring service, Fig. 9 illustrates a first part of the causal network for the example.

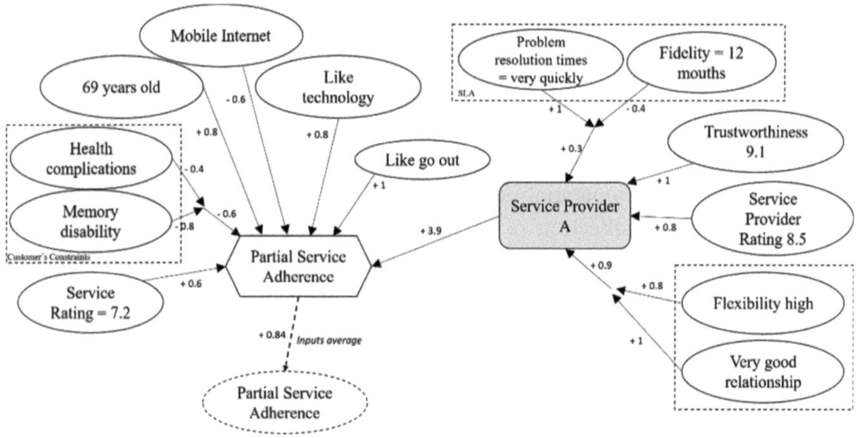

Fig. 9. Illustration of service s1 partial adherence calculation

Note that s1 requirements (defined in the first step) are compared with Mary's profile and requests. For instance, when s1 was included in the service catalogue, a recommendation was that s1 is not advised for seniors above 80 years old. As Mary is 69, her profile causally increases partial service adherence. In relation to resources, s1 requires mobile internet to make better use (although it is not mandatory). As Mary does not have mobile internet, this situation causally decreases partial service adherence. About Mary's constraints, memory disability and health complications have negative influence on the partial service adherence. The influence of these constraints is calculated as the average of the influences of the various constraints (two constraints in this example).

Regarding service provider A, nodes and their influences are identified based on the CBE management strategies. Like service provider A is aggregation node, its influence corresponds the chance nodes sum. In the example, service s1 has one service provider. If s1 had two, both would participate in the causal network and the average influence would be taken.

For s1, the partial service adherence found is 0.84 (84 %). For each service node, a *partial service adherence node* is added to the causal network, and this node will be used in the second layer.

Let's consider that by applying the fuzzy causal network to services s2 and s3, the value is 0.79 and 0.86, respectively, we can then start the second layer of the fuzzy causal network.

The Fig. 10 shows the service adherence for each single service and for the service composition possibilities. For each service coverage level a fuzzy scale (Fig. 2) was pre-established when the service was inserted in the CBE.

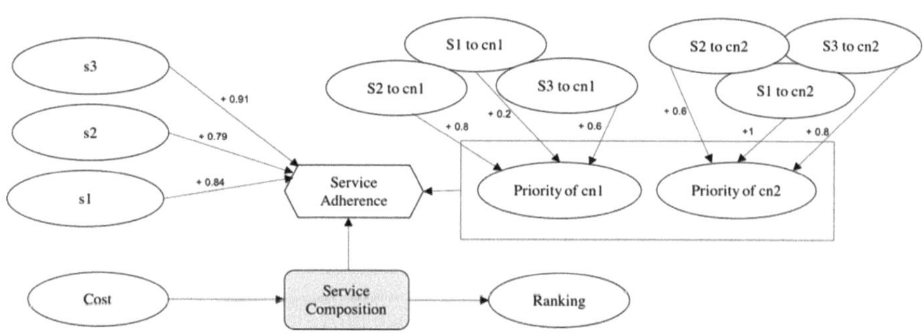

Fig. 10. Mary's service composition and ranking

The service adherence (SAD) is sum of the product between service coverage level and partial service adherence (PSA). For composite services, the service adherence is given by the maximum. As such, the following Table 2 could be generated.

Table 2. Service Adherence for single and composite services

	PSA	SCL (cn1)	SAD (cn1)	SCL (cn2)	SAD (cn2)	SAD
Single services						
S1	0,84	0,2	0,168	1	0,84	1,008
S2	0,79	0,8	0,632	0,6	0,474	1,106
S3	0,91	0,6	0,546	0,8	0,728	1,274
Composite services						
s1 and s2	–	–	0,632	–	0,84	1,472
s1 and s3	–	–	0,546	–	0,84	1,386
s2 and s3	–	–	0,632	–	0,728	1,360
s1, s2 and s3	–	–	0,632	–	0,84	1,472

For Mary seven possibilities were found. Using service adherence, cost and number of providers as criteria, the best scorers are ranked (Table 3).

Table 3. Rating of services for Mary

Rating	Services	Adherence	Cost	Number of providers
1	s1 and s2	1,472	44€	1
2	s1, s2 and s3	1,472	74€	2
3	s1 and s3	1,386	55€	2
4	s2 and s3	1,36	49€	2
5	S3	1,274	30€	1
6	S2	1,106	19€	1
7	S1	1,008	25€	1

To illustrate the multi-criteria ranking, the cost and number of providers as constrains and criteria. In this case, Mary can access to four composite services, and tree single services. Integrated services S1 and S2 have the same adherence of services s1, s2 and s3 (see column "*Adherence*" in Table 3). If only adherence is considered, they represent the first option for Mary, but the second also has higher cost. This cost can be negotiated by the coordinator of the CBE ecosystem, where multiple strategies can be applied, e.g. 10 % discount when the service pack is provided by the same provider, or this represents an agreement between providers.

Service S1 and service S2 have the same service provider (see row 1 in Table 3), so the subset of S1 and S2 is also delivered by one service provider. This can be an advantage, since an integrated service tends to be facilitated when provided by only one provider. On the other hand, it is risky, since a failure in the provision by this provider jeopardizes the provision of all services.

The service providers collaborative network for each customer is ultimately determined indirectly by services selection.

In our example scenario, care service providers for Mary depend on Mary's choice of services. If she chooses the first option, service provider is a single one. In contrast if she chooses the second option, a virtual organization (*VO*) is created with two providers (Fig. 11).

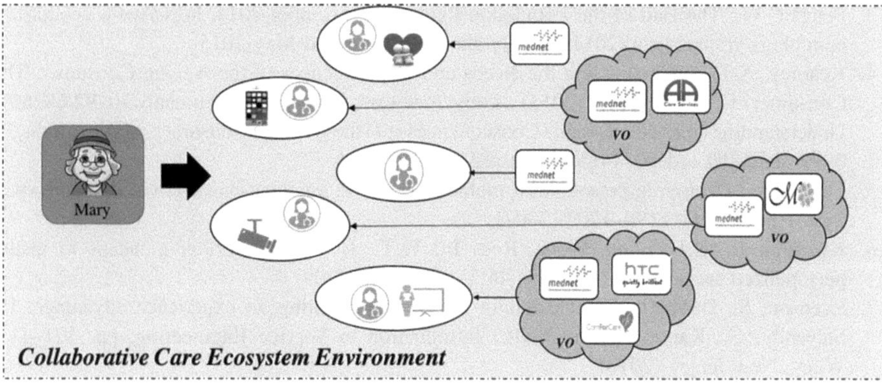

Fig. 11. Mary's potential care services providers

7 Conclusions and Future Work

Provision of personalized care services to elderly need to consider the life style aspects and the current customer's context [11]. If seniors and their family are satisfied with the provided services they will feel as unique individuals and are likely to remain loyal to the service provider [5]. Providers should seek this aspect, collecting feedback information in order to provide personalized services to their customers.

In this paper the service adherence criteria based on a fuzzy causal network for rating care services. Service adherence is part of the personalization process and represent the main criterion for finding the best personalized option to the customer.

The next phase of the work will be personalization mechanism refinement through setting multi-criteria parameters for matching between care needs and services and variable parameters like delivery time, integrated service historical data, ecosystem strategies, service loyalty time, incentives with some combined choices, etc. The last research step will address evolution mechanisms development for efficient service adaptation to evolving customer's life phase.

Acknowledgments. This work has been funded in part by the Center of Technology and Systems and the Portuguese FCT-PEST program UID/EEA/00066/2013, and by the Ciência Sem Fronteiras and Erasmus Mundi project (Brazil and European Commission).

References

1. HelpAgeInternational: Global AgeWatch Index 2014 (2014). Retrieved http://www.helpage.org/global-agewatch/. Accessed 10 Mar 2015
2. Gartner, I.: Applying Lessons From 20 Years of Hype Cycles to Your Own Innovation and Forecasting Strategies (2014). http://www.gartner.com/doc/2847417?refval=&pcp=mpe#a-1321928256. Accessed 10 Mar 2015

3. Fengler, W.: The End of the Population Pyramid, November 2014. http://www.economist.com/blogs/graphicdetail/2014/11/daily-chart-10. Accessed May 2015
4. Kearney, A.T.: Understanding the Needs and Consequences of the Ageing Consumer. The Consumer Goods Forum (2013). https://www.atkearney.com/documents/10192/682603/Understanding+the+Needs+and+Consequences+of+the+Aging+Consumer.pdf/6c25ffa3-0999-4b5c-8ff1-afdca0744fdc. Accessed 10 May 2015
5. Lee, W.-P.: Deploying personalized mobile services in an agent-based environment. Expert Syst. Appl. **32**(4), 1194–1207 (2007)
6. Kwortnik Jr., R.J., Lynn, W.M., Ross Jr., W.T.: Buyer monitoring: a means to insure personalized service. J. Mark. Res. **46**(5), 573–583 (2009)
7. Evenson, S., Dubberly, H.: Designing for service: creating an experience advantage. In: Salvendy, G., Karwowski, W. (eds.) Introduction to Service Engineering, pp. 403–413. Wiley, New Jersey (2010)
8. LeadingAge.: A Look into the Future: Evaluating Business Models for Technology-Enabled Long-Term Services and Supports (2011). http://www.leadingage.org/uploadedFiles/Content/About/CAST/CAST_Scenario_Planning.pdf. Accessed 11 April 2015
9. Hong, J., Suh, E.-H., Kim, J., Kim, S.: Context-aware system for proactive personalized service based on context history. Expert Syst. Appl. **36**(4), 7448–7457 (2009). doi:10.1016/j.eswa.2008.09.002
10. Manoharan, R., Ganesan, R., Sabarinathan, K.: Impact of hosted speech technology for health care service providers through call centers. Sch. Res. J. Interdiscip. Stud. **3**, 2712–2724 (2015)
11. Baldissera, T.A., Camarinha-Matos, L.M.: Towards a collaborative business ecosystem for elderly care. In: Camarinha-Matos, L.M., Falcão, A.J., Vafaei, N., Najdi, S. (eds.) DoCEIS 2016. IFIP AICT, vol. 470, pp. 24–34. Springer, Heidelberg (2016). doi:10.1007/978-3-319-31165-4_3
12. Camarinha-Matos, L.M., Afsarmanesh, H., Ferrada, F., Oliveira, A.I., Rosas, J.: A comprehensive research roadmap for ICT and ageing. Stud. Inform. Control **22**(3), 233–254 (2013)
13. Oliveira, A.I., Camarinha-Matos, L.M.: Negotiation support for co-design of business services. In: Camarinha-Matos, L.M., Afsarmanesh, H. (eds.) Collaborative Systems for Smart Networked Environments. IFIP AICT, vol. 434, pp. 98–106. Springer, Heidelberg (2014)
14. Afsarmanesh, H., Sargolzaei, M., Shadi, M.: A framework for automated service composition in collaborative networks. In: Camarinha-Matos, L.M., Xu, L., Afsarmanesh, H. (eds.) Collaborative Networks in the Internet of Services. IFIP AICT, vol. 380, pp. 63–73. Springer, Heidelberg (2012)
15. Camarinha-Matos, L.M., Ferrada, F., Oliveira, A.I., Rosas, J., Monteiro, J.N.: Integrated care services in ambient assisted living. In: IEEE 15th International Conference on e-Health Networking, Applications and Services (Healthcom 2013), Lisbon, pp. 197–201 (2013)
16. Kosko, B.: Neural Networks and Fuzzy Systems: A Dynamical Systems Approach to Machine Intelligence/Book and Disk, vol. 1. Prentice Hall, Upper Saddle River (1992)
17. Howard, R.A., Matheson, J.E., Miller, K.L.: Readings in Decision Analysis. Decision Analysis Group, Stanford Research Institute, Menlo Park (1977)
18. Eysenck, H.J.: A Model for Personality. Springer, Heidelberg (2012)

Information Governance as a Dynamic Capability in Service Oriented Business Networking

Mohammad R. Rasouli[1(✉)], Rik Eshuis[1], Jos J.M Trienekens[2], Rob J. Kusters[2], and Paul W.P.J Grefen[1]

[1] School of Industrial Engineering at Eindhoven, University of Technology, P.O box: 513 5600 MB Eindhoven, The Netherlands
{M.Rasouli,H.Eshuis,p.w.p.j.grefen}@tue.nl

[2] Faculty of Management Science and Technology, Open University, Heerlen, The Netherlands
{jos.trienekens,Rob.Kusters}@ou.nl

Abstract. The need for co-creating integrated solutions with customers through deep collaborations with globally distributed suppliers in the current business environment increasingly highlights the importance of service orientation in business networks (BNs). Service orientation in BNs stresses the need for composing and enacting dynamic networked business processes to support rapid responses to market opportunities. Well-established decisions for composing dynamic networked business processes and their constant enactment require high quality information exchanges among collaborating parties. Information governance (IG) is a holistic approach comprising different mechanisms that supports high quality information exchanges. In this paper the IG functionalities are identified that support ensuring high quality information exchanges among collaborating parties in service-oriented BNs. The practical relevance of the identified IG functionalities is discussed in a BN that intends to provide integrated mobility solutions. In this way, from a governance point of view, the paper intends to close the gap between information and process aspects of inter-organizational interactions among parties collaborating in dynamic value networks.

Keywords: Information governance · Service orientation · Business network · Information quality · Dynamic capability

1 Introduction

In the current business environment, organizations focusing on their core competencies collaborate with globally distributed business parties to provide products and services for customers [1]. This highlights the importance of business networking for achieving competitive advantages [2]. In this environment, competition is between business networks (BNs) rather than single organizations [3]. At the same time, emerging service-dominant logic of marketing [4] forces BNs towards service orientation through providing integrated solutions that are co-created with customers [5]. A service-oriented BN can be described as a collaborative network of independent parties within a market that co-create mass-customized packages of products and services in the form of

H. Afsarmanesh et al. (Eds.): PRO-VE 2016, IFIP AICT 480, pp. 457–468, 2016.
DOI: 10.1007/978-3-319-45390-3_39

integrated solutions [6]. Service orientation in BNs requires sensing environmental changes (e.g. customer needs) and responding to these needs rapidly through agile orchestration of resources distributed among parties. The orchestration of distributed resources is handled by networked business processes. Well-established collaborative decisions for composing dynamic networked business processes and constant interoperations through enacting composed networked business processes requires high quality information exchanges among collaborating parties. On the basis of IQ definition by [7], high quality information exchange in a BN points out providing information (by a collaborating party) that can be used properly by consumers (other collaborating parties).

Information governance (IG) is a holistic approach comprising different mechanisms that support providing high quality information [8]. In the context of service-oriented BNs, from an operational point of view, high quality information is required for decisions that support composing networked business processes. Also high quality information needs to be exchanged through networked business processes in order to prevent disruptions in operations. Although IG has been increasingly considered in recent research, it has been mainly regarded within boundaries of single organizations (see e.g. [9, 10]). On the other hand, research studies on IG in the context of BNs have been concentrated on stable BNs like conventional supply chains (e.g. [11]), and consequently emerging IG issues in dynamic BNs have not been sufficiently addressed. In order to close the described gap among the research in the context of IG and dynamic BNs, in this paper we address this research question "how IG can ensure providing high quality information for decision making and operations in service-oriented BNs?"

In this paper, to answer this research question, we characterize the functionalities of IG to enhance IQ in service-oriented BNs. To do so, we use a viewpoint based framework that enables analyzing the required functionalities within the relevant set of viewpoints. This framework is described in Sect. 2. The identified IG functionalities are explained- at a highly aggregated level- in Sect. 3. The practical relevance of the characterized IG functionalities is discussed based on a case study in Sect. 4. We discuss about the implications of the research in Sect. 5. The paper is concluded in Sect. 6.

2 A Viewpoint Based Framework for Identifying the IG Functionalities in Service-Oriented BNs

For the identification of the IG functionalities in service-oriented BNs in a structured way, we use a framework that is developed based on a viewpoint based approach (see [12]). To do so, we distinguish among two types of viewpoints, respectively, viewpoints relating to *what* needs to be governed, and viewpoints relating to *how* it can be governed. The relevant viewpoints within these two types are described in the following paragraphs.

The research question in this paper addresses governing information that is exchanged within dynamic networked business processes management. In that basis, within viewpoints relating *what* needs to be governed, we distinguish among the two relevant aspects; respectively, the information aspect and the process aspect. Differences between information and process aspects has been clearly described in the context of enterprise architecture (see e.g. [13]). The relevance of the information aspect for the identification of IG functionalities is clear. The process aspect is also relevant, because based on the research question in this paper we intend to govern information within networked business processes. In other words, governing information can require different functionalities within different steps of networked business process management (this is discussed in more detail further).

For the identification of the relevant viewpoints on *how* information can be governed, we point out two relevant views, respectively, a direction-oriented view, and a mechanism-oriented view. The direction-oriented view addresses different top-down and bottom-up approaches that can be used for governing information. Within this view, in line with governance directions proposed in related theories (see e.g. [14–16]) we consider the two main directions as an alignment direction (i.e. top-down) and an enablement direction (i.e. bottom-up). The mechanism-oriented view addresses different routines that can be used for governing information. Based on [15, 17] the three main mechanisms that can be used for governing information are characterized within structural (e.g. centralization or decentralization of roles), procedural (governance tasks), and relational mechanisms (e.g. mutual involvement practices). In this paper, based on the research question that addresses IG functionalities, we concentrate on procedural mechanisms.

In this way, the four relevant views are considered for the identification of the IG functionalities in the context of service-oriented BNs. These four views are illustrated in the following.

Information Aspect. This aspect points out information assets that are produced, stored and provided by collaborating parties in service-oriented BNs. Regarding the described research question and based on [9], the relevant domains that are considered within this aspect are specified as information product quality, information service quality, and metadata. Information product quality points of the quality attributes like completeness, accuracy, and timeliness for the information that are stored in databases. Information products are converted to information services (by software systems or manually) to be used by consumers. Information service quality addresses usefulness and usability (e.g. understandability and interpretability) of information services. Metadata, which reflects information about information, enhances semantics of information services that are exchanged among parties.

Business Process Aspect. Regarding the research question in this paper, this aspect points out networked business processes in service oriented BNs. Information services that are provided by collaborating parties are exchanged within networked business processes. Within this aspect we concentrate on managing networked business processes in the context of service-oriented BNs that embraces the two main phases, respectively, the formation and enactment of networked business processes (see[18, 19]). The formation phase reflects design-time decisions in order to set a shared objective (i.e. an expected integrated solution by a customer in service-oriented BNs), select parties that can collaborate to achieve the targeted objective, and compose networked business processes that should be executed. These decisions are supported by knowledge systems that enable to share and use accumulated knowledge and expertise within BNs (see design-time architecture in [18]). The enactment phase addresses run-time executions of networked business processes that have been composed. The enactment is supported by process systems that enable to execute intra and inter-organizational business processes.

The consideration of the process aspect is relevant in the context of the described research question, because IG functionalities differ in the design-time and the run-time phases for managing networked business processes. More precisely, the distinction of design-time and run time phases within this aspect is relevant due to the two reasons as states in the following.

Firstly, this distinction enables to distinguish between information within knowledge and process systems. The difference between these two systems has been deeply described in previous work (see e.g. [20]) and has been regarded in relevant architectures (e.g. [18]). Information in knowledge systems is shared, integrated and analyzed (e.g. within data warehouse systems) to support decision making. But, in process systems information is exchanged (e.g. among services in service oriented computing paradigm) in order to fulfil a work process (like supply chain processes). According to the Cross-Work architecture (see [18]), in design-time phases knowledge systems are used to make decisions for composing networked business processes (by using agent-based technologies). Within the run-time phase process-oriented systems are applied in order to enact composed networked business processes (by using service oriented computing technologies).

Secondly, the distinction between design-time and run-time phases within the business process aspect enables distinguishing between vertical and horizontal alignment between parties and also their assets (particularly information assets). According the alignment based perspective on IG (as described above), both of the vertical and horizontal alignments need to be considered in the context of BNs [21]. Design-time alignment of information assets implies coordination within a value network for the production of required information and also representing these information assets in way that can be used for collaborative decision making. Run-time alignment of information assets implies syntactic and semantic interoperability of information objects that are exchanged among parties.

Governance Directions View. As described, enterprise governance theories address two main directions for governance, respectively, an alignment direction and an enablement direction. In the context of this research, an alignment direction implies the adaption of information assets in order to support formed networked business processes (i.e. top-down direction. An enablement direction, on the other hand, points out the enhancement of networked business processes regarding the possibilities that are recognized within information assets (i.e. bottom-up direction). In the context of this paper, which considers dynamic interactions within service-oriented BNs, both of the mentioned directions need to be considered for governing information assets. Indeed, the alignment direction is necessary to adapt information production processes, information integration schemas, and information exchange protocols regarding emerging expectations in service-oriented BNs. The enablement direction also needs to be consider, because of the increasingly consideration of information as the driver of networked business processes in dynamic business situation (i.e. information-intensive business processes) (see e.g. [22]).

Governance Mechanisms View. As aforementioned, in this paper we rely on procedural mechanisms that can be used for governing information. According the research question in this paper, within different procedural mechanisms that can be considered, we concentrate on required functionalities that need to be realized for governing information (like [23] that proposes a set of tasks as procedural mechanisms for IG in the context of single organizations). Regarding [24], IG can be seen as higher-order abilities that direct lower-order activities for information integration and exchange. In this way, in line with [8, 24, 25] we use a dynamic capabilities perspective as a basis for the characterization of IG abilities. A dynamic capability perspective points out abilities in systems in order to govern internal resources in accordance with environmental changes [26]. It addresses the three main abilities, respectively, sensing, responding, and improving (or reconfiguring) [27]. In this way, considering the alignment and the enablement views on IG (as described above), IG abilities based on a dynamic capability perspective can be described as the ability to sense IQ related issues and possibilities, respond to these issues and possibilities in order to undergird IQ, and improve IQ based on the sensed and responded issues and possibilities.

The described views are summarized in Table 1. In order to identify IG functionalities based on these determined relevant views, firstly the information and the process aspects are integrated. The reason for this integration is that we aim to identify IG functionalities that govern information that is exchanged within networked business processes. Also, as described before, governing information in different phases of the networked business process management requires different functionalities. The integration of these two aspects results in the 6 (i.e. 3*2) sub-aspects that need to be considered for the identification of the IG functionalities.

Table 1. The views for identifying the IG functionalities

<table>
<tr><td colspan="5" rowspan="3"></td><td colspan="5"><u>How</u> it can be governed</td></tr>
<tr><td rowspan="4">Governance directions</td><td rowspan="2"></td><td colspan="3">Governance mechanisms</td></tr>
<tr><td>Sensing</td><td>Responding</td><td>Improving</td></tr>
<tr><td rowspan="5"><u>What</u> needs to be governed</td><td></td><td colspan="3">Process Aspect</td><td>Alignment</td><td colspan="3" rowspan="2">3*2=6 views</td></tr>
<tr><td></td><td></td><td>Design-time</td><td>Run-time</td><td>Enablement</td></tr>
<tr><td rowspan="3">Information aspect</td><td>Information product quality</td><td colspan="2" rowspan="3">3*2=6 views</td><td colspan="5" rowspan="3">6 *6 = 36 IG functionalities</td></tr>
<tr><td>Information service quality</td></tr>
<tr><td>metadata</td></tr>
</table>

On the other hand, the governance direction and the governance mechanisms views are also inter-related. This means that the described dynamic capabilities perspective based governance abilities can support both of the alignment and the enablement directions. In this way, regarding the characterization of the governance directions and mechanisms, we need to consider the 6 (i.e. 2*3) routines for governing information assets within networked business processes. The combination of the "what" and the "how" related views results in 36 (i.e. 6*6) functionalities that support governing information in service-oriented BNs. These identified IG functionalities are reported in http://is.ieis.tue.nl/research/bpm/raso15/?page_id=77. In the next section an aggregated set of the identified IG functionalities are described.

3 Aggregated IG Functionalities to Enhance IQ in Service-Oriented BNs

In this section the identified IG functionalities are briefly described within six aggregated IG functionalities. For aggregating the identified IG functionalities, we focus on the three IG mechanisms (i.e. the governance mechanisms view) that need to be applied within design-time and run-time networked business process management (i.e. the process aspect). Therefore we aggregate the remaining information aspect and the governance direction view. This leads to three design-time and three run-time IG functionalities. The design-time IG functionalities refer to the quality of information that is stored and used by knowledge systems for the detection of market opportunity, the formation of a service-oriented BN (e.g. in the form of instant virtual enterprise) and the composition of networked business processes to respond to detected market opportunities. The run-time IG functionalities pertain to the quality of information that is exchanged among process systems (e.g. global workflow management systems or e-sourcing middlewares) to enact a networked business process. The first three IG functionalities that are elaborated in the sequel of this section address IQ in design-time. The second three IG functionalities point out IQ in run-time.

Sensing IQ Issues and Possibilities in Design-Time Knowledge Systems: according to [28] examples of conventional IQ issues that can arise in knowledge systems due to the dynamism of service-oriented BNs are inaccuracy of information on a customer experience stored in a knowledge base (resulting from the change of customer expectations) or incompleteness of information due to the disappearance of a relevant information product (resulting from dynamic partnering). An information governor should be able to sense these issues to prevent low quality decisions.

Responding IQ Issues and Possibilities in Design-Time Knowledge Systems: sensed IQ issues and possibilities need to be respectively encountered and exploited. Encountering sensed IQ issues requires adapting information integration approaches including evolving collaborative metadata, updating integration schemas, or updating quality requirements of information services that are provided by collaborating parties. Exploiting sensed IQ issues points out redesigning composed networked business processes based on higher quality information on environment (e.g. parties or customers).

Improving Design-Time Knowledge Systems to Support Quality Decisions: knowledge systems (including knowledge bases and decision making agents) that are used for the composition of a networked business processes require to be improved based on the sensed IQ issues. This improvement need to be conducted in used knowledge bases, e.g. by information refreshment, and also in decision support systems that are used, e.g. the decision making logic that is used for adaptive partnering.

Detecting IQ Issues and Possibilities in Run-Time Process Systems: run-time quality issues are usually arisen due to the violating the design-time quality agreements, but it also can result from run-time changes in environment (like changes of customer expectations during the usage of services). IQ possibilities also can arise due to the provision of higher quality information by a collaborating party (e.g. fresher information on customer expectations in run-time). These quality issues and possibilities need to be detected during the enactment of networked business processes.

Reacting on Detected IQ Issues and Possibilities in Run-Time Process Systems: this reaction can imply reconfiguring running networked business process (e.g. through run-time switching parties), but also can be handled through interaction protocol adaptions (e.g. to handle syntactic and semantic inconsistencies among information services) or by adjusting run-time information services that are exchanged.

Enhancing Process Systems to Handle Quality Networked Business Processes: based on the sensed IQ issues and possibilities, this functionality addresses the enhancement of the networked business process patterns repositories and also the refreshment of business rules that are regarded during run-time process systems.

4 Evaluation of Practical Relevance of the Identified IG Functionalities

In this section the practical relevance of the described IG functionalities in service-oriented BNs is evaluated. Indeed, we investigate "why service-oriented BNs need to fulfil the described IG functionalities in order to make-quality decisions and access quality information within networked business processes?" In other words, we probe if the described IG functionalities address recognized IQ issues resulting from service-orientation in real-life BNs. This means that, for the evaluation of the practical relevance of the IG functionalities we need to investigate the recognition of according IQ issues in real-life service-oriented BNs. To do so, we conduct a case study research in a service-oriented BN that has been formed by a car leasing organization in order to provide customer-centric mobility solutions. Within this BN that is orchestrated by the car leasing organization different mobility experience related parties like car dealer, car rental organizations, car manufacturers, car insurers, public transportation service providers, and car maintainers collaborate. The objective is to provide a mass-customize mobility solution for a customer (i.e. service-oriented value) rather than providing a car.

According to the distinction between design-time and run-time IG functionalities in Sect. 3, we select the two units of analysis within the described BN. The first unit, which is related to design-time phase, addresses a collaborative decision making for offering a mobility solution for a customer. In this collaborative decision making, the car leasing organization uses information that are gathered and shared by all collaborating parties to shape the most attractive mobility proposition for a customer. The second unit, which is related to run-time phase, points out the enactment of customer invoicing process. This process is executed in order to issue an invoice for a customer including all services that have been provided by all collaborating parties during a specific time period.

Regarding the case study objective, we intend to identify IQ issues resulting from the dynamism that is required for service-orientation in the BN. To do so, we conduct three in-depth interviews with the IT-manager, the enterprise architect and the mobility business model developer of the car leasing organization. These three in-depth interviews are based on a semi-structured questionnaire. According to the IQ domains, questions are classified within information product quality, information service quality, and metadata. Within each of these domains we investigate the practical relevance of the theoretically explored IQ issues resulting from service-orientation that are reflected in the citations [28, 29].

For the investigation of the practical relevance of the IG functionalities, we discuss how these functionalities enable to deal with the practically recognized IQ issues resulting from service-orientation in the BN. According the run-time and the design-time phases, the next two paragraphs respectively discuss the relevance of the IG functionalities to counter IQ issues within the decision making for proposing a mobility solution for a customer and also the networked business process for customers invoicing.

As mentioned above, the car leasing organization requires to integrate information relating customers' mobility experience to be able propose tailored mobility solutions. Since a customer interacts with different parties within the mobility BN, information on customer experience is distributed among parties (e.g. in CRM systems that are used by car rental organizations or by car dealers). Because of the dynamism in the BN, collaborating parties within this BN are loosely coupled. In this way the car leasing organization is not able to use a shared database for gathering and integrating all information relating customers' experiences. Due to this nature of the BN different IQ issues are recognized like inaccuracy of information on customer experience (usually is recognized though mobility propositions those are not exciting for customers) and incompleteness of information (usually is recognized when a customer has more mobility requirements than what have been reflected by existing information). Sensing these IQ issues resulting from changes in the BN enables the car leasing organization to deploy a relevant reaction. For instance, when a customer reflects dissatisfaction about a proposed mobility solution, the sensing functionality enables the identification of IQ issues within the knowledge base that supports proposing the mobility solution. Also, the sensing functionality supports tracing changes on customer experience that are recognized by other parties. The car leasing organization uses an integration schema for integrating information on customer experience that has been based on the conceptualization of mobility solutions (see examples in [30]). Responding sensed IQ issues addresses updating these integration schemas in logical and physical views. The improvement functionality implies refreshing the knowledge base that is used by the car leasing organization in order to avoid occurrence of the same low-quality decision (e.g. proposing the same mobility solution for the customer that previously has reflected his/her dissatisfaction).

The customer invoice networked process is enacted by the car leasing organization. In doing so, according to different mobility solutions that are proposed, there is a different composed networked process (because collaborating parties and engaged services are different within each proposed mobility solution). However, due to service-orientation, customers can change the proposed and agreed mobility solution during the usage of solution (i.e. run-time customer dynamism). Also, it happens that some parties (especially car rental organizations) cannot provide the planned facilities or services on time, which necessitates switching parties in run-time. These changes necessitate run-time adaption of the customer invoice process. However, this adaption results in IQ issues like inconsistency of financial information formats that are used by switching parties, or untimeliness of financial information due to the lack of synchronization with new collaborating parties. These IQ issues can lead to invoices that are objected by customers or omit provided services. The run-time IQ detection functionality enables to discern emerging IQ issues resulting from run-time changes of the enacted customer invoice process. The detected run-time IQ issues can be reacted by the adaption of the enactment of the customer invoice process. This adaption can be handled by event-driven process control approaches or by updating business rules that are considered. The detected and reacted IQ issues enable to improve customer invoice networked process composition in design-time, which enhances customer invoice patterns that are defined in the process repository.

The findings from the conducted case study clearly shows that countering the IQ issues resulting from the dynamisms in the service-oriented mobility BN requires applying the identified IG functionalities. However, our findings mostly concentrate on the alignment view of the IG functionalities, which implies countering with the IQ issues resulting from the service-orientation. The enablement view on the IG functionalities is not considered in this case study, because data-driven approaches for decision making, e.g. BI solutions for offering mobility solutions or data-driven service composition tools, have not been yet used in this BN.

5 Discussions

The described IG functionalities enable dealing with emerging IQ issues in dynamic inter-organizational interactions in service-oriented BNs. Indeed, although service-orientation in BNs raises the ability for offering more competitive value propositions, it causes emerging risks from information exchange point of view (i.e. IQ issues) [31]. However, regarding our implications from the case study, since service-orientation is mainly triggered by innovative business models developed by marketing experts, the relating risks-especially from information exchange point of view- are neglected. This can lead to un-managed emerging risks that can disrupt operations in service-oriented BNs. IG, as described within concrete functionalities in this paper, enables to exploit service-orientation business advantages without damaging from resulting risks arisen by emerging IQ issues.

However, the realization of the IG functionalities is tough in real-life BNs. The difficulties of the realization of IG within the boundaries of a single organization, due to its multi-disciplinary nature, have been clearly reported in previous research (see e.g. [23]). These difficulties are intensified in the context of BNs, particularly service-oriented BNs, because of the independence of parties, lack of a central governance power, and the engagement of collaborating parties from various business contexts.

From a structure point of view, the implementation of the IG functionalities directly depends on the structure of networks governance. According to network governance structures, IG can be organized within centralized, decentralized, and hybrid structures. Governing information in centralized structures may be easier, because the authorities and responsibilities to apply relevant mechanisms, like standardization, can be clearly defined. However, service-orientation leads network governance from centralized structures towards distributed structures (i.e. actor to actor relations [4]). Implementing IG in distributed structures with high independence of parties that are loosely coupled seems more difficult. This situation highlights the need for IT-enabled distributed solutions that support the realization of IG functionalities. However, IT-enabled solutions supporting dynamic business networking do not clearly address IQ issues[32]. On the other hand, IT-enabled solutions for managing IQ do not consider concretely dynamic business networking requirements.

According to the technological basis for managing dynamic networked business processes in CrossWork architecture [19], the identified IG functionalities can be fulfilled by using a multi-agent system (MAS) platform as the basis for fulfilling design-time functionalities and service-oriented computing (SOC) technology as the basis for realizing run-time IG functionalities. The buildability of the component for networked business process composition (by using a MAS platform) and the component for networked business process enactment (by using SOC through employing technology from the Web service stack) is described elsewhere [19]. In this way, the identified IG functionalities can be considered as a basis to enrich the described architecture by adding components supporting quality of information for collaborative decision-making for composing networked business processes and global enactment of composed processes.

6 Conclusions

In this paper, IG functionalities to enhance IQ in service-oriented BNs are identified in a structured way. The practical relevance of the identified IG functionalities is discussed in a BN that intends to provide integrated mobility solutions for customers. The identified IG functionalities enable to handle risks concerning emerging IQ issues in service-oriented BNs. They also enable to exploit business opportunities through quality information sharing within collaborative value networks. These functionalities also provide a well-established basis for in-depth considering IG as a critical necessity within architectural solutions supporting dynamic business networking.

The findings from the mobility BN sufficiently support the practical relevance of the identified IG functionalities. However, since this BN is in transition from product-centered business model towards completely service-centered business model, we deal with limitations for the evaluation of the identified IG issues based on the observed facts. In this way, more empirical research, especially in BNs that are more service-centered, can enhance the confidence of the practical relevance of the identified IG functionalities. The future research can concentrate on the development of architectural solutions that enhance IG in service-oriented BNs based on the identified functionalities.

References

1. Coe, N.M., Dicken, P., Hess, M.: Global production networks: realizing the potential. J. Econ. Geogr. **8**, 271–295 (2008)
2. Gereffi, G., Humphrey, J., Sturgeon, T.: The governance of global value chains. Rev. Int. Polit. Econ. **12**, 78–104 (2005)
3. Zhang, D.: A network economic model for supply chain versus supply chain competition. Omega **34**, 283–295 (2006)
4. Vargo, S.L., Lusch, R.F.: Evolving to a new dominant logic for marketing. J. Mark. **68**, 1–17 (2004)
5. Camarinha-Matos, L.M., Afsarmanesh, H., Oliveira, A.-I., Ferrada, F.: Collaborative business services provision. In: Proceedings of ICEIS 2013–15th International Conference on Enterprise Information Systems, Angers, France, 4–7 Jul 2013, vol. 2, pp. 382–392 (2013)
6. Rasouli, M.R., Kusters, R.J., Trienekens, J.J., Grefen, P.W.: Service orientation in demand-supply chains: towards an integrated framework. In: Camarinha-Matos, L.M., Afsarmanesh, H. (eds.) Collaborative Systems for Smart Networked Environments. IFIP AICT, vol. 434, pp. 182–193. Springer, Heidelberg (2014)
7. Wang, R.Y.: A product perspective on total data quality management. Commun. ACM **41**, 58–65 (1998)
8. Kooper, M.N., Maes, R., Lindgreen, E.R.: On the governance of information: introducing a new concept of governance to support the management of information. Int. J. Inf. Manage. **31**, 195–200 (2011)
9. Khatri, V., Brown, C.V.: Designing data governance. Commun. ACM **53**, 148–152 (2010)
10. Young, A., McConkey, K.: Data governance and data quality: Is it on your agenda? J. Inst. Res. **17**, 69–77 (2012)
11. Hüner, K.M., Schierning, A., Otto, B., Österle, H.: Product data quality in supply chains: the case of Beiersdorf. Electron. Markets. **21**, 141–154 (2011)
12. Kotonya, G., Sommerville, I.: Requirements engineering with viewpoints. Softw. Eng. J. **11**, 5–18 (1996)
13. Dietz, J., Proper, E., Tribolet, J., Halpin, T., Hoogervorst, J., Op't Land, M., Ross, R.G., Winter, R.: The Enterprise Engineering Series. Springer, Heidelberg (2005)
14. Hoogervorst, J.A.: Enterprise Governance and Enterprise Engineering. Springer, Heidelberg (2009)
15. Van Grembergen, W., De Haes, S.: Enterprise Governance of Information Technology: Achieving Strategic Alignment and Value. Springer, New York (2009)
16. Henderson, J.C., Venkatraman, N.: Strategic alignment: leveraging information technology for transforming organizations. IBM syst. J. **32**, 4–16 (1993)
17. Tallon, P.P., Ramirez, R.V., Short, J.E.: The information artifact in IT governance: toward a theory of information governance. J. Manage. Inf. Syst. **30**, 141–178 (2013)
18. Grefen, P., Eshuis, R., Mehandjiev, N., Kouvas, G., Weichhart, G.: Internet-based support for process-oriented instant virtual enterprises. IEEE Internet Comput. **13**, 65–73 (2009)

19. Norta, A., Grefen, P., Narendra, N.C.: A reference architecture for managing dynamic inter-organizational business processes. Data Knowl. Eng. **91**, 52–89 (2014)
20. Alavi, M., Leidner, D.E.: Review: knowledge management and knowledge management systems: conceptual foundations and research issues. MIS Q. **25**(1), 107–136 (2001)
21. Gong, Y., Janssen, M.: An interoperable architecture and principles for implementing strategy and policy in operational processes. Comput. Ind. **64**, 912–924 (2013)
22. Aarikka-Stenroos, L., Jaakkola, E.: Value co-creation in knowledge intensive business services: a dyadic perspective on the joint problem solving process. Ind. Mark. Manage. **41**, 15–26 (2012)
23. Weber, K., Otto, B., Österle, H.: One size does not fit all—a contingency approach to data governance. J. Data Inf. Qual. (JDIQ) **1**(1), 4 (2009)
24. Sambamurthy, V., Zmud, R.W.: Arrangements for information technology governance: a theory of multiple contingencies. MIS Q. **23**(2), 261–290 (1999)
25. Otto, B.: On the evolution of data governance in firms: the case of johnson & johnson consumer products North America. In: Sadiq, S. (ed.) Handbook of Data Quality, pp. 93–118. Springer, Heidelberg (2013)
26. Winter, S.G.: Understanding dynamic capabilities. Strateg. Manage. J. **24**, 991–995 (2003)
27. Teece, D.J.: Explicating dynamic capabilities: the nature and microfoundations of (sustainable) enterprise performance. Strateg. Manage. J. **28**, 1319–1350 (2007)
28. Rasouli, M.R., Kusters, R.J., Trienekens, J.J., Grefen, P.W.: Information governance requirements in dynamic business networking. Industrial Management and Data Systems Special Issue on IT governance for IoT supply chains (2016)
29. Rasouli, M.R., Eshuis, R., Trienekens, J.J., Kusters, R.J., Grefen, P.: Information quality in dynamic networked business process management. In: Debruyne, C., Panetto, H., Meersman, R., Dillon, T., Weichhart, G., An, Y., Ardagna, C.A. (eds.) On the Move to Meaningful Internet Systems: OTM 2015 Conferences. LNCS, vol. 9415, pp. 202–218. Springer, Switzerland (2015)
30. Lüftenegger, E.: Service-dominant business design. Eindhoven University of Technology (2014)
31. Tallon, P.P.: Corporate governance of big data: Perspectives on value, risk, and cost. Computer **46**, 32–38 (2013)
32. Rasouli, M.R., Eshuis, R., Trienekens, J.J., Grefen, P.W.: Information governance requirements for architectural solutions supporting dynamic business networking. In: Norta, A., Gaaloul, W., Gangadharan, G.R., Dam, H.K. (eds.) ICSOC 2015 Workshops. LNCS, vol. 9586, pp. 184–189. Springer, Heidelberg (2016). doi:10.1007/978-3-662-50539-7_15

An Exploratory Method to Clarify Business Potential in the Context of Industrial Internet – A Case Study

Maarit Tihinen[1(✉)], Marika Iivari[2], Heikki Ailisto[1], Marjaana Komi[1], Jukka Kääriäinen[1], and Irina Peltomaa[1]

[1] VTT Technical Research Centre of Finland Ltd, PO Box 1100, 90571 Oulu, Finland
{Maarit.Tihinen,Heikki.Ailisto,Marjaana.Komi, Jukka.Kaariainen,Irina.Peltomaa}@vtt.fi

[2] Oulu Business School, Martti Ahtisaari Institute, University of Oulu, PO Box 4600, 90014 Oulu, Finland
Marika.Iivari@oulu.fi

Abstract. This paper introduces a study that was executed to detect business opportunities of the case companies in the context of Industrial Internet. An exploratory "scenario method" was chosen due to its ability to provide collaborative decision-making tool in a new business context. The study reveals four key perspectives identified together with case companies when looking for new business potential. Furthermore, the findings highlight the vital role of new business models and the need for transformation actions from product based business to service business. Rapid technology development and maturation provide basis for new service-focused business opportunities however companies need to be aware of new market dynamics and synergy advantages. In this study, future scenarios method was proven to be useful tool in both increasing awareness as well as in assisting to recognise the existing business potential in this new context.

Keywords: Business opportunity · Future scenario · Exploratory · Industrial internet

1 Introduction

Digital revolution is an ongoing megatrend continually changing and evolving. Ubiquitous, increasing presence of digital technologies and Industrial Internet and the Internet of Things (IoT) have attracted increasing attention in both academia and practice [1]. Industrial Internet is included in the group of the fast emerging digital ecosystems, along with smart cities [2]. Accordingly, constant change in business environment in a form of globalization, digitalization and technology development has changed the position of companies towards collaboration: no company is an island [3, 4]. Close interaction and collaboration are seen as essential mode of operation of business ecosystems [3, 5–7].

During the last decade, impressive improvements in information, communication, and connectivity technologies have unleashed new business opportunities. The reported and forecasted benefits of Industrial Internet building on these core

H. Afsarmanesh et al. (Eds.): PRO-VE 2016, IFIP AICT 480, pp. 469–478, 2016.
DOI: 10.1007/978-3-319-45390-3_40

technologies include huge opportunities reported as boosting economic growth, optimizing value chains, streamlining information flows, enabling real-time decisions, enhancing customer satisfaction and loyalty, improving on-time delivery performance, enabling higher quality, enhancing marketing, lowering costs, optimizing assets, and increasing revenues [8]. Products and services are merged with digital technologies; it is becoming increasingly difficult to disentangle digital products and services from their underlying IT infrastructures [9].

As the pace of technological development has been rapid there is a lot of confusion on how to define the terms of Industrial Internet and Internet of Things (IoT). These terms are often used interchangeably, but do not mean the same. Furthermore, a third concept, namely Industry 4.0 or Industrie 4.0 in German is relevant to the digitalization of industry. However, Industry 4.0 differs from IoT and Industrial Internet in that it focuses more on using digital and information technologies in supply chain, manufacturing and distribution [10, 11] where as IoT and Industrial Internet focus more on the use, operation and maintenance of smart products during their whole lifecycle.

One rationale for conducting this study was the recognition of terminology discontinuity; the use of various definitions does not only relate to literature, but also extends to practice. This confusion also impacts on how business potential is understood. Accordingly, the purpose of this study is to clarify using case-study method what kind of business potential relates to Industrial Internet. The research questions are identified as follows: (1) *What are the characteristics of Industrial Internet*, and (2) *How to collaboratively discover its new business potential.*

In order to answer these research questions, this study uses an exploratory scenario method [12, 13]. This method is a collaborative decision-making tool in building common understanding and identifying new business potential. Building scenarios was executed through a workshop carried out among four business enterprises in Finland during Spring 2015.

This paper is structured in the following way. In the second chapter background information about the context of Industrial Internet are introduced and the term Industrial Internet is defined. The third chapter presents the research approach of the conducted case study. In the fourth chapter, the findings of the case study are introduced. The fifth chapter provides discussion on research findings and the last chapter concludes the study.

2 Background

As the pace of changes is increasing, constant development of products and services is required from companies. Companies need to utilise novel and agile ways of working across ecosystems composed of looser, partner-based collaboration [2]. Continuous innovation and global dissemination of new technologies and tools provides tools enabling better connectivity, collaboration, and co-creation across multiple businesses [14]. Ecosystems often exist on top of a platform [7]. Platform ecosystems have driven up productivity of economies in multiple ways, for example providing efficient matching, supporting more efficient asset utilization and acting as sources of innovation [15]. Actors of ecosystem create, offer and maintain products and services that are complementary to one another. This leads to network effects where more value is extracted as more users take part [15, 16].

The terms IoT and Industrial Internet are often used interchangeably, although they do not mean the same. Techopedia [17] defines Industrial Internet to be "the integration and linking of big data, analytical tools and wireless networks with physical and industrial equipment, or otherwise applying meta-level networking functions, to distributed systems". Similarly, IoT Agenda [18] adds in machine learning and M2M communication. These definitions keep Industrial Internet as narrow particle of IoT. On the other hand, the Industrial Internet Consortium (IIC) defines Industrial Internet as a broader concept than IoT, where machines, computers and people enable intelligent industrial operations using advanced data analytics for transformational business outcomes [19]. The definition of IIC is based on whitepaper by GE [15], stating that three elements, which embody the essence of the Industrial Internet are Intelligent machines, Advanced Analytics and People at work. These definitions reflect the sight where the target is to gain greater effectiveness and new business, and the wider internet-economic characteristics must be considered. This means for instance, openness and the ability of third-party business partners to provide their added value to company's platform product. We see this collaborative, ecosystemic view of Industrial Internet as the current step in the evolution chain illustrated in Fig. 1.

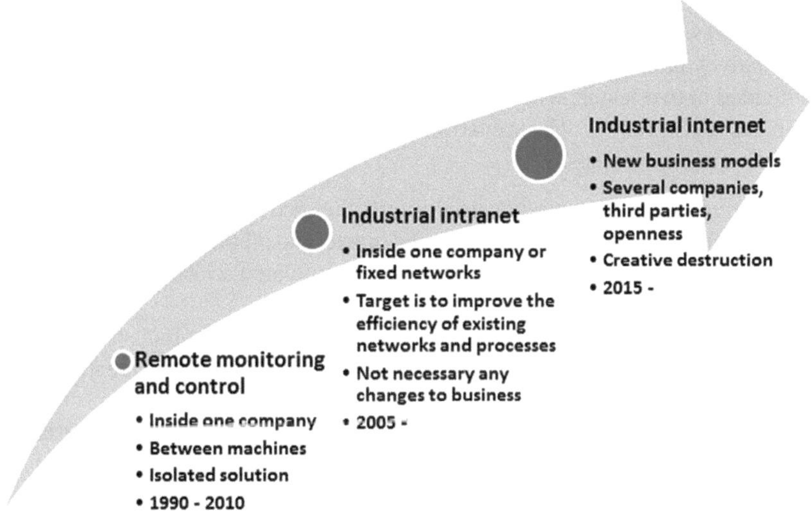

Fig. 1. Industrial internet expands business potential.

The evolution started from company-internal *remote monitoring and control* solutions. Next step were *industrial intranet* solutions that served a company or fixed network of partners. The current step in this evolution is Industrial Internet. In this article we define that ***Industrial Internet*** *automates and rationalizes operations as well as enables new business in the industrial ecosystem by connecting intelligent machines,* *equipment, users and organizations together so that decision making can be improved by using advanced data-analytics methods.* The fundamental difference with earlier generations of automation and rationalization is the scalable nature of networks, both from data and business viewpoints, enabled by dramatically improved communication, computing and data management capability – the internet. This difference is exemplified as a transformation from industrial *intranet* thinking towards industrial *internet* thinking in Fig. 1.

3 Exploratory Futures Research Approach

This study applies a futures perspective into Industrial Internet and utilises a qualitative, exploratory future scenario method [12, 13]. Future scenarios-method was chosen, as it is can be utilized as a participatory, collaborative decision-making tool in the process of exploring possible outcomes and building common view of a specific context. Exploratory scenarios describe events, trends and choices as they might evolve based on alternative assumptions on how these events, trends and choices potentially influence the future [20]. In this study, the scenario method was utilized in particular to explore, outline and assess business potential in the context of Industrial internet.

The data for the alternative Industrial Internet future scenarios presented were mapped within the TINTTI project, IT Houses to boost Industrial Internet research project. The scenarios were generated in early 2015 in one facilitated full-day (8 h) scenario workshop by a group of 12 professionals including researchers, industrial representatives and business managers from both large and small firms. The participants were divided in two teams, where each team ensured maximum variation based on the participants' backgrounds. The scenario work process discussed in this study consisted of the following main steps:

1. identifying and evaluating Industrial Internet related trends, and choosing the most the critical ones based on their anticipated impact and predictability of consequences;
2. setting up the scenario logic by selecting two unrelated scenario dimensions out of critical trends;
3. creating the scenarios by building on different perspectives of Industrial Internet and identifying drivers, limitations, and challenges emerging from the created scenarios; and
4. assessing the scenarios based on their probability, plausibility, and preferability. In total, eight alternative scenarios were generated by the workshop participants in two teams composed. These results are presented in the following chapter.

4 Industrial Internet Future Scenarios

4.1 The Scenario Dimensions

In the first step of the scenario work process the most critical scenarios were recognized and evaluated. These scenario dimensions are based on the main drivers the teams identified, where the dimensions are seen to include two extreme opposite ends, i.e. two possible alternatives. These dimensions are summarized in the following Table 1 and further elaborated in Sect. 4.2.

Table 1. Critical change dimensions for the scenarios

End 1	*Dimension*	End 2
Legislation B2C	*Security*	Case-based B2B
Experimentation, technical	*Organizational capabilities*	Risk mgmt. functional
Do it yourself (DIY) Technical	*Partnerships*	Seeking partners Commercial
Data ownership Increasing performance	*Ownership and use of knowledge*	Open data Creating new business
Separate	*Integration of systems*	Standardised
Pay-per-use; Product-based	*Logic of revenue*	Subscription; Service-based
Attitude: Excel-world	*IoT readiness*	Hype, Technically up-to-date
Contract-based Preventing	*Legal issues*	Open data Enabling

The extensive discussions during the selection of dimensions for the scenarios reflect the discussions in academic literature, hence indicating the validity of research outcomes. Some thematic overlapping also occurred, particularly in reference to the role of data ownership and legal issues around it, integration issues and the readiness and capabilities for the extensive spread of Industrial Internet solutions, both technically and commercially.

4.2 The Alternative Scenarios

The results of both teams are presented as they were formed, including the original names created to describe the scenarios. Hence, in this study, the description and analysis of the results is based on how the possible outcomes of the future were discussed at the workshop, and how the groups outlined and assessed the scenarios created. Thus, as a participatory approach, the scenario method includes the evaluation and analysis of the scenarios as they are created in practice. The rationale for needing to choose unrelated dimensions is that if one dimension can explain the existence of another, the scenario is not possible to build, hence diminishing its probability, plausibility and also preferability. The future scenarios created by the two teams during the workshop are presented below in Fig. 2.

The first team (Team I) built their Industrial Internet future scenarios based on security where they viewed the main critical dimensions for security to be either legislation-driven or case by case determined) and organisational capabilities where experimentation and risk taking culture were highlighted and on the opposite end where risk management dominated.

The IoT Garage scenario involved experimentative and innovative organization culture. This scenario was considered the "wild west of global start-ups". As security is

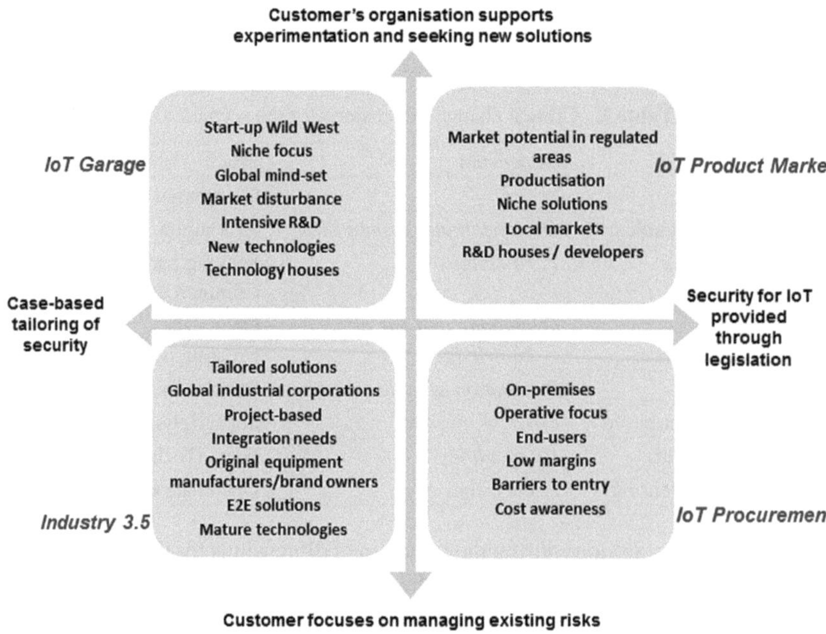

Fig. 2. Team I industrial internet scenario matrix

mainly case or customer-based rather than determined through law, a lot of niche solutions exist. This creates constant disturbance on the markets, as predictability for general directions is difficult.

The IoT Product Market scenario presents business potential mainly in regulated areas, as despite seeking new solutions, legislation sets boundaries for business development. Direction for business is easier to predict, but this scenario is very much product-oriented, aiming to serve local markets.

IoT Procurement is mainly operatively focused, with on-premises IoT solutions, and mature technologies. This scenario is based on regulated security and organisation's focus on managing existing risks rather than seeking new innovative solutions. Hence, existing, large organisations dominate and market is difficult for new companies to enter.

Industry 3.5 scenario is highlighted with global industrial enterprises; hence, the needs for integration are also high. This business is mainly project-based with customized solutions as security is mainly provided based on the customer. Therefore, original equipment manufacturers and brand owners dominate in this scenario.

The second team (Team II) chose organisational readiness towards Industrial Internet solutions as one dimension, where critical opposite ends were old-fashioned corporate culture perspective on one side, and hype and first mover attitude one the other side. Legal issues opposite ends were considered to be either publicly available open data – based or individual, contract-based, as presented in Fig. 3.

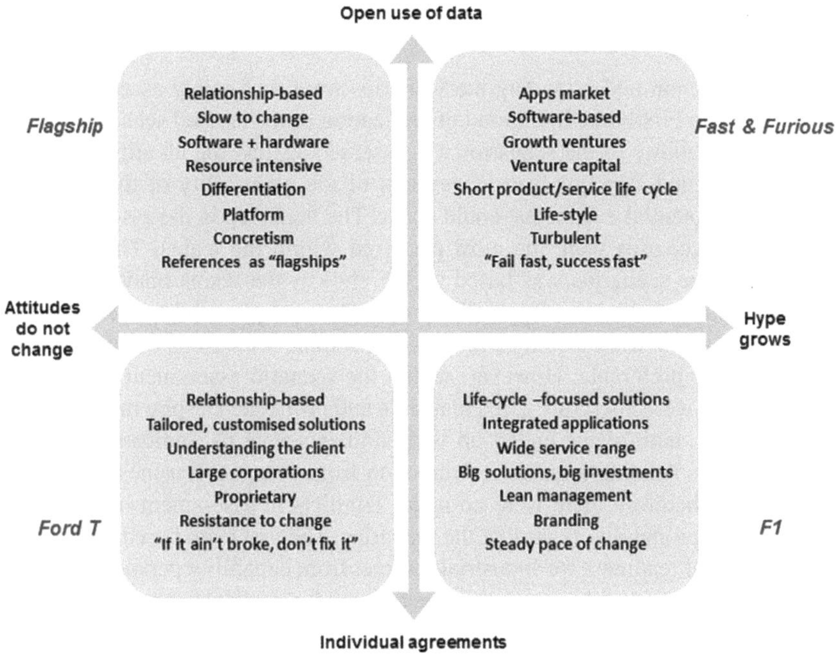

Fig. 3. Team II industrial internet scenario matrix

Flagship scenario was considered as the current state Industrial Internet is at the moment. Although opportunities for open use of data are plenty, large organisations are slow to change their attitudes and methods of operation. Trust is built through long-term business relationships as this is still very resource intensive environment.

Fast & Furious scenario is built around the hype of Industrial Internet and open use of data. This scenario is characterized with rapid change, turbulence and the rise and death of start-ups, mainly in software and application-based businesses. Product and service life-cycles are short; therefore ability to scale up the business is the key to success.

Within F1 scenario, even though the hype is high and people are interested in what Industrial Internet may provide, the need to individually agree on legal issues around products, services, security and use of data forces organisations to think not only the opportunities but also the risks involved. In this scenario, start-ups often act as service providers.

Ford T scenario is the most challenging one. In this excel-world, "if it ain't broke, don't fix it" becomes highlighted even more. Successful business can be built from thorough understanding of the customers' needs and long term business relationships with tailored, personalised solutions, but the phase of development is very slow, demanding not only financial resources but also "evangelist" work.

5 Discussion

In building common understanding the scenarios were thoroughly assessed at the end of the workshop. Firstly the likelihood of realization of the created scenarios was evaluated. The probability of the scenarios was assessed against the identified influencing factors. The second step involved assessment of the plausibility of the scenarios by looking at the potential events that could occur. The final step in the assessment was to sort out what scenarios were the most preferred within the teams. The preferability assessment of the scenarios was based on the choices the teams made regarding the alternative future predictions. Typically, probability and plausibility are often clearly correlating, whereas what would be the most preferable scenario is usually considered less plausible or preferable. However, within the scenario assessment the most preferable scenarios were also considered plausible and probable. Despite the different critical dimensions, both teams ended up with similar scenarios, indicating that digital transformation is heading to preferred direction from company business development point of view; therefore there were no major conflicts in assessment of preferability, plausibility and probability regarding the scenarios. The first team based their scenarios on organizational readiness for Industrial Internet from capability perspective, whereas the second team considered speed as one determinant for readiness. Another overlapping element was the role of law, which Team I viewed from security perspective, and Team II from contractual perspective. The outcome of this research identifies business potential to emerge through ecosystemic collaboration, total service solution, through branding and through integration of systems. These areas provide challenges but also act as drivers for new service innovations. Findings highlighted also both the need and potentiality for transformation from product based business to service business [21]. Legal issues were considered fundamental in this transformation. They impact the pace of general development, as they have the power to both enable and hinder the pursuing of business potential within Industrial Internet. These aforementioned bring focus to the need for creating new kinds of business models so that emerging opportunities and business potential of Industrial Internet can fully be utilised. Service providers still struggle with lack of awareness on the benefits of digitalisation among industrial clientele, accompanied with old-fashioned mind-sets regarding the available possibilities. Therefore the benefits of digitalisation need to be explicit and concretely stated.

6 Conclusion

This paper introduced a case study that was carried out in Spring 2015 for clarifying business potential of case companies in the context of Industrial Internet. Because of confusion on how the terms of Industrial Internet and IoT were understood and used in literature and in practice, we first defined the term Industrial Internet as follows: Industrial Internet automates and rationalizes operations as well as enables new business in the industrial ecosystem by connecting intelligent machines, equipment, users and organizations together so that decision making can be improved by using advanced data-analytics methods.

In this paper we point out an ecosystemic view of Industrial Internet. The used research method, the exploratory scenario method, was chosen because it supports the process as being collaborative decision-making tool while providing future scenarios. In total, four key perspectives were identified regarding the choices for assessing the business potential in the context of Industrial Internet. Future scenarios method was proven to be useful tool in both building a common perspective on the context as well as in assisting in the recognition of business potential in the context of Industrial Internet where technology lays the foundation for service-focused business opportunities.

Acknowledgments. The authors would like to acknowledge the consortium of the TINTTI project.

References

1. Turber, S., Smiela, C.: A business model type for the internet of things. In: Twenty Second European Conference on Information Systems, 9–11 June, Tel Aviv (2014)
2. Accenture 2016: Trend 3 – Platform Economy: Technology-driven business model innovation from the outside in. Accenture Technology Vision (2016). https://www.accenture.com/t20160125T111719__w__/us-en/_acnmedia/Accenture/Omobono/TechnologyVision/pdf/Platform-Economy-Technology-Vision-2016.pdf. Accessed 15 Apr 2016
3. Moore, J.F.: Predators and prey: a new ecology of competition. In: Harvard Business Review (May/June), pp. 75–86 (1993)
4. Adner, R., Oxley, J.E., Silverman, B.S.: Introduction: collaboration and competition in business ecosystems. Advances in Strategic Management, vol. 30. Emerald Group Publishing Limited (2013)
5. Fragidis, G., Koumpis, A., Tarabanis, K.: The impact of customer participation on business ecosystem. In: Camarinha-Matos, L., Afsarmanesh, H., Novais, P., Analide, C. (eds.) Establishing the Foundation of Collaborative Networks. IFIP, vol. 243, pp. 399–406. Springer, US (2007)
6. Russell, M.G., Huhtamäki, J., Still, K., Rubens, N., Basole, R.C.: Relational capital for shared vision in innovation ecosystems. Triple Helix **2**, 8 (2015)
7. Kelly, E.: Introduction–business ecosystems come of age. In: Canning, M., Kelly, E. (eds.) Business Ecosystems Come of Age. IFIP, vol. 243, pp. 399–406. Springer, US (2015)
8. SAP Value Views: The CEO Perspective: The Internet of Things for Industrial Machinery and Components (2014). http://go.sap.com/docs/download/2014/10/d4d37b23-0a7c-0010-82c7-eda71af511fa.pdf. Accessed 10 June 2016
9. Bharadwaj, A., El Sawy, O.A., Pavlou, P.A., Venkatraman, N.: Digital business strategy: toward a next generation of insights. MIS Q. **37**(2), 471–482 (2013)
10. Brettel, M., Friederichsen, N., Keller, M., Rosenberg, M.: How virtualization, decentralization and network building change the manufacturing landscape: an industry 4.0 perspective. Int. J. Mech. Ind. Sci. Eng. **8**(1), 37–44 (2014)
11. Lasi, H., Fettke, P., Kemper, H.G., Feld, T., Hoffmann, M.: Industry 4.0. Bus. Inf. Syst. Eng. **6**(4), 239–242 (2014)
12. Van Notten, P., van Rotmans, J., Asselt, M., Rothman, D.: An updated scenario typology. Futures **35**, 423–443 (2003)
13. Stewart, C.C.: Integral scenarios: reframing theory, building from practice. Futures **40**, 160–172 (2008)

14. Kelly, E., Marchese, K.: Supply chains and value Webs. In: Canning, M., Kelly, E. (eds.) Business Ecosystems Come of Age. Part of the Business Trends series, p. 120. Deloitte University Press (2015)
15. Evans, P.C., Annunziata, M.: Industrial Internet: Pushing the Boundaries of Minds and Machines. Whitepaper, GE (2012). www.ge.com/docs/chapters/Industrial_Internet.pdf. Accessed 15 Apr 2016
16. Seppälä, T., Halén, M., Juhanko, J., Korhonen, H., Mattila, J., Parviainen, P., Talvitie, J., Ailisto, H., Hyytinen, K.-M., Kääriäinen, J., Mäntylä, M., Ruutu, S.: The Platform – History, Characteristics, and the Definition. ETLA Reports No 47 (2015). https://www.etla.fi/wp-content/uploads/ETLA-Raportit-Reports-47.pdf. Accessed 15 Apr 2016. (in Finnish)
17. Techopedia. Definition - What does Industrial Internet mean? https://www.techopedia.com/definition/30044/industrial-internet. Accessed 15 Apr 2016
18. IoT Agenda: What is Industrial Internet of Things (IIoT)? (2016). http://internetofthingsagenda.techtarget.com/definition/Industrial-Internet-of-Things-IIoT. Accessed 15 Apr 2016
19. IIC - Industrial Internet Reference Architecture Technical Report Version 1.1 (2015). http://www.iiconsortium.org/IIRA.htm. Accessed 15 Apr 2016
20. Ahokangas, P., Perälä-Heape, M., Jämsä, T.: Alternative futures for individualized connected health. In: Gurtner, S., Soyez, K. (eds.) Challenges and Opportunities in Health Care Management, pp. 61–74. Springer International Publishing, Switzerland (2014)
21. Hui, G.: How the Internet of Things Changes Business Models. Harvard Business Review, 29 July 2014. https://hbr.org/2014/07/how-the-internet-of-things-changes-business-models. Accessed 15 Apr 2016

Services and Cloud - Cloud Technology Aspects for Vos

Do Cloud Computing Tools Support the Needs of Virtual Enterprises?

Andre F. Ruaro and Ricardo J. Rabelo(✉)

Department of Automation and Systems Engineering,
Federal University of Santa Catarina, Florianopolis, SC, Brazil
andrefruaro@gmail.com, ricardo.rabelo@ufsc.br

Abstract. Virtual Enterprise (VE) is a prominent strategy for leveraging new sustainable models to SMEs. A VE is as temporary network of enterprises that collaborate via the Internet towards achieving common goals, sharing assets, costs, risks and benefits. However, VE members do not use to share ICT assets and infrastructures in the collaboration. Cloud computing has emerged as option for that. Research works have developed prototypes and cloud-based environments to support very specific issues within given VE scenarios. However, it is important that SME managers have a broader perception about at which extent commercial cloud computing tools can indeed support the usual VE needs. This is the essential goal of this paper. The needs of VEs and performance indicators to evaluate cloud tools have been identified, and two commercial SaaS, PaaS and IaaS tools have been evaluated. Conclusions are provided in the end.

Keywords: Cloud computing · Virtual enterprises · SME

1 Introduction

SMEs (Small and Medium sized Enterprises) have gradually looked for establishing network-centric and collaborative-based strategic alliances as a means to leverage new sustainable models that allow them to more effectively cope with the increasingly and variable market demands [1].

Collaborative Networks (CN) basically is represented by a group of autonomous and heterogeneous organizations that have the willingness to collaborate with each other towards reaching common goals [2]. There are different types of CN. This paper focuses on the type Virtual Enterprise (VE). A VE is a temporary and dynamically CN formed by a group of enterprises that join competences, capacities and resources with the aim of sharing risks, costs and benefits when coping with given demands [2].

One of the most basic requirements for the realization of the VE concept is that the communication among its members should fundamentally be carried out via computer networks and proper ICT tools [2].

During the VE *life cycle* [3], VE members have different needs regarding the many types of business processes to support. On one hand, this demands adopting proper ICTs by the VE members. On the other hand, this demands investments in such ICTs, including in people to maintain them. This may become a problem as ICT is usually not part of the SMEs' core businesses and they are very limited in terms of financial and

H. Afsarmanesh et al. (Eds.): PRO-VE 2016, IFIP AICT 480, pp. 481–493, 2016.
DOI: 10.1007/978-3-319-45390-3_41

human resources [4]. Regarding that VE concept involves *per se* sharing of assets, it is relevant to extend collaboration at the ICT level so as to provide SMEs with more rational use of the general ICT infrastructure [3].

In this direction, Cloud computing technology [5] has increasingly been adopted by SMEs as a strategy to outsource ICT, under the on-demand and pay-per-use modes [6]. Some research have been done developing cloud-based prototypes for VEs looking at engineering solutions for very specific problems, including its use as an "integration middleware" among VE members and their systems (e.g. [7]). Regarding the impact the shift to cloud computing can represent to companies, it is important for SME managers to have a broader perception about at which degree the commercial cloud computing tools can indeed support VE requirements.

This represents the main objective of this paper. It shows results of an evaluation of some SaaS, IaaS and PaaS cloud tools available in the market, mostly from the end user (company) point of view. This experimental work has also provided elements for better understanding these tools' features and limitations regarding VE needs.

This paper is organized as follows. Section 1 has introduced the problem and the paper's goal. Section 2 briefly presents the research methodology. Section 3 summarizes the main foundations used in this work. Section 4 gives an outline of the literature related to the research methodology. Section 5 presents the evaluation results with the selected cloud tools. Section 6 presents some conclusions and next steps.

2 General Research Methodology and Delimitation

This work does not propose a model. Instead, it corresponds to a descriptive and applied research carried out to evaluate the phenomenon related to cloud tools, mainly in terms of their deployment and further execution. It has been focused on the *SaaS, IaaS* and *PaaS* type of cloud tools regarding the usual need of companies' processes. The tools were analyzed fundamentally considering the VE needs in the *Operation* phase of the VE life cycle [2].

This research was carried out in some steps considering the paper's goal. The *Systematic Literature Review* (SLR) methodology was applied in different steps of this research. First, the ICT requirements to support the transactions among VE members were compiled from a number of papers and further generalized. Second, performance indicators to evaluate cloud computing tools against such requirements were investigated and elicited (the results of these two steps are showed in Sect. 4).

Given the large number of commercial cloud computing tools available in the market, only two tools of SaaS, PaaS and IaaS were evaluated in the first phase of this research. Actually, a preliminary subset of tools was initially and roughly evaluated. For SaaS: *OneDrive, Google Drive, DropBox, Office 365, Google Apps,* and *Google Apps for Work.* For PaaS: *Google App Engine, Microsoft Azure Platform,* and *AWS Elastic Beanstalk.* For IaaS: *Amazon EC2, Google Compute Engine,* and *Microsoft Azure Platform.*

The final tools selection tried to consider the SMEs' reality and their usual behavior when selecting ICT tools: (i) *free* or *low-cost tools*: most of SMEs are financially very limited, which is a problem due to ICT-related costs (software and hardware acquisition, training, maintenance, updating, etc.); (ii) *well-known tools*: they use to be more robust, consolidated, documented, and easier to find training programs as well as experienced people on that; (iii) *open tools*: they are less difficult to integrate and interoperate with enterprises' systems as well as with other systems at the VE level (which in turn can also be deployed in a cloud). Open tools can save integration costs and time as well as mitigate the problem of technology lock-in.

Once selected, the cloud tools were evaluated in a transversal way, executing the experiments in a single moment. The tools were deployed and executed in a controlled environment so as to systematically observe them regarding the elicited VE requirements against the selected performance indicators. The results were annotated and analyzed in way to respond to pre-established purposes, i.e. if cloud computing tools could support the VE needs.

3 Basic Foundations

3.1 Cloud Computing

Cloud computing can be defined as a set of resources with processing power, storage, connectivity, platforms, applications and services that are available over the Internet. Its main characteristics are: on-demand self-services, resource pooling, broad network access, rapid elasticity and measured services [5, 8]. There are four basic cloud models [5, 8]: *private cloud*, *public cloud*, *community cloud*, and *hybrid cloud*.

The main cloud models are [8]:

- SaaS (*Software as a Service*) – on-demand access to application software, usually under a pay-per-use basis. Cloud providers manage the infrastructure and platforms that run the applications.
- PaaS (*Platform as a Service*) – offering of development and deployment environments and interfaces to developers of (usually SaaS) applications.
- IaaS (*Infrastructure as a Service*) – availability of infrastructure services for using computing resources, scaling, security, backup, among others.

An important element in cloud is the SLA (Service Level Agreement). It refers a guarantee, in the form of contracts, which are provided by the services providers to its consumers defining access conditions and quality levels of the provided services [8].

In the context of networked organizations, there are some issues about cloud computing that are considered as more sensitive to de treated than in single enterprises, like governance, integration/interoperability, security, data privacy, compliance, trust and dependability, at different levels of the global systems architecture [9–11].

3.2 Collaborative Networks

CN encompasses strategic alliances that are focused on the intense and fluid collaboration among autonomous organizations. The vision relies on allowing organizations to keep focused on their core skills, aggregating competencies and sharing resources with each other in order to better meet market requirements [2].

A VE can be characterized as a temporary alliance formed by autonomous and heterogeneous organizations that join their complementary core-competencies and resources to satisfy given demands, dismantling itself after all legal obligations have been met. VEs are classically originated from a VBE (Virtual organization Breeding Environment). A VBE can be defined as a long-term association of organizations which have the willingness and enough pre-conditions to collaborate towards creating VEs with the most adequate partners in a more agile and trustful way [2].

The collaboration within a VE is carried out along a lifecycle [2]: *Creation* (the VE is enacted, partners are selected and the network is configured); *Operation* (when the VE effectively runs, executing and managing the required activities and partners towards reaching its goals); *Evolution* (performed when problems take place during the *Operation* and that can jeopardize the VE's success); *Dissolution* (the VE is ended. This can either happen when the VE goals are achieved successfully or due to severe problems along its execution which lead it to abandon its business goal).

Each of such stages imposes different requirements from cloud computing tools. A wide scope of activities have to be supported, like information requests from one enterprise to another, services invocations, VE project management, distributed and cooperative (re)planning/(re)scheduling; discussions among distributed partners and decision-making, execution supervision, product development, among many others.

4 Summary of Literature Review

4.1 VE Requirements

According to the performed SLR (see Sect. 2), nine general requirements were considered as the main ones to be provided by cloud tools to support VE needs. They were elicited based on a careful generalization of fourteen papers taken as a reference for that [6, 9–21]:

- *Standards and Functionalities*: support for standard specifications, advanced features, and aspects related to ownership.
- *Multi-tenancy*: support for data privacy, user access control, access management and multi-user architecture.
- *Scalability and elasticity*: support for dynamic scalability and transparent load balancing and clustering.
- *Extensibility and openness*: licensing and rights support, modular architecture, access to documentation, forums, communities and training.
- *Security and reliability*: support for users authenticating, SLAs and reliability aspects.
- *Access control*: support for QoS management, measurement mechanisms, and billing.
- *Development tools*: support for developers, including *plugins*.
- *Management and operation*: access to management interfaces and APIs.
- *Interoperability*: supporting business process interoperability, web services, common and configured adapters, and messaging mechanisms.

These requirements are, however, generic as they do not consider the different VE needs in respect to SaaS, PaaS and IaaS types of tools. Taking those fourteen papers once again as a basis, a set of "business cases" were extracted and generalized in order to have a more concrete idea about which "VE situations" would be more representative to be observed when evaluating the cloud tools:

- *SaaS tools*: office and storage functionalities, involving the creation and sharing of documents in different formats, as contracts, budget spreadsheets, materials lists, list of VE members, working schedules, engineering projects, engineering projects, governance model and other VE configuration-related information, photos and videos. This also includes the access to systems - when offered under a SaaS model - like ERP modules and CRM.
- *IaaS tools*: supporting functionalities to deploy a web server allowing hosting an application and a database, including a virtual machine and regarding different operating systems. This also includes the request for extra memory to run enterprises' applications (like ERP modules and CRM) or to store their data.
- *PaaS tools*: supporting functionalities to develop and host applications (including databases), e.g. applications for control and VE monitoring. From a more end-user perspective (focus of this paper), PaaS seems to be the less important type of cloud tool and even not necessary for some companies. It might be important, for example, in the case a third part is hired to develop some specific software to support the achievement of the VE's goals.

4.2 Performance Indicators for Cloud Computing Tools

A second SLR was performed to identify which indicators use to be adopted when evaluating cloud tools. Among many found works, two of them [22, 23] were taken as the reference for this research, generating a list of 27 indicators. Due to space restrictions, these indicators are shown directly via the tables that present the evaluation of the selected tools (e.g. Tables 2, 3 and 4).

The next step of the work involved the mapping of every single business case (previous section) of each type of cloud tool against each indicator, i.e. which VE need a given indicator will measure.

For example, for *SaaS*, the indicators 'data privacy', 'storage capacity', 'management interfaces' and 'general and personalized adapters' were the ones considered as suitable to be applied to evaluate the VE need 'creation and sharing of documents in different formats'. This example means evaluating a given SaaS tool in terms of e.g. how good it is when dealing with the 'sharing of documents' need from the 'data privacy' point of view/indicator. Actually a subset of those nine basic VE requirements was considered to evaluate each business case. In this example, for instance, 'data privacy' is related to the 'multi-tenancy' requirement, 'storage capacity' to 'scalability and elasticity', 'management interfaces' to 'management and operation', and 'general and personalized adapters' to 'interoperability'.

For *PaaS*, for instance, the indicators 'modular architecture', 'storage capacity' and 'plugins IDE' were the ones considered as suitable to evaluate e.g. the VE need of 'the creation and execution of applications'.

For *IaaS*, for instance, the indicators 'modular architecture', 'storage capacity', 'processing capacity', 'memory capacity', 'management interfaces' and 'plugins IDE' were the ones chosen to evaluate e.g. the VE need of 'deploying a web server allowing hosting an application and a database'.

This mapping was done empirically, considering the authors' experience with cloud computing and VEs. Besides that, the more precise meaning of indicator varies a bit depending on the type of tool and hence to be contextualized during the evaluation task.

5 Experiments and Results

A local controlled computing environment was deployed to test the tools, emulating and instantiating all the mentioned business cases in each type of cloud tool.

A *weight* dimension was added in the analysis and had two objectives. The first one refers to the fact that the elicited 27 performance indicators for cloud tools are generic. Therefore, they had to be somehow "filtered", i.e. weighted about its importance or applicability according to the type of tool (SaaS, PaaS and IaaS). The second one refers to a greater focus on the VE *operation* phase regarding the research delimitation (see Sect. 2). This means a *subjective* qualification of importance (weight) of each indicator in the context of that VE phase. In the tables, "●" indicates that the given criterion (the performance indicator) is very important to be considered; "◍" that it is barely important; and "○" that it is few important or not applicable.

Inspired in [23], still *qualitatively* and *subjectively*, each indicator has received a number of stars in terms of its general performance evaluation when coping with the given VE need: *excellent* (5 stars); *good* (4 stars); *regular* (3 stars); *bad* (2 stars); *very bad* (1 star), and zero star when the given VE tool *does not support* or offer elements to evaluate it from the given indicator, or this indicator is *not applicable*.

Complementarily and also inspired in [23], but now *quantitatively*, stars were also assigned to indicators according to the following parameters (Table 1):

Table 1. Classification of quantitative indicators

Classification	Value	Storage capacity (TB)	CPU capacity (Un)	Memory capacity (GB)	Level of cryptography (Key size)
Excellent	★★★★★	100-1000	24-32	100-1000	265
Good	★★★★☆	10-100	12-24	10-100	192
Regular	★★★☆☆	0-10	0-12	0-10	128
Not support	☆☆☆☆☆	No support or no means to measure it			

As explained in the Sect. 2, two cloud tools of each type were selected out of a number of existing ones. They are the tools provided by *Google* and *Microsoft*:

- SaaS: *Google Drive* and Google Docs from Google [24], and OneDrive and Office 365 from Microsoft [25];
- PaaS: Google App Engine from Google [24], and Windows Azure (App Web) from Microsoft [25];

– IaaS: Google Compute Engine from Google [24], and Windows Azure (VM) from Microsoft [25].

Tables 2, 3 and 4 show the evaluation of such tools. Due to space restrictions, the analysis of each tool is just generally presented instead of per indicator, individually.

Table 2. SaaS tools evaluation

Performance Indicator	Weight	*Google Drive & Google Docs*	*OneDrive & Office 365*
Patterns & specifications	◐	★★★★☆	★★★★☆
Advanced functionalities	◐	★★★★★	★★★★★
Tool's ownership	◐	★★☆☆☆	★★☆☆☆
Data privacy	●	★★★★☆	★★★★☆
Management of users' access	◐	★★★★☆	★★★★☆
Multi-user architecture	●	★★★★☆	★★★★☆
Dynamic scalability	◐	★★★★☆	★★★★☆
Transparent scalability	◐	★★★☆☆	★★★☆☆
Load balancing & clustering	○	☆☆☆☆☆	☆☆☆☆☆
Storage capacity	●	★★★★★	★★★☆☆
Processing capacity	○	☆☆☆☆☆	☆☆☆☆☆
Memory capacity	○	☆☆☆☆☆	☆☆☆☆☆
Tool's licensing	◐	★★★☆☆	★★★☆☆
Modular architecture	○	★★★★☆	★★★★☆
Documentation, forums and training	●	★★★☆☆	★★★★★
Users' authentication	●	★★★★☆	★★★★☆
SLA	●	★★★★☆	★★★★☆
Dependability	●	★★★★☆	★★★★☆
Cryptography & security	●	★★★★★	★★★★★
QoS control	◐	☆☆☆☆☆	☆☆☆☆☆
Billing mechanisms	◐	★★★★☆	★★★★☆
Support to developers	○	★★★☆☆	★★★☆☆
Plugins IDE	◐	★★★★★	★★★★★
Management interfaces	◐	★★★★☆	★★★★★
Master API	◐	★★★☆☆	★★★★☆
Interoperability	●	★★★★☆	★★★★☆
Customized adapters	◐	★★★★★	★★★★★

Table 3. PaaS tools evaluation

Performance Indicator	Weight	*Google App Engine*	*Windows Azure* (App Web)
Patterns & specifications	○	★★★☆☆	★★★★★
Advanced functionalities	○	★★★★★	★★★★★
Tool's ownership	○	★★☆☆☆	★★☆☆☆
Data privacy	●	★★★★☆	★★★★☆
Management of users' access	○	★★★★☆	★★★★☆
Multi-user architecture	●	★★★★☆	★★★★☆
Dynamic scalability	●	★★★★☆	★★★★☆
Transparent scalability	○	★★★☆☆	★★★☆☆
Load balancing & clustering	○	★★★★☆	★★★★☆
Storage capacity	●	★★★☆☆	★★★☆☆
Processing capacity	○	☆☆☆☆☆	★★★☆☆
Memory capacity	○	☆☆☆☆☆	★★★★☆
Tool's licensing	○	★★★☆☆	★★★☆☆
Modular architecture	○	★★★★☆	★★★★★
Documentation, forums and training	●	★★★★☆	★★★★★
Users' authentication	●	★★★★☆	★★★★☆
SLA	●	★★★★☆	★★★★☆
Dependability	●	★★★★☆	★★★★☆
Cryptography & security	●	★★★★★	★★★★★
QoS control	○	★★★★☆	★★★★☆
Billing mechanisms	○	★★★★★	★★★★★
Support to developers	●	★★★☆☆	★★★☆☆
Plugins IDE	●	★★★☆☆	★★★★☆
Management interfaces	○	★★★★☆	★★★★★
Master API	○	★★★☆☆	★★★★☆
Interoperability	●	★★★★☆	★★★★☆
Customized adapters	○	★★☆☆☆	★★★★☆

Table 4. IaaS tools evaluation

Performance Indicator	Weight	*Google Compute Engine*	*Windows Azure* (VM)
Patterns & specifications	○	★★★★☆	★★★★★
Advanced functionalities	○	★★★★★	★★★★★
Tool's ownership	○	★★☆☆☆	★★☆☆☆
Data privacy	●	★★★★☆	★★★★☆
Management of users' access	○	★★★★☆	★★★★☆
Multi-user architecture	●	★★★★☆	★★★★☆
Dynamic scalability	●	★★★★☆	★★★★☆
Transparent scalability	○	★★★☆☆	★★★☆☆
Load balancing & clustering	○	★★★☆☆	★★★☆☆
Storage capacity	●	★★★★☆	★★★★☆
Processing capacity	●	★★★★★	★★★★★
Memory capacity	●	★★★★★	★★★★★
Tool's licensing	○	★★★☆☆	★★★☆☆
Modular architecture	○	★★★★☆	★★★★★
Documentation, forums and training	●	★★★★☆	★★★★★
Users' authentication	●	★★★★☆	★★★★☆
SLA	●	★★★★☆	★★★★☆
Dependability	●	★★★★☆	★★★★☆
Cryptography & security	●	★★★★★	★★★★★
QoS control	○	★★★★☆	★★★★☆
Billing mechanisms	○	★★★★★	★★★★★
Support to developers	○	★★☆☆☆	★★☆☆☆
Plugins IDE	●	★★★★☆	★★★★★
Management interfaces	○	★★★★★	★★★★★
Master API	●	★★★★☆	★★★★☆
Interoperability	●	★★★★☆	★★★★☆
Customized adapters	○	★★★☆☆	★★★☆☆

As it can be observed, both tools are in general equivalent. Some advantages of one to another also depend on the weights assigned to indicators. However, some pros are important to mention. In the Microsoft tools, to highlight the quality of the documentation (written in many different idioms), their master API, and the general management interface. The integration with other storage-related functionalities is intuitive and integrated with the Microsoft's desktop tools. Google tools provide a much larger storage capacity besides an interface with voice recognition capabilities.

Although with some degree of subjectivity, Microsoft's PaaS tools presented clearer advantages against Google in some indicators, besides providing more powerful and intuitive equivalent functionalities. To highlight the several customized adapters, a better hardware configuration for storage, memory and processing, the possibility of using plugins IDE other than Visual Studio (Google only supports Eclipse), on-line files synchronization (Google does that manually), among other advantages.

IaaS tools from Microsoft and Google can also be considered as equivalent at a general level. However, Microsoft tools showed sound advantages in some indicators. Microsoft tools offer much more possibilities and customizations to instantiate, configure and execute the tools, including many plugins IDE. While Microsoft offers more than 3 thousand supporting software, Google offers few more than 140. By default, Microsoft offers 448 GB of memory against 208 GB of Google. Yet, Microsoft allows execution also via the Visual Studio environment, whereas Google does that only via a browser.

After all this analysis of SaaS, PaaS and IaaS tools, the impression is that while Microsoft tools seem to be designed for enterprises usage and their integration with back-end systems (and users, of course), Google's seems to focus more on ordinary Internet end-users.

6 Conclusions

This paper has presented an experimental work with some SaaS, PaaS and IaaS cloud tools aiming at evaluating at which extent they fit the requirements of Virtual Enterprises (VE). A literature review has been made to ground the elicitation of the VE needs and performance indicators to be adopted upon cloud tools.

Given the relatively large number of tools available in the market, a number of tools were pre-evaluated. The tools from Google and Microsoft were selected and more deeply evaluated for VE purposes. This selection tried to consider the reality of SMEs, given the tools' costs, wider acceptance and openness.

The evaluation of the tools provided a more comprehensive understanding about the features, possibilities and limitations of the tools, even though considering some subjective analysis in the some cases. Due to the controlled testing environment and considering that the performance measurement was carried out in single moments, some indicators could not be properly evaluated. An example of this is the tools' resilience capability, both during their normal operation and when an intensive and transparent scalability is required. Moreover, billing issues were evaluated based on the tools' documentations available at their official sites.

As the general conclusion, it was observed that the selected cloud tools available in the market support the VE needs in the elicited representative "daily" situations. Besides their functionalities themselves, they in general present good usability and are not so complex from the user point of view. Therefore, cloud computing approach seems a technically feasible approach to be adopted by SMEs in the context of VEs. Thus SMEs might invest resources and efforts in their core areas instead of in ICT.

The access to enterprise applications (like ERP, CRM, etc.) that can be offered as-a-service is included in those situations. However, the general quality of such applications (their processes/services) and respective cloud providers could not be evaluated in this work as this varies from vendor to vendor.

One can point out that part of the tools evaluation work was carried out with some level of subjectivity. Although it was tried to consider representative VE situations and authors' experience when filling out the evaluation tables, they should not be taken literally, but rather as a general reference. Therefore, more particular analyses should be performed by each company regarding its business profile.

It was also noticed that the general VE needs for cloud-based tools are basically the same than individual "non-VE" enterprises. Therefore, it seems to be more about how sensitive and often enterprises' collaborative-related operations should be executed over the net and hence to get dependent on the general quality and security of cloud tools. Related to this matter, some aspects are important to highlight. For example, depending on the enterprises' sector, the data volume and size of 'packages' can be very large, as happens in engineering firms that intensively exchange CAD models using collaborative tools. This can overload the network and can then require very robust local network infrastructures, which can sometimes be not available at all locally or to be too expensive for a SME to support.

It is also important to stress that a VE scenario implies a very dynamic integration among enterprises, many of them by the first time. So, whenever a VE is created, the appropriate systems of the involved enterprises have to be rapidly integrated to the selected cloud tools (and then with the enterprises' systems themselves), generating a complex demand in terms of e.g. interoperability, standardization, governance and security. In addition, the work of setting up the VE's business environment should be performed whenever new VEs are created, changed and dissolved, which also demands good usability and agility from the cloud tools' environments and interfaces.

Next step of this research includes the evaluation of more cloud tools, a separated tools' evaluation for each phase of the VE life cycle, and the elaboration of a kind of tools' benchmarking for SMEs when they look at working in a VE scenario.

References

1. Myers, J.: Future value systems: next generation economic growth engines & manufacturing. In: IMS Vision Forum 2006, IMS International, Seoul, pp. 30–47 (2006)
2. Camarinha-Matos, L.M., Afsarmanesh, H.: Collaborative networks: a new scientific discipline. J. Intell. Manuf. V **16**(4–5), 439–452 (2005)

3. Cancian, M.H., Rabelo, R.J., von Wangenheim, C.G.: Supporting processes for collaborative SaaS. In: Camarinha-Matos, L.M., Scherer, R.J. (eds.) PRO-VE 2013. IFIP AICT, vol. 408, pp. 183–190. Springer, Heidelberg (2013)
4. Westphal, I., Thoben, K.D., Seifert, M.: Managing collaboration performance to govern virtual organizations. J. Intell. Manuf. **21–3**, 311–320 (2010)
5. Erl, T.: Cloud Computing–Concepts Technology & Architecture. Prentice Hall, Upper Saddle River (2014)
6. Jingjing, C., Haitao, S.: Industrial clusters information based on SaaS model. In: Proceedings of the International Conference on Business Management and Electronic Information, pp. 28–31 (2011)
7. Hyvonen, T., Jarvinen, J., Pellinen, J.: A virtual integration-the management control system in a multinational enterprise. Manage. Account. Res. **19**, 45–61 (2008)
8. NIST (National Institute of Standards and Technology). US Cloud Computing Technology Roadmap (2014). http://nvlpubs.nist.gov/nistpubs/SpecialPublications/NIST.SP.500-293.pdf
9. Zhang, K., Ma, B., Dong, P., Tang, B.: Research on producer service innovation in home-textile industrial cluster based on cloud computing platform. In: Proceedings of the 2010 IEEE International Conference on Service Operations and Logistics and Informatics, pp. 155–160 (2010)
10. Li, J., Li, B., Du, Z.: CloudVO: building a secure virtual organization for multiple clouds collaboration. In: Proceedings of the 11th ACIS International Conference on Software Engineering, Artificial Intelligence, Networking and Parallel/Distributed Computing, pp. 181–186 (2010)
11. Gao, J., Ma, J., Zhang, X.: Cloud computing based logistics resource dynamic integration and collaboration. In: Proceedings of the IEEE 16th International Conference on CSCW, pp. 939–943 (2012)
12. Mvelase, P., Dlodlo, N., Williams, Q., Adigun, M.: Virtual enterprise model for enabling cloud computing for SMEs. In: Proceedings of the 2011 International Conference on Intelligent Semantic Web-Services and Applications, paper no. 13 (2011)
13. Lai, I.K.W., Tam, S.K.T., Chan, M.F.S.: Knowledge cloud system for network collaboration: a case study in medical service industry in China. Expert Syst. Appl. **39** (15), 12205–12212 (2012)
14. Jiang, N., Xu, L., de Vrieze, P., Lim, M.-G., Jarabo, O.: A cloud based data integration framework. In: Camarinha-Matos, L.M., Xu, L., Afsarmanesh, H. (eds.) Collaborative Networks in the Internet of Services. IFIP AICT, vol. 380, pp. 177–185. Springer, Heidelberg (2012)
15. Kourtesis, D., Bratanis, K., Bibikas, D., Paraskakis, I.: Software co-development in the Era of cloud application platforms and ecosystems: the case of CAST. In: Camarinha-Matos, L. M., Xu, L., Afsarmanesh, H. (eds.) Collaborative Networks in the Internet of Services. IFIP AICT, vol. 380, pp. 196–204. Springer, Heidelberg (2012)
16. Münch, T., Buchmann, R., Pfeffer, J., Ortiz, P., Christl, C., Hladik, J., Ziegler, J., Lazaro, O., Karagiannis, D., Urbas, L.: An innovative virtual enterprise approach to agile micro and SME-based collaboration networks. In: Camarinha-Matos, L.M., Scherer, R.J. (eds.) PRO-VE 2013. IFIP AICT, vol. 408, pp. 121–128. Springer, Heidelberg (2013)
17. Mvelase, P., Sibiya, G., Dlodlo, N., Oladosu, J., Adigun, M.: A comparative analysis of pricing models for enterprise cloud platforms. Proc. AFRICON **2013**, 1–7 (2013)
18. Bandinelli, R., D'Avllio, E., Rinaldi, R.: Assessing the maturity of collaborative networks: a case study analysis in the Italian fashion SMEs. In: 20th IEEE International Conference on Engineering, Technology and Innovation, pp. 1–9 (2014)

19. Camarinha-Matos, L.M., Afsarmanesh, H., Oliveira, A.I., Ferrada, F.: Cloud-based collaborative business services provision. In: Hammoudi, S., Cordeiro, J., Maciaszek, L. A., Filipe, J. (eds.) ICEIS 2013. LNBIP, vol. 190, pp. 366–384. Springer, Heidelberg (2014)
20. Mezgar, I., Rauschecker, U.: The challenge of networked enterprises for cloud computing interoperability. Comput. Ind. **65**, 657–674 (2014)
21. Gueye, A.D., Sanogo, I., Ouya, S., Saliah-Hassane, H., Lishou, C.: Proposal for a cloud computing solution and application in a pedagogical virtual organization. In: Proceedings of the International Conference on Information Technology, INEER, pp. 349–359 (2014)
22. Binz, T., Exertier, F., Krebs, R., Le Jeune, G., Pelletier, B., Rodero-Merino, L., Niemoller, J.: 4CaaST - Building the PaaS Cloud of the Future. Immigrant PaaS Technologies: Scientific and Technical Report. European Union's Seventh Framework Programme (2011)
23. Veloudis, S., Paraskakis, I., Petsos, C.: Cloud service brokerage: strengthening service resilience in cloud-based virtual enterprises. In: Camarinha-Matos, L.M., Bénaben, F., Picard, W. (eds.) Risks and Resilience of Collaborative Networks. IFIP AICT, vol. 463, pp. 122–135. Springer, New York (2015)
24. Google, Inc.: Google Cloud Platform. http://cloud.google.com/
25. Microsoft, Inc.: Microsoft Corporation. http://www.microsoft.com/pt-br/

Towards Vendor-Agnostic IT-System of IT-Systems with the CEDE Platform

A. Luis Osório(✉)

ISEL - Instituto Superior de Engenharia de Lisboa,
Instituto Politécnico de Lisboa, and POLITEC&ID, Lisbon, Portugal
lo@isel.ipl.pt

Abstract. The increasing capabilities and quality of information technology has thrown integration endeavour to a top priority (total integration trend). However, the lack of time to mature consensus and the market dynamics, has led to technological dependencies (vendor lock-in). Over the past few years, a variety of new concepts, paradigms, methodologies and technologies have contributed to unique information technology (IT) solutions. One main research question is how to establish an open development landscape for the emergent complex integrated IT system of systems under vendor agnostic models (openness). The Collaborative Enterprise Development Environment (CEDE) is a research effort towards a unified development culture (based on conformity certifications). The strategy is complementary to existing standardizations processes and is based on promoting an open (unified) collaborative development environment.

Keywords: Collaborative networks · System of systems · Modularity framework · Collaborative development

1 Introduction

As end-users of information and technology systems (IT-systems) public and private organizations, are facing a crescent problem on how to govern their IT assets under a sustainable model, i.e., how can they ensure that the life cycle management of their assets is under a market competition model? This establishes the vendor-agnostic goal, making a technology landscape potentially sourced from competing suppliers without substitution constraints. At present such substitution is not, in most of the cases, easy or even possible. The IT-systems, potentially needed customizations/configuration efforts after acquisition, in most of the cases, involving considerable costs. These efforts strongly depend on the specific culture of the supplier of the acquired IT-System. IT-systems like enterprise resource planning (ERP), customer relationship management (CRM), supply chain management (SCM), are based on different development strategies (architecture and technologies, and parametrization issues) depending on its supplier. Important standardization efforts, like the business process model and notation (BPMN) from Object Management Group (OMG) are not an answer to avoid the need for specificities associated to technology bindings, as one of the problems that makes a

H. Afsarmanesh et al. (Eds.): PRO-VE 2016, IFIP AICT 480, pp. 494–505, 2016.
DOI: 10.1007/978-3-319-45390-3_42

substitution of a system a complex and costly process. No standards (complete) approaches are known as addressing the current handcrafted configuration efforts, by establishing specific bindings between models and implementation structures.

This problem has been addressed by both the research community and the industry in a number of projects and standardization efforts targeted to (re)think the IT landscape. The FIWARE European initiative is an example of such an effort to promote the substitutability of the (computational) responsibility of IT-systems by assuring that the substitute completely replaces the existing system without the need for any additional configuration/adaptation effort. The FIWARE initiative establishes the Generic Enabler and the reference implementation (GEri) concepts as an external modularity strategy. The GE abstracts a specialized computational responsibility through a set of interfaces for the cooperation with other IT-systems. This means that a FIWARE enabled product shall be conform a GEri used in the validation process (conformity certification) [18]. This initiative assumes however that the approach needs further efforts on defining the complete standards suite able to make the vision an effective contribution for a multi-supplier framework. The IT4IT is another effort from the well-recognized normalization body OpenGroup aiming at establishing "A Reference Architecture for Managing the Business of IT" under a main motivation of working across the recognized silos and the need for novel value chain where the substitutability is facilitated [12]. However, even if vendor-agnostic is declared as an important concern, in IT4IT reference architecture it is assumed that beyond the level 3 (levels 4 and 5) the approaches are vendor specific, Fig. 1.

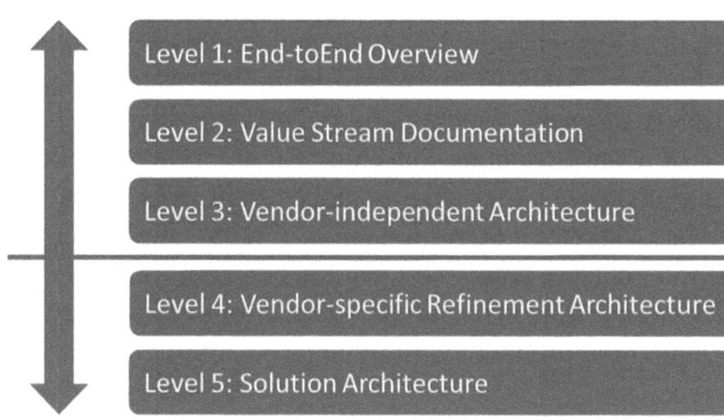

Fig. 1. IT4IT reference architecture levels [12]

This and other efforts demonstrate a crescent concern about the lock-in problem. They represent strategies to reduce cross border silos and the related risks, and added costs difficult to moderate (coordinate). At least for critical systems, there is a trend to adopt monolithic solutions under a unique responsibility from a single supplier, as a strategy to guarantee minimal risks.

This paper discusses the CEDE research as a contribution for the vendor-agnostic of IT-system of IT-systems, under an open research challenge, considering both open modularity, and a unified development culture. Both approaches are related to previous research work and productized IT solutions, adopted by the industry.

2 Open Complex System of Systems Research

The development of complex systems is a long discussed research and industry community concern. In 1972 Liskov [8] discussed reliability and complexity associated to the software developments. The concern was not at that time the vendor-agnostic but rather the complexity of developing reliable software systems. The introduction of the term complexity refers to, in the one hand "*...there are many system states in such a system, and it is difficult to organize the program logic to handle all states correctly*" and on the other hand "*... the efforts of many individuals must be coordinated in order to build the system*". It is quite interesting that more than four decades later we are discussing more or less the same problem. While nowadays the complexity might have increased, and the state of the knowledge about computer science and engineering and the available resources have evolved under paramount dimensions, we still are on difficulties to offer reliability for the new integrated and distributed system of systems. Or at least, such reliability is difficult to guarantee in a multi-supplier environment where suppliers holding different process and technology culture, collaborate to the life cycle of integrated IT-system of IT-systems (SoS).

The panoply of languages, development frameworks and paradigms are one main reason for the need for common methodologies, tools and resources able to cope with the required holistic (systemic) approaches. In fact, if considering the two technology specific main lines, the leaded by Microsoft (.NET, WCF, C#, etc.) and the Java and open source world (RMI, OSGi, Java, etc.) there is a consensus about the advantage (less risks) to adopt the unified Microsoft culture. There are a number of potential suppliers offering development services certified under this development and execution environments culture (proprietary). For what is mentioned as the open source java world (involving a diversity of many other paradigms), the situation is different; it is of high risk the adoption of a single (unique) development and process cultures. For the open source world such diversity of paradigms induce high risks when there is a need to change the supplier. There is a high probability that the new subcontracted company needs extra time to understand the assets and the potential founded need to move parts to its own development culture. This has led to situations where reutilization of existing assets is not possible or at least, is not of the interests of the new subcontracted development culture.

This situation can be in a large extent reduced if adopting certified competencies on proprietary technology landscapes (Microsoft, SAP, TIBCO, Oracle, Cisco, and many other proprietary cultures). When the strategy is to adopt open source and open specifications not leaded by a unique technology supplier it is more difficult to find competing companies able to support and evolve assets in such open worlds.

There are a number of integrated development environments (Eclipse, NetBeans, IntelliJ, among other), code generation and dependencies management (Maven, Ivy, Grape, Gradle, Buildr, STB, Leiningen, and more will appears with some justified advantage), issues and project management tools (Redmine, Bugzilla, Mantis, Trac, ProjectLibre, LibrePlan, OpenProject, MyCollab, Odoo, from many other), and well known proprietary tools like the suite offered by Atlassian. This diversity makes the potential advantages from adopting open crowdsourcing dynamics a risk to generate vendor dependencies, potentially worst that those associated to proprietary cultures. Furthermore, for large end-users the contracting of innovative start-ups is associated to a potential risk of adopting fashion technologies, development paradigms and methodologies. Such diversity makes difficult to construct consistent integration strategies for complex IT-systems, considering that these start-up, as potential competing suppliers, tend to adopt their own development culture.

Therefore, as standards are not complete to establish such a required open common culture for the development and life cycle management of complex integrated system of systems, there is a need to establish a common informatics engineering culture. One informatics engineering culture, means the establishment of standard technology, procedures, methodologies, tools, and a modularity framework, making specific development easily managed by competing suppliers. Such a convergence is expected to be accelerated and pulled by the end-users, driven by their need for competitive IT supplying markets, in particular governments. Wherever possible, the convergence shall be based on standard products, at least for the specialized IT-system infrastructure level systems (Radars, Road Side Units, things, controllers, etc.). However for higher level back-office and enterprise IT department systems, the efforts to converge to standards are commonly not enough to completely answer to evolving requirements. This has been motivating the development of common platforms like the COMPASS project that challenged a Collaborative Development Environment as an alternative to the existing Integrated Development Environments (IDE) [2]. The proposed COMPASS tool set is based on a triangular approach based on the Systems Modelling Language (SysML) a dialect of the Unified Modelling Language (UML) generating a COMPASS Modelling Language (CML) based on the Artisan product, the Java based COMPASS Overture toll [7] and the runtime tester (RT-Tester) for tests automation tasks. While arguing that is a formal contribution to open SoS, the adoption of the proprietary Artisan Studio from Atego raises the question about the openness of the approach. The modular open systems approach (MOSA) for the military industry, a program of the US department of defence (DoD), is grounded on five principles (i) establishment of an enabling environment, (ii) employ modular design, (iii) designate key interfaces, (iv) use open standards, and (v) certify conformance, as a strategy for a unified contractual framework for an open life cycle management of system of systems (complex warfighting systems) [15].

More recent theoretical works about component substitutability considers a dynamic reconfigurations of components evolving dynamically by adjusting capabilities on answering requirements changes. The adjustments are based on software component's level and structured on primitive operations like, instantiation, destruction, addition, removal, binding, unbinding, starting, stopping, and parameter's adaptation [6]. Nevertheless, while important for a scientific foundation of system of systems (or at a lower level, component of components or composites), a practical application is only viable if a unified culture is developed to accommodate such diversity of contributions for the development of reliable complex IT-system of IT-systems.

The System of systems and in particular IT-system of IT-systems concept, has been adopted along the last two or three decades as an idea of structuring the growing complexity. The Greek origin for system means a whole composed of many parts and is adopted for social, mathematical, healthcare, transport, logistics and other systems [5].

It is related to a strategy to get some form or cohesion through the composition of a diversity of parts (subsystems) coordinated for some value production.

3 The CEDE Strategy as Part of the MDEOS Program

The research to achieve a vendor-agnostic approach leads to the definition of Open System of systems, in a slightly different form but similar in objectives to the well-known Open System Interconnection (OSI) to the network/communication level. In fact, the most challenging goal is to achieve a systemic IT approach, based on a composite of IT-systems where for each subsystem the principle of substitutability shall apply. To better clarify the concept lets define IT-system of IT-system as a set S of IT-systems $S = \{S_1, S_2, \ldots, S_n\}$ where for each S_i there exist at least two potential suppliers guaranteeing a plug-and-play substitution. The definition of open IT-system of IT-systems (for simplicity SoS) diverge from what industry usually presents as open systems, which is centred on its promptness to integrate with any existing or legated system. In fact, any IT-system is (or should be) developed under architectural concerns on how to decompose the system into subsystems, guided by an internal reutilization strategy. A complex IT-system product is organized following such a modularity strategy under the culture of the developer company. This application of engineering best practice is classified as internal modularity, considering that such division of responsibilities is internal to the developer company. Two system architects will arrive, for sure, to different division of responsibilities (modularity framework) unless a same reference architecture is followed. In the open IT-system of IT-system formulation, each subsystem should be considered under an external modularity, meaning that it implements open (standard/ public domain) interfaces. The design of such a SoS under external modularity requires the architecture derives from a reference architecture and is conform to the open specifications. The research challenge is in fact to establish an equivalent open IT-system where the end-user is more "owner", and has the governance control of the It-system of IT-systems, Fig. 2.

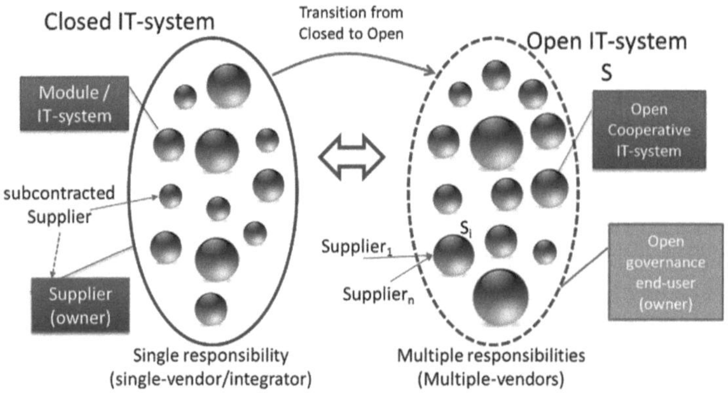

Fig. 2. Open IT-system of IT-systems

The approach to this endeavour starts from a more general strategic vision to address the upcoming complex IT-systems where the today dependencies are not acceptable, considering the dependencies they impose to the innovation processes (lock to unique suppliers). The Model Driven Engineering Open Systems (MDEOS) initiative frames the CEDE platform and a previous research, the Cooperation Enabled System (CES) [13]. The CES modularity framework, aiming at establish an external modularity framework for SoS, was strategically postponed by the difficulties to operationalize the proposed model. The reference implementation started to get too complex and the number and diversity of adopted open source contributions has generated a complex implementation difficult to validate and to be accepted by the market as an open reference modularity framework. The MDEOS program, Fig. 3, was established on the assumption there exists a gap between processes and technology that needs to be shortened and, if possible, removed through the establishment of a suite of coordinated model driven tools.

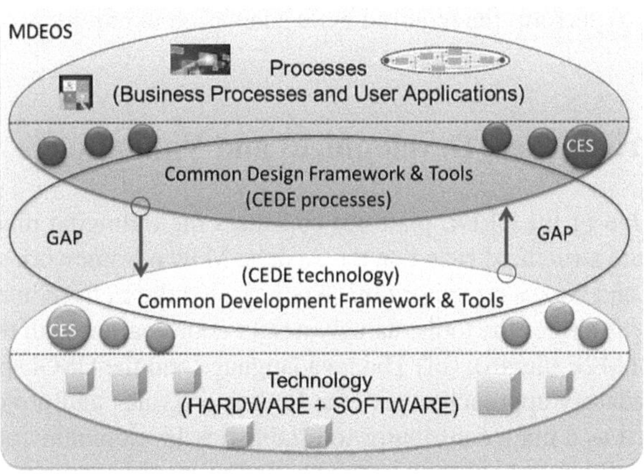

Fig. 3. Open IT-system of IT-systems

The gap between processes and technology has long been recognized as a major challenge for information intensive companies [9]. The model driven engineering (MDE) and model driven development (MDD) research, motivated in part from the Model Driven architecture (MDA) principles as formulated by OMG [11], have been contributing to reduce the gap by helping to automate the bridge between de platform independent models (PIM) and the platform specific ones (PIM). However, in spite of the number of contributions related to the MDA challenge, the dependencies from specific organization's models and meta-models and technology approaches, remains as a main obstacle for the establishment of open system of systems and this way contribute to reduce the gap between processes and IT technology.

Among the research towards the establishment of accurate models, a valuable contribution to reduce the gap between models and implementations is proposed by the Object-Process Methodology (OPM) [17]. Considering its simplicity and the mechanisms provided to describe complex system of systems, it is planned to include this modelling tool into the CEDE paradigms portfolio.

Both CEDE and CES are research contributions, as convergence efforts for the reduction of such a gap, by promoting, in the one hand, a unified development environment (CEDE) and, on the other hand, by establishing a high abstraction level to encapsulate computational responsibilities. This CES research aims at establish a complete and consistent vendor-agnostic suite of capabilities able to commit to the substitutability principle (open modularity framework).

The CEDE implementation is under development and validation, and in this phase it is focused on the selection of methodologies, technologies and tools by establishing this way a common standard development framework for the technology perspective. A more long term objective is to extend the CEDE platform to contribute for the other line of the gap with an enhanced version offering a common design framework and tools for the processes domain (as a strategy to reduce it). The idea is to offer two main groups of specialized tools, one for technology developments and the other for accessing process experts to perform the required agile adaptation to requirements change.

4 CEDE Framework Development and Validation

The initial version of the CEDE platform considers the following mandatory options: (i) the projects are structured based on the Apache Maven framework supported by Git version control and Nexus repository management; (ii) the Eclipse integrated development environment unifies the tools, namely a tight coordination with the Maven mechanisms (through M2E plugin); (iii) The java language and the OSGi specification were selected as mandatory approaches; (iv) the Redmine[1] issues and project management tool was selected as a main contributor to establish a development collaborative environment, eventually enhanced with specialized plug-ins; and (v) a federated authentication and authoring infrastructure based on LDAP directory unifies access control. The selection of technology paradigms and tools were guided by openness and a founded recognition by both the industry and research community. For the potential question, about why adopting OSGi and not other modularity framework, the reason is associated to its intrinsic potential and recognition based on a crescent adoption by the industry. Even if the OSGi specification is focused on Java, there are research works evaluating the possibility to bind this framework to other programming languages, e.g. C#/.NET as discussed in [3]. Following similar founded decisions, the construction of the CEDE platform is based on a Linux server (Ubuntu), and it is planned to be deployed from a reference implementation able to speed-up its adoption. The CEDE servers might be running on premises or on the cloud, as a resource dedicated to manage and coordinate collaborative developments for complex large scale IT-systems, Fig. 4.

[1] Redmine - http://www.redmine.org/.

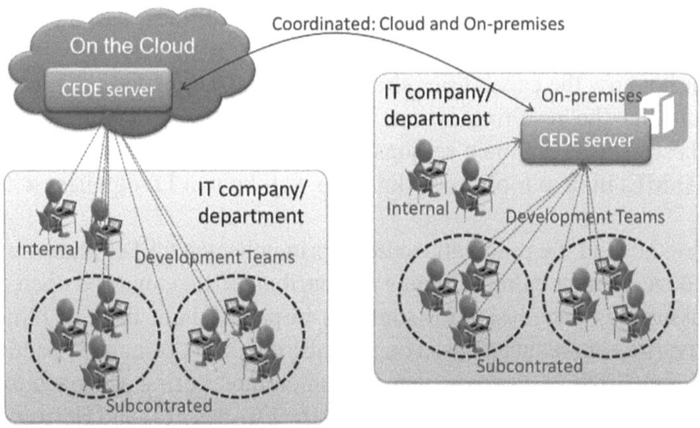

Fig. 4. The new PCS IT-system wraps the legated PSW/JUP

The selection of specific frameworks or computing paradigms is difficult to decide when there are more than one, with strong valuable arguments. One extreme example about such decision difficulties is the adoption by the OSGi standardization of two competing paradigms: i) the Blueprint Container (osgi.121, BC) and the Declarative Services (osgi.112, DS) as frameworks realizing the dependency injection and inversion of control patterns (DI/IoC). While being argued for the structuration of large scale object-oriented applications [1], the OSGi standard seems however to be conditioned by industry investments and even if the Declarative Services (DS) paradigm is getting momentum, any product that is developed on Blueprint Container is also conform to the standard. This is an example of the extreme difficulties to converge to consensus on deciding for single approaches when many options have their own arguments to be the selection one.

The CEDE platform is therefore a strategy for the development of open complex large scale IT-system of IT-systems grounded on an enhanced collaborative ecosystem. It is grounded on simple basic principles: (i) an open unified culture established by the suite of adopted concepts, implementations, technologies, methodologies, tools, and techniques; (ii) a concretization through a CEDE server with a reference implementation from where platform instances can be derived; and (iii) a competencies certification process both for developers and for companies. One main objective is to establish a vender-neutral IT-system development culture and this way reduce the tacit knowledge common to software development processes. As a knowledge intensive activity, many strategies have been researched namely the adoption of a robust transitive memory systems (TMS) to support the knowledge sharing among software development teams [16].

Furthermore, the tacit knowledge associated to the software development process is not only a problem for IT product development companies but also for the end-users. The lack of standard off-the-shelf IT-systems results on the need for specific developments, as the current and most usual strategy to make capabilities to fully match the requirements. The end-user companies, public organizations and authorities have many difficulties to establish competitive tenders for IT capabilities, based on the discussed risks of dependencies they might induce. The public tenders usually specify what is required but not how the capabilities should be organized, making this way budgeting very difficult and the resulting system dependent from the culture of the winning supplier. These aspects are main reasons to pretermit start-ups and small and medium companies (SME) in favour of less risky large well known IT suppliers with their own culture.

Therefore, beyond the pragmatic suite of principles the CEDE platform establishes an open IT development culture. It aims at contribute to an enhanced open competitive market, making this way easier for start-ups to prove about the capabilities of their products. The risks are reduced based on the substitutability principle resulting from the adoption of the CEDE IT development unified culture. A first approach to the CEDE platform is being validated by the migration of the ECoNet [14] and Horus projects. The Horus project developed the Petrol Distributed Open Service Bus (PDOSBus) as a suite of cooperative services to manage post-payments in a gas-station forecourt. The Horus IT-system obtains the vehicle identification through automatic licence plate recognition (ALPR) and registers and manage payment incidents when the vehicles leave the forecourt without paying. When a vehicle with a payment incident is positioned to feel the gas-tank and a person removes the nozzle, the point-of-sale subsystem (POS) asks a specialized Horus service for any payment incident for that vehicle. If there is a pending payment the POS operator is presented with a special warning symbol making him to initiate the suggestion for a pre-payment procedure to that vehicle. While not a too complex IT-system of IT-systems the participation of two start-ups (Exploitsys and Makewise), a large IT supplier for the POS subsystem (Gasodata/Dresser Wayne) and two large end-users companies (Galp and BP) makes the case well suited for an initial validation.

The CEDE platform while based on a suite of well-known tools, as above discussed, is planned to have a main entrance portal from where collaborating companies and individual developers can access to perform their contributions. The main modules of CEDE

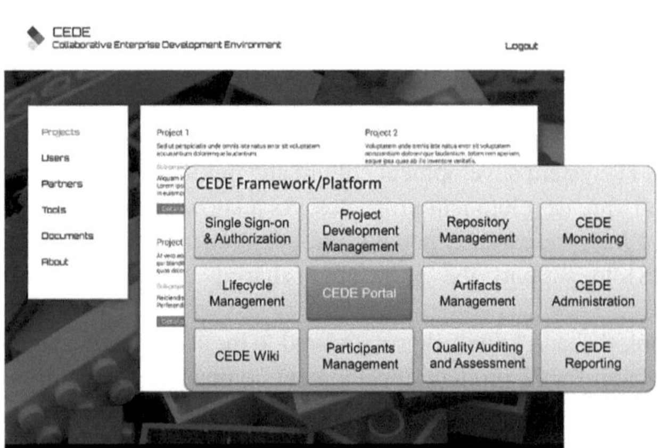

Fig. 5. A first approach to the CEDE unified collaborative development environment

platform include: (i) a single sign-on and authorization module, based on LDAP and a federated identity management); (ii) project and issues management (based on Redmine); (iii) a repository management (based on Nexus) and Git versioning system; and other governance, documentation, and management tools, Fig. 5.

As a turnaround approach to answer the lack of an effective multi-supplier (open) modularity framework, the CEDE platform aims at establish an open collaborative space. Such unified collaborative development space aims to establish a unified development environment based on a pre-established suite of standards mechanisms, technologies, patterns, and theories able to promote an enhanced competitive ecosystem for the life cycle management of open large scale complex IT-system of IT-systems. The CEDE research is aligned to the Software Engineering Method And Technology (SEMAT) concerns about the lack of solid scientific foundations for the new complex IT-system (of systems) development [4, 10]. While the SEMAT concerns are focused on software development, and the challenged program is of paramount importance, the CEDE in particular and the MDEOS program in general advocates for an IT system thinking at a different level, complementary to the software engineering layer. It is difficult to maintain a robust modularity bases when process requirements are mapping directly to software development decisions.

The CEDE platform was motivated by the difficulty large IT development companies have to manage the subcontracted partners to answer specific development projects. It is not easy for the development manager to establish reutilization strategies when the subcontracted companies hold different process and development cultures. While large companies impose their own development culture to networked partners, the model while common, has the drawback to establish proprietary solutions. Like it happened in other industries, e.g. the automotive industry, it is expected a convergence for a hierarchical market structure where larger companies positioned themselves as integrators responsible for IT-system of IT-systems based on a network of smaller specialized companies as suppliers of IT-systems to incorporate composites under the responsibility of the larger IT integrator company. The CEDE research aims at contribute for an open approach equivalent to the already existing based on proprietary cultures.

While partial contributions were identified (FIWARE, MDA, SEMAT, from other), no other known approach was found to answer similar objectives. A huge number of open source initiatives are following partial approaches to get visibility and the credibility from the market (e.g. the case of the openHAB - a vendor and technology agnostic open source automation software for your home). While many are getting succcss, most of them are not able to get momentum, a risk that might be reduced if adopting an open IT-systems development culture.

5 Conclusions and Further Research

The Collaborative Enterprise Development Environment (CEDE) research, while part of the more ambitious Model Driven Open Systems (MDEOS) program is being founded on the experiences and drawback from previous research (CES, ECoNet, Horus,

ITSIBus, and PDOSBus) sponsored by large public and private companies (Brisa, Galp, BP, APL and APDL - Administrations of Port of Lisbon and of Leixões) and governmental agencies (INIR/SIEV, ANSR). It is founded on the need for an open development culture, at both IT systems and software development levels and also at business process application domain (functional areas). The research question, how to develop open multi-supplier IT-system of Systems able to cope to the crescent complexity associated to total integration of intra and inter organization (collaborative) processes was partially answered by the proposal of the CEDE strategy. The concept of internal and external modularity were defined, being that external modularity plays a key role on the development of open SoS. By committing to external modularity principles, it means an IT-system is able to be substituted by a competitor, i.e., it is prepared for the cooperation and to be dynamically plugged to a composite making a system of systems (SoS). The unification of the development culture is also a key approach as a contribution for an ecosystem made of pluggable IT-systems and developments under specific requirements.

One main open research question is how the collaborative networks can contribute to the structuration of the underlying complex interactions among companies participating in the development of complex large scale integrated IT-systems. The collaborative developments are expected to play a major role by promoting value creation networks where companies of different sizes, from start-up to large suppliers collaborate on the development of complex critical IT-systems.

Acknowledgements. This work has been partially supported by Administration of the Port of Lisbon and Leixões through the MIELE project, Brisa Innovation and Technology, through a yearly research grant, Galpgest and BP through the Horus project and ANSR (National Road Security Authority) through the SINCRO project. The reference implementations has been supported by a group of fellowships, Paula Graça, Inês Guilherme, Paulo Borges, Victor Camargo, and Calmenelias Freitas. The participation of Exploitsys and Makewise IT companies is of paramount importance.

References

1. Alshara, Z., Seriai, A.-D., Tibermacine, C., Bouziane, H.L., Dony, C., Shatnawi, A.: Migrating large object-oriented applications into component-based ones: instantiation and inheritance transformation. In: Proceedings of the 2015 ACM SIGPLAN International Conference on Generative Programming: Concepts and Experiences, GPCE 2015, pp 55–64. ACM, New York (2015)
2. Coleman, J.W., Malmos, A.K., Larsen, P.G., Peleska, J., Hains, R., Andrews, Z., Payne, R., Foster, S., Miyazawa, A., Bertolini, C., Didierk, A.: Compass tool vision for a system of systems collaborative development environment. In: 2012 7th International Conference on System of Systems Engineering (SoSE), pp. 451–456, July 2012
3. Escoffier, C., Donsez, D., Hall, R.S.: Developing an osgi-like service platform for .net. In: 3rd IEEE Consumer Communications and Networking Conference, CCNC 2006, vol. 1, pp 213–217, January 2006

4. B Ivar and Richard. The semat-software engineering method and theory-vision satement (2009). http://semat.org/documents/20181/27952/SEMAT-vision.pdf/16059a36-a0ba-4405-b883-4a11a2131cea
5. Karcanias, N., Hessami, A.G.: Complexity and the notion of system of systems: part (i): general systems and complexity. In: 2010 World Automation Congress (WAC), pp. 1–7, September 2010
6. Lanoix, A., Kouchnarenko, O.: Component substitution through dynamic reconfigurations. In: Proceedings of 11th International Workshop on Formal Engineering Approaches to Software Components and Architectures, FESCA 2014, Grenoble, France, 12 April 2014, pp. 32–46 (2014)
7. Larsen, P.G., Battle, N., Ferreira, M., Fitzgerald, J., Lausdahl, K., Verhoef, M.: The overture initiative integrating tools for vdm. SIGSOFT Softw. Eng. Notes **35**(1), 1–6 (2010)
8. Liskov, B.H.: A design methodology for reliable software systems. In: Proceedings of the 5–7 December 1972, Fall Joint Computer Conference, Part I, AFIPS 1972 (Fall, part I), pp. 191–199. ACM, New York (1972)
9. Martin, V.A., Lycett, M., Macredie, R: Exploring the gap between business and it: an information culture approach. In: Proceeding in Action in Language, Organisations and Information Systems, ALOIS (2003)
10. Myburgh, A.: Situational software engineering complex adaptive responses of software development teams. In: 2014 Federated Conference on Computer Science and Information Systems (FedCSIS), pp. 841–850, September 2014
11. OMG-MDA. Model driven architecture (mda), mda guide rev. 2.0, June 2014. http://www.omg.org/cgi-bin/doc?ormsc/14-06-01.pdf. OMG Document ormsc/2014-06-01
12. The OpenGroup. The IT4IT Reference Architecture, Version 2.0. Number C115 in Open Group Standard. Van Haren, October 2015
13. Osório, A., Camarinha-Matos, L.M., Afsarmanesh, H.: Cooperation enabled systems for collaborative networks. In: Camarinha-Matos, L.M., et al. (eds.) PRO-VE 2011. IFIP AICT, vol. 362, pp. 400–409. Springer, Heidelberg (2011)
14. Osório, L.A., Camarinha-Matos, L.M., Afsarmanesh, H.: ECoNet platform for collaborative logistics and transport. In: Camarinha-Matos, L.M., et al. (eds.) PRO-VE 2015. IFIP AICT, vol. 463, pp. 265–276. Springer, Heidelberg (2015). doi:10.1007/978-3-319-24141-8_24
15. Rendon, R.G.: Using a modular open systems approach in defense acquisitions: implications for the contracting process. In: 2007 IEEE International Conference on System of Systems Engineering, SoSE 2007, pp. 1–6, April 2007
16. Ryan, S., OConnor, R.V.: Acquiring and sharing tacit knowledge in software development teams: an empirical study. Inf. Softw. Technol. **55**(9), 1614–1624 (2013)
17. Soffer, A.: Bridging information gaps in an OPM-based system development lifecycle. In: Meersman, R., Tari, Z., Corsaro, A. (eds.) OTM-WS 2004. LNCS, vol. 3292, pp. 787–797. Springer, Heidelberg (2004)
18. Zahariadis, T., Papadakis, A., Alvarez, F., Gonzalez, J., Lopez, F., Facca, F., Al-Hazmi, Y.: Fiware lab: managing resources and services in a cloud federation supporting future internet applications. In: Proceedings of the 2014 IEEE/ACM 7th International Conference on Utility and Cloud Computing, UCC 2014, pp. 792–799. IEEE Computer Society, Washington (2014)

Validating Policies for Dynamic and Heterogeneous Cloud Environments

Simeon Veloudis(✉), Iraklis Paraskakis, and Christos Petsos

International Faculty of the University of Sheffield, South East European Research Centre (SEERC), CITY College, 24 Proxenou Koromila St, 54622 Thessaloniki, Greece
{sveloudis,iparaskakis,chrpetsos}@seerc.org

Abstract. With the pervasion of cloud computing, virtual enterprises (VEs) are anticipated to increasingly rely on ecosystems of highly distributed, task-oriented, and collaborative cloud services for their operations. In order to manage the complexity inherent in such ecosystems, VEs are expected to increasingly depend upon policies that regulate the deployment and delivery of these services. Nevertheless, the heterogeneity inherent in cloud services hinders the formulation of effective and interoperable such policies. This calls for a policy validation mechanism that is able to automatically evaluate the correctness of these policies. This paper proposes such a validation mechanism, one which is underpinned by a generic representation of the *knowledge* that lurks behind policies and thus is orthogonal to any particular cloud service delivery platform.

Keywords: Virtual enterprises · Cloud computing · Policies · Ontologies · Linked USDL

1 Introduction

Cloud computing introduces a paradigm whereby infrastructure, platform, and application resources are abstracted as services and delivered remotely over the Internet by a multitude of providers [1, 2]. These services allow enterprises to realise significant savings while accelerating, at the same time, the development and deployment of new applications. Naturally, cloud computing is expected to impact the manner in which enterprises cooperate in a distributed collaborative network [2]. In particular, activities accomplished in the frame of a virtual enterprise (VE) may include utilisation of cloud services spanning different administrative domains and levels of capability (IaaS, PaaS and SaaS). For example, consider the scenario (adapted from [3]) whereby a scientific consortium is formed in order to collaboratively run a large cascade of meteorological and hydrological computational models for flood forecasting. Such processing utilises SaaS components offered by different consortium participants. Each such component may be deployed on a participant's proprietary infrastructure, or on infrastructure provisioned as a cloud service (IaaS offering). The computation also requires new specialised software that is developed on a software platform that is too provisioned as a service (PaaS offering).

H. Afsarmanesh et al. (Eds.): PRO-VE 2016, IFIP AICT 480, pp. 506–517, 2016.
DOI: 10.1007/978-3-319-45390-3_43

Cloud-based VEs are therefore rapidly being transformed into complex ecosystems of heterogeneous, externally-sourced services. As the number of these services increases, keeping track of when and how they evolve over time, e.g. as a result of intentional or unintentional changes, becomes an increasingly challenging process. The situation is further perplexed by the dynamic nature of VEs as new enterprises may be added or existing ones leave.

In order to deal with this complexity, VEs are anticipated to rely on *policies* that regulate the deployment and delivery of cloud services. This calls for mechanisms that are able to generically evaluate the conformance of services with these policies, as well as to validate the correctness of the policies. We argue that, in order to deal with the dynamic nature of cloud-based VEs, as well as with the heterogeneity of the cloud services that they employ, these mechanisms must advocate a clear separation of concerns whereby policies are expressed orthogonally to the code used for enforcing them. This brings about a number of positive effects: (i) it keeps the mechanisms independent of any particular cloud delivery platform; (ii) it enables them to deal with a wide range of heterogeneous policies and services; (iii) it allows reasoning about policy interrelations (e.g. conflicting or overlapping policies).

In this respect, in [5] we proposed SC^3: a mechanism for automatically evaluating the compliance of cloud services with preset policies concerning their business aspects of delivery. In this paper, we go a step further and propose a *policy validation* mechanism for evaluating the *correctness* of the policies themselves. The mechanism is underpinned by an ontology able to accurately capture the seminal characteristics of the policies. By shifting the locus of effort from software development to the creation of knowledge structures, our ontology introduces an extra layer of abstraction which enables the formal representation of the concepts that lurk behind business policies. It thereby disentangles the definition of policies from the code employed for enforcing them. The proposed ontology draws upon Linked USDL [6] – an ontological framework which readily provides the necessary structures for accommodating the required concepts. Finally, it is to be noted that the proposed mechanism forms part of a broader mechanism that is being developed as part of the PaaSword project [7] and which aims at validating a wide range of policies, including security policies, in heterogeneous and dynamic cloud environments.

The rest of this paper is structured as follows. Section 2 presents related work. Section 3 outlines a motivating usage scenario and presents a particular categorisation of policies, namely state-oriented policies. Section 4 outlines an ontological model for state-oriented policies and presents the policy validation mechanism. Section 5 presents conclusions and future work.

2 Related Work

Several works have attempted to address the shortcomings entailed by the lack of separation of concerns between policy specification on the one hand, and policy enforcement on the other [8–14]. These works generally utilise custom languages, and ontologies, for capturing policies which are subsequently enforced at run-time through a reference monitor. In [8], the authors propose PONDER – a purpose-made domain specific language for modelling security and management policies; [9–11] advocate the use of markup languages for the specification of access control policies. However, such syntactic descriptions fail to capture the knowledge that lurks behind policies: they are simply data models that lack semantic interoperability.

Closer to our work are the approaches reported in [12–14]. These are based on Semantic Web representations for representing the knowledge lurking behind *action-oriented* policies, i.e. policies that regulate when an actor can perform a particular action on a particular resource (see Sect. 3). In [12], the authors present KAoS – a policy enforcement and governance framework which advocates a 3-layered architecture consisting of: (i) a human interface layer; (ii) a policy management layer, which captures policies in OWL; (iii) a policy monitoring and enforcement layer, which converts policies expressed in OWL to a programmatic format suitable for policy enforcement. The work reported in [13] proposes Rei – a rule-based policy framework that permits the declarative specification of heterogeneous policies. Rei policies specify those actions that *can* be performed, and those actions that *should* be performed, by a named entity. It therefore allows the specification of a desirable set of behaviours which are understandable – and enforceable – by autonomous entities in dynamic cloud environments. The work in [14], proposes POLICYTAB for supporting trust negotiation in dynamic Web environments. POLICYTAB embraces an ontology-based approach for capturing policies that guide a trust negotiation process for providing regulated access to Web resources.

Although they do achieve, to different extents, a separation of concerns between policy representation and policy enforcement, the approaches above rely on custom ontologies for modelling policies. Despite the fact that such ontologies may be suitable for capturing action-oriented policies, they generally lack the expressivity for addressing the *state-oriented* business policies on which this work reports (see Sect. 3). In this respect, instead of extending – or adapting – the ontologies defined in [12–14], we opt for Linked USDL: an easily extensible and diffused vocabulary of concepts and their associations that readily provides the necessary constructs for capturing the seminal characteristics of state-oriented policies. In addition, the reliance of the approaches in [12–14] on OWL [15], raises concerns about performance when they are used for checking the compliance of increasing loads of cloud services. Our work alleviates these concerns through the use of the lightweight RDF-based [16] vocabulary offered by Linked USDL.

3 Policies for Cloud Service Quality Assurance

We are interested in determining, in a generic manner, a set of *business constraints* that any service aspiring to be used by a VE must satisfy. In our framework, these constraints take the form of *business policies*. Next we demonstrate such policies through the example of Sect. 1. Let *CPMeteo* be a cloud delivery platform that hosts various services for the flood forecasting computation. These services are developed either by the scientific consortium that performs these computations, or by third-party providers. Suppose that an ecosystem partner, or third-party provider, offers a new service to CPMeteo, call it *Meteo@Cloud*, which encrypts, stores and provides access to intermediate results of the various phases of the flood forecasting computation. For the new service to become available on CPMeteo, certain criteria must be satisfied. These essentially represent a set of *service-level objectives* (SLOs) that are expressed in terms of constraints on relevant *service-level attributes*; Table 1 summarises the service-level attributes, and their corresponding SLOs, considered for the purposes of this example. These SLOs form CPMeteo's *business policy* (BP) with respect to deploying Meteo@Cloud. The BP additionally incorporates a set of *service-level profiles* (SLPs). These are essentially sets of SLOs that formulate different 'deployment schemes' offered by CPMeteo. For instance, a 'gold' SLP may group together the 'gold' SLOs of each of the service-level attributes of Table 1[1].

Table 1. Entry-level criteria

Service-level attribute	Acceptable values	SLO	Comments
`storage`	[100,1000)	Gold storage	Size in TB
	[10,100)	Silver storage	
	[1,10)	Bronze storage	
`encryption`	256	Gold encryption	Key-length in bits
	192	Silver encryption	
	128	Bronze encryption	

We assume that the service provider who offers Meteo@Cloud provides a service description (SD) that specifies the manner in which Meteo@Cloud is to be offered through CPMeteo. This SD must be compliant with CPMeteo's business policy. For instance, an SD which fails to specify a value for the `storage` attribute, or one which specifies a value lesser than 1 TB, cannot be considered compliant with the BP.

3.1 State-Oriented Policies vs Action-Oriented Policies

The works in [11–13] focus on *action-oriented* policies, i.e. policies that control the conditions under which an actor can perform an action on a particular resource. Clearly, an indispensible ingredient of action-oriented policies is the specification of the actor who initiates the action, as well as of the action itself. The ontologies proposed in [11–13] naturally provide constructs for the specification of these ingredients. In contrast, as it becomes evident from Sect. 3.1, the kind of policies that our framework focuses on does not place any emphasis on specifying the actor that potentially initiates a particular action, or on the nature of the action itself: the actor may be *any* service provider, whereas

[1] Of course, the number of SLPs offered by CPMeteo, and the SLOs that these comprise, is an application-specific issue determined by CPMeteo itself. For instance, CPMeteo may choose to define a 'gold' SLP as an SLP that comprises either 'gold'-only SLOs, or two 'gold' and a 'silver' SLO; alternatively, it may choose to define the latter grouping as a 'silver' SLP.

the action is *invariably* the on-boarding of a service on a cloud service delivery platform. Our *business* policies predominantly focus on the conditions that must be met for a service to be on-boarded on such a platform. These conditions entail a set of artefacts that an SD must encompass. In this respect, they essentially formulate a set of *guaranteed states* which are represented through the SLOs and the SLPs that the business policies comprise. We shall term such policies *state-oriented.* Clearly, such a shift in focus from action-oriented to state-oriented business policies calls for a novel approach to the ontological modelling of policies, one which provides the necessary constructs for representing the artefacts that an SD must encompass. In this paper we propose such an approach based on Linked USDL [6]: an ontology framework which provides the necessary concepts for capturing SLPs and SLOs. In the following section we provide an outline of our approach. A brief account of the reasons that lead us to opt for Linked USDL is first in order.

3.2 Linked USDL

Linked USDL is a re-modelled version of USDL [17]. It draws upon the experience gained with USDL, as well as with other research efforts in the realm of Semantic Web Services and business ontologies [18, 19]. It builds upon the principles of Linked Data in order to endorse its use in a 'web of data'. In this respect, it models specifications in an RDF vocabulary that better supports the generic representation of web and cloud services. The adoption of Linked USDL brings about the following advantages [19]. Firstly, its reliance on existing widely-used RDF vocabularies, such as GoodRelations [21] the Simple Knowledge Organization System (SKOS) ontology [22], and FOAF [23]. In this respect, it promotes knowledge sharing whilst it increases the interoperability, and thus the reusability and generality, of our security policies. Secondly, by offering a number of different profiles, Linked USDL provides a holistic and generic solution able to adequately capture a wide range of business details. In addition, Linked USDL is designed to be easily extensible through linking to further existing, or new, ontologies.

4 Representation and Validation of State-Oriented Policies

Linked USDL comprises a Core schema which in our model encodes certain invariable characteristics of a BP. From this Core schema a number of extension schemata hinge addressing diverse business aspects of a BP, such as pricing, SLA, security, and IPR; for the purposes of this paper, we focus on the SLA schema. Sections 4.1 and 4.3 below describe, with reference to the scenario of Sect. 3.1, how state-oriented policies are modelled within the Core and SLA schemata respectively. Sections 4.2 and 4.4 describe how the *correctness* of state-oriented policies is evaluated by the policy validation mechanism.

4.1 Linked USDL Core

We use Linked USDL's Core schema in order to formally capture the following two facts about a BP: (i) the identity of the *business entity* which is responsible for defining the BP (i.e. CPMeteo, in the case of the scenario of Sect. 3.1); (ii) the *role* in the capacity of which this business entity acts when defining the BP. To this end, we utilise the USDL Core classes and properties depicted in Fig. 1[2].

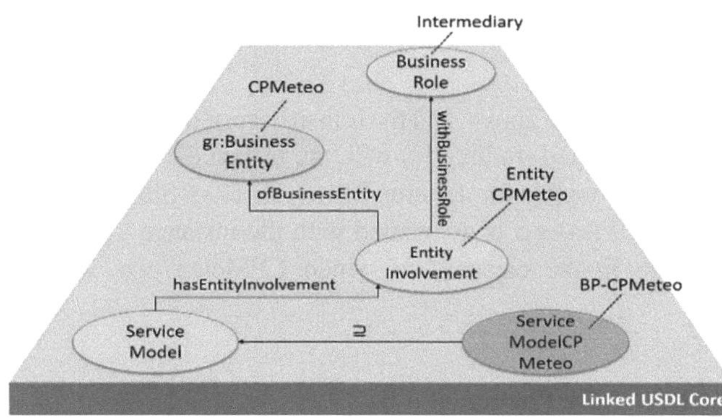

Fig. 1. Linked USDL core classes, interrelations and instances

More specifically, a BP is identified by an instance of the USDL Core class `ServiceModel`. For example, in the scenario of Sect. 3.1, the BP is identified by the instance `BP-CPMeteo` depicted in Fig. 1. In fact, `BP-CPMeteo` is an instance of a particular subclass of `ServiceModel`, namely of the subclass `ServiceMo-delCPMeteo`, which is specifically introduced into our model for accommodating all of CPMeteo's BPs[3]. Now, in order to capture the aforementioned two facts we:

2 This is by no means the complete set of the classes and properties offered by USDL Core, but rather an appropriate subset discerned for the purposes of this paper. Note that in order to reduce notational clutter we avoid specifying namespaces for classes and properties, unless a class or property comes from an external ontology (e.g. the GoodRelations ontology). In addition, the following conventions are used in the figures of this paper: a class is represented by an oval; a property is represented by an arrow decorated with the name of the property; a subclass relation is represented by an arrow decorated with the subset symbol (⊆); instance-class associations are represented with perforated lines.

3 Although we concentrate here on a single BP, CPMeteo may be associated with a number of different BPs, each represented by a distinct instance of the class `ServiceModelCP-Meteo`.

1. Associate the instance BP-CPMeteo with an instance, say EntityCPMeteo, of the class EntityInlvolvement through the property hasEntity Involvement.
2. Associate the instance EntityCPMeteo with the instance CPMeteo of the class grBusinessEntity via the property ofBusinessEntity. Note that the instance CPMeteo identifies the business entity which is responsible for defining the BP.
3. Associate the instance EntityCPMeteo with the instance Intermediary of the class BusinessRole via the property withBusinessRole. Note that the instance Intermediary identifies the role in the capacity of which CPMeteo acts when defining the BP.

By virtue of steps 1 and 2 above, and the transitivity of object properties, the instance BP-CPMeteo is associated (indirectly) with the instance CPMeteo, thus identifying the business entity responsible for defining BP-CPMeteo. Similarly, by virtue of steps 1 and 3 above, BP-CPMeteo is associated with the instance Intermediary, thus identifying the role in the capacity of which CPMeteo acts when defining BP-CPMeteo.

4.2 Validating the Core Portion of a BP

Our aim is to verify that the Core portion of a BP correctly captures the two facts mentioned in Sect. 4.1, namely the business entity responsible for defining the BP, as well as the role in the capacity of which this business entity acts when defining the BP. First, however, we need to ensure that there indeed exists an instance of the class ServiceModel which identifies the BP. To this end, the policy validation mechanism uses the Apache Jena Java API in order to obtain all those resources that are defined as subclasses of the class ServiceModel, as well as all the instances that are encompassed in these subclasses. The mechanism then ensures that there exists exactly one instance in the subclass ServiceModelCPMeteo (i.e. the BP-CPMeteo instance of Fig. 1) which identifies the BP.

Turning next to verifying that the BP correctly captures the two facts mentioned in Sect. 4.1, the validation mechanism uses again the Jena Java API in order to check that: (i) BP-CPMeteo is associated with exactly one instance of the class EntityInvolvement via the hasEntityInvolvement property; (ii) this EntityInvolvement instance is associated with the instance CPMeteo of the class gr:BusinessEntity, and with no other instances from that class; (iii) the same EntityInvolvement instance is associated with the instance Intermediary of the class BusinessRole, and with no other instances from that class. In case any of these checks fails, the validation process fails.

4.3 Linked USDL SLA

USDL SLA provides an adequate ontological framework for modelling the knowledge that lurks behind a BP, i.e. the particular characteristics that a service must exhibit in order to be on-boarded on a cloud platform. As discussed in Sect. 3, these characteristics are formulated in terms of SLPs and SLOs. Below we outline how these SLPs and SLOs are modelled in USDL SLA[4].

SLPs are expressed as instances of the USDL SLA `ServiceLevelProfile` class (see Fig. 2). For example, the SLPs of the scenario of Sect. 3.1 are expressed as instances of a particular subclass of the class `ServiceLevelProfile`, namely `SLP-CPMeteo`, which encompasses all SLPs offered by CPMeteo. Thus, the instance `SLP-Gold` depicted in Fig. 2, represents CPMeteo's 'gold' profile. The class `SLP-CPMeteo` is associated with the BP (i.e. with the instance `BP-CPMeteo` that identifies the BP) through the property `hasSLPCPMeteo` (see Fig. 2). This is a sub-property of the USDL SLA property `hasServiceLevelProfile` which associates the USDL Core class `ServiceModel` with the USDL SLA class `ServiceLevelProfile`.

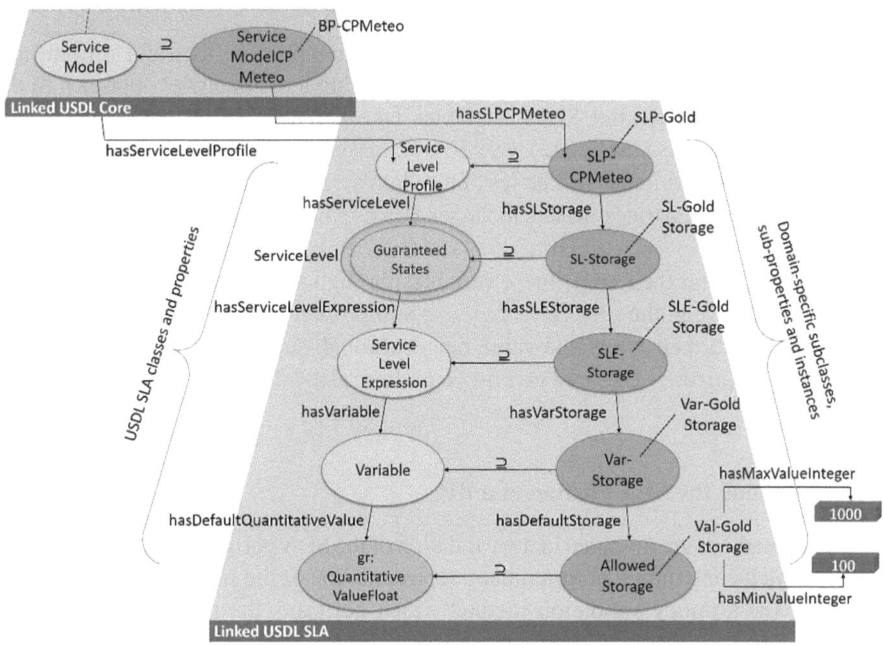

Fig. 2. Linked USDL SLA framework

As reported in Sect. 3.1, each SLP comprises an SLO for each of the service-level attributes of Table 1. In our framework, the SLOs corresponding to a particular attribute are expressed as instances of a suitable subclass of the USDL SLA `Guaranteed-States` class (see Fig. 2). For example, the SLOs of the attribute `storage`, i.e. the

[4] The modelling of SLPs and SLOs in Linked USDL was presented in [5]; it is repeated here for completeness. Recall from Sect. 3 that SLOs express entry-level criteria that must be satisfied in order for a service to be on-boarded on CPMeteo. Also recall that SLPs are groupings of SLOs that represent different 'deployment packages' offered by CPMeteo.

'gold storage', 'silver storage', and 'bronze storage' SLOs of Table 1, appear as instances of the subclass `SL-Storage` (for instance the instance `SL-GoldStorage` depicted in Fig. 2)[5]. An SLP is related to the SLOs that it comprises through suitable sub-properties of the property `hasServiceLevel`. For instance, an SLP is associated with the SLOs of the `storage` attribute through the sub-property `hasSLStorage`; in Fig. 2, this sub-property interrelates the instances `SLP-Gold` and `SL-GoldStorage`.

Now, each SLO is expressed in terms of a *service-level expression* (SLE) which articulates those conditions that must be met for the SLO to be achieved. An SLE is represented as an instance of an appropriate subclass of the class `ServiceLevelExpression` (see Fig. 2). For instance, the SLEs corresponding to the storage SLOs take the form of instances of the class `SLE-Storage` (cf. `SLE-GoldStorage` of Fig. 2). SLOs are related to their SLEs through suitable sub-properties of the property `hasServiceLevelExpression`. For instance, the storage SLOs are related to their SLEs via the property `hasSLEStorage` depicted in Fig. 2.

Finally, each SLE is associated with a *variable* that represents a certain attribute and is linked with an allowable range of values. Following a symmetrical approach to the one provided for SLOs and SLEs, variables take the form of instances of suitable subclasess of the class USDL SLA `Variable` class. Similarly, value ranges take the form of instances of suitable subclasses of the class `gr:Quantitative ValueInteger`. Figure 2 illustrates these subclasses (`Var-Storage`, `AllowedStorage`), and instances (`Var-GoldStorage`, `Val-GoldStorage`), for the 'gold' storage attribute. SLEs bind their constituent variables through sub-properties of the property `hasVariable` (e.g. the `hasVarStorage` sub-property of Fig. 2). Similarly, variables are linked to their allowable value ranges through sub-properties of the property `hasDefaultQuantitativeValue` (e.g. the `hasDefaultStorage` sub-property of Fig. 2).

4.4 Validating the SLA Portion of a BP

Two main methods are involved in the validation of the SLA portion of a BP: (i) a parsing method which constructs a programmatic representation of the framework described in Sect. 4.3; (ii) a policy validation method which performs the necessary correctness checks.

Programmatically Representing the SLA Portion of a BP. Each of the USDL-SLA classes depicted in Fig. 2 is represented programmatically in terms of an appropriate in-memory data structure. Subsequently, for each such class S, the validation mechanism discovers all the domain-specific subclasses C of S that are encompassed in the BP. It then populates the data structure corresponding to S with these subclasses. For example, it populates the data structure corresponding to the USDL-SLA class `ServiceLevelProfile` with the `SLP-CPMeteo` subclass and the data structure corresponding

---

[5] Similarly, the SLOs of the `encryption` attribute, i.e. the 'gold encryption', 'silver encryption', and 'bronze encryption' SLOs of Table 1, appear as instances of an analogous subclass, say `SL-Encryption` (not shown in Fig. 2).

to the USDL-SLA class `ServiceLevel` with the `SL-Storage` subclass. The same applies for the data structures corresponding to the rest of the USDL SLA classes depicted in Fig. 2. Each discovered subclass *C* is also represented programmatically in terms of an appropriate in-memory structure. For each such subclass *C*, the validation mechanism proceeds to discover all those properties that are defined in the BP, along with their linked ranges, which happen to have as the subclass *C* as their domain. It then populates the data structure corresponding to *C* with these properties. These properties are effectively all the *sub-properties* of the USDL SLA properties that are encountered in the BP. By the end of this process, we have a complete in-memory representation of the model depicted in Fig. 2.

Validating the SLA Portion of a BP. The policy validation method operates on the in-memory data structures constructed by the parsing method above. More specifically, it checks that: (i) at least one instance exists in each of the subclasses of the `ServiceLevelProfile` class (e.g. the instance `SLP-Gold` depicted in Fig. 2); (ii) the instance `BP-CPMeteo` (that identifies the BP) is associated with such an instance through a sub-property of the property `hasServiceLevelProfile`. Subsequently, the validation method checks that: (i) each SLP instance is associated with at least one SLO instance, i.e. with at least one instance from the subclasses of the `GuaranteedStates` class that were discovered by the parsing process; (ii) these associations take place through distinct sub-properties of the USDL SLA property `hasServiceLevel`. In an entirely symmetrical manner, the validation mechanism then checks that: (i) each SLO (i.e. each subclass of the class `GuaranteedStates`) is associated with at least one SLE (i.e. with at least one subclass of `ServiceLevelExpression`) via a distinct sub-property of `hasServiceLevelExpression`; (ii) each SLO instance is associated with at least one SLE instance. An analogous set of checks applies for the associations between SLEs and variables. Furthermore, the mechanism checks that there exists an one-to-one correspondence between variables and quantitative (or qualitative) values. In addition, it checks that: (i) all quantitative value instances are associated with minimum and maximum values via the properties `gr:hasMinValueInteger`, `gr:hasMaxValueInteger`; (ii) each quantitative value instance is associated with an appropriate unit of measurement via `gr:hasUnitOfMeasurement`.

Testing the Validation Mechanism. In order to increase our assurance on the policy validation mechanism, a *test harness* has been developed for potentially discovering invalid BPs that may go undetected by the mechanism. The harness automatically injects errors into the BP and observes whether these are detected by the validation mechanism. More specifically, for every triple *T* in the BP, it extracts the subject T_S, the predicate T_P, and the object T_O, of *T*. It then generates a new triple T' by introducing an error in T_S (e.g. a typo) and runs the validation mechanism with *T* being replaced by T'. It follows the same procedure for T_P and T_O. The test harness revealed a number of bugs that led to failure in detecting certain erroneous BPs. For example, a significant bug that was discovered was that the validation mechanism failed to check whether certain object properties interconnecting instances in the BP were in fact sub-properties of the correct Linked USDL properties.

5 Conclusions and Future Work

We have presented a *policy validation* mechanism which automatically assesses the *correctness* of *state-oriented policies*. This ensures that cloud services are checked for compliance against *correctly-formed* policies. We believe that such a mechanism is a vital ingredient of any framework aspiring to provide policy-based quality assurance of cloud services. Our policy validation mechanism has been used in conjunction with the SC^3 mechanism that we have developed for evaluating the quality of cloud services. Both mechanisms have been successfully used for assessing CRM services on-boarded on an exising commercial cloud application platform – namely the CAS Open platform [18].

As part of future work, we intend to extend our mechanism to cover a wider range of policies including action-oriented policies. Such an extension will enable us to model policies articulating the actions that need to be taken in case one or more SLOs are violated (or are about to be violated) *during* the consumption of a service. In addition, we are already extending our mechanism to cope with context-aware security policies in highly-dynamic and heterogeneous cloud environments.

Acknowledgements. The research leading to these results has received funding from the European Union's Horizon 2020 research and innovation programme under grant agreement No. 644814.

References

1. Foster, I., Zhao, Y., Raicu, I., Lu, S.: Cloud computing and grid computing 360-degree compared. In: IEEE Grid Computing Workshop 2008, pp. 1–10. IEEE (2008)
2. Cloud computing reference architecture. Technical report, NIST (2011)
3. Veloudis, S., Paraskakis, I., Friesen, A., Verginadis, Y., Patiniotakis, I., Rossini, A.: Continuous quality assurance and optimisation in cloud-based virtual enterprises. In: Camarinha-Matos, L.M., Afsarmanesh, H. (eds.) PRO-VE 2014. LNCS, vol. 434, pp. 621–632. Springer, Heidelberg (2014)
4. Yi, S.: Virtual organization based distributed environmental spatial decision support systems: applications in watershed management. Ph.D. thesis, Michigan State University, 3348219 (2008)
5. Veloudis, S., Paraskakis, I., Petsos, C.: Cloud service brokerage: strengthening service resilience in cloud-based virtual enterprises. In: Camarinha-Matos, L.M., et al. (eds.) PRO-VE 2015. LNCS, vol. 463, pp. 122–135. Springer, Heidelberg (2015)
6. Linked USDL. http://www.linked-usdl.org/
7. PaaSword project. http://www.paasword.eu/
8. Damianou, N., Dulay, N., Lupu, E., Sloman, M.: The ponder policy specification language. In: Sloman, M., Lobo, J., Lupu, E. (eds.) Proceedings of the International Workshop on Policies for Distributed Systems and Networks (POLICY 2001), pp. 18–38. Springer-Verlag, London (2000)
9. eXtensible Access Control Markup Language (XACML) Version 3.0, 22 January 2013. OASIS Standard. http://docs.oasis-open.org/xacml/3.0/xacml-3.0-core-spec-os-en.html

10. Security Assertions Markup Language (SAML) Version 2.0. Technical Overview, 25 March 2008. OASIS Standard (2008). https://www.oasis-open.org/committees/download.php/27819/sstc-saml-tech-overview-2.0-cd-02.pdf
11. WS-Trust 1.3. 19 March 2007. OASIS Standard (2007). http://docs.oasis-open.org/ws-sx/ws-trust/200512/ws-trust-1.3-os.doc
12. Uszok, A., Bradshaw, J., Jeffers, R., Johnson, M., Tate, A., Dalton, J., Aitken, S.: KAoS policy management for semantic web services. IEEE Intel. Syst. **19**(4), 32–41 (2004)
13. Kagal, L., Finin, T., Joshi, A.: A policy language for a pervasive computing environment. In: 4th IEEE International Workshop on Policies for Distributed Systems and Networks (POLICY 2003), pp. 63–74. IEEE Computer Society, Washington, DC (2003)
14. Nejdl, W., Olmedilla, D., Winslett, M., Zhang, C.C.: Ontology-based policy specification and management. In: Gómez-Pérez, A., Euzenat, J. (eds.) ESWC 2005. LNCS, vol. 3532, pp. 290–302. Springer, Heidelberg (2005)
15. OWL Web Ontology Language Reference. W3C Recommendation, 10 February 2004. http://www.w3.org/TR/owl-ref/
16. RDF 1.1 XML Syntax. W3C Recommendation, 10 February 2004. http://www.w3.org/TR/rdf-syntax-grammar/
17. Barros, A., Oberle, D.: Handbook of Service Description: USDL and Its Methods. Springer, New York (2012)
18. Cardoso, J., Pedrinaci, C., Leidig, T., Rupino, P., Leenheer, P.: Foundations of open semantic service networks. Int. J. Serv. Sci. Manage. Eng. Technol. **4**(2), 1–16 (2013)
19. Cardoso, J., Pedrinaci, C., Leidig, T.: Linked USDL: a vocabulary for web-scale service trading. In: 11th Extended Semantic Web Conference (ESWC) (2014)
20. GoodRelations: The Professional Web Vocabulary for E-Commerce. http://www.heppnetz.de/projects/goodrelations/
21. SKOS Simple Knowledge Organization System. http://www.w3.org/2004/02/skos/
22. The FOAF Project. http://www.foaf-project.org
23. CAS CRM. http://www.cas-crm.com/

Design Science and Business Models - Design Science Research

Managing Actors, Resources, and Activities in Innovation Ecosystems – A Design Science Approach

Katri Valkokari[1(✉)], Cristina C. Amitrano[2], Francesco Bifulco[2], and Tiina Valjakka[1]

[1] VTT, Technical Research Centre of Finland, PL1000, 02044 Espoo, Finland
{katri.valkokari,tiina.valjakka}@vtt.fi
[2] University of Naples Federico II, Campus Monte S. Angelo, 26 via Cinthia, 80126 Naples, Italy
{cristinacaterina.amitrano,francesco.bifulco}@unina.it

Abstract. Through a design science approach, the paper explores how actors in a network create and sustain competitive advantage independently and through participation in a system of actors (i.e., a collaborative network) who are not hierarchically managed but, rather, act toward their own goals within the innovation ecosystem. In accordance with design studies, the relevance of research and its quality are evaluated against practice. The two cases discussed in the paper highlight that, in practice, innovation ecosystem actors must manage activities and relationships at the level of both individual and organisation. This finding has interesting research implications, as innovation ecosystems have been studied mostly at either macro or interpersonal (micro) level while the organisation (meso) level is seldom discussed. Furthermore, the findings should help managers to strive for and utilise innovation ecosystems better and to evaluate their ability and potential to survive via internal and external collaboration aimed at innovation.

Keywords: Innovation ecosystems · Collaborative networks · Innovation management · Design science · ARA (Actors Resources and Activities) model

1 Introduction

Innovation is increasingly perceived as collaboration beyond organisational boundaries rather than intra-organisation action. Nonetheless, only around a third of innovating companies drew on external development or knowledge sources from 2010 to 2012 [1]. Therefore, huge potential remains in innovation ecosystems that are able to integrate diverse actors for collaborative innovation [2] in today's business environment, wherein knowledge is highly dispersed and complexity is growing all the time. Therefore, we wish to draw attention to the dynamic, hyperconnected, and networked but often loosely bound *ecosystems* that enable collaborative innovation.

The ecosystem view offers a systems approach to innovation management by focusing on how actors in a network create and sustain competitive advantage independently and as participants in a system of actors who, rather than being hierarchically managed, each act in pursuit of their own goals [3, 4]. In other words, the concept of ecosystems emphasises that the relationships constantly co-evolve through the actions

H. Afsarmanesh et al. (Eds.): PRO-VE 2016, IFIP AICT 480, pp. 521–530, 2016.
DOI: 10.1007/978-3-319-45390-3_44

and interactions of the actors involved. These collaborative systems of innova-tion, wherein the actors co-produce the outcome of innovation follow dynamic and multi-faceted models. Thus, the multiplicity of participant types, roles, and inter-dependencies implies that ecosystem management is a challenging task and that possibilities for ecosystem management are not equally distributed among participants. Hence, *innovation ecosystem management* is simultaneously an engrossing academic research question and a practical challenge for all actors involved in collaborative innovation systems. *Design science* was, therefore, a natural choice for the research approach for our study of two emerging innovation ecosystems, in Finland and Italy.

2 A Design Science Approach to Innovation Ecosystem Management

2.1 Current Understanding of Innovation Ecosystems

The ecosystem approach represents a departure from existing literature on innovation and network management. The ecosystem should be understood as a context wherein there is ongoing interplay among actors taking a variety of roles – for instance, as keystones, dominators, or niche players [5]. The logic of action differs by ecosystem type, with business ecosystems focusing on co-creation of value for customers, co-generation of new knowledge constituting the main activity in a knowledge ecosystem, and innovation ecosystems positioned between the two [4]. In other words, as pointed out by Autio and Thomas [6], 'the defining element of innovation ecosystems is not a given product, but rather a coherent set of inter-related technologies and associated organizational competencies that glue a variety of participants together to co-produce a set of offerings for different user groups and uses' (p. 208). Clarysse et al. (2014) have stated that knowledge ecosystems are formed around a university or public research organisation (PRO) whereas large companies are the leaders of business ecosystems [7]. It also has been shown that national and city governments are becoming increasingly important in influencing innovation, and they can support the knowledge flows between large corporations and start-ups to speed up innovation [8]. The multiplicity of participant types, roles, and interdependencies implies that the possibilities and the challenges ecosystem management entails are not equally distributed across participants [9].

The concept of ecosystems emphasises that the relationships are constantly co-evolving through actions and interactions of the actor taking part [4, 6]. Interaction within and beyond (organisational) boundaries is essential to innovation ecosystems [10]. The results of the collaborative innovation arise from the dynamics of strategic manoeuvring amongst actors, and, therefore, the key factor for success is their ability to manage dynamic strategic interactions related to innovation [11]. Instead of aiming to avoid uncertainty, all actors must be flexible and prepared to make adjustments; the connection with each other implies that a decision or action taken by one influences all the others – but not in any uniform manner [4].

Still, most research on business systems (including innovation perspectives) has stressed gaining of individual-level benefits over system-level value creation and innovation. That is, the focus has been on company strategies in innovation ecosystems instead of system innovations. The study described here, in contrast, calls attention to the ways in which total value creation can be increased through joint activities by the key actors and, furthermore, distributed fairly among them.

2.2 The Logic of Collaborative Networks

The study approached innovation ecosystems from the meso (organisational) level. When the ecosystem approach is applied in discussion of collaborative networks, it becomes clear that each network member has its own reasons to collaborate. In the ecosystem approach, collaborative networks are defined as autonomous, geographically distributed, and heterogeneous [12]. Thus, the concept of collaborative network organisations (CNOs) highlights that there is an organisation overarching the participants' activities, roles, and shared governance rules. While CNOs are dynamic and often temporary in nature, innovation ecosystems are even more loosely structured, and participants' individual interests bring constant changes. On the other hand, the concept of virtual organisation breeding environment (VBE) represents the more loosely coupled co-operation setting found with a puddle of organisations and their related supportive institutions and hence is better suited to addressing innovation ecosystems. However, long-term co-operation agreements and interoperable infrastructure are mentioned as a 'base' also for breeding environments [12]. Therefore, we prefer to use the idea of the *innovation ecosystems* to capture a dynamic, temporary, continuously changing, hyper-connected, and networked assemblage that enables collaborative innovation.

2.3 The Design Science Approach

Design-focused professionals, such as architects, engineers, lawyers, and managers, face growing pressure to find new ways to solve nested problems – i.e., to act and decide on the basis of a systematic body of evidence [13]. In management and business studies, design science holds a steady but minor position on the sidelines of mainstream descriptive studies. There are some examples of problem-solving and of bridging between theory and practice through design science, in the operations management [14] and information systems fields [15]. Design science can be linked to several other qualitative approaches too, such as action research, participatory case studies, academia–industry partnership, and constructive approaches. With the lens of design science, the common goal in these exploratory approaches should be the researcher developing a 'means to an end', an artefact to solve a practical problem [14]. In our study, the practical managerial challenge and the research question were both 'How are the innovation ecosystems created and managed – and by whom?' The result of this study is a conceptual artefact [16], i.e. a collaborative model for innovation ecosystems evaluated in two case studies. The type of knowledge contribution can be described as exaptation, meaning known solutions extended to new problems [15], as the solution is based on the ARA model. The design science research process utilised in this study is illustrated at the Fig. 1. The process is based on the DSRM Process presented by Peffers et al. 2012 [16]. Hence, the demonstration and evaluation phases are integrated as the conceptual artefact's use and test occur through the case studies. The first two phases (problem identification and setting the objectives of a solution) were carried through during the program preparations.

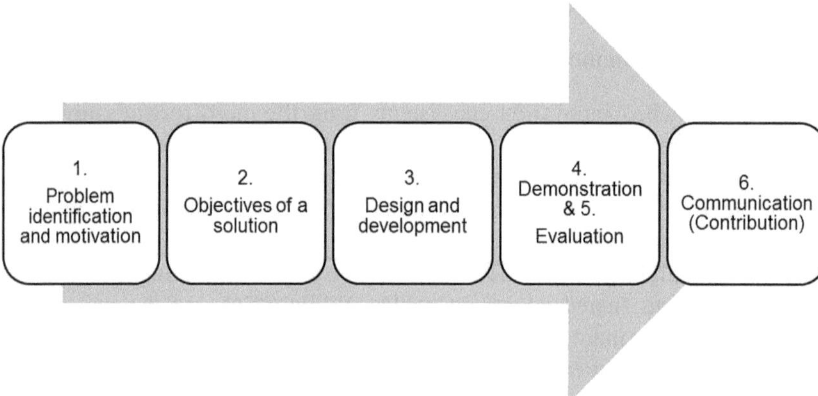

Fig. 1. Design science research process in this study.

In other words, through the case studies, the practitioners and researchers strove to jointly build and evaluate a design science research artefact, a collaborative model for innovation ecosystems (Fig. 2). This kind of approach also suggests that research is not just about under-standing and explaining issues and phenomena but also about changing them [17] and affecting creation of new ideas and innovation. Therefore, a

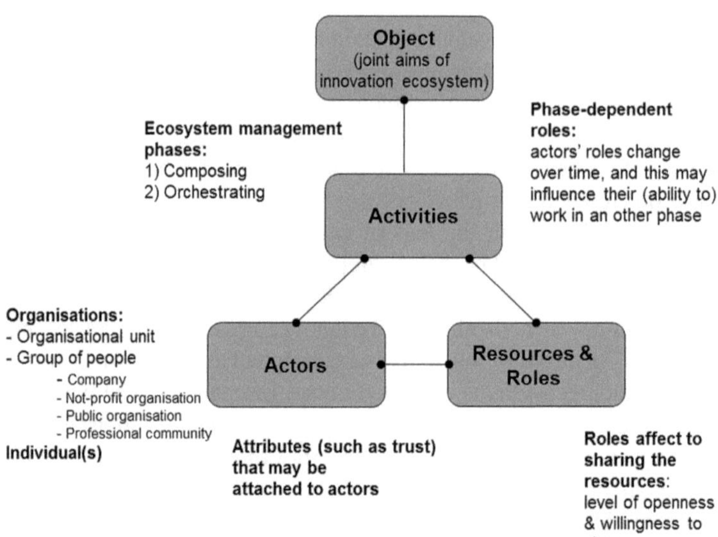

Fig. 2. Collaborative model for innovation ecosystems (built on the basis of the ARA model).

joint project (or process) of researchers and practitioners – companies or other organisations – and close co-operation throughout the problem-solving are necessary in such a research setting.

2.4 A Preliminary Artefact for the Joint Solution – a Collaborative Model for Innovation Ecosystems

In our study, the above-mentioned practical managerial challenge and research question were addressed via a systemic approach to innovation management. Together we worked to build a conceptual artefact, the collaborative model for how a network of actors creates and sustains competitive advantage independently and as participants in a system of actors who, rather than being hierarchically managed, pursue their own goals [3, 4]. In other words, the objectives of the solution were qualitative, i.e., describe how this new artefact is expected to support solutions to problems related to collaboration in innovation ecosystems. The main research question, 'How are the innovation ecosystems created and managed – and by whom?', was broken down into three sub-questions:

- Who are the *main actors* in an innovation ecosystem?
- What kinds of *resources* are needed to integrate key actors in an innovation ecosystem?
- What are the *key activities* of the various actors within the innovation ecosystems?

This division into sub-questions was theoretically grounded in the well-known actors, resources, and activities (ARA) model, introduced by Håkansson and Johanson [18]. This particular theoretical model was chosen for several reasons. Firstly, the ARA model describes the in-built dynamics of a network, its actors, and its resources, which makes it a suitable concept for use in a study approaching innovation eco-systems at organisation level. Furthermore, it is in line with the practical managerial questions raised by all actors involved in the research process. In addition, the ARA model's way of approaching networks is closely related to the concept of interaction and knowledge as a dynamic resource, which formed an important practical and theoretical starting point for our study. Finally, the ARA model highlights the ever-evolving and emergent nature of the networks so is a good fit for studies of systemic innovation activities. A challenge becomes clear at this juncture: the latter aspect of the networks makes it hard to address our study's managerial perspective, with the question of whether an innovation ecosystem is manageable or not.

3 The Research Design for Demonstration and Evaluation

Design science was a natural choice for the research approach in our study of two emerging innovation ecosystems, from Finland and Italy: *innovation ecosystem management* is both a fascinating question for academic research and a practical challenge for the many actors involved in collaborative innovation systems. Since creation of innovation ecosystems and their management is a newly developing phenomenon and area of research, we consider qualitative methods to be appropriate.

Both interviews and focus groups were utilised for describing actors and their roles, relationships, and activities in the two emerging innovation ecosystems examined. Table 1 presents a summary of the data sources used for evaluation as well as building the artefact (see the Design Science Research Process at Fig. 1). The informants (interviewees or focus-group members and workshop participants) held senior corporate management, R&D, business unit, or innovation management positions. The workshops focused especially in building and demonstrating the artefact, i.e. the collaborative model for innovation ecosystems.

Table 1. Summary of the data sources.

Case	Interviews	Focus groups	Workshops
Finland	In all, 17 interviews, at 11 companies, five research institutes, and one facilitator organisation	Problem-solving-based group discussions of four subprojects	Two workshops on innovation ecosystem building
Italy	In all, 20 interviews, at 18 companies, one research institute, and one regional competence centre	Problem-solving-based group discussions of two subprojects	Two workshops on actor dynamics and resources' integration

The empirical material was collected and analysed by four researchers, the authors of this paper. The cases selected were chosen because through the joint development programmes the researchers and practitioners shared the challenge of innovation ecosystem creation and management. Furthermore, the two cases chosen enable exploration that involves comparison between two national systems of innovation. The multiple-case-study approach is well suited to new research areas when new perspectives are sought and when there is little knowledge available about the complex phenomenon being studied [19].

Most of the organisations involved were established, globally operating Finnish and Italian companies and public organisations – i.e., public research institutes, universities, and regional development agencies. The ecosystems represented various fields of industry and organisation sizes, bringing diversity to the problem-solving and increasing the learning and variety. Our data analyses for joint problem-solving were based on the above-mentioned ARA model [15], which helped researchers and practitioners alike to gain a holistic, general view of the two innovation ecosystems and their characteristics. The focus-group meetings and workshops were organised as a means of joint problem-solving and to assist in the data analysis and test the preliminary findings from the interview data.

4 Findings from Evaluation

There were both similarities and differences between the two innovation ecosystems and between their respective actors, resources, and activities.

Actors. The main difference was in the ecosystems' size, the number of actors involved. The Italian ecosystem, DATABENC, consists of 48 actors whereas the Finnish programme (REBUS) has 31 actors formally involved. The DATABENC ecosystem featured a large number of SMEs (77 % of the actors), while there were mainly larger companies in the REBUS ecosystem. In both ecosystems, the informants agreed that several other actors should be more fully involved. Specifically, the participants recognised that in the ecosystem composition phase, it is important to confirm the involvement of a broad spectrum of actors, while membership dynamics (i.e., entry and exit of actors) were emphasised in the orchestration phase. For instance, funding institutions were not actively involved in either ecosystem, although they could be important in the commercialisation of innovations created by actors in the ecosystem.

Resources and roles. In the Italian ecosystem, two universities, a national research centre, and a regional competence centre have a pivotal role in bringing together all the actors, while a local institution (in the Campania region) acts as a facilitator. Similarly, the six universities, the research institute, and the national open innovation company (FIMECC) in the REBUS ecosystem have a significant role in integrating the actors' efforts and facilitating collaboration among the various organisations involved. Both cases show that public organisations can have the role of a keystone in innovation ecosystems. Furthermore, more than one actor may act in this kind of role. Accordingly, technological competition and similarities in resources were identified also as motivation for exiting the DATABENC ecosystem.

Activities. For both ecosystems, the participants suggested that having various kinds of joint activities – such as joint discussions and operations – and shared resources was critical. In this connection, face-to-face discussions were considered to be important. Also, the need for networking via development forums (in relation to Open Source initiatives and innovation platforms) was highlighted as a means to ensure collaboration for innovation by increasing commitment. Developing clear joint rules was seen as an especially strong way to increase trust in a situation wherein the relationship does not necessarily have a long history. Furthermore, the presence of SMEs active in the cultural heritage sector in the DATABENC ecosystem showed their important role as the 'glue' between education and knowledge through monitoring and fruition activities.

Structure. The ecosystem structure differed between the two cases. The four sub-projects of REBUS form quite independently operating sub-ecosystems that have their own goals while at the same time collaborating with other stakeholders, who were not directly involved. There were four sub-projects also in the DATABENC ecosystem, but they were closely linked to one another. They sought to reach complementary goals that merge in the strategic purposes of the entire ecosystem – namely, the implementation of an integrated system of knowledge, the development of diagnostic monitoring, and advancing of technologies for a sustainable future.

Joint Configuration of the Artefact – A Collaborative Model for Innovation Ecosystem Management. The ARA model supported joint problem-solving between the practitioners and researchers, along with developing the collaborative model for an innovation ecosystem (see Fig. 2). Firstly, the work identified the *main actors* in the innovation ecosystem and also the changes in actors as a baseline for manage-ment. The findings highlighted that management needs and governance possibilities in innovation ecosystems differ from those in direct business relationships, such as dyadic supplier–purchaser relationships. In innovation ecosystems, the relationships are not typically governed with contracts, and this renders the role of relational governance mechanisms important. Secondly, recognising the *resources* of actors was a starting point for a negotiation process aimed at balancing out the self-interest of the actors involved. Accordingly, the practitioners pointed out that, in addition to their resources, it is important to understand the *roles of actors*. The role, which is closely linked to the relevant actor's business model, affects what resources that actor is ready to bring and on what kind of terms. Finally, portraying the *key activities* of the various actors within the innovation ecosystems proved to be the most case-specific element and depended on the goals of the development programme.

The key activities related to management of the innovation ecosystem were similar between the two cases and consistent with the view of interactions implied by the ecosystem concept; i.e., relationships between actors proved to be the primary mechanism for managing the actors in the ecosystem. Finding a balance between the interests of the individual actors involved is critical, and, therefore, motivating the actors to put effort into the joint activities and the whole ecosystem is vital.

5 Conclusions

Our work makes two main contributions to innovation management literature and practice: firstly, we have proposed an initial, explorative taxonomy of actors and pointed to a need to understand the respective roles, and, secondly, we have identified key activities for developing and managing actors through their relationships within innovation ecosystems. Furthermore, the work underscores that actors need to manage activities and relationships at both individual and organisation level. This has interesting research implications, as innovation ecosystems have been studied mostly at either the macro or the interpersonal (micro) level, while little attention is devoted to organisation level. It is vital for actor organisations to understand and manage the inter-organisational and the interpersonal level at the same time.

How the Design Science Approach Works. By adopting problem-solving as the main *modus operandi* for the development programmes and the research work, we attempted to achieve simultaneous attainment of efficiency and innovation. Although conducting such explorative research to address ill-structured managerial problems involves many methodological challenges, we found three benefits arising from that choice.

Firstly, a common well-defined problem served effective co-ordination of knowledge originating from various disciplines and communities of practice. Secondly, innovativeness cannot be programmed beforehand. That is, a waterfall-type planned programme would hardly have created innovative and feasible solutions. In contrast, an iterative and incremental problem-solving process allowing learning and redefinition offered greater possibilities for doing so. Thirdly, when one runs large programmes that involve several parties and highlight research–practice co-operation, there is a danger of project execution getting bogged down in the realities faced in the participant organisations' day-to-day practice, so we needed to avoid this. To that end, we paid particular attention to project-execution flow, which was defined as the speed of the problem-solving process. We arrived at a feasible goal of achieving 3–6-month process cycles in task-specific problem-solving processes, with the timing dependent on ambition level, the iterations needed, and case-specific scheduling.

Thus, the study highlighted how identifying the problems and objectives is itself a challenge. The joint process before creation of the actual artefact (i.e., the innovation ecosystem) forms a key stage in which the translation of knowledge between research and practice occurs. However, it is not at all certain that the new kinds of artefacts required by the design science research approach can be innovated and discovered. The discussion above should help managers in their search for better innovation ecosystems and their utilisation of these, while simultaneously assisting them in evaluating the ecosystems' ability and potential to survive by means of internal and boundary-spanning collaboration for innovation. In summary, it should help them better understand how to collaborate for innovation, with whom, and why.

There is significant room for fruitful research, though it is clear that no 'one size fits all' solution exists for the management of innovation ecosystems. These ecosystems and their models of operation differ from each other in the forms of joint processing, their rules of participation, and the ownership of results. Thus, the conceptual artefact, the collaborative model for innovation ecosystems, build and evaluated in this study opens several avenues for further research. Although, the evaluation was done in two innovation ecosystems the co-evolution within these ecosystems is still on-going and the study can provide only a snap-shot to this process. Therefore, one obvious need for further research would be follow-up of these ecosystems. Another important dimension for future research would be a quantitative approach in order to test the net types and differences and their impacts on a larger scale. Furthermore, innovation ecosystems influence in the creation of innovative start-ups or spin-offs should also be explored as the current studies focus more on roles of well-established companies and research institutes in the two emerging innovation ecosystems.

Acknowledgements. The authors would like to thank all actors in the two innovation ecosystems: their willingness to collaborate and share ideas enabled the design science approach adopted in the study. The research work in the context of the Finnish case forms part of the research programme Towards Relational Business Practices (REBUS), one of the research programmes of the Finnish Metals and Engineering Competence Cluster, FIMECC. The research work related to the Italian case forms part of the High Technology Consortium for Cultural Heritage (DATABENC - Distretto ad Alta TecnologiA per i BENi Culturali), supported by the Italian National Operative Programme 2007–2013.

References

1. OECD Science, Technology and Innovation Scoreboard 2015: Innovation for Growth and Society. Organisation for Economic Co-operation and Development (OECD) Publishing, Paris (2015)
2. Bifulco, F., Tregua, M., Amitrano, C.C.: Smart cities and innovation: a multi-stakeholder perspective. J. Manag. Mark. **2**(1), 27–33 (2014)
3. Russo-Spena, T., Tregua, M., Amitrano, C.C., Bifulco, F.: Smart technologies and service ecosystems: a focus on social and material aspects of innovation. In: Spender, J.C., Schiuma, G., Albino, V. (eds.) Proceedings 10th IFKAD. Culture, Innovation and Entrepreneurship: Connecting the Knowledge Dots, Bari, Italy, pp. 1898–1914 (2015)
4. Valkokari, K.: Business, innovation, and knowledge ecosystems: how they differ and how to survive and thrive within them. Technol. Innov. Manag. Rev. **5**(8), 17–24 (2015)
5. Iansiti, M., Levien, R.: The Keystone Advantage: What the New Dynamics of Business Ecosystems Mean for Strategy, Innovation, and Sustainability. Harvard Business School Press, Boston (2004)
6. Autio, E., Thomas, L.D.: Innovation ecosystems: implications for innovation management. In: Dodgson, M., Gann, D.M., Phillips, N. (eds.) The Oxford Handbook of Innovation Management, pp. 204–228. Oxford University Press, Oxford (2014)
7. Clarysse, B., Wright, M., Bruneel, J.: Creating value in ecosystems: crossing the chasm between knowledge and business ecosystems. Res. Policy **43**, 1164–1176 (2014)
8. Lerner, J.: The Architecture of Innovation. Harvard Business Review Press, Watertown (2012)
9. Adner, R., Kapoor, R.: Value creation in innovation ecosystems: how the structure of technological interdependence affects firm performance in new technology generations. Strateg. Manag. J. **31**, 306–333 (2010)
10. Pisano, G.P., Verganti, R.: Which kind of collaboration is right for you? Harvard Bus. Rev. **86**(12), 80–86 (2008)
11. Paasi, J., Luoma, T., Valkokari, K., Lee, N.: Knowledge and intellectual property management in customer-supplier relationships. Int. J. Innov. Manag. **14**(4), 629–654 (2010)
12. Camarinha-Matos, L.M., Afsarmanesh, H.: Collaborative Networks: Reference Modeling. Springer, New York (2008)
13. Van Aken, J.E., Romme, G.: Reinventing the future: adding design science to the repertoire of organization and management studies. Organ. Manag. J. **6**, 5–12 (2009)
14. Holmström, J., Ketokivi, M., Hameri, A.-P.: Bridging practice and theory: a design science approach. Decis. Sci. **40**(1), 1540–5915 (2009)
15. Gregor, S., Hevner, A.R.: Positioning and presenting design science research for maximum impact. MIS Q. **37**(2), 337–355 (2013)
16. Peffers, K., Rothenberger, M., Tuunanen, T., Vaezi, R.: Design science research evaluation. In: Peffers, K., Rothenberger, M., Kuechler, B. (eds.) DESRIST 2012. LNCS, vol. 7286, pp. 398–410. Springer, Heidelberg (2012)
17. Burke, W.: Organization Change: Theory and Practice. SAGE Publications, Thousand Oaks (2002)
18. Håkansson, H., Johanson, J.: A model of industrial networks. In: Axelsson, B., Easton, G. (eds.) Industrial Networks: A New View of Reality, pp. 28–36. Routledge, London (1992)
19. Yin, R.K.: Case Study Research, 3rd edn. Sage Publication, Thousand Oaks (2003)

Situating Case Studies Within the Design Science Research Paradigm: An Instantiation for Collaborative Networks

Eric Costa[1,2(✉)], António Lucas Soares[1,2], and Jorge Pinho de Sousa[1,2]

[1] INESC TEC – INESC Technology and Science, Campus da FEUP, Rua Dr. Roberto Frias 378, 4200-465 Porto, Portugal
{eric.m.costa,jsousa}@inesctec.pt

[2] FEUP – Faculty of Engineering, University of Porto, Rua Dr. Roberto Frias S/N, 4200-465 Porto, Portugal
als@fe.up.pt

Abstract. A rigorous evaluation of an artifact is one of the fundamental aspects to be considered in Design Science Research projects. This evaluation part becomes even more difficult when a large variety of artifacts must be designed for a project. This can be a challenge for the field of Collaborative Networks, which involves knowledge from several scientific disciplines. Case studies are one of the evaluation methods in Design Science Research that are used for an *ex-post* evaluation of artifacts. However, we argue that this method can also be used for the *ex-ante* evaluation, mainly when multidisciplinary research is being carried out. Therefore, the main objective of this paper is to present and discuss a multidisciplinary project of Collaborative Networks using case studies before and after the design of the artifacts. On top of the Design Science Research guidelines, this research is supported by knowledge from Business and Management Studies on how to effectively design and perform Case Study Research for artifact evaluation.

Keywords: Design science research · Case study research · Collaborative networks · Multidisciplinary research

1 Introduction

Design Science Research (DSR) is a well-established research paradigm within the Information Systems (IS) community [1, 2]. In Business and Management Studies (BMS) management is viewed, more and more, as a design science, in an attempt to balance description and prescription-driven research approaches [3]. However, there is still much to explore regarding the applicability of DSR in other research areas, especially in how it can frame multidisciplinary research. A particular challenge to the DSR approaches and methods occurs in the field of Collaborative Networks (CNs) that require the design of a large variety of artifacts, involving several scientific disciplines.

To perform a good DSR project some fundamental aspects must be considered, such as the construction of a viable artifact [1], the rigorous evaluation of this artifact [4, 5],

H. Afsarmanesh et al. (Eds.): PRO-VE 2016, IFIP AICT 480, pp. 531–544, 2016.
DOI: 10.1007/978-3-319-45390-3_45

and the knowledge contribution of the DSR project [2]. In fact, the evaluation of artifacts represents an essential element of DSR, but even so there is still a need for guidance and support on how to design this component of a DSR approach.

Many DSR works point out case studies as one possible approach for the *ex-post* evaluation of the artifact [4–6]. However, in multidisciplinary research (for example in the intersection between IS and BMS) case studies can be used before the design of the artifact, to evaluate some preliminary forms or some parts of the artifact, i.e. meta-artifacts [7]. This approach can be applied for collecting data (through interviews, questionnaires, etc.) that will be used as an input for the construction of the artifact, and also to support its *ex-ante* validation/evaluation. However, most of the studies in DSR referring the use of case studies as an evaluation method still fail to provide clear directions on how to effectively design and perform case studies.

The main objective of this study is to discuss a different possibility for using Case Study Research (CSR) within the DSR paradigm in multidisciplinary research. The research question is:

- How can CSR be effectively integrated within the DSR paradigm in multidisciplinary research?

Therefore, a research framework is presented for performing a multidisciplinary study, in the field of CNs, which uses DSR and CSR. Using an illustrative example developed on an ongoing doctoral project, it is argued that both conceptions of case studies from the areas of IS and BMS can be adopted in multidisciplinary research, by using CSR at the *ex-ante* stage of the artifact design, and also by selecting case studies for an *ex-post* evaluation. This is a research in progress work, where some parts of this project were already completed, such as the literature review and some exploratory study using empirical data. The next planned parts are the case studies and artifact development. The context under analysis are internationalization processes with the aim of establishing CNs between industrial enterprises associations (IEAs) and their associated small and medium enterprises (SMEs).

The paper aims at contributing to the area of IS and DSR, using knowledge from BMS on how to effectively design and perform CSR for artifact evaluation. Moreover, the results of this study can be relevant for BMS by providing new ways of doing case-based research [8], and also for researchers designing artifacts of CNs, with knowledge from different scientific disciplines. Another contribution to the field of CNs is to present a different context, i.e. the context of CNs between IEAs and SMEs to optimize internationalization processes.

For this purpose, literature on DSR and CSR is first analyzed in Sect. 2, by considering the fundamental aspects of each paradigm/methodology and by showing how case studies are performed in both IS and BMS. Then, the research framework is presented in Sect. 3, along with a multidisciplinary project of CNs designed using the developed framework. This case shows a possible way of performing multidisciplinary research, and focus on understanding how CSR can be effectively integrated with DSR. Finally, Sect. 4 presents a discussion and the main conclusions of this study.

2 Literature Review

2.1 Fundamentals of Design Science Research

Undoubtedly, the important work by Hevner et al. [1] has been inspiring many research contributions in the area of DSR. These authors provide new insights for IS researchers and practitioners on how to effectively conduct, evaluate and present DSR. This work is mostly influenced by the seminal thinking of Simon [9] about the design theory and the design process. The main goal of DSR is to create innovative artifacts addressing unsolved problems in organizations [10]. Such artifacts may include:

- conceptual artifacts, such as constructs, models, methods, and frameworks [4];
- formal logical instructions, such as algorithms and instantiations [4];
- system design, language/notation, guidelines, requirements, patterns, and metrics [11];
- social innovations [3];
- new properties of technical, social, or informational resources [12];
- architectures, design principles, and design theories [13].

Hevner [14] develops an approach based on a complementary 3-cycle model (Fig. 1): (1) *relevance cycle* – to bridge the contextual environment with the design science activities; (2) *rigor cycle* – to connect the design science activities with the knowledge base (from scientific foundations, experience, and expertise); and (3) *design cycle* – to iterate between the core activities of developing and evaluating the design artifact.

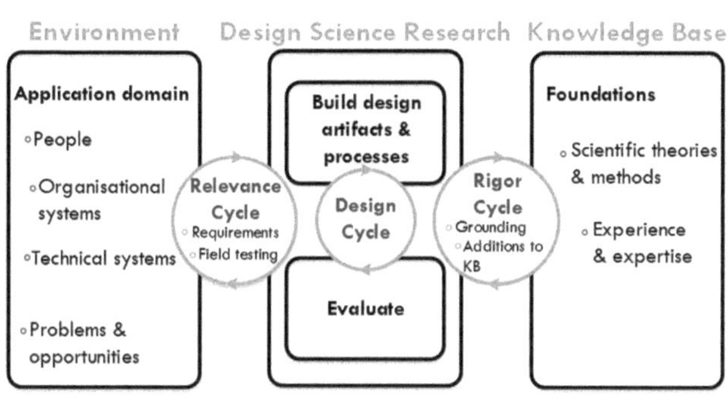

Fig. 1. The 3-cycle model of design science research [14]

Well designed and developed artifacts are expected to contribute with new knowledge to the body of scientific evidence and to real-world applications [10]. Gregor and Hevner [2] identify four types of knowledge contributions, based on the existing state of knowledge, in both the problem and the solution domains: (i) invention (new solutions for new problems); (ii) improvement (new solutions for known problems); (iii) exaptation (known solutions extended to new problems; and (iv) routine design (known solutions for known problems). To conduct proper DSR in IS, Peffers et al. [15] develop and evaluate a methodology (DSRM) consisting of six steps: (i) problem identification and motivation; (ii) definition of the objectives for a solution; (iii) design and development; (iv) demonstration; (v) evaluation; and (vi) communication.

2.2 Design Science and Multidisciplinary Research

Many knowledge regarding DSR has been developed in other research areas, such as architecture and engineering disciplines. Some examples of recent studies have been done in the social domain [16], as well as in the engineering domain, with specific focus on requirements engineering [17], ontology engineering [18], and production engineering [19].

Some important contributions have also been made in BMS. The work of van Aken [3], developed in the same year as the renowned paper by Hevner et al. [1], makes a distinction between description- and prescription-driven research, discussing management as a design science. The author suggests that the traditional description-driven research in BMS (based on the paradigm of the explanatory sciences) must be balanced with more prescription-driven research (based on the paradigm of the design sciences) in order to mitigate relevance and utilization problems. Denyer et al. [20] also make important contributions to this area presenting a DSR approach to management, with a discussion of prescriptive knowledge in the form of design propositions following the so-called CIMO-logic. CIMO-logic combines problematic *Contexts* with certain *Intervention* types to deliver specific *Outcomes*, following generative *Mechanisms*. Holmstrom et al. [21] propose a design science approach to bridge practice to theory rather than theory to practice in Operations Management. Finally, Hodgkinson and Starkey [22] make a critical assessment of contributions from the British Academy of Management, suggesting that design science and critical realism have the potential to face the existing relevance problem in the area.

Nevertheless, more contributions from other research areas are needed, especially in what concerns multidisciplinary research.

2.3 Case Studies as an Evaluation Method and Case Study Research

The evaluation of artifacts represents an essential element of DSR [1, 15]. However, with the exception of a few recent works, there is still the need for more guidance on how to design the evaluation component of DSR [4–6]. Peffers et al. [4] perform a review on 148 DSR articles to analyze the "artifact/evaluation method" combination in order to support researchers in the evaluation method selection. Venable et al. [23] develop a comprehensive framework for evaluation in DSR, comprising a four-step methodology and making an important distinction between "*ex-ante vs. ex-post*" evaluation and "*artificial vs. naturalistic*" evaluation. Prat et al. [6] present a holistic view of artifact evaluation in IS, resulting in a high-level abstraction model of evaluation methods and in some instantiations of this model through a set of generic evaluation methods.

All of these works point out case studies as one of the typical naturalistic evaluation method in DSR, to be used for the artifact *ex-post* evaluation. However, in multidisciplinary research, for example in the intersection between IS and BMS, case studies can be used before the design of the artifact. The present paper aims at demonstrating a possible way of doing this, by evaluating some preliminary forms or some parts of the artifact, i.e. meta-artifacts [7]. Therefore, we argue that case studies can be applied as a method for collecting data (through interviews, questionnaires, etc.) that will function as an input for the construction of the artifact, and its subsequent *ex-ante* validation/evaluation. In addition, most of the work in IS referring the use of case studies as an evaluation method still fail to provide clear directions on how to effectively design and perform the case studies themselves.

Case Study Research in Business and Management Studies. In BMS, particularly in the case of Operations Management, CSR is a reputable and widely-accepted research methodology. It gained importance in these areas mainly with the seminal works by Yin [24] and Eisenhardt [25], and later by Voss et al. [26]. In fact, Ketokivi and Choi [27] reinforce this growing interest by stating that a renaissance of CSR in Operations Management occurred in the last twenty-five years. Case studies are preferred in general when [24]: (i) "how" or "why" questions are used; (ii) the researcher has no control or little control over events; or (iii) the focus is on a contemporary phenomenon within a real-life context.

However, many authors argue that CSR should be used not only for inductive research, as recommended by Yin [24] and Eisenhardt [25], but also for deductive research [28] or for abductive research [29]. Therefore, Ketokivi and Choi [27] propose three different methodological approaches to CSR, in order to analyze its methodological diversity and to increase its transparency: (i) theory generation (inductive research); (ii) theory testing (deductive research); and (iii) theory elaboration (abductive research). Each approach has its peculiarities, mainly concerning the emphasis and interplay between theory and practice, as described in Fig. 2 by the thickness of the arrows.

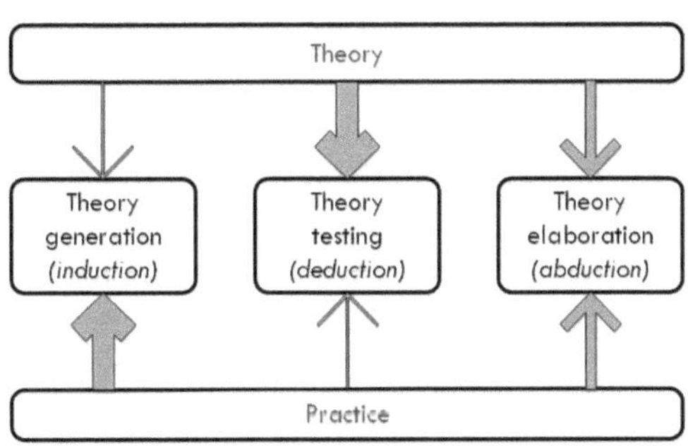

Fig. 2. Three methodological approaches to CSR (adapted from Ketokivi and Choi [27])

An effective design of case studies is a fundamental part of any CSR project [24]. Voss et al. [30] revisit case research in OM, giving important recommendations for effectively designing CSR: (i) have knowledge about the theoretical and empirical contexts; (ii) ensure (internal, construct, and external) validity and reliability of the CSR; (iii) select an appropriate research logic (theory generation, theory testing or theory elaboration); (iv) select cases (single or multiple; holistic or embedded); and (v) develop a research protocol (phenomena under study, unit of analysis, research instruments, procedures, etc.). After successfully designing the CSR, the next stages are to conduct, analyze, and report case research [24, 26, 28].

Different Perspectives for Using Case Studies. In BMS, a case study is presented as an empirical description of a contemporary phenomenon within its real-life context, and it is typically based on a variety of data sources [24]. In DSR, case studies are viewed as observational methods for the application and the evaluation of an artifact to a real-world context [1, 4, 5]. These two definitions are in some way similar but also different, essentially in what concerns the methodological approach, these differences being perceptible in some specific cases in the literature.

Barratt and Barratt [31] present a comprehensive case study to explore internal and external supply chain linkages. Although focusing on a single case, these authors develop a set of research propositions that provide important insights to extend the supply chain visibility. Before presenting their findings, a detailed description of the methodology is presented. They start to describe the methodology with the background and motivation of the study, referring the duration and the procedures followed. Then, they justify the rationale of using a single case study, arguing that even though a single case may offer only limited generalizability, it allows for a more in-depth exploration and understanding of the phenomena. Additionally, other important aspects are described in detail: (i) the sampling approach (qualitative design with embedded multiple units of analysis); (ii) the unit of analysis (information-based supply chain linkage) and informants (e.g. supply chain and logistics directors, and account managers); (iii) the data sources (semi structured interviews, documentation, and observation); and (iv) the data analysis (transcription of interviews, construct and validity, and data triangulation). Finally, the resulting propositions are viewed in a theory generation perspective, providing relevant contributions for theory and practice. However, the authors also recognize some lack of external validity (limited generalizability) that is typical in inductive studies [24].

The study of Barratt and Barratt [31] is a good example of a rigorous case study design. The authors present a sound description of the CSR approach, addressing all the main factors described in the literature for successfully conducting case studies. In contrast, looking at the design science literature, many authors refer the use of case studies for the artifact evaluation stage but without a clear detail on how the whole CSR has been conducted. Some studies naturally present the selected cases in a detailed way, as well as the informants and the data sources used [15]. However, other important aspects are not clarified, such as the validity and reliability of the CSR approach, the research logic (if it is inductive, deductive or abductive), the nature of the case (if it is holistic or embedded), and the detail of the CSR protocol.

2.4 Concluding Remarks

From the analyzed literature on case studies in IS and BMS, it is clear that, in practice, researchers use quite different methodological approaches. From one side, CSR represents a rigorous methodology in BMS, with a set of steps and requirements that need to be followed for obtaining more robust cases and for contributing to theory and practice.

From the other side, case studies are a typical evaluation method in IS, mainly used to observe if an artifact is valid in a specific empirical context. These definitions are valid for a particular research area where the study occurs. However, the problem still remains for researchers that are working with DSR in a multidisciplinary context, as it is the case presented in this paper, for example, with the intersection of IS and BMS. In these cases, the questions are whether a researcher needs to consider all the rigor that is imposed in BMS, or if case studies can only be used for an *ex-post* evaluation of the artifact. This gives room for the following research question: How can CSR be effectively integrated within the DSR paradigm in multidisciplinary research?

It is not the purpose of this study to compare DSR with CSR, as this comparison was already made by previous research, e.g. [19, 32, 33]. Instead, the objective here is to respond to the previously stated research question and to understand the interplay between these two methodologies/paradigms in multidisciplinary studies. As referred above, we argue that case studies can be used not only after the development of the artifact but also for an *ex-ante* evaluation, by evaluating meta-artifacts that will function as an input to build the final artifact. The rigor of the design process must be present during the entire study, not only at the design stage of the artifact. A rigorous design of the CSR approach is also important. Therefore, using knowledge from both DSR and CSR, a research framework for a multidisciplinary project of CNs is presented in the next section.

3 Design of a Multidisciplinary Project of Collaborative Networks

3.1 Context

This project presented in this section is an ongoing multidisciplinary doctoral project, developed on the intersection of two main research areas: (i) International Business (IB); and (ii) Information Management (IM). This doctoral project will study different IEAs that act as an institutional network support for the internationalization of their associated SMEs. Despite receiving some support from governments and from other institutional entities, many SMEs still face difficulties in managing their internationalization processes [34]. In some cases, they have a restricted access to relevant information or limited contact with knowledge and experience from key players, reducing the chance of entering in new markets with success [35]. In other cases, the poor information management capability of SMEs represents another hindrance for their internationalization processes [36].

Therefore, the objective is to understand the problems and the needs from both IEAs and SMEs, as well as to analyze the network dynamics that are formed through this institutional-based business environment. The ultimate goal is to design new information and knowledge management solutions and artifacts, following the DSR paradigm. The expected result is to improve the decision-making capability of SMEs to internationalize and to empower IEAs for acting as a fundamental institutional support by establishing CNs to optimize internationalization processes.

CNs are networks of organizations that are formed by different and autonomous geographically distributed entities, which are heterogeneous regarding operating environment, culture, social capital, and goals [37]. These CNs allow companies and organizations to share risks and benefits [38], representing also important sources of information and knowledge [34]. Interactions and collaborative processes in CNs are most of the times supported and mediated by information and communication technologies [39] and differ from other network forms (supply chains, virtual enterprises, clusters, etc.). This because collaboration is "an intentional property that derives from the shared belief that together the network members can achieve goals that would not be possible or would have a higher cost if attempted by them individually." [37].

The aim in this section is to show how this multidisciplinary project was designed, giving more detail in parts such as the design of the CSR, the description of the artifact, and the DSR knowledge contribution.

3.2 Research Framework

Based on the theoretical background of Sect. 2 and on the proposed research questions, the aim was to build a multidisciplinary research framework encompassing knowledge and contributions both from IS, with focus on DSR [15], and from BMS, with focus on CSR [24]. This doctoral project is a possible way of doing multidisciplinary research, focused on understanding how DSR can frame this kind of research and on showing how CSR can be integrated with DSR.

The result is then a doctoral project divided in three main stages of research (Fig. 3): (i) *ex-ante* stage (define the problem and express the motivation for the study; define the objectives of the artifact and perform an *ex-ante* evaluation); (ii) artifact design stage (design and develop the artifact); (iii) *ex-post* stage (demonstrate the artifact and perform an *ex-post* evaluation; report and communicate the results).

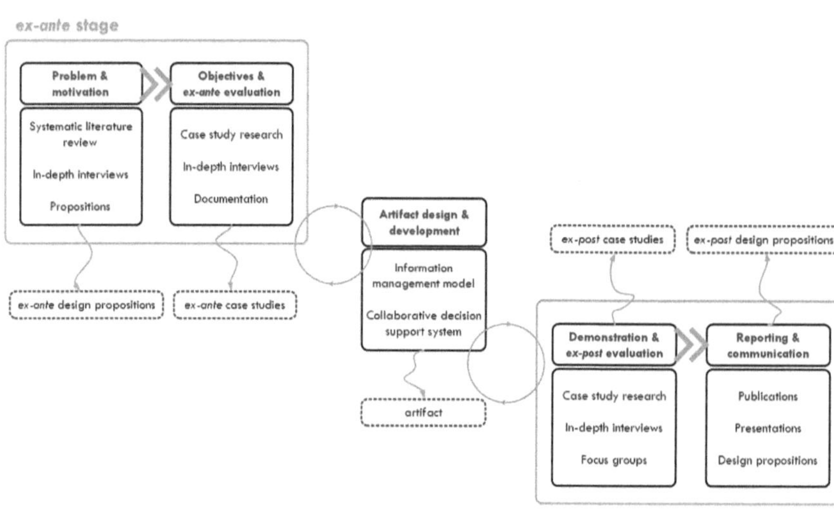

Fig. 3. Research framework of this doctoral project (based on Peffers et al. [15])

The design process is always present along all stages of the project, i.e. design propositions will be developed and case studies will be designed before and after the design/ development of the artifact. Two artifacts will be designed and developed: (i) an information management model; and (ii) a collaborative decision support system. Naturally, some iterative processes may occur during the course of this project, such as reporting and communication of some early results or iterations, leading to the re-definition of objectives and to new processes for artifact design and development (to improve effectiveness). Currently, this project is at the *ex-ante* stage, more precisely at the definition of the specific artifacts to be developed.

3.3 Research Activities

Problem and Motivation. A systematic literature review (SLR) was first performed, as a way to analyze the scientific relevance of the research, and to define the problem scope and the motivation of this study. This form of research synthesis is common in organization and management studies [20]. Accordingly, the SLR was done to investigate the role of information, knowledge and collaboration in internationalization decisions of SMEs, as well as to understand the state-of-the-art of approaches to tackle these issues. The main findings obtained with this SLR were [40]: (i) there is no detailed systematic analysis on the specific content and scope of the information required for making decisions in internationalization; (ii) there is a lack of comprehensive and systematic studies addressing how SMEs manage internationalization information generated in collaborative contexts; (iii) there is no evidence on how SMEs can convert information into knowledge to support decision-making in internationalization processes. In order to guarantee the practical relevance of the research, and to better define the problem and the motivation of the study, interviews with IEAs were performed. The main goal of these interviews was to provide an in-depth analysis on the relation and the impact of IEAs in internationalization processes of SMEs. This part of the research is completed. The ongoing part is to use the results both from the SLR and from the exploratory study to develop a theoretical/conceptual framework, together with some design propositions (*ex-ante* design propositions). This framework and these design propositions will be then tested in the next stage of the research, providing the contextual knowledge for the design of the CSR and of the artifact to be developed, which represent the next planned parts of this project.

Objectives and *Ex-ante* Evaluation. To help in the definition of the desired objectives for the solutions to be developed, a more focused research will be performed using a CSR. As mentioned earlier, in DSR, case studies are only pointed out to be used at the *ex-post* evaluation stage of a specific artifact [4, 5]. However, considering the multidisciplinary nature of this project, CSR will be used for both *ex-ante* and *ex-post* evaluation of the artifact. Therefore, a qualitative design of a multiple embedded case study will be used to describe the existing relationships between information, collaboration and knowledge creation, in the internationalization processes of SMEs. The main goal will be to specify the requirements for an effective transformation of information into knowledge on internationalization, mediated through collaborative processes and tools.

This CSR will be developed following the recommendations for effectively designing CSR [8, 27, 28, 30]. Table 1 summarizes the CSR design applied at this stage of the research.

Table 1. Summary of the CSR design

Recommendation	Description
Knowledge on the theoretical context	SLR, conceptual framework and design propositions prior to the CSR
Knowledge on the empirical context	Interviews with IEAs prior to the CSR
Sampling	Qualitative design of a multiple embedded case study
Unit of analysis	Two IEAs and some of their associated SMEs
Informants	Personnel working in internationalization processes and owners/managers of IEAs and SMEs
Data sources	In-depth semi-structured interviews, documentation and observations
Data analysis	Transcription and coding of interviews with MAXQDA, and cross-case analysis, until reaching a point of data saturation
Research logic	General theory and empirical context balanced, following an abductive research for theory elaboration
Construct validity	Transcripts of interviews sent back to the informants for corroboration, responses from the informants supported by documents and observations (data triangulation), and diversity of informants (role and position)
External validity	Replication logic of the multiple-case studies to different contexts or to the same context of internationalization but in different countries, cultures, and industrial sectors
Reliability	Case study protocol to repeat the data collection procedures

Therefore, the design of the CSR is ready and the next stages will be to conduct, analyze and report the results [24]. These results will also be used to test and refine the design propositions developed in the previous research stage (*ex-ante* design propositions). With this CSR it will be possible to define the objectives for the solution to be developed, as well as to perform a naturalistic *ex-ante* evaluation of the artifact. Therefore, the meta-artifacts will be designed and developed in parallel with the CSR.

Artifact Design and Development. This stage of the research will follow the design cycle of the DSR paradigm, taking place in parallel with the CSR, as a way to iterate between the design and the evaluation of the artifact. Therefore, at some points in time, data will be collected from the informants of IEAs and SMEs who will be involved in discussing and giving feedback on intermediate concepts of the artifact (meta-artifacts). The expected result is the design of two artifacts intended to be used as core components for the development or configuration of socio-technical systems supporting the internationalization processes of SMEs in an IEA context. This result will be a combination of conceptual artifacts, i.e. models and methods. As described in Peffers et al. [4], a method represents actionable instructions that are conceptual (not algorithmic). A model is a simplified representation of reality documented through a formal notation or language. The specific objectives of this research stage are:

- to perform a requirements gathering process for designing the artifacts;
- to design an information management model adaptable to the processes of internationalization in collaboration, mediated by IEAs (artifact 1);
- to design a collaborative decision support system to explore the information management model and capitalize internationalization knowledge (artifact 2).

In terms of contribution for DSR knowledge (Sect. 2.1), the final artifact will represent a mix of: (i) improvement (new solutions for known problems), by the information management model; and (ii) exaptation (known solutions extended to new problems), by the decision support system.

Demonstration and *Ex-post* Evaluation. To perform the demonstration and *ex-post* evaluation of the artifact, CSR and focus groups will be used. The procedures to perform this new CSR will be the same applied in the *ex-ante* evaluation, regarding the data sources, data analysis and validity ensuring. The difference here is that new informants and new SMEs will be interviewed, with modifications and improvements being made according to the feedback obtained. The *ex-post* evaluation of the artifact will also include focus groups with IEAs and SMEs of different industrial sectors. This will allow to strengthen the validation of the artifact, as well as the generalization of the findings.

Reporting and Communication. The scientific and practical contributions of this doctoral project will be reported in international peer-reviewed journals and in international refereed conferences, on selected areas from the following broader domains: Information Management, Information Systems, Business Management, International Business, and Collaborative Networks. The scientific and technical results of this doctoral project will be communicated in international and national refereed conferences, doctoral consortiums, workshops, and meetings with interested individuals. These results will include the final theoretical/conceptual framework and theory, as well as the final design propositions (*ex-post* design propositions). Moreover plans for the evolution and sustainability of the artifact will also be developed and disseminated.

4 Discussion and Final Considerations

The DSR paradigm is very useful to be used when the objective of a specific project is to create innovative artifacts, in order to contribute in a balanced way for both the scientific knowledge and the empirical part that is under study. Particularly in the case of IS, DSR has been proving its importance and it is consensual that it is now a well-established and reliable research paradigm in this area. However, like any other research area, there is always aspects that need to be discussed and improved to increase validity and reliability. In this paper, two research gaps related with DSR were considered: (i) more DSR studies are needed from other research areas (outside IS), particularly in what concerns multidisciplinary research; (ii) although representing a typical evaluation method, researchers in DSR fail to provide clear insights on how to effectively design and perform case studies; moreover, case studies are only pointed out for the *ex-post* evaluation of the artifact, leaving aside the use of this evaluation method for the *ex-ante* evaluation. These identified gaps allowed to define the following research question: How can CSR be effectively integrated within the DSR paradigm in multidisciplinary research?

This paper shows how case studies can be designed in DSR bringing important guidelines and considerations from BMS on how to effectively design CSR, a reputable research methodology in this area. Therefore, a research framework of an ongoing doctoral project that uses DSR and CSR in the multidisciplinary field of CNs is presented. In this project, DSR is adopted as the main research paradigm to better connect the knowledge base with the environment of the different multidisciplinary contexts involved. Results show that, in fact, CSR may be used for both the *ex-ante* and *ex-post* evaluation of the artifact to be developed, when considering this specific multi-disciplinary research.

One limitation of this study is the generalization of this specific research framework. Every project has its own needs and peculiarities, especially in the case of projects involving knowledge from different research areas, and it is difficult to design a general research framework to be adapted in many different contexts. Therefore, for this research framework, the methods and techniques have to be adapted to the specific context under study. Yet, this paper brings new insights on understanding the interplay between DSR, from IS, and CSR, from BMS. Analyzing the developed research framework, it is possible to realize the importance of a rigorous design of the CSR, mainly in what concerns the research logic (inductive, deductive or abductive research) and the case nature (holistic or embedded), as well as ways of ensuring its validity and reliability. These aspects are most of the times not considered in DSR works that make the use of case studies. A rigorous design of the artifact is one of the fundamental aspects of DSR projects. Nonetheless, we argue that this rigor on the design must happens at all stages of the project, including when designing the CSR approach.

This paper can contribute first to the area of IS and DSR, using knowledge from BMS on the effective and rigorous design of case studies for artifact evaluation. Moreover, the results obtained can also be relevant for researcher in BMS. As stated by Spring and Santos [8], new ways of doing CSR are needed to fully understand the changes that are happening in the Operations Management field. So, we believe that DSR can be relevant to these areas because it can be used as a more cyclical research design, ensuring a balanced interplay between theory and the CSR (important aspects indicated by Spring and Santos [8]). Finally, this paper can also contribute for researchers that are designing artifacts involving CNs, by showing an illustrative example on how to design a multi-disciplinary project of CNs. Moreover, the context of internationalization and the establishment of CNs between IEAs and SMEs to improve these processes is a different CN context, which represents a new contribution to the field of CNs.

Acknowledgments. This research was funded by the Portuguese funding agency, Fundação para a Ciência e a Tecnologia (FCT), through the Ph.D. Studentship SFRH/BD/110131/2015.

References

1. Hevner, A., March, S., Park, J., Ram, S.: Design science in information systems research. MIS Q. **28**, 75–105 (2004)
2. Gregor, S., Hevner, A.: Positioning and presenting design science research for maximum impact. MIS Q. **37**, 337–355 (2013)
3. van Aken, J.E.: Management research based on the paradigm of the design sciences: the quest for field-tested and grounded technological rules. J. Manag. Stud. **41**, 219–246 (2004)
4. Peffers, K., Rothenberger, M., Tuunanen, T., Vaezi, R.: Design science research evaluation. In: Peffers, K., Rothenberger, M., Kuechler, B. (eds.) DESRIST 2012. LNCS, vol. 7286, pp. 398–410. Springer, Heidelberg (2012)
5. Venable, J., Pries-Heje, J., Baskerville, R.: A comprehensive framework for evaluation in design science research. In: Peffers, K., Rothenberger, M., Kuechler, B. (eds.) DESRIST 2012. LNCS, vol. 7286, pp. 423–438. Springer, Heidelberg (2012)
6. Prat, N., Comyn-Wattiau, I., Cnam, C.: Artifact evaluation in information systems: design science research – a holistic view. In: 19th Pacific Asia Conference on Information Systems (2014)
7. Vahidov, R.: Representing meta-artifacts. In: Design-Type Research in Information Systems: Findings and Practices, pp. 115–134. IGI Global (2012)
8. Spring, M., Santos, J.B.: Case study research in operations management: new contexts, new theories, new approaches. In: 22nd International Annual EurOMA Conference (2015)
9. Simon, H.A.: The Sciences of the Artificial. MIT Press, Cambridge (1996)
10. Hevner, A., Chatterjee, S.: Design Research in Information Systems: Theory and Practice. Springer Science and Business Media, New York (2010)
11. Offermann, P., Blom, S., Schönherr, M., Bub, U.: Artifact types in information systems design science – a literature review. In: Winter, R., Zhao, J., Aier, S. (eds.) DESRIST 2010. LNCS, vol. 6105, pp. 77–92. Springer, Heidelberg (2010)
12. Järvinen, P.: Action research is similar to design science. Qual. Quant. **41**, 37–54 (2007)
13. Vaishnavi, V.K., Kuechler, W.J.: Design Science Research Methods and Patterns. CRC Press, Taylor & Francis Group, Boca Raton (2015)
14. Hevner, A.: A three cycle view of design science research. Scand. J. Inf. Syst. **19**, 87–92 (2007)
15. Peffers, K., Tuunanen, T., Rothenberger, M.A., Chatterjee, S.: A design science research methodology for information systems research. J. Manag. Inf. Syst. **24**, 45–77 (2007)
16. van Aken, J.E.: Developing generic actionable knowledge for the social domain: design science for use in the swamp of practice. Methodol. Rev. Appl. Res. **2**, 9–25 (2015)
17. Plachkinova, M., Peffers, K., Moody, G.: Communication artifacts for requirements engineering. In: 10th International Conference on Design Science Research in Information Systems and Technology, DESRIST 2015 (2015)
18. Ostrowski, L., Helfert, M., Gama, N.: Ontology engineering step in design science research methodology: a technique to gather and reuse knowledge. Behav. Inf. Technol. **33**, 443–451 (2014)
19. Lacerda, D.P., Dresch, A., Proença, A., Antunes Júnior, J.A.V.: Design science research: A research method to production engineering. Gestão & Produção **20**, 741–761 (2013)

20. Denyer, D., Tranfield, D., van Aken, J.E.: Developing design propositions through research synthesis. Organ. Stud. **29**, 393–413 (2008)
21. Holmstrom, J., Ketokivi, M., Hameri, A.-P.: Bridging practice and theory: a design science approach. Decis. Sci. **40**, 65–87 (2009)
22. Hodgkinson, G.P., Starkey, K.: Not simply returning to the same answer over and over again: reframing relevance. Br. J. Manag. **22**, 355–369 (2011)
23. Venable, J., Pries-heje, J., Baskerville, R.: FEDS: a framework for evaluation in design science research. Eur. J. Inf. Syst. 1–13 (2014)
24. Yin, R.K.: Case study research: Design and methods. SAGE Publications, Thousand Oaks (2009)
25. Eisenhardt, K.M.: Building theories from case study research. Acad. Manag. Rev. **14**, 532–550 (1989)
26. Voss, C., Tsikriktsis, N., Frohlich, M.: Case research in operations management. Int. J. Oper. Prod. Manag. **22**, 195–219 (2002)
27. Ketokivi, M., Choi, T.: Renaissance of case research as a scientific method. J. Oper. Manag. **32**, 232–240 (2014)
28. Barratt, M., Choi, T.Y., Li, M.: Qualitative case studies in operations management: trends, research outcomes, and future research implications. J. Oper. Manag. **29**, 329–342 (2011)
29. Dubois, A., Gadde, L.E.: Systematic combining: an abductive approach to case research. J. Bus. Res. **55**, 553–560 (2002)
30. Voss, C., Johnson, M., Godsell, J.: Revisiting case research in operations management. In: 22nd International Annual EurOMA Conference (2015)
31. Barratt, M., Barratt, R.: Exploring internal and external supply chain linkages: evidence from the field. J. Oper. Manag. **29**, 514–528 (2011)
32. Dresch, A., Lacerda, D., Miguel, P.A.: A distinctive analysis of case study, action research and design science research. Rev. Bus. Manag. **17**, 1116–1133 (2015)
33. Nabukenya, J.: Combining case study, design science and action research methods for effective collaboration engineering research efforts. In: 45th Hawaii International Conference on System Sciences (2012)
34. Costa, E., Soares, A.L., Sousa, J.P.: A new insight in the SMEs internationalization process. In: 16th IFIP WG 5.5 Working Conference on Virtual Enterprises, PRO-VE 2015 (2015)
35. Hsu, W.-T., Chen, H.-L., Cheng, C.-Y.: Internationalization and firm performance of SMEs: the moderating effects of CEO attributes. J. World Bus. **48**, 1–12 (2013)
36. Rodriguez, V., Barcos, L., Jesús Álvarez, M.: Managing risk and knowledge in the internationalisation process. Intang. Cap. **6**, 202–235 (2010)
37. Camarinha-Matos, L., Afsarmanesh, H.: Collaborative networks: a new scientific discipline. J. Intell. Manuf. **16**, 439–452 (2005)
38. Parung, J., Bititci, U.: A metric for collaborative networks. Bus. Process Manag. J. **14**, 654–674 (2008)
39. Carneiro, L.M., Soares, A.L., Patrício, R., Azevedo, A.L., Pinho de Sousa, J.: Case studies on collaboration, technology and performance factors in business networks. Int. J. Comput. Integr. Manuf. **26**, 101–116 (2013)
40. Costa, E., Soares, A.L., Sousa, J.P.: Information, knowledge and collaboration management in the internationalisation of SMEs: a systematic literature review. Int. J. Inf. Manage. **36**, 557–569 (2016)

Layout Design and Reconfiguration in a Collaborative Manufacturing Network

Maria Manuela Azevedo[1,2(✉)], José António Crispim[2,3], and Jorge Pinho de Sousa[1,2]

[1] Faculty of Engineering, University of Porto, Rua Dr. Roberto Frias, 4200-465 Porto, Portugal

[2] INESC TEC, Rua Dr. Roberto Frias, 4200-465 Porto, Portugal
{maria.m.azevedo, jorge.p.sousa}@inesctec.pt

[3] School of Economics and Management, University of Minho, Campus de Gualtar, 4710-057 Braga, Portugal
crispim@ee.uminho.pt

Abstract. This study explores strategic agility of an automotive corporate group and its influence on facility layouts and operational performance. Strategic agility is viewed here as a firm's strategic intent to achieve agile operations through collaboratively deploying the layouts of a set of facilities, driven by a management focus on improving its responsiveness and adaptability to customers' requirements. Our "collaborative multi-facility layout problem" involves the physical organization of departments between and inside several facilities geographically dispersed, that collaborate in manufacturing a complex product in a given time window. The model proposed in this work allows us to analyse the benefits of new horizontal collaboration forms with respect to several objectives, namely costs (material handling inside and between facilities, re-layout) and adjacency between departments. A case study of a first tier supplier in the automotive industry shows the applicability potential of the approach to real-life problems. The results show that horizontal collaboration among the facilities can positively influence the performance of the corporate group as a whole, and that of each firm individually.

Keywords: Agile operations · Multi-facility layout problems · Multi-objective optimization · Reconfigurable layouts · Collaboration

1 Introduction

In a more and more competitive world, companies easily recognize they need to permanently develop new and more sophisticated strategies, in order to maintain and increase their performance. The reconfiguration and continuous optimization of resources and production processes can be a way to reduce costs and increase their opportunities and profit [1]. The integration in Collaborative Networks (CN) can also be an important step to make organizations more effective and agile as part of broader manufacturing systems, and this may be specially important for SMEs, due to their reduced dimensions and high vulnerability. In this context, one of the current big challenges for industry is clearly the permanent need for rapid reconfiguration of

H. Afsarmanesh et al. (Eds.): PRO-VE 2016, IFIP AICT 480, pp. 545–556, 2016.
DOI: 10.1007/978-3-319-45390-3_46

manufacturing enterprises, in response to changing requirements and opportunities [2]. In practice, the configuration of facility layouts comprises the physical organization (of departments, machines, workstations, storage spaces, etc.) inside a plant, thus facilitating production and material handling, and allowing flexible and efficient operations [3].

In a more ambitious way, and as proposed in this work, the combination of design and reconfiguration of layouts for collaborative networks of facilities, can in fact help companies to be more flexible and competitive. Therefore, the main research question of this work can be stated as follows: "in a dynamic network of factories, what impact can sharing departments among facilities have on the flexibility level of this network and on each factory individually?"

To answer this question, we propose a mathematical model (a quadratic integer program) to be used in assigning projects of complex products to networks of facilities and in designing the layout of each specific facility. These networks can be viewed as a kind of Virtual Enterprises (VE). In fact, in our particular case, the facilities are part of a corporate group, and even if they are not fully independent from each other, they own all the other main characteristics of a VE.

The next section of the paper presents a brief state of the art on facility layout and network collaboration, as a way to position the contributions of the proposed model and to highlight its innovation. In the following sections the problem under study is described, followed by a presentation of the model. Then preliminary computational results are presented. The paper ends with some conclusions on the presented approach and with topics for future research.

2 Literature Review

The concept of *Collaborative Network (CN)* is currently widely disseminated and recognized as an important instrument for the competitiveness and survival of organizations, specially in periods of turbulent socio-economic changes [2]. A CN is a network of a variety of entities (e.g. organizations and people), largely autonomous, geographically distributed, and heterogeneous in terms of operating environment, culture, social capital and goals, but that collaborate to better achieve common or compatible goals, thus jointly generating value, with interactions supported by computer networks [2]. In CNs, *Virtual Organizations (VOs)* are an important class, characterized in four dimensions as follows: space (physically dispersed), time (asynchronous), mode of interaction (electronic networks) and individual diversity (different) [4]. A particular case of VO is the *Virtual Enterprises (VE)*, representing a temporary alliance of enterprises that come together to share skills or core competences and resources in order to better respond to business opportunities, and whose cooperation is supported by computer networks [2].

A rapid formation of VOs, when needed, and their adjustments to the specific requirements of a given emerging opportunity is of great importance and is frequently viewed as a requirement for agility, and used as a survival mechanism in face of market/society turbulence [1].

Strategic agility is viewed in the literature from quite different managerial perspectives (e.g., operations, information systems, marketing, human resources) [5]. For example [6] define agility as “a successful exploration of competitive bases (speed, flexibility, innovation proactivity, quality and profitability) thought the integration of reconfigurable resources and knowledge management to provide customer driven products and services in a fast changing market environment”. Recently, [7] consider that agility is the project team’s ability to quickly change the project plan as a response to customer or stakeholders needs, market or technology demands in order to achieve better project and product performance in an innovative and dynamic project environment.

In fact, given today’s frequency of changes in business environments, it is more and more important for companies to be flexible as a way to respond quickly and dynamically to those changes. This response capability should also exist at a higher, corporate level, combining a plant-level and a network-level analysis that aims at understanding the continuous interaction between individual plants and their constituent networks [8].

In the context of this work, we aim at applying these concepts to extended facility layout problems (FLP), that in fact encompass various types of situations, such as the allocation of departments inside facilities [9] or machines inside departments [10]. This area has been studied from several different points of view, considering: the type of layout configuration (single row [11], multi-rows [12], multi-floor [13], cellular [12], …); the type of problem (department/machine allocation, product flows [10], routing [14], …); the objectives (single [12] or multiple [15], minimizing costs [12] or distances [16], or maximizing adjacencies [17], profits [18], …) and constraints (overlap, budget [18], areas [19], …); the nature of the problem (static [10] or dynamic [17]) and solved by a large variety and combination of resolution approaches (exact methods [20], heuristics [21], …).

Due to the large impact that the layout has in a manufacturing company, recent studies tend to add more and more features to the basic, traditional problems. This is e.g. the case of [10] that integrates the layout design (by the location of unequal-area machines with duplicates) and the product flows assignment problem (by assigning products to machines according to the product process route). The work by [17] is another example, they proposes a dynamic allocation of departments, considering multiple objectives (minimize total material handling costs (MHC) and re-layout costs, and maximize adjacencies), solving the problem with classical optimization methods and with population-based metaheuristics.

Although the FLP has been extensively studied (for some surveys see for example [11, 22, 23]), the majority of works deal with the design and reconfiguration of layouts at a single facility. The model proposed in this work intends to cover this gap, by simultaneously designing the layout of a group of facilities, and performing the allocation of products considering the whole network. Therefore, an innovation of our research comes from considering capacities in the transport of materials between facilities, and from allowing the possibility of performing changes along time. Moreover, the model allows the addition or removal of departments and facilities at different periods, thus providing a higher level of flexibility.

3 Problem Description

The automotive industry works with "projects" that are associated with specific models of a car. A project comprises several parts that are themselves composed by a group of materials or components (see Fig. 1).

The mathematical model proposed in this work considers a set of geographically separated facilities that can produce and store the same type of products and components. Each facility has more or less the same department structure, with the same type of equipment and machines. These facilities are served (and linked) by a distribution system that uses trucks to move the raw materials, components and products between the factories.

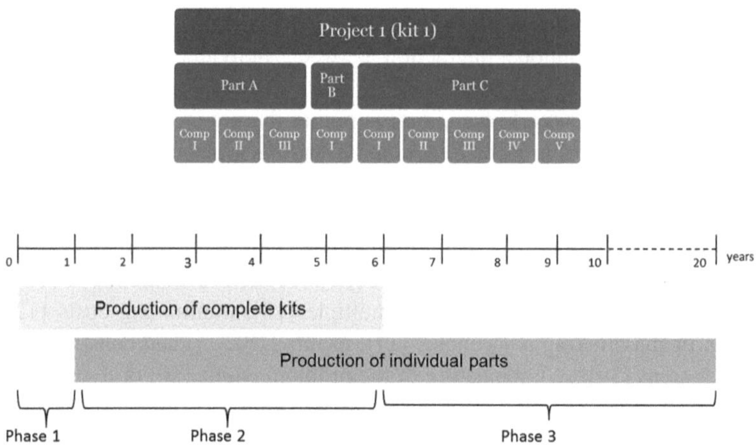

Fig. 1. Product complexity.

Given the high complexity of products, and the variety of requests from customers, in general collaboration between facilities is needed, with the formation of networks that change dynamically for each project.

In this context, our "collaborative multi-facility layout problem" involves the physical organisation of departments between and inside several geographically dispersed facilities, that collaborate in manufacturing a complex product in a given time window. The problem consists therefore in finding the best global layout for a given project. In order to optimise operations, we can use the flexibility of the system to exchange the location of departments between the facilities in different periods of time.

4 Model Description

The model developed in this work (Fig. 2) provides firms with the ability to dynamically modify or reconfigure individual business processes to accommodate their actual and potential needs [24] by determining the best layout configuration of each facility, taking into account the project needs in each period, the available production capacity and the transportation capacities between facilities. The model also considers the possibility, along time, of adding or closing facilities (departments and sites), thus creating the flexibility for firms to quickly respond, by continuously adapting to changing business environments [25].

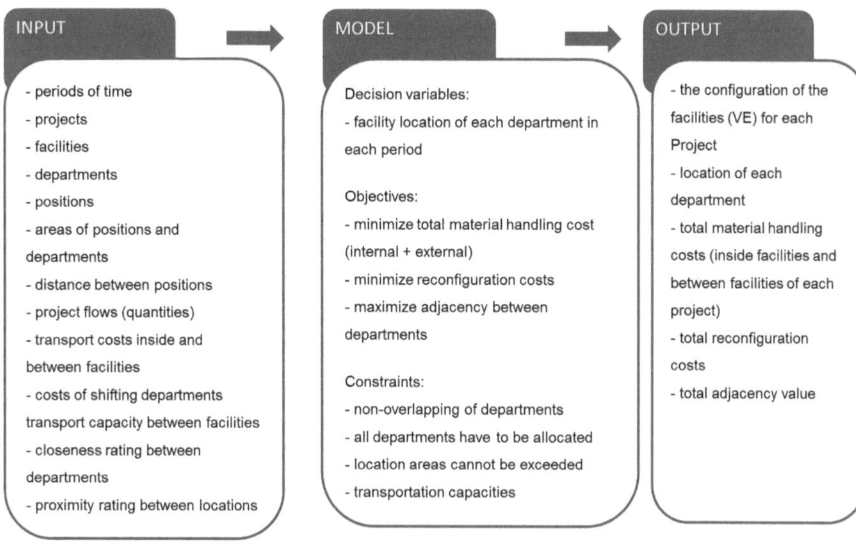

Fig. 2. Proposed model.

The formulation considered in this work is based on the Quadratic Assignment Problem (QAP), commonly used for dynamic layout problems [22]. Multiple objectives are considered, as defined by expression (1).

$$Min\ Z = \alpha\,\mathrm{MHC} + \beta\,\mathrm{RC} - \gamma\,\mathrm{Adj}. \tag{1}$$

The objective *"minimizing the total material handling costs (MHC)"* is commonly used in the literature of the unequal area FLP [17, 26]). As [27] we assume fixed dimensions for facilities and the existence of several departments to be located inside facilities. We consider the total MHC as the sum of the internal and the external MHC of each project. This model considers also the "*minimization of reconfiguration costs (RC)"* frequently used for layout reconfigurations (see e.g. [28] or [29]).

The objective *"maximization of adjacency (Adj)"* of the departments is based on a *closeness rating* (defining the importance of closeness between departments as proposed by [15]) and the *proximity* between the locations to where the departments are assigned. This is an important feature of the problem, due to the fact that when departments are allocated to different buildings, the relationships between them can be conditioned in different ways (e.g. imposing constraints on sharing the same specialized equipment or the same workers).

Our model adapts the constraints usually applied in the literature to solve unequal FLPs [21] to this multi-facility dynamic layout problem, namely: ensure that each position in a facility has at most one department, in each period; guarantee that each department is assigned only to one position, in each period; ensure that the area of a position is never exceeded by the department area assigned to it, in consecutive periods [20]; ensure that the existing capacity for transportation between facilities is never exceeded; check that the total number of existing locations is higher or equal to the total number of existing departments in each period; and confirm that only active departments are assigned to active locations in each period.

5 Computational Results

The performance of the proposed model was tested on some numerical instances based on a real case study briefly described below. Two situations have been considered, defined on the current case: first, by adding a new facility (test1); and, second, by closing one facility (test2). All the tests were made with the optimization software IBM ILOG Cplex V12.6, with a limit running time of 6 h.

5.1 Problem Data

The case study motivating this work is based on a corporate group that produces plastic parts for the automotive industry. Initially (*t1*) there are 2 facilities (*f1* and *f2*), and since *t2* we consider a new facility (*f3*), with in total 13 locations to position the departments (Fig. 3). The distance between *f1* and *f2* is 30, as well as between *f2* and *f3*; the distance between *f1* and *f3* is 50 unit of distance.

For executing the movements between departments, we consider a distribution (transport) system based on the following assumptions: *internal transport costs* are constant along time and do not depend on the distances (5 cost units/unit of flow);

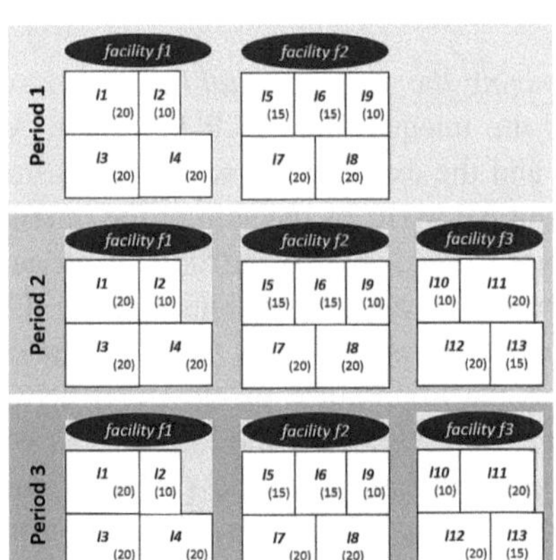

Fig. 3. Available area for the different facilities in each period of the horizon.

external transport costs vary with time (t1 = 20, t2 = 22, t3 = 25). The capacity of transport between facilities also vary (t1 = 800, t2 = 1000 and t3 = 800).

There are 5 different types of departments: raw material warehousing; injection; assembly; painting; and product warehousing (Table 1). Due to characteristics and organization of the production, the areas assigned to each department can change in each period. We also consider that there some advantages in having departments of the same type (e.g. injection – A, B, C) together in the same facility (closeness level equal to 5).

Table 1. Departments in the case study.

Departments		**Raw material warehouse**			**Injection**			**Assembly**			**Painting**	**Product warehouse**		
		A	**B**	**C**	**D**	**E**	**F**	**G**	**H**	**I**	**J**	**K**	**L**	**M**
Re-layout cost		5000			20 000			10 000			80 000	5000		
Active departments	t1	0	1	1	0	1	1	0	1	1	1	0	1	1
	t2	1	1	1	1	1	1	1	1	1	1	1	1	1
	t3	1	1	1	1	1	1	1	1	1	1	1	1	1
Area	t1	0	10	20	0	20	20	0	15	10	20	0	15	20
	t2	10	20	20	15	20	20	10	15	10	20	15	15	20
	t3	10	20	15	15	20	15	5	15	5	20	15	15	20

We consider there are 4 projects, in different life cycle phases: *project 1* and *2* have a continuous production along the planning horizon; *project 3* finishes in period *t2*; and *project 4* starts in period *t2* (Table 2).

Table 2. Project flows in each period.

Periods			**Project**	**Flows between departments**			
t1	t2	t3					
✓	✓	✓	P1	C - > F (500)	F - > J (350)	J - > H (200)	H - > M (200)
✓	✓	✓	P2	B - > E (100)	E - > J (150)	J - > H (150)	H - > L (50)
✓	✓		P3	C - > F (100)	F - > I (100)	I - > M (50)	
	✓	✓	P4	A - > D (50)	D - > G (150)	G - > K (100)	

Concerning the relative importance of the different objectives, we have considered the following weights (that should later be subject to some kind of sensitivity analysis): 35 % for MHC; 35 % for reconfiguration costs; and 30 % for adjacency.

5.2 Adding Facilities

The occurrence of a new project (P4) in t2 allows us to explore the recourse to a new facility. Table 3 and Fig. 4(test1) show the results obtained for this situation. Analysing these results, it is possible to conclude that:

- Department J (painting) does not change along the horizon;
- Facilities tend to become specialized in some phase of production (e.g. *facility 2* focus on Assembly, Painting and Product warehouse; *f1* and *f3* focus on the first production phases, with Raw material warehouse, and Injection; and *f1* at *t3* deals with all the product warehouses);
- *project 4* rotates among the 3 facilities, apparently due to the smaller quantities to be produced;
- flows inside facilities are naturally higher, because the distances are lower, and the capacity to transport is not constrained, as it is the case for the transport between facilities;
- external MHC costs (1 542 400) are considerably larger than internal MHC costs (34 500);
- there are 3 reconfigurations occurring inside facilities, and 10 between facilities, with a total reconfiguration cost of 165 000 and an adjacency value of 1015.

Table 3. Results of test 1 – adding facility *f3* at *t2*.

Project	Network structure	Flows inside facilities			Flows between facilities					Total MHC
		f1	*f2*	*f3*	*f1–f2*	*f1–f3*	*f2–f1*	*f2–f3*	*f3–f2*	
P1	***f1, f2, f3***									**650 150**
t1	*f1, f2*	500	400		350					
t2	*f3, f2*		400	500					350	
t3	*f2, f1*		1050		200					
P2	***f1, f2, f3***									**373 900**
t1	*f1, f2*	100	200		150					
t2	*f1, f2*	100	200		150					
t3	*f3, f2*		150	100				50	150	
P3	***f1, f2, f3***									**108 650**
t1	*f1, f2*	100	50		100					
t2	*f3, f2*			200					50	
P4	***f1, f2, f3***									**444 200**
t2	*f1, f2, f3*					50	100		150	
t3	*f1, f2, f3*			50			100		150	
		800	**2450**	**850**	**950**	**50**	**200**	**50**	**850**	**1 576 900**
	Re-layout costs 165 000				**Adjacency 1015**					

5.3 Eliminating Facilities and Departments

In order to understand the impact of eliminating a facility, we will consider that *project 3* finishes in period *t2* (thus making departments B, E, I and L unnecessary) –see Table 4 and Fig. 4(test2). Analysing these results, it is possible to conclude that:

- facility f2 has always 3 types of departments for the last phases of production (Assembly, Painting, and Product warehouse);
- departments J and D do never change along the planning horizon; and departments B, E, M, H and K only change inside the same facility;
- flows (see Table 4) are similar to *test 1*, for each facility and between facilities;
- external MHC costs (1 399 900) decrease and internal MHC costs (11 650) decrease too, when compared with test1;
- this solution has less reconfigurations (5 inside facilities and 5 between facilities), with smaller reconfiguration costs than test1 (115 000), and a lower value of adjacency (895).

Table 4. Results of test 2 – close facility *f1* at *t3*.

Project	Network structure	Flows inside facilities			Flows between facilities					Total MHC
		f1	*f2*	*f3*	*f1–f2*	*f1–f3*	*f2–f1*	*f2–f3*	*f3–f2*	
P1	***f1, f2, f3***									**766 800**
t1	*f1, f2*	500	400		350					
t2	*f3, f2*		400	500					350	
t3	*f2, f3*		900						350	
P2	***f1, f2, f3***									**247 450**
t1	*f1, f2*	100	200		150					
t2	*f1, f2*	100	150		150		50			
P3	***f1, f2, f3***									**143 900**
t1	*f1, f2*	100	50		100					
t2	*f3, f2*		50	100					100	
P4	***f1, f2, f3***									**253 400**
t2	*f1, f2, f3*			150		50			100	
t3	*f2, f3*		100	50					150	
		800	**2250**	**800**	**750**	**50**	**50**	**0**	**1050**	**1 411 550**
Re-layout cost 115 000					**Adjacency 895**					

5.4 Assessing Network Collaboration

This model allows companies to evaluate, in different ways, the performance of the generated configurations: both for each facility and for the network formed for each project (in terms of flows, costs and time evolution) (see Fig. 5).

Despite their preliminary nature, the results show the potential of inter facilities collaboration in manufacturing systems, and its role in dynamically adjusting the

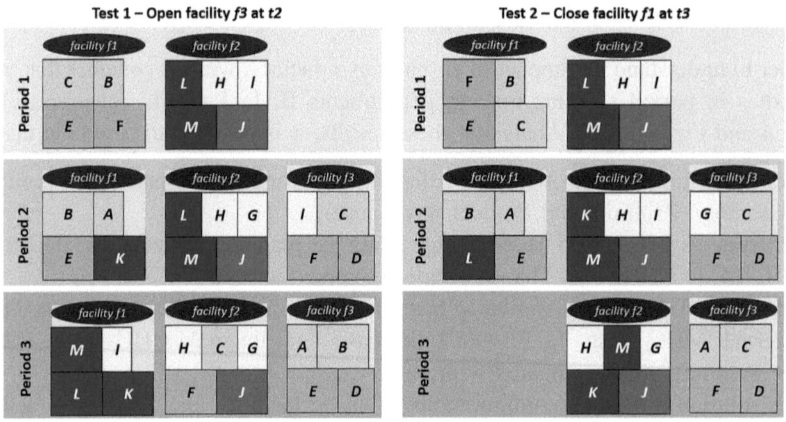

Fig. 4. Configuration of facilities, in test1 and in test2.

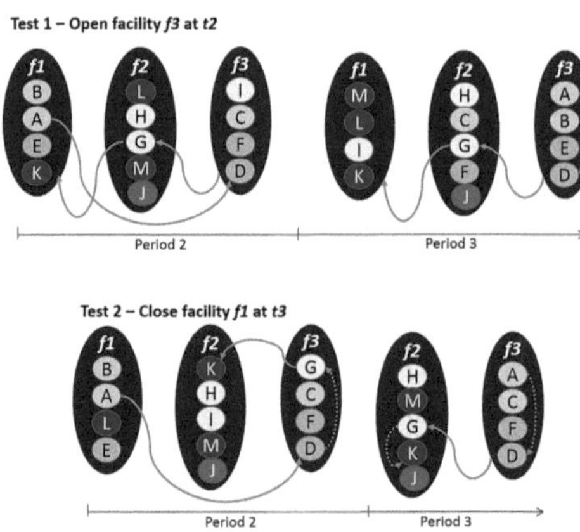

Fig. 5. Flows between facilities at Network of project p4.

network structure to take into account the flows requirements in different periods of the planning horizon. These experiments also show the developed model can be used to adjust the firm's strategy in response to internal or external changes through facility layout collaboration.

6 Conclusions

This paper presents a model for supporting the definition of a collaboration strategy of different facilities or companies in a corporate group, to enhance its agility and responsiveness. For illustrative purposes, a case study was defined based on a first tier supplier in the automotive industry. The formation of collaborative networks involving the companies of the group may clearly improve manufacturing performance for the products and components of the different projects.

The model proposed in this work determines the layout configuration of all facilities, taking into consideration the flows between departments induced by the different projects. The model considers three objectives (minimize *total material handling costs*, minimize *re-layout costs,* and maximize the *adjacency* between departments) in order to better reflect the main prevailing concerns in real situations. The model was tested with two simplified instances inspired by real situations, namely: the emergence of a new project that requires a new partner; and the conclusion of a project leading to the end of that collaboration. These changes lead to the implementation of some layout reconfigurations, in different periods of the planning horizon.

In general terms, the model can be used to support the design and deployment of new configurations and layouts, based on advanced forms of collaboration, and thus promote the strategic agility of a corporate group. This will allow a higher adaptability to customer requirements (better handling demand fluctuations or changing location of facilities to be closer to customers) certainly improving global performance.

Acknowledgments. This research was partially financed by the North Portugal Regional Operational Programme (NORTE 2020), under the PORTUGAL 2020 Partnership Agreement, and through the European Regional Development Fund (ERDF), within the project "TEC4-Growth - Pervasive Intelligence, Enhancers and Proofs of Concept with Industrial Impact/NORTE-01-0145-FEDER-000020". The first author was also funded by the Ph.D. grant SFRH/BD/33731/2009 from FCT, the Portuguese Foundation for Science and Technology (MIT Portugal Program).

References

1. Afsarmanesh, H., Camarinha-Matos, L.M., Msanjila, S.S.: On management of 2nd generation virtual organizations breeding environments. Annu. Rev. Control **33**(2), 209–219 (2009)
2. Camarinha-Matos, L.M., Afsarmanesh, H., Galeano, N., Molina, A.: Collaborative networked organizations - concepts and practice in manufacturing enterprises. Comput. Ind. Eng. **57**(1), 46–60 (2009)
3. Azevedo, M.M., Crispim, J.A., de Sousa, J.P.: Flexible and reconfigurable layouts in complex manufacturing systems. In: Emmanouilidis, C., Taisch, M., Kiritsis, D. (eds.) Advances in Production Management Systems. IFIP AICT, vol. 397, pp. 484–493. Springer, Heidelberg (2013)
4. Vartiainen, M.: The functionality of virtual organizations. In: Proceedings of T-world 2001, Helsinki, 13 September 2001, pp. 273–292 (2001)
5. Li, X., Goldsby, T.J., Holsapple, C.W.: Supply chain agility: scale development. Int. J. Logist. Manag. **20**(3), 408–424 (2009)
6. Yusuf, Y.Y., Sarhadi, M., Gunasekaran, A.: Agile manufacturing: the drivers, concepts and attributes. Int. J. Prod. Econ. **62**(1), 33–43 (1999)
7. Conforto, E.C., Amaral, D.C., Silva, S.L., Di Felippo, A., Kamikawachi, D.S.L.: The agility construct on project management theory. Int. J. Proj. Manag. **34**(4), 660–674 (2016)

8. Cheng, Y., Farooq, S., Johansen, J.: International manufacturing network: past, present and future. Int. J. Oper. Prod. Manag. **35**(3), 392–429 (2015)
9. Aiello, G., Enea, M., Galante, G.: A multi-objective approach to facility layout problem by genetic search algorithm and electre method. Robot. Comput. Integr. Manuf. **22**(5–6), 447–455 (2006)
10. Taghavi, A., Murat, A.: A heuristic procedure for the integrated facility layout design and flow assignment problem. Comput. Ind. Eng. **61**(1), 55–63 (2011)
11. Keller, B., Buscher, U.: Single row layout models. Eur. J. Oper. Res. **245**(3), 629–644 (2015)
12. Kia, R., Baboli, A., Javadian, N., Tavakkoli-Moghaddam, R., Kazemi, M., Khorrami, J.: Solving a group layout design model of a dynamic cellular manufacturing system with alternative process routings, lot splitting and flexible reconfiguration by simulated annealing. Comput. Oper. Res. **39**(11), 2642–2658 (2012)
13. Kia, R., Khaksar-Haghani, F., Javadian, N., Tavakkoli-Moghaddam, R.: Solving a multi-floor layout design model of a dynamic cellular manufacturing system by an efficient genetic algorithm. J. Manuf. Syst. **33**(1), 218–232 (2014)
14. Kulturel-Konak, S., Smith, E., Norman, B.: Layout optimization considering production uncertainty and routing flexibility. Int. J. Prod. Res. **42**(21), 4475–4493 (2004)
15. Jaafari, A.A., Krishnan, K.K., Doulabi, S.H.H., Davoudpour, H.: A multi-objective formulation for facility layout problem. In: World Congress on Engineering and Computer Science, vol. II (2009)
16. Koşucuoğlu, D., Bilge, U.: Material handling considerations in the FMS loading problem with full routing flexibility. Int. J. Prod. Res. **50**(22), 6530–6552 (2012)
17. Emami, S., Nookabadi, A.S.: Managing a new multi-objective model for the dynamic facility layout problem. Int. J. Adv. Manuf. Technol. **68**(9–12), 2215–2228 (2013)
18. Şahin, R., Ertoğral, K., Türkbey, O.: A simulated annealing heuristic for the dynamic layout problem with budget constraint. Comput. Ind. Eng. **59**(2), 308–313 (2010)
19. Kulturel-Konak, S., Konak, A.: Unequal area flexible bay facility layout using ant colony optimisation. Int. J. Prod. Res. **49**(7), 1877–1902 (2011)
20. Lacksonen, T.A.: Preprocessing for static and dynamic facility layout problems. Int. J. Prod. Res. **35**(4), 1095–1106 (1997)
21. Wang, M.J., Hu, M.H., Ku, M.Y.: A solution to the unequal area facilities layout problem by genetic algorithm. Comput. Ind. **56**(2), 207–220 (2005)
22. Drira, A., Pierreval, H., Hajri-Gabouj, S.: Facility layout problems: a survey. Annu. Rev. Control **31**(2), 255–267 (2007)
23. Moslemipour, G., Lee, T.S., Rilling, D.: A review of intelligent approaches for designing dynamic and robust layouts in flexible manufacturing systems. Int. J. Adv. Manuf. Technol. **60**, 11–27 (2011)
24. Raschke, R.L. David, J.S.: Business Process Agility Business Process Agility (2005)
25. Ganguly, A., Nilchiani, R., Farr, J.V.: Evaluating agility in corporate enterprises. Int. J. Prod. Econ. **118**(2), 410–423 (2009)
26. Bozorgi, N. Abedzadeh, M. Zeinali, M.: Tabu search heuristic for efficiency of dynamic facility layout problem. Int. J. Adv. Manuf. Technol. **77**, 689–703 (2014)
27. Wong, K.Y.: Applying ant system for solving unequal area facility layout problems. Eur. J. Oper. Res. **202**(3), 730–746 (2010)
28. Shahin, A., Poormostafa, M.: Facility layout simulation and optimization: an integration of advanced quality and decision making tools and techniques. Mod. Appl. Sci. **5**(4), 95 (2011)
29. McKendall, A.R., Hakobyan, A.: Heuristics for the dynamic facility layout problem with unequal-area departments. Eur. J. Oper. Res. **201**(1), 171–182 (2010)

Design Science and Business Models - Business Models in Hyperconnected Context

Business Models Based on Co-opetition in a Hyper-Connected Era: The Case of 5G-Enabled Smart Grids

Sara Moqaddamerad(✉), Yueqiang Xu, Marika Iivari, and Petri Ahokangas

Oulu Business School, University of Oulu, Pentti Kaiteran katu 1, 90014 Oulu, Finland
{Sara.Moqaddamerad,Yueqiang.Xu,Marika.Iivari,
Petri.Ahokangas}@oulu.fi

Abstract. This paper aims at introducing a new perspective on devising business models based on the logic of the networked and hyperconnected technological and business environment. The empirical data combines two technological areas: 5G and smart grids. The 5G technology provides rudimentary knowledge about how to create a networked infrastructure for ubiquitous, reliable, and high-speed connectivity. The outcome will enable the utilization of innovative and hyper-connected technologies in the smart grid sector. In the context of the smart grid, we apply a 4C-layered business model that builds on the functional logic of the commercialization of technologies in the 5G era. This eco-systemic business model illustrates how different actors interact in each layer, giving the possibility to identify existing and potential smart grid applications that could be enabled by 5G. We expanded hyperconnectivity into four dimensions, including hyper-connectability, hyper-memorisability, hyper-diffusibility, and hyper-scalability, through an empirical study that can further be developed for a stronger theoretical model of hyperconnectivity.

Keywords: Hyperconnectivity · Business models · Co-opetition · 5G · Smart grid

1 Introduction

Entering the era of information supported by big data, the Internet, digitalization, and information and communication technology (ICT) has deeply impacted human society [5, 17]. Consequently, the demand for technological advancement that can sustain all the kinds of services needed for people's lives is growing exponentially. To address this need, ICT's evolution created an integrated, fast-moving, ubiquitous, and hyperconnected world in which the temporal and spatial boundaries of doing business are vanishing through virtualization [1, 17].

Enabling ICT technologies have also facilitated many new opportunities in traditional industrial sectors [18, 21], such as utilities and energy, where smart grids have emerged as an "Energy Internet" [15, 29]. A smart grid can be defined as a two-way communication infrastructure of information and energy flows, allowing the integration of distributed energy resources, storage, consumption, and flexible demand [35].

H. Afsarmanesh et al. (Eds.): PRO-VE 2016, IFIP AICT 480, pp. 559–568, 2016.
DOI: 10.1007/978-3-319-45390-3_47

For these industrial energy players, the upcoming fifth generation of mobile networks (5G) is becoming a pivotal enabler for hyperconnectivity, as it aims to create more intelligent technologies and integrated networks with real-time control, lower latency, and a higher data rate [4]. Future 5G networks ought to enable innovative ways of connecting, sharing, and allocating infrastructure and other resources [23] that—together with the new smart grid platform and technologies—can open a myriad of new opportunities for businesses, consumers, and decision makers [15]. This highlights business modelling as a crucial part of integrated networks such as smart grids [29].

The use of an ecosystemic business model in the smart grid domain could unlock five main types of value across the energy industry and society: (1) economic value (i.e., value through avoiding unnecessary costs and investment in constructing excess generation capacity), (2) environmental value (i.e., value created by retiring the fossil fuel power plants and integrating renewables), (3) reliability value (i.e., value created by using next-generation communication technology to improve network reliability), (4) energy security value (i.e., value created by ramping up distributed generation to reduce reliance on depleting fossil fuel resources), and (5) engagement and interaction value (i.e., value created by enabling consumers and prosumers to actively participate in the energy market) [36].

On top of that, 5G networks should bear multiple services and integrate multiple technologies to fulfill a wide variety of demands, including user experience enhancement and rapid business development. It is expected that 5G will remove the barriers related to connectivity capacity (creating a wireless connected world) and network performance (information can be accessed smoothly and constantly), as well as to resource optimization (by intelligently and dynamically allocating the scare resources such as infrastructure and spectrum) [10].

In a hyperconnected context, absorbing and integrating others' resources leads to accelerating the development of new products, easy market access, and eventually to obtaining knowledge and resources that otherwise require strenuous effort and a heavy cost in order to be achieved without collaboration and sharing [13]. Conversely, the extent to which organizations have adapted to hyperconnectivity is limited [30, 31]. Additionally, most modern business model frameworks lack such a holistic perspective on interdependency in the industry [25]. Furthermore, within hyperconnected contexts, firms do not only cooperate and collaborate but also compete to gain advantage [7, 9], while the uncertainty, risk, and open competition that characterize the 5G business environment make sustaining competitive advantage problematic.

The advent of the smart grid can be seen as an evolutionary development from the traditional, centralized production and distribution energy system to a modern energy network that incorporates two-way, end-to-end communication and decentralized operations of generation, transmission, and distribution [38]. It is argued that when analyzing the transition of utility-led centralized energy systems to a distributed smart grid system, the traditional single-actor-focused business model conceptualizations and tools are not applicable [36]. This research gap is rarely studied in general business model literature, nor has it been addressed in hyperconnectivity studies. Based on this gap in current knowledge in empirical and theoretical studies, this study seeks to explore how hyperconnectivity within 5G-enabled smart grids affects business modelling in such a networked environment. Hence, this study specifically asks '*How can business models be applied in co-opetition-based value creation and capture in the context of a hyper-connected business ecosystem?*'

The study is organized as follows. First, the peculiarities of the hyperconnected business context are discussed. Then, the concept of a co-opetition-based business model approach is introduced. The last section presents our framework for a 5G-supported co-opetitive smart grid, with accompanying discussion and conclusions.

2 Background

2.1 The Context of Hyperconnectivity

Hyperconnectivity can be considered as the inclusion of people-to-machine and machine-to-machine communications, supporting the development of the IoT [32]. Hyperconnectivity is defined as a state of stimulus associated with the near-constant contact with others. They view the Internet, mobile technologies (such as smartphones), and increasingly ubiquitous electronic networks as the key enablers of hyperconnectivity [14]. The 5G networks aim at revolutionizing the quality and efficiency of hyperconnectivity by enabling higher frequencies, allowing greater device densities; providing greater bandwidths, and building the utmost base station and antennas which are highly integrative in comparison with the previous four generations [4].

The territory of hyper-connection expands in two dimensions: (1) hyper-memorisability, where all the information is stored in huge databases and is accessible anytime from anywhere, and (2) hyper-diffusibility, where all the thinking and thoughts can be massively reproduced, communicated and diffused in a network, without physical limits [17]. The combination of hyperconnectivity, and big data and analytics could empower economies in three key ways: through the ability to know, the ability to have dialogue, and the ability to innovate [22]. Thus, hyperconnectivity is the main factor of change [17], as it has the power to profoundly modify the network of interindividual relations and society as a whole [31].

2.2 Co-opetition-Based Business Models

Business models covey the logic and architecture of how economic value is created and captured [12]. As emphasized by [16], a business model entails the value proposition (i.e., products and services), customer relationship, and the network of partners as well as cost and revenue structure [40]. Exploiting the business potential of created innovations requires new organizational activities through which the resources are selected and arranged [27]. Indeed, firms should identify the ways of managing their resources beyond their current business model in order to respond to the challenges of today's turbulent business environment [11].

Therefore, firms should build up different and actually more complex but beneficial relationships where they simultaneously cooperate and compete with each other (i.e., create a co-opetitive business design). According to [7], as the need for acquiring external resources increases, those companies that hold a strong position in the industry will likely cooperate with their competitors and as a result will adopt a co-opetition strategy. This strategy leads to enhancing the dynamic development and competitive advantage of the firm since it can cooperate with one competitor while competing with another, or simultaneously cooperate and compete with the same partner [8, 9, 19].

A digital, hyperconnected economy creates a specific and unique form of value creation wherein the firm and its partners generate value for various users in the networked market [39]. The value proposition offered by companies in the era of 5G and hyperconnectivity is accessibility-based business models for peer-to-peer (P2P) markets. In virtual markets, value can be created through the novel integration of information, products, and services; an innovative transaction mechanism; and the recombination of resources, capabilities, and reshaping of the relationships among the partners, suppliers, and customers [2] within the value network regarding the focus, locus, and modus of activities [28]. This P2P collaboration results in sustainability and economic benefit since the resources can be obtained easily and cheaply.

The focus of innovative 5G business models, for instance, is to create and capture value and new pricing models through multi-partnerships [23]. Hence, the business model describes how a focal firm may tap into its value network or ecosystem in order to perform the activities that are necessary to fulfill the perceived customer needs as the business model focuses on the activities performed by the subset of actors within the focal firm's collaborative network [3]. This builds the theoretical foundations of business models for a hyperconnected 5G-enabled smart grid. Building on this theoretical understanding, the next section presents our research design and methodology.

3 Research Design and Methodology

This study adopts an action-based research methodology for data collection within two techno-social collective innovation projects: one studies the P2P technical and market design of smart grids as part of European Union–level energy innovation research, and the other one is a Finnish-American research cooperation on 5G networks and how they enables key sectors such as smart grids.

Referring to [6], an action research methodology in management science leads to producing scientific knowledge that can serve the action; it enables the formalization and contextualization of models and tools, leading to the production of new knowledge capable of facilitating organizational change. The action research approach was supported by stakeholder consultation, embodied through an ecosystem actor workshop organized in Finland in 2015. A stakeholder workshop can facilitate the process of identifying the underlying connections and tensions by creating conditions in which the participants can "*co-creatively meet their individual and collective needs*" [24]. This approach has been employed in a number of techno-economic researches, especially as described in energy and smart grid literature [20].

To analyze the smart grid business context, we apply a 4C-layered business model typology (which is appropriate for a 5G business environment) presented by [34]. The 4C typology classifies Internet age businesses through four basic prototypical business models, each with varying value propositions and revenue models [34]: connection, content, context, and commerce. The 4C framework was applied by [37] for spectrum sharing in the telecom industry. Due to having an ecosystemic feature, the 4C framework is suitable for the context of a smart grid and 5G. The underlying logic of this model suggests that the upper layers can be supported and enabled by lower layers, that value can be offered in multiple layers, and that different combinations of layers can be utilized for creating value propositions. In other words, the 4C model describes the structure of the ecosystem and how different layers and models can interact [37].

In the 5G-enabled smart grid context, the use of a 4C ecosystemic model gives a comprehensive view on how the value of smart grids and hyperconnectivity is created through collaborative, competitive, and co-opetitive activities. The layers are organized into four horizontals and four verticals. The horizontals start from the connection layer on the left and end in the commerce layer on the right. The connection layer, for instance, is described as the infrastructure of the business. The verticals cover four technological layers including infrastructure and hardware, platforms and data, equipment and devices (plus user interface), and applications and services, as proposed by [38]. This framework, shown in Fig. 1, is elaborated in the following section.

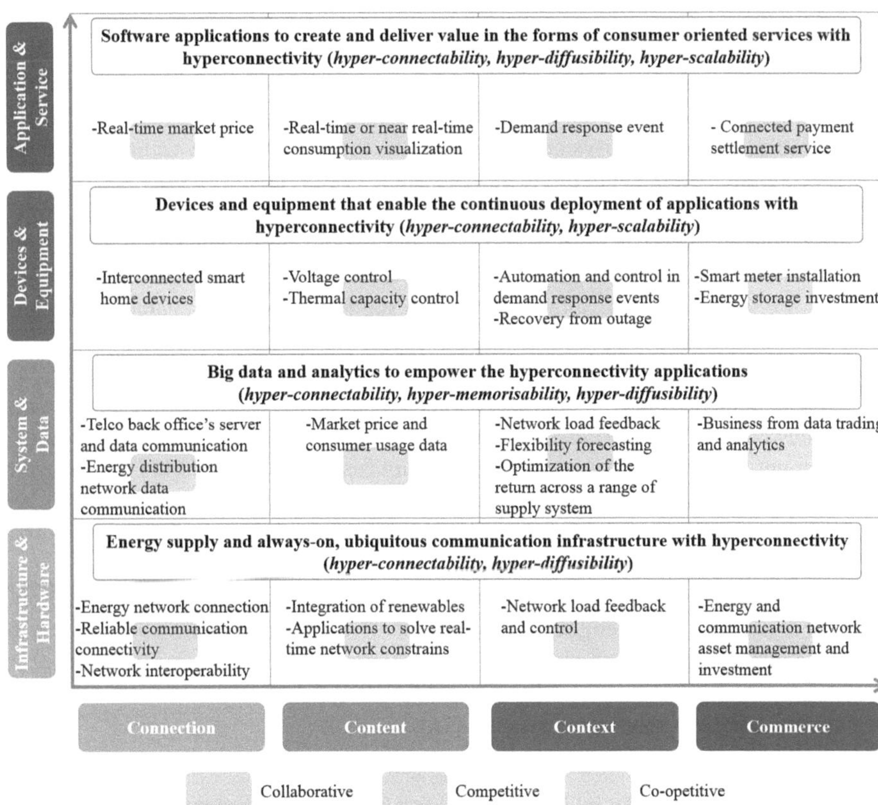

Fig. 1. The 4C ecosystemic business model for P2P smart grids.

4 Results

4.1 The Context of 5G and Smart Grid Projects

The aim of the 5G project is twofold: technology-wise it aims at investigating and improving the technologies related to spectrum and content sharing; and economics-wise it aims at creating transformative business models and regenerating the future market for mobile operators. Therefore, we attempt to design creative models that encapsulate both technology and business/economic performance. The assumption is that the success of 5G technological applications rests on the economic value that it brings for a wide variety of stakeholders—including content providers, regulatory agencies, service providers, and users—by enhancing the interaction among them. The experimental data has been collected from an ongoing joint Finnish-American project (JointMacs). In this paper, we applied the theoretical basis of the 5G networks derived from the literature, as well as the business model that we designed for the 5G ecosystem. Future smart grids require 5G-based infrastructure design to perform safely and efficiently; therefore, the same business model design that is applicable to 5G ecosystem is needed for the smart grids to create economic value.

For the smart grid context, this study utilizes data collected from 'P2P SmarTest', a European Horizon 2020 project researching a smarter P2P-based energy system integrated with 5G communication, regional markets, and innovative business models. This project builds upon an ecosystemic perspective, incorporating the technological and social-economic components of smart grids such as ICT for the energy sector, micro grids, and power system economics. The P2P concept proposed by this research project can find its applications in both large-scale distributed energy generation and smaller energy systems, such as micro grids. To develop a holistic view on the potential business models, services, and applications that can be supported by a 5G-enabled P2P smart grid, the ecosystemic business model was adopted.

A smart grid is one of the 5G-enabled energy use cases. Information brokerage for the content, context, and connection layers can be affected by 5G; besides, it provides continuous connectivity and lower latency. Smart generation and the application of a large amount of data are empowered by 5G; it builds a unified and flexible infrastructure to ensure the deployment of virtual network functions, technological performance, and a reliable communication solution for the services in smart grids. For instance, in urban areas 5G can provide dedicated communication for smart meters [33].

In spite of the value that can be created through a 5G-enabled smart grid, a number of barriers may pose challenges to the adoption of smart grids. These barriers can be classified into four groups: the lack of regulatory framework and open standards, technology and infrastructure immaturity, low public awareness and behavioral barriers, and commercial risks and market uncertainty [26].

4.2 The 4C Business Model Framework for 5G-Enabled Smart Grids

The role of an infrastructure business is to build and manage facilities for high-volume operations, such as maintaining data networks, back-office transactional services, and communications through a 5G network. The requirements of an infrastructure business are about the economics of scale, reliability, and security, thus 5G plays a critical enabling role. As ascending upwards along the smart grid technical layer in Fig. 1, there is a trend among the ecosystem actors to move from collaborative oriented activities to competitive activities. It is especially interesting to point out that although smart home device businesses are currently focusing on creating complementary value and service offerings, there is an emerging movement steering towards more co-opetitive and competitive directions as the market gets saturated.

The content layer presents concrete offerings provided by different parties, including power quality, renewable energy integration, grid control, and monitoring and consumption feedback, none of which would happen without a communication network with ultra-reliability and ultra-low latency to facilitate the safety, control, and monitoring aspects of wireless automation applications. Balancing energy supply and network constraints are the prime focus, and therefore the ecosystem needs to exhibit more collaborative behavior. However, as customer usage data is becoming crucial to the further development of smart grid services and applications, a high degree of competitive activities can be observed in this layer.

Moving beyond the content layer, contextual value is created and captured in the context layer. Flexibility is the key concern, this requiring hyperconnected actors and coordination of activities among the ecosystem stakeholders. When reaching the commerce layer, the data from P2P smart grid project depicts a high degree of competition along all the technological layers. However, it is noteworthy that the smart meter market shows more cooperative behavior. This is largely due to the adopted policy as in many countries (especially in the EU member states) smart meter rollout is mandated and driven by policies and regulations.

By looking at the 4C model as a whole, hyperconnectivity dimensions can be observed in the technological layers or horizons of the ecosystemic model. Clearly, hyper-connectability, enabled by 5G (as one of the key components of hyperconnectivity), has presence in all four technological layers of the smart grid. Hyper-memorisability and hyper-diffusibility are highly associated with how energy information is communicated, diffused, and stored in the data infrastructure in order to improve the distribution network-balancing capability of a smart grid as opposed to the traditional grid. At the same time, hyper-scalability plays a key role in the case of Automated Demand Response such as 'OpenADR', enabling highly scalable responses to network peak reduction events.

Overall, the smart grid ecosystemic model shows different dynamics across the layers, where the development of smart home devices, smart meter and storage installation, big data businesses, and renewable generation show a clear co-opetitive pattern. At a systemic level, the P2P smart grid as a whole can be seen as co-opetitive.

5 Conclusions

A critical understanding of hyperconnectivity and its implication for the new generation of business models is not possible without taking into account an ecosystemic perspective.

Assuming that hyperconnectivity is a fundamental aspect for the organization of networked industries. This study conducted an empirical investigation on the 5G-enabled smart grids in hyperconnectivity contexts. One theoretical contribution of the paper lies in the discovery of four dimensions of hyperconnectivity (hyper-connectability, hyper-memorisability, hyper-diffusibility, and hyper-scalability) through an empirical study that can serve as a starting point and overarching theme when developing a stronger theoretical model of hyperconnectivity. One of the practical implications of the study relates to the typological proposition of hyperconnectivity's four dimensions, which could support system design in various hyperconnectivity enabled domains, such as industrial internet and smart energy systems.

Hence, the research contributions of this work relate mainly to the literature on business models, smart grid innovation, and system design but they also have implications for the literature on business ecosystems and strategic management from a co-opetition perspective. One possible limitation is that the P2P SmarTest project could only evaluate 5G's potential in existing and known smart grid applications, thus the unforeseeable applications that might emerge cannot be covered in the project's scope.

Acknowledgments. The authors would like to acknowledge and thank the support of JointMacs, P2P SmarTest, TINTTI, and Core++ project consortiums.

References

1. Amer, A., Yahya, S., Jani, S.H., Sembilan, N., Khusus, D.: Research on hyper-connectivity element and its utilization in electronic channels marketing: a literature analysis. In: International Symposium on Management and Social Science (ISMSS) (2014)
2. Amit, R., Zott, C.: Value creation in e-business. Strateg. Manag. J. **22**, 493–520 (2001)
3. Amit, R., Zott, C.: Crafting business architecture: the antecedents of business model design. Strateg. Entrepreneurship J., 1–20 (2015). http://wileyonlinelibrary.com, doi:10.1002/sej.1200
4. Andrews, J.G., Buzzi, S., Choi, W., Hanly, S., Lozano, A., Soong, A.C.K., Zhang, J.C.: What will 5G be? IEEE J. Sel. Areas Commun. **32**(6), 1065–1082 (2014). doi:10.1109/JSAC.2014.2328098
5. Atzori, L., Iera, A., Morabito, G.: The internet of things: a survey. Comput. Netw. **54**, 2787–2805 (2010)
6. Bahari, N., Maniak, R., Fernandez, V.: Ecosystem business model design. In: XXIVe Conférence Internationale de Management Stratégique, pp. 1–18. AIMS, Paris (2015)
7. Bengtsson, M., Kock, S.: Co-opetition in business networks: to cooperate and compete simultaneously. Ind. Mark. Manag. **29**, 411–426 (2000)
8. Bengtsson, M., Eriksson, J., Wincent, J.: Co-opetition dynamics: an outline for further inquiry. Int. Bus. J. **20**(2), 194–214 (2010)
9. Brandenburger, A.M., Nalebuff, B.J.: Co-opetition. Currency/Doubleday, New York (1996)
10. Chen, M., Zhang, L.U., Taleb, T.: Cloud-based wireless network: virtualization, reconfigurable, smart wireless network to enable 5G technologies. Mob. Netw. Appl. **20**(6), 704–7012 (2015)
11. Chesbrough, H.W., Rosenbloom, R.S.: The role of the business model in capturing value from innovation: evidence from Xerox Corporation's technology spinoff companies. Ind. Corp. Change **11**(3), 529–555 (2002)

12. Chesbrough, H.: Business model innovation: opportunities and barriers. Long Range Plan. **43**(2–3), 354–363 (2010)
13. Chesbrough, H., Vanhaverbeke, W., West, J.: New Frontiers in Open Innovation. Oxford University, Oxford (2014)
14. Collins, P., Kolb, D.: Hyper-connectivity: how choice, response norms and technology do (and don't) matter. Acad. Manag. Proc. **2013**, 15245 (2013)
15. Cowan, K.R.: A new roadmapping technique for creatively managing the emerging smart grid. Creativity Innov. Manag. **22**(1), 67–83 (2013)
16. Dubosson-Torbay, M., Osterwalder, A., Pigneur, Y.: E-business model design, classification, and measurements. Thunderbird Int. Bus. Rev. **44**(1), 5–23 (2002)
17. Ganascia, J.-G.: Views and examples on hyper-connectivity. In: Floridi, L. (ed.) The Onlife Manifesto: Being Human in a Hyperconnected Era, pp. 65–85. Springer, Heidelberg (2015)
18. Glova, J., Sabol, T., Vajda, V.: Business models for the internet of things environment. Procedia Econ. Finan. **15**, 1122–1129 (2014)
19. Gnyawali, D.R., Park, B.J.: Co-opetition between giants: collaboration with competitors for technological innovation. Res. Policy **40**, 650–663 (2011)
20. Grunewald, P.H., Cockerill, T.T., Contestabile, M., Pearson, P.J.G.: The socio-technical transition of distributed electricity storage into future networks-system value and stakeholder views. Energy Policy **50**, 44–457 (2012)
21. Gubbi, J., Buyya, R., Marusic, S., Palaniswami, M.: Internet of Things (IoT): a vision, architectural elements, and future directions. Future Gener. Comput. Syst. **29**, 1645–1660 (2013)
22. Hagström, M., Gill, N.: The wisdom of the cloud: hyperconnectivity, big data, and real-time analytics. In: Dutta, S., Bilbao-Osorio, B. (eds.) The Global Information Technology Report 2012, pp. 97–103. World Economic Forum, Geneva (2012)
23. Hamari, J., Sjöklint, M., Ukkonen, A.: The sharing economy: why people participate in collaborative consumption. J. Assoc. Inf. Sci. Technol. (2015). doi:10.1002/asi.23552. http://ssrn.com/abstract=2271971
24. Holman, P., Devane, T., Cady, S., Adams, W.A.: The Change Handbook: The Definitive Resource on Today's Best Methods for Engaging Whole System. BerrettKoehler Publishers, San Francisco (2007)
25. Iivari, M., Ahokangas, P., Komi, M., Tihinen, M., Valtanen, K.: Toward ecosystemic business models in the context of industrial internet. J. Bus. Models **4**(2), 42–59 (2016)
26. Luthra, S., Kumar, S., Kharb, R., Ansari, M.F., Shimmi, S.L.: Adoption of smart grid technologies: an analysis of interactions among barriers. Renew. Sustain. Energy Rev. **33**, 554–565 (2014)
27. Noda, T., Collis, D.: The evolution of intra-industry firm heterogeneity: insight from a process study. Acad. Manag. J. **44**, 897–925 (2001)
28. Onetti, A., Zucchella, A., Jones, M.V., McDougall-Covin, P.P.: Internationalization, innovation and entrepreneurship: business models for new technology-based firms. J. Manag. Gov. **16**, 337–368 (2010)
29. Rohrbeck, R., Konnertz, L., Knab, S.: Collaborative business modeling for systemic and sustainability of innovations. Int. J. Technol. Manag. **63**(1/2), 4–23 (2013)
30. Sandulli, F., Chesbrough, H.: The Two Sides of Open Business Models. Available at SSRN (2009). http://dx.doi.org/10.2139/ssrn.1325682
31. The Economist: The Hyper-connected Economy: Phase 2 Hyper-connected Organizations, How Businesses Are Adapting to the Hyper-connected Age (2015)
32. The Global Information Technology Report: Living in a Hyperconnected World. World Economic Forum, Geneva (2012)

33. Thrybom, L., Kapovits, Á.: Eurescom: 5G and Energy. 5G–Infrastructure-Association. Version 1 (2015). www.5g-ppp.eu
34. Wirtz, B.W., Schilke, O., Ullrich, S.: Strategic development of business models: implications of the web 2.0 for creating value on the internet. Long Range Plan. **43**(2–3), 216–226 (2010)
35. Wolsink, M.: The research agenda on social acceptance of distributed generation in smart grids: renewable as common pool resources. Renew. Sustain. Energy Rev. **16**, 822–835 (2012)
36. Xu, Y., Kopsakangas-Savolainen, M., Ahokangas, P., Li, F.: Ecosystemic business model and value in the peer-to-peer smart grid. In: Global Energy Interconnection, pp. 858–871. Global Energy Interconnection, Beijing (2016)
37. Yrjölä, S., Ahokangas, P., Matinmikko, M.: Evaluation of recent spectrum sharing concepts from business model scalability point of view. In: IEEE DySPAN – Dynamic Spectrum Access Networks, Stockholm (2015)
38. Yu, Y., Yang, J., Chen, B.: The smart grids in china: a review. Energies **5**, 1321–1338 (2012)
39. Zott, C., Amit, R.: Business model design: an activity system perspective. Long Range Plan. **43**(2–3), 216–226 (2010)
40. Zott, C., Amit, R., Massa, L.: The business model: recent developments and future research. J. Manag. **37**(4), 1019–1042 (2011)

A Collaborative Decisional System to Support a Business Model for the Development of Charging Infrastructure

Giuseppe Ianniello[1,2,3], Michela Piccarozzi[1,2,3], Ilaria Baffo[1,2,3](✉), Giuseppe Stecca[1,2,3], and Pasquale Carotenuto[1,2,3]

[1] DEIM – Industrial Engineering School, University of Tuscia, Largo dell'Università snc, 01100 Viterbo, Italy
ilaria.baffo@unitus.it

[2] Istituto di Analisi dei Sistemi ed Informatica "Antonio Ruberti" (IASI), National Research Council (CNR), Via dei Taurini, 19, 00185 Rome, Italy

[3] Istituto per le Applicazioni del Calcolo "M. Picone"(IAC), National Research Council(CNR), Via dei Taurini, 19, 00185 Rome, Italy

Abstract. The obstacles to the E-Mobility (EM)'s development are widely discussed both in scientific and in industrial fields. Approaches to overcome these obstacles are still not consolidate. At the same time, it is not so clear, what Business Models (BM) are more sustainable for the owners of Charging Infrastructure (CI). With the aim to support the development of charging network (CN), the authors propose a new BM based on intelligent, collaborative and digital services for all actors of the value chain. The implementation of this BM starts with the development of a decisional structure (DS) and the sharing of data and information among all operators that are involved into the charging process. The main elements of the model are explained and the first results of implementation are given. Future development are discussed to enrich the research and to supply at industrial field a useful tool to face decisions in the real context of CNs.

Keywords: Collaborative business models · Service systems ICT oriented · Optimization · Decision support system

1 Introduction

The de-carbonisation of the transport sector is a priority goal of the whole European Commission (EC), that has been proved through several efforts, such as the Kyoto Protocol, the European plan on climate change (2009, 20-20-20 goals) and its related white papers. With respect to the targets imposed by the EC on the reduction of CO_2 emissions, especially in the transport sector, the development of electric vehicles represents an important key driver towards achieving the prefixed objectives. Despite the fact that the benefits related to the diffusion of EM in both urban and/or extra-urban contexts are well known, with reference to their environmental, social and economic impacts, the development of such a market still presents significant impediments, widely discussed in the scientific literature. In particular, the main obstacles are related to the long battery charging time, scepticism among potential end-users [3], high costs of electric cars with

H. Afsarmanesh et al. (Eds.): PRO-VE 2016, IFIP AICT 480, pp. 569–578, 2016.
DOI: 10.1007/978-3-319-45390-3_48

respect to traditional combustion engine vehicles [22] and, as here studied, the lack of a widespread, accessible and homogeneous recharge infrastructure. The objective of this work is to create a digital and collaborative system to support the decisional processes for the development of new BM for charging services at national and international level.

Adopting the point of view of [13], this article does not claim to deliver detailed solutions for all the decisions on different business levels. Rather, it aims to create a structured approach, which can be used as decision support when developing of BM for the owners of charging stations. Today the decision to invest into this sector is limited by a too high degree of uncertainty with respect to demand of users, the payback time and the profitability linked with the CI. For this reason, the authors here propose a structured BM based on an engineering approach able to reduce this degree of uncertainty and to support the development of intelligent and collaborative CNs. The assumptions made in this work could support the creation of a new BM based on digital services for CIs. This kind of offering, nowadays represents an innovation for the global market and could help the investors to create a "Blue Ocean" in the field of e-stations. The remainder of the paper is so structured: Sect. 2 explores the most recent scientific contributions on EM field from point of view of developed BM and implemented DS. Section 3 explains in detail the proposed BM based on three levels of DS. Finally, conclusions and future works suggested.

2 Literature Review

Hybrid Electric Vehicle (HEV) and full Electric Vehicle (EV) have been developed rapidly in the last years in order to counteract the CO_2 emissions and the liveability of crowded and polluted urban areas. The great part of efforts made into industrial and scientific field to support this development are linked to technological aspects of sector, first of all on battery durations. Unfortunately, these efforts have been not sufficient to overcome all obstacles to the development of the EM. Only recently, researchers and managers are developing the fundamental elements aimed at supporting the EM sector's progression. Among them the lack of a homogenous CI represents the main problem still un-solved in some European countries. But why there aren't enough investors for this market? For the authors of this work the reasons are to be found in: (*i*) degree of uncertainty on real demand of charging during the next five years, (*ii*) lack of new BM for the investors; (*iii*) lack of decision support systems to manage the CN. Strategies aimed to contrast the aforementioned points, will result in more profitable BM for EM.

The two following paragraphs reassume the collected scientific contributions in this field. In particular, the cited works highlight the steps made forward and the questions still open from both industrial and scientific point of view. Among them, particular emphasis is given to gaps, above mentioned, for the development of CIs.

2.1 Business Model for E-Mobility Market

The uncertainty, regarding the development of EM sector, creates obstacles about the decision of how to enter and how to manage a profitable business for this market.

Car manufacturers, batteries producers, utilities, charging services providers, oil and gas companies, public authorities at national and international level, are among the potential players involved in the process of developing the culture of EM that ultimately pertains to car drivers. Some previous research on the perspective of car manufactures [10] and charging service providers [11] show that different approaches can be implemented for managing a business linked to EM. For this reason, the role of BM is a key element in exploring the business possibilities stemming from the EM field. In general, the relevance of BM as public information in annual reports published by corporations is a topic of emergent interest [12].

In a context where a continuous evolving technology allows for a lower cost of information to find customer solutions, innovative companies need to think about their role in capturing value in providing new products or services, satisfying customers need and if possible with benefits for the society at large. For this reason, a BM and a Decision Support Tool (DSS) may provide support for business pioneers in this field. "A business model articulates the logic and provides data and other evidence that demonstrates how a business creates and delivers value to customers. It also outlines the architecture of revenues, costs, and profits associated with the business enterprise delivering that value [23]. From this definition, we can draw different elements. The starting point is the product or service with specific technological features to deliver to customers. The second element is the benefits to the customers, and if possible to the society at large, stemming from using the product/service. The third element is the market where to sell the product/service. The 4th element is the possible revenues configuration in connections with the costs structure of a business entity, and as a consequence the design of a mechanism able to capture value. In a definition, "a business model defines how the enterprise creates and delivers value to customers, and then converts payments received to profits [23].

The lack of a generally accepted theoretical background for BMs in economic theory drives researchers toward methodology based on case studies often involving a multidisciplinary approach. Contributions devoted to EM and BMs come from different areas: economics, business administration, accounting, engineering, environmental sciences. The effort is made for defining the main components and operating procedures for this business area. For example, [5] analyses the opportunity to implement a specific BM related to the question of "range anxiety" and battery pack charging in Denmark.

Authors in [1] attempts to generate BM innovations in the field of EM, using the idea of systematically combining five dimensions of the values concept (often a key concept in any BM). This approach is expression of a need to explore new patterns in an innovative business field. [1] underlines that BM patterns such as disintermediation, product-to-service, and leasing have been already implemented in the automotive industry. Some of them, for example car sharing (product-to-service BM) may get additional boost in the context of EM. In designing BMs in the field of EM, it seems there is space for different players, such as car manufactures and service providers. In this context of uncertainty, there is a need for simulation "in order to identify the most suitable model from the perspective of the actors involved in the automotive network. This often represents an academic exercise. Certainly, the simulation cannot be carried out without making assumptions about the BMs of the other players, the development of the market for EM, and the dynamics of technology development. In addition, as in the near future we will have a situation, in which conventional, hybrid and electric cars are co-existing, it is very important to think of transition scenarios that consider these patterns of technologies." [1].

The need to use simulation with the DSS tool stems from the idea that the typical BM described by some authors [2, 14, 25] largely used for combustion engine vehicles, cannot be transferred to EM concepts because of technological restrictions. For this reason, an effort is required to explore BMs for EM, trying to understand which of the classic BM components are needed and what factors must be integrated.

BMs in the EM field are also influenced by regulation at national and international level regarding the distribution grid, the standardization of CIs, the localization and the quantity of charging points/stations. Therefore, new mobility concepts and BMs should be integrated in the regulatory framework and public policy for transforming the technological advantages of electric vehicles (EV) into value added for the customers [13]. A key point in solving this problem is the way (and where) energy is delivered to EV drivers, since this decision may create space for new agents. Authors in [19] discuss the role played by the "EV supplier-aggregator" considered a competitive business as other trading activities in the market, selling electricity to EV owner. What kind of charging technology and where to locate charging points are relevant elements in designing a BM in the EM field?

2.2 Location Problems Modelling and Algorithms

Despite the problem of location of stations for charging is widely discussed in the scientific literature, there is a gap of useful tools for this specific aim and where present, often they are too complex to become efficient solutions in a business context. Traditionally, discrete location problems deal with the decision about which site(s) select for opening or establishing facilities able to serve commodities to satisfying a given demand, with the goal to minimize fixed installation and variable (transportation) costs. Discrete location problems are usually modelled using graphs and integer programming. Even simplest classes of discrete location problems such as the un-capacitated facility location problem (UFLP) are proven to have exponential complexity (UFLP is NP-Complete), although several efficient solution procedures can be found in literature [15]. Facility location problems are applied to a wide range of disciplines such as location of plants, telecommunication networks, rescue facilities [21], and so on. Recently, a growing trend can be observed where facility location problems are applied to the optimization of green logistics and sustainable mobility. [7] surveys the peculiarities of network design for plug-in hybrid electric vehicles (PHEV). According to the authors, the most important characterizing features of PHEV to be considered in network design are: the driving patterns, the charging characteristics, the number of vehicles on the network. A critical factor is the stochastic behaviour of the system. [24] proposes an integer formulation for location of recharging stations to serve electric scooters, considering constrains related to the charging time. [25] uses a simulation and optimization based technique to define optimal location of charging stations for private owned electric vehicles. The work in [9] compares different location models and considers institutional requirements for charging stations network design in an application case of Bejing, China. In [27] the location problem for charging station is expanded to consider the capacity of each station with the aim to design the number of recharging station in each facility. The surveyed literature shows a growing coverage of location problems considering more and more the particularities of electric mobility as an integration of the classical facility problem. In most of the surveyed works, the problem instances are not too big and standard commercial solvers adopting branch and bound based algorithm is used.

3 The Collaborative and Digital Decisional System to Support a New Business Model for the Development of Charging Infrastructure

The proposed collaborative and digital DS for supporting the creation of a new BM for the development of CNs, is able to support the owners, managers and operators on three decisional level: strategic, tactical and operative. The authors propose to face the uncertainty of persons that invest into infrastructure of charging into three different layers corresponding with three different decision makers or three different roles into the value chain. At the same time, the flow of the business is divided into five steps, at each one

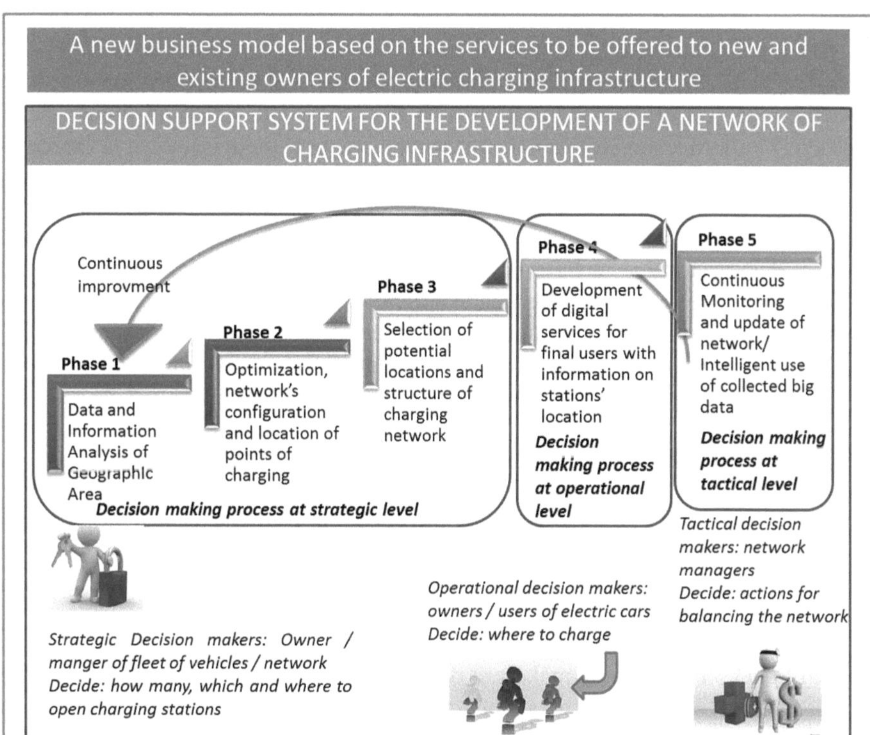

Fig. 1. Proposed structure for new BM based on decisional process system

a digital service has to be implemented and a collaborative procedure has to be developed for the sharing of information and data. The business idea is based on the offer of a set of digital services able to support the decision making process, under explained, at different levels. The framework is sketched in Fig. 1 and detailed in the following.

Strategic Level. The decision maker at this level is usually the owner or the manager of fleet of areas for position of stations, vehicles or of commercial distribution chain, or of fuel stations. Typically, he can decide how many, which and where to open charging stations. These decisions fall back into the classification of strategic decisions as they involve an amount of resources and time that cannot be changed in easy way and in fast manner. The proposed BM offers for this kind of actors a decision support system including 3 phases corresponding to actions to develop:

Phase 1: Collection of data and information about the geographic area object of analysis. For example, thanks to this action the decision maker collects data as traffic information, proximity of Point of Interests (PoIs), proximity of parking, proximity of other charging stations, behaviours of potential users, et others;

Phase 2: During this phase, a feasibility analysis is performed. At this point of decisional process, the decision maker makes a selection of potential sites for the installation of charging station. This action is important to discard unrealizable projects and to focus the efforts towards objectives more achievable.

Phase 3: On basis of acquired data, this action puts in place an optimization process to select the best network's configuration with the location of charging points. In the proposed DS, this decision is taken thanks to mathematical models known in Operation Research and their relative implementation.

Operational Level. The decision makers at this level are the operators, the owners or drivers of electric cars that, on basis of digital supplied services, they decide where going to charge their electric vehicle. These decisions fall back into the classification of operational decisions as they involve an amount of limited economic resources and limited time. The decision can be changed abruptly without involving great amount of resources and time. At this level one activity or phase has to be developed:

Phase 4: In this phase the proposed BM foresees the development of digital services for final users thank to information on location of charging stations. This kind of services includes the possibility to book charging, direct the car to the nearest station, receive the invoice of recharges and others. This process can be monitored and checked at the same time by the owner of the network such as by the final user, thanks to sharing of data-base for single client.

Tactical Level. The decision makers at this level are the directors of the network that on basis of users' behaviours can adopt actions for balancing the network applying for example strategies of marketing or pricing. These decisions fall back into the classification of tactical decisions as they involve an amount of resources that can be changed in a medium term horizon. For this level one phase has to been implemented:

Phase 5: The last phase of proposed structure is relative to monitoring and update of CN. Moreover, an intelligent use of collected big data is desirable to enrich the availability of data relative to e-mobility sector. Thanks to elaboration of these data the managers, the directors and the operators can adopt decision more efficient thank to a continue set of updated data. The framework underline the importance for the BM, of the use of hyper-connected data along all the decisional phases for all the decision makers which have to coordinate in order to execute the process. The study presented in this paper presents the preliminary steps for the creation of this DS for development of a new BM able to support the increase of CI at national and international level. In particular, the following paragraph describe implementation details both with respect to BM and to respect to the phase 1 and 2 of DS.

3.1 Elements for Designing a New Business Model

The literature put in evidence as many authors agree that the elements on which BMs for EM are based are: vehicles, their autonomy and batteries [6]; CI [4, 13]; System integration of EV into the energy system [4, 8]. The market of digital services for the managing of charging process is not yet sufficiently developed, especially regarding the CIs. For them, key elements are the accessibility to the charging stations, the type of connection and the communications links [13]. Efficient combinations of these variables can be numerous. The charging stations can be public, private or semi-public, and can have different recharging speed. Moreover, the type of connection can be unidirectional, which can only deliver power in one direction, or bidirectional, which transmit electricity in both directions. Infrastructure maturity and connected services increase the efficiency and operation of the model, so we can consider also the power connection, the information flow, the type of operator and the type of billing. Others services that have to been developed are related to drive the car to the nearest station on basis of traffic information and charge information. To do it, the shortest path algorithm that characterizes many navigators has to consider not only the distance of the route but also the need charge to reach the destination. Moreover, the users should have the possibility to booking the charge and to have real-time information on the status of station. Thanks to this kind of managing of the charging process, monitored and checked by a shared database, will be possible in few time to create also ad hoc services for specific kind of clients. From this consideration, the owners of CN could implement a different pricing policy for users and a set of marketing strategies able to increase the demand of charging in shortly time. Shifting the focus, from the technological problems to management and commercial ones, it will allow to move the efforts toward projects today more needed such as: (*i*) the development of communication plans; (*ii*) dissemination of information on incentives for the use of EV; (*iii*) the implementation of services that enable the accessibility to charging points; (*iv*) the definition of pricing policy cheaper respect to traditional fuel; (*v*) the introduction of strategies for the storage/production of energy with renewable sources, and of procedures for an intelligent use of energy on the line (smart grid technologies); (vi) the production of a continue flow of information for the mangers and the clients/users. The combination of these smart and digital solutions could be the turning point for the crossing of obstacles to changing from traditional car to electric car. Thanks to the proposed DS structure will be possible to create a data base and a set of collaborative procedure to create and to manage the CN in intelligent and digital way. As consequence, the manager could propose a set of commercial offers for each users and check the profitable of each action made, improving continuously its business implementation. In the following paragraph the phase 1 and 2 of DS are explained in details and discussed.

3.2 Proposed Optimization Tool for the Positioning of Charging Stations

Traditionally, location problems are used to decide where and which plants to open in order to satisfy a given demand localized into a geographical area. The decision maker, on the basis of a preliminary analysis, selects a set of potential sites to activate. In the same way, the owner or manager of the CN collects data and information on geographical area where he has interest to put in place a set of CIs (**Phase 1**). During the **Phase 2**, the information on demands of charging, traffic information, presence of competitors, are elaborated and inserted as input into the mathematical model such as proposed by [17, 20]. The optimization model has been designed and implemented considering: (*i*) The as-is scenario coming from mapping the location of existing charging stations; (*ii*) Charging demands; (*iii*) Electricity network loads or the possibility to power the charging station from renewable energy sources; (*iv*) Availability of areas in order to mark them as potential sites for charging-stations. A first release of the described decisional tool for the charging-stations positioning has been successfully implemented for the city of Viterbo, a small town of 65,000 citizens localized in the centre of Italy. The demand of electric charging has been estimated on the busiest streets of the city, estimating a number of EV equal to 1 % of vehicles on the road. The potential locations have been selected on the basis of market's needs, with an estimation of 20 available potential location sites, such as: (*i*) Parking of shopping centres; (*ii*) Parking of schools, universities, courts, town hall etc.; (*iii*) Parking for mobility interchange (rail, metro, bus); (*iv*) Fuel stations located on the routes to entry at the city. On the basis of the estimated demand and of the potential sites where to install a charging station, the tool returns the best solution in terms of number of stations and their locations. In the implemented test, 11 has been the exact number of infrastructures needed to satisfy the demand of charging. The problem has been modelled and solved at its optimality by using the Cplex® solver, considering several variants of the model depending for example from budget, from number of stations, or from maximum distance between each customer respect to the charging station. For brevity of discussion complete test results are omitted; a set of 20 tests have been carried out for each type of proposed model, while the solver returned in a few seconds the optimal solution to the problem.

4 Conclusion

Currently, the offer of ICT services for e-mobility is lower of its demand and collaborative and integrated solutions are lacking. The authors believe that moving the attention from technological point of view toward managerial one, may help the e-mobility market to explode in the short term. For helping in this aim, they propose in this work a new BM based on a three level DS for the development of CIs and their relative integrated digital services. The paper focused in particular on detailing the first two steps of the framework. The authors are actually working on the other phases proposing intelligent approaches for the problem solving procedures for each actors of the value chain. As last step, when the data base will be built and the collaborative procedure defined, the authors could build the BM based on structured DS and on available information coming from data warehouse. In future works, the authors want to put in evidence the great potentiality offered by the proposed model, enriching it of new algorithms and new models able to increase the ability to create/incentive charging demand and to manage in a profitable way the charging process.

Acknowledgments. The authors would like to thank Spin8, an Italian spin off and e-mobility provider, born with the aim to create business solutions in this field. The company is supporting researches for the development of recharge infrastructure and ICT services for users. In particular, Karin Fischer (CEO of Spin8), Prof. Stefano Ubertini and Prof. Fabrizio Rossi (Tuscia University) that have encouraged this work.

References

1. Abdelkafi, N., Makhotin, S., Posselt, T.: Business model innovations for electric mobility – what can be learned from existing business model patterns? Int. J. Innov. Manag. **17**(1), 1–41 (2013)
2. Afuah, A.: Business Models: A Strategic Management Approach. McGraw-Hill/Irwin, Boston (2004)
3. Brooker, A., Thornton, M., Rugh, J.: Technology improvement pathways to cost-effective vehicle electrification: preprint (2010)
4. Brown, S., Pyke, D., Steenhof, P.: Electric vehicles: the role and importance of standards in an emerging market. Energy Policy **38**(7), 3797–3806 (2010)
5. Christensen, T.B., Wells, P., Cipcigan, L.: Can innovative business models overcome resistance to electric vehicles? Better place and battery electric cars in Denmark. Energy Policy **48**, 498–505 (2012)
6. Delucchi, M.: An analysis of the retail and life cycle cost of battery-powered electric vehicles. Transp. Res. Part D: Transp. Environ. **6**(6), 371–404 (2011)
7. Green, R.C., Wang, L., Alam, M.: The impact of plug-in hybrid electric vehicles on distribution networks: a review and outlook. Renew. Sustain. Energy Rev. **15**(1), 544–553 (2011)
8. Guille, C., Gross, G.: A conceptual framework for the vehicle-to-grid (V2G) implementation. Energy Policy **37**(11), 4379–4390 (2009)

9. He, S.Y., Kuo, Y.H., Wu, D.: Incorporating institutional and spatial factors in the selection of the optimal locations of public electric vehicle charging facilities: a case study of Beijing, China. Transp. Res. Part C: Emerg. Technol. **67**, 131–148 (2016)
10. Ianniello, G., Piccarozzi, M., Rossi, F.: La Mobilità Elettrica negli Annual Report delle Aziende Automobilistiche: Rischi, Strategie e Ambiente, working paper (2015). https://www.spin8.eu/wp-content/uploads/EMobility-Annual-report_wp_2015.pdf. Accessed 6 Apr 2016
11. Ianniello, G., Piccarozzi, M., Stefanoni, A.: The role of charging service provider to support electric mobility, in atti del XXVII Congresso Nazionale di Scienze Merceologiche "Qualità & Innovazione per una economia circolare ed un futuro sostenibile" Viterbo 2 – 4 March (2016). ISBN 978 88 941647 0 1
12. ICAEW, 2010. Business Models in Accounting: The theory of the firm and financial reporting, Institute of Chartered Accountants of England and Wales (2016). http://ssrn.com/abstract=2335875. Accessed 6 Apr 2016
13. Kley, F., Lerch, C., Dallinger, D.: New business models for electric cars - a holistic approach. Energy Policy **39**(6), 3392–3403 (2011). ISSN 0301-4215
14. Matzen, D., Ronald, A., Andreasen, M.M.: Product/service-systems: proposal for models and terminology. Technical report, Neukirchen (2005)
15. Mirchandani, P.B., Francis, R.L.: Discrete Location Theory. Wiley, Hoboken (1990)
16. Osterwalder, A., Pigneur, Y.: Creare Modelli di Business. Edizioni FAG Milano, Assago (2010)
17. Revelle, C.S., Laporte, G.: The plant location problem: new models and research prospects. Oper. Res. **44**(6), 864–874 (1996)
18. Rezania, R., Prüggler, W.: Business models for the integration of electric vehicles into the Austrian energy system. In: 2012 9th International Conference on the European Energy Market (EEM), pp. 1–8. IEEE (2012)
19. San Roman, T.G., Momber, I., Abbad, M.R., Miralles, A.S.: Regulatory framework and business models for charging plug-in electric vehicles: infrastructure, agents, and commercial relationships. Energy Policy **39**, 6360–6375 (2011)
20. Silva, F.J.F., De la Figuera, D.S.: A capacitated facility location problem with constrained backlogging probabilities. Int. J. Prod. Res. **45**(21), 5117–5134 (2007)
21. Stecca, G., Puliafito, A., Simonetti, M., Mariotta, G., Sciuto, P.: A cloud-based system to protect against industrial multi-risk events. Procedia CIRP **41**, 650–654 (2016)
22. Tate, E.D., Harpster, M.O., Savagian, P.J.: The Electrification of the Automobile: From Conventional Hybrid, to Plug-In Hybrids, to Extended-Range Electric Vehicles. SAE International, Warrendale (2008)
23. Teece, D.J.: Business models, business strategy and innovation. Long Range Plann. **43**(2–3), 172–194 (2010)
24. Wang, Y.W.: An optimal location choice model for recreation-oriented scooter recharge stations. Transp. Res. Part D: Transp. Environ. **12**(3), 231–237 (2007)
25. Wise, R., Baumgartner, P.: Godownstream—the new profit imperative in manufacturing. Harvard Bus. Rev. **77**(5), 133–141 (1999)
26. Xi, X., Sioshansi, R., Marano, V.: Simulation–optimization model for location of a public electric vehicle charging infrastructure. Transp. Res. Part D: Transp. Environ. **22**, 60–69 (2013)
27. Zhu, Z.H., Gao, Z.Y., Zheng, J.F., Du, H.M.: Charging station location problem of plug-in electric vehicles. J. Transp. Geogr. **52**, 11–22 (2016)

Business Model Boutique: A Prêt-à-Porter Solution for Business Model Innovation in SMEs

Sander Smit[1], Garyfallos Fragidis[2], Siegfried Handschuh[3], and Adamantios Koumpis[3(✉)]

[1] BM-Change, 5081 CS Hilvarenbeek, The Netherlands
sander@bm-change.nu
[2] Institute of Service Science, University of Geneva, 1227 Carouge, Switzerland
garyf@teicm.gr
[3] Fakultät für Informatik und Mathematik, Universität Passau, 94032 Passau, Germany
{siegfried.handschuh,adamantios.koumpis}@uni-passau.de

Abstract. We introduce the concept of a Business Model Boutique as a means to support business model innovation in SMEs for the improvement of their competitiveness and growth. The Business Model Boutique aims to support the improvement of the competiveness of SME's by increasing their awareness and knowledge of business modelling techniques and business model innovation concepts and by facilitating their business model innovation processes. Finally, we present empirical results from an application of our approach for the case of a new generation of Rollators to help older people cope with challenges of everyday life and mobility in urban areas.

Keywords: Business model innovation · Business Model Canvas · Small and medium-sized enterprises (SMEs) · Entrepreneurship · Value co-creation · Conceptual modelling

1 Introduction

The role of SMEs in economic growth is critical (European Commission 2013). In Europe, 99.8 % of the 20 million enterprises are SME's. Together they employ 86.8 million people, which represents 66.5 % off all European jobs, while 80 % of new jobs are created by SME's (European Commission 2014). The recovery of the European economy is largely based on the growth of SME's. The development, management and growth of an SME is much more difficult than it may seem from a distance. Some major difficulties that entrepreneurs face when they execute their business are related to the urgent need for adaptability to a fast changing environment, the lack of guidelines for the implementation of changes, the lack of knowledge and processes for the adaption or the transformation of their business model, and the lack of resources to keep up with the state-of-the art in business model innovation (Schneider 2011).

However, current approaches and tools for business modeling and business model innovation operate mainly on a conceptual level and they often fail to reach the practical

H. Afsarmanesh et al. (Eds.): PRO-VE 2016, IFIP AICT 480, pp. 579–587, 2016.
DOI: 10.1007/978-3-319-45390-3_49

needs of SME's, the workaday circumstances and the concrete challenges they face. In particular, many business model frameworks leave out a great part of idiosyncratic factors and parameters that are crucial for a successful implementation. As a result, they are seen again as having only theoretical value, but impractical and irrelevant to the needs of SME's. In general, the lack of knowledge and awareness on business model innovation and the lack of validated and targeted information, tools and processes for successfully innovating one's business model causes sub-optimal growth of SME's. The result is companies that are not as responsive and as successful as they could be and inertia, inability to exploit opportunities or even failures and unnecessary bankruptcies, which entails loss of capital, productive resources and jobs. In this paper we present the concept of the a 'Business Model Boutique' as a place that entrepreneurs can find a variety of services and tools that can be used for successfully conceiving and transforming their business models to keep them current, relevant to the competition and responsive to the emerging trends and challenges.

In an age characterised by hyperconnectivity, SMEs that exhibit reduced access to financial, human and knowledge resources are finding themselves with a relatively low or no barriers to innovate in terms of changing their business models, risking synergies and cross-overs in areas that haven't yet been explored or areas that they may have traditionally been considered as out of scope for their existing core business profile.

The Business Model Boutique aims to support the improvement of the competiveness of SME's by increasing their awareness and knowledge of business modelling techniques and business model innovation concepts and by facilitating in general their business model innovation processes. In this respect, the aim of the Business Model Boutique is to help SME's to adapt and innovate their business model in a timely and effective way. The research approach is based on the concepts of user-centred service design and context mapping, ensuring that the needs and demands of business owners are properly addressed in the development of the business modelling concepts, the support services and the tools. The concept of organisational lifecycle is used for the development of adjusted strategic services for the business model innovation of SMEs.

1.1 Business Model Innovation by SMEs: Mission Impossible

There are many business support initiatives available for companies in many countries, most of which aim to stimulate entrepreneurship and start-ups and put an emphasis to the growth of SMEs. However, research in 10 European regions shows that effective business support services are lacking, with most stakeholders stating that there is insufficient availability of effective services in their region (Probst 2013). A wide range of methods and tools is used in these business support initiatives. The latest generation of tools use design principles, experimentation, visualisation and lean methodologies as described in (Amit 2011). And while there has been 'published a lot of scientific and practical contributions to business model innovation literature' which should have been considered in the present paper as one of our anonymous reviewers has stated, there are not sufficient transitions from a theoretical concept to a computer-based implementation that would facilitate wide uptake of the methodology by an audience of adopters that might be (some of them) willingly ignorant of the intrinsics of the methodology, however extremely convinced to use it in case there would be evidence of positive prior usage. Throughout the world, experiments are being held with this more creative and explorative way of re-organizing existing business and start-up new business (Ries 2011). Many of these tools are proprietary and developed within consultancy companies, but many free alternatives are available. Table 1 summarizes some of the most influential methods and tools for the support of in the business initiatives.

Table 1. Overview of existing business model innovation tools and methods.

Method	Origin	Remarks
Business Model Canvas (Osterwalder 2010)	Osterwalder	Creative commons
Value proposition canvas (Osterwalder 2004)	Osterwalder	Creative commons
St. Gallen Business Model Navigator (Gassman 2013)	St. Gallen Univ.	Proprietary
Business Model Diamond/STOF (Bouwman 2012)	Novay	Proprietary
4I-Framwork (Frankenberger 2013)	St. Gallen Univ.	Method
Fluidminds way to business model innovation (Fluidminds, 2014)	Fluidminds	Method, free templates
Business model brainstorm kit (BOA 2013)	Board of Innovat.	Board game, free e-version
BMA Elements/BMA Buildng Site (BMA 2013)	Busin Mod Archit	Board game

2 The Business Model Boutique Concept and Services

The Business Model Boutique is the place that entrepreneurs visit to find a variety of tailored-made solutions about business model innovation that can be used for successfully conceiving and transforming their business models to keep them current, relevant to the competition and responsive to the emerging trends and challenges. The entrepreneurs who come to the Business Model Boutique can choose tools and services or further adjust them to their specific needs. The solutions offered are tailored to the specific needs and the profile of certain types of entrepreneurs/companies with the use of a user-centred approach and co-design processes with a target group of entrepreneurs. The Business Model Boutique is supported in its operation by the Business Model Research Lab, which captures, stores and analyses business models and business model transformations. To be able to identify the key success factors of a specific business model, information about its operational context in which it was deployed, will also be captured, stored and analysed. The Business Model Boutique is envisaged to provide the following services:

- Business modelling: the development of business models as visual representations.
- Business model innovation: the development of improved business models, with input from user requirement, business model patterns and other methodological patterns.

- Value proposition analysis: analysis of the value proposition and its relationship with the customer and the other elements of the business model (e.g. to identify opportunities or inconsistencies).
- Sensitivity analysis: analysis of the impact of trends and events on the business model.
- Business ecosystem analysis: analysis of the impact of the evolutionary patterns of business ecosystem on specific business models.
- Business model transformation analysis: analysis of the requirements of the transformation process from an existing business model to a new one.

A variety of tools will be necessary to support the delivery of services and solutions provided by the Business Model Boutique. For instance, business modelling will require a manual for explaining the concept of business modelling and applications and tools for helping business owners understand, describe and represent their business model. Or the analysis of value proposition will require tools that support business owners to anticipate on changing customer needs and demands, and determine the impact on their business model. A business game will also serve reconsidering and better understanding one's business model, as well as developing and experimenting with new business models or business ideas. First of all, it will enable the business owners to learn or get deeper in the concepts and methods of business modelling. The most typical example of services provided through the Business Model Boutique is the improvement of an existing business model, for instance as a result of the development of new trends in the environment or the emergence of new technologies. The service process is envisaged as such:

1. The user begins with the description of the different aspects of his/her business, which ends with the depiction of the existing business model.
2. Next, the user may proceed with the analysis of the value proposition of the business model, to identify opportunities or inconsistencies, and sensitivity analysis, to estimate the impact of new trends and events.
3. Based on this, an improved business model is developed, analysed and enhanced with the use of different concepts and tools that will be developed in the Business Model Boutique.
4. At the end a business model transition path can be developed that will guide the business transformation process.

In general, business owners need to learn when to use business model innovation as a tool for improving the performance of their organisation. The time to invest is when an organisation is impacted by a game-changing event such as new customer needs or expectations, the approaching of a new, different market, some unexpected significant economic downturn, a new business owner with different ideas or a changing competitor landscape. Such events can be mapped on the different phases of an organisational lifecycle. The service concepts developed within Business Model Boutique address the different phases as well as the level of awareness of the business owner.

2.1 Practical Aims and Application Potential

With the Business Model Boutique we aim to bring together business model analysis with business model innovation methods. Business Model boutique aspires to democratise the access to business model innovation support tools and methods further and develop services that teach entrepreneurs how to work with and how to apply existing methods and tools. Business Model Boutique will elaborate on that and develop tools that are easy and fun to use and visually appealing. In areas where no free tools are available, Business Model Boutique will develop tools that are easy and fun to use and visually attractive. In Table 2 below we outline the current problems for entrepreneurs and SMEs, the existing tools and services to overcome these problems and the Business Model Boutique approach, which aspires to develop a next generation of tools and services for the support of business model innovation.

Table 2. Problems, offerings and the Business Model Boutique ambition.

Problems	Current offering	Business Model Boutique's ambition
Entrepreneurs, pre-starters and independent professionals: - Operate individually - Are looking for funding - Focus on product and service innovation - Are looking for partners - Lack education in business strategy and innovation - Need to adapt faster to a changing business environment	- Awareness meetings and information sessions for pre-starters - Coaching - Network meetings, business clubs - Courses and training in class teaching - Consulting services from experts	- Provide tools and learning material for understanding and using business model innovation - Develop or adapt tools that show the relation between one's business model and its operational context - Develop or adapt business model innovation tools that link to issues specific for the phase the organisation is in. - Help entrepreneurs with understanding and managing their business ecosystem - Connect entrepreneurs - Provide examples and best practices in business model innovation from various industries

3 An Example Application

We present empirical results of an application case related to an innovation we have worked together to introduce in the market of what one would describe as assistive technologies but from our side we regard as a mainstream consumer product, namely what we call the *'Swinging Semantic Rollators'*.

Rollators have been designed for first time in Germany before exactly 100 years and they appear in their existing form since 1978 after a new design implemented in Sweden. In Germany especially their use is extremely wide, with products that are covering the entire spectrum of low-end/low-cost to high-end/high cost products covering different needs (i.e. standard, lightweight, foldable, suitable for shopping, etc.). For senior citizens, even a trip to a bakery at the same neighborhood can be a challenge. Only assembling sensors and monitoring systems will not help if the technology is not well and easily accepted by the user.

Our idea for what for the *'Swinging Semantic Rollators'* aspires to transform rollators into a mobile smart environment with sensoring capabilities to help increase mobility, guidance and fun for moving to older persons. We solve this problem by developing a smart assistance focused on speech-recognition for command and communication with the user, image processing for obstacles detection and user's facial expressions, and open data for route planning, safe navigation and location monitoring. Capabilities such as vital signs monitoring, proximity sensors, automatic brakes and emergency signaling call can be implemented separately and integrated with the semantic system.

Our differential is the use of open data and semantic technologies to facilitate elderly technology usage. Similar attempts have been implemented; see (Martini 2014), (Schwan 2010) and (Kuusisto 2015), however they all were primarily focused on monitoring sensors for spatial environmental objects, user's physical conditions and daily activities to provide a safely guide for people with cognitive limitations. Therefore, all solutions do not present capabilities to lower the barrier between technology and senior citizens.

In the Swinging Rollators venture we regard rollators as a special type of 'exoskeletons' with the capacity to take several of today's robot companions functions related to guidance, interaction and communication to support a multitude of older people's needs like emergency service request, navigation in the city, goal oriented search, as well as to enable an interaction with grandchildren and fitness motivation. To the latter, as part of the services we shall deploy in the initial 6 month timeframe of the venture are included 3 'Semantic Rollator Games' which are: (a) Rewards for walking (Get Out of Home), (b) City Trivia (Basic city policing and care for the others), (c) Capture The Flag (Scavenger Hunt).

In the venture we make intensive use of open data to facilitate mobility with traffic, weather, public events management, community city maps, terrain conditions and public transportation. A senior citizen can say "I want to go to the bakery", the weather forecast will be accessed to confirm whether it will rain or the temperature is adequate (neither too hot for the summer, nor too cold with snow or ice in the winter), check for a safe and with lower slope route, considering the terrain conditions and community city maps as well as accessibility criteria. If a bus or train is required, the offered service will check the next times and locations. As a live system, is possible to detect streets and sidewalks in maintenance avoiding this path and redirecting the users to an alternative way. If the citizen says "I am not feeling well" the Swinging Semantic Rollator can automatically send an alarm message to the family with the current location, a message to the ambulance service and an alarm sound to catch the attention of people around. Finally, the Rollator shall offer the ability to the family members and the medical doctor and carers to trace the route and have access to the activities undertaken by the user - this feature offers the capability to easily locate a person in case it is lost or has not contacted their family for some time. All speech interaction will be using IntelliSem's in house Natural technology (IntelliSem 2016).

For the city of Passau and for an entire population of about 17,000 rollator users there is a clear incremental trend for the aging population that is above the national average and is comparable to this of the city of Hamburg that is the national champion in the number of older persons. We estimate to attract as pilot users and testers in the initial phase of the venture 100 to 150 users for what we expect to be on a daily intensive use of more than 5 h per day. We regard them as the 'seed capital' for the spread through word of mouth and attraction of new users. Though there are no official statistics for the number of Rollators that are currently in use in Europe and Germany in particular though there is an estimate of about half a million new Rollator users each year (Straßmann 2013) and (Sheeley 2013), Germany is accepted as a lead market (Levsen 2015).

4 Conclusions

We applied our approach towards a business model boutique for use by SMEs in the case of designing a new advanced model for a Rollator. We engaged in the process companies that were active as OEMs in the area together with IT companies and defined a new type of product that we call the Swinging Semantic Rollator. Having in mind the low degree of innovation in this market where manufacturers mainly gave emphasis in the improvement of the design of their products with advancements in e.g. the brakes, a lighter structure with use of titanium, our results offer the opportunity of validating the theoretical concept of a business model boutique with a very practical and hands-on oriented approach. The positive effects of the application of the Business Model Boutique in the case of the Swinging Semantic Rollators venture have as follows:

(a) We introduced a new concept for an existing product; (b) We redefined the main value proposition offered by that product to its traditional market (in our case this is older people with mobility difficulties). (c) We improved the profile of the product to attract attention by other audiences and stakeholders such as telecommunications and mobile service providers, App and service developers, game companies, etc. (d) We created a field for new dynamic collaborations with actors that havent been together before: companies that are offering daily care products for elderly persons who will co-develop with game company a new App to incentivise older persons to leave their home and participate in a Scavenger Hunt ('Capture The Flag') game, and finally (e) We contributed to the demand for Rollators that will look like the conventional ones but will offer a multitude of IT-enabled connectivity with a wide range of surveillance, health status and monitoring, personal mobility assistance, intelligent route planning and advice for any personal matter, etc.

Acknowledgements. The research leading to these results has received partly funding from the European Union Horizons 2020 – the Framework Programme for Research and Innovation

(2014-2020) under grant agreement 643808 Project MARIO 'Managing active and healthy aging with use of caring service robots' and grant agreement 645425 Project SSIX 'Social Sentiment analysis financial IndeXes'.

References

de Ruyter, B., van Loenen, E., Teeven, V.: User centered research in ExperienceLab. In: Schiele, B., Dey, A.K., Gellersen, H., de Ruyter, B., Tscheligi, M., Wichert, R., Aarts, E., Buchmann, A.P. (eds.) AmI 2007. LNCS, vol. 4794, pp. 305–313. Springer, Heidelberg (2007)

BOA 2013: Board of Innovation, Business model brainstorm kit. http://www.boardofinnovation.com/business-model-templates-tools/. Accessed 12 Mar 2015

BMA 2013: BMA Elements/BMA Building Site. http://businessmodelarchitect.eu/products/business-model-architect-building-site/. Accessed 12 Mar 2015

Niitamo, V.-P., Kulkki, S., Eriksson, M., Hribernik K.A.: State-of-the-art and good practice in the field of living labs. In: Proceedings of the 12th International Conference on Concurrent Enterprising: Innovative Products and Services through Collaborative Networks, Milan, Italy, 2006, pp. 349–357 (2006)

Probst, L., Monfardini, E., Frideres, L., Bohn, N.U.: European Cluster Excellence Scoreboard, Pilot Version, September 2013, Extension of the European Cluster Observatory, Promoting better policies to develop world-class clusters in Europe, European Commission (2013)

Vargo, S.L., Lusch, R.F.: Service-dominant logic: continuing the evolution. J. Acad. Mark. Sci. **36**(1), 1–10 (2008)

Amit, R., Zott, C.: Creating value through business model innovation. MIT Sloan Manag. Rev. **53**, 40–50 (2011)

Bouwman, H.: Business models tooling and a research agenda. In: 25th Bled e-conference (2012)

European Commission: A recovery on the horizon? Annual report on European SME's 2012/2013 (2013)

European Commission: Innovation Union scoreboard 2014 (2014)

Frankenberger, K., Weiblen, T., Csik, M., Gassmann, O.: The 4I-framework of business model innovation: a structured view on process phases and challenges. Int. J. Prod. Dev. **18**(3/4), 249–273 (2013)

Gassman, O., Frankenberger, K., Csik, M.: The St. Gallen business model navigator. Working paper, University of St. Gallen (2013)

Fluidminds: Business Model Innovation (2014). http://www.fluidminds.ch/en/what-we-do/business-model-innovation.htm. Accessed 21 Apr 2015

Osterwalder, A.: The business model ontology: a proposition in a design science approach. Doctoral dissertation, Université de Lausanne, Switzerland (2004)

Osterwalder, A.: Business model generation (2010, self published)

Ries, E.: The Lean Startup, How Constant Innovation Creates Radically Successful Businesses. Penguin Book, Baltimore (2011)

Schneider, B.: This Is Service Design Thinking. BIS Publishers, Amsterdam (2011)

IntelliSem: Natural technology (2016). http://intellisem.libbn.org/?page_id=17. Accessed 5 June 2016

Sheeley, A.: Over Two Million Rollators Now in Use in Germany (2013). http://justwalkers.com/mobility-blog/over-two-million-rollators-now-in-use-in-germany/#.V12WB_l95hF. Accessed 4 June 2016

Straßmann, B.: Es rollt: Die Generation Gehwagen macht mobil – nicht nur Rollatoren werden technisch anspruchsvoll und chic (2013). http://www.zeit.de/2013/12/Rollatoren. Accessed 4 June 2016

Martini, F.: Gehhilfe als digitaler Gehilfe (2014). http://www.siemens.com/innovation/de/home/pictures-of-the-future/digitalisierung-und-software/digitale-assistenten-gehhilfe-als-digitaler-gehilfe.html. Accessed 2 June 2016

Schwan, B.: Der intelligente Rollator (2010). http://www.heise.de/tr/artikel/Der-intelligente-Rollator-990514.html. Accessed 2 June 2016

Kuusisto, O.: Smart rollators with VTT technology (2015). http://www.vttresearch.com/media/news/smart-rollators-with-vtt-technology. Accessed 2 June 2016

Levsen, N.: Lead Markets in Age-Based Innovations: Demographic Change and Internationally Successful Innovations. Springer, Heidelberg (2015)

A Framework for Applying Data Integration and Curation Pipelines to Support Integration of Migrants and Refugees in Europe

Oya Deniz Beyan[1], Siegfried Handschuh[2], Adamantios Koumpis[2(✉)], Garyfallos Fragidis[3], and Stefan Decker[1]

[1] RWTH Aachen University, Informatik 5, Aachen, Germany
{beyan,decker}@dbis.rwth-aachen.de
[2] Fakultät für Informatik und Mathematik, Universität Passau, Passau, Germany
siegfried.Handschuh@uni-passau.de,
adamantios.koumpis@uni-passau.de
[3] Institute of Service Science, University of Geneva, Geneva, Switzerland
gary.fragidis@gmail.com

Abstract. We investigate the benefit of data integration and curation services for the current refugee crisis and proposed an architecture to support development of innovative solutions. We focus on developing a multi- /cross-lingual semantic data curation pipeline enriched with natural language processing capabilities in order to (a) improve decision making capabilities of public authorities with data driven dashboards; (b) stimulate the development of innovative application and services supporting integration of refugees; and (c) improve the use of open data for tackling the societal challenges.

Keywords: Data curation of semi-structured and unstructured data · Big data analytics · Technology integration · Migration and refugee crisis · Social integration · Data lakes

1 Introduction

Open data initiatives and big data technologies can help EU economy to create better solutions for effective use of infrastructure such as housing and education, delivery of integration services for various domains including public health management and social cohesion, and developing a workforce to move towards a skill based economy [1, 2]. Moreover, mobile technologies and web based services can exploit the rich open data sources to create innovative products [3]. Despite of being a tremendous resource, open data, especially open government data, is yet largely untapped [9]. According to an assessment carried out by the European Data Portal team Open Data Maturity is just 44 % whereas Open Data readiness is 45 % in member states [10]. Although Open Data can help overcome certain economic constraints, developers tended benefit only small range of it, most limited with transportation and mobility.

H. Afsarmanesh et al. (Eds.): PRO-VE 2016, IFIP AICT 480, pp. 588–596, 2016.
DOI: 10.1007/978-3-319-45390-3_50

The major obstacle to develop innovative knowledge services and applications by exploiting the open data is related with the lack of the data integration and curation services [4]. Today, many service and mobile app developers requires access to timely and interpretable data to address raising societal needs and challenges. Most of the times they experience difficulties to identify data sources, understand the data representation schemas and accessing requirements, interpret different formats and merge into single usable schema, moreover deal with multilingual data [5]. All these preprocessing steps does not fit the real life requirements of entrepreneurs. In most of the cases, companies are under pressure to deliver their products in short time to answer raising demand. Moreover, their human capital and expertise in technologies are shaped around their core business, which not necessarily capable of dealing with data integration challenges. Therefore, next generation companies will need supporting data curation services to exploit the open data in their product development cycle.

In this research, we investigate the benefit of data integration and curation services for the current refugee crisis and proposed an architecture to support development of innovative solutions.

2 Refugee Crisis and Promises of Data Driven Services

The unprecedented human crisis generated by the wars in European Union neighborhood such as Libya, Syria, Iraq as well as further conflicts in Africa -Somalia or Middle East - Afghanistan have put a tremendous pressure on EU social and political system, with refugee waves never encountered since the Second World War. According to the International Organization for Migrants (IOM), since January 2015, 1.103.496 migrants, including asylum seekers, are reported to have arrived to Europe by land and sea routes [11]. Only in 2015 Germany alone received ~1.1M refugees [12]. The current humanitarian crisis is unprecedented with an appalling cost in short run, whereas in the long-run, much will depend on how well successful refugees are integrated [6].

The influx of refugees and migrants into Europe is conjuring new frontiers: a unique feature of most adult refugees is the connectivity of these refugees via smartphones that functions as their main lifeline to the wider world [7]. To this, several apps have been launched to help refugees integrate in recent months while activists have turned to crowdfunding and other online initiatives to help refugees find housing or jobs [13–15]. However, what may look, at first sight, like a lively ecosystem is only a collection of apps that have been developed independently and will disappear unexpectedly because of absence of use, leaving an empty space that will be difficult to be covered by a second generation of applications or services.

What we see as an unprecedented opportunity is in case we can come up with the necessary business model innovations that will help shift the balance from burden to benefit by making use of data driven decision making and service provision. In this scope our aim is to support independently developed applications and to strengthen the sustainability of the adhocracy of the existing ‘ecosystem’ by means of offering a systematized support for curating data.

From our side we consider that it is in the interest of all data users, i.e., not only the refugees, asylum seekers and migrants themselves but also the authorities in the several countries of EU as well as non-governmental organisations (NGOs) and activists to be able to access high-quality data which have integrity.

There are a set of challenges to produce and maintain high-quality data which goes beyond the capabilities of any independent app creator. First challenge is regarding accessing data required for smart policy making at governmental and administrative level. Although there are considerable amount of open data initiatives in EU, it is difficult to collect and curate data required planning for basic needs of refugees such as housing, employment and education. Next challenge is the variety of the data sources including websites, social media, open government portal provides wide range of structured, semi structured and unstructured data. Lastly cross lingual support is a challenge since the source and receiver of information requires different language sets.

3 Scope and Underlying Technologies

The main objective of our work is develop a multi-cross lingual semantic data curation pipeline enriched with natural language processing capabilities in order to (a) improve decision making capabilities of public authorities with data driven dashboards; (b) stimulate the development of innovative application and services supporting integration of refugees; and (c) improve the use of open data with semantic services for tackling the societal challenges. Such a data curation pipeline provides multilingual data integration services for data driven product development and will offer APIs to any end user that wants to connect and provide applications for the needs of migrants and refugees as well as for the need of governments and NGOs.

This poses the need for taking a more holistic approach to the entire data value chain that our research addresses, as described in the next section. In particular, our work concentrates on collecting, aggregating and integration data from a multitude of sources, which broadly fall into three categories:

- *Closed data sources:* private data which is available within the member organisations of the consortium such as refugees' personal health records [16]. This private data has to be protected against both accidental data leakages and unauthorized access.
- *Open data sources:* sources with data which has been made available to the public due to legislation such as the "freedom of information" act. This data mostly includes statistical data. Examples include World Health Organization's global health observatory data, European Union Open Data Portal, data sets from open health data, European Data Portal, World Bank Health Data, open government data portals [17–22].
- *Social media sites:* user generated content from social media sites has to be accessed and integrated on a per-site basis. Data from such sites will provide knowledge about refugees.

Most of the aforementioned data sources contain also geospatial data for which the data fusion process has more specialized requirements. Due to the nature of the data, the geographical data points have to be combined based on geographical features such as e.g. proximity. In addition, the temporal nature of e.g. movement data needs to be preserved.

Linked Data and Semantic Web technologies simplify data integration for knowledge-intensive applications by enabling a Web of interoperable and machine-readable data based on formal and explicit descriptions of the structure and semantics of the data [23]. The fundamental building blocks for Linked Data are the graph-based data model of RDF [24], the Linked Data principles [25], and formal and domain specific semantics [26]. The benefits of Semantic Web technologies include simplification of information retrieval [27], information extraction [28] and data integration [29].

The Linked Data principles have been adopted by an increasing number of data providers, especially from the Linking Open Data community, which makes free and public data available as Linked Data. At the time of writing, approximately 300 different sources following the Linked Data principles are available. Specifically linked open government data promises an opportunity for people and companies to earn money and reap value from this high-quality and free information out there [8].

For many organizations who publishes open data there is a tradeoff between high quality data generation (requiring non-trivial human expert input) and massive data generation (requiring low human processing cost) [18]. As low cost open data publishing becomes more predominant, the urge for advanced data integration and curation approaches increases. In this sense, Linked Data and related Semantic technologies provide the foundational infrastructure to enable data fusion using data from different sources. Linked Data allows for addressing the structural, syntactic or semantic heterogeneity of data resulting from data access to multiple data sources with different formats, schemas or structure [30, 31].

4 Requirements and Design Principles

The proposed semantic data curation pipeline architecture aims to provide a service integration and collaboration platform for small and medium size enterprises to foster the development of data driven services and products. Today big data start to transforms businesses in all over the world and already many entrepreneurs created business models reliant on data. Although big data offers substantial value to organizations, it also brings many challenges to deal with data variety and quality issues. Addressing societal challenges with big data driven solutions may depend on consuming third party generated data created in diverse contexts with different set of goals. Adaptation and repurposing of the third party data requires specific expertise and in most cases involvement diverse technologies at the different stages of the data curation pipeline. The semantic data curation pipeline will enable emergence of high quality data driven business models for knowledge organizations. It will serve to companies, local and central governments and NGOs to build their data driven services and products to tackle social, economic and health care challenges of migrants and refugees. Smart application related with housing or job allocation, multi lingual screening programs related with emerging public health threats, targeted training and education programs to build qualified workforce can be mentioned among them.

The core value of the semantic data curation pipeline will be improving data quality and completeness as well as ensuring the verifiability and data provenance. Trustable and high quality data sets will have a positive impact on businesses by improving decision making capabilities based on big data analysis, It will also serve as a collaboration framework for small and medium size businesses to build their products in a value change, such as integrating cloud storage solution, multilingual translation services and data analysis solution from different partners within a single production line. In our work we have defined four guiding design principles for the semantic data curation pipeline to meet specified requirements of businesses:

(1) To facilitate the orchestration of mature and readily available technologies
The proposed semantic framework should support service integration for delivering high quality and verifiable data. It should allow for 3rd parties i.e. government organizations and NGOs to introduce, test and validate their Apps or systems as a part of the curation pipeline. Introduced technologies can support one or more curation level which comprises different roles as follows:
   (a) Discovery and acquisition of structured and unstructured data typically by registering to the Data Lakes (see also [32]); (b) Interpretation, annotation and providing multilingual support. Also includes indexing of collected, analyzed and curated data for efficient querying, metadata maintaining and semantic linking; (c) Analyzing data for posterity ensuring reliability, accessibility and retrieval capacity for future use and reuse; (d) Storing data for long term access, use and reuse; (e) providing access to external parties with a focus of selling integrated data and offering data driven services and products
(2) To improve the availability of multilingual machine discoverable data
Lack of multilingual machine discoverable data sets is one of the major shortcomings for stakeholders who are tackling challenges related with migration issues at large. The semantic data curation pipeline and big data platform should help to create large-scale, multilingual, semantically interoperable integrated data assets that will be of value and utility to the following perspectives:
   (a) *IT Environment Set-up:* By allowing connection to data lake API, to enable NGOs, Governments and European companies to build innovative multilingual products and services to help various groups of migrants and refugees understand the basics they can avail in each EU country. (b) Social objectives: to support refugees and migrants in their adaptation and integration, and facilitate public authorities and NGOs in optimizing their resources by data driven decision making.
(3) To create a multi sectoral value chain to address the needs of refugees
The value of the aspired infrastructure will be serving as a one-stop service platform to support needs of refugees and migrants. The value chain should be achieved by integrating and linking multi sectoral data by developing a contextual model to address social and economic needs of refugees. A contextual model for life events of targeted population can facilitate integrating information around needs in regard to immediate health risks, education, social support and employment. Our aim is to specify, develop and evaluate a life-event oriented, integrated, interoperable Pan-European platform for online one-stop analysis, filtering and visualization of added

value information and provision of services for refugees. Such a platform would be accompanied by a coherent services and products for realising and exploiting refugees' needs.

(4) To accelerate the development of new products and services
The curation pipeline can accelerate development of new products and innovative reuse of existing ones by supplying high quality curated data sets. The various use cases can demonstrate how a data management or data analytics product successfully marketed in another domain can benefit from data curation to extend its market. Products that applies the big data analytics solutions in various domains can be easily adopted to provide solutions for refugee crisis.

5 The Proposed Data Value Chain

We propose a five layer semantic data curation pipeline to meet above mentioned requirements and principles of value chain. It should be noted that the aforementioned requirements are not author-driven i.e. they were not dictated by the authors of this article but were acquired through the exploratory phase of our research to reflect real needs that have appeared either from the demand side namely the refugees themselves or the supply side namely the companies or the organisations that have offered Apps and services to satisfy such needs. The data value chain consists of 5 stages spanning from the data acquisition phase to the data usage phase. Layers and corresponding set of technologies is involved for extracting and integrating data from a variety of open data sources and delivering semantically enriched data to consumers as follows:

1. *Data Acquisition:* Technology responsible for discovering and registering structured and unstructured data from open data sources like Pan-European Open Data, Twitter, Facebook, etc. With this technology, an archiving platform will retrieve, structure and process large amounts of web content applying intelligent harvesting operations over hypertext, images, linked files, among other associated contents.
2. *Data Interpretation and Multilingual Interoperability:* Technology responsible to ensure multilingual translation of discovered and registered data from open data sources, building upon metadata management an indexing system for efficient querying and browsing over the data collected. Within this technology, proposed industry standard formats such as TMX will be applied for creation and maintenance of translation memories.
3. *Data Analysis and Curation:* Technology responsible for enabling the extraction of annotated datasets from structured and unstructured data, providing a semantic enrichment over the data which enhances the data usage and analysis. Within this technology a suite of statistical services will be provided as the tools to analyse, explore and extract insights based on prediction and correlation of data.
4. *Data Storage:* Technology responsible for the provision of a public-facing web repository, providing a scalable and secure storage system of the collected data, and an archiving mechanism, enabling an easy way to preserve, view, interrogate and reuse the content data.

5. *Data Usage:* This step comprises an API layer, localization service, and an analytics and decision making platform for data consumption.
   - *API engine:* This technology will be responsible for providing and managing accesses to external players consuming the curated data.
   - *Localization services:* This technology will be used to translate information into languages used by major migrant groups.
   - *Analytics and decision making platform:* This technology will be used for consuming the curated data and supporting employment and recruitment needs for refugees, migrants and asylum seekers, exploring information of various European countries and regions.

6 Conclusions

Currently, the use of publicly available data to facilitate interactions between public administrators, business and refugees is limited. Mostly the refugees use very specific applications developed in each country. Typical functionalities offered by existing applications allow refugees to access very particular information. Our proposed semantic curation pipeline will improve comprehension and increase accessibility of open data for developing services to tackle integration problems of refugees, thereby ensuring effective transparency of information. In order to accomplish this vision, we will realize an integrated five step technical solution so that at the end refugees will receive valuable information about their life-events. For this goal, we have developed a framework to provide a systematic transfer of information and technology across different sectors and a developed a data sharing and linking culture.

The benefits we see from the proposed system are related at a large extent to the benefits of any system that makes use of open public data in terms of fostering innovation. However, early adopters of open data driven solution should be aware of three possible pitfalls, namely: "(1) thinking of open data as a technical process rather than a culture change or innovation process; (2) getting trapped in outdated business models of data sale as revenue; (3) starting with the data rather than specific issues or challenges" [33]. In our case, we believe that targeting the societal challenge that Europe faces nowadays will lead the proposed framework in a sustainable innovation platform and open new opportunities for solving business and societal challenges.

References

1. Parycek, P., Hochtl, J., Ginner, M.: Open government data implementation evaluation. J. Theor. Appl. Electron. Commer. Res. **9**(2), 80–99 (2014)
2. Chen, H., Chiang, R.H.L., Storey, V.C.: Business intelligence and analytics: from big data to big impact. MIS Q. **36**(4), 1165–1188 (2012)
3. Lee, M., Almirall, E., Wareham, J.: Open data and civic apps: first-generation failures, second-generation improvements. Commun. ACM **59**(1), 82–89 (2015)

4. Lee, G., Kwak, Y.H.: An open government maturity model for social media-based public engagement. Gov. Inf. Q. **29**(4), 492–503 (2012)
5. Cavanillas, J.M., Curry, E., Wahlster, W.: New Horizons for a Data-Driven Economy, A Roadmap for Usage and Exploitation of Big Data in Europe. Springer, Heidelberg (2016)
6. OECD Migration Policy Debates, "Is this humanitarian migration crisis different?", N7, September 2015. https://www.oecd.org/migration/. Accessed: 22 Apr 2016
7. CBC News "For Syrian refugees, smartphones are a lifeline. http://www.cbc.ca/news/world/for-syrian-refugees-smartphones-are-a-lifeline-not-a-toy-1.3221349. Accessed 02 May 2016
8. Bizer, C., et al.: The meaningful use of big data: four perspectives–four challenges. ACM SIGMOD Rec. **40**(4), 56–60 (2012)
9. Ding, L., et al.: TWC data-gov corpus: incrementally generating linked government data from data. gov. In: Proceedings of the 19th International Conference on World wide web. ACM (2010)
10. Open Data Maturity in Europe 2015: Insights into the European state of play, European Union (2015)
11. World Migration Report 2015 – Migrants and Cities: New Partnerships to Manage Mobility, International Organization for Migration (2016)
12. 476.649 Asylanträge im Jahr 2015. https://www.bamf.de/SharedDocs/Meldungen/DE/2016/201610106-asylgeschaeftsstatistik-dezember.html. Accessed 24 Apr 2016
13. Ankommen: The guide for your first weeks in Germany. https://www.ankommenapp.de/
14. http://www.refugeespeaker.org/. Accessed 24 Apr 2016
15. http://www.universaldoctor.com/prod/en_GB/153/UniversalDoctor+Speaker+Web.html
16. European Commission Directorate-General for Health and Food Safety, Personal health record. http://ec.europa.eu/dgs/health_food-safety/docs/personal_health_record_english.pdf. Accessed 21 Apr 2016
17. Global Health Observatory, The data repository. http://www.who.int/gho/database/en/. Accessed: 27 Apr 2016
18. https://open-data.europa.eu/en/data
19. OpenDataHealth. http://openhealthdata.metajnl.com/. Accessed 22 Apr 2016
20. EuropeData Portal. https://publicdata.eu/. Accessed 22 Apr 2016
21. Health Data, The World Bank. http://data.worldbank.org/topic/health. Accessed 27 Apr 2016
22. Opening Up Government. https://data.gov.uk/. Accessed 30 Apr 2016
23. Berners-Lee, T., Hendler, J., Lassila, O.: The semantic web. Sci. Am. **284**(5), 28–37 (2001)
24. Decker, S., et al.: The semantic web: the roles of XML and RDF. IEEE Internet Comput. **4**(5), 63–73 (2000)
25. Berners-Lee, T.: Linked data-design issues. W3C (2006). Accessed 24 Apr 2016
26. Bizer, C., Heath, T., Berners-Lee, T.: Linked data-the story so far. Semant. Serv. Interoper. Web Appl. Emerg. Concepts **5**, 205–227 (2009)
27. van Elst, L., Dignum, V., Abecker, A.: Towards agent-mediated knowledge management. In: van Elst, L., Dignum, V., Abecker, A. (eds.) AMKM 2003. LNCS (LNAI), vol. 2926, pp. 1–30. Springer, Heidelberg (2004)
28. Fonseca, F.T., et al.: Using ontologies for integrated geographic information systems. Trans. GIS **6**(3), 231–257 (2002)
29. Fensel, D., et al.: OIL: an ontology infrastructure for the semantic web. IEEE Intell. Syst. **2**, 38–45 (2001)
30. Doan, A., Halevy, A.Y.: Semantic integration research in the database community: a brief survey. AI Mag. **26**(1), 83 (2005)
31. Moon, J.Y., Sproull, L.: Essence of distributed work: the case of the Linux Kernel. In: Hinds, P., Kiesler, S. (eds.) Distributed Work, pp. 381–404. The MIT Press, Cambridge (2002)

32. Stein, B., Morrison, A.: "The enterprise data lake: Better integration and deeper analytics". Technology Forecast: Rethinking integration Issue 1. http://www.pwc.com/us/en/technology-forecast/2014/cloud-computing/assets/pdf/pwc-technology-forecast-data-lakes.pdf. Accessed 4 May 2016
33. Carolan, L.: "The challenges and pitfalls from the use of open data". Harvesting Open Data for Nutrition Security, ILSI Research Foundation, ILSI Annual Meeting 2016, St. Petersburg, Florida, 25 January 2016

Emerging Applications - Agribusiness Value Chain

The Electronic Product Code Information Services (EPCIS) is a standard that provides specifications to assure product traceability [4]. The collection and analysis of product information allows supply chains to be virtualized and remotely monitored, optimized and controlled [5]. However, tracking a product is not enough to grant its quality. All the roles involved have to incrementally provide additional information regarding the product stages. EPCIS proposes a mechanism to exchange and share data but the semantics of data is informally defined and its interpretation is left up to the individual implementing engines [6].

Works presented in literature are mainly focused on enabling technologies, without addressing the usage of the generated information for control at a supply chain level. In this paper, a collaborative architecture is presented, which allows the traceability of information throughout the entire supply chain. Such architecture exploits the EPCIS standard to capture events related to products and a non-relational database to store them.

The paper is structured as follows. Section 2 revises the main literature available on this topic. Section 3 defines the food supply chain and presents the transparency problem. Section 4 describes the EPCIS standard by highlighting its capabilities and possible extensions. In Sect. 5, the collaborative architecture to grant transparency in supply chain is proposed, while Sect. 6 reports an application to a case study. Finally, Sect. 7 illustrates conclusions and states future works.

2 Related Works

Several researchers related to food traceability have already been done, especially related to the introduction of RFID technology in the agrifood industry [7]. Works on virtualized supply chains exploited to design traceability systems for foods provide systems to track the location of certain items and trace their history [5].

Examples of application of EPCIS for food product traceability are described in several works for different products. RFID technology was used together with wireless sensor networks in the wine production for monitoring the vineyards [8]. In the fish market, traceability systems based on EPCIS to store and manage fish information from farmer to retailer were studied [9, 10].

In the meat supply chain, due to recent meat crises and scandals, reference architectures based on EPCIS standard to grant transparency were presented [11–13]. Some works also investigate the best way of representing EPCIS events to enhance query efficiency, e.g., by means of a graph structure [14].

The EPCIS standard is also adopted for traceability of other kinds of products, e.g. in the pharmaceutical domain, to grant the security of the drug supply chain [15, 16].

3 Transparency Problem in Food Supply Chain

Different kinds of companies are involved in a food supply chain, each of them operating in different markets and selling different products [17]. The food supply chain includes five main stages, as shown in Fig. 1: production, processing, storage, distribution and retail. Physical items are exchanged among the stages (solid lines), while data collected in each stage are not exchanged neither follow a coherent standard.

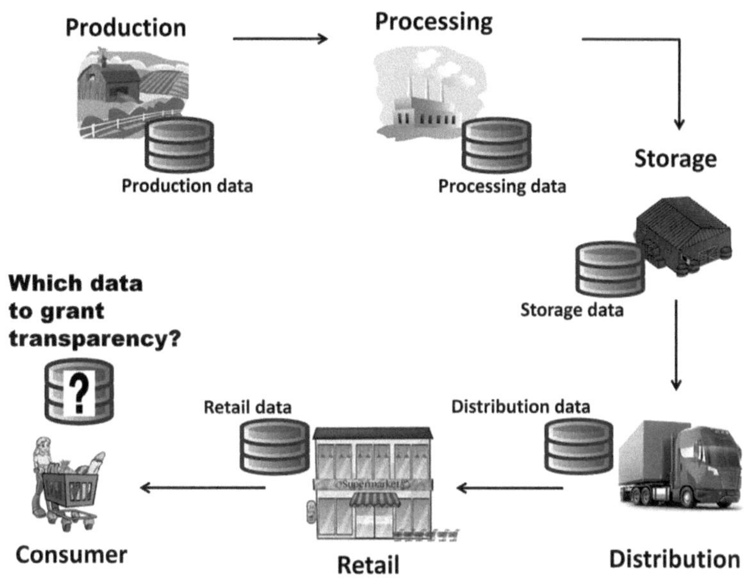

Fig. 1. Sectors included in the food supply chain.

As a result, the consumer is not aware of the process followed by the product during the previous stages, but also that production or processing companies do not have information regarding storage, distribution and retail.

The lack of communication across the stages clearly affect the trust of the chain, since each actor is not aware of the history of the product during the other stages. In fact, the managers of the companies in the production or processing stages are interested in knowing if the products are correctly stored and distributed along the supply chain. Thus, they need to know when their products arrive to the storages, how long remain there, how long is the journey to the retails, etc. Also the managers of retail companies are interested in information collected during other stages, such as the origin of the products they sell in order to trust their quality. Furthermore, all these information are of interest also for the final customer.

4 EPCIS Standard for Product Tracking

The Electronic Product Code Information Services (EPCIS) is a standard defined by GS1, a not-for-profit international organization which provides specifications for the representation of product traceability information. It also develops several global standards to facilitate end-to-end traceability and information sharing [4].

EPCIS provides a data model serialized as an XML schema for capturing information artefacts that encapsulate the geographical progress and status of an item or set of items during the different phases of the supply chain. This is achieved by capturing data generated through the scanning of a barcode or RFID tag and encapsulating it as an event.

4.1 EPCIS Events

Accordingly to EPCIS 1.1 [18] four core event types are defined:

- *ObjectEvent*, used to register a general event occurring to a physical or digital object;
- *AggregationEvent*, used to indicate a physically aggregation objects (i.e., objects that are physically constrained to be in the same place at the same time, such as items in a pallet);
- *TransformationEvent*, used when a set of input objects are consumed and transformed in output objects;
- *TransactionEvent*, used when one or more objects are linked or delinked with business transactions.

The field of each event represent the four possible dimensions of an EPCIS event (i.e., what, when, where and why). Particularly they contain information regarding (1) the physical or digital objects participating in the event, (2) the period of time in which the event occurred, (3) the location in which the event was registered, and (4) the business context of the event. The meaning of the dimensions varies depending on the event type.

In addition to the basic EPCIS types, the standard can be extended by specific organizations to make it more suitable to their business. In fact, every event has an extension point, which can be used to attach additional data. Even if EPCIS specification proposes a mechanism to exchange and share data, the XML schema defines only the structure of the data to be recorded, while the semantics of data is informally defined and its interpretation is left up to the individual implementing engines [6]. Therefore, additional information regarding the four dimensions of the event (e.g., temperature, humidity, etc.) can be collected and stored.

4.2 Core Business Vocabulary

Together with EPCIS, GS1 defined the Core Business Vocabulary (CBV), which defines specific data values to populate part of the EPCIS data model. CBV includes two different vocabularies, Standard Vocabulary and User Vocabulary.

The definition and meaning of the elements of the Standard Vocabulary are agreed in advance by the partners compliant with the standard. For example, the EPCIS standard defines the field "business step," whose possible values (e.g., shipping, receiving) are defined in the Standard Vocabulary. Standard Vocabularies are defined for the following fields of EPCIS: business steps, dispositions, business transaction types, and source and destination types.

On the contrary, the vocabularies of the User Vocabulary are controlled by a single organization, which has not constraints in deciding their meaning. While the CBV does not specify particular user vocabulary elements, it recommends syntax templates for the end users in defining their own elements. User Vocabularies can be defined for the following fields of the EPCIS standard: physical or digital objects, locations including both read points and business locations, business transaction identifiers, source/destination identifiers, and transformation identifiers.

5 Collaborative Architecture to Grant Transparency

The collaborative architecture proposed to grant transparency across the supply chain is shown in Fig. 2. In addition to the solid lines showing the item flow, the information flows are shown as dotted lines. Red thin dotted lines represent exchange of EPCIS events, while green large dotted lines represent exchange of transparency information. Each actor involved in the supply chain uses the EPCIS standard to capture events related to products. The captured EPCIS events are sent to the Product tracking platform, where they are stored and analyzed.

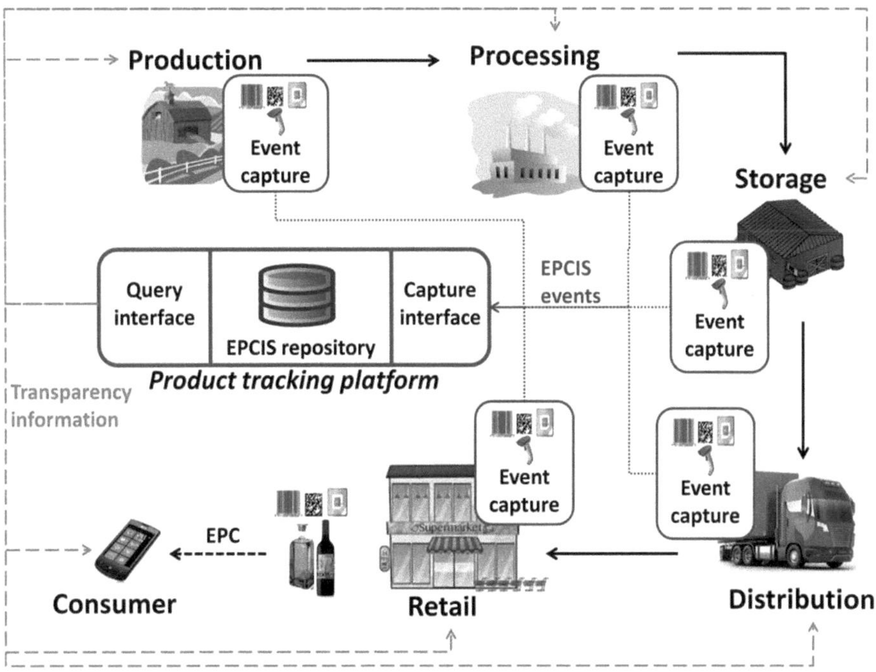

Fig. 2. Collaborative architecture based on a EPCIS product tracking platform.

The product tracking platform consists of three main elements: the event capturing interface, the EPCIS data repository and the query interface. The capture interface receives the EPCIS events captured by the companies in the supply chain. Procedures of event captures are custom logic specific for each company. An EPCIS event, while containing the information regarding the product identifier, also includes information regarding the business context in which data is obtained.

The captured EPCIS events are stored in a data repository. Due to the fact that EPCIS events can be easily translated into JSON format [14] and that the efficiency of non-relational versus relational databases in managing EPCIS data was recently proven [19], the data repository is implemented in a NoSQL database, particularly MongoDB [20].

Through the query interface, the applications interact with the data repository in which all the EPCIS events are stored and organized. Through a mobile App the consumer is able to read the EPC of the product of interest and consult the transparency information stored related to the product. Some information are valid for each product, such as the times and places the product crossed during its lifetime Other information vary from one product to another. For example, for a frozen food, the temperature range at which the product was kept can be retrieved.

Not only the customer can access to the stored information, but also all the other companies of the supply chain can control the events occurred to the products during the previous or following stages. In this way the transparency of the supply chain is granted not only for the consumer but also to all the companies involved.

6 Application

An example of the XML document used to capture an EPCIS event related to the creation of a wine bottle is shown in the following.


```
<?xml version="1.0" encoding="UTF-8" standalone="yes"?>
 <epcis:EPCISDocument xmlns:epcis="urn:epcglobal:epcis:xsd:1"
xmlns:xsi="http:// www.w3.org/2001/XMLSchema-instance"
schemaVersion="1">
  <EPCISBody>
    <EventList>
      <ObjectEvent>
        <eventTime>2016-08-14T18:34:20Z</eventTime>
        <recordTime>2016-08-14T18:34:20Z </recordTime>
        <eventTimeZoneOffset>-02:00</eventTimeZoneOffset>
        <epcList>
          <epc>urn:epc:id:sgtin:0814141.181335.234</epc>
        </epcList>
        <action>ADD</action>
        <bizStep>urn:epcglobal:cbv:bizstep:commissioning
        </bizStep>
        <disposition>urn:epcglobal:cbv:disp:active</disposition>
        <readPoint>
          <id>urn:epc:id:sgln:0814141.00300.1</id>
       </readPoint>
       <bizLocation>
          <id>urn:epc:id:sgln:0814141.00300.0</id>
       </bizLocation>
       <bizTransactionList>
          <bizTransaction type="urn:epcglobal:cbv:btt:po"> urn:
           epc:id:gdti:0814141.05432.2345 </bizTransaction>
          </bizTransactionList>
       <extensions>
          <temperature> 25 </temperature>
       </extensions>
     </ObjectEvent>
   </EventList>
 </EPCISBody>
</epcis:EPCISDocument>
```

In the body of the document, a list of EPCIS event can be registered. In this case a single EPCIS event is represented. In an event, a list of product can be involved, but in this case a single product is considered. The product is identified by its EPC, which is codified through the Serialized Global Trade Item Number (SGTIN) standard. For each event the kind of action (add, delete or observe) is specified.

Then, information regarding the business stem (bizStep) and disposition are given, accordingly to the CBV definitions. The identification of the EPC reader (readPoint) and of the location at which the event is registered are also reported. To each event, a set of transaction can be associated, identified by their Global Document Type Identifier (GDTI). Finally, the user-defined extensions can be set. In this case, the additional information coming from a temperature sensor is included.

The EPCIS event is translated into a JSON document to be stored in MongoDB. The JSON document corresponding to the previous XML document is the following.


```
{
"_id": ObjectId(""),
"eventType": "ObjectEvent",
"eventTime": ISODate("2016-08-14T18:34:20Z"),
"recordTime": ISODate("2016-08-14T18:34:20Z"),
"eventTimeZoneOffset": -02:00,
"epcList": [
        "urn:epc:id:sgtin:0814141.181335.234"
 ],
"action" : "ADD",
"bizStep" : "urn:epcglobal:cbv:bizstep:commissioning",
"disposition" : "urn:epcglobal:cbv:disp:active",
"readPoint" : "urn:epc:id:sgln:0814141.00300.1",
"bizLocation" : "urn:epc:id:sgln:0814141.00300.0"",
"bizTransactionList": [
              {
              "type" : "urn:epcglobal:cbv:btt:po",
              "value": urn:epc:id:gdti:0814141.05432.2345
}
 ],

 "extensions" : [
              {
              "name" : "temperature",
              "value": 25
              }
  ]
 }
```


```
  "extensions" : [
               {
               "name" : "temperature",
               "value": 25
               }
   ]
  }
```

Modelling Pricing Policy Based on Shelf-Life of Non Homogeneous Available-To-Promise in Fruit Supply Chains

Hanzel Grillo(✉), M.M.E. Alemany, and A. Ortiz

Centro de Investigación de Gestión e Ingeniería de Producción (CIGIP), Universitat Politècnica de València, Camino de Vera S/N, 46022 Valencia, Spain
hangries@upvnet.upv.es
grillo7@gmail.com

Abstract. Fruit Supply Chains (SCs) are influenced by uncontrollable natural factors causing heterogeneity in their products, as regards certain attributes that are relevant to customers and vary over time because of the shelf-life. As a consequence customers should be served not only with the required quantity and due date as usual, but also with the quality, freshness and homogeneity specified in their orders. The order promising process (OPP) is based on the uncommitted availability of homogeneous product quantities in planned lots (ATP) that are uncertain. Therefore, there is a risk of not being reliable in the commitments because of discrepancies between the real and planned homogeneous quantities. Furthermore, due to the shelf-life (SL), serving customers with the freshest product introduce the risk of increasing waste because of the aging process. To efficiently manage these risks, this work proposes a mathematical model for handling the heterogeneous ATP in fruit SCs and a pricing policy based on the product SL in the moment of delivery. In order to illustrate the application of the modelling approach, a short numerical example is introduced. The example evidences a conflictive situation when optimizing the assignation of homogeneous ATP between serving orders with fresh and more valuable product, what could lead to increase the risk of having waste because of expiration, and consequently, more costs and less profit.

Keywords: Order-promising process · Available-To-Promise · Lack of homogeneity in the product · Fruit supply chain · Perishability

1 Introduction

The order promising process (OPP) presents special features and more complexity in fruit supply chains (SCs), where uncontrollable natural factors like weather, land, water drought, etc. are present. That kind of factors can confer heterogeneity to units of the same product as regards certain attributes relevant to customers. Additionally, due to the perishability, products are not just affected by the non homogeneity but also for the aging process. The order proposals of these SCs require homogeneity in units of the same product, and normally, customers expect to be served with the freshest product, with the quality required, but with a reasonable price. For this reason, the pricing policy

H. Afsarmanesh et al. (Eds.): PRO-VE 2016, IFIP AICT 480, pp. 608–617, 2016.
DOI: 10.1007/978-3-319-45390-3_52

can be directly based on the status of the product at the time of delivery. These aspects become a problem when customer orders are promised based on future planned homogeneous quantities; because final characteristics are not known certainly until the product is harvested, classified, packed and transported to the customer. Then, fruit supply chains have inherent uncertainty in the handling of the available to promise (ATP) quantities, due to not just the homogeneity in the product, but also to the shelf life (SL). One of the main challenges when modelling the OPP in fruit SCs, is firstly to estimate the homogeneous ATP quantities derived from the master plan in advanced to be produced and classified. Secondly, due to perishability, those homogeneous ATP quantities deteriorate over time being necessary to provide traceability. Thirdly, the harvesting time and SL, become critically important in terms of the freshness of the product in the moment of delivery. Consequently, it also affects earns obtained, in case the pricing policy is directly linked with the product freshness. Therefore, the main contribution of this paper is to include these challenges combined into the OPP for fruit SCs. To properly handle them, a mathematical programming model for supporting the OPP has been formulated that takes into account the homogeneity required in the ATP, the dynamism conferred to it by the SL and a proper pricing policy linked to the perishability of the product.

The rest of the paper is organized as follows: Sect. 2 presents a short summary of the related work founded. Sections 3 and 4 describes the proposed way to model the ATP in fruit SCs and the modelling of the SL, respectively. Section 5 describes the link assumed between the remaining SL and the pricing policy for the ATP. Section 6 presents a numerical example to show the conflict when freshness and benefit are both them combined for being optimized. Finally, Sect. 7 exposes the main conclusions and future research lines.

2 Related Work

This work aims to introduce less investigated characteristics in the OPP, such as the homogeneous ATP quantities and their perishability in fruit SCs. The homogeneous ATP concept is included in the so called lack of homogeneity in the product (LHP). LHP is defined as the absence of uniformity among units of the same product, that can originate from the incorporation of raw materials directly derived from nature, and/or production processes features that confer heterogeneity to it (Alarcon et al. (2011), Alemany et al. (2013, 2015), Mundi et al. (2016) and Grillo et al. (2016)). Improper management of non-homogeneous units of the same product and its inherent uncertainty can impact very negative on customer service level. It is established that, due to inherent LHP uncertainty, the planned size of homogeneous sublots and the real ones can differ once produced and classified into subtypes. A variety of other studies, like Lin et al. (2010), have dealt with some characteristics related with the LHP without explicitly mention it. In the specific case of fruit SCs, the lack of literature is even more evident, being Kilic et al. (2010) the closest case validated in the food processing sector. In this paper, the main LHP characteristic appear randomly in raw materials with a strong effect over the finished product. The perishability (SL consuming) is identified as one of LHP types (Grillo et al. 2016), and as a cause of conflictive price range of the served orders with the product SL at delivery time. In Sects. 4 and 5 we will introduce the concepts and explain how to model this approach.

4 Modelling the Shelf-Life

One strategic issue on modelling the ATP for fruit supply chains is the perishability. This factor makes ATP characteristics of each subtype defined in Eq. (1) to change over time while the SL is consuming. If we assume that the SL is pre-defined for each subtype, the freshness of products committed with customers will depend on the remaining SL in the moment of delivery to customer. To maintain a traceability of the remaining SL is necessary in fruit SC for different reasons: (1) customer satisfaction is strongly influenced by the freshness of the product, (2) in case the freshness will be lower than expected, a discount in the price can restore a proper level of customer satisfaction, and finally, (3) because of the perishability, product waste should occur if its SL is exhausted and it has not been assigned to any customer order. Therefore, to mathematically describe the relationship of homogeneous ATP with its selling price, it is necessary to first calculate the SL. When reserving homogeneous ATP in a specific time period, to be delivered in the customer's place on a due date (dd_o), the SC must take into account the time required for transporting the product from the harvesting point to the packing plants where the classifications and packing operations take place, as well as the transporting time since the product is shipped from the plant until it is delivered to the customer. This is necessary to deliver the product with the minimum portion of its SL (sl_{ib}) already consumed. In terms of calculation, we can define the fraction of already lost SL (LSL^{ob}), of the ATP in the moment of the delivery to the customer as follows:

$$LSL^{ob} = \sum_{p,h,t,r,i} \left(\frac{(dd_o - h) Y_{ib}^{ophtr}}{sl_{ib}} \right) \qquad \forall o, b \tag{3}$$

Where dd_o is the due date expected for the subtype b requested in the order proposal o. Consequently, the remaining shelf life (RSL^{ob}) as:

$$RSL^{ob} = 1 - LSL_{ob} \qquad \forall o, b \tag{4}$$

Figure 1 shows a short example about the way of calculate Eqs. (3) and (4).

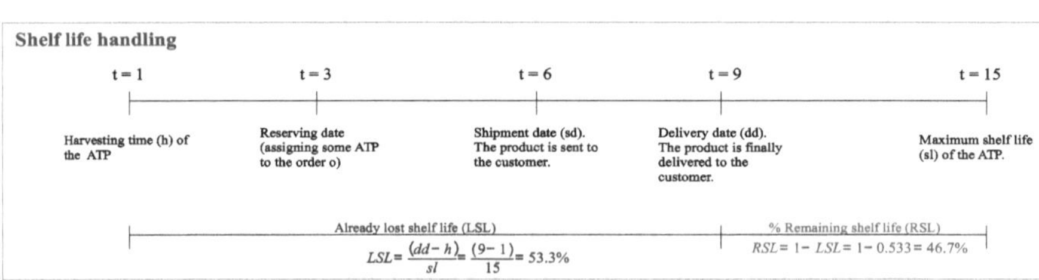

Fig. 1. Example of shelf life calculation

5 Shelf Life-Based Pricing Policy

It is usual in fruit SCs that products maintain their initial classification over time once classified and packed. This means that no quality level changes are considered. Instead, the selling price of the product is adjusted according to the aging process until the delivery date. This adjustment is made on a discrete basis, where prices are set based on predefined remaining SL intervals.

Let us consider the example in Fig. (2), where there are three price ranges of the ATP based on three predefined limits of the already lost shelf life (ms), and a fourth limit where the product is considered waste. Then, if the product has not overpass the first limit of the price range 1 (ms1), the selling price applied will be the highest one. With time passing the product gradually loses part of its SL until reaching the second limit. When overpassing this second limit, the selling price applied should be the second one and so on, until the product becomes waste. Therefore, the SL-based pricing policy for the assignation of homogeneous ATP should include as minimum, the following components:

ms^{rb} Maximum percentage of LSL^{ob} for each price range level r. These percentages are defined when the price of ATP lowers from lower ranges to higher ones.

sp^{r}_{ib} Selling price of product i, belonging to the subtype b, according to price range r.

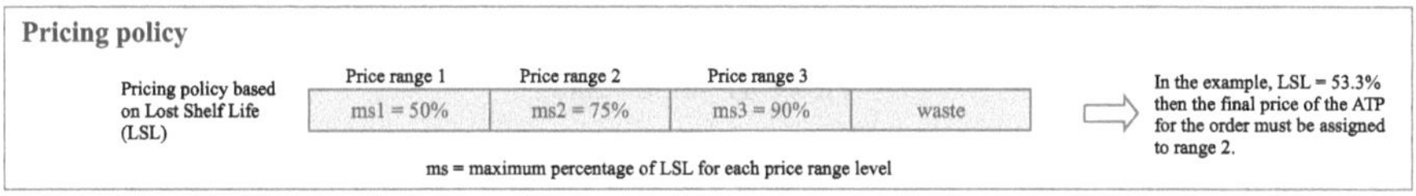

Fig. 2. Pricing policy schema

Maximise

$$\sum_{o,i,b} \sum_{p,h,t,r} rq^{o}_{ib} sp^{r}_{ib} Y^{ophtr}_{ib} \tag{5}$$

Subject to: Eqs. (1)–(2) and

$$LSL^{ob} = \sum_{p,h,t,r,i} \left(\frac{(dd_o - h) Y^{ophtr}_{ib}}{sl_{ib}} \right) \quad , \quad \forall o, b \tag{6}$$

$$LSL^{ob} - ms^{rb} \leq 1 - \sum_{p,h,t,i} Y^{ophtr}_{ib} \quad , \quad \forall o, b, r \tag{7}$$

$$ms^{rb} - LSL^{ob} \leq 1 - \sum_{p,h,t,i,r=r+1} Y^{ophtr}_{ib} \quad , \quad \forall o, b, r < nr \tag{8}$$

$$ms^{rb} \geq LSL^{ob} \quad , \quad \forall o, b, r = nr \tag{9}$$

In the above model, Eq. (5) aims to maximise the total sells of the product. Equations (1) and (2) specify the computation of the available to promise, while Eq. (6) calculates the remaining SL for the product used to fulfill each specific incoming order. Equations (7) and (8) oblige the binary variable to set just one price range for the subtype of product used to fulfil each specific order. Finally, Eq. (9) establishes that product used to fulfil orders cannot exceed the last price range, otherwise it becomes waste.

6 Numerical Example

The objective of the numerical example presented in this section is twofold. On one hand, it is shown the utility of the above equations for computing the incomes in case the product price depends on the product's freshness. On the other hand, it is shown that only maximizing incomes through serving customers with the most fresh product at the best price, presents the risk of increasing the waste. This could make impossible to serve future incoming orders. Let us assume the case of one packing plant that has to process four production lots of just one fruit (master plan) during the planning horizon composed by eight periods of time. Each lot is classified into 3 subtypes (b1, b2, b3) according to the β_{ib}^{pt} parameter (Table 1).

Table 1. Input data

		Period (t)							
		1	2	3	4	5	6	7	8
Master plan (mps_i^{pht})		350			500		400		200
β_{ib}^{pt}	b1	0,5			0,6		0,4		0,7
	b2	0,3			0,3		0,3		0,2
	b3	0,2			0,1		0,3		0,1
atp_{ib}^{pht}	b1	175			300		160		140
	b2	105			150		120		40
	b3	70			50		120		20
Harvesting time (h)		1			3		5		8
Period of becoming waste		5			7		9		12

At the beginning of the OPP, we assume that no order has been already committed. Suppose a maximum shelf life of 5 periods for all subtype, a pricing policy with 3 ranges (Table 2) and cost of 5€ per unit of product expired. Based on the harvesting time, the SL, the last price range, and Eq. (4), it is possible to compute the period at which each lot becomes waste (Table 1). This means that the ATP quantities derived from each lot may only be used to serve orders with a due date before the period at which it expires. Furthermore, due to customer homogeneity requirements, it is not possible to accumulate discrete ATP to serve the same order (Eqs. (1)–(2)). Suppose the sequential arrival of five customer order proposals requesting certain quantities of subtype b1 for different due dates. It is our aim to analyse the results of committing these orders on-line under two different policies: (a) to serve orders with the freshest product (Table 3), that is equivalent to sell the product at the highest price range and

(b) to serve orders with the less fresh product (Table 4). To implement the first policy, it is necessary to reserve the product from the ATP quantity as near as possible from the due date of the order. The column “Lot” in Tables 3 and 4, show the value of the lot in which the corresponding variable Y_{ib}^{ophtr} should have a value of 1. The huge issue in fruit supply chains is that the effect of the non homogeneous product combined with the perishability, brings out an enormous risk of having waste (since the remains of the ATP cannot be mixed in order to have more quantity to fulfill new orders). As it can be seen in Table 3, the first policy maximizes the incomes per order but at the same time presents two important drawbacks. First, it is not possible to serve the last order because there is not enough unexpired homogeneous product. Second, if we assume that no more orders arrive during the planning horizon, the remaining ATP of periods 1 and 4 will expire in periods 5 and 7, respectively. Consequently, this first policy originates a negligible waste of 300 units with a total cost of €1.500.

Table 2. Selling price based on price ranges.

Price Range	ms^{rb}	Selling price €/unit
r1	0,3	10 €
r2	0,6	8 €
r3	0,8	5 €

Table 3. Serving orders from the freshest product (highest price range/Last-In-First-Out)

							$UATP_{ib}$								
Order	Subtype	Quantity	Due date	Lot(Y_{ib}^{ophtr})	Lost Shelf Life (LSL_i^o)	Price range	1	4	6	8	Selling income				
1	b1	100	8	8	0,0%	r1	175	300	160	40	1.000 €				
2	b1	125	5	4	40,0%	r2	175	175	160	40	1.000 €				
3	b1	150	6	6	20,0%	r1	175	175	10	40	1.500 €	Waste			
4	b1	50	4	4	20,0%	r1	175	125	10	40	500 €	5	7	Total	Total Profit
5	b1	130	7				175	125	10	40		175	125	300	
Total							175	125	10	40	**4.000 €**	875 €	625 €	**1.500 €**	**2.500 €**

Table 4. Serving order from the less fresh product (lowest price range/First-In-First-Out)

							$UATP_{ib}^{pht}$								
Order	Subtype	Quantity	Due date	Lot(Y_{ib}^{ophtr})	Lost Shelf Life (LSL_i^o)	Price range	1	4	6	8	Selling income				
1	b1	100	8	6	60,0%	r2	175	300	60	140	800 €				
2	b1	125	5	1	80,0%	r3	50	300	60	140	625 €				
3	b1	150	6	4	60,0%	r2	50	150	60	140	1.200 €	Waste			
4	b1	50	4	1	60,0%	r2	0	150	60	140	400 €	5	7	Total	Total Profit
5	b1	130	7	4	80,0%	r3	0	20	60	140	650 €	0	20	20	
Total							0	20	60	140	**3.675 €**	0 €	100 €	**100 €**	**3.575 €**

On the contrary, in order to implement the second policy it is necessary to reserve product from the ATP as far as possible from the due date, but without being expired (Table 4). Through this second policy, it is possible to serve all customer order proposals. Although the incomes per sales are lower as compared with the first policy, the total profit is higher for the second policy because the waste is considerably reduced (only 20 units for a total cost of €100).

Then, there is a conflictive situation when deciding on the best balance between being careful in sell out the product as it is near to the maximum shelf life, knowing that it implies to lose a portion of profit, and achieving higher incomes by selling more fresh product but with the risk of not being able to serve some future orders and having more waste. This conflictive decision (due to the LHP, the perishability, and the expected selling prices linked with the shelf life), and the uncertainty involved in its solution, are important issues during the OPP optimization in fruit supply chains.

7 Conclusion

To better analyse fruit supply chains and the corresponding order promising process, it is needed to consider the non homogeneity in the product as an inherent characteristic from nature. Subdivision of the ATP into homogeneous sublots has to be performed. Another factor is the perishability that makes even more complicated the analysis because of the risk of having wasted product. Since the customer normally need fresher product, then the pricing policy can be adjusted to the shelf life. This paper describes an approach for modelling the splitting of the ATP into homogeneous sublots can be done, how to calculate the shelf life of the product at the moment of delivery, and based on that, an expected selling price. A numerical example shows a strong conflictive situation when the OPP must decide between the prioritization between profit (as a balance of sells income and waste cost) and the customer service (as a requirement of always have fresh and homogeneous product). To better analyse this conflictive situation, uncertainty methods could be used in future research work.

Acknowledgement. This research has been supported by the Ministry of Science, Technology and Telecommunications, government of Costa Rica (MICITT), through the program of innovation and human capital for competitiveness (PINN) (PED-019-2015-1).

References

Alarcon, F., Alemany, M.M.E., Lario, F.C., Oltra, R.F.: The lack of homogeneity in the product (LHP) in the ceramic tile industry and its impact on the reallocation of inventories. Boletin Soc. Espanola Ceram. Vidr. **50**, 49–57 (2011). doi:10.3989/cyv.072011

Alemany, M.M.E., Grillo, H., Ortiz, A., Fuertes-Miquel, V.S.: A fuzzy model for shortage planning under uncertainty due to lack of homogeneity in planned production lots. Appl. Math. Model. (2015). doi:10.1016/j.apm.2014.12.057

Alemany, M.M.E., Lario, F.-C., Ortiz, A., Gomez, F.: Available-To-Promise modeling for multi-plant manufacturing characterized by lack of homogeneity in the product: an illustration of a ceramic case. Appl. Math. Model. **37**, 3380–3398 (2013). doi:10.1016/j.apm.2012.07.022

Blanco, A.M., Masini, G., Petracci, N., Bandoni, J.A.: Operations management of a packaging plant in the fruit industry. J. Food Eng. **70**, 299–307 (2005). doi:10.1016/j.jfoodeng.2004.05.075

Grillo, H., Alemany, M.M.E., Ortiz, A.: A review of mathematical models for supporting the order promising process under Lack of Homogeneity in Product and other sources of uncertainty. Comput. Ind. Eng. **91**, 239–261 (2016)

Kilic, O.A., van Donk, D.P., Wijngaard, J., Tarim, S.A.: Order acceptance in food processing systems with random raw material requirements. Spectrum **32**, 905–925 (2010). doi:10.1007/s00291-010-0213-4

Lin, J.T., Hong, I.H., Wu, C.H., Wang, K.S.: A model for batch available-to-promise in order fulfillment processes for TFT-LCD production chains. Comput. Ind. Eng. **59**, 720–729 (2010). doi:10.1016/j.cie.2010.07.026

Maihami, R., Karimi, B.: Optimizing the pricing and replenishment policy for non-instantaneous deteriorating items with stochastic demand and promotional efforts. Comput. Oper. Res. **51**, 302–312 (2014). doi:10.1016/j.cor.2014.05.022

Mundi, M.I., Alemany, M.M.E., Poler, R., Fuertes-Miquel, V.S.: Fuzzy sets to model master production effectively in Make to Stock companies with Lack of Homogeneity in the Product. Fuzzy Sets Syst. **293**, 95–112 (2016). http://dx.doi.org/10.1016/j.fss.2015.06.009

Tsao, Y.-C., Sheen, G.-J.: Dynamic pricing, promotion and replenishment policies for a deteriorating item under permissible delay in payments. Part Spec. Issue Top. Real-Time Supply Chain Manag. **35**, 3562–3580 (2008). doi:10.1016/j.cor.2007.01.024

and learning processes (Middel et al. 2006). The knowledge compiled by researchers after these projects can be discussed and shared with other companies and researchers (Alvesson 1996; Coughlan and Coghlan 2002), especially in the field of supply chain management (Näslund et al. 2010).

The collaboration project, led by the authors of this paper, has been carried out in the region of Galicia (Northwest Spain) and has been supported by the Food Cluster of Galicia (CLUSAGA; www.clusteralimentariodegalicia.org). The food sector is one of the strategic sectors in Galicia both for its size and for its economic and social significance.

Ten food companies participated in this project (4 dairy companies, 2 meat companies, 2 fruits and vegetables companies, 1 wine company and 1 dough company). Likewise, an association representing five small agriculture cooperatives participates in the project. The geographical location of these companies is presented in Fig. 1. Almost all companies are small or medium sized companies.

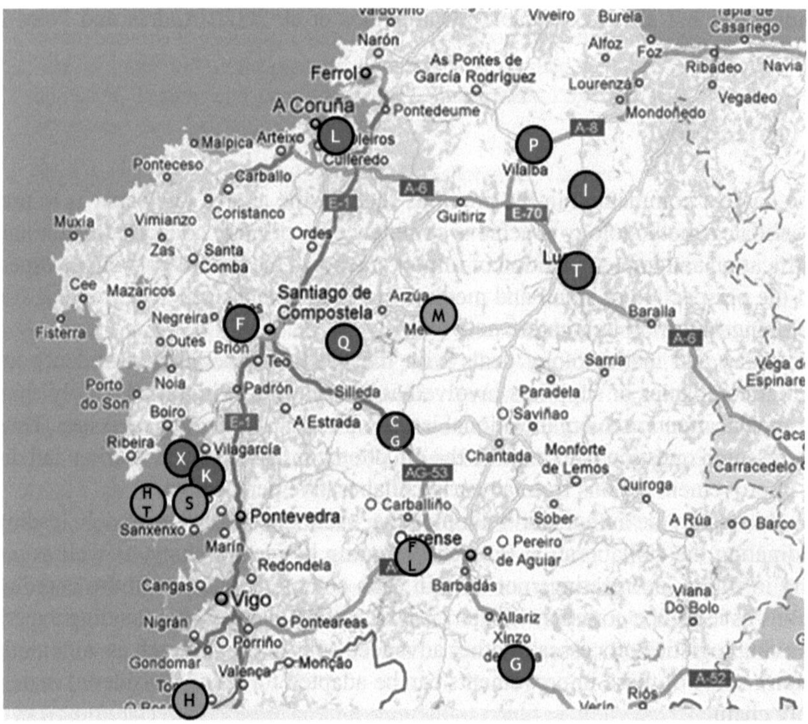

Fig. 1. Geographical location of companies (red) and agriculture cooperatives (green) in the project (Galicia; Northwest Spain) (Color figure online)

Although some companies develop their activities in the same type of food subsector, only some companies of dairy and agricultural subsectors could be considered as competitors.

3 The Methodology and the Project

The collaboration process began with a visit of the authors to each company and cooperative in order to know and understand their logistics and productive problems.

Then, three sessions of work were developed on the premises of each company and cooperative to deepen the analysis and diagnosis. The purpose of this phase was not only to identify and to classify potential improvements in the supply chain management, but also to implement some of them. A summary of this individual diagnosis was shared electronically among all companies of the project.

Simultaneously, three specific sessions of joint work with all companies and cooperatives were developed in order, not only to exchange and share examples of individual improvements in each company (to encourage similar changes in other companies), but also to explore joint collaboration actions. The project was developed during four months.

The members of the project team were the authors of the paper (the coordinators and leaders) and those responsible for logistics and/or production management in each company. As some of the companies are small companies, in some cases, the CEOs participated directly in the project. The involvement of main directors and some CEOs reinforces their commitment with the project.

Likewise, between meetings, the authors coordinated the development of proposed actions by telephone and e-mail. In each company, the authors identified opportunities for improvements and implemented them after. These individual improvements could be grouped into three big areas:

- The packaging rationalization from a logistics point of view. For example, in one meat company, thanks to the redesign of one box has been possible the reduction of its cost (the amount of paperboard used is reduced a 12 %, but also it is reduced the amount of waste). Additionally, this improvement increases the number of boxes per EUR pallet (from 80 to 120; a 50 % without increasing the height of the pallet), so the logistics costs are lower.
- The improvement of warehouse management. For example, changing the warehouses layout, the procedures of warehouses processes (receiving, putaway, storage, picking, replenishment or shipping), the definition of requirements for WMS (Warehouse Management Systems) implementation or the adoption of EAN 128 labels in unit loads and boxes.
- The improvement of transport management. For example, redesigning the internal transport routes, implementing KPIs for measuring efficiency in transport, analyzing the suitability of adopting internal o outsourced transport.

As it was commented previously, the individual actions in each company were presented at the joint meetings as an example for other companies in the project. These sessions were important in order, not only to share and discuss results and experiences of improvement, but also to achieve confidence between participants. The common type of individual improvements adopted seems to confirm this last statement. Likewise, it was important to understand the problems and conditions of each company for identifying feasible actions in collaboration. Additionally, this confidence was critic for developing the stage of joint improvements and going beyond to establish the basics of potential "collaboration networks" in the future.

So, also in these meetings, different improvement in logistics management alternatives were explored from a collaborative perspective. Thus, thanks to this primary collaborative analysis, three main areas for improvement were identified:

- The combined transport between companies to reach markets and common retailers. In this regard, two options were selected: one with three routes in the Galicia area; another with three routes to deliver products from Galicia to other areas of Spain.
- The placement of a joint warehouse in the area of Madrid for delivery products to central, south and east markets in Spain. In this regard, four companies initially had outsourced small stores in the surroundings of Madrid. Likewise, 10 companies delivered their products via Madrid, so the use of one joint warehouse as a cross-docking point was also a potential improvement for companies.
- The joint purchase and negotiation of products and logistics services, particularly, packaging material, labels, fuel, parcel services and the "pool" of reusable packaging. For example, the yearly number of cardboard boxes used by 10 companies exceeds the 2.4 million units. Likewise, in these 10 companies the yearly consumption of labels and plastic film for pallets exceeds, respectively, the 15 million of units and the 1.2 million of meters.

These areas of improvement have currently different levels of implementation. Four of the six proposed transport routes are running today (including the example of the next section). Regarding Madrid Warehouse, three of the companies are sharing the same premise. Finally, five companies are purchasing some logistics products and components together. Clusaga and the authors are working to include in this process new companies.

In the assessment of the interest of implementing each of these joint improvements three major groups of difficulties were found (especially at transport and storage):

- The retailers and customers´ requirements. For example, the time of loading/unloading or the combination of internal and outsourced transport resources.
- The legal requirements; for example, the temperature range of products, the incompatibilities between products, the restrictions on driving hours, or the limitations in the capacity of trucks (weight and volume; all companies distribute their products in pallets).
- The quality of the available information (the lack of information, the lack of structured information, the lack of reliability of the information or the variability of information).

Regarding this last point, further efforts to align and structure the information are still needed to make an electronic platform that eases central purchases and sharing transport and storage resources. Anyway, the first steps to develop a "collaboration network" in the future have been established.

4 An Example of Joint Transport Improvement

To illustrate an example of joint action among companies, the analysis of a transport route (from the South to the North of Galicia) for the distribution of products at a controlled temperature is presented (see Fig. 2). The ultimate goal of this shared route was to improve standards of quality, service and cost associated with the transport of distribution to customers in northern Galicia (therefore compatible with the schedules of loading and unloading of each supplier and retailer).

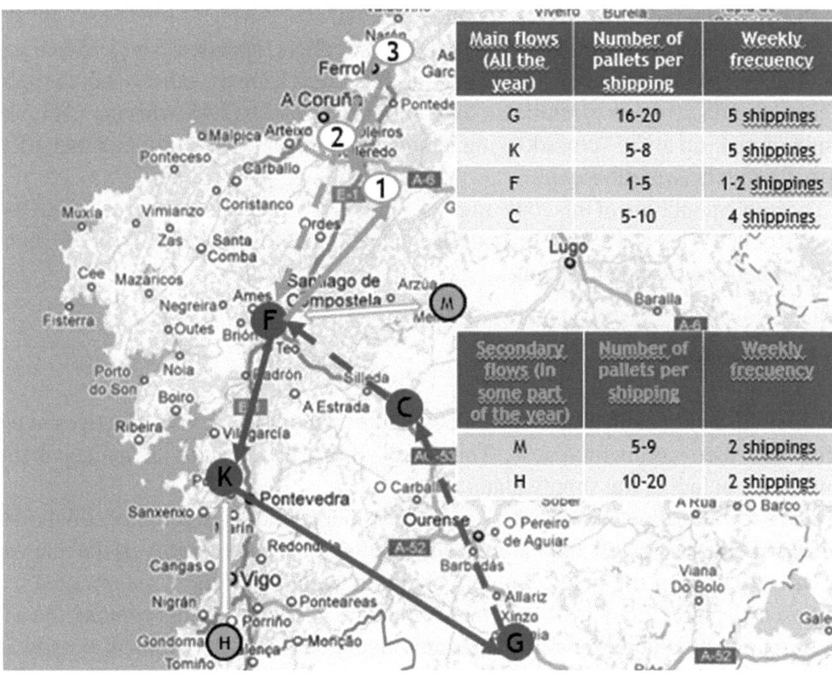

Fig. 2. Description of one joint route proposed by companies

Specifically, after considering six different options, a system of joint transport arises from the companies “C”, “G”, “K” and “F” (main flow) to the warehouses of three retailers in northern Galicia (retailers: “1”, “2” and “3”). Likewise, in some periods of the year, the main flow is supplemented with flows coming from the cooperatives “M” and “H” (secondary flows).

To implement this proposal, two coordinate daily routes have been adopted. On the one hand, a model “milk run” product collection from Santiago de Compostela (center of Galicia) following the “K”, “G”, “C” and “F” sequence (this sequence eases the availability of the goods in each company). On the other hand, a circuit from Santiago de Compostela to the three retailers´ stores.

The authors of this paper play the role of negotiators with retailers. Thanks to this proposal, the retailers can reduce the number of trucks received in their warehouses, without compromising agreed delivery times.

In this sense, to make possible the proposal, the company "F" (located in the surroundings of Santiago de Compostela) is used as a "crossdocking" point for the other companies. Likewise, this "crossdocking" point ("F") is used to integrate the secondary flow that comes from the cooperative "M" (the cooperative itself moves their goods to "F" with their own transport resources).

Something similar has been adopted with the company "K" used as "crossdocking" point to integrate the flow from the cooperative "H".

The first of the trucks (pallet collection from suppliers) spends 9.5 h (5.75 h of transport (402 km); 45 min per stop and 45 min of legal break). On the other hand, the second of the trucks (distribution to retailers), the route spends 9.45 h (3.45 h driving (241.4 km), 45 min of pick-up at the "crossdocking" point "F", a legal break of 45 min and 4.5 h of stops at retailers´ warehouses).

The implementation of this route implies a 20 to 50 % reduction of the cost of delivery of each pallet. The extra cost of handling the products in the crossdocking point is included in these estimated savings.

5 Conclusions

Nowadays in a very competitive world, companies have to propose alternatives in order to improve their competitiveness. This need affects to all areas of management in companies, including the supply chain management.

This paper has aimed to contribute to a better understanding of primary collaboration when companies are small and medium sized without a clear visibility of the interest of this collaboration in the field of supply chain management ("the common goal") and when no many structured information resources are available. In this context, the adoption of this methodology for deploying individual and joint improvement is especially significant in order to achieve confidence between companies and as a previous step for adopting "collaboration networks".

Going beyond, the role of the authors acting as "agent of change" in this methodology, according to the Action Research approach should be highlighted. This involvement allows the identification of potential joint improvements, easing the achievement of confidence among companies. Likewise, the authors supply the vision of changes and improvements adopted successfully in other supply chains. These efforts could allow the foundation of the pillars of future collaborative networks.

References

González-Loureiro, M., Dabic, M., Puig, F.: Global organizations and supply chain: new research avenues in the international human resource management. Int. J. Phys. Distrib. Logist. Manag. **44**(8/9), 689–712 (2014)

García-Arca, J., González-Portela Garrido, A.T., Prado-Prado, J.C.: "Packaging Logistics" for improving performance in supply chains: the role of meta-standards implementation. Production **26**(2), 261–272 (2016)

Huo, B.: The impact of supply chain integration on company performance: an organizational capability perspective. Supply Chain Manag. Int. J. **17**(6), 596–610 (2012)

Wiengarten, F., Longoni, A.: A nuanced view on supply chain integration: a coordinative and collaborative approach to operational and sustainability performance improvement. Supply Chain Manag. Int. J. **20**(2), 139–150 (2015)

Pérez-Mesa, J.C., Galdeano-Gómez, E.: Collaborative firms managing perishable products in a complex supply network: an empirical analysis of performance. Supply Chain Manag. Int. J. **20**(2), 128–138 (2015)

Barratt, M.: Understanding the meaning of collaboration in the supply chain. Supply Chain Manag. Int. J. **9**(1), 30–42 (2004)

Wilhelm, M.M.: Managing co-opetition through horizontal supply chain relations: linking dyadic and network levels of analysis. J. Oper. Manag. **29**(7/8), 663–676 (2011)

Choi, T.Y., Wu, Z.: Triads in supply networks: theorizingbuyer–supplier–supplier relationships. J. Supply Chain Manag. **45**(1), 8–25 (2009)

Camarinha-Matos, L.M., Afsarmanesh, H.: Collaborative networks: a new scientific discipline. J. Intell. Manuf. **16**, 439–452 (2005)

Matopoulos, A., Vlachopoulou, M., Manthou, V., Manos, B.: A conceptual framework for supply chain collaboration: empirical evidence from the agri-food industry. Supply Chain Manag. Int. J. **12**(3), 177–186 (2007)

Andres, B., Poler, R.: Computing the strategies alignment in collaborative networks. In: Mertins, K., Bénaben, F., Poler, R., Bourrières, J.-P. (eds.) Enterprise Interoperability VI, pp. 29–40. Springer International Publishing, Cham (2014)

Andres, B., Sanchis, R., Poler, R.: A cloud platform to support collaboration in supply networks. Int. J. Prod. Manag. Eng. **4**(1), 5–13 (2016)

Wu, Z., Choi, T., Rungtusanatham, M.J.: Supplier–supplier relationships in buyer–supplier–supplier triads: implications for supplier performance. J. Oper. Manag. **28**(2), 115–123 (2010)

Rapoport, R.N.: Three dilemmas of action research. Hum. Relat. **23**, 499–513 (1970)

Raelin, J.A., Coghlan, D.: Developing managers as learners and researchers: using action learning. J. Manag. Educ. **30**(5), 670–689 (2006)

Middel, R., Coghlan, D., Coughlan, P., Brennan, L., McNichols, T.: Action research in collaborative improvement. Int. J. Technol. Manag. **33**(1), 67–91 (2006)

Alvesson, M.: Leadership studies: from procedure and abstraction to reflexivity and situation. Leadersh. Q. **7**(4), 455–485 (1996)

Coughlan, P., Coghlan, D.: Action research for operations management. Int. J. Oper. Prod. Manag. **22**(2), 220–240 (2002)

Näslund, D., Kale, R., Paulraj, A.: Action research in supply chain management—a framework for relevant and rigorous research. J. Bus. Logist. **31**(2), 331–355 (2010)

Mapping Multidimensional Value(s) for Co-creation Networks in a Circular Economy

Anna Aminoff(✉), Katri Valkokari, and Outi Kettunen

VTT, Technical Research Centre of Finland, PL1000, 02044 Espoo, Finland
{anna.aminoff,katri.valkokari,outi.kettunen}@vtt.fi

Abstract. The transition towards a circular economy cannot be achieved if individual organizations advance their own interests independently. Companies need to build new collaborative networks for value co-creation. Therefore, identification of what kind of value will be created or destroyed for different partners in the networks is critical. In this paper, we propose a framework for mapping multidimensional value in co-creation networks by combining streams of literature on three topics: (1) Circular Economy, (2) Co-Creation and Collaborative networks, (3) Sustainable value creation. The specific contribution of the framework is that it recognizes that the value created in different parts of networks is linked, and the change of value in one link influences others. Moreover, the approach of the paper adds the dimension of circularity into analyses of value creation.

Keywords: Circular economy · Multidimensional value · Co-creation · Collaborative networks

1 Introduction

If the current consumption trend continues, the Earth's carrying capacity will be greatly exceeded. Recently, the Circular Economy (CE) has attracted increasing interest as a way to overcome the problems of the current production and consumption model [1]. CE refers to a concept which aims at creating a system that is restorative by design [1, 2]; and recently, emphasizes economic aspect, seeing CE business models as enablers to create competitive advantage [3]. The CE enables future growth through a supportive relationship with ecological and social systems [2]. The CE cannot be achieved if individual actors advance their own interests independently. The transition towards the CE will require new value chain partners, or new roles of existing partners and a new kind of collaboration between the participating partners. Companies need to build new collaborative networks for value co-creation. Therefore, identification of what kind of value will be created or destroyed for different partners in the networks, aiming to create win-win-win business models, is critical [4]. With "win-win-win" we refer to the possibility that more than bilateral value can be created.

In this paper, we propose a systematic approach for identifying multidimensional value in co-creation networks. The paper addresses the following research questions:

H. Afsarmanesh et al. (Eds.): PRO-VE 2016, IFIP AICT 480, pp. 629–638, 2016.
DOI: 10.1007/978-3-319-45390-3_54

(1) How can multidimensional value(s) be identified for the actors' co-creation networks? (2) How are the multidimensional values linked together from the viewpoint of different actors? The aim of the framework developed in this paper is twofold. First, the aim is to provide rich data for the research to develop an understanding of value creation in a CE. Second, the aim is to guide managers to recognize the implications of novel CE business models for different actors in a co-creation network.

2 Research Design

For our research design, we first advance a conceptual framework of mapping multidimensional value in a CE by combining streams of literature on three topics: (1) Circular Economy, (2) Co-creation and Collaborative networks, (3) Sustainable value creation. This is presented in Sect. 3.

We chose a qualitative case study design to match the state of current theory and the exploratory goals of the study, as suggested by [5]. A case study design is applicable for identifying emerging themes and patterns as it allows for acquiring rich and detailed data of the studied phenomenon. Our unit of analyses is 'a value proposition for the business model (of a network)'. As cases, we sought companies that are putting effort into developing a circular business, and who already have at least some experience of CE business. For particular cases, we selected business models that focal companies can see will create competitive advantage. This enabled us to get rich and relevant data. The cases are presented in Table 1. The main data collection method was workshops with companies. The selected participants in the workshops were mostly from a focal company, but in one workshop there were also stakeholders (see Table 1). One workshop lasted for three hours, and was led by two or three researchers.

Table 1. Description of the cases

Case	Company	Tentative business model of a network	Workshop participants
Case A	Company 1: SME	Profitable processing of mixed construction site waste into secondary raw material	Managing Director Head of production Head of R&D Quality manager
Case B	Company 1:	High-quality sorting including data bank, collection equipment and methods, and logistics centers close to the waste source	Managing Director Head of production Head of R&D Quality manager
Case C	Company 2: Startup, social enterprise Service provider, digitalization	Digitalized concept, which enables recycling centers to digitalize the process, and add value-added services	CEO (owner) Chairman of the board, Investors (2)

We used the data from cases for two purposes; (1) to empirically test the framework, and (2) to illustrate the framework with one of these cases. So far, we have tested the framework in three cases. We selected one case, Case A, to illustrate the framework.

3 The Framework for Identifying Multidimensional Value in Co-creation Networks

3.1 Circular Economy

A CE is an industrial system that is restorative or regenerative by intention and design [2]. Current trends, such as growing consumption, new generations of consumers, technological leaps, and urbanisation are accelerating the transformation towards a CE. The CE discussion has recently started to highlight the economic aspect, seeing CE business models as enablers to create a competitive advantage [6, 7]. The circular concept is proposed to give an even greater competitive advantage in the future as it generates more value from each unit of resource than the traditional 'take-make-dispose' model [2].

The CE sets new expectations on business network actors related to present product and service deliveries. The future business models will be radically different compared to current models, and the value of the material itself can increase instead of diminishing. These will affect the roles of actors as well as value distribution among the actors. Therefore, the transformation towards a CE sets challenges, especially for established companies as it may destroy the usefulness of their existing capabilities and business models, and require changes to their business networks. Previous literature has presented several approaches to CE business models and for evaluating product sustainability. One of the most recognized is the 6R methodology. The six R's come from the words *reduce, reuse, recycle, recover, redesign* and *remanufacture*. The methodology represents a 'science-based, comprehensive and quantitative' framework for the evaluation of product sustainability [8]. Promoting 6R sustainable manufacturing practices will require collaboration and integration across businesses in the product life-cycle stages, which all must be considered holistically if sustainability benefits are to be derived [9]. EMF [10], in turn, includes in the value circle five activities: share, maintain/prolong, reuse/redistribute, refurbish/remanufacture and recycle.

3.2 Co-creation and Collaboration Networks

The co-creation paradigm highlights interactions, joint resource bases, engagement platforms and an ecosystemic approach as new means for business [11]. Therefore, collaborative networked organisations (CNOs) show a high potential as drivers of value co-creation [12]. A distinction has been made between different types of co-creation in networks, and the characteristics are summarized in 3C's as: *cooperative, coordinative,* and *collaborative* [13]. Collaborative networks (CN) are defined as autonomous, geographically distributed, and heterogeneous, dynamic and often temporary in their nature [14]. Further, the concept of CNO's highlights that there is an organization responsible for the participants' activities, roles and shared governance rules. To summarize, these categorizations of co-creation and collaborative networks distinguish the network models based on the interdependency of the participants and levels of co-creation. A co-creation network can be distinguished from the value network based on the development orientation, i.e., a co-creation network aims to generate new business opportunities, whereas a value network focuses on the present supplier – customer deliveries.

Based on the literature of collaborative networks, Romero and Molino [15] *have introduced the concept of A Green Virtual Enterprise Breeding Environment (GVBE)* as a model for reaching sustainable development through collaboration. The GVBE is defined as a long-term strategic alliance of green enterprises. In the area of CN there are several tools and methods developed that can assist the commitment and interaction of the multiple stakeholders [16]. Thus, more studies focusing specifically on *dynamics of collaborative co-creation networks* (i.e., building and re-building them) are needed for further advancement of the existing literature.

In this study, we define the *circular economy co-creation network* as a dynamic network including both the actors of the *core business value network* and other relevant *stakeholders.* The key element of co-creation is that actors have a shared, jointly generated purpose, i.e., a CE business innovation case that can be based on 6R strategies, sharing assets or providing services [9, 10]. Figure 1 illustrates the actors and their relationships in the layered circular economy co-creation network.

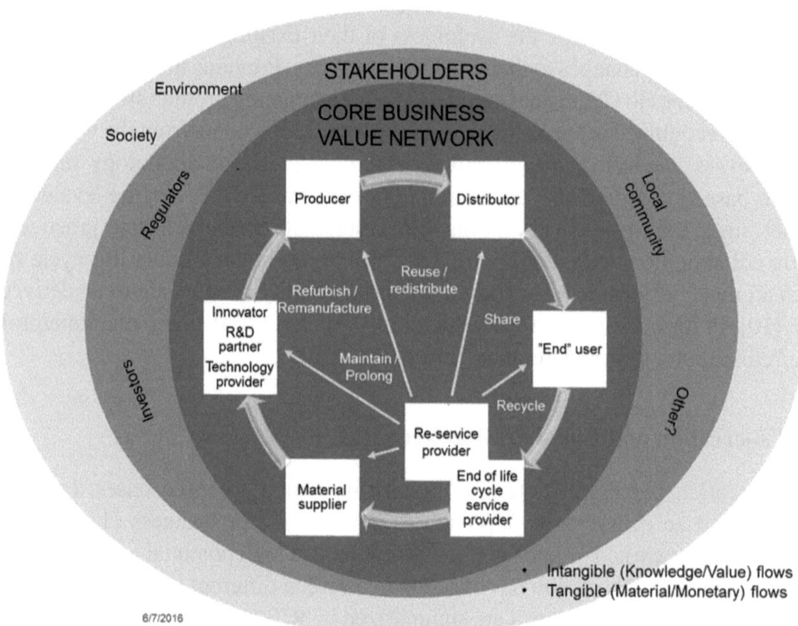

Fig. 1. Actors in the circular economy co-creation network

Here, the circular economy co-creation network consists of two main types: actors in the core business value network and other stakeholders such as regulators and investors. In addition to them, environment and society are highlighted as beneficiaries in line with the sustainability paradigm [17, 18]. The challenge of co-creation, which is required in CE, is to find the 'win-win-win' setting and therefore value for each of these stakeholder groups as well as members of core-business network needs to be identified [4]. This includes identification of both intangible and tangible flows [19] between the actors. In a CE, value is not created in a firm in isolation, but firms and their stakeholders acting together. There are often game-changing changes in business models [20] and the considerations of value for the broad range of new network actors and stakeholders become vital.

3.3 Sustainable Value Creation and Value Creation in a CE

Sustainable value creation and value creation in a CE are closely linked research streams, but as the research of value creation in a CE is still in its infancy, we base the framework mainly on sustainable value creation. Traditionally, value has been treated only as revenues from customers minus the costs incurred [21]. Businesses have rarely approached environmental and social topics from a value perspective, but have treated them as peripheral matters [22]. Sustainable value creation recognizes the three bottom lines, i.e., economic, environmental and social aspects of value creation [23]. Porter and Kramer [22] introduce a shared value concept which refers to creating economic value in a way that also creates value for society by addressing its needs. Here, value is defined as benefits relative to cost. Sustainable value creation includes a consideration of value to different actors of a business network, and other stakeholders such as investors, shareholders as well as government and regulators [24, 25]. In sustainable business thinking, also the environment and society are considered stakeholders [24].

Bocken et al. [22] recognize four different forms of value that enhance the balance between the self-interests of involved actors and facilitate collaboratively shaping the value for different stakeholders. The forms are: value captured, value missed, value destroyed and new value opportunities. Value captured represents the positive benefits delivered to stakeholders. Value missed refers to situations where stakeholders fail to capitalize on existing assets, capabilities and resources. Value destroyed represents negative outcomes of the business, and usually concerns the forms of damaging environmental or social impact. In the CE, the same principles can be applied; however, more research is needed to elaborate the different aspects of value. CE emphasize the multidimensional aspects of value creation, as achieving only economic benefits doesn't guarantee the business to be restorative and regenerative [2].

3.4 The Preliminary Framework for Mapping Multidimensional Value(S) for Co-creation Networks in a Circular Economy

The framework adapts a qualitative approach to identifying the multidimensional forms of value for different actors in the co-creation network, aiming to provide rich data. This includes three steps in order to coordinate and guide the work. *The first step* in the

Figure 3 presents the results of using the framework in Case A.

1 DEFINING THE PRELIMINARY VALUE PROPOSITION OF THE NETWORK:
Profitable processing of mixed construction site waste into raw material

2 IDENTIFICATION OF ACTORS OF THE (PROSPECTIVE) NETWORK AND ITS VIEW

Innovators: Universities, own expertise
Raw-material suppliers: Construction and transportation companies
Producer: Company A
Distributor: Future wholesaler/distributor of renewable materials. Raw material stock for secondary raw materials.
End users: Producers of secondary raw materials products. Manufacturers of goods from secondary raw materials. Energy plants.
Others Energy plants, waste processing plants

What enhances?
- Changes in the values of people and companies
- Regulation
- Technological advancements
- Waste reception costs

What hinders?
- Increasing amount of plants burning waste

3 VALUE HUNTING

Company A		Potential value sources and value for core actors	Possible missed or destroyed value
What enhances? • Regulation • Traceability of materials • Technologies • Competition and competitors • Awareness of consumers • Owners and the strategies of the company • Awareness of new possibilities	What hinders? • Dirty and mixed waste • Our own limited thoughts • Competition of the construction waste • Analysis costs of materials • Expensive treatment processes and equipment • Increase in the waste burning cacpacity	• Streghtening the upstream and downstream business chain • Business expansion to new markets	• The value decreases since most of the material is burned or directed to the competitors for treatment • Obsolence increases over time • Transportation costs

Other actors	Potential value sources and value for core actors	Possible missed or destroyed value
Society as a whole	Raw material and energy self-sufficiency	
Raw material supplier	Raw material quality and efficient material procurement Efficient processes	Need for warehousing permices of non-separeted waste diminishes
End user (Company A's customer)	Increased quality of raw material	
Extensive delivery network	Increased business opportunities	
Machine and equipment suppliers	Separation equipment IT providers	
Energy production plants and waste treatment plants		Waste as a fuel for energy plants diminishes Waste material for traditional waste treatment plants diminishes

Fig. 3. Illustration of the framework based on Case A

5 Discussion and Conclusions

Collaboration across a wide set of stakeholders is necessary in transformation towards CE [3, 26]. However, currently, there is a lack of a framework for aiding the companies to identify the multidimensional value in a CE. Based on the previous literature, we develop a systematic approach to identifying multidimensional values for their co-creation networks, emphasizing interlinkages of values and actors, and to understand the new roles of the existing and new partners. The specific contribution of the approach we propose is that it recognizes that the value created in different parts of a network is linked, and the change of benefits and costs in one link influences others. Moreover, the previous literature has studied both value creation and capture in a linear way – in value chains or networks. The approach of the paper adds the dimension of circularity.

The framework will both guide the companies in developing a circular business and achieving win-win-win business models as well as researchers in creating novel knowledge of value creation in a CE. We tested the conceptual framework in three cases, and based on the feedback it was seen as valuable by the companies, the main value being adding the understanding of the implication towards the co-creation network as a whole. For research, the use of a framework offers many possibilities. The framework will allow us to further analyze what kind of value is created in a CE and further categorize this value. This forms the basis for the research of CE business models. We will also be able to form archetypes of co-creation networks in different kinds of business models. Moreover, applying a framework in data collection will also enable the creation of knowledge of what kind of value is missed today and what are the major value creation opportunities in a CE.

The proposed framework focuses on the very first phase in developing and implementing networked CE business models and building a circular economy co-creation network. As the next phase, the identified key players of the network will be motivated for actual collaboration, in order to address the possibilities, challenges and value issues together at network level.

References

1. Lieder, M., Rashid, A.: Towards circular economy implementation: a comprehensive review in context of manufacturing industry. J. Clean. Prod. **115**, 36–51 (2015)
2. Ellen MacArthur Foundation: Towards the Circular Economy: Accelerating the Scale-Up Across Global Supply Chains, vol. 3 (2014)
3. Ghisellini, P., Cialani, C., Ulgiati, S.: A review on circular economy: the expected transition to a balanced interplay of environmental and economic systems. J. Clean. Prod. **114**, 11–32 (2015)
4. Antikainen, M., Valkokari, K.: Framework for Sustainable Circular Business Model Innovation, pp. 13–16. ISPIM Innov. Forum, Boston, March 2016
5. Yin, R.: Case Study Research: Design and Methods (Applied Social Research Methods), 5th edn. SAGE Publications, Thousand Oaks (2013)
6. Wijkman, A., Kristian, S.: The Circular Economy and Benefits for Society – Swedish Case Study Shows Jobs and Climate as Clear Winners. Club of Rome (2015)
7. Srivastava, S.: Network design for reverse logistics. Omega **36**, 535–548 (2008)
8. Joshi, K., Venkatachalam, A., Jaafar, I.H., Jawahir, I.: A new methodology for transforming 3R concept into 6R concept for improved product sustainability. In: Global Conference on Sustainable Product Development and Life Cycle Engineering, Sao Paulo, Brazil, October 2006
9. Badurdeen, F., Iyengar, D., Metta, H.: Extending total life-cycle thinking to sustainable supply chain design. Int. J. Prod. Lifecycle Manag. **4**, 49–67 (2010)
10. Ellen MacArthur Foundation: Intelligent Assets: Unlocking the Circular Economy Potential (2016)
11. Ramaswamy, V., Ozcan, K.: The Co-creation Paradigm. Standford Business Books, Redwood City (2014)
12. Romero, D., Molina, A.: Collaborative networked organisations and customer communities: value co-creation and co-innovation in the networking era. Prod. Plan. Control **22**, 447–472 (2011)
13. Brown, K., Keast, R.: Citizen-government engagement: community connection through networked arrangements. Asian J. Publ. Adm. **25**, 107–132 (2003)
14. Camarinha-Matos, L., Afsarmanesh, H.: Collaborative Networks – Reference Modelling. Springer, New York (2008)
15. Romero, D., Molina, A.: Green virtual enterprises and their breeding environments. In: Camarinha-Matos, L.M., Boucher, X., Afsarmanesh, H. (eds.) Collaborative Networks for a Sustainable World. PRO-VE 2010 IFIP AICT, pp. 25–35. Springer, Heidelberg (2010)

16. Camarinha-Matos, L.M., Afsarmanesh, H., Boucher, X.: The role of collaborative networks in sustainability. In: Camarinha-Matos, L.M., Boucher, X., Afsarmanesh, H. (eds.) PRO-VE 2010. IFIP AICT, vol. 336, pp. 1–16. Springer, Heidelberg (2010)
17. Freeman, R.E., Wicks, A.C., Parmar, B.: Stakeholder theory and the corporate objective revisited. Organ. Sci. INFORMS **15**(3), 364–369 (2004)
18. Schenkel, M., Krikke, H., Caniëls, M.C.J., van der Laan, E.: Creating integral value for stakeholders in closed loop supply chains. J. Purchasing Supply Manag. **41**(3), 155–166 (2015)
19. Allee, V.: Value network analysis and value conversion of tangible and intangible assets. J. Intellect. Capital **9**, 5–24 (2008)
20. Beattie, V., Smith, S.J.: Value creation and business models: refocusing the intellectual capital debate. Br. Acc. Rev. **45**, 243–254 (2013)
21. Lindgreen, A.: Value in business and industrial marketing. Value Bus. Ind. Mark. **41**, 4–7 (2012)
22. Porter, M.E., Kramer, M.R.: Creating Shared Value. Harvard Bus. Rev. **89**, 62–77 (2011)
23. Elkington, J.: Cannibals with Forks: The Triple Bottom Line of 21st Century Business. An Introduction to Sustainable Development. Capstone Publishing Ltd, Oxford (2006)
24. Bocken, N., Rana, P., Short, S.W.: Value mapping for sustainable business thinking. J. Ind. Prod. Eng. **32**, 67–81 (2015)
25. Donaldson, T., Preston, L.: The stakeholder theory of the corporation: concepts, evidence and implications. Acad. Manag. Rev. **20**, 65–91 (1995)
26. Lacy, P., Rutqvist, J.: Waste to Wealth: The Circular Economy Advantage, 1st edn. Palgrave Macmillan, Basingstoke (2015)

Green Virtual Business Network for Managing and Reusing Waste Between Partner Organizations

Ahm Shamsuzzoha[1,2(✉)], Petri Helo[2], and Maqsood Sandhu[3]

[1] Department of Mechanical and Industrial Engineering, Sultan Qaboos University, PO Box 33, 123 Muscat, Oman
ahsh@squ.edu.om

[2] Department of Production, University of Vaasa, PO Box 700, 65101 Vaasa, Finland
{ahm.shamsuzzoha, petri.helo}@uwasa.fi

[3] Department of Business Administration, United Arab Emirates University, Al Ain, UAE
maqsoods@uaeu.ac.ae

Abstract. Today, industry is under intense pressure to stay competitive in market segment with limited resources. To withstand such challenges manufacturing organizations need to be collaborative. This collaboration not only benefits many aspects in their daily businesses but contributes other aspects like waste management. In this research, especial focus is given on managing industrial wastes through recycling and reuse between partner organizations as resources within a business network. This concept turns out mutual benefits between partners and managing Eco-friendly business environment based on substituting a new resource by an undervalued resource such as waste. This paper also presents a modelling approach for industrial wastes management within business network, which intends to support the identification of wastes substitution opportunities.

Keywords: Business network · Waste reuse · Industrial ecology · Sustainable environment

1 Introduction

The green virtual business network is an environment where companies cooperate with each other for achieving mutual benefits. Such network can be built both physically collocated and virtually distributed regionally or globally. The objective of either form of network is to share resources and expertise within the networked partners under mutual trust. The trust plays the main role to be successful of such networks.

There are various forms and formats of business network with different goals. From literature, it is noticed that most of the business network is mainly focused on developing collaborative products and/or services to gain competitive power over competitors [1, 2]. However, little or no research is done so far with the issue of managing waste collaborate within the green virtual business network. With the view to fulfill

H. Afsarmanesh et al. (Eds.): PRO-VE 2016, IFIP AICT 480, pp. 639–651, 2016.
DOI: 10.1007/978-3-319-45390-3_55

such objective this is concentrated on managing industrial waste through forming and executing collaborative business network. The objective of this research can be categorized as follows:

(1) To propose a methodology to support formation and execution of a business network for mutual benefits
(2) To investigate the possibility to managing wastes within collaborative partners
(3) To promote environmental sustainability through green virtual business network.

The paper is structured as follows: Sect. 3 illustrates relevant literature in the proposed field, while Sect. 3 highlights the research methodology. Section 4 concentrates to demonstrate the life cycle of business collaboration. Brief explanation of industrial waste is outlined in Sect. 5, whereas; Sect. 6 states the techniques of collaborative waste management in industry. A framework of networked waste management is illustrated in Sect. 7, while, mapping of waste management between companies are defined along with mathematical model to calculate the waste-resource analysis within a business network in stated in Sect. 8. This research is concluded with future research directions in Sect. 9.

2 Literature Review

Today's emerging concept of circular economy motivates global companies to be sustainable in production process and innovation [1]. To achieve sustainability within manufacturing companies need to focus various perspectives. Waste reduction or make the waste reusable as resource is one of an important way. This waste reuse as resource can be done within individual companies or group of companies forming a virtual business network. This kind of network can be termed as green virtual business network [15].

Formation of green virtual business network to improve customer services is a growing trend between companies [15, 16]. This trend is helping today's business domain in various ways to be competitive in the market segment [1, 2].

Managing waste as a result from industrial operations is nowadays is a huge environmental concern. Manufacturing companies are forced by rules to obey global environmental regulations [3, 4]. It is therefore become an obligation for companies to invest resources to manage or treat their waste properly. However, often it becomes difficult for companies to manage waste individually but it asks for cooperation with other companies, which motivates the company to form a business network. This network not only gives added business benefits but also support to manage each other's waste cooperatively.

The application of business network to manage waste is not widely analyzed and found in the literature [5, 14, 16–18]. Most of the networks are confined with to achieve business benefits through developing products or processes through collaboration and not management of wastes. This research gaps is identified from literature survey and this research presented a guidelines and aspects to manage industrial waste collaboratively.

3 Research Methodology

The methodology of this research is highlighted with various stages as displayed in Fig. 2. From Fig. 1 it is noticed that the first step in the methodology is to identify the problem specification, which is followed by developing the green virtual business network based on the specified problem. When the green virtual business network is formed, in the next available stage of the methodology is to collect necessary data from the case companies within the virtual business network. Initially, five case companies were selected based on their products, whose by-products or wastes can be used between each other as potential resources after necessary treatments. Necessary wastes data were collected through physical visits to the selected case companies' premises, which were mostly historical records from the companies. All the collected data will be analyzed based on its suitability to solve the identified problem.

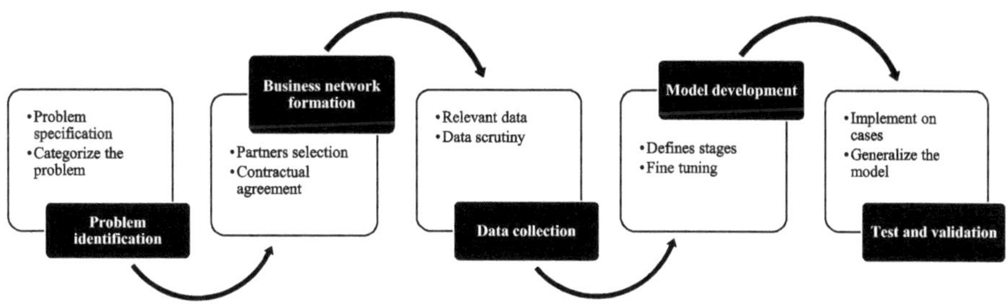

Fig. 1. Stages within research methodology

At the third stage, a model will be developed which is basically a problem solving framework defining each stages how to solve the identified problem. This model will then be tested and validated through implementing it to solve real life case examples. If the model is validated successfully, a generic theory will be proposed to be used to solve specific problem.

4 Virtual Business Network for Mutual Benefits

The concept of virtual business network comes from the theme where manufacturing companies are formed through the implementation of information and communication technology (ICT). This ICT framework supports the selection of partners, formation of the partnership network, communication between partner organizations and execution of the collaborative network [6, 7].

A leading partner known as 'Initiator Company', after rigorous market survey, starts this business network after identifying business opportunities. After identifying the business opportunities, the initiating partner company looks for the possible partner organizations within similar business domain. When the partners are selected based on predefined criterions, an agreement is signed between the partner companies, where

6 Collaborative Waste Management: Potential for Mutual Resources

It is become important for manufacturing companies to abide by environmental rules and regulations. To respect such rules and regulations manufacturing managers need to adopt various strategies to limit the impact of their operations and products on the natural environment. Manufacturing companies produces huge amount of wastes that affects environment if they are not treated or recycled properly. These wastes need to be managed effectively and efficiently for the benefits of companies themselves, diverse stakeholder groups, including end-customers, industrial customers, suppliers and financial institutions [3].

Manufacturing companies are evolved with various environmental aspects such green purchasing [4], reverse logistics [9], product stewardship [10], etc. All such activities involve varying degree of interaction with the companies in manufacturing domain from suppliers to end customers. The limited knowledge and understanding of individual companies for environmental awareness has hampered the development of widely accepted model or framework to manage costly environment. Although, several business networking or collaboration can be found in the literature, however, few researches found on collaborative management of environment.

The level of wastes as manufacturing companies are producing in their daily production lines often become cumbersome and unmanageable by individual company's efforts. In such challenging situation, combined effort to manage such wastes can offer companies economic benefits as well. In collaborative way, wastes can be treated internally by the knowledge and expertise from partner companies or can be treated in a common place for mutual efforts. The way of waste treatment may be varied from company to company but the objective will be same to get benefit from it. There are some ways already exists, where partner companies can manage their wastes in collaboration. Some of the ways to waste management is highlighted in Table 2.

Table 2. Various ways to collaborative waste management

Collaborative waste management	Brief description
Industrial symbiosis [11, 12]	It is associated with the concept to utilize each other's by-products and otherwise share resources within the business collaboration
Industrial eco-park [13]	With this concept business partners cooperate with each other and with the local community to reduce waste and pollution by efficiently sharing resources
Waste-to-feed exchange	In this concept, one company's by products are used as resources to other company through mutual agreement through forming the business network
Business ecosystem [14]	In this business domain, collaborative partners shares both resources as well as wastes between each other to stay environment friendly

(*Continued*)

Table 2. (*Continued*)

Collaborative waste management	Brief description
Systematic approach	In this approach, collaborative partners take the form of waste cascading, shared logistics for building green retrofits and new strategies in existing industrial developments
Waste-to-energy	At this concept, collaborative partners attract complementary businesses to use the waste to produce energy between each other that could benefit from eco-industrial strategies
Eco-industrial park [13, 15]	In this concept, partner companies are collocated in a certain geographic location to participate in the industrial waste management system with the objective to reduce environmental impact

From Table 2 it is noticed that the waste can be managed through several organizational forms and processes. In case of organizational forms, such as industrial symbiosis, eco-industrial parks, etc., wastes are managed through collaboration and such synergistic possibilities are offered by geographic proximity. Whereas, in case of processes, such as recycling, reuse, etc., wastes are treated depending on the wastes natures. For instance, in waste recycling the process can be up-cycling or down-cycling and for reuse case, it can be direct reuse or use as second-hand, which is dependent on the waste nature.

7 A Framework for Collaborative Waste Management: Green Virtual Business Network View

Although, several researches are done on virtual business networks successes and limitations but limited researches are done on green virtual networks directly involved with managing industrial wastes [16, 17]. Several IT-based tools are available to manage waste in general but due to cost and complexity they may not be suitable for many companies, especially small and medium size enterprises (SMEs) [18]. Most of the individual company treats its by-products or wastes separately, which may not be very cost effective and efficient. In such circumstances, companies (SMEs) can collaborate by forming a green virtual business network with the objective to monitor and manage their wastes and look for the possibilities to exchange or recycle\reuse of wastes as resources among each other.

Green virtual business network can play an important role in managing and reusing/recycling industrial waste among the network chain. This kind of network can be defined specifically to focus on inter-organizational goal setting, shared environmental planning and to work together to reduce environmental damage through wastes treatment processes like industrial ecology, industrial symbiosis, reuse/recycling/discard, etc. These practices with the objective to reduce environmental impact can be directed either upstream toward partner organizations or downstream toward customers. The upstream practices are closely linked with process-based performance monitoring, management, while downstream practices are related with product-based performance monitoring, and management.

To maintain industrial ecology, it is necessary to build collaborative effort within companies. Such collaborative effort supports to enhance waste management through recycling, reuse and discard. In order to fulfill such objectives, companies need to follow a framework that guidelines companies step-by-step to manage their harmful wastes. The framework can be based on both physical network within companies and/or green virtual network. This kind of network helps to utilize each other's by-products, otherwise, share as resources into economic products among the partner organizations.

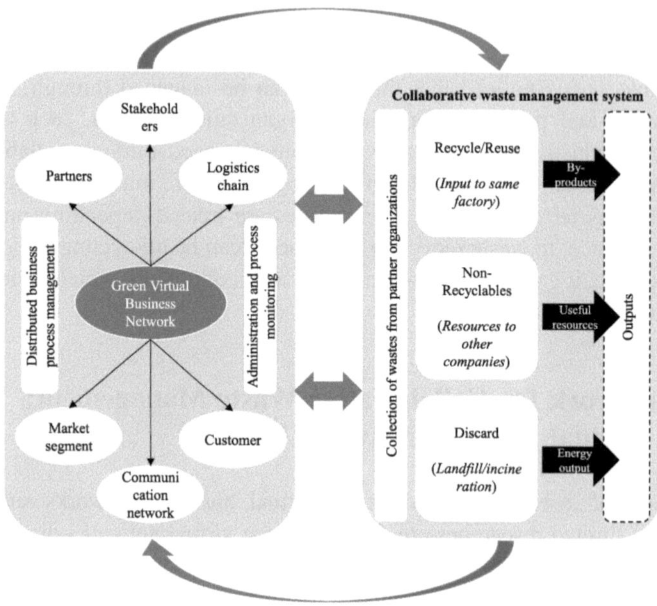

Fig. 3. Collaborative waste management framework

A framework for green virtual business network to manage waste is displayed in Fig. 3. From Fig. 3 it is noticed that there is an iterative relationship between the business network and the waste management system. The basic functionally of the business network is to manage distributed business processes, which are supported by necessary administration and process monitoring. The green virtual business network is tightly coupled with partners, stakeholders, logistics chain, market segment, communication network and customer as highlighted in Fig. 3.

In addition to managing the business processes, the green virtual business network is interacting with the collaborative waste management system. This waste management system has three formats such as recycle/reuse, non-recyclables and discard. In the recycle/reuse phase, collected wastes from the partner companies are treated and the by-products are used internally. In the non-recyclable phase, the collected wastes are used as possible resources within the network partner organizations. In the discard phase, recyclable and non-recyclable wastes are used as landfills/incineration as depicted in Fig. 3. The framework as outlined in this research can be successfully implemented to manage collaborative industrial wastes and keep the costly environment clean for human being.

8 Networked Waste Management: Illustrative Business Cases

(a) Mapping of Waste Management Among the Green Virtual Business Network

As explained earlier, the networked waste management is an idea, where one company's waste within a business network can be a useful resource for other company. This concept contributes to the input-output matching approaches by including different types of resource substitutions. It can be demonstrated as the modelling approach, which is used for identifying potential waste, which is considered as output from an industry, and use as input resource to other industry. This type of waste management technique can be successfully implemented in a green virtual business network, where the collaboration starts after identifying business opportunity to exchange waste between partners.

Figure 4 demonstrates an idea of waste management through mapping among collaborative partner organizations within a business network. As seen from Fig. 4, the

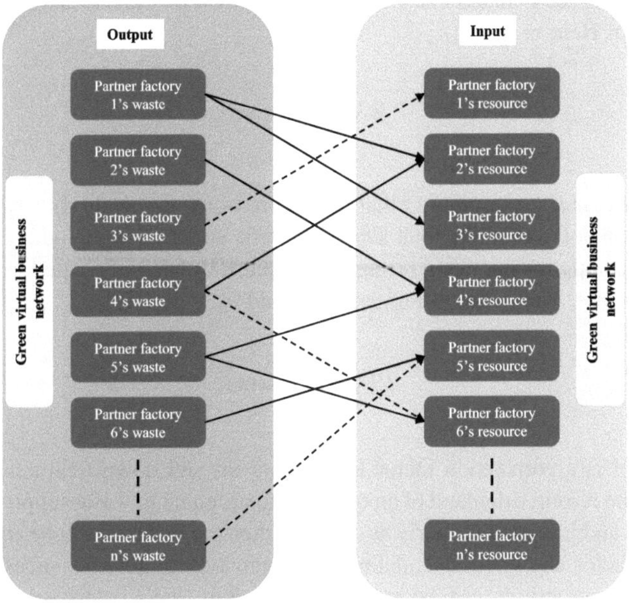

Fig. 4. Mapping of waste reuse within a green virtual business network

wastes from one or more partner organizations can be successfully used as resources for the other company or companies depending on their matching and suitability. From Fig. 4, it can also be noticed that all the companies within the business network may not exchange wastes among each other due to unsuitable, or individual company might be specialized to treat its wastes for internal use. For instance, from Fig. 4 it is seen partner factory 3's waste may be or may not be used or suitable as an input resource for partner factory one. Most of the cases, some wastes might be needed some kinds of processing before using them as resources by the other partners companies. This collaboration practices support network partners to minimize and reuse their waste effectively and efficiently and promote to maintain environmental sustainability.

Often such wastes might need to be processed within the network partners to them useful resources. Such processes can be incineration, waste symbiosis, departed, sorting, recycling, etc. In case of the reprocessing needs, individual partner organization or group of similar kind of waste producing partners can collaborate with each other with their skills and expertise to treat such wastes useful. There should be balanced between supply wastes and resources demand. In case of overstocked wastes can be discarded by the partners in an environmental friendly ways.

(b) Mathematical Model of Collaborative Waste Management

The exchange of waste and resource is of course depends of the demand-supply relationships between the companies. Each of the waste to be used as resource has a quantity. The amount of supply of waste cannot exceed the available demand as resource. In case of mismatch between supply and demand, priority will be given on the first come first serve basis. Even waste exchange policy can be formulated based on the evaluation on which waste demand can give better use to the waste. This waste supply and resource demand can be presented as of a mathematical model as follows (adapted from Hein et al. [5]):

$$WS_{ij} \geq \sum_{j=1}^{n} ws_{ij}$$

Where, ws_{ij} is a waste supply i that meets a resource demand j. In any situation, the sum of ws_{ij} cannot exceed the total available waste supply WS_{ij}. In addition to that, the sum of waste supplies ws_{ij} for a resource demand RDj has to be equal or less than the resource demand. This relationship can be stated as:

$$RD_j \geq \sum_{i=1}^{m} c_i ws_{ij}$$

Where, ci is a conversion factor for treating up and downstream substitutes. For example, if the resource demand of an organization is equal to waste supply from another organization and it is used properly as resource then the c_j factor will be equal to 1. This conversion factor allows for calculating the summation of new resources that are substituted. Three criterions can be used for evaluating the waste-resource conversion within green virtual business network:

- Maximize the quantity of substituted new resources ws_{ij}
- Maximize net profit by substituting earn revenue ER_{ij} minus operating cost OC_{ij} for a match WS_{ij}
- Minimize capital investment CI_{ij} for a technology to transfer ws_{ij}

The cost of capital investment can be CI_{ij} due to cost incurred to transportation cost to transfer waste from one factory to another one, waste conversion or recycling cost to make it useable resource for other factory if needed, cost for CO_2 emission process if there is any, etc. In order to calculate cost-revenue balance sheet, it is useful to formulate multi-objective optimization problem with the objective functions as of:

$$\sum_{i=1}^{m}\sum_{j=1}^{n} c_i ws_{ij} = maximum$$

$$\sum_{i=1}^{m}\sum_{j=1}^{n} (ER_{ij} - OC_{ij}) = maximum$$

$$\sum_{i=1}^{m}\sum_{j=1}^{n} CI_{ij} = minimum$$

Subject to the constraints:

$$\sum_{j=1}^{n} \mathrm{ws}_{ij} - \mathrm{WS}_i \leq 0$$

and

$$\mathrm{ws}_{ij} \geq 0$$

The waste data from the case organizations are to be analyzed following the above-mentioned mathematical model and multi-objective optimization in order to make the waste management process economically feasible for the organizations within a business network. The analysis will be done in a manner as highlighted in Table 3.

Table 3. Exchange of waste-resource with quantity within a collaborative business network

Waste supplier	Waste receiver as a resource	Resource name	Quantity
Organization 1	Organization 3	TBA	TBA
Organization 2	Organization 1	TBA	TBA
Organization 3	Organization 2	TBA	TBA
Organization … n	Organization … m	TBA	TBA

Based on the predefined objective functions total amount of waste from one organization as the replacement of resource for other organization, capital investment and net profit can be calculated and summed up as presented in Table 4 as sample. It is noted that only profitable waste-resource exchange (feasible solutions) will be allowed and non-profitable scenarios will be discarded from consideration.

Establishing Networks for the Treatment of WEEE Components

Mohammadtaghi Falsafi[1,2(✉)] and Rosanna Fornasiero[1]

[1] ITIA-CNR Institute of Industrial Technologies and Automation, Via Corti 12, 20133 Milan, Italy
{mohammadtaghi.falsafi,rosanna.fornasiero}@itia.cnr.it
[2] Department of Mechanical Engineering, Politecnico Di Milano, Via La Masa 1, 20157 Milan, Italy

Abstract. This paper analyzes different approaches for managing Waste Electronic and Electrical Equipment (WEEE) in order to reduce the economic and environmental impacts and in particular how to manage collaborative networks. The classifications are made based on the review of the recent and related literature in WEEE treatment and show the impacts on different cases studied in the literature. In addition, a simulation model is proposed to study the practical impact of improving the capability of a Region to treat WEEE components.

Keywords: Waste Electrical and Electronic Equipment (WEEE) · Supply chain models · Simulation

1 Introduction

The aim of this study is to propose an innovative model to evaluate the cost of implementing networks to recover/recycle Waste of Electronic and Electrical Equipment (WEEE) components. To reach this aim, it is first studied different models of WEEE supply chain management from literature from which some important parameters for the evaluation of the cost of the networks emerge. Most of the models consider distance between treatment centres and collection centres, type of vehicles to use in transportation of WEEE, type of supply chain structure and also agents to collect the WEEE as well as the product residual value. Some of these criteria have been taken into consideration for the creation of the model to analyse the costs of the creation of a WEEE components treatment network.

This paper describes a detailed analysis of the creation of collaborative networks for handling the flow of WEEE in an Italian region and consider the re- and de-manufacturing process of one important component which is the Printed Circuit Board (PCB). The proposed model allows to evaluate the costs for establishing a collaborative network where treatment centres and de-manufacturing plants can work together to improve the capability of a Region to recycle components from End-of-Life products. In particular, in Sect. 2, the proposed classification of the models for WEEE treatment in the present literature is explained which are chosen based on the scope of this paper. In Sect. 3, a

H. Afsarmanesh et al. (Eds.): PRO-VE 2016, IFIP AICT 480, pp. 652–660, 2016.
DOI: 10.1007/978-3-319-45390-3_56

simulation model is described and applied to a specific case related to the Italian WEEE treatment activity and in Sect. 4 results of the proposed model are discussed. Finally, Sect. 5 explains the final remarks and proposed suggestions for the future improvement in this context.

2 Literature Review of Supply Chain Models for WEEE Management

In literature there are different approaches and definitions for distinguishing treatment centers and collection centers. In general, collection centers are the points where WEEE is collected from different sources (private citizens, communities, electric equipment retailers with the duty to assure a certain percentage of collection upon what they sell) and sometimes disassembled to main components; treatment centers are specialized in disassembly of WEEE and WEEE components and also in some occasions these centers are referred to as treatment plants where the recycling and re-manufacturing of WEEE is implemented.

2.1 Models to Identify the Critical Factors for WEEE Management

In literature, it is possible to find several studies defining the critical factors for the management of WEEE. In Kim et al. [1], the re-manufacturing process of reusable parts in reverse logistics is discussed; manufacturer has two options as providing the components from the suppliers or recover its own products. In this study, critical factors are identified as the type of collected products from customers, the quantity of parts required by manufacturing plants, the parts for assembling each product, the products to go to the subcontractor for re-manufacturing as outsourcing, the refurbished parts from re-manufacturing operations, the parts purchased from external supplier, and the number of disposed parts. Considering these critical factors, it is proposed a model which determines the number of remanufactured components in order to reduce the costs.

In case of Gobbi [2], the role of the product residual value (PRV) and the loss of value over time of returned products are considered critical factors in the context of reverse logistics while in Luglietti et al. [3], the environmental and economic impacts of engine re-manufacturing process is based on three options for EOL automotive engine as reuse, re-manufacturing and material recovery.

The concepts of collaboration and collaborative networks are considered important in reverse logistics according to what Romero and Molina [4] have discussed and in Frayret et al. [5] have emphasized this role in the collaborative programs implemented in business practices. There are other important aspects of collaborative networks in reverse logistics which are analysed like the impact of sustainability [6] and the impact of IT [7] and both of them can give some suggestions for this work. In Bigum et al. [8], metal recovery from high-grade WEEE is discussed and the results of the study show that the environmental impacts could be positively justified and applied.

2.2 Facility Location Models of WEEE Collection Points

Another important issue in reverse supply chain management is finding the best location for collection points. In Barba-Gutiérrez et al. [9], the importance of WEEE transportation and its effect on environment is discussed and for the specific case, it is suggested to keep the distance below 500 km, in order to have recycling activities which are economically and environmentally efficient.

More recently in Vidovic et al. [10], a novel approach to position the collection points of end-of-life vehicles (ELVs) is introduced based on the concept of multiple service zones. The service zones are obtained based on centroids of each area with one collection point and this approach has been partially applied also to this work as a way to define where to locate the new plants. Grunow and Gobbi [11] present three different models based on optimization for managing WEEE collection in Denmark and analyze the location of the collection points to guarantee the dispersion of collection points in a small scale problem.

Melo et al. [12] analyze the facility location model based on strategic planning and define four key characteristics which can be useful also for this paper which are: multi-layer facilities, multiple commodities, single/multiple period(s), and the use of deterministic/stochastic parameters.

In Queiruga et al. [13] it is suggested a model to rank allocation of Spanish municipalities based on factors like land costs, personnel costs, energy prices, and facility access. The result shows that the large cities have priority in this case while by considering other factors other different results are obtained. In Ponce-Cueto et al. [14] an optimization model is analyzed for a location and allocation problem in different dimensions (local, regional, central) in the context of reverse logistics. Their aim is to minimize the total cost by considering facility operation, waste handling, transportation, and disposal.

2.3 Models to Close the Loop of the Supply Chain of WEEE

This section considers the models which study closed-loop of the WEEE supply chain management. In Savaskan et al. (2001) [15] considering different take-back channel structures, the best agent to collect WEEE is explored. Three scenarios are defined as: the manufacturer is responsible for the reverse flow of the products, the retailers are responsible to take the products back to the cycle, and to outsource the recycling activities. In the context of decentralized system, the authors conclude that the coordination of manufacturer and retailers is the best scenario.

Implication of different types of supply chain mentioned above is studied in Savaskan et al. (2004) [16] where the models are compared with respect to the wholesale price, the retail price, the product return rate, and the total supply chain profits. The study defines that the optimal product return rate of the coordinated channel is the highest followed by retailers, manufacturers and third parties respectively. It is shown that the coordinated channel is more effective than the decentralized channel. Other models in Yang et al. (2009) [17] analyzes the supply chain in different tiers as supplier, manufacturer, retailer, consumer and recovery centers while in Cardoso et al. (2013) [18] it is defined the capacity and location of the plants for closed-loop supply chain in order to maximize the net present value.

The impact of ecological and technological issues in closed-loop supply chain with recycling activities are the two other aspects considered in Georgiadis et al. (2008) [19]. From the other point of view in a collection – re-manufacturing scheme, these EOL products can generate new profits. Also analytical models are used for reverse logistics to improve the efficiency and effectiveness of the whole system [20] while in Koh et al. (2012) [21], it is discussed that environmental issues can be dealt such that all the players in the network can collaborate in a beneficial way.

2.3.1 Simulation Models for Supply Chain Configuration

Among the different quantitative approaches for managing supply chain configuration, simulation has several advantages since it gives the possibility to have a realistic observation of the dimensions to be considered when studying the characteristics of the supply chain [22] and analyse the network along a certain period of time. Therefore it can result in strategic approaches which could be useful for decision making policies [23]. In the past, several simulation approaches have been proposed for solving different types of problems related to supply chain configurations. Cigolini et al. (2014) [24] used discrete-event simulation to analyze different supply chain configurations in terms of stocks and stock-out by evaluating if intermediaries influenced product quality and costs. Ramanathan (2014) [25] implemented a simulation method by considering several performance indicators to evaluate the importance of collaboration in a supply chain, while Bottani and Montanari (2010) [26] proposed a simulation model where information sharing mechanisms in a supply chain are considered to be a way to support demand forecast.

Camarinha-Matos (2013) [6] has analyzed the Factories of the Future (FoF) in the roadmap of horizon 2020. Simulation is a subset of "customer focused manufacturing" which could also affect collaborative networks in the category of "collaborative and mobile enterprises". In literature, there are numerous studies for network configuration in reverse logistics. Some focus on the simulation (like Kara, Rugrungruang et al. (2007) [27]) Also there are some papers that analyze both the simulation and optimization together (e.g. Topcu, Benneyan et al. 2013 [28], Sadjadi, Soltani et al. 2014 [29], Martinsen, Gulbrandsen-Dahl 2015 [30]).

3 The Model for De-manufacturing Network

In Italy, a pilot plant has been developed to handle one important part of WEEE, which is the Printed Circuit Board (PCB). The plant is proposed to re- and de-manufacture PCBs with dedicated innovative machines [31] to recycle metal and plastic from the PCBs of WEEEs and remanufacture the automotive PCBs. Apart from the technological improvement held by this kind of pilot plant, it emerged as important to study how such kind of technologies can change the established networks for WEEE management in a certain area and how collaboration can change among the actors in terms of exchanging materials and information.

In order to analyze the characteristics of the system, simulation is used. The simulation model developed in this work considers different types of nodes:

- Source nodes: Treatment centers where the WEEE is dismantled to its raw material. The model assumes that there are treatment centers that have only WEEE with low value from where only PCBs and other treatment centers from where PCBs with high value can arrive.
- Re- and de-manufacturing plants: These plants are to be located in the existing local network and in the model it is assumed that they are located close to some treatment centers.
- Sinks: They are the plants that are potential destinations for the output of re- and de-manufacturing plants. The outputs are metal and plastic. The location of the plants is based on the plants already exist in the region that have the potentiality or readiness to collect the outputs.
- PCBs with low value will follow only the de-manufacturing process while PCBs with high value will follow first a verification on their residual value and then in case it is high, they go to the re-manufacturing process; otherwise they go to the de-manufacturing process.

It is assumed that each entity (transportable unit) in the simulation corresponds to the truck capacity; all the trucks start from the same node (home node); when the simulation starts running all the trucks start travelling from that node and when they are idle they go back until next load is available. The logic of choosing the home node is related to the density of plants and treatment centers in the region; more specifically, the de-manufacturing plant which has more density compared to the other plants is the home node.

When a truck loads in a treatment center, it goes to the assigned plant to unload, then if any output is ready for pick-up at the plant, the truck loads it and take it to the destinations, otherwise it travels to the closest treatment centers. When a truck unloads in the destinations, it checks for any loads ready in treatment centers or plants. There is no constraint for the trucks to move between different plants and treatment centers in all the network and regardless of the clusterization of the network.

The different what-if scenarios are built by changing number of trucks in the model and the capacity of the trucks in order to evaluate performance of the system in terms of travelling distance, truck utilization and plant capacity utilization.

3.1 Input Data

Since there are no official data on PCBs flows, this study considers that the amount of PCBs to be handled is on average 4.5 % of the total weight of WEEE as suggested in Grosso, Rigamonti (2014) [32].

The location of the de-manufacturing plants and destinations is studied and obtained by the model proposed by Falsafi, Fornasiero (2016) [33]. For estimating the flows of PCBs for each plant, which are going to operate in the future, we need to foresee the future trends. These flows are calculated assuming the 5 % yearly increase of the WEEE production, attracting the flows which are currently transported to developing countries, attracting the flows which currently go to the landfill, and the ability to import WEEEs from other regions in Italy [32].

From the PCB treatment process to be handled in the plants, it will be possible to obtain 30 % of metal and 70 % of plastic as output to be recycled [32]. Economies of scale are also considered and the unitary cost (cost per ton) for both re- and de-manufacturing plants is linked to the plant capacity.

4 Results

Figure 1 shows the network view in the simulation model for de-manufacturing plants, which is done by SIMIO software. The picture shows the location of 21 treatment centers and 3 plants of an Italian Region with the two destinations for the outputs of metal and plastic. The model was tested with the current flows and with a scenario increasing the flow in the next 10 years according to the rate of increase of WEEE explained in Sect. 3.1.

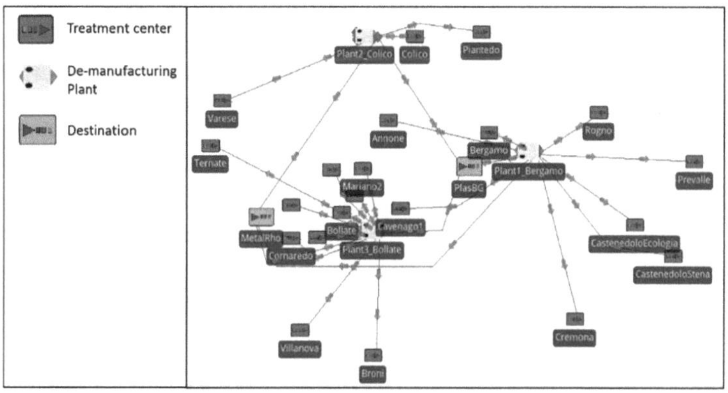

Fig. 1. Simulation overview in Simio

Table 1 shows the results of the simulation for the current and future flows for de-manufacturing plant. The trucks' utilizations are 80 % and 92 %, which are reasonably high. In addition, by increasing the flow by 4.33 times (from current to future flow), the increase in total costs is 3 % less than the increase in the total flow; this 3 % stems from the more efficient performance of the plants whose costs increases by 5 % less than the increase of the total flow.

Furthermore, in order to analyse the feasibility of the proposed model, it is useful to consider the inventory situation of the treatment centres and plants. The maximum average PCBs waiting at treatment centres is 3 tons approximately. The maximum average queue in the plants is 16 tons, which is relatively high and therefore, should be considered for further analysis in managing the inventories in the plants. In addition, on average each load is held around 1 working day or less (depending on the 3 plants based on the "average holding time") and this shows that the proposed configuration and the operation of the plants are in the feasible criteria.

26. Bottani, E., Montanari, R.: Supply chain design and cost analysis through simulation. Int. J. Prod. Res. **48**(10), 2859–2886 (2010)
27. Kara, S., Rugrungruang, F., Kaebernick, H.: Simulation modelling of reverse logistics networks. Int. J. Prod. Econ. **106**(1), 61–69 (2007)
28. Topcu, A., Benneyan, J.C., Cullinane, T.P.: A simulation-optimisation approach for reconfigurable inventory space planning in remanufacturing facilities. Int. J. Bus. Perform. Supply Chain Model. **5**(1), 86–114 (2013)
29. Sadjadi, S.J., Soltani, R., Eskandarpour, A.: Location based treatment activities for end of life products network design under uncertainty by a robust multi-objective memetic-based heuristic approach. Appl. Soft Comput. **23**, 215–226 (2014)
30. Martinsen, K., Gulbrandsen-dahl, S.: Use of post-consumer scrap in aluminium wrought alloy structural components for the transportation sector. Procedia CIRP **29**, 686–691 (2015)
31. Fideas project. http://www.fideas.industries/?lang=en
32. Grosso, M., Rigamonti, L.: Valutazione di sostenibilità ambientale della la gestione di una categoria di rifiuto speciale in Lombardia: il caso dei RAEE. Technical report of the Lumbardy Region (2014)
33. Falsafi, M., Fornasiero, R.: Network configuration for re- and de-manufacturing: a case study in Italy. In: Proceedings of 23rd Euroma conference, Trondheim, Norway, June 2016

orward supply chain process of remanufactured products has in many cases the tures as normal supply chains of new manufactured products to customers. The es of distribution systems and partners can be involved. A challenge for rema- ing is to efficiently arrange the reverse chain, involving the difficulty of g the number of cores coming back from customer.

emanufacturing internal processes contain the necessary physical manufac- ps to recondition the incoming cores to the required quality level. The generic) remanufacturing process is described in Fig. 4 [7]. When a core undergoes a cturing process, it may pass through a number of specific operations. In no rder, these are: inspection, cleaning, disassembly, reprocessing, reassembly, d storage.

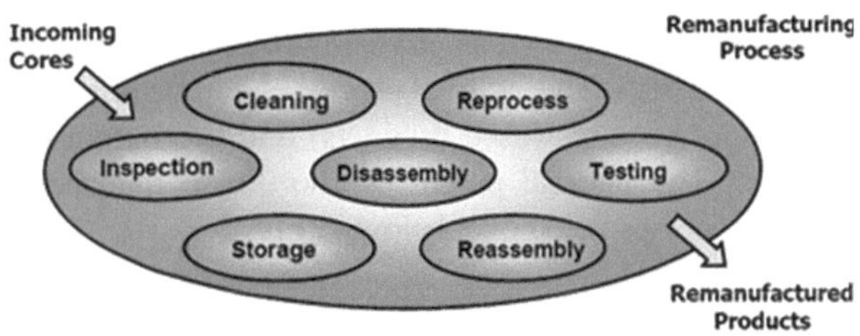

Fig. 4. Generic remanufacturing internal process [7]

are different types of companies that perform remanufacturing (internal These companies can be classified according to their relationship to the product urer, i.e. the Original Equipment Manufacturer (OEM); (1) the OEM itself, (2) d "official" contractors, and (3) independent remanufacturers.

first two cases, OEMs retain at least some control over both the numbers and y of the remanufactured products. Relationships between contractors and n involve mutually beneficial information flows regarding both original design ons and product failure modes and frequencies [11].

ternal processes can be difficult for the remanufacturing company to organise ge. Logistics operators, core collection, storage and warehousing are often n the networks. A more detailed analysis of potential networking forms can n [12] including *Industry-specific remanufacturing networks, Location-based cturing networks, Remanufacturing parks* and *Remanufacturing ecosystems.*

efits from Remanufacturing

nufacturing benefits are manifold. Remanufacturing it is good for:

rs. Remanufactured parts and components provide same as original perform- reliability at costs typically only 50–80 % of a new. Instant availability gives rs more options at repair and overhaul time. The results are maximum produc- d lower costs.

Circular Economy in Shipbuilding and Marine Networks – A Focus on Remanufacturing in Ship Repair

Kim Jansson(✉)

VTT Technical Research Centre of Finland Ltd, Vuorimiehentie 3,
P.O. Box 1000 02044 Espoo, Finland
Kim.Jansson@vtt.fi

Abstract. There are about 85,000 ships in the world, with 82 % being at least 5 years old, and over half at least 15 years old [4]. All of these ships require, or will require, regular repair and maintenance. The European shipbuilding and marine industry is highly networked. The EU-28 marine supplies industry's 1st and 2nd tier enterprises employed about 390,000 people in up to about 30,000 companies [10].

In short remanufacturing is an industrial process of restoring used products to an 'as new' condition. Remanufacturing is a key strategy within the circular economy and an important technology for reducing CO_2 emission, saving material, labour, energy and prolonging the "end-of life" of products, components and systems.

The paper describes different types of ship repair activities, their frequency and the collaborative networks involved. Furthermore, for each type of repair activity the paper reports the potential of applying remanufacturing approaches, involved companies and their role in a remanufacturing process.

Keywords: Circular economy · Remanufacturing · Marine industry · Shipyards · Ship repair · Collaborative networked in remanufacturing

1 Introduction

In December 2015, the European Commission published *Closing the loop — An EU action plan for the circular economy*, a new strategy that aims to support the transition to a circular economy in the EU [1]. According to the action plan, the transition to a more circular economy is an essential contribution to the EU's efforts to develop a sustainable, low carbon, resource-efficient and competitive economy. The action plan sets out a large number of initiatives that address all stages of the product life cycle.

Also, the maritime industries need products with reduced environmental impact and less emissions, involving components suitable for a prolonged lifetime. IMO (the International Maritime Organization), the United Nations specialized agency with responsibility for the safety and security of shipping and the prevention of marine pollution by ships, has introduced regulations that shipowners need to adhere to. One example of these initiatives is the establishment of the Emission Control Areas (ECA) to limit the

H. Afsarmanesh et al. (Eds.): PRO-VE 2016, IFIP AICT 480, pp. 661–671, 2016.
DOI: 10.1007/978-3-319-45390-3_57

emission of SOx by limiting the maximum sulphur content of the fuel oils used on-board. Other actions are the proper control and management of ships' ballast water that has become a major challenge for the global shipping industry. These imposed regulations will have a positive environmental impact, but in addition voluntary measure are also needed. This requires understanding how the circular economy can be implemented and promoted in the maritime industry, and how companies can assess their potential for circular economy forms. In recent decades, European maritime industry has been dealing with increased competition from shipyards in Asia, forcing Europeans to specialize in the construction and production of cruise ships, ferries, special purpose ships and luxury yachts.

2 Circular Economy and Remanufacturing

The circular economy is a generic term for an industrial economy that produces neither waste nor pollution. More precisely, according to the Ellen MacArthur Foundation [2] "*A circular economy is restorative and regenerative by design, and aims to keep products, components, and materials at their highest utility and value at all times. It replaces the 'end-of-life' concept with restoration, shifts towards the use of renewable energy, eliminates the use of toxic chemicals, and aims for the elimination of waste through the superior design of materials, products and production systems.*"

Remanufacturing is a key strategy within the circular economy. There are many definition of remanufacturing. According to the Automotive Parts Remanufacturers Association [5], remanufacturing is the process of returning a used product to at least its original performance with a warranty that is equivalent to or better than that of the newly manufactured product. From a customer viewpoint, the remanufactured product can be considered the same as a new product. Figure 1 positions remanufacturing in the waste hierarchy and in Fig. 2 remanufacturing is shown within the circular economy.

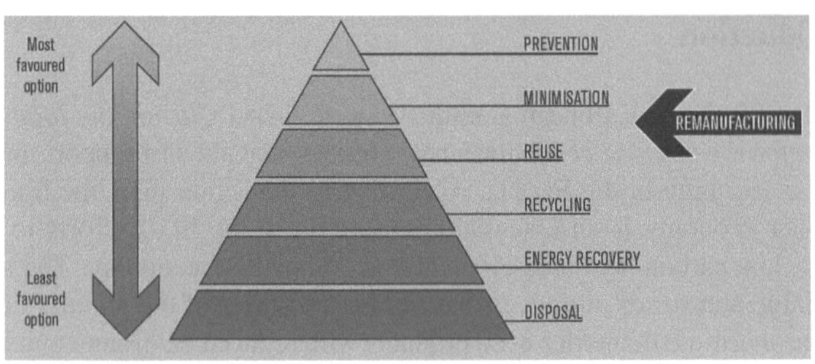

Fig. 1. Remanufacturing in the waste hierarchy [3]

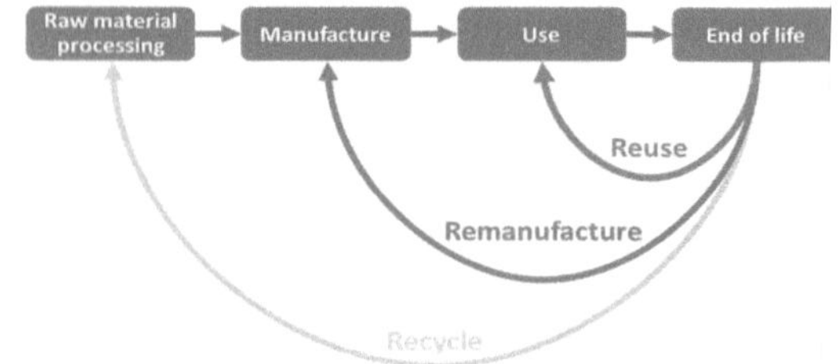

Fig. 2. Remanufacturing in the context of the circul

2.1 Remanufacturing Processes

Remanufacturing systems can be seen as consisting of two
external and *internal* processes. The external processes can b
of coordinating the input of cores (used products) and the
products to customers. The internal processes coordinate
"factory walls". The processes are shown below in Fig. 3.

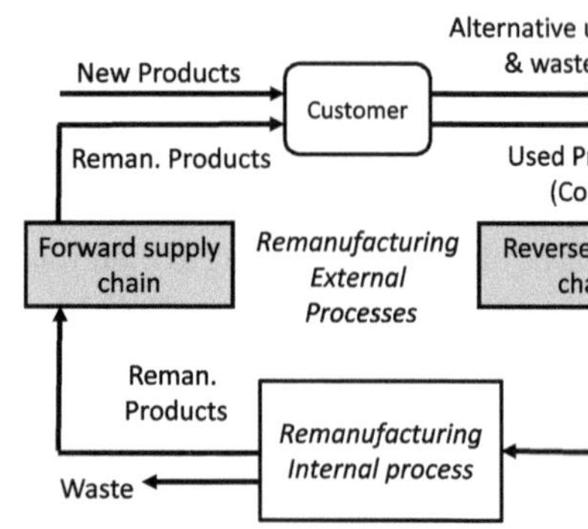

Fig. 3. External and internal processes of remanufacturing

The external processes in a remanufacturing system
output from the actual remanufacturing (internal) processe
remanufactured products through different manufacturing
ment of components, Fig. 3.

From a logistics perspective, the logistical system spa
ations can be referred to as a restorative closed-loop sup
covers the flow of physical products from producer to cust
consists of the flow of physical products from customer
facturing system is a typical representation of the Circula

The
same fe
same ty
nufactu
predicti
The
turing s
(interna
remanu
specific
testing

Ther
process)
manufac
contract
In the
the qual
OEMs c
specifica
The e
and man
included
be found
remanuf

2.2 Be

The Rem

Custon
ance an
custom
tivity a

Business. Remanufacturing is based on an exchange system where customers return cores in exchange for our remanufactured products. Remanufacturing is an additional option to support customers and help lower owning and operating costs. Profit margins are often bigger for remanufactured products than for new products.
Environment. The business of returning end of life components to same as original condition, reduce waste and minimize the need for raw material to produce new parts, keeping non-renewable resources in circulation for multiple lifetimes, and reduces energy consumption and greenhouse gas emissions. Material and energy savings are up to 90 %.
Society. Remanufacturing creates a large number of job positions, requiring skilled personnel.

Remanufacturing thus support circular economy in it's all three dimensions, economic, environmental and social.

3 Remanufacturing in the Shipbuilding and Marine Industry

3.1 The European Shipbuilding Industry

The European shipbuilding industry is the global leader in the construction of complex vessels such as cruise ships, ferries, mega-yachts and dredgers. It also has a strong position in building submarines and other naval vessels. The European marine equipment industry is a world leader for a wide range of equipment needed on-board ships and in harbours, ranging from propulsion systems, through large diesel engines and environmental and safety systems, to cargo handling and electronics systems.

Ship repair is an important part of the marine industry. Ship repair does not necessarily require dry docking, as work can be undertaken alongside the vessels at berths or at sea, Table 1 gives an overview of different types of ship repair activities. Normally ships are dry docked for maintenance and overhaul at regular time intervals e.g. every 2–3 years. Larger ship conversion services alter the structure or configuration of vessels so as to enable them to carry out a different purpose than was originally intended when the vessel was built. Some special characteristics of the ship repair business include:

- Significant planning and scheduling activity well in advance rather than *ad hoc* or unplanned activities.
- Short delivery times – an intensive short period to mitigate the earning opportunities lost while the ship is unable to generate sales.
- Use of a variety of skilled labour in collaborative networks
- Labour-intensive i.e. low level of automation.
- Involving a wide variety of products.
- One-off large ships, but many small components and work objects.

Table 1. Different types of ship repair activities, their frequency, typical location and duration.

	Milestones of ships Lifecycle	Frequency	Location	Duration
1	Maintenance	Continuous	Any	n/a
2	Small-scale voyage repairs	Occasionally	At sea	hours
3	On-Board repair	Occasionally	Harbour	hours, days
4	Planed dry-docking, ship overhaul	2 times in 5 years	Repair Yard	~ 2 weeks
5	Large-scale Retrofit & Refurbishment.	After 10 – 15 years of operation	Repair Yard	~ 3-4 weeks
6	Modernisation extends the commercial life by an other 20 years.	First lifetime is usually 20 – 30 years	Repair Yard	~ 3-4 weeks
7	Conversion, Lengthening, Transformation to other usage	n/a	Repair Yard	~ 1-3 months
8	Emergency repair & damage repair	No scheduled	Any	variable

3.2 Circular Economy in the Marine Industry

Ships have always been recycled. The material used for building ships, in the old days wood, or nowadays steel has always been valuable. In recycling, the shipping industry is a forerunner of other industries, such as the automotive and aviation sectors. Some 95–98 % of ship materials by weight are recycled [9]. However, the majority of ship demolitions take place in what can only be called horrific circumstances in Asia, where ships are pulled up on muddy beaches (beaching) [8]. The demolition is dangerous, costs many lives and is very polluting.

Referring to Fig. 1, recycling is not the most favourable form of circular economy. Reuse, repair, retrofit, refurbish and remanufacturing are forms of circular economy where not only the material is used, but also other value in form a labour and energy. Using the above-mentioned forms of circular economy, are ways to prolong the lifetime of a marine structure.

Ship repair is an industrial branch that is not very often addressed in the "Remanufacturing community". Table 2 below gives an overview of European Remanufacturing intensity in different industrial sectors according to a recent study in the ERN project [4].

From the table, we can see that the remanufacturing intensity (share of business domain) in the marine sector is very low. Although complete ships are not remanufactured in the sense that they are not restored to an 'as new' condition, the principles of remanufacturing can be applied to small sections, components and other marine equipment. As the marine remanufacturing typically occurs at the component level, there is potential for 'leakage' in the numbers to other sectors. For example, remanufacturers of diesel engines may identify themselves as being in the machinery of the HDOR sector.

Examples of this type of repair activity are corrective maintenance, e.g. breakdown maintenance, spare parts and component replacement and HVAC system maintenance, but also planned maintenance, predictive maintenance and preventive maintenance.

Remanufacturing in Planned Dry-Dockings and Ship Overhauls. These types of ship repair require the involvement of a ship repair yard and typically also dry docking of the ship. The frequency of planned dry-docking is approximately 2 times in 5 years. Figure 6 illustrates the corresponding roles in the potential remanufacturing process. In this case, the cores are collected at the repair yard and sent to a remanufacturing company for reconditioning. The remanufactured product is then used at other yards (or in other business domains). In some cases the product used can be used for other purposes after processing (second life). An example of an external remanufacturing company (OEM) could be a diesel engine manufacturer using remanufactured components such as cylinder covers, pistons, piston crowns, piston rods, exhaust valves, cylinder covers or connecting rods.

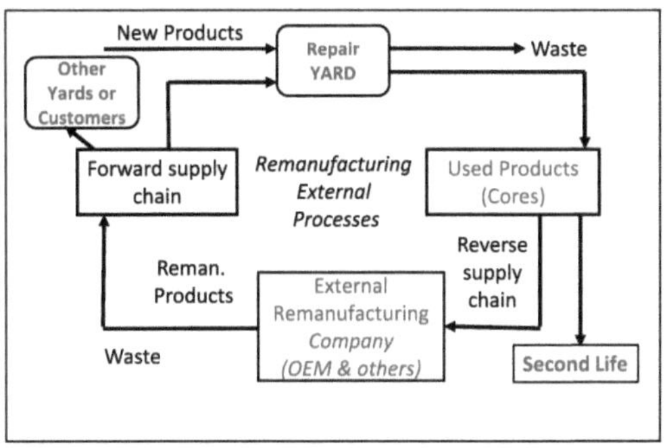

Fig. 6. Remanufacturing in planned dry-docking.

Remanufacturing in Large Scale Ship Repair and Refurbishments. This type of passenger ship repair is typically performed after 10–15 years of operation. It involves a ship repair yard and often also a specialised turnkey provider for refurbishment

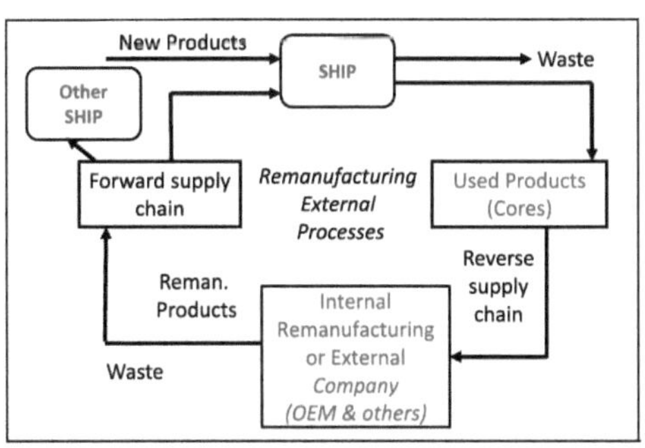

Fig. 7. Remanufacturing in large scale ship retrofit and refurbishment.

Table 2. Summary of European remanufacturing activities across industry sectors [4]

Sectors	Turnover (€bn)	Firms	Employment ('000)	Cores ('000)	Intensity
Aerospace	12.4	1,000	71	5,160	11.5%
Automotive	7.4	2,363	43	27,286	1.1%
EEE	3.1	2,502	28	87,925	1.1%
Furniture	0.3	147	4	2,173	0.4%
DOR	4.1	581	31	7,390	2.9%
Machinery	1.0	513	6	1,010	0.7%
Marine	0.1	7	1	83	0.3%
Medical equipment	1.0	60	7	1,005	2.8%
Rail	0.3	30	3	374	1.1%

4 Opportunities for Remanufacturing in Ship Repair

Below we review the different types of ship repair activities according to Table 1. We also use the generic remanufacturing process, with its external and internal processes (Fig. 3), to analyse the roles played by the shipyard and the ship (shipowner) in the remanufacturing processes.

Remanufacturing in Small Scale Ship Repair. The first three types of ship repair activities (maintenance, small scale voyage repairs and on-board repair) according to Table 1 are typically small and do not require dry docking. Figure 5 illustrates the potential roles of the remanufacturing product customer, core supplier and process owner. The cores are collected from the ship and sent to a remanufacturing company for reconditioning. The remanufactured product is then used in other ships (or in other business domains).

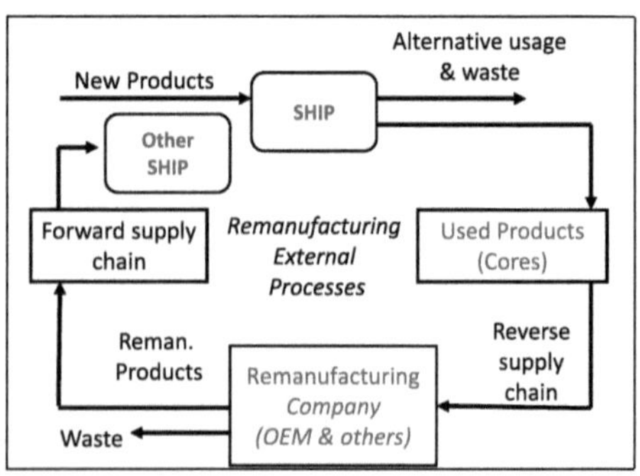

Fig. 5. Remanufacturing in small scale ship repair activities.

Circular Economy in Shipbuilding and Marine Networks – A Focus on Remanufacturing in Ship Repair

Kim Jansson(✉)

VTT Technical Research Centre of Finland Ltd, Vuorimiehentie 3,
P.O. Box 1000 02044 Espoo, Finland
Kim.Jansson@vtt.fi

Abstract. There are about 85,000 ships in the world, with 82 % being at least 5 years old, and over half at least 15 years old [4]. All of these ships require, or will require, regular repair and maintenance. The European shipbuilding and marine industry is highly networked. The EU-28 marine supplies industry's 1st and 2nd tier enterprises employed about 390,000 people in up to about 30,000 companies [10].

In short remanufacturing is an industrial process of restoring used products to an 'as new' condition. Remanufacturing is a key strategy within the circular economy and an important technology for reducing CO_2 emission, saving material, labour, energy and prolonging the "end-of life" of products, components and systems.

The paper describes different types of ship repair activities, their frequency and the collaborative networks involved. Furthermore, for each type of repair activity the paper reports the potential of applying remanufacturing approaches, involved companies and their role in a remanufacturing process.

Keywords: Circular economy · Remanufacturing · Marine industry · Shipyards · Ship repair · Collaborative networked in remanufacturing

1 Introduction

In December 2015, the European Commission published *Closing the loop — An EU action plan for the circular economy*, a new strategy that aims to support the transition to a circular economy in the EU [1]. According to the action plan, the transition to a more circular economy is an essential contribution to the EU's efforts to develop a sustainable, low carbon, resource-efficient and competitive economy. The action plan sets out a large number of initiatives that address all stages of the product life cycle.

Also, the maritime industries need products with reduced environmental impact and less emissions, involving components suitable for a prolonged lifetime. IMO (the International Maritime Organization), the United Nations specialized agency with responsibility for the safety and security of shipping and the prevention of marine pollution by ships, has introduced regulations that shipowners need to adhere to. One example of these initiatives is the establishment of the Emission Control Areas (ECA) to limit the

H. Afsarmanesh et al. (Eds.): PRO-VE 2016, IFIP AICT 480, pp. 661–671, 2016.
DOI: 10.1007/978-3-319-45390-3_57

emission of SOx by limiting the maximum sulphur content of the fuel oils used on-board. Other actions are the proper control and management of ships' ballast water that has become a major challenge for the global shipping industry. These imposed regulations will have a positive environmental impact, but in addition voluntary measure are also needed. This requires understanding how the circular economy can be implemented and promoted in the maritime industry, and how companies can assess their potential for circular economy forms. In recent decades, European maritime industry has been dealing with increased competition from shipyards in Asia, forcing Europeans to specialize in the construction and production of cruise ships, ferries, special purpose ships and luxury yachts.

2 Circular Economy and Remanufacturing

The circular economy is a generic term for an industrial economy that produces neither waste nor pollution. More precisely, according to the Ellen MacArthur Foundation [2] "*A circular economy is restorative and regenerative by design, and aims to keep products, components, and materials at their highest utility and value at all times. It replaces the 'end-of-life' concept with restoration, shifts towards the use of renewable energy, eliminates the use of toxic chemicals, and aims for the elimination of waste through the superior design of materials, products and production systems.*"

Remanufacturing is a key strategy within the circular economy. There are many definition of remanufacturing. According to the Automotive Parts Remanufacturers Association [5], remanufacturing is the process of returning a used product to at least its original performance with a warranty that is equivalent to or better than that of the newly manufactured product. From a customer viewpoint, the remanufactured product can be considered the same as a new product. Figure 1 positions remanufacturing in the waste hierarchy and in Fig. 2 remanufacturing is shown within the circular economy.

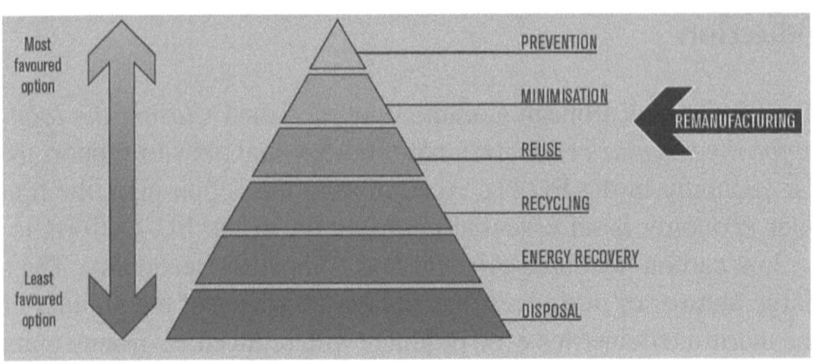

Fig. 1. Remanufacturing in the waste hierarchy [3]

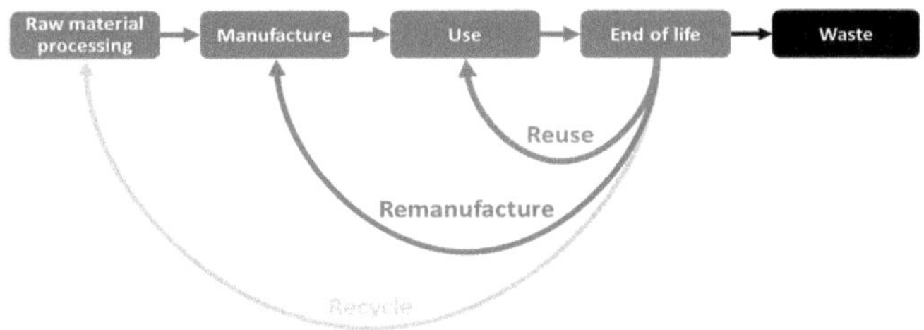

Fig. 2. Remanufacturing in the context of the circular economy [4]

2.1 Remanufacturing Processes

Remanufacturing systems can be seen as consisting of two interrelated processes, the *external* and *internal* processes. The external processes can be referred to as the process of coordinating the input of cores (used products) and the output of remanufactured products to customers. The internal processes coordinate the operations within the "factory walls". The processes are shown below in Fig. 3.

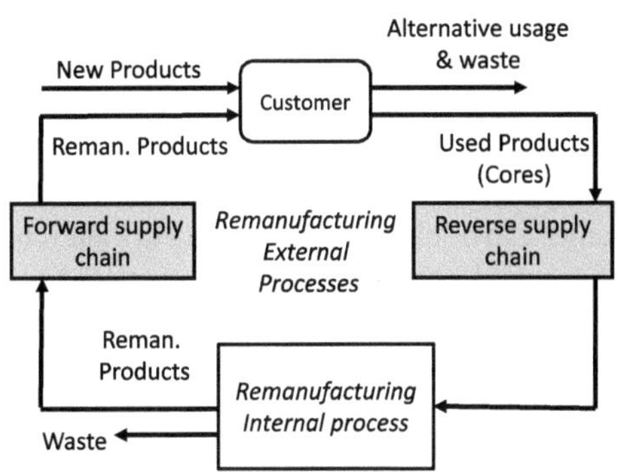

Fig. 3. External and internal processes of remanufacturing systems (adapted from [6])

The external processes in a remanufacturing system are limited to the input and output from the actual remanufacturing (internal) processes, which transform cores into remanufactured products through different manufacturing operations and the replacement of components, Fig. 3.

From a logistics perspective, the logistical system spanning product recovery operations can be referred to as a restorative closed-loop supply chain. The forward chain covers the flow of physical products from producer to customer, while the reverse chain consists of the flow of physical products from customer to producer. Thus a remanufacturing system is a typical representation of the Circular Economy.

The forward supply chain process of remanufactured products has in many cases the same features as normal supply chains of new manufactured products to customers. The same types of distribution systems and partners can be involved. A challenge for remanufacturing is to efficiently arrange the reverse chain, involving the difficulty of predicting the number of cores coming back from customer.

The remanufacturing internal processes contain the necessary physical manufacturing steps to recondition the incoming cores to the required quality level. The generic (internal) remanufacturing process is described in Fig. 4 [7]. When a core undergoes a remanufacturing process, it may pass through a number of specific operations. In no specific order, these are: inspection, cleaning, disassembly, reprocessing, reassembly, testing and storage.

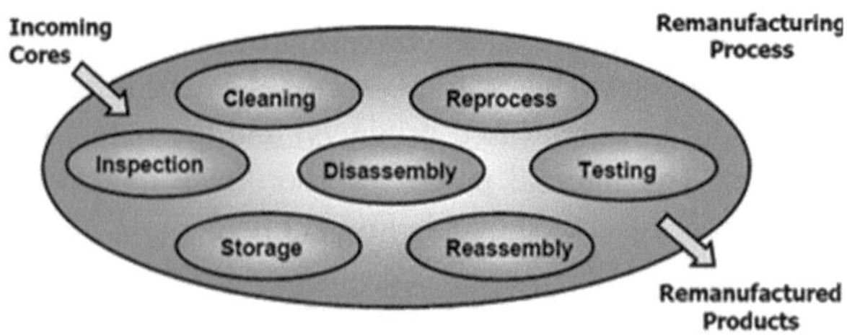

Fig. 4. Generic remanufacturing internal process [7]

There are different types of companies that perform remanufacturing (internal process). These companies can be classified according to their relationship to the product manufacturer, i.e. the Original Equipment Manufacturer (OEM); (1) the OEM itself, (2) contracted "official" contractors, and (3) independent remanufacturers.

In the first two cases, OEMs retain at least some control over both the numbers and the quality of the remanufactured products. Relationships between contractors and OEMs can involve mutually beneficial information flows regarding both original design specifications and product failure modes and frequencies [11].

The external processes can be difficult for the remanufacturing company to organise and manage. Logistics operators, core collection, storage and warehousing are often included in the networks. A more detailed analysis of potential networking forms can be found in [12] including *Industry-specific remanufacturing networks, Location-based remanufacturing networks*, *Remanufacturing parks* and *Remanufacturing ecosystems*.

2.2 Benefits from Remanufacturing

The Remanufacturing benefits are manifold. Remanufacturing it is good for:

Customers. Remanufactured parts and components provide same as original performance and reliability at costs typically only 50–80 % of a new. Instant availability gives customers more options at repair and overhaul time. The results are maximum productivity and lower costs.

services. Figure 7 illustrates the corresponding roles in the potential remanufacturing process. The cores are collected from the ship and internally reconditioned at the yard or sent to a turnkey provider for reconditioning. The remanufactured product is then used in other ships (or in other business domains).

An example of this is remanufacturing of a complete cabin (*restoring it to "as new" condition) or remanufacturing of cabin components,* including re-upholstery of soft goods, textiles (draperies, head boards, refinishing of fixed furniture, new wall, floor and ceiling surfaces, bathroom floors and walls, bathroom furniture and fittings, technical electrical, HVAC and piping, etc.

Remanufacturing in Ship Conversions. These types of major ship repair and modification activities (modernisation, extending the ship's commercial life by approx. 20 years and conversion, lengthening, transformation to other usage) can be performed, although not for all ships, after the first ship lifetime e.g. usually after 20–30 years. Figure 8 illustrates the corresponding roles in the potential remanufacturing process.

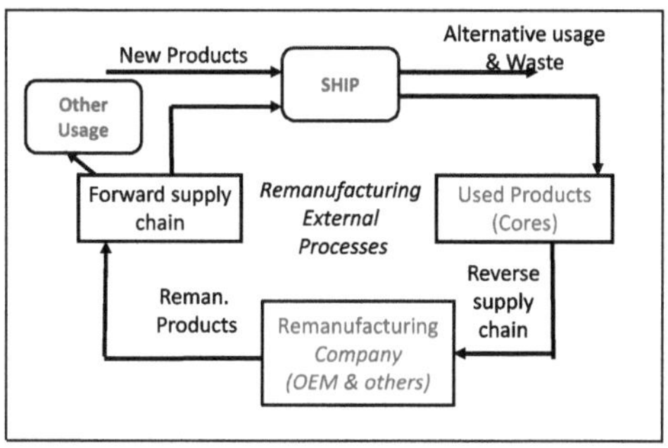

Fig. 8. Remanufacturing in major ship transformation and modification activities.

Table 3 lists the different ship repair activities together with their potential for remanufacturing.

Table 3. Remanufacturing opportunities in ship repair.

	Milestones of ships Lifecycle	Reman. Opportunity	Role of Ship (Ship Owner)	Role of Repair Yard
1	Maintenance	Yes	Core supplier	n/a
2	Small-scale voyage repairs	Yes	Core supplier	n/a
3	On-board repair	Yes	Core supplier	n/a
4	Planed dry-docking, ship overhaul	Yes	Customers of reman parts	Core collection, Prepare 2nd life
5	Large-scale Retrofit & Refurbishment	Yes	Customer of reman parts	Remanufacturer
6	Modernisation extend the commercial life by another 20 years.	Minor	Core supplier	Core collector
7	Conversion, Lengthening, Transformation to other usage	Minor	Core supplier	Core collector
8	Emergency & damage repair	n/a	n/a	n/a

4.1 Challenges and Opportunities of Applying Remanufacturing in Ship Repair

From Figs. 5, 6, 7, 8 and Tables 1 and 3 we can conclude that remanufacturing opportunities are more evident in ship repair activities focused on component level and smaller operations. There are many challenges involved, for example:

- There are few standard products
- The uncertain timing and quantity of returned cores
- Reverse logistics: from different locations. Small quantity of products collected from each source.
- Difficulty in achieving an economy of scale.
- Employees' knowledge and skills in remanufacturing
- Finding a suitable customer (ship) for the refurbished parts.

On the other hand there are also potential opportunities for profitable remanufacturing, e.g.

- Ship series, sister ships
- Big ships, more similar components
- Partnership with OEMs for components and systems
- Upgrade of technology to the latest standard
- Response to environmental legislation
- Better reputation, attract workforce

4.2 Growing Markets

The number of seagoing vessels is continuously increasing. Especially the number of passenger ships in the cruise industry has grown considerably. Ship repair is a permanent element of the maritime industry. It will always be needed. Periodic and emergency maintenance and repair work are essential so as to keep vessels operable and attractive for cruise passengers. All vessels must undergo special surveys every five years, in addition to regular repairs, in order to remain seaworthy and fulfil regulatory requirements. Economically, many ship owners have found it more profitable to increase the life of their existing fleet due to the high building costs of a new vessel. Furthermore ship-owners are reluctant to sell their older tonnage on the second hand market. The owners would rather keep their high quality cruise vessels than sell them to future competitors. Environmental issues caused by accidents and oil spills put pressure on ship owners to improve their maintenance standards. The results are increased maintenance and repair work for the yards. All in all, there is a positive outlook for remanufacturing as a part of circular economy in the ship repair industry.

5 Conclusions

Remanufacturing represents a "win-win-win" situation: customers need to pay less for the remanufactured products or components; remanufacturing companies earn more and there are environmental benefits. As a whole, remanufacturing is expected to contribute to all three dimensions of sustainability (environment, economy, society). Remanufacturing saves material and energy resources, prevents waste, creates skilled jobs and produces substantial savings compared to new goods with new components. It makes products available at lower prices; it makes a contribution to conservation of materials and energy, and it provides employment opportunities. Thus through becoming more common, remanufacturing can contribute to the circular economy in Europe.

The paper discusses how remanufacturing could be applied in the different types of ship repair activities. The yard could take different roles in the remanufacturing value chain and reverse logistics operations. The paper reviews challenges and opportunities of applying the remanufacturing concepts in the marine domain. There is evidence of a potential for growth in applying remanufacturing in ship repair activities.

Acknowledgement. This work was partly funded by the European Commission through the Project ERN: "The European Remanufacturing Network - Coordinating and Supporting European Remanufacturers", Grant agreement no: 645984.

References

1. The European Union: Closing the loop – an EU action plan for the Circular Economy. Brussels, COM (2015) 614/2
2. Ellen MacArthur Foundation: Towards a circular economy. Economic and business rationale for an accelerated transition (2012)
3. Benoy, A.-M., Owen, L., Folkerson, M.: Triple Win – The Social, Economic and Environmental Case for Remanufacturing. All-Party Parliamentary Sustainable Resource Group and All-Party Parliamentary Manufacturing Group. UK 2014. European Remanufacturing Network: Remanufacturing Market Study (2015). ERN-Project, Horizon 2020, grant agreement no. 645984. http://www.remanufacturing.eu/
4. APRA, Automotive Parts Remanufacturers Association. http://www.apra-europe.org
5. Östlin, J.: On remanufacturing systems - analysing and managing material flows and remanufacturing processes. Linköping Studies in Science and Technology, Thesis No. 1192, Department of Mechanical Engineering, Linköping University, SE-581 83 Linköping, Sweden (2008)
6. Sundin, E.: Product and process design for successful remanufacturing, in production systems. Dissertation No. 906, Linköping University, Linköping, Sweden (2004)
7. Lloyd's Register: Ship Recycling: Practice and Regulation Today. London, UK, June 2011
8. Jansson, K.: Remanufacturing & Ship Repair Possibilities, Networking and Outlook. World Remanufacturing Summit, Shanghai (2013)
9. ECORYS SCS Group: Study on the Competitiveness of the European Shipbuilding Industry (2009)
10. Karvonen, I., Jansson, K., Tonteri, H., Vatanen, S., Uoti, M.: Enhancing remanufacturing - studying networks and sustainability to support Finnish industry. J. Remanufacturing **5** (2015). Springer
11. Karvonen, I., Jansson, K., Uoti, M.: Promoting remanufacturing through collaboration. In: Camarinha-Matos, L.M., Scherer, R.J. (eds.) PRO-VE 2013. IFIP AICT, vol. 408, pp. 599–608. Springer, Heidelberg (2013)

Author Index

Abreu, António 241
Adamiak, Katarzyna 87
Afsarmanesh, Hamideh 87, 110, 350
Ahokangas, Petri 559
Ailisto, Heikki 469
Alemany, M.M.E. 608
Aminoff, Anna 629
Amitrano, Cristina C. 521
Andres, Beatriz 228
Anquetil, Anne-Ghislaine 3
Antonelli, Dario 24
Arvanitakis, Angelos 361
Askounis, Dimitrios 361
Astanin, Sergey 24
Ávila, Paulo 420
Azevedo, Américo 274, 420
Azevedo, Maria Manuela 545

Baffo, Ilaria 569
Baldissera, Thais Andrea 443
Barata, José 313
Barros, Ana Cristina 60, 73, 178
Bassanino, May 385
Bastos, João 420
Batres, Rafael 327
Bednar, Slavomir 411
Benaben, Frederick 156
Beyan, Oya Deniz 588
Bifulco, Francesco 521
Bilecki, Luís Felipe 200
Biliri, Evmorfia 361
Borges, Michele Andréia 137
Bruno, Giulia 24, 599

Camarinha-Matos, Luís M. 253, 350, 443
Campos, Pedro 148
Carotenuto, Pasquale 569
Cenedese, Claudio 313
Chavarria-Barrientos, Dante 327
Correia, Ana 373
Costa, Eric 60, 531
Crispim, José António 545
Crossley, Andrew 189

Dandolini, Gertrudes Aparecida 137
Danese, Pamela 433
Daudi, Morice 215
Dawes, Tom 73
de Sousa, Jorge Pinho 531, 545
de Vrieze, Paul 124
Decker, Stefan 588
Di Orio, Giovanni 313
Díaz-Madroñero, Manuel 228

Edwards, Rhian 189
El Asri, Ikram 289
Eshuis, Rik 457

Falsafi, Mohammadtaghi 652
Faria, José 274
Fernandes, Renato 148
Fernando, Terrence 385
Ferrada, Filipa 350
Ferreira, Filipe 274
Fertier, Audrey 156
Fiorese, Adriano 200
Fontanili, Franck 3
Fornasiero, Rosanna 433, 652
Fragidis, Garyfallos 579, 588

García-Arca, Jesús 618
González-Portela, A. Trinidad 618
Graça, Paula 253
Grefen, Paul W.P.J. 457
Grillo, Hanzel 608

Handschuh, Siegfried 579, 588
Harney, Owen 48
Hauge, Jannicke Baalsrud 215
Hayka, Haygazun 302
Helo, Petri 639
Hogan, Michael 48
Hurrell, Sue 189

Ianniello, Giuseppe 569
Iivari, Marika 469, 559

Inomata, Danielly Oliveira 60
Iram, Shamaila 385

Jansson, Kim 340, 661
Jassbi, Javad 313
Jullien, Nicolas 35

Kääriäinen, Jukka 469
Karvonen, Iris 340
Kerzazi, Noureddine 289
Kettunen, Outi 629
Kokkinakos, Panagiotis 361
Komi, Marjaana 469
Korhonen, Heidi 340
Koumpis, Adamantios 579, 588
Krylatov, Alexander 265
Kusters, Rob J. 457

Lampathaki, Fenareti 361
Lauras, Matthieu 3
Lünnemann, Pascal 302
Lynch, Jane 189

Macchion, Laura 433
Malekan, Hodjat Soleimani 87, 110
Marques, Ana Luísa 274
Matei, Oliviu 313
Mazzaroto, Solange 60
Messina, Dario 178
Michalitsi-Psarrou, Ariadni 361
Modrak, Vladimir 411
Molina, Arturo 327
Montarnal, Aurelie 156
Moqaddamerad, Sara 559
Mula, Josefa 228

Nagorny, Kevin 373
Neumeyer, Sebastian 302
Nizamani, Qurat-Ul-Ain 165

Ojo, Adegboyega 48
Oliveira, Ana Inês 350
Ortiz, A. 608
Osagie, Edobor 48
Osório, A. Luis 494

Paraskakis, Iraklis 506
Peltomaa, Irina 469
Perez, Roberto 327
Petersen, Sobah Abbas 101
Petsos, Christos 506
Petychakis, Michael 361
Piccarozzi, Michela 569
Poler, Raul 228
Popov, Ivan 265
Porwol, Lukasz 48
Prado-Prado, J. Carlos 618
Puhar, Primoz 101

Rabelo, Ricardo J. 481
Rajper, Noor Jehan 165
Rasouli, Mohammad R. 457
Reiff-Marganiec, Stephan 165
Rezazade Mehrizi, Mohammmad H. 110
Rezgui, Amira 35
Roseira, Catarina 148
Ruaro, Andre F. 481
Ryynänen, Tapani 340

Sanchis, Raquel 228
Sandhu, Maqsood 639
Santos, Cláudio 60, 73
Schoen, Quentin 3
Scholze, Sebastian 373
Shafahi, Mohammad 350
Shamsuzzoha, Ahm 639
Smit, Sander 579
Soares, António Lucas 60, 73, 137, 178, 531
Soares, Carlos 13
Sorouri, Majid 394
Spindler, Philipp 373
Stark, Rainer 302
Stasiewicz, Arkadiusz 48
Stecca, Giuseppe 569
Stokic, Dragan 373

Teixeira, Sónia A.C. 148
Thoben, Klaus-Dieter 215
Tihinen, Maarit 469
Trienekens, Jos J.M. 457
Truptil, Sébastien 3, 156

Urze, Paula 241

Valjakka, Tiina 521
Valkokari, Katri 521, 629
van der Kooij, Rimmert 101
Varvakis, Gregorio 60
Veloudis, Simeon 506
Vinelli, Andrea 433

Viola, Vincenzo 599
Vyatkin, Valeriy 394

Wang, Wei Min 302
Waqar, Mohammad 48
Wright, Paul K. 327

Xu, Lai 124
Xu, Yueqiang 559

Zakharov, Victor 265
Zarmehri, Mohammad Nozari 13
Zeleti, Fatemeh Ahmadi 48